KT-237-661

72 ●

"HANK WILLIAMS MEMORIAL ALBUM"

VIJ-5001M

JAZZ AT MASSEY HALL

PERFORMANCE/JAMES FOX · MICK JAGGER

STEREO STX-4134

JOHN LEE HOOKER

THAT'S WHERE IT'S AT!

3 C 054 - 10534

TTL & DUKE REID · GOLDEN HITS

THE GOLDEN GATE QUARTET

MOTOWN®

THE TEMPTATIONS

POWER

ARPO

LBY 1174 F · EDDIE COCHRAN

SCRATCH HITS

OTIS BLUE

EAGLES

KAY CHARLES

RAY CHARLES/THE RIGHT TIME

THE GENIUS OF RAY CHARLES

Million Sellers by Fats Domino — Vol. I

FATS DOMINO ★ BOOGIE WOOGIE BABY

James Brown at "THE APOLLO"

The Hits Of Marvin Gaye

CALL ON ME/THAT'S THE WAY LOVE IS

GEORGE JONES VOLUME 2

BOBBY BLAND

MAKE ME STRONG

BIG BILL BROONZY Midnight steppers    BT 2001

FOR LP FANS ONLY    ELVIS PRESLEY    ELVIS PRE

ELVIS PRESLEY

BILLIE HOLIDAY 1942-1951-1954

2 C 068-86527 M

GOLDEN RECORDS

THE ORIGINAL FIVE BLIND BOYS OF ALABAMA — Marchi

McLEMORE AVENUE

BLIND SONNY TERRY & WOODY GUTHRIE with ALEC STEWART

WOODY GUTHRIE

ARETHA FRANKLIN / ARETHA'S GOLD

BOOKER T. & THE M.G.'S

THE BLUES — VOL. I

2138

AAR

LE

MCA-270

LP 190

34A

GETS REDDING

OTIS REDDING

HISTORY OF RHYTHM & BLUES VOL

CHECKER ■ DALE HAWKINS ■ "SUZIE Q" - BEST OF DALE HAWKINS ■

HISTORY OF RHYTHM & BLUES VOL 4

JA

BOB DYLAN

HIGHWAY 61 REVISITED

THE GOLDEN YEARS 1953-55

THE BIG BEAT 1956-60

LITTLE MILTON · HISH & LOW · 1 SHO

39

# LIFE

# Keith Richards

# LIFE

## WITH James Fox

Weidenfeld & Nicolson

LONDON

First published in Great Britain in 2010
by Weidenfeld & Nicolson

10 9 8 7 6 5 4 3 2 1

Copyright © 2010 by Mindless Records, LLC

All rights reserved. No part of this publication may be reproduced, stored in a retrieval system, or transmitted, in any form or by any means, electronic, mechanical, photocopying, recording or otherwise, without the prior permission of both the copyright owner and the above publisher.

The right of Keith Richards to be identified as the author of this work has been asserted in accordance with the Copyright, Designs and Patents Act 1988.

A CIP catalogue record for this book is available from the British Library.

ISBN (hardback): 978 0 297 85439 5
ISBN (export trade paperback): 978 0 297 86308 3

The author is grateful for permission to quote lyrics from the following songs: "(I Can't Get No) Satisfaction." Written by Mick Jagger & Keith Richards. © 1965 Renewed, ABKCO Music, Inc. www.abkco.com. Used with permission. All rights reserved. "Get off of My Cloud." Written by Mick Jagger & Keith Richards. © 1965 Renewed, ABKCO Music, Inc. www. abkco.com. Used with permission. All rights reserved. "Gimme Shelter." Written by Mick Jagger & Keith Richards. © 1970 Renewed, ABKCO Music, Inc. www.abkco.com. Used with permission. All rights reserved. "Yesterday's Papers." Written by Mick Jagger & Keith Richards. © 1967 Renewed, ABKCO Music, Inc. www.abkco.com. Used with permission. All rights reserved. "Salt of the Earth." Written by Mick Jagger & Keith Richards. © 1969 Renewed, ABKCO Music, Inc. www.abkco.com. Used with permission. All rights reserved. "As Tears Go By." Written by Mick Jagger, Keith Richards & Andrew Oldham. © 1964 ABKCO Music, Inc. Renewed U.S. © 1992 and all publication rights for U.S.A. and Canada — ABKCO Music, Inc. / Tro-Essex Music Inc. Used by permission. International © secured. "Can't Be Seen." Written by Mick Jagger and Keith Richards. Published by Promopub B.V. "Torn and Frayed." Written by Mick Jagger and Keith Richards. Published by Colgems-EMI Music Inc. "Casino Boogie." Written by Mick Jagger and Keith Richards. Published by Colgems-EMI Music Inc. "Happy." Written by Mick Jagger and Keith Richards. Published by Colgems-EMI Music Inc. "Before They Make Me Run." Written by Mick Jagger and Keith Richards. Published by Colgems-EMI Music Inc. "All About You." Written by Mick Jagger and Keith Richards. Published by Colgems-EMI Music Inc. "Fight." Written by Mick Jagger, Keith Richards and Ron Wood. Published by Promopub B.V. and Halfhis Music. "Had It with You." Written by Mick Jagger, Keith Richards and Ron Wood. Published by Promopub B.V. and Halfhis Music. "Flip the Switch." Written by Mick Jagger and Keith Richards. Published by Promopub B.V. "You Don't Have to Mean It." Written by Mick Jagger and Keith Richards. Published by Promopub B.V. "How Can I Stop." Written by Mick Jagger and Keith Richards. Published by Promopub B.V. "Thief in the Night." Written by Mick Jagger, Keith Richards and Pierre de Beauport. Published by Promopub B.V. and Pubpromo Music.

Book design by Fearn Cutler de Vicq
Printed in Great Britain by CPI Mackays, Chatham ME5 8TD

The Orion Publishing Group's policy is to use papers that are natural, renewable and recyclable and made from wood grown in sustainable forests. The logging and manufacturing processes are expected to conform to environmental regulations of the country of origin.

Weidenfeld & Nicolson
Orion Publishing Group Ltd, Orion House,
5 Upper Saint Martin's Lane, London WC2H 9EA
An Hachette UK Company
www.orionbooks.co.uk

*For Patricia*

---

# Photographs

# LIFE

# Chapter One

In which I am pulled over by police officers in Arkansas during our
1975 US tour and a standoff ensues.

W hy did we stop at the 4-Dice Restaurant in Fordyce,
Arkansas, for lunch on Independence Day weekend? On
any day? Despite everything I knew from ten years of driving through
the Bible Belt. Tiny town of Fordyce. Rolling Stones on the police
menu across the United States. Every copper wanted to bust us by any
means available, to get promoted and patriotically rid America of
these little fairy Englishmen. It was 1975, a time of brutality and confrontation. Open season on the Stones had been declared since our last
tour, the tour of '72, known as the STP. The State Department had
noted riots (true), civil disobedience (also true), illicit sex (whatever
that is), and violence across the United States. All the fault of us, mere
minstrels. We had been inciting youth to rebellion, we were corrupt-
ing America, and they had ruled never to let us travel in the United
States again. It had become, in the time of Nixon, a serious political
matter. He had personally deployed his dogs and dirty tricks against
John Lennon, who he thought might cost him an election. We, in
turn, they told our lawyer officially, were the most dangerous rock-
and-roll band in the world.

In previous days our great lawyer Bill Carter had single-handedly slipped us out of major confrontations devised and sprung by the police forces of Memphis and San Antonio. And now Fordyce, small town of 4,837 whose school emblem was some weird red bug, might be the one to take the prize. Carter had warned us not to drive through Arkansas at all, and certainly never to stray from the interstate. He pointed out that the state of Arkansas had recently tried to draw up legislation to outlaw rock and roll. (Love to see the wording of the statute — "Where there be loudly and insistently four beats to the bar...") And here we were driving back roads in a brand-new yellow Chevrolet Impala. In the whole of the United States there was perhaps no sillier place to stop with a car loaded with drugs — a conservative, redneck southern community not happy to welcome different-looking strangers.

In the car with me were Ronnie Wood; Freddie Sessler, an incredible character, my friend and almost a father to me who will have many parts in this story; and Jim Callaghan, the head of our security for many years. We were driving the four hundred miles from Memphis to Dallas, where we had our next gig the following day at the Cotton Bowl. Jim Dickinson, the southern boy who played piano on "Wild Horses," had told us that the Texarkana landscape was worth the car ride. And we were planed out. We'd had a scary flight from Washington to Memphis, dropping suddenly many thousands of feet, with much sobbing and screaming, the photographer Annie Leibovitz hitting her head on the roof and the passengers kissing the tarmac when we landed. I was seen going to the back of the plane and consuming substances with more than usual dedication as we tossed about the skies, not wanting to waste. A bad one, in Bobby Sherman's old plane, the *Starship*.

So we drove and Ronnie and I had been particularly stupid. We pulled into this roadhouse called the 4-Dice where we sat down and ordered and then Ronnie and I went to the john. You know, just start me up. We got high. We didn't fancy the clientele out there, or the food, and so we hung in the john, laughing and carrying on. We sat there for forty minutes. And you don't do that down there. Not then. That's what excited and exacerbated the situation. And the staff called the cops. As we pulled out, there was a black car parked on the side, no number plate, and the minute we took off, twenty yards down the road, we get sirens and the little blinking light and there they are with shotguns in our faces.

I had a denim cap with all these pockets in it that were filled with dope. Everything was filled with dope. In the car doors themselves, all you had to do was pop the panels, and there were plastic bags full of coke and grass, peyote and mescaline. Oh my God, how are we going to get out of this? It was the worst time to get busted. It was a miracle we had been allowed into the States at all for this tour. Our visas hung on a thread of conditions, as every police force in the big cities also knew, and had been fixed by Bill Carter with very hard long-distance footwork with the State Department and the Immigration Service over the previous two years. It was obviously condition zero that we weren't arrested for possession of narcotics, and Carter was responsible for guaranteeing this.

I wasn't taking the heavy shit at the time; I'd cleaned up for the tour. And I could have just put all of that stuff on the plane. To this day I cannot understand why I bothered to carry all that crap around and take that chance. People had given me all this gear in Memphis and I was loath to give it away, but I still could have put it on the plane and driven clean. Why did I load the car like some pretend dealer? Maybe I woke up too late for the plane. I know I spent a long time opening up the panels, stashing this shit. But peyote is not particularly my line of substances anyway.

In the cap's pockets there's hash, Tuinals, some coke. I greet the police with a flourish of the cap and throw pills and hash into the bushes. "Hello, Officer" (flourish). "Oh! Have I broken some local law? Pray forgive me. I'm English. Was I driving on the wrong side of the road?" And you've already got them on the back foot. And you've got rid of your crap. But only some of it. They saw a hunting knife lying on the seat and would later decide to take that as evidence of a "concealed weapon," the lying bastards. And then they made us follow them to a car park somewhere beneath city hall. As we drove they watched us, surely, throwing more of our shit into the road.

They didn't do a search immediately when we got to the garage. They said to Ronnie, "OK, you go into the car and bring out your stuff." Ronnie had a little handbag or something in the car, but at the same time, he tipped all the crap he had into a Kleenex box. And as he got out, he said to me, "It's under the driver's seat." And when I go in, I didn't have anything in the car to get, all I've got to do is pretend that I have something and take care of this box. But I didn't know what the fuck to do with it, so basically I just scrunched it up a bit and I put it under the backseat. And I walked out and said well I don't have anything. The fact that they didn't tear the car apart is beyond me.

By now they know who they've got ("Weeeell, looky here, we got some live ones"). But then they suddenly didn't seem to know what to do with these international stars stuck in their custody. Now they had to draft in forces from all over the state. Nor did they seem to know what to charge us with. They also knew we were trying to locate Bill Carter, and this must have intimidated them because this was Bill Carter's front lawn. He had grown up in the nearby town of Rector and he knew every state law enforcement officer, every sheriff, every prosecuting attorney, all the political leaders. They may have started to regret that they'd tipped off the wire services to their catch. The national news media were gathering outside the courthouse — one Dallas TV station had hired a Learjet to get pole position on the story. It was Saturday afternoon and they were making calls to Little Rock to get advice from state officials. So instead of locking us up and having that image broadcast to the world, they kept us in loose "protective custody" in the police chief's office, which meant we could walk about a bit. Where was Carter? Offices shut during the holiday, no cell phones then. It was taking some time to locate him.

In the meantime we're trying to get rid of all this stuff. We're festooned. In the '70s I was flying high as a kite on pure, pure Merck cocaine, the fluffy pharmaceutical blow. Freddie Sessler and I went to the john, we weren't even escorted down there. "Jesuschrist," the phrase that preceded everything with Freddie, "I'm loaded." He's got bottles full of Tuinal. And he's so nervous about flushing them down that he loses the bottle and all the fucking turquoise-and-red pills are rolling everywhere and meanwhile he's trying to flush down coke. I popped the hash down and the weed, flushed it, the fucking thing won't flush, there's too much weed, I'm flushing and flushing and then suddenly these pills come rolling there under the cubicle. And I'm trying to pick 'em up and fling 'em in and everything, but I can't because there's another cubicle in between the one Freddie's in and the one I'm in, so there's fifty pills lying stranded on the floor in the middle cubicle. "Jesuschrist, Keith." "Keep your cool, Freddie, I've got all the ones out of mine, have you got all the ones out of yours?" "I think so, I think so." "OK, let's go in the middle one and get rid of them." It was just raining with fucking shit. It was unbelievable, every pocket or place you looked...I never knew I had that much coke in my life!

The sleeper was Freddie's briefcase, which was in the trunk of the car, as yet unopened and we knew he had cocaine in there. They couldn't fail to find it. Freddie and I decided we should disown Freddie strategically for that afternoon and say he was a hitchhiker, but one to whom we were happy to extend the powers of our legal adviser, if need be, when he finally appeared on the scene.

Where was Carter? It took some time to marshal our forces, while the population of Fordyce was swelling to riot-size proportions. People from Mississippi, Texas, Tennessee—all coming in to watch the fun. Nothing would happen until Carter was located, and he was on the tour, he wasn't far away, just having a deserved day off. So there was time to reflect how I had dropped my guard and forgotten the rules. Don't break the law and get pulled over. Cops everywhere, and certainly in the South, have a whole range of quasi-legal tricks to bust you if they feel like it. And they could put you away for ninety days then, no problem. That's why Carter told us to stick to the interstate. The Bible Belt was a lot tighter in those days.

We did many miles on the ground in those early tours. Roadhouses were always an interesting gamble. And you better get ready for it—and be ready for it. You try going to a truck stop in 1964 or '65 or '66 down south or in Texas. It felt much more dangerous than anything in the city. You'd walk in and there's the good ol' boys and slowly you realize that you're not going to have a very comfortable meal in there, with these truckers with crew cuts and tattoos. You nervously peck away—"Oh, I'll have that to go, please." They'd call us girls because of the long hair. "How you doing, girls? Dance with me?" Hair... the little things that you wouldn't think about that changed whole cultures. The way they reacted to our looks in certain parts of London then was not much different from the way they reacted to us in the South. "Hello, darling," and all that shit.

When you look back it was relentless confrontation, but you're not thinking about it at the time. First off these were all new experiences and you were really not aware of the effects it might or might not have on you. You were gradually growing into it. I just found in those situations that if they saw the guitars and knew you were musicians, then suddenly it was totally OK. Better take a guitar into a truck stop. "Can you pick that thing, son?" Sometimes we'd actually do it, pull out the guitars, sing for our supper.

But then all you had to do was cross the tracks and you'd get a real education. If we were playing with black musicians, they'd look after us. It was "Hey, you wanna get laid tonight? She'll love you. She ain't seen anything like you before." You got welcomed, you got fed and you got laid. The white side of town was dead, but it was rockin' across the tracks. Long as you knew cats, you was cool. An incredible education.

Sometimes we'd do two or three shows a day. They wouldn't be long shows; you'd be doing twenty minutes, half an hour three times a day, waiting for the rotation because these were mostly revue shows, black acts, amateurs, local white hits, whatever, and if you went down south, it was just endless. Towns and states just went by. It's called white-line fever. If you're awake you stare at the white lines down the middle of the road, and every now and again somebody says "I need a crap" or "I'm hungry." Then you walked into these brief bits of theater behind the road. These are minor roads in the Carolinas, Mississippi and stuff. You get out dying for a leak, you see "Men's" and some black bloke is standing there saying "Coloreds only," and you think "I'm being discriminated against!" You'd drive by these little juke joints and there's this incredible music pumping out, and steam coming out the window.

"Hey, let's pull over here."

"Could be dangerous."

"No, come on, listen to that shit!"

And there'd be a band, a trio playing, big black fuckers and some bitches dancing around with dollar bills in their thongs. And then you'd walk in and for a moment there's almost a chill, because you're the first white people they've seen in there, and they know that the energy's too great for a few white blokes to really make that much difference. Especially as we don't look like locals. And they get very intrigued and we get really into being there. But then we got to get back on the road. Oh shit, I could've stayed here for days. You've got to pull out again, lovely black ladies squeezing you between their huge tits. You walk out and there's sweat all over you and perfume, and we all get in the car, smelling good, and the music drifts off in the background. I think some of us had died and gone to heaven, because a year before we were plugging London clubs, and we're doing all right, but actually in the next year, we're somewhere we thought we'd never be. We were in Mississippi. We'd been playing this music, and it had all been very respectful, but then we were actually there sniffing it. You want to be a blues player, the next minute you fucking well are and you're stuck right amongst them, and there's Muddy Waters standing next to you. It happens so fast that you really can't register all of the impressions that are coming at you. It comes later on, the flash-backs, because it's all so much. It's one thing to play a Muddy Waters song. It's another thing to play with him.

Bill Carter was finally tracked down to Little Rock, where he was having a barbecue at the house of a friend of his who happened to be a judge, a very useful coincidence. He would hire a plane and be there in a couple of hours, bringing the judge with him. Carter's judge friend knew the state policeman who was going to search the car; told him that he thought the police had no right to do it and warned him to hold off a search until he got there. Everything froze for two more hours.

Bill Carter had grown up working on the local political campaigns from when he was in college, so he knew almost everybody of impor-tance in the state. And people he had worked for in Arkansas had now become some of the most powerful Democrats in Washington. His mentor was Wilbur Mills, from Kensett, chairman of the House Ways and Means Committee, second most powerful man after the president. Carter came from a poor background, joined the Air Force at the time of Korea, paid for law studies with his GI money until it ran out, when he joined the Secret Service and ended up guarding Kennedy. He wasn't in Dallas that day — he was on a training course — but he'd been everywhere with Kennedy, planned his trips, and knew all the key officials in every state Kennedy had visited. He was close to the center. After Kennedy's death he was an investigator on the Warren Commission and then started his own law practice in Little Rock, becoming a kind of people's lawyer. He had a lot of balls. He was passionate about the rule of law, the correct way of doing things, the Constitution — and he taught police seminars on it. He'd gone into the defense attorney business he told me because he'd got fed up with policemen routinely abusing their power and bending the law, which meant almost all of them he encountered on tour with the Rolling Stones, in almost every city. Carter was our natural ally.

His old contacts in Washington had been his ace card when we were refused visas to tour in the United States in 1973. What Carter found when he first went to Washington on our behalf late that year was that the Nixon dictum prevailed and ran through the bureaucracy down to the lowest level. He was told officially that the Stones would never tour in the United States again. Apart from our being the most dangerous rock-and-roll band in the world, inciting riots, purveying gross misconduct and contempt for the law, there was widespread anger that Mick had appeared on stage dressed as Uncle Sam, wearing the Stars and Stripes. That by itself was enough to refuse him entry. It was bunting! You had to guard yourself against being attacked from that area. Brian Jones got pulled in because he picked up an American flag that was lying around backstage in the mid-'6os in Syracuse, New York, I think it was. He put it over his shoulder, but a corner of it touched the ground. This was after the show and we were making our way back and the police escort barged us all into an office and started screaming, "Dragging the flag on the ground. You're demeaning my nation, an act of sedition."

Then there was my record — no getting away from it. It was also widely known — what else did the press write about me? — that I had a heroin addiction. I'd just had a conviction in the UK for possession of drugs, in October 1973, and I had been convicted of possession in France in 1972. Watergate was heating up when Carter began his campaign — some of Nixon's henchmen had been jailed and Nixon was soon to fall along with Haldeman, Mitchell and the rest — some of whom had been involved personally with the FBI in the underhanded campaign against John Lennon.

Carter's advantage at the immigration department was that he was one of the boys, he came from law enforcement, he had respect for having been with Kennedy. He did an "I know how you boys feel" and just said he wanted a hearing because he didn't think we were being treated fairly. He worked his way in; many months of slogging. He paid attention particularly to the lower-level staff, who he knew could obstruct things on technicalities. I underwent medical tests to prove that I was drug free, from the same doctor in Paris who had given me many a clean bill of health. Then Nixon resigned. And then Carter asked the top official to meet Mick and judge for himself, and of course Mick puts on his suit and charms the pants off him. Mick is really the most versatile bloke. Why I love him. He can hold a philosophical discussion with Sartre in his native tongue. Mick's very good with the locals. Carter told me he applied for the visas not in New York or Washington but in Memphis, where it was quieter. The result was an astonishing turnaround. Waivers and visas were suddenly issued on one condition: that Bill Carter toured with the Stones and would personally assure the government that riots would be prevented and that there would be no illegal activities on the tour. (They required a doctor to accompany us — an almost fictional character who appears later in the narrative, who became a tour victim, sampling the medication and running off with a groupie.)

Carter had reassured them by offering to run the tour Secret Service–style, alongside the police. His other contacts also meant that he would get a tip-off if the police were planning a bust. And that's what saved our asses on many occasions.

Things had hardened up since the 1972 tour, with all the demonstrations and antiwar marches and the Nixon period. The first evidence of this was in San Antonio on June 3. This was the tour of the giant inflatable cock. It came rising up from the stage as Mick sang "Starfucker." It was great was the cock, though we paid for it later in Mick's wanting props at every tour after that, to cover his insecurities. There was a huge business of getting elephants on stage in Memphis until they ended up crashing through ramps and shitting all over the stage in rehearsals and were abandoned. We never had a problem with the cock in our opening shows at Baton Rouge. But the cock was a lure to the coppers who had given up trying to bust us in the hotel or while we were traveling or in the dressing room. The only place they could get us was on stage. They threatened to arrest Mick if the cock rose that night, and there was a mighty standoff. Carter warned them that the kids would burn down the arena. He'd taken the temperature and realized the kids weren't going to stand for it. In the end Mick decided to defer to the sentiments of the authorities, and it didn't erect itself in San Antonio. In Memphis when they threatened to arrest Mick for singing the lyrics "Starfucker, starfucker," Carter stopped them in their tracks by producing a playlist from the local radio station that showed they'd been playing it on the air without any protest for two years. What Carter saw and was determined to fight every inch of the way was that every time the police moved, in every city, they violated the law, acted illegally, tried to bust in without warrants, made searches without probable cause.

So there was some form on the books already by the time Carter finally got to Fordyce, with the judge under his arm. A great press corps was established in town; roadblocks had been erected to stop more people coming in. What the police wanted to do was to open the trunk, where they were sure they would find drugs. First they charged me with reckless driving because my tires had squealed and kicked up gravel as I left the restaurant car park. Twenty yards of reckless driving. Charge two: I had a "concealed weapon," the hunting knife. But to open the trunk legally they needed to show "probable cause," meaning there had to be some evidence or reasonable suspicion that a crime had been committed. Otherwise the search is illegal and even if they find the stuff the case will be thrown out. They could have opened the trunk if they'd seen contraband when they looked through the car window, but they hadn't seen anything. This "probable cause" business was what generated the shouting matches that frequently erupted now between the various officials as the afternoon wore on. First off, Carter made it clear that he saw a trumped-up charge. To invent a probable cause, the cop who stopped me said that he smelled marijuana smoke coming through the windows as we left the car park and this was their cue to open the trunk. "They must think I fell off a watermelon truck," Carter told us. The cops were trying to say that in the minute between leaving the restaurant and driving out of the car park there was time to light up a spliff and fill the car with enough smoke that it could be smelled many yards away. This was why they had arrested us, they said. That alone destroyed the credibility of the police evidence. Carter discussed all this with an already enraged chief of police, whose town was under siege, but who knew he could stop our sold-out concert the following night at the Cotton Bowl in Dallas by keeping us in Fordyce. In Chief Bill Gober, Carter saw and we saw the archetype redneck cop, the Bible Belt version of my friends from Chelsea police station, always prepared to bend the law and abuse their powers. Gober was a man personally enraged by the Rolling Stones — their dress, their hair, what they stood for, their music and above all their challenge to authority, as he saw it. Disobedience. Even Elvis said "Yes, sir." Not these long-haired punks. So Gober went ahead and opened the trunk, warned by Carter that he would challenge him all the way to the Supreme Court. And when the trunk was opened that was the real creamer. It was legs-in-the-air laughter.

When you crossed the river from Tennessee, then mostly a dry state, into West Memphis, which is in Arkansas, there were liquor stores selling what was basically moonshine with brown paper labels. Ronnie and I had gone berserk in one of them, buying every bizarre bottle of bourbon with a great label, Flying Cock, Fighting Cock, the Grey Major, little hip flasks with all of these exotic handwritten labels on them. We had sixty-odd in the trunk. So now we were suddenly suspected of being bootleggers. "No, we bought them, we paid for them." So I think all of that booze confused them. This is the '70s and boozers are not dopeheads, in those days there was that separation. "At least they're men and drink whiskey." Then they found Freddie's briefcase, which was locked, and he told them he'd forgotten the combination. So they smacked it open and there, sure enough, were two small containers of pharmaceutical cocaine. Gober thought he had us, or at least he had Freddie, cold.

It took some time to find the judge, now late in the evening, and when he arrived he'd been out on the golf course all day, drinking, and by this time he was flying.

Now we have total comedy, absurdity, Keystone Kops as the judge takes to his bench and the various lawyers and cops try to get him to follow their versions of the law. What Gober wanted to do was to get the judge to rule that the search and the finding of the coke were legal and that all of us would be detained on felony charges—i.e., put in the slammer. On this little point of law, arguably, hung the future of the Rolling Stones, in America at least.

What then happened is pretty much as follows, from what I overheard and from Bill Carter's later testimony. And this is the quickest way to tell it, with apologies to Perry Mason.

**The Cast:**
  Bill Gober. Police Chief. Vindictive, enraged.
  Judge Wynne. Presiding judge in Fordyce. Very drunk.
  Frank Wynne. Prosecuting attorney. The judge's brother.
  Bill Carter. Well-known, aggressive criminal lawyer, representing the Rolling Stones. Native of Arkansas, from Little Rock.
  Tommy Mays. Prosecuting attorney. Idealistic, fresh out of law school.
  Others present: Judge Fairley. Brought along by Carter to witness fair play and to keep him out of jail.

**Outside Courthouse:** Two thousand Rolling Stones fans who are pressed against barricades outside the town hall, chanting "Free Keith. Free Keith."

**Inside Courtroom:**
  **Judge:** Now, I think what we are judging here is a felony. A felony, gennnmen. I will take summmissions. Mr. Attorney?
  **Young Prosecuting Attorney:** Your Honor, there is a problem here about evidence.

**Judge:** Y'all have to excuse me a minute. I'll recess.

[Perplexity in court. Proceeding held up for ten minutes. Judge returns. His mission was to cross the road and buy a pint bottle of bourbon before the store closed at ten p.m. The bottle is now in his sock.]

**Carter** [on telephone to Frank Wynne, the judge's brother]: Frank, where are you? You'd better come up. Tom's intoxicated. Yeah. OK. OK.

**Judge:** Proceed, Mr. . . . ah . . . proceed.

**Young Prosecuting Attorney:** I don't think we can legally do this, Your Honor. We don't have justification to hold them. I think we have to let them go.

**Police Chief** [to judge, yelling]: Damn we do. You gonna let these bastards go? You know I'm gonna place you under arrest, Judge. You damn right I am. You are intoxicated. You are publicly drunk. You are not fit to sit on that bench. You are causing a disgrace to our community. [He tries to grab him.]

**Judge** [yelling]: You sonofabitch. Gerraway from me. You threaten me, I'm gonna have your ass outta . . . [A scuffle.]

**Carter** [moving to separate them]: Whoa. Now, boys, boys. Let's stop *squabbling*. Let's keep *talking*. This is no time to get the liver out and put the knives in ha ha . . . We got TV, the world's press outside. Won't look good. You know what the governor's going to say about this. Let's proceed with the business. I think we can reach some agreement here.

**Courtroom Official:** Excuse me, Judge. We have the BBC on live news from London. They want you now.

**Judge:** Oh yeah. 'Scuse me a minute, boys. Be right back. [He takes a nip from the bottle in his sock.]

**Police Chief** [still yelling]: Goddamn circus. Damn you, Carter, these boys have committed a felony. We found cocaine in that damn car. What more do you want? I'm gonna bust their asses. They gonna play by our rules down here and I'm gonna hit 'em where it hurts.

How much they payin' you, Hoover boy? Unless I get a ruling that the search was legal, I'm gonna arrest the judge for public drunk.

**Judge** [v/o to BBC]: Oh yeah, I was over there in England in World War Two. Bomber pilot, 385th Bomb Group. Station Great Ashfield. I had a helluva time over there.... Oh, I love England. Played golf. Some of the great courses I played on. You got some great ones there.... Wennnworth? Yeah. Now to inform y'all, we're gonna hold a press conference with the boys and explain some of the proceedings here, how the Rolling Stones came to be in our town here an' all.

**Police Chief:** I got 'em here and I'm holding 'em. I want these limeys, these little fairies. Who do they think they are?

**Carter:** You want to start a riot? You seen outside? You wave one pair of handcuffs and you will lose control of this crowd. This is the Rolling Stones, for Christ sakes.

**Police Chief:** And your little boys will go behind bars.

**Judge** [returned from interview]: What's that?

**Judge's Brother** [taking him aside]: Tom, we need to confer. There is no legal cause to hold them. We will have all hell to pay if we don't follow the law here.

**Judge:** I know it. Sure thing. Yes. Yes. Mr. Carrrer. You will all approach the bench.

The fire had gone out of all except Chief Gober. The search had revealed nothing that they could legally use. There was nothing to charge us with. The cocaine belonged to Freddie the hitchhiker and it had been illegally discovered. The state police were mostly now on Carter's side. With much conferring and words in the ear, Carter and the other lawyers made a deal with the judge. Very simple. The judge would like to keep the hunting knife and drop the charge on that — it hangs in the courtroom to this day. He would reduce the reckless driving to a misdemeanor, nothing more than a parking ticket for which I would pay $162.50. With the $50,000 in cash that Carter had brought down with him, he paid a bond of $5,000 for Freddie and the cocaine, and it was agreed that Carter would file to have it dismissed on legal grounds later — so Freddie was free to go too. But there was one last condition. We had to give a press conference before we went and be photographed with our arms around the judge. Ronnie and I conducted our press conference from the bench. I was wearing a fireman's hat by this time and I was filmed pounding the gavel and announcing to the press, "Case closed." Phew!

It was a classic outcome for the Stones. The choice always was a tricky one for the authorities who arrested us. Do you want to lock them up, or have your photograph taken with them and give them a motorcade to see them on their way? There's votes either way. In Fordyce, by the skin of our teeth, we got the motorcade. The state police had to escort us through the crowds to the airport at around two in the morning, where our plane, well stocked with Jack Daniel's, was revved up and waiting.

In 2006, the political ambitions of Governor Huckabee of Arkansas, who was going to stand in the primaries as a contender for the Republican presidential nomination, extended to granting me a pardon for my misdemeanor of thirty years previous. Governor Huckabee also thinks of himself as a guitar player. I think he even has a band. In fact there was nothing to pardon. There was no crime on the slate in Fordyce, but that didn't matter, I got pardoned anyway. But what the hell happened to that car? We left it in this garage loaded with dope. I'd like to know what happened to that stuff. Maybe they never took the panels off. Maybe someone's still driving it around, still filled with shit.

# Chapter Two

---

Growing up an only child on the Dartford marshes. Camping holidays in Dorset with my parents, Bert and Doris. Adventures with my grandfather Gus and Mr. Thompson Wooft. Gus teaches me my first guitar lick. I learn to take beatings at school and later vanquish the Dartford Tech bully. Doris trains my ears with Django Reinhardt and I discover Elvis via Radio Luxembourg. I morph from choirboy to school rebel and get expelled.

For many years I slept, on average, twice a week. This means that I have been conscious for at least three lifetimes. And before those lifetimes there was my childhood, which I ground out east of London in Dartford, along the Thames, where I was born. December 18, 1943. According to my mother, Doris, that happened during an air raid. I can't argue. All four lips are sealed. But the first flash of memory I have is of lying on the grass in our backyard, pointing at the droning airplane in the blue sky above our heads, and Doris saying, "Spitfire." The war was over by then, but where I grew up you'd turn a corner and see horizon, wasteland, weeds, maybe one or two of those odd Hitchcock-looking houses that somehow miraculously survived. Our street took a near hit from a doodlebug, but we weren't there. Doris said it bounced along the curbstones and killed everyone on either side of our house. A brick or two landed in my cot. That was evidence that Hitler was on my trail. Then he went to plan B. After that, my mum thought Dartford was a bit dangerous, bless her.

Doris and my father, Bert, had moved to Morland Avenue in Dartford from Walthamstow to be near my aunt Lil, Bert's sister, while Bert was called up. Lil's husband was a milkman, who'd been moved there on his new round. Then, when the bomb hit that end of Morland Avenue, our house wasn't considered safe and we moved in with Lil. When we came out of the shelter after a raid one day, Lil's roof was on fire, Doris told me. But that's where our families were all stuck together, after the war, in Morland Avenue. The house that we used to live in was still there when I first remember the street, but about a third of the street was just a crater, grass and flowers. That was our playground. I was born in the Livingstone Hospital, to the sound of the "all clear"—another of Doris's versions. I'll have to believe Doris on that one. I wasn't really counting from day one.

My mother had thought she was going somewhere safe, moving to Dartford from Walthamstow. So she had moved us to the Darent Valley. Bomb Alley! It contained the biggest arm of Vickers-Armstrongs, which was pretty much a bull's-eye, and the Burroughs Wellcome chemical firm. And on top of that it was around Dartford where German bombers would get cold feet and just drop their bombs and turn around. "Too heavy round here." *BOOM.* It's a miracle we didn't get it. The sound of a siren still makes the hair on the back of my neck curl, and that must be from being put in the shelter with Mum and the family. When the sound of that siren goes off, it's automatic, an instinctive reaction. I watch many war movies and documentaries, so I hear it all the time, but it always does the trick.

My earliest memories are the standard postwar memories in London. Landscapes of rubble, half a street's disappeared. Some of it stayed like that for ten years. The main effect of the war on me was just that phrase, "Before the War." Because you'd hear grown-ups talking about it. "Oh, it wasn't like this before the war." Otherwise I wasn't particularly affected. I suppose no sugar, no sweets and candies, was a good thing, but I wasn't happy about it. I've always had trouble scoring. Lower East Side or the sweet shop in East Wittering, near my home in West Sussex. That's the closest I get nowadays to visiting the dealer — the old Candies sweet shop. I drove over there at 8:30 one morning not long ago with my mate Alan Clayton, singer of the Dirty Strangers. We'd been up all night and we'd got the sugar craving. We had to wait outside for half an hour until it opened. We bought Candy Twirls and Bull's-Eyes and Licorice & Blackcurrant. We weren't going to lower ourselves and score at the supermarket, were we?

The fact that I couldn't buy a bag of sweets until 1954 says a lot about the upheavals and changes that last for so many years after a war. The war had been over for nine years before I could actually, if I had the money, go and say, "I'll have a bag of *them*" — toffees and Aniseed Twists. Otherwise it was "You got your ration stamp book?" The sound of those stamps stamping. Your ration was your ration. One little brown paper bag — a tiny one — a *week*.

Bert and Doris had met working in the same factory in Edmonton — Bert a printer and Doris working in the office — and they had started out together living at Walthamstow. They had done a lot of cycling and camping during their courtship before the war. It brought them together. They bought a tandem and used to go riding into Essex and camping with their friends. So when I came along, as soon as they could, they used to take me on the back of their tandem. It must have been very soon after the war, or maybe even during the war. I can imagine them driving through an air raid, plowing ahead. Bert in front, Mum behind and me on the back, on the baby seat, mercilessly exposed to the sun's rays, throwing up from sunstroke. It's been the story of my life ever since — on the road again.

In the early part of the war — before my arrival — Doris drove a van for the Co-op bakers, even though she told them she couldn't drive. Luckily, in those days there were almost no cars on the road. She drove the van into a wall when she was using it illegally to visit a friend, and they still didn't fire her. She also drove a horse and cart for bread deliveries closer to the Co-op, to save the wartime fuel. Doris was in charge of cake distribution for a big area. Half a dozen cakes for three hundred people. And she would be the decider of who would get them. "Can I have a cake next week?" "Well, you had one last week, didn't you?" A heroic war. Bert was in a protected job, in valve manufacturing, until D-day. He was a dispatch rider in Normandy just after the invasion, and got blown up in a mortar attack, his mates killed around him. He was the only survivor of that particular little foray, and it left a very nasty gash, a livid scar all the way up his left thigh. I always wanted to get one when I grew up. I'd say, "Dad, what's that?" And he'd say, "It got me out the war, son." It left him with nightmares for the rest of his life. My son Marlon lived a lot with Bert in America for some years, while Marlon was growing up, and they used to go camping together. Marlon says Bert would wake up in the middle of the night, shouting, "Look out, Charlie, here it comes. We're all goners! We're all goners! Fuck this shit."

Everyone from Dartford is a thief. It runs in the blood. The old rhyme commemorates the unchanging character of the place: "Sutton for mutton, Kirkby for beef, South Darne for gingerbread, Dartford for a thief." Dartford's big money used to come from sticking up the stagecoach from Dover to London along the old Roman road, Watling Street. East Hill is very steep. Then suddenly you're in the valley over the River Darent. It's only a minor stream, but then you've got the short High Street and you've got to go up West Hill, where the horses would drag. Whichever way you're coming, it's the perfect ambush point. The drivers didn't stop and argue — part of the fare would be the Dartford fine, to keep the journey going smoothly. They'd just toss out a bag of coins. Because if you didn't pay going down East Hill, they'd signal ahead. One gunshot — he didn't pay — and they'd stop you at West Hill. So it's a double stickup. You can't get out of it. That notion had pretty much stopped when trains and cars took over, so probably by the middle of the nineteenth century they're looking for something else to do, some way of carrying on the tradition. And Dartford has developed an incredible criminal network — you could ask some members of my extended family. It goes with life. There's always something fallen off the back of a lorry. You don't ask. If somebody's just got a nice pair of diamond somethings, you never ask, "Where did they come from?"

For over a year, when I was nine or ten, I was waylaid, Dartford-style, almost every day on my way home from school. I know what it is like to be a coward. I will *never* go back there. As easy as it is to turn tail, I took the beatings. I told my mum that I had fallen off my bike again. To which she replied, "Stay off your bike, son." Sooner or later we all get beaten. Rather sooner. One half are losers, the other half bullies. It had a powerful effect on me and taught me some lessons for when I grew big enough to use them. Mostly to know how to employ that thing little fuckers have, which is called speed. Which is usually "run away." But you get sick of running away. It was the old Dartford stickup. They have the Dartford tunnel now with tollbooths, which is where all the traffic from Dover to London still has to go. It's legal to take the money and the bullies have uniforms. You pay, one way or another.

My backyard was the Dartford marshes, a no-man's-land that stretches three miles on either side along the Thames. A frightening place and fascinating at the same time, but desolate. When I was growing up, as kids we'd go down to the riverbank, a good half an hour ride on a bike. Essex County was on the other side of the river, the northern shore, and it might as well have been France. You could see the smoke of Dagenham, the Ford plant, and on our side the Gravesend cement plant. They didn't call it Gravesend for nothing. Everything unwanted by anyone else had been dumped in Dartford since the late nineteenth century—isolation and smallpox hospitals, leper colonies, gunpowder factories, lunatic asylums—a nice mixture. Dartford was the main place for smallpox treatment for all of England from the time of the epidemic of the 1880s. The river hospitals overflowed into ships anchored at Long Reach—a grim sight in the photographs, or if you were sailing up the estuary into London. But the lunatic asylums were what Dartford and its environs were famous for—the various projects run by the dreaded Metropolitan

Asylums Board for the mentally unprepared people, or whatever they call it these days. The deficient in brain. The asylums drew a belt around the area, as if somebody had decided, "Right. This is where we're going to put the loonies." There was a massive one, very grim, called Darenth Park, which was a kind of labor camp for backward children until quite recent times. There was Stone House Hospital, whose name had been changed to something more genteel than the City of London Lunatic Asylum, which had Gothic gables and a tower and observation post, Victorian-style—where at least one suspect for Jack the Ripper, Jacob Levy, was imprisoned. Some of the nuthouses were for harder cases than others. When we were twelve or thirteen, Mick Jagger had a summer job at the Bexley nuthouse, the Maypole, as it was called. I think they were a bit more upper-class nutters—they got wheelchairs or something—and Mick used to do the catering, taking round their lunches.

Almost once a week you'd hear sirens going—another loony escaped—and they'd find him in the morning in his little nightshirt, shivering on Dartford Heath. Some of them escaped for quite a while, and you'd see them flitting through the shrubbery. It was a feature of life when I was growing up. You still thought you were at war, because they used the same siren if there was a breakout. You don't realize what a weird place you're growing up in. You'd give people directions: "Go past the loony bin, not the big one, the small one." And they'd look at you as if you were from the loony bin yourself.

The only other thing that was there was the Wells firework factory, just a few little isolated sheds on the marsh. It blew itself up one night in the '50s, and a few guys with it. Spectacular. As I looked out my window, I thought the war had started again. All the factory was making then was your tuppenny banger, your Roman candles and your golden shower. And your jumping jacks. Everybody from around there remembers that—the explosion that blew the windows out for miles around.

One thing you've got is your bike. Me and my mate Dave Gibbs, who lived on Temple Hill, decided it would be cool if we put those little cardboard flappers on the back wheel so it sounded like an engine when the spokes went round. We'd hear "Take that bloody thing away. I'm trying to get some sleep around here," so we used to ride down to the marshes and the woods by the Thames. The woods were very dangerous country. There were buggers in there, hard men who'd scream at you. *"Fuck off."* We took the cardboard flappers out. It was a place of madmen and deserters and tramps. Many of these guys were British Army deserters, a little like the Japanese soldiers who still thought the war was on. Some of them had been living there for five or six years. They'd cobbled together maybe a caravan or some tree house for shelter. Vicious, dirty swine they were too. The first time I got shot was by one of those bastards — a good shot, an air gun pellet on the bum. One of our hangs was a pillbox, an old machine gun post, of which there were many along the tideway. We used to go and pick up the literature, which was always pinups, all crumpled up in the corner.

One day we found a dead tramp in there, huddled up, covered in bluebottles. A dead para-fin. (Paraffin lamp, rhyming slang for tramp.) Filthy magazines lying around. Used rubbers. Flies buzzing. And this para-fin had croaked. He'd been there for days, weeks even. We never reported it. We ran like the fucking Nile.

I remember going from Aunt Lil's to infant school, to West Hill school, screaming my head off. "No way, Mum, no way!" Howling and kicking and refusing and refusing to go, but I did go. They had a way about them, grown-ups. I put up a fight, but I knew it was a full-on moment. Doris felt for me, but not that much. "This is life, boy, something we can't fight." I remember my cousin, who was Aunt Lil's son. Big boy. He was at least fifteen, with a charm that cannot be imagined. He was my hero. He had a check shirt! And he went out when he wanted. I think he was called Reg. Cousin Kay was their daughter. She pissed me off because she had really long legs, could always run faster than me. I came in a valiant second every time. She was older than me, though. We rode my first horse together, bareback. A great old white mare that barely knew what was going on, that had been put out to pasture, if you could call it that round where we lived. I was with a couple of mates and Cousin Kay, and we got on the fence and managed to get on the horse's back, and thank God she's a sweet mare, otherwise if she had taken off I would have gone for a loop. I had no rope.

I hated infant school. I hated all school. Doris said I was so nervous she remembered bringing me home on her back because I couldn't walk, I was trembling so hard. And this was before the stick-ups and the bullying began. What they fed you was awful. I remember at infant school being forced to eat "Gypsy Tart," which revolted me. I just refused it. It was pie with some muck burned into it, marmalade or caramel. Every schoolkid knew this pie and some actually liked it. But it wasn't my idea of a dessert, and they tried to force me to eat it, threatening me with punishment or a fine. It was very Dickensian. I had to write out "I will not refuse food" three hundred times in my infantile hand. After so many times I had it down. "I,I,I,I,I,I,I . . . will,will,will,will . . ."

I was known to have a temper. As if nobody else has one. A temper that was aroused by Gypsy Tart. In retrospect, the British education system, reeling from the war, had not much to work with. The PT master had just come from training commandos and didn't see why he shouldn't treat you the same as them even though you're five or six years old. It was all ex-army blokes. All these guys had been in WWII and some of them were just back from Korea. So you were brought up with this kind of barking authority.

I should have a badge for surviving the early National Service dentists. The appointments were I think two a year—they had school inspections—and my mum had to drag me screaming to them. She'd have to spend some hard-earned money to buy me something afterwards, because every time I went there was sheer hell. No mercy. "Shut up, kid." The red rubber apron, like an Edgar Allan Poe horror. They had those very rickety machines in those days, '49, '50, belt-drive drills, electric-chair straps to hold you down.

The dentist was an ex-army bloke. My teeth got ruined by it. I developed a fear of going to the dentist with, by the mid-'70s, visible consequences — a mouthful of blackened teeth. Gas is expensive, so you'd just get a whiff. And also they got more for an extraction than for a filling. So everything came out. They would just yank it out, with the smallest whiff of gas, and you'd wake up halfway through an extraction; seeing that red rubber hose, that mask, you felt like you were a bomber pilot, except you had no bomber. The red rubber mask and the man looming over you like Laurence Olivier in *Marathon Man*. It was the only time I saw the devil, as I imagined. I was dreaming, and I saw the three-pronged fork and he was laughing away, and I wake up and he's going, "Stop squawking, boy. I've got another twenty to do today." And all I got out of it was a dinky toy, a plastic gun.

After a time the town council gave us a flat over a greengrocer's in a little row of shops in Chastilian Road, two bedrooms and a lounge — still there. Mick lived one street away, in Denver Road. Posh Town, we used to call it — the difference between detached and semidetached houses. It was a five-minute bike ride to Dartford Heath and only two streets away from my next school, the school Mick and I both went to, Wentworth Primary School.

I went back to Dartford to breathe the air not long ago. Nothing much had changed in Chastilian Road. The greengrocer's is now a florist called the Darling Buds of Kent, whose proprietor came out with a framed photograph for me to sign, almost the moment I'd stepped onto the pavement. He behaved as if he was expecting me, the picture ready, as unsurprised as if I came every week, whereas I hadn't been around there for thirty-five years. As I walked into our old house, I knew exactly the number of stairs. For the first time in fifty years I entered the room where I lived in that house, where the florist now lives. Tiny room, exactly the same, and Bert and Doris in the tiny room across a three-foot landing. I lived there from about 1949 to 1952.

Across the street there were the Co-op and the butcher's—that's where the dog bit me. My first dog bite. It was a vicious bugger, tied up outside. Finlays tobacconist was on the opposite corner. The post box was still in the same place, but there used to be a huge hole on Ashen Drive where a bomb dropped, which is now covered over. Mr. Steadman used to live next door. He had a TV and he used to open the curtains to let us kids watch. But my worst memory, the most painful that came back to me, standing in the little back garden, was the day of the rotten tomatoes. I've had some bad things happen, but this is still one of the worst days of my life. The greengrocer used to stack old fruit crates in the back garden, and a mate and I found all these far-gone tomatoes. We just squidged the whole packet up. We started having a rotten-tomato fight and we splashed them every-where, tomatoes all over the place, including all over myself, my mate, the windows, the walls. We were outside, but we were bombing each other. "Take that, swine!" Rotten tomato in your face. And I went inside and my mum scared the shit out of me.

"I've called the man."

"What are you talking about?"

"I've called the man. He's going to take you away, because you're out of control."

And I broke down.

"He's coming here in fifteen minutes. He'll be here any minute now to take you away into the home."

And I shat myself. I was about six or seven.

"Oh, Mum!" I'm on my knees, I'm pleading and begging.

"I've had it up to here with you. I don't want you anymore."

"No, Mum, please..."

"And on top of that, I'm going to tell your dad."

"Oh, *Muuuuuum*."

That was a cruel day. She was relentless. She kept it going for about an hour too. Until I cried myself to sleep and realized eventually that there was no man at all and that she had been putting me on. And I had to figure out why. I mean, a few rotten tomatoes? I guess I needed a lesson: "You don't do that around here." Doris was never strict. It was just "This is the way it is, this is what's going to happen and you're going to do this and do that." But that's the only time she put the fear of God into me.

Not that we ever had the fear of God in our family. There's nobody in my family that ever had anything to do with organized religion. None of them. I had a grandfather who was a red-blooded socialist, as was my grandmother. And the church, organized religion, was something to be avoided. Nobody minded what Christ said, nobody said there wasn't a God or anything like that, but stay away from organizations. Priests would be considered with much suspicion. See a bloke in a black frock, cross the road. Mind out for the Catholics, they're even dodgier. They had no time for it. Thank God, otherwise Sundays would have been even more boring than they were. We never went to church, never even knew where it was.

I went down to Dartford with my wife, Patti, who had never been there, and my daughter Angela, who was our guide, being a native of the place and brought up, like me, by Doris. And while we were standing there in Chastilian Road, out of the next-door shop, a unisex hairdresser's called Hi-Lites that only had room for about three customers, came what seemed like fifteen young female assistants of an age and type I recognized. It would have been nice if it had been there when I was there. Unisex salon. I wonder what the greengrocer would have had to say about that?

In the next minutes or so, the dialogue went along these familiar lines.

**Fan:** Can we have your autograph, please? It's to Anne and all the girls at Hi-Lites. Come into the hairdresser's, have your hair cut. Are you going to Denver Road where Mick lived?

**KR:** That's the next one up, right?

**Fan:** And I want you to sign one to my husband.

**KR:** Oh, you married? Oh, shit.

**Fan:** Why you asking? Come into our salon.... Got to get a piece of paper. My husband's not going to believe this.

**KR:** I'd forgotten what it was like to be mobbed by Dartford girls.

**Older Fan:** These are all too young to appreciate it. We remember you.

**KR:** Well, I'm still going. Whatever you're listening to now, they wouldn't have been there without me. I'm going to have dreams about this place tonight.

**Fan:** Did you ever imagine, in that little room?

**KR:** I imagined everything. I never thought it would happen.

There was something intrinsically Dartford about those girls. They're at ease, they hang together. They're almost like village girls — in the sense that they belong to one small place. Still, they give that feeling of closeness and friendliness. I used to have a few girlfriends in Chastilian Road days, though it was purely platonic at the time. I always remember one gave me a kiss. We were about six or seven. "But keep it dark," she said. I still haven't written that song. Chicks are always miles ahead. Keep it dark! That was the first girlfriend thing, but I was mates with a lot of girls as I grew up. My cousin Kay and I, we were friends for quite a few years. Patti and Angela and I drove past Heather Drive, near the heath. Heather Drive was really upscale. This is where Deborah lived. I got this incredible fixation on her when I was eleven or twelve. I used to stand there looking at her bedroom window, like a thief in the night.

The heath was only a five-minute bike ride away. Dartford's not a big place, and you could go out of it, out of town and out of mind, within a few minutes into that piece of Kentish scrub and woodland, like some medieval grove where one tested one's biking skills. The glory bumps. You used to be able to drive your bike through these hills and deep craters under low trees, zoom about and fall over. What a great name, the glory bumps. I've had many since, but none as big as those. You could hang there all weekend.

In Dartford in those days, and maybe still, you turned one way to the west, and there was the city. But if you went east or south, you got deep country. You were aware you were right at the very edge. In those days, Dartford was a real peripheral suburb. It also had its own character; it still does. It didn't feel part of London. You didn't feel that you were a Londoner. I can't quite remember any civic pride in Dartford when I was growing up. It was somewhere to get out of. I didn't feel any nostalgia when I went back that day, except for one thing — the smell of the heath. That brought back more memories than anything else. I love the air of Sussex, where I live, to death, but there's a certain mixture of stuff on Dartford Heath, a unique smell of gorse and heather that I don't get anywhere else. The glory bumps had gone, or were grown over or weren't as big as I thought they were, but walking through that bracken took me back.

London to me when I grew up was horse shit and coal smoke. For five or six years after the war there was more horse-drawn traffic in London than there was after the First World War. It was a pungent mixture, which I really miss. It was a sort of bed you lay in, sensory-wise. I'm going to try and market it for the older citizens. Remember this? London Pong.

London hasn't changed that much to me except for the smell, and the fact you can now see how beautiful some of the buildings are, like the Natural History Museum, with the grime cleaned off and the blue tiles. Nothing looked like that then. The other thing was that the street belonged to you. I remember later on seeing pictures of

Chichester High Street in the 1900s, and the only things in the street are kids playing ball and a horse and cart coming down the road. You just got out the way for the occasional vehicle.

When I was growing up, it was heavy fog almost all winter, and if you've got two or three miles to walk to get back home, it was the dogs that led you. Suddenly old Dodger would show up with a patch on his eye, and you could basically guide your way home by that. Sometimes the fog was so thick you couldn't see a thing. And old Dodger would take you up and hand you over to some Labrador. Animals were in the street, something that's disappeared. I would have got lost and died without some help from my canine friends.

When I was nine they gave us a council house in Temple Hill, in a wasteland. I was much happier in Chastilian Road. But Doris considered we were very lucky. "We've got a house" and all of that crap. OK, so you drag your arse to the other side of town. There was, of course, a serious housing crisis for a few years after the war. In Dartford many people were living in prefabs in Princes Road. Charlie Watts was still living in a prefab when I first met him in 1962 — a whole section of the population had put down roots in these asbestos and tin-roof buildings, lovingly cared for them. There wasn't much the British government could do after the war except try and clean up the mess, which you were part of. They glorified themselves in the process, of course. They called the streets of this new estate after themselves, the Labour Party elite, past and present — a little hastily in the latter category, maybe, given that they had been in power only six years before they were out again. They saw themselves as heroes of a working-class struggle — one of whose militants and party faithful was my own granddad Ernie Richards, who had, with my grandmother Eliza, more or less created the Walthamstow Labour Party.

The estate had been opened in 1947 by Clement Attlee, the post-war prime minister and Ernie's friend, one of those who had a street named after him. His speech is preserved in the ether. "We want people to have places they will love; places in which they will be happy and where they will form a community and have a social life and a civic life.... Here in Dartford you are setting an example of how this should be done."

"No, it wasn't nice," Doris would say. "It was rough." It's a lot rougher now. Parts of Temple Hill are no-go areas, real youth gang hell. It was still under construction when we moved in. There was a building shed on the corner, no trees, armies of rats. It looked like a moonscape. And even though it was ten minutes from the Dartford that I knew, the old Dartford, it sort of made me feel for a while, at that age, that I'd been transported to some sort of alien territory. I felt like I'd been moved to some other planet for at least a year or so before I could get to know a neighbor. But Mum and Dad loved the council house. I had no choice but to bite my tongue. As a semidetached goes, it was new and well built, but it wasn't ours! I thought we deserved better. And it made me bitter. I thought of us as a noble family in exile. Pretentious! And I sometimes despised my parents for accepting their fate. That was then. I had no concept of what they'd been through.

Mick and I knew each other just because we happened to live very close, just a few doors away, with a bit of schooling thrown in. But then once we moved from near my school to the other side of town, I became "across the tracks." You don't see anybody; you're not there. Mick had moved from Denver Road to Wilmington, a very nice suburb of Dartford, whereas I'm totally across town, across the tracks. The railway literally goes right through the center of town.

Temple Hill — the name was a bit grand. I never saw a temple all the time I was there, but the hill was the only real attraction for a kid. This was one very steep hill. And it's amazing as a kid what you can do with a hill if you're willing to risk life and limb. I remember I used to get my *Buffalo Bill Wild West Annual* and put it on a roller skate, widthwise, and then sit on it and just zoom down Temple Hill. Too bad if anything was in the way — you had no brakes. And at the end there was a road that you had to cross, which meant playing chicken with cars, not that there were many cars. But I can't believe this hair-raising ride. I'd be sitting two inches or less off the ground, and God help the lady with the pram! I used to yell, "Look out! Pull over." Never got stopped for doing it. You got away with things in those days.

I have one deep scar from that period. The flagstones, big heavy ones, were laid out beside the road, loose, not yet bedded in concrete. And of course thinking I was Superman, I just wanted, with a friend, to get one of them out of the way because it was ruining our football game. Memory is fiction, and an alternative fiction of that event is from my friend and playmate Sandra Hull, consulted all these years later. She remembers that I offered gallantly to move the flagstone for her because the gap was too wide for her to leap between them. She also remembers much blood as the flagstone dropped and squashed my finger and I raced to the sink indoors, where it flowed and flowed. And then there were stitches. The result over the years — mustn't exaggerate — may well have affected my guitar playing, because it really flattened out the finger for pick work. It could have something to do with the sound. I've got this extra grip. Also, when I'm finger-picking it gives me a bit more of a claw, because a chunk came out. So it's flat and it's also more pointed, which comes in handy occasionally. And the nail never grew back again properly, it's sort of bent.

It was a long way back and forth to school, and to avoid the steep gradient of Temple Hill, I'd walk round the back, right around the hill. It was called the cinder path and it was level, but it meant walking around the back of the factories, past Burroughs Wellcome and Bowater paper mill, past an evil-smelling creek with all the green and yellow shit bubbling. Every chemical in the world had been poured into this creek, and it's steaming, like hot sulfur springs. I held my breath and walked quicker. It really looked like something out of hell. At the front of the building there was a garden and a beautiful pond with swans floating about, which is where you learned about "more front than Harrods."

I kept a notebook for songs and ideas on the last tour we did, while

I was thinking about these memoirs. There's an entry that reads, "A snapshot of Bert & Doris leapfrogging in the '30s, I found in my gander bag. Tears to the eyes." The pictures actually show them doing a kind of calisthenics — Bert doing handstands on Doris's back, both of them doing cartwheels and tableaux, Bert particularly showing off his physique. Bert and Doris seemed, in those early photographs, to be having a wonderful time together, going camping, going to the sea, having so many friends. He was a real athlete. He was an Eagle Scout too, which is the highest you can get in scouting. He was a boxer, Irish boxer. Very physical, my dad. In that way I think I've inherited that thing of "Oh, come on, what do you mean you're not feeling well?" The body, you take that for granted. Doesn't matter what you do to it, it's supposed to work. Forget about taking care of it. We have that constitution where it's unforgivable for it to break down. I've stuck to it. "Oh, it's just a bullet, just a flesh wound."

Doris and I were close, and Bert was excluded in a way, simply because he wasn't there half the time. Bert was a fucking hardworking man, silly sod, for twenty-odd quid a week, going up to Hammersmith to work for General Electric, where he was a foreman. He knew a lot about valves — the loading and transporting of them. You can say what you like about Bert, he wasn't a man of ambition. I think because he grew up through the Depression, his idea of ambition was getting a job and holding on to it. He got up at 5:00, back home at 7:30, went to bed at 10:30, which gave him about three hours a day with me. He tried to make it up to me at weekends. I'd go to his tennis club with him or he'd take me up the heath and we'd play soccer a bit or we'd work our garden allotment. "Do this, do that." "All right, Dad." "Wheelbarrow, hoe this, weed this." I liked to watch the way things grow and I knew my dad knew what he was on about. "We've got to get these spuds in now." Just the basic stuff. "Nice runner beans this year." He was pretty distant. There wasn't time to be close, but I was quite happy. To me he was a great bloke; he was just me dad.

Being an only child forces you to invent your world. First you're living in a house with two adults, and so certain bits of childhood will go by with you listening almost exclusively to adult conversation. And hearing all these problems about the insurance and the rent, I've got nobody to turn to. But any only child will tell you that. You can't grab hold of a sister or a brother. You go out and make friends, but playtime stops when the sun goes down. And then the other side of that, with no brothers or sisters and no immediate cousins in the area— I've got loads of extended family, but they weren't there—was how to make friends and who to make friends with. It becomes a very important, a vital part of existence when you're that age.

Holidays were particularly intense from that point of view. We'd go to Beesands in Devon, where we used to have a caravan. It was next to a village called Hallsands, which had fallen into the sea, a ruined village, which was very interesting to a young kid. It was really *Five Go Mad in Dorset*. All these dilapidated houses, and half of them you can see under the water. These weird, romantic ruins right next door. Beesands was an old fishing village, right on the beach, where fishing boats were pulled up. To me when I was a kid, it was a great community because you got to know everybody within two or three days. Within four days I'm talking with a deep Devon burr and relishing being a local. I'd meet tourists: "Which way's Kingbridge?" "Ooh, where ye be goin'?" Very Elizabethan turn of phrase, still talking very ancient English.

Or we'd go camping with tents, which is what Bert and Doris had always done. How to light the Primus; how to put the flysheet up, the groundsheet down. I'm with just Mum and Dad, and when I'd get there I'd look to see if there was anybody to hang with. And I'd get a bit wary, if I was the only one...and I'd get a bit jealous sometimes when I saw a family with four brothers and two sisters. But at the same time it makes you grow up. In that you're basically exposed to the adult world unless you create your own. The imagination comes into play then, and also things to do by yourself. Like wanking. It was very intense when I did make friends. Sometimes I'd meet a great bunch of brothers or sisters in some other tent and I'd always be heart-broken when it was over, gone.

Their big thing, my parents, was Saturday and Sunday at the Bexley tennis club. It was an appendix to the Bexley Cricket Club. There was always this feeling at the tennis club, because of Bexley Cricket Club's magnificent and beautiful nineteenth-century pavilion, that you were the poor cousin. You never got invited over to the cricket club. Unless it was pissing with rain, every weekend that was it — straight to the tennis club. I know more about Bexley than I do about Dartford. I would follow on the train after lunch with my cousin Kay and meet my parents there, every weekend. Most of the other people there were definitely on another strata, English class–wise, at that time. They had cars. We went on bikes. My job was to pick up the balls that went over the railway line at the cost of nearly getting electrocuted.

For companionship I kept pets. I had a cat and a mouse. It's hard to believe that's what I had — it may explain a little of what I am. A little white mouse, Gladys. I would bring her to school and have a chat in the French lesson when it got boring. I'd feed her my dinner and lunch, and I'd come home with a pocketful of mouse shit. Mouse shit doesn't matter. It comes out in hardened pellets, there's no pong involved, it's not squidgy or anything like that. You just empty your pockets and out come these pellets. Gladys was true and trusted. She very rarely poked her head out of the pocket and exposed herself to instant death. But Doris had Gladys and my cat knocked off. She killed all my pets when I was a kid. She didn't like animals; she'd threatened to do it and she did it. I put a note on her bedroom door, with a drawing of a cat, that said "Murderer." I never forgave her for that. Doris's reaction was the usual: "Shut up. Don't be so soft. It was pissing all over the place."

Doris's job when I was growing up and almost from the time the machines were invented was washing-machine demonstrator — specifically a Hotpoint specialist — at the Co-op in Dartford High

Street. She was very good at this; she was an artist at demonstrating how they worked. Doris had wanted to be an actress, to be on the stage, to dance. It ran in the family. I'd go in and stand amongst the crowd circled around her, watch her demonstrate how fantastic the new Hotpoint was. She didn't have one herself; it took her ages to get her own. But she could make a real show out of how to load a Hotpoint. They didn't even have running water. You had to fill them and empty them with a bucket. They were new things in those days, and people would say, "I'd love a machine to wash my clothes, but Jesus, it's like rocket science to me." And my mum's job was to say, "No, it's not. It's this easy." And when later on we were living skint and nasty in the peeling refuse bin of Edith Grove, before the Stones took off, we always had clean clothes because Doris would demonstrate them, iron them and send them back with her admirer, Bill, the taxi driver. Send them in the morning, back at night. Doris just needed dirty material. Can we provide, baby!

Years later Charlie Watts would spend day after day in Savile Row with his tailors, just feeling the quality, deciding which buttons to use. I couldn't go there at all. Something to do with my mother, I think. She was always going into drapery stores looking for curtains. And I had no say in it. I'd just be parked on a chair or bench or shelf or something, and I'd watch Mum. She's got what she wanted and they're wrapping it up, and then, oh no! She suddenly turns round and sees something else she wants, pushing the man to the limit. At the cash-and-carry the money went through those tubes in a little canister. I used to sit there watching for hours while my mother decided what she couldn't afford to buy. But what can you say about the first woman in your life? She was Mum. She sorted me out. She fed me. She was forever slicking my hair and straightening my clothes, in public. Humiliation. But it's Mum. I didn't realize until later that she was also my mate. She could make me laugh. There was music all the time, and I do miss her so.

\* \* \*

How my mum and dad got together is a miracle—something so random, the random of opposites, in their backgrounds and personalities. Bert's family were stern, rigid socialists. His father, my grandfather Ernest G. Richards, known locally as Uncle Ernie, was not just a Labour Party stalwart. Ernie was up in arms for the working man, and when he started there was no Socialist movement, there was no Labour Party. Ernie and my grandmother Eliza were married in 1902, at the very beginning of the party—they had two MPs in 1900. And he won that part of London for Keir Hardie, the party's founder. He would hold that fort for Keir come what may, day in, day out, canvassing and recruiting after the First World War. Walthamstow was fertile Labour territory then. It had taken in a big working-class exodus from the East End of London and a new rail commuter population—the political front line. Ernie was staunch in the real meaning of that word. No backing down, no retreat. Walthamstow became a Labour stronghold, a safe enough seat for Clement Attlee, who'd put Churchill out as prime minister in 1945 and who was the MP for Walthamstow in the 1950s. He sent a message when Ernie died, calling him "the salt of the earth." And they sang "The Red Flag" at his funeral, a song they have only just stopped singing at the Labour Party conferences. I'd never taken in the touchiness of the lyrics.

> *Then raise the scarlet standard high,*
> *Within its shade we'll live and die,*
> *Though cowards flinch and traitors sneer,*
> *We'll keep the red flag flying here.*

And Ernie's job? He was a gardener, and he worked for the same food-production firm for thirty-five years. But Eliza, my grandmother, was, if anything, saltier—she was elected a councillor before Ernie, and in 1941 she became the mayor of Walthamstow. Like Ernie she had risen through the political hierarchy. Her origins were Bermondsey working class, and she more or less invented child welfare for

Walthamstow — a real reformer. She must have been a piece of work — she became chairman of the housing committee in a borough that had one of the biggest programs of council house expansion in the country. Doris always complained that Eliza was so upright she wouldn't let her and Bert have a council house when they were first married — wouldn't push them up the list. "I can't give you a house. You're my daughter-in-law." Not just strict but rigid. So it's always intrigued me: the unlikelihood of somebody from that family getting together with this other lot of libertines.

Doris and her six sisters — I come from a matriarchy on both sides of my family — grew up in two bedrooms, one for them and another for my grandparents Gus and Emma, in Islington. That's tight accommodation. One front room that was only used on special days and a kitchen and parlor in the back. That whole family in those rooms and that small kitchen; another family living upstairs.

My grandfather Gus — God bless him — I owe so much of my love of music to him. I write him notes frequently and pin them up. "Thanks, Granddad." Theodore Augustus Dupree, the patriarch of this family, surrounded by women, lived near Seven Sisters Road, with seven daughters, at 13 Crossley Street, N7. And he'd say, "It's not just the seven daughters, with the wife that makes eight." His wife was Emma, my long-suffering grandmother, whose maiden name was Turner, and who was a very good piano player. Emma was really a step above Gus — very ladylike, spoke French. How he got his hands on her I don't know. They met on a Ferris wheel at the agricultural fair in Islington. Gus was a looker, and he always had a gag; he could always laugh. He used that humor, that habit of laughing, to keep everything alive and going in dire times. Many of his generation were like that. Doris certainly inherited his insane sense of humor, as well as his musicality.

We're supposed not to know where Gus came from. But then none of us know where we come from — the pits of hell, maybe. Family rumor is that that elaborate name wasn't his real name. For some weird reason none of us ever bothered to find out, but there it is on the census form: Theodore Dupree, born in 1892, from a large family in Hackney, one of eleven children. His father is listed as "paper hanger," born in Southwark. Dupree is a Huguenot name, and many of those came originally from the Channel Islands — Protestant refugees from France. Gus had left school at thirteen and trained and worked as a pastry cook around Islington and learned to play violin from one of his father's friends in Camden Passage. He was an all-round musician. He had a dance band in the '30s. He played saxophone then, but he claimed he got gassed in the First World War and couldn't blow afterwards. But I don't know. There are so many stories. Gus managed to cover himself in cobwebs and mists. Bert said he was in the catering detachment — from his trade as a pastry cook — and he wasn't in the front line. He was just baking bread. And Bert said to me, "If he got gassed it was in his own oven." But my aunt Marje, who knows everything and still lives as this is written, aged ninety-something, says that Gus was called up in 1916 and was a sniper in WWI. She said that whenever he talked about the war he always had tears in his eyes. Didn't want to kill anybody. He was wounded in the leg and shoulder either at Passchendaele or the Somme. When he couldn't play the saxophone he took up the violin again and the guitar; his wound aggravated his bowing arm, and a tribunal awarded him ten shillings a week for the wounding. Gus was a close friend of Bobby Howes, who was a famous musical star of the 1930s. They were in the war together and they did a double act in the officers' mess and cooked for them. So they had a better chance to feed themselves than the average soldier. So says Auntie Marjie.

By the 1950s he had a square dance band, Gus Dupree and His Boys, and used to do well playing the American air bases, playing hoedowns. He'd work in a factory in Islington in the day and play at night, getting up in a white-fronted shirt, a "dickey." He played Jewish weddings and Masonic do's, and he brought cakes back in his violin case; all my aunts remember that. He must have been very hard up — he never, for example, bought new clothes, only secondhand clothes and shoes.

Why was my grandmother long-suffering? Apart from being in various states of pregnancy for twenty-three years? Gus's great delight was to play violin while Emma played piano. But during the war she caught him bonking an ARP warden in a blackout, caught him up to the usual. On the piano too. Even worse. And she never played piano for him again. That was the price. And she was very stubborn — in fact she was very unlike Gus, not attuned to his artist's temperament. So he roped his daughters in, but it was "never quite the same, Keith," he would tell me. "Never quite the same." With the stories he told me, you'd think Emma was Arthur Rubinstein. "There was nothing like Emma. She could play," he'd say. He turned it into a long-lost love, a yearning. Unfortunately that hadn't been his only infidelity. There were lots of little rumpuses and walkouts. Gus was a ladies' man and Emma just got fed up.

The fact is that Gus and his family were a very rare thing for those days — they were about as bohemian as you could get. Gus encouraged a kind of irreverence and nonconformity, but it was in the genes too. One of my aunts was in repertory, into amateur dramatics. They were all artistically inclined in one way or another, depending on their circumstances. Given the times we're talking about, this was a very free family — very un-Victorian. Gus was the kind of guy that, when his daughters were growing up and they'd be called on by four or five of their boyfriends and their boyfriends would be sitting down on the sofa opposite the window and the girls would be sitting across from them, would go up to the john and unload a piece of string with a used rubber on it and dangle it in front of the boys, and the girls couldn't see it. That was his sense of humor. And all the boys would be going red and cracking up, and the girls wouldn't know what the hell for. Gus liked to make a little commotion. And Doris said how horrified her mother, Emma, was by the scandal that two of Gus's sisters, Henrietta and Felicia, who lived together in Colebrooke Row, were — she would say it in a whisper — "on the game." Not all Doris's sisters were like her — with such a spicy tongue, you might say. Some of them were upright and proper like Emma, but no one denied the fact of Henrietta and Felicia.

My earliest memories of Gus were the walks we took, the sorties we made, mostly I think for him to get out of the house of women. I was an excuse and so was the dog called Mr. Thompson Wooft. Gus had never had a boy in the house, son or grandchild, until I came along, and I think this was a big moment, a big opportunity to go for walks and disappear. When Emma wanted him to do household chores, he invariably replied, "I'd love to, Em, but I've got a hole in my bum." A nod and a wink and take the dog for a walk. And we'd go for miles and sometimes, it seemed, for days. Once on Primrose Hill we went to look at the stars, with Mr. Thompson, of course. "Don't know if we can make it home tonight," said Gus. So we slept under a tree.

"Let's take the dog for a walk." (That was the code for we're moving.)

"All right."

"Bring your mac."

"It's not raining."

"Bring your mac."

Gus once asked me (when I was about five or six years old) while out for a stroll:

"Have you got a penny on you?"

"Yer, Gus."

"See that kid on the corner?"

"Yer, Gus."

"Go give it to him."

"What, Gus?"

"Go on, he's harder up than you."

I give the penny.

Gus gives me two back.

The lesson stuck.

Gus never bored me. On New Cross station late at night in deep fog, Gus gave me my first dog end to smoke. "No one will see." A familiar Gusism was to greet a friend with "Hello, don't be a cunt all yer life." The delivery so beautifully flat, so utterly familiar. I loved the man. A cuff round the head. "You never heard that." "What, Gus?"

He would hum entire symphonies as we walked. Sometimes to Primrose Hill, Highgate or down Islington through the Archway, the Angel, every fucking where.

"Fancy a saveloy?"

"Yer, Gus."

"You can't have one. We're going to Lyons Corner House."

"Yer, Gus."

"Don't tell your grandmother."

"OK, Gus! What about the dog?"

"He knows the chef."

His warmth, his affection surrounded me, his humor kept me doubled up for large portions of the day. It was hard to find much that was funny in those days in London. But there was always MUSIC!

"Just pop in here. I've got to get some strings."

"OK, Gus."

I didn't say a lot; I listened. Him with his cheesecutter, me with my mac. Maybe from him I got the wanderlust. "If you've got seven daughters off the Seven Sisters Road and with the wife it makes eight, you get out and about." He never drank that I can recall. But he *must* have done something. We never hit pubs. But he would disappear into the back rooms of shops quite frequently. I perused the merchandise with glowing eyes. He'd come out with the same.

"Let's go. Got the dog?"

"Yer, Gus."

"Come along, Mr. Thompson."

You had no idea where you'd end up. Little shops around the Angel and Islington, he'd just disappear into the back. "Just stay here a minute, son. Hold the dog." And then he'd come out saying, "OK," and we'd go on and end up in the West End in the workshops of the big music stores, like Ivor Mairants and HMV. He knew all the makers, the repair guys there. He'd sit me up on a shelf. There'd be these vats of glue and instruments hung up and strung up, guys in long brown coats, gluing, and then there'd be somebody at the end testing instruments; there'd be some music going on. And then there'd be these little harried men coming in from the orchestra pit, saying, "Have you got my violin?" I'd just sit up there with a cup of tea and a biscuit and the vats of glue going *blub blub blub* like a mini Yellowstone Park, and I was just fascinated. I never got bored. Violins and guitars hung up on wires and going around on a conveyor belt, and all these guys fixing and making and refurbishing instruments. I see it back then as very alchemical, like Disney's *The Sorcerer's Apprentice*. I just fell in love with instruments.

Gus was leading me subtly into getting interested in playing, rather than shoving something into my hand and saying, "It goes like this." The guitar was totally out of reach. It was something you looked at, thought about, but never got your hands on. I'll never forget the guitar on top of his upright piano every time I'd go and visit, starting maybe from the age of five. I thought that was where the thing lived. I thought it was always there. And I just kept looking at it, and he didn't say anything, and a few years later I was still looking at it. "Hey, when you get tall enough, you can have a go at it," he said. I didn't find out until after he was dead that he only brought that out and put it up there when he knew I was coming to visit. So I was being teased in a way. I think he studied me because he heard me singing. When songs came on the radio, we'd all start harmonizing; that's just what we did. A load of singers.

I can't remember when it was that he took the guitar down and said, "Here you go." Maybe I was nine or ten, so I started pretty late. A gut-string classical Spanish guitar, a sweet, lovely little lady. Although I didn't know what the hell to do with it. The smell of it. Even now, to open a guitar case, when it's an old wooden guitar, I could crawl in and close the lid. Gus wasn't much of a guitar player himself, but he knew the basics. He showed me the first licks and chords, the major chord shapes, D and G and E. He said, "Play 'Malagueña,' you can play anything." By the time he said, "I think you're getting the hang of it," I was pretty happy.

My six aunts, in no special order: Marje, Beatrice, Joanna, Elsie, Connie, Patty. Amazingly, at the time of writing, five of them are still alive. My favorite aunt was Joanna, who died in the 1980s of multiple sclerosis. She was my mate. She was an actress. A rush of glamour came into the room when Joanna arrived, black hair, wearing bangles and smelling of perfume. Especially when everything else was so drab in the early '50s, Joanna would come in and it was as if the Ronettes had arrived. She used to do Chekhov and stuff like that at Highbury Theatre. She was also the only one that never married. She always had boyfriends. And she too, like all of us, was into music. We would harmonize together. Any song that came on the radio, we'd say, "Let's try that." I remember singing "When Will I Be Loved," the Everly Brothers song, with her.

The move to Spielman Road on Temple Hill, across the tracks and into the wasteland, was a catastrophe for me for at least one whole year of living dangerously and fearfully, when I was nine or ten. I was a very small guy in those days — I grew into my rightful size not until I was fifteen or so. If you're a squirt like I was you're always on the defensive. Also I was a year younger than everybody else in my class, because of my birthday, December 18. I was unfortunate in that respect. And a year at that age is enormous. I loved to play football, actually; I was a good left winger. I was swift and I tried to shoot my passes. But I'm the smallest fucker, right? One bang into a back and I'm down in the mud, a solid tackle from a guy that's a year older than me. If you're that small and they're that tall, you're a football yourself.

You're always going to be a squirt. So it was "Oh hello, little Richards." I was called "Monkey" because my ears stuck out. Everybody was called something.

The route to my school from Temple Hill was the street without joy. Up to the age of eleven I'd bus it there and walk it back. Why didn't I bus it back? *No fucking money!* I'd spent the bus fare, spent the haircutting money, done it myself in front of the mirror. Snip, snip, snip. So I had to make my way across town, totally the opposite side of town, about a forty-minute walk, and there's only two ways to go, Havelock Road or Princes Road. Toss a coin. But then I knew that the minute I got out of school, this guy would be waiting for me. The guy always guessed which way I was going. I'd try to figure out new routes, get busted in people's gardens. I'd spend the whole day wondering how to get home without taking a beating. Which is hard work. Five days a week. Sometimes it didn't happen, but at the same time you're sitting in the classroom churning inside. How the hell do I get past this guy? This guy would be merciless. There was nothing I could do about it and I would live in fear all day, which ruined my concentration.

When I got a black eye from being beaten up, I'd go home to Doris, and she'd say, "Where did you get that from?" "Oh, I fell over." Otherwise you'd get the old lady wound up about "Who did it?" It was better to say you fell off your bike.

Meanwhile I'm getting these terrible school reports, and Bert's looking at me: "What's going on?" You can't explain that you spend the whole day at school worrying how to get home. You can't do that. Wimps do that. It's something you've got to figure out for yourself. The actual beating was not the problem. I learned how to take beatings. I didn't really get that hurt. You learn how to keep your guard up, and you learn how to make sure that somebody thinks they've done far more damage to you than they really have. "Aaaaaah"—and they think, "Oh my God, I've really done some harm."

And then I wised up. I wish I'd thought of it sooner. There was this very nice bloke, and I can't remember his name now, he was a bit of an oaf, he wasn't made for the academic life, let's put it like that, and he was big and he lived on the estate — and he was so worried about his homework. I said, "Look, I'll do your fucking homework, but you come home with me. It's not that far out of your way." So for the price of doing his history and geography, suddenly I had this minder. I always remember the first time, couple of guys waiting for me as usual, and they saw him coming. And we beat the shit out of them. It only took two or three times and a little ritual bloodletting and victory was ours.

It wasn't until I got to my next school, Dartford Tech, that things, by a great fluke, righted themselves. By the time of the 11-plus exam, Mick had already gone to Dartford Grammar School, which is "Ooh, the ones in the red uniforms." And the year after that was my turn, and I failed miserably but not miserably enough to go to what then was known as secondary modern. It's all changed now, but if you went there under that archaic system, you were lucky if you got a factory job at the end. You were not going to be trained for anything more than manual labor. The teachers were terrible and their only function was to keep this mob in line. I got into that middle ground of technical school, which is, in retrospect, a very nebulous phrase, it means you didn't make grammar, but there's something worthwhile in there. You realize later on that you're being graded and sifted by this totally arbitrary system that rarely if ever takes into account your whole character, or "Well, he might not be very good in class, but he knows more about drawing." They never took into account that hey, you might be bored because you know that already.

The playground's the big judge. That's where all decisions are really made between your peers. It's called play, but it's nearer to a battlefield, and it can be brutal, the pressure. There's two blokes kicking the shit out of some poor little bugger and "Oh, they're just letting off steam." In those days it was pretty physical at times, but most of it was just taunts, "pansy" and all of that.

It took me a long time to figure out how to knock somebody else out instead of me getting it. I'd been an expert at taking beatings for quite a long time. Then I had a lucky break where I did a bully in by total sheer luck. It was one of those magical moments. I was twelve or thirteen. One minute I'm the mark, and with just one swift move, I put the big man in school down. Against the rockery and the little flower bed, he slipped and fell over and I was on him. When I fight, a red curtain comes down. I don't see a thing, but I know where to go. It's as if a red veil drops over my eyes. No mercy, mate, the boot went in! Pulled off by the prefects and all of that. How are the mighty fallen! I can still remember the astounding surprise when this guy went down. I can still see the little rockery and the pansies he fell over in, and after that I didn't let him up.

Once he was down, the whole atmosphere in the schoolyard changed. A huge cloud seemed to be lifted from me. My reputation after that suddenly released me from all that angst and stress. I'd never been aware the cloud was so large. It was the only time I started to feel good about school, mostly because I was able to repay a few favors some other guys had done for me. An ugly little sod called Stephen Yarde, "Boots" we used to call him, because of his huge feet, was the favorite to be picked on by the bully boys. He was being taunted all the time. And knowing what it was like to be waiting for a beating, I stood up for him. I became his minder. It was "Don't fuck with Stephen Yarde." I never wanted to get big enough to beat up other people; I just wanted to get big enough to stop it happening.

With that weight off my mind, my work improved at Dartford Tech. I was even getting praise. Doris kept some of my reports: *Geography 59%, a good exam result. History 63%, quite good work.* But against the science subjects on the report sheet the form master put a single bracket that enclosed them all—there was no daylight between them for abjectness—and he wrote them all off with *no improvement* in mathematics, physics and chemistry. Engineering drawing was *still rather beyond him.* That report on science subjects contained the story of the big betrayal and of how I was turned from a reasonably compliant student into a school terrorist and a criminal, with a lively and lasting rage against authority.

There is a photograph of our group of schoolboys standing in front of a bus, smiling for the camera, in the company of one schoolmaster. I am standing in the front row, wearing shorts, aged eleven. It was taken in 1955 in London, where we had gone to sing at a concert at St. Margaret's Church in Westminster Abbey — a choir competition between schools, performed in front of the queen. Our school choir had come a long way, a bunch of Dartford yokels who were winning cups and prizes for choral work on a national level. The three sopranos were Terry and Spike and me — the stars, you might say, of the show. And our choirmaster, pictured by the bus, the genius who had forged this little flying unit out of such unpromising material, was called Jake Clare. He was a mystery man. I found out only many years later that he'd been an Oxford choirmaster, one of the best in the country, but he was exiled or degraded for boinky boink with little boys. Given another chance in the colonies. I don't want to sully his name, and I have to say this is only what I heard. He'd certainly had better material to work with than us — what was he doing down here? Around us, anyway, he kept his hands clean, although he was famed for playing with himself through his trouser pocket. He hammered us into shape to the point where we were clearly one of the best choirs in the country. And he picked out the three best sopranos that he was given. We won quite a few trophies, which hung in the assembly hall. I've still never played a better gig prestige-wise than Westminster Abbey. You got the taunts: "Oh, choirboy, are we? Fantsy pantsy." It didn't bother me; the choir was wonderful. You got coach trips to London. You got out of physics and chemistry, and I would have done anything for that. That's where I learned a lot about singing and music and working with musicians. I learned how to put a band together — it's basically the same job — and how to keep it together. And then the shit hit the fan.

Your voice breaks, aged thirteen, and Jake Clare gave the three of us sopranos the pink slip. But they also demoted us, kept us down one class. We had to stay down a year because we hadn't got physics and chemistry and hadn't done our maths. "Yeah, but you let us off that because of choir practice. We worked our butts off." That was a rough thank-you. The great depression came right after that. Suddenly at thirteen I had to sit down and start again with the year under. Redo a whole school year. This was the kick in the guts, pure and unmixed. The moment that happened, Spike, Terry and I, we became terrorists. I was so mad, I had a burning desire for revenge. I had reason then to bring down this country and everything it stood for.

I spent the next three years trying to fuck them up. If you want to breed a rebel, that's the way to do it. No more haircuts. Two pairs of trousers, the skin-tight ones under the regulation flannels, which came off the minute I was out the gate. Anything to annoy them. It didn't get me anywhere; it got me a lot of black looks from my dad, but even that didn't stop me. I really didn't like to disappoint my dad, but... sorry, Dad.

It still rankles, that humiliation. It still hasn't gone out, the fire. That's when I started to look at the world in a different way, not their way anymore. That's when I realized that there's bigger bullies than just bullies. There's *them,* the authorities. And a slow-burning fuse was lit. I could have got expelled easily after that, in any different way, but then I'd have had to face my dad. And he would have spotted that immediately — that I'd manipulated it. So it had to be a slow-moving campaign. I just lost total interest in authority or trying to make good under their terms. School reports? Give me a bad one, I'll forge it. I got very good at forgery. *He could do better.* Somehow I managed to find the same ink, make it *He could* not *do better.* My dad would look at it. *"He could not do better.* Why does he give you a B-minus?" Pushing my luck a bit there. But they never detected the forgeries. I was actually hoping they would, because then I could be done, expelled for forgery. But apparently it was too good, or they decided that that one is not going to work, boy.

I lost total interest in school after choir went down the tube. Technical drawing, physics, mathematics, a yawn, because it doesn't matter how much they try to teach me algebra, I *just don't get it,* and I don't see why I should. I'll understand at gunpoint, on bread and water and a whip. I would learn it, I could learn it, but there's something inside of me saying this is going to be no help to you, and if you do want to learn it, you'll learn it by yourself. At first, after the voice broke and we were given that boot down, I stuck very close together with the guys I used to sing with, because we all felt the same burning resentment for winning them all the medals and shields that they were always so proud of in their assembly hall. Meanwhile, we're cleaning their bloody shoes round the back, and that's the thanks you get.

You cut some rebel style. In the High Street there was Leonards, where they sold very cheap jeans, just as jeans were becoming jeans. And they would sell fluorescent socks around '56, '57 — rock-and-roll socks that glow in the dark so she always knows where I am, with black musical notes on them, pink and green. Used to have a pair of each. More daring still, I'd have pink on one foot and green on the other. That was really, like, wow.

Dimashio's was the ice cream parlor–coffee shop. Old Dimashio's son went to school with us, big fat Italian boy. But he could always make plenty of friends by bringing them down to his dad's joint. There was a jukebox there, so it was a hang. Jerry Lee Lewis and Little Richard, apart from a load of schlock. It was the one little bit of Americana in Dartford. Just a little store, counter down the left side, jukebox, some seats and tables, the ice cream machine. At least once a week, I went to the cinema and usually to the Saturday morning pictures, either at the Gem or the Granada. Like Captain Marvel. SHAZAM! If you said it right, it might actually happen. Me and my mates in the middle of the field, going, "SHAZAM! We're not saying it right!" Other blokes laughing behind our heads. "Yeah, you're not going to laugh when I get it right. SHAZAM!" Flash Gordon, those little puffs of smoke. He had bleached-blond hair. Captain Marvel.

You could never remember what it was about, it was more about the transformation, about just a regular guy who says one word and suddenly he's gone. "I want to get that down," you'd think. "I want to get out of this place."

And as we got bigger and a little brawnier, we started to swing our weight about a bit. The ludicrous side to Dartford Tech was its pretensions to being a public school (that's what they call private schools in England). The prefects had little gold tassels on their caps; there was East House and West House. It was trying to recapture a lost world, as if the war hadn't happened, of cricket, cups and prizes, schoolboy glory. All of the masters were totally substandard, but they were still aiming for this ideal as if it were Eton or Winchester, as if it were the '20s or the '30s or even the 1890s. In the midst of this there was, in my middle years there, soon after the catastrophe, a period of anarchy that seemed to go on for a very long time — a prolonged period of chaos. Maybe it was just one term in which, for whatever reason, these mad mass bundles would go on in the playing fields. There were about three hundred of us, everybody leaping around. It is strange, thinking back, that nobody stopped us. There were probably just too many of us running about. And nobody got hurt. But it allowed a certain degree of anarchy to the point that when the head prefect did come along and try to stop us one day, he was set upon and lynched. He was one of those perennial martinets, captain of sport, head of school, the most brilliant at all things. He swung his weight around, he would be really officious to the younger kids, and we decided to give him a taste. His name was Swanton — I remember him well. And it was raining, very nasty weather, and we stripped him and then chased him until he climbed a tree. We left him with his hat with the little gold tassels, that's all he had left on. Swanton came down from the tree and rose to become a professor of medieval studies at the University of Exeter and wrote a key work called *English Poetry Before Chaucer*.

Of all the schoolmasters, the one sympathetic one, who didn't bark out orders, was the religious instruction teacher, Mr. Edgington. He used to wear a powder blue suit with cum stains down the leg. Mr. Edgington, the wanker. Religious instruction, forty-five minutes, "Let's turn to Luke." And we were saying, either he's pissed himself or he's just been round the back shagging Mrs. Mountjoy, who was the art mistress.

I had adopted a criminal mind, anything to fuck them up. We won cross-country three times but we never ran it. We'd start off, go and have a smoke for an hour or so and then chip in towards the end. And the third or fourth time, they got wise and put monitors down the whole trail, and we weren't spotted along the other seven miles. *He has maintained a low standard* was the six-word summary of my 1959 school report, suggesting, correctly, that I had put some effort into the enterprise.

I was taking in a lot of music then, without really knowing it. England was often under fog, but there was a fog of words that settled between people too. One didn't show emotions. One didn't actually talk much at all. The talk was all *around* things, codes and euphemisms; some things couldn't be said or even alluded to. It was a residue of the Victorians and all brilliantly portrayed in those black-and-white movies of the early '60s — *Saturday Night and Sunday Morning, This Sporting Life*. And life was black-and-white; the Technicolor was just around the corner, but it wasn't there yet in 1959. People really do want to touch each other, to the heart. That's why you have music. If you can't say it, sing it. Listen to the songs of the period. Heavily pointed and romantic, and trying to say things that they couldn't say in prose or even on paper. Weather's fine, 7:30 p.m., wind has died down, P.S. I love you.

Doris was different — she was musical, like Gus. At three or four or five years old, at the end of the war, I was listening to Ella Fitzgerald, Sarah Vaughan, Big Bill Broonzy, Louis Armstrong. It just spoke to me, it was what I listened to every day because my mum played it.

My ears would have gone there anyway, but my mum trained them to go to the black side of town without her even knowing it. I didn't know whether the singers were white, black or green at the time. But after a while, if you've got some musical ears, you pick up on the difference between Pat Boone's "Ain't That a Shame" and Fats Domino's "Ain't That a Shame." Not that Pat Boone's was particularly bad, he was a very good singer, but it was just so shallow and produced, and Fats's was just so natural. Doris liked Gus's music too. He used to tell her to listen to Stéphane Grappelli, Django Reinhardt's Hot Club—that lovely swing guitar—and Bix Beiderbecke. She liked jazzy swing. Later on she loved going to hear Charlie Watts's band at Ronnie Scott's.

We didn't have a record player for a long time, and most of it, for us, was on the radio, mostly on the BBC, my mother being a master twiddler of the knobs. There were some great British players, some of the northern dance orchestras and all of those that were on the variety shows. Some great players. No slouches. If there was anything good she'd find it. So I grew up with this searching for music. She'd point out who was good or bad, even to me. She was musical, musical. There were voices she would hear and she'd say "screecher" when everyone else would think it was a great soprano. This was pre-TV. I grew up listening to really good music, including a little bit of Mozart and Bach in the background, which I found very over my head at the time, but I soaked it up. I was basically a musical sponge. And I was just fascinated by watching people play music. If they were in the street I'd gravitate towards it, a piano player in the pub, whatever it was. My ears were picking it up note for note. Didn't matter if it was out of tune, there were notes happening, there were rhythms and harmonies, and they would start zooming around in my ears. It was very like a drug. In fact a far bigger drug than smack. I could kick smack; I couldn't kick music. One note leads to another, and you never know quite what's going to come next, and you don't want to. It's like walking on a beautiful tightrope.

I think the first record I bought was Little Richard's "Long Tall Sally." Fantastic record, even to this day. Good records just get better with age. But the one that really turned me on, like an explosion one night, listening to Radio Luxembourg on my little radio when I was supposed to be in bed and asleep, was "Heartbreak Hotel." That was the stunner. I'd never heard it before, or anything like it. I'd never heard of Elvis before. It was almost as if I'd been waiting for it to happen. When I woke up the next day I was a different guy. Suddenly I was getting overwhelmed: Buddy Holly, Eddie Cochran, Little Richard, Fats. Radio Luxembourg was notoriously difficult to keep on station. I had a little aerial and walked round the room, holding the radio up to my ear and twisting the aerial. Trying to keep it down because I'd wake Mum and Dad up. If I could get the signal right, I could take the radio under the blankets on the bed and keep the aerial outside and twist it there. I'm supposed to be asleep; I'm supposed to be going to school in the morning. Loads of ads for James Walker, the jewelers "in every high street," and the Irish sweepstakes, with which Radio Lux had some deal. The signal was perfect for the ads, "and now we have Fats Domino, 'Blueberry Hill,'" and shit, then it would fade.

Then, "Since my baby left me" — it was just the sound. It was the last trigger. That was the first rock and roll I heard. It was a totally different way of delivering a song, a totally different sound, stripped down, burnt, no bullshit, no violins and ladies' choruses and schmaltz, totally different. It was bare, right to the roots that you had a feeling were there but hadn't yet heard. I've got to take my hat off to Elvis for that. The silence is your canvas, that's your frame, that's what you work on; don't try and deafen it out. That's what "Heartbreak Hotel" did to me. It was the first time I'd heard something so stark. Then I had to go back to what this cat had done before. Luckily I caught his name. The Radio Luxembourg signal came back in. "That was Elvis Presley, with 'Heartbreak Hotel.'" Shit!

Around 1959, when I was fifteen, Doris bought me my first guitar. I was already playing, when I could get one, but you can only tinker when you haven't got one of your own. It was a Rosetti. And it was about ten quid. Doris didn't have the credit to buy it on hire purchase, so she got someone else to do it, and he defaulted on the payment — big kerfuffle. It was a huge amount of money for her and Bert. But Gus must have had something to do with it too. It was a gut-string job. I started where every good guitar player should start — down there on acoustic, on gut strings. You can get to wire later on. Anyway, I couldn't afford an electric. But I found just playing that Spanish, an old workman, and starting from there, it gave me something to build on. And then you got to steel strings and then finally, wow! Electricity! I mean, probably if I had been born a few years later, I would have leapt on the electric guitar. But if you want to get to the top, you've got to start at the bottom, same with anything. Same with running a whorehouse. I would just play every spare moment I got. People describe me then as being oblivious to my surroundings — I'd sit in a corner of a room when a party was going on or a family gathering, and be playing. Some indication of my love of my new instrument is Aunt Marje telling me that when Doris went to hospital and I stayed with Gus for a while, I was never parted from my guitar. I took it everywhere and I went to sleep with my arm laid across it.

I have my sketchbook and notebook of that year. The date is more or less 1959, the crucial year when I was, mostly, fifteen years old. It's a neat, obsessive piece of work in blue Biro. The pages are divided by columns and headings, and page two (after a crucial page about Boy Scouting, of which more later) is called "Record List. 45 rpm." The first entry: "Title: Peggy Sue Got Married, Artiste(s): Buddy Holly." Underneath that, in a less neat scrawl, are the encircled names of girls. Mary (crossed out), Jenny (ticked), Janet, Marilyn, Veronica. And so on. "Long Players" are *The Buddy Holly Story, A Date with Elvis, Wilde about Marty* (Marty Wilde, of course, for those who don't know), *The "Chirping" Crickets.* The lists include the usuals — Ricky Nelson, Eddie Cochran, Everly Brothers, Cliff Richard ("Travellin' Light") — but also Johnny Restivo ("The Shape I'm In"), which was number three on one of my lists, "The Fickle Chicken" by the Atmospheres, "Always" by Sammy Turner — forgotten jewels. These were the record lists of the Awakening — the birth of rock and roll on UK shores. Elvis dominated the landscape at this point. He had a section in the notebook all to himself. The very first album I bought. "Mystery Train," "Money Honey," "Blue Suede Shoes," "I'm Left, You're Right, She's Gone." The crème de la crème of his Sun stuff. I slowly acquired a few more, but that was my baby. As impressed as I was with Elvis, I was even more impressed by Scotty Moore and the band. It was the same with Ricky Nelson. I never bought a Ricky Nelson record, I bought a James Burton record. It was the bands behind them that impressed me just as much as the front men. Little Richard's band, which was basically the same as Fats Domino's band, was actually Dave Bartholomew's band. I knew all this. I was just impressed by ensemble playing. It was how guys interacted with one another, natural exuberance and seemingly effortless delivery. There was a beautiful flippancy, it seemed to me. And of course that goes even more for Chuck Berry's band. But from the start it wasn't just the singer. What had to impress me behind the singer would be the band.

But I had other preoccupations. One of the best things that happened to me at that time, believe it or not, was joining the Boy Scouts. Its leader, Baden-Powell, a genuinely nice man who was well tuned in to what small boys liked doing, did believe that without the scouts the empire would collapse. This is where I came in, as a member of the Seventh Dartford Scouts, Beaver Patrol, although the empire was showing signs of collapsing anyway for reasons that had nothing to do with character and tying knots. I think my foray into scouting must have happened just before the guitar really set in — or maybe before I owned one — because when I really started playing the guitar, that was my other world.

Scouting was a separate thing from music. I wanted to know how to survive, and I'd read all of Baden-Powell's books. And now I've got to learn all these tricks. I want to know how to find out where I am; I want to know how to cook something underground. For some reason I needed survival skills and I thought it was important to learn. I already had a tent in the back garden, where I would sit for hours, eating raw potatoes and such. How to pluck a fowl. How to gut things. What bits to leave in and what bits to leave off. And whether to keep the skin or not. Is it any use? Nice pair of gloves? It was kind of miniature SAS training. It was mainly a chance to swagger around with a knife on your belt. That was the attraction for a lot of us. You didn't get the knife until you got a few badges.

Beaver Patrol had its own shed — one of the other dads' unused garden shed, which we took over and where we had planning meetings about what the patrol was going to do. You're good at that, you're good at that. We'd sit around and talk and have a smoke, and we went on field trips to Bexleyheath or Sevenoaks. Scout Leader Bass was the scoutmaster, who seemed ancient at the time but was probably only about twenty. He was a very encouraging guy. He'd say, "All right, tonight is knotting. The sheepshank, the bowline, the running bowline." I had to practice at home. How to start a fire without matches. How to make an oven, how to make a fire without smoke. I'd practice in the garden all week. Rubbing two sticks together — forget about it. Not in that climate. It might work in Africa or some other un-humid area. So it was basically the magnifying glass and dry twigs. Then suddenly, after only three or four months, I've got four or five badges and I'm promoted to patrol leader. I had badges all over the place, unbelievable! I don't know where my scout shirt is now, but it's adorned, stripes and strings and badges all over the place. Looked like I was into bondage.

All that boosted my confidence at a crucial moment, after my ejection from the choir, especially the fact that I was promoted so fast. I think it was more important, that whole scouting period, than I've ever realized. I had a good team. I knew my guys and we were pretty solid. Discipline was a little lax, I must admit, but when it came to

"This is the task for today," we did it. There was the big summer camp at Crowborough. We'd just won the bridge-building competition. That night we drank whiskey and had a fight in the bell tent. It's pitch-black, there's no light, everybody's just swinging, breaking things, especially themselves — first bone I ever broke was hitting the tent pole in the middle of the night.

The only time I pulled rank was when my scouting career came to an end. I had a new recruit, and he was such a prick, he couldn't get along with anybody. And it was like "I've got an elite patrol here and I've got to take this bum in? I'm not here to wipe snot. Why'd you dump him on me?" He did something, and I just gave him a whack. Bang, you cunt. Next thing I know I'm up before the disciplinary board. On the carpet. "Officers do not slap" and all that bullshit.

I was in my hotel room in Saint Petersburg, on tour with the Stones, when I found myself watching the ceremony commemorating the hundredth anniversary of the Boy Scouts. It was at Brownsea Island, where Baden-Powell started his first camp. All alone in my room, I stood up, made the three-fingered salute and said, "Patrol leader, Beaver Patrol, Seventh Dartford Scouts, sir." I felt I had to report.

I had summer jobs to while away the time, usually working behind the counter in various stores, or loading sugar. I don't recommend that. In the back of a supermarket. It comes in great big bags, and sugar cuts you up like a motherfucker and it's sticky. You do a day's loading of sugar and you're humping it on your shoulder and you're bleeding. And then you package it. It should have been enough to put me off the stuff, but it never did. Before sugar, I did butter. Today you go in the shop and look at that nice little square, but the butter used to come in huge blocks. We used to chop it up and wrap it up there in the back of the shop. You were taught how to do the double fold, and the correct weight, and to put it on the shelf and go, "Doesn't it look nice?" Meanwhile there are rats running around the back, and all kinds of shit.

I had another job around that time, early teens. I did the bakery, the bread round at weekends, which was really an eye-opener at that age, thirteen, fourteen. We collected the money. There were two guys and a little electric car, and on Saturday and Sunday it's me with them trying to screw the money out. And I realized I was there as an extra, a lookout, while they say, "Mrs. X . . . it's been two weeks now." Sometimes I'd sit in the truck, freezing cold and waiting, and then after twenty minutes the baker would come out red faced and doing his flies up. I started slowly to realize how things were paid for. And then there were certain old ladies who were obviously so bored, the highlight of their week was being visited by the bread men. And they'd serve the cakes they'd bought from us, have a nice cup of tea, sit around and chat, and you realize you've been there a bloody hour and it's going to be dark before you finish the round. In the winter I looked forward to them, because it was kind of like *Arsenic and Old Lace,* these old ladies living in a totally different world.

While I was practicing my knots I wasn't noticing — in fact I didn't piece it together until years later — some swift moves Doris was making. Around 1957, Doris took up with Bill, now Richards, my stepfather. He married Doris in 1998, after living with her since 1963. He was in his twenties and she was in her forties. I just remember that Bill was always there. He was a taxi driver, and he was always driving us about, always willing to take on anything that involved driving. He even drove us on holiday, me, Mum and Dad. I was too young to know what the relationship was. Bill to me was just like Uncle Bill. I didn't know what Bert thought and I still don't know. I thought Bill was Bert's friend, a friend of the family.

He just turned up and he had a car. That's partly what did it for Doris, back in 1957. Bill had first met her and me in 1947, when he lived opposite us in Chastilian Road, working in the Co-op. Then he joined a firm of taxi drivers and didn't reappear until Doris came out of Dartford station one day and saw him. Or, as Doris told it, "I only knew him from living opposite him, and he was at the cab one day, and I came off the station and I went, 'Hello.' And he came running after me and said, 'I'll take you home.' I said, 'Well, I don't mind,' because I would have had to wait for a bus otherwise, and he took me home. And then it started and I can't believe it. I was so brazen."

Bill and Doris had to get up to some deception, and I feel for Bert if he knew. One of their opportunities was Bert's passion for tennis. It left Doris and Bill free to have a date out together. Then, according to Bill, they'd somehow get in a position to see Bert leaving the tennis club on his bike and race back in Bill's taxi to get Doris home before him. Doris reminisced, "When Keith started with the Stones, Bill used to take him here and everywhere. If it wasn't for Bill, he couldn't have gone anywhere. Because Keith used to say, 'Mick says I've got to get to so-and-so.' And I'd say, 'How are you going to get there, then?' And Bill would say, 'I'll take him.'" That's Bill's so far unheralded role in the birth of the Rolling Stones.

Still, my dad was my dad, and I was scared shitless of facing him come the day I got expelled, which is why it had to be a long-term campaign — it couldn't be done in one swift blow. I would just slowly have to build up the bad marks until they realized that the moment had come. I was scared not from any physical threat, just of his disapproval, because he'd send you to Coventry. And suddenly you're on your own. Not talking to me or even recognizing I was around was his form of discipline. There was nothing to follow it up; he wasn't going to whip my arse or anything like that; it never came into the equation. The thought of upsetting my dad still makes me cry now. Not living up to his expectations would devastate me.

Once you'd been shunned like that you didn't want it to happen again. You felt like you were nothing, you didn't exist. He'd say, "Well, we ain't going up the heath tomorrow" — on the weekend we used to go up there and kick a football about. When I found out how Bert's dad treated him, I thought I was very lucky, because Bert never used physical punishment on me at all. He was not one to express his emotions. Which I'm thankful for in a way. Some of the times I pissed him off, if he had been that kind of guy, I'd have been getting beatings, like most of the other kids around me at that time. My mum was the only one that laid a hand on me now and again, round the back of the legs, and I deserved it. But I never lived in fear of corporal punishment. It was psychological. Even after a twenty-year gap, when I hadn't seen Bert for all that time and when I was preparing for our historic reunion, I was still scared of that. He had a lot to disapprove of in the intervening twenty years. But that's a later story.

The final action that got me expelled was when Terry and I decided not to go to assembly on the last day of the school year. We'd been to so many and we wanted to have a smoke, so we just didn't go. And that I believe was the actual final nail in the coffin of getting me expelled. At which of course my dad nearly blew up. But by then, I think he'd written me off as any use to society. Because by then I was playing guitar, and Bert wasn't artistically minded and the only thing I'm good at is music and art.

The person I have to thank at this point — who saved me from the dung heap, from serial relegation — is the fabulous art instructor Mrs. Mountjoy. She put in a good word for me to the headmaster. They were going to dump me onto the labor exchange, and the headmaster asked, "What's he good at?" "Well, he can draw." And so I went to Sidcup Art College, class of 1959 — the musical intake.

Bert didn't take it well. "Get a solid job." "What, like making lightbulbs, Dad?" And I started to get sarcastic with him. I wish I hadn't. "Making valves and lightbulbs?"

By then I had big ideas, even though I had no idea how to put them into operation. That required meeting a few other people later on. I just felt that I was smart enough, one way or another, to wriggle out of this social net and playing the game. My parents were brought up in the Depression, when if you got something, you just kept it and you held it and that was it. Bert was the most unambitious man in the world. Meanwhile, I was a kid and I didn't even know what ambition meant. I just felt the constraints. The society and everything I was growing up in was just too small for me. Maybe it was just teenage testosterone and angst, but I knew I had to look for a way out.

# Chapter Three

In which I go to art college, which is my guitar school. I play
in public for the first time and end up with a chick that same night.
I meet Mick at Dartford Railway Station with his Chuck Berry
records. We start playing—Little Boy Blue and the Blue Boys.
We meet Brian Jones at the Ealing Club. I get Ian Stewart's approval at
the Bricklayers Arms, and the Stones form around him. We want
Charlie Watts to join but can't afford him.

I don't know what would have happened if I *hadn't* been expelled
from Dartford and sent to art college. There was a lot more
music than art going on at Sidcup, or any of the other art colleges in
south London that were turning out suburban beatniks—which is
what I was learning to be. In fact there was almost no "art" to be had
at Sidcup Art College. After a while you got the drift of what you
were being trained for, and it wasn't Leonardo da Vinci. Loads of
flash little sons of bitches would come down in their bow ties from
J. Walter Thompson or one of the other big advertisers for one day
a week to take the piss out of the art school students and try and
pick up the chicks. They'd lord it over us and you got taught how to
advertise.

There was a great feeling of freedom when I first went to Sidcup.
"You mean you can actually smoke?" You're with lots of different artists, even if they're not really artists. Different attitudes, which was
really important to me. Some are eccentrics, some are wannabes, but

they're an interesting bunch of people, and a very different breed, thank God, to what I was used to. We'd all got there out of boys' schools and suddenly we're in classes with chicks. Everybody's hair was getting long, mainly because you could, you were that age and for some reason it felt good. And you could finally dress any way you wanted; everybody had come from uniforms. You actually looked forward to getting on the train to Sidcup in the morning. You actually looked forward to it. At Sidcup I was "Ricky."

I realize now that we were getting some dilapidated tail end of a noble art-teaching tradition from the prewar period—etching, stone lithographs, classes on the spectrum of light—all thrown away on advertising Gilbey's gin. Very interesting, and since I liked drawing anyway, it was great. I was learning a few things. You didn't realize you were actually being processed into some sort of so-called graphic designer, probably Letraset setter, but that came later. The art tradition staggered on under the guidance of burnt-out idealists like the life classes teacher, Mr. Stone, who had been trained at the Royal Academy. Every lunchtime he'd down several pints of Guinness at the Black Horse and come to class very late and very pissed, wearing sandals with no socks, winter and summer. Life class was often hilariously funny. Some lovely old fat Sidcup lady with her clothes off—oooh way hay tits!—and the air heavy with Guinness breath and a swaying teacher hanging on to your stool. In homage to high art and the avant-garde that the faculty aspired to, one of the school photographs designed by the principal had us arranged like figures in a geometric garden from the big scene in *Last Year at Marienbad,* the Alain Resnais film—the height of existentialist cool and pretentiousness.

It was a pretty lax routine. You did your classes, finished your projects and went to the john, where there was this little hangout-cloakroom, where we sat around and played guitar. That was what really gave me the impetus to play, and at that age you pick up stuff at speed. There were loads of people playing guitar there. The art colleges produced some notable pickers in that period when rock and roll, UK-style, was getting under way. It was a kind of guitar workshop, basically all folk music, Jack Elliott stuff. Nobody noticed if you weren't at the college, so the local musical fraternity used it as a meeting place. Wizz Jones used to drop in, with a Jesus haircut and a beard. Great folk picker, great guitar picker, who's still playing—I see ads for his gigs and he looks similar, though the beard's gone. We barely met, but Wizz Jones to me then was like...Wizzzz. I mean, this guy played in clubs, he was on the folk circuit. He got paid! He played pro and we were just playing in the toilet. I think I learned "Cocaine" from him—the song and that crucial fingerpicking lick of the period, not the dope. Nobody, but nobody played that South Carolina style. He got "Cocaine" from Jack Elliott, but a long time before anyone else, and Jack Elliott had got it from the Reverend Gary Davis in Harlem. Wizz Jones was a watched man, watched by Clapton and Jimmy Page at the time too, so they say.

I was known in the john for my rendition of "I'm Left, You're Right, She's Gone." They sometimes got at me because I still liked Elvis at the time, and Buddy Holly, and they didn't understand how I could possibly be an art student and be into blues and jazz and have anything to do with that. There was this certain "Don't go there" with rock and roll, glossy photographs and silly suits. But it was just music to me. It was very hierarchical. It was mods and rockers time. There were clear-drawn lines between the "beats," who were addicted to the English version of Dixieland jazz (known as traditional), and those into R&B. I did cross the line for Linda Poitier, an outstanding beauty who wore a long black sweater, black stockings and heavy eyeliner à la Juliette Gréco. I put up with a lot of Acker Bilk—the trad jazzers' pinup—just to watch her dance. There was another Linda, specs, skinny but beauty in the eyes, who I clumsily courted. A sweet kiss. Strange. Sometimes a kiss is burned into you far more than whatever comes later. Celia I met at a Ken Colyer Club all-nighter. She was from Isleworth. We hung all night, we did nothing, but for that brief moment it was love. Pure and simple. She lived in a detached house, outta my league.

Sometimes I still visited Gus. By that time, because I'd been playing for two or three years, he said, "Come on, give me 'Malagueña.'" I played it for him and he said, "You've got it." And then I started to improvise, because it's a guitar exercise. And he said, "That's not how it goes!" And I said, "No, but Granddad, it's how it *could* go." "You're getting the hang of it."

In fact, early on I was never really that interested in being a guitar player. It was just a means to an end to produce sound. As I went on I got more and more interested in the actual playing of guitar and the actual notes. I firmly believe if you want to be a guitar player, you better start on acoustic and then graduate to electric. Don't think you're going to be Townshend or Hendrix just because you can go *wee wee wah wah,* and all the electronic tricks of the trade. First you've got to know that fucker. And you go to bed with it. If there's no babe around, you sleep with it. She's just the right shape.

I've learned everything I know off of records. Being able to replay something immediately without all that terrible stricture of written music, the prison of those bars, those five lines. Being able to hear recorded music freed up loads of musicians that couldn't necessarily afford to learn to read or write music, like me. Before 1900, you've got Mozart, Beethoven, Bach, Chopin, the cancan. With recording, it was emancipation for the people. As long as you or somebody around you could afford a machine, suddenly you could hear music made by people, not set-up rigs and symphony orchestras. You could actually listen to what people were saying, almost off the cuff. Some of it can be a load of rubbish, but some of it was really good. It was the emancipation of music. Otherwise you'd have had to go to a concert hall, and how many people could afford that? It surely can't be any coincidence that jazz and blues started to take over the world the minute recording started, within a few years, just like that. The blues is universal, which is why it's still around. Just the expression and the feel of it came in because of recording. It was like opening the audio curtains. And available, and cheap. It's not just locked into one community here and one community there and the twain shall never meet. And of course that breeds another totally different kind of musician, in a generation. I don't need this paper. I'm going to play it straight from the ear, straight from here, straight from the heart to the fingers. Nobody has to turn the pages.

I forgot to mention that to play the blues was like a jailbreak out of those meticulous bars with the notes crammed in like prisoners.

Like sad faces

Everything was available in Sidcup—it reflected that incredible explosion of music, of music as style, of love of Americana. I would raid the public library for books about America. There were people who liked folk music, modern jazz, trad jazz, people who liked bluesy stuff, so you're hearing prototype soul. All those influences were there. And there were the seminal sounds — the tablets of stone, heard for the first time. There was Muddy. There was Howlin' Wolf's "Smokestack Lightnin'," Lightnin' Hopkins. And there was a record called *Rhythm & Blues Vol. 1.* It had Buddy Guy on it doing "First Time I Met the Blues"; it had a Little Walter track. I didn't know Chuck Berry was black for two years after I first heard his music, and this obviously long before I saw the film that drove a thousand musicians — *Jazz on a Summer's Day,* in which he played "Sweet Little Sixteen." And for ages I didn't know Jerry Lee Lewis was white. You didn't see their pictures if they had something in the top ten in America. The only faces I knew were Elvis, Buddy Holly and Fats Domino. It was hardly important. It was the sound that was important. And when I first heard "Heartbreak Hotel," it wasn't that I suddenly wanted to be Elvis Presley. I had no idea who he was at the time. It was just the sound, the use of a different way of recording. The recording, as I discovered, of that visionary Sam Phillips of Sun Records. The use of echo. No extraneous additions. You felt you were in the room with them, that you were just listening to exactly what went down in the studio, no frills, no nothing, no pastry. That was hugely influential for me.

That Elvis LP had all the Sun stuff, with a couple of RCA jobs on it too. It was everything from "That's All Right," "Blue Moon of Kentucky," "Milk Cow Blues Boogie." I mean, for a guitar player, or a budding guitar player, heaven. But on the other hand, what the hell's going on there? I might not have wanted to be Elvis, but I wasn't so sure about Scotty Moore. Scotty Moore was my icon. He was Elvis's guitar player, on all the Sun Records stuff. He's on "Mystery Train," he's on "Baby Let's Play House." Now I know the man, I've played with him. I know the band. But back then, just being able to get through "I'm Left, You're Right, She's Gone," that was the epitome of guitar playing. And then "Mystery Train" and "Money Honey." I'd have died and gone to heaven just to play like that. How the hell was that done? That's the stuff I first brought to the john at Sidcup, playing a borrowed f-hole archtop Höfner. That was before the music led me back into the roots of Elvis and Buddy — back to the blues.

To this day there's a Scotty Moore lick I still can't get down and he won't tell me. Forty-nine years it's eluded me. He claims he can't remember the one I'm talking about. It's not that he won't show me; he says, "I don't know which one you mean." It's on "I'm Left, You're Right, She's Gone." I think it's in E major. He has a rundown when it hits the 5 chord, the B down to the A down to the E, which is like a yodeling sort of thing, which I've never been quite able to figure. It's also on "Baby Let's Play House." When you get to "But don't you be nobody's fool / Now baby, come back, baby..." and right at that last line, the lick is in there. It's probably some simple trick. But it goes too fast, and also there's a bunch of notes involved: which finger moves and which one doesn't? I've never heard anybody else pull it off. Creedence Clearwater got a version of that song down, but when it comes to that move, no. And Scotty's a sly dog. He's very dry. "Hey, youngster, you've got time to figure it out." Every time I see him, it's "Learnt that lick yet?"

The hippest guy at Sidcup Art College was Dave Chaston, a famous man of that time and place. Even Charlie Watts knew Dave, in some other jazz connection. He was the arbiter of hip, hip beyond bohemian, so cool he could run the record player. You'd get a 45 and play it and play it, again and again, almost like looping it. He had the first Ray Charles before anybody else — he'd even seen him play — and I first heard him during one of those lunchtime record breaks.

Everybody then was going for looks. You can't tell that yet from the photograph of the class of '59, my induction year; things were only just beginning. The guys look conventionally dressed in V-neck pullovers, and the teenage girls are dressed to look like women of fifty, indistinguishable from the few women teachers. In fact, everyone, of both sexes, was wearing black sweaters far too long for them, except for Brian Boyle, who was the archetypal mod, who would be changing his clothes every week. We wondered where he got the money. The half belt's back, the Prince of Wales check and the bouffant hair, and then he got a Lambretta with a little fucking furry squirrel tail on the end. Brian may have single-handedly started the mod movement, which was art college and south London in origin. He was one of the first to go to the Lyceum and to get the mod gear. He was in a frenzied fashion race at the time — the first to ditch the drape jacket and put on the short boxy one. He was definitely ahead on footwear, with pointy shoes instead of round ones, winkle pickers with Cuban heels — a big revolution. Rockers didn't get to the points until later. He went to the shoemaker and got the points extended four inches, which made it very difficult to walk. It was intense, kind of desperate, this never-ending fashion flash, but funny to watch, and he was a funny bloke too.

I couldn't afford squirrel tails. I was lucky to have a pair of trousers. The opposite of that fashionista stuff was your rockers and your motorbike racers. Nobody could quite put their finger on me. Somehow I managed to have a foot in both camps without having to split my balls. I had my own uniform, winter or summer: Wrangler jacket, purple shirt and black drainpipes. I got a reputation for being impervious to the cold, because I didn't vary my wardrobe much. As for drugs, it was before my time, except for the occasional use of Doris's period pills. The thing people had started taking was ephedrine, which was horrible, so that didn't last long. And then there were nasal inhalers, which were full of Dexedrine and smelled of lavender. You took the top off it and rolled up the cotton wool stuff and made little pills. Dexedrine for colds!

\* \* \*

The figure I'm standing next to in the school picture is Michael Ross. I can no longer listen to certain records without Michael Ross coming to mind. My first public performance was with Michael; we did a couple of school gigs together. He was a special guy, extrovert, talented, up for all risk and adventure. He was a really gifted illustrator, taught me many tricks of how to work pen and ink. And he was into music big-time. Michael and I liked the same kind of music, something that was available for us to play. That's why we gravitated to country music and blues, because we could play it with just ourselves. One's enough, so much better with two. He introduced me to Sanford Clark, a heavy-duty country singer, very like Johnny Cash, came out of the cotton fields and the air force with a US hit called "The Fool." We played his "Son of a Gun," partly because it was the only thing the instruments would bear, but a great song. We did a school party, somewhere round Bexley, in the gymnasium, sang a lot of country stuff as best as we could at the time, with only two guitars and nothing else. What I remember most about our first gig was that we pulled a couple of birds and spent the whole night in a park somewhere, in one of those shelters with a bench and a little roof over it. We didn't really do anything. I touched her breast or something. We were just snogging all night, all those tongues going like eels. And then we just slept there till morning, and I thought, "My first gig and I end up with a chick. Shit! Maybe I've got a future here."

Ross and I played more. It drifted on without any sort of concentrated thought, but you go back again next weekend and there's a bigger crowd.... And there's nothing like an audience doing that to encourage you. I guess somewhere in there was the glimmer.

I had spent my entire school life expecting to do National Service. It was in my brain—I was going to art school and then into the army. And suddenly, just before my seventeenth birthday, in November 1960, it was announced that it was over, ended forever. (The Rolling

Stones would soon be cited as the single reason why it should be brought back.) But that innocent day I remember, at art school, you could almost hear a massive exhale, a huge sense of relief that went through the school. There was no more work that day. I remember all of us guys at that age looking at one another, realizing we're not being sent to a drafty destroyer somewhere, or marching about at Aldershot. Bill Wyman did National Service, in the RAF in Germany, and he quite enjoyed it. But he's older than I am.

At the same time it was "Motherfuckers!" We'd spent all of these years with that cloud over us. Some guys round school would start to deliberately develop a twitch, working their way up to a dangerous personality disorder, so they could be let off. It was a whole built-in system, everyone comparing notes about how you could get out of it. "I've got corns, I can't march."

It changes guys. I saw my older cousins, older friends who'd been through it. They'd come out different men, basically. Left right left right. That drill. It's brainwashing. You can do it in your goddamn sleep. Sometimes these guys did. Their whole mind changed, and their sense of who they were, what level they inhabited. "I've been put in my place and I know where it is." "You're a corporal and don't think you're gonna get any higher in life." I was very aware of it with guys I knew that had done it. A lot of steam seemed to have been taken out of them. They took two years off in the National Service and came back and they're still schoolboys, but by then they're twenty.

Suddenly you felt like you had two free years, but it was a complete illusion, of course. You didn't know what to do with it. Even your parents didn't know what to do with those years, because they were expecting you to disappear at eighteen. It all happened so fast. My life had been plodding along nicely until I found out there was no National Service. There was no way I was going to get out of this goddamn morass, the council estate, the very small horizons. Of course if I'd done it, I'd probably be a general by now. There's no way to stop a primate. If I'm in, I'm in. When they got me in the scouts, I was a patrol leader in three months. I clearly like to run guys about. Give me a platoon, I'll do a good job. Give me a company, I'll do even better. Give me a division, and I'll do wonders. I like to motivate guys, and that's what came in handy with the Stones. I'm really good at pulling a bunch of guys together. If I can pull a bunch of useless Rastas into a viable band and also the Winos, a decidedly unruly band of men, I've got something there. It's not a matter of cracking the whip, it's a matter of just sticking around, doing it, so they know you're in there, leading from the front and not from behind.

And to me, it's not a matter of who's number one, it's what works.

Not long before this book went to press, a letter of mine came to light, which had been in the possession of my aunt Patty for almost fifty years and had never been seen outside my family. She was still alive when she gave it to me, in 2009. In it I describe, among other things, the moment I met Mick Jagger on the train station at Dartford in 1961. The letter was written in April 1962, only four months later, when we were already hanging out and trying to learn how to do it.

*6 Spielman Rd*
*Dartford*
*Kent*

*Dear Pat,*

*So sorry not to have written before (I plead insane) in bluebottle voice. Exit right amid deafening applause.*

*I do hope you're very well.*

*We have survived yet another glorious English Winter. I wonder which day Summer falls on this year?*

*Oh but my dear I have been soooo busy since Christmas beside working at school. You know I was keen on Chuck Berry and I thought I was the only fan for miles but one mornin' on Dartford Stn. (that's so I don't have to write a long word like station) I was holding one of Chuck's records when a guy I knew at primary school 7–11 yrs y'know came up to me. He's got every record Chuck Berry ever made and all his mates have too, they are all rhythm and blues fans, real R&B I mean (not this Dinah Shore, Brook Benton crap) Jimmy Reed, Muddy Waters, Chuck, Howlin' Wolf, John Lee Hooker all the Chicago bluesmen real lowdown stuff, marvelous. Bo Diddley he's another great.*

*Anyways the guy on the station, he is called Mick Jagger and all the chicks and the boys meet every Saturday morning in the 'Carousel' some juke-joint well one morning in Jan I was walking past and decided to look him up. Everybody's all over me I get invited to about 10 parties. Beside that Mick is the greatest R&B singer this side of the Atlantic and I don't mean maybe. I play guitar (electric) Chuck style we got us a bass player and drummer and rhythm-guitar and we practice 2 or 3 nights a week. SWINGIN.'*

*Of course they're all rolling in money and in massive detached houses, crazy, one's even got a butler. I went round there with Mick (in the car of course Mick's not mine of course) OH BOY ENGLISH IS IMPOSSIBLE.*

*"Can I get you anything, sir?"*

*"Vodka and lime, please"*

*"Certainly, sir"*

*I really felt like a lord, nearly asked for my coronet when I left.*

*Everything here is just fine.*

*I just can't lay off Chuck Berry though, I recently got an LP of his straight from Chess Records Chicago cost me less than an English record.*

*Of course we've still got the old Lags here y'know Cliff Richard, Adam Faith and 2 new shockers Shane Fenton and John Leyton SUCH CRAP YOU HAVE NEVER HEARD. Except for that greaseball Sinatra ha ha ha ha ha ha ha.*

*Still I don't get bored anymore. This Saturday I am going to an all night party.*

*"I looked at my watch*
*It was four-o-five*
*Man I didn't know*
*If I was dead or alive"*
*Quote Chuck Berry*
*Reeling and a Rocking*

*12 galls of Beer Barrel of Cyder, 3 bottle Whiskey Wine. Her ma and pa gone away for the weekend I'll twist myself till I drop (I'm glad to say).*

*The Saturday after Mick and I are taking 2 girls over to our favourite Rhythm & Blues club over in Ealing, Middlesex.*

*They got a guy on electric harmonica Cyril Davies fabulous always half drunk unshaven plays like a mad man, marvelous.*

*Well then I can't think of anything else to bore you with, so I'll sign off goodnight viewers*

*BIG GRIN*

*Luff*

*Keith xxxxx*

*Who else would write such bloody crap*

Did we hit it off? You get in a carriage with a guy that's got *Rockin' at the Hops* by Chuck Berry on Chess Records, and *The Best of Muddy Waters* also under his arm, you are gonna hit it off. He's got Henry Morgan's treasure. It's the real shit. I had no idea how to get hold of that. I realize now I'd met him once before outside Dartford Town Hall when he was selling ice creams for a summer job. He must have been about fifteen, just before he left school, about three years before we actually started the Stones, because he just happened to mention that he occasionally did a dance around there doing Buddy Holly and Eddie Cochran stuff. It just clicked in my mind that day. I bought a choc ice. I don't know, it might have been a cornet. I plead the statute of limitations. And then I didn't see him again until the fateful day on the train.

And he was carrying this stuff. "Where the hell did you get this?" It was, always, all about records. From when I was eleven or twelve years old, it was who had the records who you hung with. They were precious things. I was lucky to get two or three singles every six months or something. And he said, "Well, I got this address." He was already writing off to Chicago, and funnily enough to Marshall Chess, who had a summer job with his dad in the mail room there, and who later became the president of Rolling Stones Records. It was a mail-order thing, like Sears, Roebuck. He'd seen this catalogue, which I had never seen. And we just started talking. He was still singing in a little band, doing Buddy Holly stuff, apparently. I'd never heard about any of that. I said, "Well, I play a little." I said, "Come on round, play some other stuff." I almost forgot to get off at Sidcup because I was still copying down the matrix numbers of the Chuck Berry and Muddy Waters records he happened to have with him. *Rockin' at the Hops:* Chess Records CHD-9259.

Mick had seen Buddy Holly play at the Woolwich Granada. It's one of the reasons I cottoned to him, and because he had far more contacts than me, and because this man's got some shit! I was well out of the loop then. I was a yokel compared to Mick, in a way. He had the London thing down... studying at the London School of Economics, meeting a wider range of people. I didn't have the money; I didn't have the knowledge. I just used to read the magazines, like *New Musical Express:* "Eddie Cochran appearing with Buddy Holly." Wow, when I grow up I'll get a ticket. Of course they all croaked before then.

Almost immediately after we met we'd sit around and he'd start to sing and I'd start to play, and "Hey, that ain't bad." And it wasn't difficult; we had nobody to impress except us and we weren't looking to impress ourselves. I was learning too. With Mick and me at the beginning, we'd get, say, a new Jimmy Reed record, and I'd learn the moves on guitar and he would learn the lyrics and get it down, and we would just dissect it as much as two people can. "Does it go like that?" "Yeah, it does as a matter of fact!" And we had fun doing it. I think we both knew we were in a process of learning, and it was something that you wanted to learn and it was ten times better than school. I suppose at that time, it was the mystery of how it was done, and how could you sound like that? This incredible desire to sound that hip and cool. And then you bump into a bunch of guys that feel the same way. And via that you meet other players and people and you think it actually can be done.

Mick and I must have spent a year, while the Stones were coming together and before, record hunting. There were others like us, trawling far and wide, and meeting one another in record shops. If you didn't have money you would just hang and talk. But Mick had these blues contacts. There were a few record collectors, guys that somehow had a channel through to America before anybody else. There was Dave Golding up in Bexleyheath, who had an in with Sue Records, and so we heard artists like Charlie and Inez Foxx, solid-duty soul, who had a big hit with "Mockingbird" a little after this. Golding had the reputation for having the biggest soul and blues collection in southeast London or even beyond, and Mick got to know him and so he would go round. He wouldn't nick records or steal them, there were no cassettes or taping, but sometimes there would be little deals where somebody would do a Grundig reel-to-reel copy for you of this and that. And such a strange bunch of people. Blues aficionados in the '60s were a sight to behold. They met in little gatherings like early Christians, but in the front rooms in southeast London. There was nothing else necessarily in common amongst them at all; they were all different ages and occupations. It was funny to walk into a room where nothing else mattered except he's playing the new Slim Harpo and that was enough to bond you all together.

There was a lot of talk of matrix numbers. There would be these muttered conversations about whether you had the bit of shellac that was from the original pressing from the original company. Later on, everybody would argue about it. Mick and I were smirking at each other across the room, because we were only there to find out a bit more about this new collection of records that had just arrived that we'd heard about. The real magnet was "Hell, I'd love to be able to play like that." But the people you have to meet to get the latest Little Milton record! The real blues purists were very stuffy and conservative, full of disapproval, nerds with glasses deciding what's really blues and what ain't. I mean, these cats *know?* They're sitting in the middle of Bexleyheath in London on a cold and rainy day, "Diggin' My Potatoes"...Half of the songs they're listening to, they have no idea of what they are about, and if they did they'd shit themselves. They have their idea of what the blues are, and that they can only be played by agricultural blacks. For better or worse it was their passion.

And it certainly was mine too, but I wasn't prepared to discuss it. I wouldn't argue about it; I would just say, "Can I get a copy? I know how they're playing it, but I just need to check." That's what we lived for, basically. It was very unlikely that any chick would get in the way, at that point, of getting a chance to hear the new B.B. King or Muddy Waters.


Mick sometimes had the use of his parents' Triumph Herald at the weekend, and I remember we went to Manchester to see a big blues show, and there's Sonny Terry and there's Brownie McGhee, and John Lee Hooker and Muddy Waters. He was the one we wanted to see particularly, but also we wanted to see John Lee. There were others, like Memphis Slim. It was a whole revue that was going through Europe. And Muddy came on, acoustic guitar, Mississippi Delta stuff, and played a magnificent half an hour. And then there was an interval and he came back with an electric band. And they virtually booed him off the stage. He plowed through them like a tank, as Dylan did a year or so later at the Manchester Free Trade Hall. But it was hostile—and that's when I realized that people were not really listening to the music, they just wanted to be part of this wised-up enclave. Muddy and the band were playing great. It was a knockout band. He had Junior Wells with him; I think Hubert Sumlin was on there too. But for this audience, blues was only blues if somebody got up there in a pair of old blue dungarees and sang about how his old lady left him. None of these blues purists could play anything. But their Negroes had to be dressed in overalls and go "Yes'm, boss." And in actual fact they're city blokes who are so hip it's not true. What did electric have to do with it? Cat's playing the same notes. It's just a little louder and it's a little more forceful. But no, it was "Rock and roll. Fuck off." They wanted a frozen frame, not knowing that whatever they were listening to was only part of the process; something had gone before and it was going to move on.

Passions ran very high in those days. It wasn't just mods against bikers, or the loathing of the threatened trad jazzers for us rock and rollers. There were micro-squabbles almost unbelievable to imagine now. The BBC was giving live coverage to the Beaulieu Jazz Festival in 1961 and they had to actually shut down the broadcast when trad jazz and modern jazz fans started to beat the shit out of each other, and the whole crowd lost control. The purists thought of blues as part of jazz, so they felt betrayed when they saw electric guitars—a whole bohemian subculture was threatened by the leather mob. There was certainly a political undercurrent in all this. Alan Lomax and Ewan MacColl—singers and famous folk song collectors who were patriarchs, or ideologues, of the folk boom—took a Marxist line that this music belonged to the people and must be protected from the corruption of capitalism. That's why "commercial" was such a dirty word in those days. In fact the slanging matches in the music press resembled real political fisticuffs: phrases like "tripe mongers," "legalized murder," "selling out." There were ludicrous discussions about authenticity. Yet the fact is, there was actually an audience for the blues artists in England. In America most of those artists had got used to playing cabaret acts, which they quickly found out didn't go down well in the UK. Here you could play the blues. Big Bill Broonzy realized he could pick up a bit of dough if he switched from Chicago blues to being a folksy bluesman for European audiences. Half of those black guys never went back to America, because they realized that they were being treated like shit at home and meanwhile, lovely Danish birds were tripping over themselves to accommodate them. Why go back? They'd found out after World War II that they were treated well in Europe, certainly in Paris, like Josephine Baker, Champion Jack Dupree and Memphis Slim. That's why Denmark became a haven for so many jazz players in the '50s.

Mick and I had a totally identical taste in music. We never needed to question or explain. It was all unsaid. We'd hear something, we'd both look at each other at once. Everything was to do with sound. We'd hear a record and go, That's wrong. That's faking. *That's* real. It was either that's the shit or that isn't the shit, no matter what kind of music you were talking about. I really liked some pop music if it was the shit. But there was a definite line of what the shit was and what wasn't the shit. Very strict. First off, I think to Mick and me it was like, we've got to learn more, there's more out there, because then we branched out to rhythm and blues. And we loved the pop records. Give me the Ronettes, or the Crystals. I could listen to them all night. But the minute we went on stage trying to do one of those songs, it was like, "Go to the broom closet."

I was looking for the core of it — the expression. You would have no jazz without blues out of slavery — that most recent and particular version of slavery, not us poor Celts for example, under the Roman boot. They put those people through misery, not just in America. But there's something produced by its survivors that is very elemental. It's not something you take in in the head, it's something you take in in the guts. It's beyond the matter of the musicality of it, which is very variable and flexible. There's loads of kinds of blues. There's very light kind of blues, there's very swamp kind of blues, and it's the swamp basically where I exist. Listen to John Lee Hooker. His is a very archaic form of playing. Most of the time it ignores chord changes. They're suggested but not played. If he's playing with somebody else, that player's chord will change, but he stays, he doesn't move. And it's relentless. And the other, the most important thing apart from the great voice and that relentless guitar, was that foot stomp, a crawling king snake. He carried his own two-by-four wood block to amplify his stomps. Bo Diddley was another one who loved to do just that one elemental chord, everything on one chord, the only thing that moves is the vocal and the way you're playing it. I really only learned more about this later on. Then there was the power in people's voices, like Muddy, John Lee, Bo Diddley. It wasn't loud, necessarily, it just came from way down deep. The whole body was involved; they weren't just singing from the heart, they were singing from the guts. That always impressed me. And that's why there's a lot of difference between blues singers that don't play an instrument and blues players that do, be it piano or guitar, because they have to develop their own way of call and respond. You're going to sing something and then you've got to play something that answers or asks another question and then you resolve. And so your timing and your phrasing become different. If you're a solo singer you tend to concentrate on the singing, and most times hopefully for the better, but sometimes it can be divorced from the music in a way.

One day, very early on after we'd met up again, Mick and I went to the seaside and we played in a pub, on a trip with my mum and dad to Devon one weekend. The ghost of Doris must be summoned to recount this strange occasion, because I remember little about it. But we must have had a glimmer to have done it at all.

**Doris:** We had Keith and Mick down in Beesands in
Devon for the weekend one summer when they were sixteen,

seventeen. They used to run coaches from Dartford. Keith had his guitar with him. And Mick was bored to tears down there. "No women," he said. "No women." There was nobody down there. Beautiful place. We rented a cottage on the beach. The old boys used to go out and catch mackerel right outside the front door. They used to sell them for sixpence each. Not much for them to do. Swim ... They went to the local pub because Keith brought his guitar down. They were quite amazed how he could play then. We drove them home in the car. It was about eight or ten hours in the Vauxhall normally. Then of course the battery went, didn't it? We had no lights. I remember pulling up outside Mrs. Jagger's house at the Close. "Where were you? Why are you so late?!" What a murderous drive home.

Mick was hanging out with Dick Taylor, his mate from grammar school who was at Sidcup too. I joined them in late 1961. There was also Bob Beckwith, the guitar player who had the amplifier, which made him really important. Quite often in the early days, there was one amplifier with three guitars going through it. We called ourselves Little Boy Blue and the Blue Boys. My guitar, this time an f-hole arch-top Höfner steel string, was Blue Boy—the words written on its face—and because of that I was Boy Blue. That was my very first steel-string guitar. You'll only find pictures of it in the club gigs, before the takeoff. I bought it secondhand in Ivor Mairants, off Oxford Street. You knew it had had one owner because of the patches and sweat marks on the fret board. He's either playing up the top, the fiddly bits, or he's a chord man. It's like a map, a seismograph. And I left it either on the Victoria line or the Bakerloo line on the London Underground. But where better to bury it than the Bakerloo line? It left scars.

We gathered in Bob Beckwith's front room in Bexleyheath. Once or twice Dick Taylor used his house. At the time Dick was very studious, you'd put him in the purist vein, which didn't stop him becoming a Pretty Thing in a couple of years. He was the real thing, a good player; he had the feel. But he was very academic about his blues, and actually it was a good thing because we were all a bit off the flight. We'd just as soon break into "Not Fade Away" or "That'll Be the Day" or "C'mon Everybody," or straight into "I Just Want to Make Love to You." We saw it all as the same kind of stuff. Bob Beckwith had a Grundig, and it was on that that we made the first tape of any of us together, our first attempt at recording. Mick gave me a copy of it—he bought it back at auction. A reel-to-reel tape and the sound quality is terrible. Our first repertoire included "Around and Around" and "Reelin' and Rockin'" by Chuck Berry, "Bright Lights, Big City" by Jimmy Reed, and to put the icing on the cake, "La Bamba," sung by Mick with pseudo-Spanish words.

Rhythm and blues was the gate. Cyril Davies and Alexis Korner got a club going, the weekly spot at the Ealing Jazz Club, where rhythm and blues freaks could conglomerate. Without them there might have been nothing. It was where the whole blues network could go, all the Bexleyheath collectors. People who read the ad came down from Manchester and Scotland just to meet the faithful and hear Alexis Korner's Blues Incorporated, which also had the young Charlie Watts on drums and sometimes Ian Stewart on piano. That's where I fell in love with the men! Almost nobody was booking this kind of music in clubs at the time. It's where we all met to swap ideas and swap records and hang. Rhythm and blues was a very important distinction in the '60s. Either you were blues and jazz or you were rock and roll, but rock and roll had died and gone pop—nothing left in it. Rhythm and blues was a term we pounced on because it meant really powerful blues jump bands from Chicago. It broke through the barriers. We used to soften the blow for the purists who liked our music but didn't want to approve of it, by saying it's not rock and roll, it's rhythm and blues. Totally pointless categorization of something that is the same shit—it just depends on how much you lay the backbeat down or how flash you play it.

Alexis Korner was the daddy of the London blues scene—not a great player himself, but a generous man and a real promoter of talent. Also something of an intellectual in the musical world. He lectured on jazz and blues at such places as the Institute of Contemporary Arts. He used to work for the BBC—DJ'ing and interviewing musicians, which meant he was in close contact with God. He knew his stuff backwards; he knew every player who was worth his salt. He was part Austrian, part Greek and had been brought up in North Africa. He had a real Gypsy-looking face with long sideburns, but he spoke with a really rich "I say, old boy" voice, very precise English.

Alexis's band was damn good. Cyril Davies was a hell of a harp player, one of the best harp players you've ever heard. Cyril was a panel beater from Wembley, and his manners and his way of coming on were exactly what you'd expect of a panel beater from Wembley, with a huge thirst for bourbon. He had this aura because he'd actually been to Chicago and he'd seen Muddy and Little Walter so he came back with a halo round him. Cyril didn't like anybody. He didn't like us because he felt the winds of change coming and he didn't want it. He died very soon afterwards, in 1964, but he'd already broken away from Alexis's band in 1963 to form the R&B All-Stars, with a weekly gig at the Marquee.

The Ealing Club was a trad jazz club that Blues Incorporated took over on Saturday nights. It was a funky room, sometimes ankle deep in condensation. It was under Ealing tube station, and the roof over the stage was one of those thick glass cobbled pavements, so there's all these people walking over your head. And every now and again, Alexis would say, "You want to come up and play?" And you're playing an electric guitar and you're ankle deep in water, and you're just hoping everything's grounded right, otherwise sparks will fly. My equipment was always on a knife edge. When I got round to wire strings, they were expensive. If one broke, you'd keep another one and then loop them together and extend it and put it back on, and it would work! If the string could at least cover the fret board, you knotted it just above the nut and then extended it to cover the tuning pegs. It did affect tuning to a certain extent! Half a string here and half a string there. Thank God for scouting and knotting.

I had a thing called a DeArmond pickup. And it was unique. You could clamp it above the soundboard and it slid up and down on a spindle. You didn't have a bass pickup or a treble pickup. If you wanted a softer sound, you slid the fucker up the spindle towards the neck and so you got a bassier sound up there. And if you wanted treble, you slid it down the pole again. And of course this played havoc with its wiring. I used to carry a soldering kit for emergencies, because you'd be sliding this thing up and down, and it was just so breakable. I was always soldering and rewiring behind the amp—a Little Giant amp the size of a radio. I was one of the first to get an amp. We were all using tape recorders before that. Dick Taylor used to plug into his sister's Bush record player. My first amp was a radio; I just took that apart. My mother was pissed off. The radio's not working because I've got it apart and I'm plugging, *zzzz,* just trying to get a sound. In that respect good training for later on—honing your sound, matching guitars to amps. We started from scratch, with the tubes and valves. Sometimes if you take one valve out, you can get this really raunchy, dirty sound because you're pushing the machine and it's got to work overtime. If you put the double-A valve back in, then you've got this sweeter sound. That's how I got electrocuted so many times. I kept forgetting to unplug the fucker before I started poking around in the back.

We first met Brian Jones at the Ealing Jazz Club. He was calling himself Elmo Lewis. He wanted to be Elmore James at the time.

"You'll have to get a tan and put on a few inches, boy." But slide guitar was a real novelty in England, and Brian played it that night. He played "Dust My Broom," and it was electrifying. He played it beautifully. We were very impressed with Brian. I think Mick was the first one to go up and talk to him, and discovered that he had his own band, most of whom deserted him in the next few weeks.

Mick and I had come up together to the club and done Chuck Berry numbers, which annoyed Cyril Davies, who thought it was rock and roll and he couldn't play it anyway. When you start to play in public and you're playing with some guys that have done it before, you're low in the hierarchy and you always feel you're being tested. You've got to be there, on time, your equipment's got to be working, which it rarely was in my case. You have to measure up. Suddenly you're in with the big boys, you're not just pissing around in school gyms. Shit, this is pro. At least semipro; pro with no money.

I left art school around this time. At the end your teacher says, "Well, I think this is pretty good," and they send you off to J. Walter Thompson and you have an appointment, and by then, in a way you know what's coming — three or four real smarty-pants, with the usual bow ties. "Keith, is it? Nice to see you. Show us what you've got." And you lay the old folder out. "Hmmmm. I say, we've had a good look at this, Keith, and it does show some promise. By the way, do you make a good cup of tea?" I said yes, but not for you. I walked off with my folio — it was green, I remember — and I dumped it in the garbage can when I got downstairs. That was my final attempt to join society on their terms. The second pink slip. I didn't have the patience or the facility to be a hack in an advertising agency. I was going to end up the tea boy. I wasn't very nice to them in the interview. Basically I wanted an excuse to be thrown out on my own and thrown back on music. I think, OK, I've got two free years, not in the army. I'm going to be a bluesman.

I went to the Bricklayers Arms, a seedy pub in Soho, for the first time for the first rehearsal for what turned out to be the Stones. I think it was May of '62, lovely summer evening. Just off Wardour Street. Strip Alley. I get there, I've got my guitar with me. And as I get there the pub's just opened. Typical brassy blond old barmaid, not many customers, stale beer. She sees the guitar and says, "Upstairs." And I can hear this boogie-woogie piano, this unbelievable Meade Lux Lewis and Albert Ammons stuff. I'm suddenly transported in a way. I feel like a musician and I haven't even got there! I could have been in the middle of Chicago, in the middle of Mississippi. I've got to go up there and meet this man who's playing this, and I've got to play with him. And if I don't measure up, it's over. That was really my feeling as I walked up those stairs, *creak creak creak*. In a way I walk up those stairs and come down a different person.

Ian Stewart was the only one in the room, with this horsehair sofa that was split, horsehairs hanging out. He's got on a pair of Tyrolean leather shorts. He's playing an upright piano and he's got his back to me because he's looking out of the window where he's got his bike chained to a meter, making sure it's not nicked. At the same time he's watching all the strippers going from one club to another with their little round hatboxes and wigs on. "Phoar, look at that." All the while this Leroy Carr stuff is rumbling off his fingers. And I walk in with this brown plastic guitar case. And just stand there. It was like meeting the headmaster. All I could hope for was that my amp would work.

Stu had gone down to the Ealing Club because he'd seen an ad Brian Jones had placed in *Jazz News* in the spring of '62 for players wanting to start an R&B band. Brian and Stu started rehearsing with a bunch of different musicians; everybody would chip in two quid for an upstairs room in a pub. He'd seen Mick and me at the Ealing Club doing a couple of numbers and invited us along. In fact, to give Mick his due, Stu remembered that Mick had been coming already to his rehearsals, and Mick said, "I'm not doin' it if Keith's not doin' it." "Oh, you made it, did you?" And I started with him and he says, "You're not gonna play that rock-and-roll shit, are ya?" Stu had massive reservations and he was suspicious of rock and roll. I'm "Yeah," and then I start to play some Chuck Berry. And he's "Oh, you know Johnnie Johnson?" who was Chuck's piano player, and we started to sling the hash, boogie-woogie. That's all we did. And then the other guys slowly started to turn up. It wasn't just Mick and Brian. Geoff Bradford, a lovely slide blues guitar player who used to play with Cyril Davies. Brian Knight, a blues fan and his big number was "Walk On, Walk On." He had that down and that was it. So Stu could have played with all these other cats, and actually we were third in line for this setup. Mick and I were brought in as maybes, tryouts. These cats were playing clubs with Alexis Korner; they knew shit. We were brand-new in town in those terms. And I realized that Stu had to make up his mind whether he was going to go for these real traditional folk blues players. Because by then I'd played some hot boogie-woogie and some Chuck Berry. My equipment had worked. And by the end of the evening I knew there was a band in the making. Nothing was said, but I knew that I'd got Stu's attention. Geoff Bradford and Brian Knight were a very successful blues band after the Stones, Blues by Six. But they were basically traditional players who had no intention of playing anything else except what they knew: Sonny Terry and Brownie McGhee, Big Bill Broonzy. Stu I think that day realized by the time I'd sung him "Sweet Little Sixteen" and "Little Queenie," and he'd got behind me that somehow a deal had been made without anything being said. We just hit a chord together. "So I'll be back then, right?" "See you next Thursday."

Ian Stewart. I'm still working for him. To me the Rolling Stones is his band. Without his knowledge and organization, without the leap he made from where he was coming from, to take a chance on playing with this bunch of kids, we'd be nowhere. I don't know what the attraction was with Stu and me. But he was absolutely the main impetus behind what happened next. Stu to me was a much older man—

actually only by about three or four years, but at that time so it seemed. And he knew people. I knew nothing. I'd just come from the sticks.

I think he'd started to enjoy hanging around with us. He just felt there was some energy there. So somehow these blues players fell away and it was Brian, Mick, Stu and me, and Dick Taylor on bass. At first, that was the skeleton and we were looking for a drummer. We said, "God, we'd love that Charlie Watts if we could afford him"—because we all thought Charlie Watts was a God-given drummer—and Stu put the feelers out. And Charlie said I'd love any gigs I can get, but I need money to hump these drums on the tube. He said if you can come back to me and say you've got a couple of solid gigs a week, I'm in.

Stu was solid, formidable looking, with a huge protruding jaw, though he was a good-looking guy. I'm sure much of his character was influenced by his looks, and people's reactions to them, from when he was a kid. He was detached, very dry, down-to-earth and full of incongruous phrases. Driving at speed, for example, would be "going at a vast rate of knots." His natural authority over us, which never changed, was expressed as "Come on, angel drawers," "my little three-chord wonders" or "my little shower of shit." He hated some of the rock-and-roll stuff I played. He hated Jerry Lee Lewis for years— "Oh, it's all just histrionics." Eventually he softened on Jerry, he had to crumble and admit that Jerry Lee had one of the best left hands he'd ever heard. Flamboyance and showmanship were not in Stu's bag. You played in clubs, it had nothing to do with showing off.

By day Ian worked in a suit and tie at Imperial Chemical Industries near Victoria Embankment, and this is what helped to fund our rehearsal room fees later on. He put his money where his mouth was, at least where his heart was, because he didn't talk a lot about it. The only fantasy Stu ever had was his insistence that he was the rightful heir to Pittenweem, which is a fishing village across from St. Andrews golf course. He always felt cheated, usurped through some weird Scottish lineage. You can't argue with a guy like that. Why wasn't the piano loud enough? Look, you're talking to the laird of Pittenweem.

In other words, this is not worth discussing, you know? I once said, "What's the tartan, then, of the Stewart clan?" He said, "Ooh, black-and-white check with various colors." Stu was very dry. He saw the funny side of things. And it was Stu who had to pick up all the crap after the mayhem. There were loads of guys that were technically ten times better, but with his feel on the left hand, they could never get to where he was. He might have been the laird of Pittenweem, but his left hand came out of the Congo.

By this time Brian's got three babies with three different women and he's living in London with the latest, Pat, and the kid, having finally left Cheltenham with shotguns firing at his heels. They were living in this damp basement in Powis Square with fungus growing up the wall. And that's where I first heard Robert Johnson, and came under Brian's tutorship and delved back into the blues with him. I was astounded at what I heard. It took guitar playing, songwriting, delivery, to a totally different height. And at the same time it confused us, because it wasn't band music, it was one guy. So how can we do this? And we realized that the guys we were playing, like Muddy Waters, had also grown up with Robert Johnson and had translated it into a band format. In other words, it was just a progression. Robert Johnson was like an orchestra all by himself. Some of his best stuff is almost Bach-like in construction. Unfortunately, he screwed up with the chicks and had a short life. But a brilliant burst of inspiration. He gave you a platform to work on, no doubt as he did to Muddy and the other guys we were listening to. What I found about the blues and music, tracing things back, was that nothing came from itself. As great as it is, this is not one stroke of genius. This cat was listening to somebody and it's his variation on the theme. And so you suddenly realize that everybody's connected here. This is not just that he's fantastic and the rest are crap; they're all interconnected. And the further you went back into music and time, and with the blues you go back to the '20s, because you're basically going through recorded music, you think thank God for recording. It's the best thing that's happened to us since writing.

But real life sometimes entered our domain, and in this case Mick had come back drunk one night to visit Brian, found he wasn't there and screwed his old lady. This caused a seismic tremble, upset Brian very badly and resulted in Pat leaving him. Brian also got thrown out of his flat. Mick felt a little responsible, so he found a flat in a dismal bungalow in Beckenham, in a suburban street, and we all went to live there. It was there I went in 1962 when I left home. It was a gradual departure. A night here and there, then a week, then forever. There was no final moment of parting, of shutting the wicker gate behind me.

Doris had this to say on the subject:

**Doris:** From eighteen till he left home at twenty, Keith was in between jobs, nothing, that's why his dad got on at him. Get your hair cut and get yourself a job. I waited till Keith left before I moved out. I wouldn't go while he was at home. I couldn't leave him, could I? Break his heart. Then on the day I moved out, Bert went to work; Keith wasn't with me. I had an electric light bill in my hand, and I went out and I posted the electric light bill back in! So Bert could pay it. Nice gesture, wasn't it? Bill bought a ground-floor flat, because I told him I had to get out. They were just finishing these new flats, and he went up, done a deal with the builders and we moved in. Bill had some money. Bought it straight out. First telephone I had was when Bill bought that flat. I phoned Keith up one night. He said, "Yes?" I said, "Keith, we've moved into this flat." I said, "I've got a phone, isn't it lovely?" He wasn't that pleased.

It was here, in Beckenham, that we began mysteriously to collect this little core collection of early fans, including Haleema Mohamed, my first love. Recently someone sold back to me a diary I kept in 1963 — I think the only diary I ever wrote, more like a logbook of the Stones' progress in those dire days. I must have left it in one of the flats we were always vacating, and whoever it was held on to it for all that time. In its back pocket was a tiny picture of Lee, as I called her. She was a beauty, with a slightly Indian look about her. It was the eyes that always got me and her smile and they're both in the picture, as I remember her. She was at least two or three years younger than me, fifteen or at the most sixteen, and she had an English mother. I never saw her father, but I remember meeting the rest of her family. I remember going to pick her up and just saying hello to them in Holborn.

I was in love with Lee. Our relationship was touchingly innocent — maybe partly because if we ever got close we'd have to bunk up in a room full of other people, like Mick or Brian. And she was very young and lived with her parents in Holborn, an only child, like me. She must have put up with a lot, however fond she was of me. And it's clear that we had one breakup and then got together again. "Second time around" says the diary, bitterly.

She was one of a gang of girls who used to come around in 1962. Where they came from we never figured out, though my diary shows that we met at least once at the Ken Colyer Club. There wasn't a fan club in those days. This was the pre–fan club period. I don't even know if we'd had any gigs. We just used to sit around and practice and learn. And somehow we got invaded by a bunch of five or six cockney girls from Holborn and Bermondsey. They used to speak great cockney back slang; they were really young, but they took it on themselves to take care of us. They used to come around and do our washing and cooking and then stay overnight and do the rest. It was really no big deal. Sex then was mostly just like, it's a bit chilly, let's cuddle, the gas has gone out and no shillings left. I was in love with Lee for a long time. She was just incredibly nice to me. It wasn't a big sexual thing, we just sort of grew into each other. Maybe we were a little pissed one night, and also that shit builds up. Whenever we saw each other, we kept looking at each other and you know there's something between you, it's whether...can you get across the gap? And eventually, it usually happens. And, according to the diary, she came back a second time.

She must have been around for our first gig as "the Rollin' Stones," a band name Stu highly disapproved of. Brian, after figuring how much it would cost, called up *Jazz News,* which was a kind of "who's playing where" rag, and said, "We've got a gig at..." "What do you call yourselves?" We stared at one another. "It?" Then "Thing?" This call is costing. Muddy Waters to the rescue! First track on *The Best of Muddy Waters* is "Rollin' Stone." The cover is on the floor. Desperate, Brian, Mick and I take the dive. "The Rolling Stones." Phew!! That saved sixpence.

A gig! Alexis Korner's band was booked to do a BBC live broadcast on July 12, 1962, and he'd asked us if we'd fill in for him at the Marquee. The drummer that night was Mick Avory—not Tony Chapman, as history has mysteriously handed it down—and Dick Taylor on the bass. The core Stones, Mick, Brian and I, played our set list: "Dust My Broom," "Baby What's Wrong?" "Doing the Crawdaddy," "Confessin' the Blues," "Got My Mojo Working." You're sitting with some guys, and you're playing and you go, "Ooh, yeah!" That feeling is worth more than anything. There's a certain moment when you realize that you've actually just left the planet for a bit and that nobody can touch you. You're elevated because you're with a bunch of guys that want to do the same thing as you. And when it works, baby, you've got wings. You know you've been somewhere most people will never get; you've been to a special place. And then you want to keep going back and keep landing again, and when you land you get busted. But you always want to go back there. It's flying without a license.

*Dezo Hoffmann / Rex USA*

# Chapter Four

Mick, Brian and me in Edith Grove, summer of '62. Learning
Chicago blues. Marquee, Ealing Club, Crawdaddy Club. Turf
fights with the trad jazzers. Bill Wyman comes with his Vox.
Wongin' the pog at the Station Hotel. We get Charlie on board.
Andrew Loog Oldham signs us with Decca. First UK tour
with the Everly Brothers, Bo Diddley and Little Richard;
our music drowned in riots. The Beatles give us a song. Andrew
locks Mick and me in a kitchen and we write our first one.

The Rolling Stones spent the first year of their life hanging
places, stealing food and rehearsing. We were paying to be the
Rolling Stones. The place where we lived — Mick, Brian and I — at
102 Edith Grove, in Fulham, was truly disgusting. We almost made it
our professional business for it to be so, since we had little means to
make it otherwise. We moved in in the summer of 1962 and lived
there for a year through the coldest winter since 1740, as records
attested, and the shillings we fed into the meter for warmth, for electricity and gas, were not that easy to come by. It was mattresses and no
furniture to speak of, only a threadbare carpet. There was no fixed
rotation between the two beds and a couple of mattresses. And it
didn't really matter much; usually all three of us would wake up on
that floor, where we had the enormous radiogram that Brian had
brought with him, a great '50s warm-up number.

We'd sit around working out the music in the Wetherby Arms, in
the King's Road, Chelsea. Usually I'd go round the back and steal their

empties and then sell them back to them. You got a couple of pence on a beer bottle. Which in those times was not a lot of money. We stole empties at the parties we went to as well. Get one of us in first, and then the rest would come in in gang formation.

Edith Grove was a funny household. Three chicks underneath on the ground floor, student teachers from Sheffield; two poofters from Buxton above us. We had the middle floor. What the hell are we doing in Chelsea living between these northerners? It was a real slice of "Welcome to London," since nobody came from there.

The student teachers from Sheffield are probably headmistresses now. But at the time they were a randy bunch. Which we had very little time for. We were in and out like Flynn. Mick and Brian were down there, but I never got involved with them. I didn't fancy 'em. But I found they came in handy. They would do a bit of laundry for you. Or my mum would send the washing via Bill from her washing-machine demonstrations. The two incipient poofters hung out in the pubs in Earls Court with the Australian poofters, of which there were many at that time. Earls Court was Australia, basically. And a lot of them were wang-danglers because they could be more poofter in London than they could in Melbourne or Sydney or Brisbane. The guys above us would be talking with an Australian accent when they came back from these Earls Court outings. They're going, "Hello, cobber!" "I thought you were from Buxton."

Our flatmate was called James Phelge, the origin of half of the early pen name for our songwriting, Nanker Phelge. A "nanker" is a look — the face stretched to terrible contortions by the fingers inserted into all available orifices — a great Brian speciality. We advertised for a flatmate over the mike at the Ealing Club, someone to share the rent. Phelge must have sensed what he was getting into. He turned out to be perhaps the only person on the planet who could have lived in that terrible place with us — and even outflank us in gross and unacceptable behavior. He was in any case apparently the only one willing to live with this bunch pounding through the night, learning their crap, trying to find a gig. We were just idiotic together. We were still teen-agers at the time, although at the top end of the scale. We dared each other: who could be more disgusting than anybody else. You think you can disgust me? I'll show you. We'd get back from a gig and Phelge would be standing at the top of the stairs saying "Welcome home," stark naked with his shitty underpants on his head, or pissing on you or flobbing at you. Phelge was a serious flobber. Mucus from every area he could summon up. He loved to walk into a room with a huge snot hanging out of his nose and dribbling down his chin, but otherwise be perfectly charming. "Hello, how are you? And this is Andrea, and this is Jennifer..." We had names for all different kinds of flob: Green Gilberts, Scarlet Jenkins. There was the Gabardine Helmsman, which is the one that people aren't aware of; they snot it and it hangs on their lapel like a medal. That was the winner. Yellow Humphrey was another. The Flying V was the one that missed the handkerchief. People were always having colds in those days; things were always running out of their noses and they didn't know what to do with them. And it can't have been cocaine; it was a little too early. I think it was just bad English winters.

Because we had nothing much to do, we had very few gigs, we ended up studying people. And we'd always be nicking things from the other flats. Go down and rifle the girls' drawers while they were out, find a shilling or two. The bog was rigged up for recording. We'd just switch on if somebody went in there, especially if one of the chicks downstairs said, "Can I use your john?" because theirs was occupied. "Yes, sure." "Quick! Turn it on." And then, after every "performance," when the chain was pulled it sounded like incredible applause. We'd play it back later. After every visit there it sounded like Sunday night at the London Palladium.

The worst horror, certainly for any visitors to Edith Grove, was the pile of unwashed dishes in the "kitchen," the substances growing out of the crockery, the greasy, cold pans piled in junked pyramids of foulness that no one could bear to touch. Yet it is true that one day we looked at this mess, Phelge and I, and thought that there was perhaps nothing else to do than to clean it. Given that Phelge was one of the filthiest people in the world, that was some historic decision. But that day we were overwhelmed by the amount of rubbish and so we went downstairs and stole a bottle of washing-up liquid.

At the time, the poverty seemed constant, unmovable. To go through that winter of '62 was rough. It was a cold winter. But then Brian had this fantastic idea of bringing up his friend Dick, who had his Territorial Army bonus, and Brian was merciless towards Dick. We didn't mind because we were getting the fallout. This is when nobody's got two pennies to rub to-fucking-gether. Dick Hattrell was his name, and he was from Tewkesbury. And Brian almost killed the man. He would force him to walk behind him and pay for everything. Cruel, cruel, cruel. He would make him stand outside while we ate and he paid. Even Mick and I were shocked, and we were pretty cold-blooded. Sometimes he'd let him in for dessert. There was a streak of real cruelty in Brian. Dick Hattrell was Brian's old school friend and he was panting like a little puppy after Brian. Once Brian left the poor sod outside with no clothes on, and it's snowing and he's begging and Brian's laughing, and I'm not going to go to the window, I'm laughing too much. How could a guy let himself get into that position? Brian stole all his clothes and then sent him outside in his underpants. In a snowstorm. "What do you mean I owe you twenty-three pounds? Fuck off." He's just paid for us all evening; we've been feasting like kings. Terrible really, terrible. I said, "Brian, that's just cold-blooded, man." Brian, a cold-blooded, vicious motherfucker. Only short and blond with it. I wonder what happened to Hattrell. If he survived that, he could survive anything.

We were cynical, sarcastic and rude where necessary. We used to go to the local caff, which we called the "Ernie" because everyone in there was named Ernie, or so it seemed. "Ernie" became everybody else. "What a fucking Ernie, Christ." Anybody that insisted on doing his job without doing you a favor was a fuckin' Ernie. Ernie was the working man. Only got one thing on his mind, making another extra shilling.

If I'd had the choice of finding a diary of any three-month period of the Stones' history, it would have been this one, the moment the band was hatching. And I did find one, covering January to March of 1963. The real surprise was that I kept any record of this period. It covers the crucial span when Bill Wyman arrived, or, more important, his Vox amplifier appeared and Bill came with it, and when we were trying to snare, to coin a phrase, Charlie Watts. I even kept accounts of the money we earned at gigs, the pounds, shillings and pence. Often it just said "o" when we played for beer at tiny end-of-term school dances. But entries also show January 21, Ealing Club: o; January 22, Flamingo: o; February 1, Red Lion: £1 10s. At least we'd got a gig. As long as you've got a gig, life is wonderful. Somebody called us up and booked us! I mean, wow. We must be doing something right. Otherwise shoplifting, picking up beer bottles and hunger was the order of the day. We used to pool our money for guitar strings, mending amplifiers and valves. Just to keep what we had going was an incredible expense.

Inside the cover of the pocket diary are the heavily inked words "Chuck," "Reed," "Diddley." There you have it. That was all we listened to at the time. Just American blues or rhythm and blues or country blues. Every waking hour of every day was just sitting in front of the speakers, trying to figure out how these blues were made. You collapsed on the floor with a guitar in your hands. That was it. You never stop learning an instrument, but at that time it was still very much searching about. You had to make sounds if you wanted to play a guitar. We went for a Chicago blues sound, as close as we could get it—two guitars, bass and drums and a piano—and sat around and listened to every Chess record ever made. Chicago blues hit us right between the eyes. We'd all grown up with everything else that everybody had grown up with, rock and roll, but we focused on that. And as long as we were all together, we could pretend to be black men. We soaked up the music, but it didn't change the color of our skin. Some even went whiter. Brian Jones was a blond Elmore James from Cheltenham. And why not? You can come from anywhere and be any color. We found that out later. Cheltenham, admittedly, is a bit far-fetched. Blues players from Cheltenham, there ain't a lot. And we didn't want to make money. We despised money, we despised cleanliness, we just wanted to be black motherfuckers. Fortunately we got plucked out of that. But that was the school; that's where the band was born.

The early days of the magic art of guitar weaving started then. You realize what you can do playing guitar with another guy, and what the two of you can do is to the power of ten, and then you add other people. There's something beautifully friendly and elevating about a bunch of guys playing music together. This wonderful little world that is unassailable. It's really teamwork, one guy supporting the others, and it's all for one purpose, and there's no flies in the ointment, for a while. And nobody conducting, it's all up to you. It's really jazz — that's the big secret. Rock and roll ain't nothing but jazz with a hard backbeat.

Jimmy Reed was a very big model for us. That was always two-guitar stuff. Almost a study in monotony in many ways, unless you got in there. But then Jimmy Reed had something like twenty hits in the charts with basically the same song. He had two tempos. But he understood the magic of repetition, of monotony, transforming itself to become this sort of hypnotic, trancelike thing. We were fascinated by it, Brian and I. We would spend every spare moment trying to get down Jimmy Reed's guitar sounds.

Jimmy Reed was always pissed out of his brain. There was one famous time, he was already like an hour and forty-five minutes late for a show, finally they get him onto the stage and he goes, "This one's called 'Baby What You Want Me to Do?'" And he threw up over the whole first two rows. Probably happened many times. He always had his wife with him, whispering the lyrics in his ear. You can even hear it on the records sometimes: "Going up... going down," but it worked. He was a solid favorite to the black folks in the South, and occasionally in the whole world. It was a fascinating study in restraint.

Minimalism has a certain charm. You say, that's a bit monotonous, but by the time it's finished, you're wishing it hadn't. There's nothing bad about monotony; everyone's got to live with it. Great titles— "Take Out Some Insurance." This is not your everyday song title. And it would always come down to him and his old lady having a fight or something. "Bright Lights, Big City," "Baby What You Want Me to Do?" "String to Your Heart," wicked songs. One of Jimmy's lines was "Don't pull no subway, I rather see you pull a train." Which actually means don't go on the dope, don't go underground, I'd rather see you either drunk or on cocaine. Took me years and years to decipher this.

And I was heavily into Muddy Waters's guitarist Jimmy Rogers, and the guys that played behind Little Walter, the Myers brothers. Talk about an ancient form of weaving, they were the masters. Half of the band was the Muddy Waters band, which included Little Walter as well. But while he was making these records, he had another little team, Louis Myers and his brother David, founders of the Aces. Two great guitar players. Pat Hare used to play with Muddy Waters and also did a few tracks with Chuck Berry. One of his unreleased numbers was called "I'm Gonna Murder My Baby," dug up from the Sun vaults after he did just that, and then killed the policeman sent to investigate. He went in for life in the early '60s and died in a Minnesota jail. There was Matt Murphy and Hubert Sumlin. They were all Chicago blues players, some more solo than others. But as teams, if we keep it down to that, the Myers brothers definitely go way up to the top of the list. Jimmy Rogers with Muddy Waters, an amazing pair of weavers. Chuck Berry is fantastic, but he would weave by himself, with himself. He did great overdubs with his own guitar because he was too cheap to hire another guy most of the time. But that's just on records; you can't re-create that live. But his "Memphis, Tennessee" is probably one of the most incredible little bits of overdubbing and tinkering that I've ever heard. Let alone a sweet song. I could never overstress how important he was in my development. It still fascinates me how this one guy could come up with so many songs and sling it so gracefully and elegantly.

So we sat there in the cold, dissecting tracks for as long as the meter held out. A new Bo Diddley record goes under the surgical knife. Have you got that wah-wah? What were the drums playing, how hard were they playing...what were the maracas doing? You had to take it all apart and put it back together again, from your point of view. We need a reverb. Now we're really in the shit. We need an amplifier. Bo Diddley was high tech. Jimmy Reed was easier. He was straightforward. But to dissect how he played, Jesus. It took me years to find out how he actually played the 5 chord, in the key of E — the B chord, the last of the three chords before you go home, the resolver in a twelve-bar blues — the dominant chord, as it's called. When he gets to it, Jimmy Reed produces a haunting refrain, a melancholy dissonance. Even for non–guitar players, it's worth trying to describe what he does. At the 5 chord, instead of making the conventional barre chord, the B7th, which requires a little effort with the left hand, he wouldn't bother with the B at all. He'd leave the open A note ringing and just slide a finger up the D string to a 7th. And there's the haunting note, resonating against the open A. So you're not using root notes, but letting it fall against a 7th. Believe me, it's (a) the laziest, sloppiest single thing you can do in that situation, and (b) one of the most brilliant musical inventions of all time. But that is how Jimmy Reed managed to play the same song for thirty years and get away with it. I learned how to do it from a white boy, Bobby Goldsboro, who had a couple of hits in the '60s. He used to work with Jimmy Reed and he said he'd show me the tricks. I knew all the other moves, but I never knew that 5 chord move until he showed it to me, on a bus somewhere in Ohio, in the mid-'60s. He said, "I spent years on the road with Jimmy Reed. He does that 5 chord like this." "Shit! That's all it is?" "That's it, motherfucker. You live and learn." Suddenly, out of a bright sky, you get it! That haunting, droning note. Absolute disregard for any musical rules whatsoever. Also absolute disregard for the audience or anybody else. "It goes like this." In a way, we admired Jimmy more for that than his playing. It was the attitude. And also very haunting songs. They might be based on a seemingly simplistic bedrock, but you try "Little Rain."

One of the first lessons I learned with guitar playing was that none of these guys were actually playing straight chords. There's a throw-in, a flick-back. Nothing's ever a straight major. It's an amalgamation, a mangling and a dangling and a tangling thing. There is no "properly." There's just how you feel about it. Feel your way around it. It's a dirty world down here. Mostly I've found, playing instruments, that I actually want to be playing something that should be played by another instrument. I find myself trying to play horn lines all the time on the guitar. When I was learning how to do these songs, I learned there is often one note doing something that makes the whole thing work. It's usually a suspended chord. It's not a full chord, it's a mixture of chords, which I love to use to this day. If you're playing a straight chord, whatever comes next should have something else in it. If it's an A chord, a hint of D. Or if it's a song with a different feeling, if it's an A chord, a hint of G should come in somewhere, which makes a 7th, which then can lead you on. Readers who wish to can skip Keef's Guitar Workshop, but I'm passing on the simple secrets anyway, which led to the open chord riffs of later years — the "Jack Flash" and "Gimme Shelter" ones.

There are some people looking to play guitar. There's other people looking for a sound. I was looking for a sound when Brian and I were rehearsing in Edith Grove. Something easily done by three or four guys and you wouldn't be missing any instruments or sound on it. You had a wall of it, in your face. I just followed the bosses. A lot of those blues players of the mid-'50s, Albert King and B.B. King, were single-note players. T-Bone Walker was one of the first to use the double-string thing—to use two strings instead of one, and Chuck got a lot out of T-Bone. Musically impossible, but it works. The notes clash, they jangle. You're pulling two strings at once and you're putting them in a position where actually their knickers are pulled up. You've always got something ringing against the note or the harmony. Chuck Berry is all double-string stuff. He very rarely plays single notes. The reason that cats started to play like that, T-Bone and so on, was economics—to eliminate the need for a horn section. With an amplified electric guitar, you could play two harmony notes and you could basically save money on two saxophones and a trumpet. And my double-string playing was why, in the very first Sidcup days, I was looked on as a bit of a wild rock and roller, and not really a serious blues player. Everybody else was playing away on single strings. It worked for me because I was playing a lot by myself, so two strings were better than one. And it had the possibility of getting this dissonance and this rhythm thing going, which you can't do picking away on one string. It's finding the moves. Chords are something to look for. There's always the Lost Chord. Nobody's found it.

Brian and I, we had the Jimmy Reed stuff down. When we were really hunkering down and working, working, Mick obviously felt a little bit out of it. Also he was away at the London School of Economics for much of the day to start with. He couldn't play anything. That's why he picked up on the harp and the maracas. Brian had picked up the harmonica very quickly at first, and I think Mick didn't want to be left behind. I wouldn't be surprised if from the beginning it wasn't just from being in competition with Brian. He wanted to play in the band musically as well. And Mick turned out to be the most amazing harp player. I'd put him up there with the best in the world, on a good night. Everything else we know he can do—he's a great showman—but to a musician, Mick Jagger is a great harp player. His phrasing is incredible. It's very Louis Armstrong, Little Walter. And that's saying something. Little Walter Jacobs was one of the best singers of the blues, and a blues harp player par excellence. I find it hard to listen to him without awe. His band the Jukes were so hip and sympathetic. His singing was overshadowed by the phenomenal harp, which was based on a lot of Louis Armstrong's cornet licks. Little Walter would smile in his grave for the way Mick plays. Mick and Brian played totally different styles — Mick sucking, like Little Walter, Brian blowing, like Jimmy Reed, both bending notes. When you play like that, the Jimmy Reed style, it's called "high and lonesome," and when you hear it, it just touches the heart. Mick is one of the best natural blues harp players I've heard. His harp playing is the one place where you don't hear any calculation. I say, "Why don't you sing like that?" He says they're totally different things. But they're not — they're both blowing air out of your gob.

This band was very fragile; no one was looking for this thing to fly. I mean, we're anti-pop, we're anti-ballroom, all we want to do is be the best blues band in London and show the fuckers what's what because we know we can do it. And these weird little bunches of people would come in and support us. We didn't even know where they came from or why, or how they found out where we were. We didn't think we were ever going to do anything much except turn other people on to Muddy Waters and Bo Diddley and Jimmy Reed. We had no intention of being anything ourselves. The idea of making a record seemed to be totally out of the picture. Our job at that time was idealistic. We were unpaid promoters for Chicago blues. It was terribly shining shields and everything like that. And monastic, intense study, for me at least. Everything from when you woke up to when you went to sleep was dedicated to learning, listening and trying to find some money — a division of labor. The ideal thing was, right, we've got enough to live on, a few bob in case of emergencies, and on top of that, beautiful, these girls come round, three or four of them, Lee Mohamed and her mates, and clear up for us, cook for us and just hang about. What the hell they saw in us at that time, I don't know.

We didn't have any other interests in the world except how to keep the electricity going and how to nick a few things out of the super-market for food. Women were really third on that list. Electricity, food and then, hey, you got lucky. We needed to work together, we needed to rehearse, we needed to listen to music, we needed to do what we wanted to do. It was a mania. Benedictines had nothing on us. Any-body that strayed from the nest to get laid, or try to get laid, was a trai-tor. You were supposed to spend all your waking hours studying Jimmy Reed, Muddy Waters, Little Walter, Howlin' Wolf, Robert Johnson. That was your gig. Every other moment taken away from it was a sin. It was that kind of atmosphere, that kind of attitude that we lived with. The women around were really quite peripheral. The drive in the band was amazing among Mick, Brian and myself. It was inces-sant study. Not really in the academic sense of it, it was to get the feel of it. And then I think we realized, like any young guys, that blues are not learned in a monastery. You've got to go out there and get your heart broke and then come back and then you can sing the blues. Pref-erably several times. At that time, we were taking it on a purely musi-cal level, forgetting that these guys were singing *about* shit. First you've got to get in the shit. And then you can maybe come back and sing it. I thought I loved my mother and I left her. She still did my laundry. And I got my heart broken, but not right away. My sights were still set on Lee Mohamed.

The venues in the diary are the Flamingo Club in Wardour Street, where Alexis Korner's Blues Incorporated played; the Ealing Club, mentioned already; Richmond was the Crawdaddy Club in the Sta-tion Hotel, where we really took off; the Marquee was then in Oxford Street, where Cyril Davies's R&B All-Stars performed after he'd bro-ken away from Korner; the Red Lion was in Sutton, south London; and the Manor House was a pub in north London. The sums of money were the paltry earnings from playing our guts out, but they began to get better.

\* \* \*

I don't think the Stones would have actually *coagulated* without Ian Stewart pulling it together. He was the one that rented the first rehearsal rooms, told people to get there at a certain time; otherwise it was so nebulous. We didn't know shit from Shinola. It was his vision, the band, and basically he picked who was going to be in it. Far more than anybody actually realizes, he was the spark and the energy and the organization that actually kept it together in its early days, because there wasn't much money, but there was this idealistic hope that "we can bring the blues to England." "We have been chosen!" All that dopey sort of stuff. And Stu had such incredible enthusiasm in that way. He'd stepped out — made a split with the people he'd played with. He took a leap in the dark there, really. It was against the grain. It alienated him from his cozy little club scene. Without Stu we'd have been lost. He'd been around the club scene a lot longer — we were just new kids on the block.

One of his first strategies was to wage guerrilla war against the trad jazzers. That was a big, bitter cultural shift. The traditional jazz bands, aka Dixieland bands, semi-beatniks, were doing very, very well. "Midnight in Moscow," Acker Bilk, the whole goddamn lot of them. They flooded the market. Very good players, Chris Barber and all of those cats. They ran the scene. But they couldn't understand that things were moving and that they should incorporate something else into their music. How could we dislodge the Dixieland mafia? There seemed to be no chinks in their armor. It was Stu's idea that we play the interval at the Marquee, while Acker was having a beer. No money in it, but the interval was the thin end of the wedge. Stu figured out that strategy. He would just turn up and say, no money, but interval at the Marquee, or the Manor House. Suddenly the interval became more interesting than the main event. You put the interval band on, and they're playing Jimmy Reed. Fifteen minutes. And it was really only a matter of months before that traditional-jazz monopoly faded away. There was bitter hatred of us. "I don't like your music. Why don't you play in ballrooms?" "You go! We're staying." But we had no idea that the ground was shifting at the time. We weren't that arrogant. We were just happy to get a gig.

There is a parable on film of the changeover of power between jazz and rock and roll, in *Jazz on a Summer's Day* — a hugely important film for aspiring rock musicians at the time, mostly because it featured Chuck Berry at the Newport Jazz Festival in 1958, playing "Sweet Little Sixteen." The film had Jimmy Giuffre, Louis Armstrong, Thelonious Monk, but Mick and I went to see *the man*. That black coat. He was brought on stage — a very bold move by someone — with Jo Jones on drums, a jazz great. Jo Jones was, among others, Count Basie's drummer. I think it was Chuck's proudest moment, when he got up there. It's not a particularly good version of "Sweet Little Sixteen," but it was the attitude of the cats behind him, solid against the way he looked and the way he was moving. They were laughing at him. They were trying to fuck him up. Jo Jones was raising his drumstick after every few beats and grinning as if he were in play school. Chuck knew he was working against the odds. And he wasn't really doing very well, when you listen to it, but he carried it. He had a band behind him that wanted to toss him, but he still carried the day. Jo Jones blew it, right there. Instead of a knife in the back, he could have given him the shit. But Chuck forced his way through.

A description of the early days of bookings and of my amazement and excitement that we were starting to be a working band comes in another letter to my aunt Patty, astonishing to find, which came to light while I was writing this book.

*Wednesday 19th Dec.*                                    *Keith Richards*
                                                          *6, Spielman Rd*
                                                          *Dartford*

*Dear Patty,*

*Thanks for birthday card. Arrived on the correct day 18th full marks.*

*Hope you are both keeping well and all that, chiz, chiz.*

*I'm having a ball here, I live in my friends flat in Chelsea most of the time and we are starting to make the music business quite profitable. The next big craze over here is for Rhythm & Blues and we are in demand. This week we have clinched a deal to play regularly at the Flamingo night club in Wardour Street starting next month. We were talking to an agent on Monday who reckons that we have a very commercial sound and if all goes well and he isn't another twister we could be earning £60 to £70 a week shortly, also there is a record company starting to send us letters as regards a session in the next few months. Straight up the Hot Hundred.*

*Still, enough of my antics. Everyone here is back to recovery, except that my leprosy keeps coming back and Dad's got Parkinsons disease and Mum's down with the sleeping sickness.*

*Can't think of much more so will sign off now have a luverly Xmas*

*Love from Keef X*

This is the first sighting of my nickname "Keef" and shows it didn't come originally from fans. I was known as "Cousin Beef" in my extended family, and that turned naturally to "Keef."

The short time covered by the diary ends at the exact moment when our future was assured — our getting a regular gig at the Crawdaddy Club in Richmond, from which everything sprinkled out. Fame in six weeks. To me, Charlie Watts was the secret essence of the whole thing. And that went back to Ian Stewart — "We have to have Charlie Watts" — and all the skulduggery that went down in order to get Charlie. We starved ourselves to pay for him! Literally. We went shoplifting to get Charlie Watts. We cut down on our rations, we wanted him so bad, man. And now we're stuck with him!

At first we had neither Bill nor Charlie, though Bill is mentioned in the second diary entry:

**January 1963**
**Wednesday 2**

*New bass-guitarist with Tony trying out. One of the best rehearsals ever. Bass guitar adds more power to sounds. Also secured with bass guitarist is one 100 gns Vox amplifier. Decided on programme for Marquee. Must be a knockout to secure a bigger spot.*

Bill had amplifiers! Bill came fully equipped. He was a package deal. We used to play with this guy called Tony Chapman, who was merely a fill-in, and I don't know if it was Stu or Tony, much to his own detriment, who said, "Oh, I've got this other player," which was Bill. And Bill arrived with this amplifier, believe it or not, protected by Meccano, with the green stuff on the screws. A Vox AC30 amplifier, which was beyond our means to possess. Built by Jennings in Dartford. We used to worship it. We used to look at it and get on our knees. To have an amplifier was crucial. First off I just wanted to separate Bill from his amplifier. But that was before he started playing with Charlie.

**Thursday 3**

*Marquee with Cyril*
*1 or 2½ hour sets £10–£12*
*Very good set. "Bo Diddley" received with very good applause. 612 people attended session. 1st set good warm up. 2nd set swung fabulously. Impressed some very big people. Received £2. Paul Pond:— "Knockout."*
*Harold Pendleton asked to be introduced.* [He was the owner of the Marquee! I tried to kill the guy twice, by

swinging my guitar at his head. He hated rock and roll and was always sneering.]

**Friday 4**

    *Flamingo ad: "Original Chicago R&B sound starring the Rollin' Stones."* [And we'd never been north of bloody Watford.]

    *Play Red Lion. Sutton. Pickup came unsoldered.*

    *Red Lion:— Band played poorly, nevertheless a raving reception especially "Bo Diddley" & "Sweet Little 16." Tony diabolical. Discussed presentation for "Flamingo."*

    *Good quote in MM.* [Melody Maker]

    *Came up in the afternoon. Lost wallet 30 /- in it Should be retrieved.*

And a first hint of a recording, of any sort:

**Saturday 5**

    *Got wallet back,*

    *Richmond*

    *Cock up. My pickup clapped out completely. Brian played harp and I used his guitar. "Confessin' the Blues" "Diddley-Daddy" & "Jerome" and "Bo Diddley" went well. Mad row with promoter over money. Refused to play there again. Discussed new demo disc. To be made this week with any luck. "Diddley-Daddy" looked good. With Cleo and friends as vocal group. Band earned £37 this week.*

Thirty-seven pounds for five blokes!

**Monday 7th**

    *Flamingo*

    *Must hone Stu, Tony & Gorgonzola.*

*My guitar returned in perfect working order. Flamingo
on first thought not too hot. But Johnny Gunnell more
than satisfied. Tony must go. That means Bill and Vox.
"Confessin' the Blues" went well. Lee came down. I've got
my brand.*

In which I seem to assume the mantle of musical director. Johnny
Gunnell — it was the Gunnell brothers, Johnny and Ricky, who ran
the Flamingo. And Bill and his Vox are secured. A historic day. That
last line is from Muddy Waters: "I've got my brand on you." I was
definitely hot on Lee.

**Tuesday 8**

*£30:10!!!
Ealing.
Band played quite well. "Bo Diddley" was an absolute
knockout. If we can repeat this performance at the Marquee
we'll be laughing.
Start at Ealing on Saturday. "Look What You've
Done" reasonable.
6/-!!!! 50% up on last week.*

**Thursday 10**

*£12. Tony Meehan reckoned the band. [He was the
drummer with the Shadows.]
Marquee. First set 8:30 or 9:00 musically very good but
didn't quite click. Second set 9:45–10:15 swung much
better. Brian and I rather put off by lack of volume due to
work to rule in power station. "Bo Diddley" tremendous
applause, as usual. Lee and the girls came down.
Approached Charlie for regular work.*

Halfway through the set and suddenly the power went down. We
were fucked! We were rocking! And then they put us to half power,

due to an industrial action by the electricity workers. And we're looking at one another, we're looking at our amplifiers, we're looking at the sky, the ceiling.

**Friday 11**

> *Bill agrees to stay on even if we chuck Tony.*

**Monday 14**

> *Tony sacked!!*
> *Flamingo*
> *Surprise!!! Rick & Carlo played. Without a doubt the Rollin' Stones were the most fantastic group operating in the country tonight. Rick & Carlo are 2 of the best. Audience was changed from last week which is the main thing. Money not quite so exciting. £8. Still, should rise steam now.*

Rick and Carlo! Carlo Little was a butcher, a killing drummer, great energy. And Ricky Fenson on bass, a lovely player. They had bleached their hair blond for the gig. And who did they really work for? Screaming Lord effing Sutch. From time to time they'd sit in with us—that's when Charlie still wasn't with us, and it's why he decided to join the band, because he heard we had this red-hot rhythm section. Ricky and Carlo, if they went into a solo, they would go into turbo max. The room would take off; they almost blew us off the stage they were so good. The two of them together. When Carlo set into that bass drum, this is what I'm talking about. This was rock and roll! As a kid, to play with these guys, who were only two or three years older than we were, but they had been at it a long time, was something. The first time they took me in there—"OK, it goes like this"—and I suddenly had this rhythm section behind me, whoa! That was the first time I got three feet off the ground and into the stratosphere. This was before I was working with Charlie and Bill or anything.

And from the earliest I always felt good on stage. You get nervous before you go up there before a lot of people, but to me the feeling was, let the tiger out the cage. Maybe that's just another version of butterflies. It could be. But I've always felt very comfortable on stage, even if I screw up. It always felt like a dog, this is my turf, piss around it. While I'm here, nothing else can happen. All I can do is screw up. Otherwise, have a good time.

Next day is the first mention of Charlie playing with us:

**Tuesday 15**

*All group money to be given up for at least 2 weeks to buy amp & mikes.*

*Ealing — Charlie*

*Maybe due to my cold but didn't sound right to me, but then Mick & Brian & myself still groggy from chills and fever!!!*

*Charlie swings but hasn't got right sound yet. Rectify that tomorrow!*

*Poor crowd. No money, chucking it. Have a day off.*

*Rick & Carlo to play sat & mon.*

So Charlie was coming in. We were going to try and figure out how to separate Bill from the amplifier and still end up winning. But at the same time, Bill and Charlie were starting to play together, and there was something happening here. Bill is an incredible bass player, there's no doubt about it. I discovered it gradually. Everybody was learning. Nobody had any firm ideas of what they wanted to do and everybody came from a slightly different background. Charlie was a jazzman. Bill was from the Royal Air Force. At least he'd been abroad.

Charlie Watts has always been the bed that I lie on musically, and to see that note about how to "rectify" his sound seems extraordinary. But like Stu, Charlie had come to rhythm and blues because of its jazz connection. A few days later I write, *Charlie swings very nicely but can't rock. Fabulous guy though....* He had not got rock and roll down at that time. I wanted him to hit it a little harder. He was still too jazz for me. We knew he was a great drummer, but in order to play with the Stones, Charlie went and studied Jimmy Reed and Earl Phillips, who was the drummer for Jimmy Reed, just to get the feel of it. That sparse, minimalized thing. And he's always retained it. Charlie was the drummer we wanted, but first off, could we afford him, and second off, would he give up some of his jazz ways for us?

**Tuesday 22**

> £0
>
> *Ealing — Charlie*
> *Cock up No. 2. Only 2 people turned up by 8:50 so we*
> *went home. Nevertheless we did a couple of numbers one*
> *using maracas, tambourine and wailing guitar with Charlie*
> *doing a big jungle rhythm (which just shows he can do it).*
> *Stopped by cops on way to flat. Frisked. Moaning bastards.*
> *No more work until Sat.*

The big jungle rhythm was the Bo Diddley lick — "Shave and a haircut, two bits" is what the beat's called, and what it sounds like. "Bo Diddley, Bo Diddley, have you heard? / My pretty baby said she was a bird."

As for the frisk, when I read that, I thought, "Even then?" We had nothing. Not even money. It's not surprising that when they hit on me for the real shit later, I knew about it. Frisked for no reason at all. And my reaction is still the same. Fucking moaning bastards. They always moan. You wouldn't be a cop if you weren't a moaner. "Come on, assume the position." Back then there was nothing to find. I was frisked a hundred times before I even thought, "Oh my God, I've got something on me."

**Thursday 24**

*No Marquee*

*Cyril's scared of the applause we get according to Carlo
& Rick. Laid off for month. If nothing shows up in the
meantime we'll go back. Spent day practising. Worthwhile,
I hope! Must persevere with fingerstyle. Great opportunities I feel. Bastard though. Can't control 'em. Bleedin
spider, feels like.*

**Saturday 26**

*£16*

*Ealing — Rick & Carlo*

*Band bit rusty. Quite good though. Audience up.
Sweaty and crowded. Luvly!!!*

*£2*

*Lee was there.*

*Funny, can't seem to fit all my new practiced dodgy bits
into the act. Don't relax enough. Boys a bit cynical lately.*

**Monday 28**

*Toss' sister said Lee was crazy to have me but didn't
want to make a fool of herself and would I give her some
help. I did fair I reckon.*

Lee and I had broken up and this was the rapprochement — mutu-
ally agreed on both sides. "Toss" was short for Tosca, her girlfriend.

**Saturday 2**

*£16*

*Ealing*

*Charlie & Bill*

*Fabulous evening with big crowd. Sound returned
with a bang. Charlie fabulous.*

By February 2, that night, we were playing with the final lineup and the rhythm section, Charlie and Bill. The Stones!

If it hadn't been for Charlie, I would never have been able to expand and develop. Number one with Charlie is that he's got great feel. He had it then, from the start. There's tremendous personality and subtlety in his playing. If you look at the size of his kit, it's ludicrous compared with what most drummers use these days. They've got a fort with them. An incredible barrage of drums. Charlie, with just that one classico setup, can pull it all off. Nothing pretentious, and then you hear him and it don't half go bang. He plays with humor too. I love to watch his foot through the Perspex. Even if I can't hear him, I can play to him just by watching. The other thing is Charlie's trick that he got, I think, from Jim Keltner or Al Jackson. On the hi-hat, most guys would play on all four beats, but on the two and the four, which is the backbeat, which is a very important thing in rock and roll, Charlie doesn't play, he lifts up. He goes to play and pulls back. It gives the snare drum all of the sound, instead of having some interference behind it. It'll give you a heart arrhythmia if you look at it. He does some extra motion that's totally unnecessary. It pulls the time back because he has to make a little extra effort. And so part of the languid feel of Charlie's drumming comes from this unnecessary motion every two beats. It's very hard to do — to stop the beat going just for one beat and then come back in. And it also has something to do with the way Charlie's limbs are constructed, where he feels the beat. Each drummer's got a signature as to whether the hi-hat's a little bit ahead of the snare. Charlie's very far back with the snare and up with the hi-hat. And the way he stretches out the beat and what we do on top of that is a secret of the Stones sound. Charlie's quintessentially a jazz drummer, which means the rest of the band is a jazz band in a way. He's up there with the best, Elvin Jones, Philly Joe Jones. He's got the feel, the looseness of it, and he's very economical. Charlie used to work weddings and bar mitzvahs, so he knows the schmaltz too. It comes from starting early, playing the clubs when he was really young.

A little bit of showmanship, without himself being the showman. *Bah-BAM*. And I've got used to playing with a guy like this. Forty years on, Charlie and I are tighter than we could express or even probably know. I mean, we even get daring enough to try and screw each other up sometimes on the stage.

Back then I used to rag Stu and Charlie wicked about jazz. We were supposed to be getting the blues down, and sometimes I'd catch Stu and Charlie listening to jazz on the sly. "Stop that shit!" I was just trying to break their habits, trying to put a band together, for Christ's sake. "You've got to listen to blues. You've got to listen to fucking Muddy." I wouldn't even let them listen to Armstrong, and I love Armstrong.

Bill always felt looked down upon, mainly because his real last name was Perks. And he was stuck in this dead-end job in south London. And he was married. Brian was very class conscious, you see. "Bill Perks," to him, was some lowlife. "I wish we could find a new bass player, this one's a right fucking Ernie with his greasy hair," Phelge remembers Brian saying. Bill was still a bit of a teddy boy at the time, with the quiff. But that was all so superficial. Meanwhile Brian was the king rat of the whole gang.

By February we were paying off hire purchase. I bought two guitars in the space of a month:

**Jan 25**

    *Day off*

    *Buy new guitar, Harmony or Hawk?*

    *Harmony has good price but do you get guarantee.*

*"Hawk" has and also has case supplied.*

    *Both models £84.0.0*

    *Got 2 thumbpicks — bought Harmony with two P.U.'s sunburst finish in 2-tone case £74.*

**Wednesday 13 (February)**

*Rehearsal*

*Got new gitty from Ivor's! Lovely instrument!! What a
sound!!! New nos "Who Do You Love?" & "Route 66"
Great! Revised "Crawdaddy" fabulous (all Brian's ideas).*
[At least I give credit.]

And the venues were beginning to jump.

**Saturday 9**

*18:0:0*

*Amp payments due*

*Ealing*

*Collyers' All-niter?* [crossed out]

*Must have been near record steaming hot and packed full*

*Band raved. Get real little girl fans there*

*£2*

*Stopped at flat*

*Paid Bill £6 for Vox*

**Monday 11**

*Day off. Dead bored.*

The last two entries are the key to what was happening, all of a
sudden. We were going to record and we were about to take up the
Richmond gig.

**Thursday 14**

*Manor House*

*Quite good. Small crowd. Blues by 6 frightened them
all away*

*New gitty takes some getting use to. New nos. went
well.*

*Stu says Glyn Johns will record us Mon or Thurs next*
*week with ideas of selling them to Decca.*
*£1*

**Friday 15**
*Red Lion*
*Can't get any sound out of this place.*
*Punch up during session.*
*Offered Richmond Station Hotel every sun. from coming*
*sun. Windfall.*

On the inside cover of the diary is written the phrase "Wongin' the pog." And next to that, under the personal-notes section, "In Case of Accident Please Inform," I've written, "My Mum." No details.

"Wongin' the pog" was when we'd look at all these people dancing around, hanging from rafters, going crazy. "What are they doing?" "They're wongin' the pog, ain't they?" "At least we got them wongin' the pog." It meant you got paid. The gigs were getting tight and hot. We had this groundswell going on in London. When you've got three queues going round a whole damn block waiting to get into a show, you say we've got something going here. This is no longer just us begging. All we need to do now is nurture this thing.

The spaces were small, which suited us. It suited Mick best of all. Mick's artistry was on display in these small venues, where there was barely space to swing a cat — perhaps more so than it ever was later. I think Mick's movements come a lot from the fact that we used to play these very, very small stages. With our equipment on stage, we'd sometimes have no more room than a table as a viable space to work. The band was two feet behind Mick, he was right in the middle of the band, there were no delay effects or separation, and because Mick was playing a lot of harmonica, he was part of the band. I can't think of any other singer at the time in England that played harp and was the lead singer. Because the harp was, still can be, a very important part of the sound, especially when you're doing blues.

Give Mick Jagger a stage the size of a table and he could work it better than anybody, except maybe James Brown. Twists and turns, and he's got the maracas going — c'mon, baby. We used to sit on stools and play, and he would work around us because there was no room to move. You swung a guitar, you hit somebody else in the face. He used to play four maracas while he sang. It's a long time since I've reminded him about the maracas. He was brilliant. Even at that age I was astounded by how he used that small space to do so much. It was like watching a Spanish dancer.

Richmond is where we learned the gig. That's where we realized that we really did have a good band, and we could really release people for a few hours and get that reciprocation between the stage and the audience. Because it's not an act. Whatever Mick Jagger thinks.

My favorite place, looking back, was the Station Hotel, Richmond, just because everything really kicked off from there. The Ricky Tick Club in Windsor was a damn good room to play. Eel Pie was fantastic, because basically it was the same old crowd — they just moved around wherever we were playing. Giorgio Gomelsky, there's another name that resonates from this period. Giorgio, who actually organized us and got us gigs in the Marquee and the Station Hotel, a very important person in the whole setup. A Russian émigré, a great bear of a man, with incredible drive and enthusiasm. Brian led Giorgio to believe that he was the de facto manager of something that we didn't think needed managing. He did amazing things, put us up, got us gigs, but there was nothing more to promise at the time. It was just "We need gigs, we need gigs. Spread the word." And Giorgio was very instrumental in that, very early on. He got booted out by Brian once Brian saw bigger things coming. Unbelievable how much Brian was the manipulator, thinking about these things. One had the feeling that Brian had made promises to people that nobody else had. So when the promises weren't delivered, we were all assholes. Brian was a bit free with promise land. Giorgio later became manager of the

Yardbirds, including Eric Clapton, who were already picking up our spots. And then Eric left the Yardbirds and went away on a sabbatical for six months and came back as God, which he's still trying to live down.

Mick has changed tremendously. Only thinking about this time do I remember with regrets how completely tight Mick and I were in the formation, the early years of the Stones. First off, we never had to question the aim. We were unerring in where we wanted to go, what it should sound like, so we didn't have to discuss it, just figure a way to do it. We didn't have to talk about the target, we knew what it was. It was basically just to be able to make records. The targets get bigger as things happen. Our first aim as the Rolling Stones was to be the best rhythm and blues band in London, with regular gigs every week. But the main aim was somehow to get to make records. To actually get into the portal, the holy of holies, the recording studio. How can you learn if you can't get in front of a microphone and a tape recorder in a studio? We saw this thing building up, and what's the next step? Make records, by hook or by crook. John Lee Hooker, Muddy Waters, Howlin' Wolf, they were who they were, there was no compromise. They just wanted to make records, just like me, that's one of my connections with them all. I'll do anything to make a record. It was really narcissistic in a way. We just wanted to hear what we sounded like. We wanted the playback. The payback didn't come into it, but the playback we really wanted. In a way, in those days, being able to get into the studio and get an acetate back sort of legitimized you. "You're now a commissioned officer" instead of being one of the ranks. Playing live was the most important thing in the world, but making records stamped it. Signed, sealed and delivered.

Stu was the only guy that knew somebody that could actually open a door to a studio late at night and get an hour there. In those days it was like going into Buckingham Palace or getting an entrée into the admiralty. It was nearly impossible to get into a recording studio. It's bizarre that now anybody can make a record anywhere and put it on the Internet. Then it was like leaping over the moon. A mere dream. The first studio I actually went in was IBC in Portland Place, right across the road from the BBC, but of course there was no connection. With Glyn Johns, who happened to be an engineer there and just wangled us some time. But that was just a one-gig thing.

Then came the day that Andrew Loog Oldham came to see us play at Richmond, and things began to move at devastating speed. Within something like two weeks we had a recording contract. Andrew had worked with Brian Epstein and was instrumental in creating the Beatles' image. Epstein fired Andrew because they got into some bitch argument. Andrew took a large step to the left and branched out on his own: "Right, I'll show you." We were the instrument of his revenge on Epstein. We were the dynamite, Andy Oldham the detonator. The irony is that Oldham, at the start, the great architect of the Stones' public persona, thought it was a disadvantage for us to be considered long-haired and dirty and rude. He was a very pristine boy himself at the time. The whole idea of the Beatles and the uniforms, keeping everything uniform, still made sense to Andrew. To us it didn't. He put us in uniforms. We had those damn houndstooth, dogtooth check jackets on *Thank Your Lucky Stars,* but we just dumped them immediately and kept the leather waistcoats he'd got us from Charing Cross Road. "Where's your jacket?" "I dunno. My girlfriend's wearing it." And he did cotton on real quick to the fact that he'd have to go with it. What are you going to do? The Beatles are all over the place like a fucking bag of fleas, right? And you've got another good band. The thing is not to try and regurgitate the Beatles. So we're going to have to be the anti-Beatles. We're not going to be the Fab Four, all wearing the same shit. And then Andrew started to play that to the hilt. Everybody's too cute and they all wear uniforms and it's all showbiz. And it was actually Andrew that disintegrated the way you can present yourself—do everything wrong, at least from a showbiz, Fleet Street point of view.

Course we had no idea. "We're too good for this shit, man. We're blues players, you know, at all of eighteen years old. We've done Mississippi, been through Chicago." You kid yourself. But it was really flying into the face of it. And of course the timing was dead right. You've got the Beatles, mums love them and dads love them, but would you let your daughter marry *this*? And that was pretty much a stroke of genius. I don't think Andrew or any of us were geniuses, it was just a stroke that hit the mark, and once we had that down, it was OK, now we can get into this game of show business and still be ourselves. I don't have to have the same haircut as him or him. I always looked at Andrew as the absolute PR man par excellence. I saw him as a sharp blade. I liked him a lot, neurotic and sexually disoriented as he was. He'd been sent to a public school called Wellingborough, and at school in general, like me, he hadn't had a very good time. Andrew, especially in those days, was always a bit jittery, like crystal, but he was very, very sure of himself and what we should do, all the while with this certain fragility inside him. But he certainly put up a lot of front. I liked his mind; I liked the way he thought. And having done the art school bit and studied advertising, I saw the point immediately in what he was trying to do.

We signed a deal with Decca. And days after that—getting paid to do this!—we were in a studio, Olympic Studios. But most of our early stuff at this time was recorded in Regent Sounds Studio. It was just a little room full of egg boxes and it had a Grundig tape recorder, and to make it look like a studio, the recorder was hung on the wall instead of put on the table. If it was on the table, it wasn't pro. But actually, what they did there was advertising jingles—"Murray mints, Murray mints, the too-good-to-hurry mints." It was just a little jingle studio, very basic, very simple, and it made it easy for me to learn the bare bones of recording. One of the reasons we picked it was because it was mono, and what you hear is what you get. It was only a two-track tape recorder. I learned how to overdub on it, by what they call ping-ponging, where you put the track that you just recorded onto one track and then overdub. But of course you're losing generations by doing that, sound-wise.

You're letting the thing go through the mill one more time, and we found out that wasn't such a bad idea. So the first album and a lot of the second, plus "Not Fade Away," which was our first big chart climber at number three in February 1964, and "Tell Me," were made surrounded by egg boxes. Those first albums were recorded at several studios with incredible people walking in, like Phil Spector, who played bass on "Play with Fire," Jack Nitzsche playing harpsichord. Spector and Bo Diddley came around and Gene Pitney, who recorded one of the first songs I wrote with Mick, "That Girl Belongs to Yesterday."

But the Decca deal meant that Stu had to be dropped from the band. Six is too many and the obvious odd one out is the piano player. That's the brutality of the business. It was Brian's task, since he called himself the leader of the band, to break it to Stu. It was a very hard thing. He wasn't surprised, and I think he'd already made his own decision about what he would do about it if it turned up. He understood it totally. We expected Stu to go, "Fuck you. Thanks a lot." That was where the largeness of Stu's heart really displayed itself. From then on, OK, I'll drive you about. He was always on the records; he was only interested in the music.

To us he never was fired. And he understood it totally. "Don't look the same as you, do I?" He had the largest heart in the world, man. He was instrumental in putting us together and he wasn't about to let us drop because he was put in the background.

The first single came out rapidly after the signing of the contract— everything moving in days, not weeks. It was a very deliberately commercial pitch—"Come On," by Chuck Berry. I didn't think it was the best thing we could have done, but I did know it was something that would make a mark. As a recording it's probably better than I thought it was at the time. But I have a feeling we thought that was the only shot we had in our locker then. It was not something that we'd ever played in the clubs. It was nothing to do with what we were doing. At the time there was a purist strain running through the band, which I obviously was not on top of. I loved my blues, but I saw the potential of other things. And also I loved pop music. I quite cold-bloodedly saw this song as just a way to get in. To get into the studio and to come up with something very commercial. It's very different from Chuck Berry's version; it's very Beatle-ized, in fact. The way you could record in England, you couldn't get fussy, you went in and did it. I think everybody thought it stood a good shot. The band itself were like "We're making a record, can you believe this shit?" There was also a sense of doom. Oh my God, if the single makes it, we've got two years and that's it. Then what are we going to do? Because nobody lasted. Your shelf life in those days, and a lot even now, was basically two and a half years. And apart from Elvis, nobody had proved that wrong.

The weird thing is that when that first record came out, we were still basically a club band. I don't think we had played anything bigger than the Marquee. The record wormed its way into the top twenty, and suddenly, in a matter of a week or so, we'd been transformed into pop stars. This is very difficult with a bunch of guys that are really like "get outta here," you know, "fuck off." And suddenly they're dressing us up in dogtooth-check fucking suits and we're rushed along on the tide. It was like a tsunami. One minute, hey, you wanted to make a record, you've made a record and it's in the goddamn top twenty, and now you've got to do *Thank Your Lucky Stars*. TV you'd never thought about. We were propelled into show business. Because we were so anti-showbiz, it was the cold shoulder to us, enough already. But then we realized that we did have to make certain concessions.

Now we had to figure out how to work it. The jackets didn't last long. Maybe it was a good move for the first record, but by the second record, there was none of that. The crowds at the Crawdaddy Club had got so huge Gomelsky moved the club to the Athletic Ground, Richmond. July 1963, we actually moved out of London for a gig, for the first time ever — to Middlesbrough, Yorkshire, and a first taste of the bedlam. Between then and 1966 — for three years — we played virtually every night, or every day, sometimes two gigs a day. We played well over a thousand gigs, almost back to back, with barely a break and perhaps ten days off in that whole period.

Maybe if we'd been wearing our houndstooth jackets and looking like little dolls we wouldn't have outraged the males in the audience at the Wisbech Corn Exchange in Cambridgeshire in July 1963. We were city boys, and this music is what's happening in the city. But you try playing Wisbech, in 1963, with Mick Jagger. You got a totally different reaction. All of these hayseeds literally chewing on straw. The Wisbech Corn Exchange, out in the goddamn marshes. And a riot was started because the local yokels, the boys, couldn't stand the fact that all of their chicks were gawping and blowing themselves out about this bunch of fags, as far as they were concerned, from London. "Eee by gum." That was a very good riot, which we were lucky to escape from. By the greatest contrast known to rock-and-roll audiences, the previous night we'd played a debutante ball at Hastings caves, for someone called Lady Lampson, all via Andrew Oldham, an awfully super-duper, upper-crusty affair doing a lowlife bash in Hastings caves, which are quite big. And we were just part of the entertainment. We were told when we were not working to go into the catering area. That got our backs up, but we were playing it cool until one of them came up to Ian Stewart and said, "I say, piano chappie, can you play 'Moon River'?" Bill decked him or took him out one way or another. Lord Lampson, or whoever it was at the time, said, "Who's that horrid little man?" You can play at our parties, but we'll treat you like a black man. It was all right for me, I felt very proud, I mean I love to be treated as black. But it was Stu that had to take the first remark. "I say, piano chappie..."

At first, our audiences were female driven, until towards the end of the '60s, when it evened out. These armies of feral, body-snatching girls began to emerge in big numbers about halfway through our first UK tour, in the fall of 1963. That was an incredible lineup: the Everly Brothers, Bo Diddley, Little Richard, Mickie Most. We felt like we were in Disneyland, or the best theme park we could imagine. And at the same time we had this unique opportunity to check out the top cats. We used to hang from the rafters in the Gaumonts and the Odeons to watch Little Richard, Bo Diddley and the Everlys at work. It was a five-week tour. We went everywhere, Bradford, Cleethorpes, Albert Hall, Finsbury Park. Big gigs, small gigs. There was that amazing feeling of, wow, I'm actually in a dressing room with Little Richard. One part of you is the fan, "Oh, my God," and the other part of you is "You're here with the man and now you better be a man." The first time we went up on that first stage, at the New Victoria Theatre in London, it went to the horizon. The sense of space, the size of the audience, the whole scale, was breathtaking. We just felt so puny up there. Obviously we weren't that bad. But we all looked at one another with shock. And the curtains opened and aaaaghh. Working the Coliseum. You get used to it pretty quick, you learn. But that first night I felt so miniature. And of course we're not sounding like we usually are in a small room. Suddenly we're sounding like little tin soldiers. There were so many things to learn, real quick. That was the biggest deep end, really. We were probably disastrously horrible in some of those shows, but by then there was a buzz going on. The audience was louder than we were, which certainly helped. Great backup vocals of chicks screaming. So in a way, we learned through this barrage of shrieking.

Little Richard's stage presentation was outrageous, and brilliant. You never knew which way he was going to arrive. He had the band thumping out "Lucille" for almost ten minutes, which is a long time to keep that riff going. The whole place blacked out, nothing to see but the exit signs. And then he'd come out of the back of the theater. Other times he'd run on stage and then disappear again and come back. He had a different intro almost every time. What you realized was that Richard had checked the theater, talked to the lighting people — Where can I come from? Is there a doorway up there? — and figured out how he could get the most effective intro possible.

Whether it's bang, straight in, or whether to let the riff roll for five minutes and then turn up from the loft. Suddenly you're not just playing a club, where presentation means nothing, where there's no room to move, no way of doing anything. Suddenly to see stage work going on, with Bo Diddley too, it was mind-blowing, like you'd been elevated, somehow, by a miracle and allowed to talk to the gods. On and on went "Lucille," thumping away, until you wondered if he'd ever show up. And suddenly there's a spotlight on the balcony, and the Reverend is alive! Reverend Penniman. And the riff is on. So we learned their showmanship. And after all, Little Richard was one of the best masters we could have learned from.

I used this trick a lot with the X-Pensive Winos, where we'd black out the stage and the whole band would sit in a circle, smoking a joint and having a drink. And people didn't know we were there. And then the lights go up and we break. That came from Little Richard.

The Everly Brothers come out and there's a soft light, the band plays very quietly, and their voices, that beautiful, beautiful refrain — almost mystical. "Dream, dream, dream...," slipping in and out of unison and harmony. Load of bluegrass in those boys. The best rhythm guitar playing I ever heard was from Don Everly. Nobody ever thinks about that, but their rhythm guitar playing is perfect. And beautifully placed and set up with the voices. They were always very polite, very distant. I knew their band better — Joey Page, he was the bass player; Don Peake on guitar; and on drums was Jimmy Gordon, who was out of high school doing that. He was also Delaney & Bonnie's drummer and Derek and the Dominos' drummer. Eventually he hacked his mother to death in a schizophrenic rage and was sentenced to life in California. But that's another story. Later on I knew the Everlys were having problems, that they always did. There was something a little analogous to Mick and me in that brotherhood. You've been through thick and thin, and then it gets really big and you have the time and space to figure out what it is you don't like about each other. Yeah, more of that later on.

There was an unforgettable dressing-room scene during that tour. I like Tom Jones. I first met him on that tour with Little Richard. I'd been on the road with Little Richard for three or four weeks, and Richard was not hard to get along with and still isn't, and we'd have a laugh together. But in Cardiff, guys like Tom Jones and his band the Squires were still living five years behind. They all walk into Little Richard's dressing room, and they've still got the leopard-skin coats with the black velvet collars, and the drapes—a procession of teddy boys all bowing and scraping. And Tom Jones actually kneels in front of Little Richard as if he's the pope. And of course Richard rises right to the occasion: "My boys!" They don't realize that Richard is a screaming fag. So they don't know how to take this. "Well, baybee, you're a Georgia peach." This total culture clash, but they were so in awe of Richard that they would take anything he would say. And he's giving me a nod and a wink. "I love my fans! I love my fans! Ohh, baby!" The Reverend Richard Penniman. Never forget he comes from the gospel church, like most of them do. We all sang Hallelujah at one time or another. Al Green, Little Richard, Solomon Burke, they all got ordained. Preaching is tax free. Very little to do with God, a lot to do with money.

Jerome Green was Bo Diddley's maracas shaker. He'd been with him on all the records and he was sloppy drunk, one of the sweetest motherfuckers you could ever meet. He would just fall into your arms. He was almost Bo's partner; they'd been together through everything. There was a lot of call-and-response going on, "Hey, man, your old lady's so ugly, I had to chase her away with an ugly stick." Jerome must have been an important part of Bo's life for Bo to keep him on. But the maracas were amazing. He used to play four in each hand, eight maracas, very African. And the sound was incredible, pissed or not. That would be his thing: "I can't go on, I'm not drunk."

I took over the job of being Jerome's roadie for some reason. We liked each other a lot, and he was great fun. He was a big guy, looked a little like Chuck Berry. Suddenly there'd be this cry backstage, anybody seen Jerome? And I'd say, I bet I know where he is. He'll be in the nearest pub from backstage. In those days, I wasn't that famous; people wouldn't recognize me. I'd zip round to the pub closest to the backstage and there'd be Jerome and he'd be talking to the locals and they'd all be buying him drinks because they didn't often meet a six-foot black man from Chicago. I was his minder: "Jerome, you're on. Bo's looking for you." "Oh Christ, I'll be right back."

By the end of the tour he fell pretty ill. That's when I learned to call up doctors and get organized. I had him living at my apartment. "I've given up on this English food, man. Where can I get some god-damn American food round here? I wanna hamburger." So I'd go round Wimpy's to get him one. "Call this a hamburger?" "Sorry, Jerome." In a way I did it just because he was always such a laugh, and also he really was such a charming guy. Didn't mind taking you for a few bucks either. But you felt if you weren't there, he'd fall under a bus or flush himself down the toilet if possible. He left Bo's band not long after this.

That first tour was bizarre. I was never that confident about my own playing, but I knew that between us we could do things and that there was something happening. We started off opening the show, and then we got to ending the intermission, and then we got to open-ing up the second half, and within six weeks, the Everly Brothers were virtually saying, hey, you guys better top the bill. Within six weeks. Something happened as we were going round England. The chicks started screaming. It was teenyboppers! And to us, being "bluesmen," this was, well, we're really going downhill here. We don't want to be some fucking ersatz Beatles. Shit, we've worked this hard to be a very, very good blues band. But the money's better, and suddenly with the size of the audience, like it or not, you're no longer just a blues band, you're now what they're going to call a pop band, which we despised.

In a matter of weeks, we went from nowhere to London's crown-ing triumph. The Beatles couldn't fill in all of the spots on the charts. We filled in the gaps for the first year or so. You can put it down to

Bob Dylan's "The Times They Are A-Changin'." You knew it, you sniffed it in the air. And it was happening fast. The Everly Brothers, I mean, I loved them dearly, but they smelled it too, they knew something was happening, and as great as they were, what are the Everly Brothers gonna do when there's suddenly three thousand people chanting, *"We want the Stones. We want the Stones"*? It was so quick. And Andrew Loog Oldham was the one that grabbed the moment; he was right on top of it. We knew that we'd set something on fire that I still can't control, quite honestly.

All we knew was that we were on the road every day of the week. Maybe a day off here and there to get somewhere else. But we could tell from on the street, all over England and Scotland, Wales. Six weeks ahead you could feel it in the air. We got bigger and bigger and more and more crazy, until basically all we thought about was how to get into a gig and how to get out. The actual playing time was probably five to ten minutes at max. In England for eighteen months, I'd say, we never finished a show. The only question was how it would end, with a riot, with the cops breaking it up, with too many medical cases, and how the hell to get out of there. The biggest part of the day was planning the in and the out. The actual gig you didn't even get to know much about. It was just mayhem. We came there to listen to the audience! Nothing like a good ten, fifteen minutes of pubescent female shrieking to cover up all your mistakes. Or three thousand teenage chicks throwing themselves at you. Or being carried out on stretchers. All the bouffants awry, skirts up to their waists, sweating, red, eyes rolling. That's the spirit, girl. That's the way we like 'em. On the set list, for what it was worth, we had "Not Fade Away," "Walking the Dog," "Around and Around," "I'm a King Bee."

Sometimes chief constables would devise these ridiculous plans. I remember once in Chester, after a show that had ended in a riot, following the chief constable of Chester police over the rooftops of Chester city as in some weird Walt Disney film, with the rest of the band behind me, and him in full uniform, with a constable at his side. And then he loses his fucking way, and we're perched on the top of Chester city, while his great "Escape from Colditz" plan disintegrates. Then it starts to rain. It was like something out of *Mary Poppins*. The uniform with the baton, the whole bit, and this was his great master plan. In those days at my age you thought the cops knew how to deal with everything; you were supposed to believe that. But you soon realized that these guys had never dealt with anything like this. It was as new to them as it was to us. We're all babes in the wood here.

We used to play "Popeye the Sailor Man" some nights, and the audience didn't know any different because they couldn't hear us. So they weren't reacting to the music. The beat maybe, because you'd always hear the drums, just the rhythm, but the rest of it, no, you couldn't hear the voices, you couldn't hear the guitars, totally out of the question. What they were reacting to was being in this enclosed space with us — this illusion, me, Mick and Brian. The music might be the trigger, but the bullet, nobody knows what that is. Usually it was harmless, for them, though not always for us. Amongst the many thousands a few did get hurt, and a few died. Some chick third balcony up flung herself off and severely hurt the person she landed on underneath, and she herself broke her neck and died. Now and again shit happened. But the limp and fainted bodies going by us after the first ten minutes of playing, that happened every night. Or sometimes they'd stack them up on the side of the stage because there were so many of them. It was like the western front. And it got nasty in the provinces — new territory for us. Hamilton in Scotland, just outside of Glasgow. They put a chicken wire fence in front of us because of the sharpened pennies and beer bottles they flung at us — the guys that didn't like the chicks screaming at us. They had dogs parading inside the wire. The wire mesh was quite common in certain areas, especially around Glasgow at that time. But it was nothing new. You could see the same thing going on in clubs in the South, the Midwest. "Midnight Hour" Mr. Wilson Pickett, his stage set consisted of a rack of shotguns this side and a rack of shotguns that side. And the shotguns weren't there as props. They were loaded, probably with rock salt, no heavy-duty stuff. But to look at it was enough to put anybody off throwing things at the stage or going berserk. It was just a measure of control.

One night somewhere up north, it could have been York, it could have been anywhere, our strategy was to stay behind in the theater for a couple of hours and have dinner there, just wait for everybody to go to bed and then leave. And I remember walking back out onto the stage after the show, and they'd cleaned up all of the underwear and everything, and there was one old janitor, night watchman, and he said, "Very good show. Not a dry seat in the house."

Maybe it happened to Frank Sinatra, Elvis Presley. I don't think it had ever reached the extremes it got to around the Beatles and the Stones time, at least in England. It was like somebody had pulled a plug somewhere. The '50s chicks being brought up all very jolly hockey sticks, and then somewhere there seemed to be a moment when they just decided they wanted to let themselves go. The opportunity arose for them to do that, and who's going to stop them? It was all dripping with sexual lust, though they didn't know what to do about it. But suddenly you're on the end of it. It's a frenzy. Once it's let out, it's an incredible force. You stood as much chance in a fucking river full of piranhas. They were beyond what they wanted to be. They'd lost themselves. These chicks were coming out there, bleeding, clothes torn off, pissed panties, and you took that for granted every night. That was the gig. It could have been anybody, quite honestly. They didn't give a shit that I was trying to be a blues player.

For a guy like Bill Perks, when suddenly there it is in front of you, it's unbelievable. We caught him in the coal pile with a chick, somewhere in Sheffield or Nottingham. They looked like something out of *Oliver Twist*. "Bill, we've got to go." It was Stu that found him. What are you going to do at that age when most of the teenage population of everywhere has decided you're it? The incoming was incredible. Six months ago I couldn't get laid; I'd have had to pay for it.

\* \* \*

One minute no chick in the world. No fucking way, and they're going la la la la la. And the next they're sniffing around. And you're going wow, when I changed from Old Spice to Habit Rouge, things definitely got better. So what is it they want? Fame? The money? Or is it for real? And of course when you've not had much chance with beautiful women, you start to get suspicious.

I've been saved by chicks more times than by guys. Sometimes just that little hug and kiss and nothing else happens. Just keep me warm for the night, just hold on to each other when times are hard, times are rough. And I'd say, "Fuck, why are you bothering with me when you know I'm an asshole and I'll be gone tomorrow?" "I don't know. I guess you're worth it." "Well, I'm not going to argue." The first time I encountered that was with these little English chicks up in the north, on that first tour. You end up, after the show, at a pub or the bar of the hotel, and suddenly you're in the room with some very sweet chick who's going to Sheffield University and studying sociology who decides to be really nice to you. "I thought you were a smart chick. I'm a guitar player. I'm just going through town." "Yeah, but I like you." Liking is sometimes better than loving.

By the late '50s, teenagers were a targeted new market, an advertising windup. "Teenager" comes from advertising; it's quite cold-blooded. Calling them teenagers created a whole thing amongst teenagers themselves, a self-consciousness. It created a market not just for clothes and cosmetics, but also for music and literature and everything else; it put that age group in a separate bag. And there was an explosion, a big hatch of pubescents around that time. Beatlemania and Stone mania. These were chicks that were just dying for something else. Four or five skinny blokes provided the outlet, but they would have found it somewhere else.

The power of the teenage females of thirteen, fourteen, fifteen, when they're in a gang, has never left me. They nearly killed me. I was never more in fear for my life than I was from teenage girls. The ones that choked me, tore me to shreds, if you got caught in a frenzied crowd of them — it's hard to express how frightening they could be. You'd rather be in a trench fighting the enemy than to be faced with this unstoppable, killer wave of lust and desire, or whatever it is — it's unknown even to them. The cops are running away, and you're faced with this savagery of unleashed emotions.

I think it was Middlesbrough. And I couldn't get in the car. It was an Austin Princess, and I'm trying to get in the car and these bitches are ripping me apart. The problem is if they get their hands on you, they don't know what to do with you. They nearly strangled me with a necklace, one grabbed one side of it, the other grabbed the other, and they're going, "Keith, Keith," and meanwhile they're choking me. I get hold of the handle and it comes off in my hand, and the car goes zooming off, and I'm left with this goddamn handle in my hand. I got left in the lurch that day. The driver panicked. The rest of the guys had gotten in the car, and he just wasn't going to stick around any longer. So I was left in this pack of female hyenas. Next thing, I woke up in this back alley stage door entrance, because the cops had obviously moved everyone on. I'd passed out, I'd suffocated, they were all over me. What are you going to do with me now you've got me?

I remember one scene of real contact with these girls — a completely unexpected moment, a vignette.

The sky is sullen. It's a day OFF! Suddenly the storm breaks viciously! Outside I see three die-hard fans. Their bouffants are succumbing to nature's forces. But they stay! What can a poor boy do? "Get in here, dopes." My tiny cubicle is filled with three drowned brats. They steam, trembling. They drench my room. The hairdos are done. They are trembling from the storm and from suddenly being in their (or one of their) idol's room. Confusion reigns. They don't know whether to squat or go blind. I'm equally confused. It's one thing to play on stage to them, it's another to be face-to-face. Towels become an important issue, as does the john. They make a poor attempt to resurrect themselves. It's all nerves and tension. I get them some coffee laced with a little bourbon, but sex is not even in the air. We sit and talk and laugh until the sky clears. I get them a cab. We part as friends.

September 1963. No songs, at least none that we thought would make the charts. Nothing in the ever-depleting R&B barrel looked likely. We were rehearsing at Studio 51 near Soho. Andrew had disappeared to walk about and absent himself from this gloom and he'd walked into John and Paul, getting out of a taxi in the Charing Cross Road. They had a drink and they detected Andrew's distress. He told them: no songs. They came back to the studio with him and gave us a song that was on their next album but wasn't coming out as a single, "I Wanna Be Your Man." They played it through with us. Brian put on some nice slide guitar; we turned it into an unmistakably Stones rather than Beatles song. It was clear that we had a hit almost before they'd left the studio.

They deliberately aimed it at us. They're songwriters, they're trying to flog their songs, it's Tin Pan Alley, and they thought this song would suit us. And also we were a mutual-admiration society. Mick and I admired their harmonies and their songwriting capabilities; they envied us our freedom of movement and our image. And they wanted to join in with us. The thing is, with the Beatles and us, it was a very friendly relationship. It was also very cannily worked out, because in those days singles were coming out every six, eight weeks. And we'd try and time it so that we didn't clash. I remember John Lennon calling me up and saying, "Well, we've not finished mixing yet." "We've got one ready to go." "OK, you go first."

When we first took off we were too busy playing on the road to think about writing songs. Also we reckoned it wasn't our job; it hadn't occurred to us. Mick and I considered songwriting to be some foreign job that somebody else did. I rode the horse and somebody else put the shoes on. Our first records were all covers, "Come On," "Poison Ivy," "Not Fade Away." We were just playing American music to English people, and we could play it damn good, and some American people even heard. We were already shocked and stunned to be where we were, and we were very happy as interpreters of the music that we loved. We thought we had no reason to step outside. But Andrew was persistent. Strictly pressure of business. You've got an incredible thing going here, but without more material, and preferably new material, it's over. You've got to find out if you can do that, and if not, then we've got to find some writers. Because you can't just live off cover versions. That quantum leap into making our own material, that took months, though I found it a lot easier than I expected.

The famous day when Andrew locked us in a kitchen up in Willesden and said, "Come out with a song"—that did happen. Why Andrew put Mick and me together as songwriters and not Mick and Brian, or me and Brian, I don't know. It turned out that Brian couldn't write songs, but Andrew didn't know that then. I guess it's because Mick and I were hanging out together at the time. Andrew puts it this way: "I worked on the assumption that if Mick could write postcards to Chrissie Shrimpton, and Keith could play a guitar, then they could write songs." We spent the whole night in that goddamn kitchen, and I mean, we're the Rolling Stones, like the blues kings, and we've got some food, piss out the window or down the sink, it's no big deal. And I said, "If we want to get out of here, Mick, we better come up with something."

We sat there in the kitchen and I started to pick away at these chords.... "It is the evening of the day." I might have written that. "I sit and watch the children play," I certainly wouldn't have come up with that. We had two lines and an interesting chord sequence, and then something else took over somewhere in this process. I don't want to say mystical, but you can't put your finger on it. Once you've got that idea, the rest of it will come. It's like you've planted a seed, then you water it a bit and suddenly it sticks up out of the ground and goes, hey, look at me. The mood is made somewhere in the song. Regret, lost love. Maybe one of us had just busted up with a girlfriend. If you can find the trigger that kicks off the idea, the rest of it is easy. It's just hitting the first spark. Where that comes from, God knows.

With "As Tears Go By," we weren't trying to write a commercial pop song. It was just what came out. I knew what Andrew wanted: don't come out with a blues, don't do some parody or copy, come out with something of your own. A good pop song is not really that easy to write. It was a shock, this fresh world of writing our own material, this discovery that I had a gift I had no idea existed. It was Blake-like, a revelation, an epiphany.

"As Tears Go By" was first recorded and made into a hit by Marianne Faithfull. That was only weeks away. After that we wrote loads of airy-fairy silly love songs for chicks and stuff that didn't take off. We'd give them to Andrew and, amazing to us, he got most of them recorded by other artists. Mick and I refused to put this crap we were writing with the Stones. We'd have been laughed out of the goddamn room. Andrew was waiting for us to come up with "The Last Time."

Songwriting had to be fitted in. After a show was sometimes the only time. It was impossible on the road. Stu would drive us, and he was merciless. We'd be stuck in the back of this Volkswagen, sealed in, one window at the back, and you sat on the engine. Most important was the gear, the amplifiers and the microphone stands and the guitars, and then, once that was loaded, "wedge yourselves in." Find some room, and if you wanted to stop for a pee, forget about it. He'd pretend he couldn't hear you. And he had a huge stereo, mobile sounds forty years ahead of what they've got now. Two huge JBLs next to his ears in his driving cabin. A traveling prison.

\* \* \*

The Ronettes were the hottest girl group in the world, and early in 1963 they'd just released one of the greatest songs ever recorded, "Be My Baby," produced by Phil Spector. We toured with the Ronettes on our second UK tour, and I fell in love with Ronnie Bennett, who was the lead singer. She was twenty years old and she was extraordinary, to hear, to look at, to be with. I fell in love with her silently, and she fell in love with me. She was as shy as I was, so there wasn't a lot of communication, but there sure was love. It all had to be kept very quiet because Phil Spector was and notoriously remained a man of prodigious jealousy. She had to be in her room all the time in case Phil called. And I think he quickly got a whiff that Ronnie and I were getting on, and he would call people and tell them to stop Ronnie seeing anybody after the show. Mick had cottoned to her sister Estelle, who was not so tightly chaperoned. They came from a huge family. Their mother, who had six sisters and seven brothers, lived in Spanish Harlem, and Ronnie had first stepped out onto the Apollo stage when she was fourteen years old. She told me later that Phil was acutely conscious of his receding hairline and couldn't stand my abundant barnet (London rhyming slang for hair: Barnet Fair). This insecurity was so chronic that he would go to terrible lengths to allay his fears — to the point where, after he married Ronnie in 1968, he made her prisoner in his California mansion, barely allowing her out and preventing her from singing, recording or touring. In her book she describes Phil taking her to the basement and showing her a gold coffin with a glass top, warning her that this was where she would be on display if she strayed from his rigorous rules. Ronnie had a lot of guts at that young age, which didn't, however, get her out of Phil's grip. I remember watching Ronnie do a vocal at Gold Star Studios: "Shut up, Phil. I know how it should go!"

Ronnie remembered how we were on that tour together:

**Ronnie Spector:** Keith and I made ways to be together — I remember on that tour, in England, there was so much fog that the bus had to actually stop. And Keith and I got out and we went over to this little cottage and this old lady came to the door, sort of heavy and so sweet — and I said, "Hi, I'm Ronnie of the Ronettes" and Keith said, "I'm Keith Richards of the Rolling Stones and we can't move our bus because we can't see any farther than our hands...." So she says, "Oh! Come on in, kids, I'll give you something!" and she gave us scones, tea and then she gave us extra ones to bring back to the bus and to be honest, those were the happiest days of my entire career.

We were twenty years old and we just fell in love. What do you do when you hear a record like "Be My Baby" and suddenly you are? But same old story, can't let anybody else know. So it was a terrible thing in a way. But basically, it was just hormones. And sympathy. Without us even thinking about it, we both realized that we were awash in this sea of sudden success and that other people were directing us and we didn't like it. But nothing much you can do about it. Not on the road. But then, we would never have met if we had not been in this weird situation. Ronnie only wanted the best for people. And never quite got the best for herself. But her heart was definitely in the right place. I went to the Strand Palace Hotel and looked her up early one morning. "Just want to say hello." The tour was about to leave for Manchester or somewhere, we had to all get on the bus, so I just figured I'd pick her up before. Nothing happened then. I just helped her to pack. But it was a very bold move for me, because I'd never put the come-on to any chick. We were reunited in New York not long after this, as I will tell. And I've always kept in touch with Ronnie. On the day of 9/11 we were recording together, a song called "Love Affair," in Connecticut. It is a work in progress.

In the arrogance of youth, the idea of being a rock star or a pop star was taking a step down from being a bluesman and playing the clubs. For us to have to dip our feet into commercialism, in 1962 or '63, was for a small while distasteful. The Rolling Stones, when they started, the limits of their ambition was just to be the best fucking band in London. We disdained the provinces; it was a real London mind-set. But once the world beckoned, it didn't take long for the scales to fall from the eyes. Suddenly the whole world was opening up, the Beatles were proving that. It's not that easy being famous; you don't want to be. But at the same time you've got to be in order to do what you're doing. And you realize you've already made the deal at the crossroads. Nobody said this was the deal. But within a few weeks, months, you realize that you've made the deal. And that you are now set on a path that is not your aesthetically ideal path. Stupid teenage idealisms, purisms, bullshit. You're now set on the path, along with all those people that you wanted to follow anyway, like Muddy Waters, Robert Johnson. You've already made the fucking deal. And now you have to follow it, just like all your brothers and sisters and ancestors. You are now on the road.

Michael Cooper / Raj Prem Collection

# Chapter Five

The Stones' first tour of the USA. Meeting Bobby Keys at the San Antonio State Fair. Chess Records, Chicago. I hook up with the future Ronnie Spector and go to the Apollo in Harlem. Fleet Street (and Andrew Oldham) provide our new popular image: long-haired, obnoxious and dirty. Mick and I write a song we can give the Stones. We go to LA and record with Jack Nitzsche at RCA. I write "Satisfaction" in my sleep, and we have our first number one. Allen Klein becomes our manager. Linda Keith breaks my heart. I buy my country house, Redlands. Brian begins to melt down—and meets Anita Pallenberg.

The first time the Stones went to America, we felt we'd died and gone to heaven. It was the summer of '64. Everybody had their own little thing about America. Charlie would go down to the Metropole when it was still swinging, and see Eddie Condon. The first thing I did was visit Colony Records and buy every Lenny Bruce album I could find. Yet I was amazed by how old-fashioned and European New York seemed—quite different to what I'd imagined. Bell-boys and maître d's, all that sort of thing. Unnecessary fluff and very unexpected. It was as if somebody had said, "These are the rules" in 1920 and it hadn't changed a bit since. On the other hand, it was the fastest-moving modern place you could be.

And the radio! You couldn't believe it after England. Being there at a time of a real musical explosion, sitting in a car with the radio on was beyond heaven. You could turn the channels and get ten country stations, five black stations, and if you were traveling the country and they faded out, you just turned the dial again and there was another great song. Black music was exploding. It was a powerhouse. At Motown they had a factory but without turning out automatons. We lived off Motown on the road, just waiting for the next Four Tops or the next Temptations. Motown was our food, on the road and off. Listening to car radios through a thousand miles to get to the next gig. That was the beauty of America. We used to dream of it before we got there.

I knew Lenny Bruce might not be every American's sense of humor, but I thought from there I could get a thread to the secrets of the culture. He was my entrée into American satire. Lenny was the man. *The Sick Humor of Lenny Bruce;* I'd taken him in long before I got to America. So I was well prepared when on *The Ed Sullivan Show* Mick wasn't allowed to sing "Let's Spend the Night Together," we had to sing "Let's Spend Some Time Together." Talk about shades and nuances. What does that mean, especially to CBS? A night is not allowed. Unbelievable. It used to make us laugh. It was pure Lenny Bruce—"Tittie" is a dirty word? What's dirty? The word or the tittie?

Andrew and I walked into the Brill Building, the Tin Pan Alley of US song, to try and see the great Jerry Leiber, but Jerry Leiber wouldn't see us. Someone recognized us and took us in and played us all these songs, and we walked out with "Down Home Girl," by Leiber and Butler, a great funk song that we recorded in November 1964. Looking for the Decca offices in New York on one of our adventures, we ended up in a motel on 26th and 10th with a drunken Irishman called Walt McGuire, a crew cut guy who looked as if he'd just gotten out of the American navy. This was the head of the US Decca office. And we suddenly realized the great Decca record company was actually some warehouse in New York. It was a card trick. "Oh yes, we have big offices in New York." And it was down on the docks on the West Side Highway.

We were listening to chick songs, doo-wop, uptown soul: the Marvelettes, the Crystals, the Chiffons, the Chantels, all of this stuff coming in our ears, and we're loving it. And the Ronettes, the hottest girl group around. "Will You Love Me Tomorrow" by the Shirelles. Shirley Owens, their lead singer, had an almost untrained voice, beautifully balanced with a fragility and simplicity, almost as if she wasn't a singer. All this stuff you heard — no doubt the Beatles had an effect — "Please Mr. Postman," and "Twist and Shout" by the Isley Brothers. If we'd tried to play anything like that down at the Richmond Station Hotel it would have been *"What?* They've gone mad." Because they wanted to hear hard-duty Chicago blues that no other band could play as well as we could. The Beatles certainly could never have played it like that. At Richmond it was our workmanlike duty not to stray from the path.

The first show we ever did in America was at the Swing Auditorium in San Bernardino, California. Bobby Goldsboro, who taught me the Jimmy Reed lick, was on the show, and the Chiffons. But earlier we'd had the experience of Dean Martin introducing us at the taping of the *Hollywood Palace* TV show. In America then, if you had long hair, you were a faggot as well as a freak. They would shout across the street, "Hey, fairies!" Dean Martin introduced as something like "these long-haired wonders from England, the Rolling Stones.... They're backstage picking the fleas off each other." A lot of sarcasm and eyeball rolling. Then he said, "Don't leave me alone with *this,"* gesturing with horror in our direction. This was Dino, the rebel Rat Packer who cocked his finger at the entertainment world by pretending to be drunk all the time. We were, in fact, quite stunned. English comperes and showbiz types may have been hostile, but they didn't treat you like some dumb circus act. Before we'd gone on, he'd had the bouffanted King Sisters and performing elephants, standing on their hind legs. I love old Dino. He was a pretty funny bloke, even though he wasn't ready for the changing of the guard.

On to Texas and more freak show appearances, in one case with a pool of performing seals between us and the audience at the San Antonio Texas State Fair. That was where I first met Bobby Keys, the great saxophone player, my closest pal (we were born within hours of each other). A soul of rock and roll, a solid man, also a depraved maniac. The other guy on that gig was George Jones. They trailed in with tumbleweed following them, as if tumbleweed was their pet. Dust all over the place, a bunch of cowboys. But when George got up, we went whoa, there's a master up there.

You have to ask Bobby Keys how big Texas is. It took me thirty years to convince him that Texas was actually just a huge landgrab by Sam Houston and Stephen Austin. "No fucking way. How dare you!" He's red in the face. So I laid a few books on him about what actually happened between Texas and Mexico, and six months later he says, "Your case seems to have some substance." I know the feeling, Bob. I used to believe that Scotland Yard was lily-white.

But Bobby Keys should be allowed to tell the tale of our first meeting, since this is a Texan story. He flatters me, but in this case I have allowed it.

**Bobby Keys**: I first met Keith Richards physically in San Antonio, Texas. I was so biased against that man before I actually met him. They recorded a song, "Not Fade Away," by a guy named Buddy Holly, born in Lubbock, Texas, same as me. I said, "Hey, that was Buddy's song. Who are these pasty-faced, funny-talking, skinny-legged guys to come over here and cash in on Buddy's song? I'll kick their asses!" I didn't care much for the Beatles. I kind of secretly liked them, but I saw the death of the saxophone unraveling before my eyes. None of these guys have saxes in their bands, man! I'm going to be playing Tijuana Brass shit for the rest of my life. I didn't think, "Great, we're going to be on the same show." I was playing with a guy named Bobby Vee, who had a hit at the time called "Rubber Ball" ("I keep bouncing back to you"),

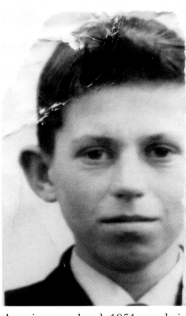

Mum and Dad, late 1930s.

At primary school, 1951, aged eight.

Aged four, on my first tricycle, at Southend-on-Sea.

On the south coast of England, 1956, aged twelve.

Beesands, Devon, with my parents, 1950s.

First love, Haleema.

Right: 1964

Terry O'Neill

Seated, right to left: Doris, grandfather Gus, grandmother Emma, aunt Marjorie. Standing, left to right: aunts Elsie, Joanna, Patty, Connie, Beatrice.

At RCA Studios, Hollywood, with Mick and Andrew Oldham, 1965.

*Bob Bonis/NotFadeAwayGallery.com*

Munich, September 14, 1965. First trip to West Germany. The night Anita met Brian Jones.

*Bob Bonis/NotFadeAwayGallery.com*

1963

*Philip Townsend*

Bob Bonis/NotFadeAwayGallery.com

Early US tour, where the audiences were kept well away.
Ratcliffe Stadium, Fresno, California, May 1965.

Gered Mankowitz

RCA Studios, Sunset and Ivar, Hollywood, 1965, working on *Aftermath*.

Mick and me at Redlands, 1967.

A nice cup of tea with Charlie outside court after being charged with "insulting behaviour" — urinating in a garage forecourt — July 1965.

*Dennis Hart/Rex USA*

A friendly greeting from the Jack Tar Hotel, Clearwater, Florida, May 1965.

*Bob Bonis/NotFadeAwayGallery.com*

*Gered Mankowitz*

1965 US tour. The show was stopped by the sheriff for rowdiness. This is just before the restart, which didn't go any better.

Blue Lena, my
Bentley Continental
Flying Spur.

Publicizing *Between the Buttons,* January 1967.

*Popperfoto/Getty Images*

John Knoote/Rex USA

Chichester Magistrates' Court, where we opted to go to trial for the Redlands bust, May 10, 1967.

Laid up in Achmed's shop in Tangier, Morocco. Background: Marianne, Mick; middle, left to right: Robert Fraser, Brian Jones, Achmed; foreground, back to camera: Anita.

Michael Cooper/Raj Prem Collection

With Anita
at the Venice
Film Festival,
soon after
her role in
*Barbarella.*

*Dezo Hoffmann/Rex USA*

California, 1968. Left to right: me, Gram Parsons, Tony Foutz, Anita, and Phil Kaufman, Gram's manager.

*Michael Cooper/Raj Prem Collection*

Stones, 1969, with new guitarist Mick Taylor.

Arrival of Marlon,
King's College
Hospital, London,
August 10, 1969.

Harris/Rex USA

Madison Square Garden, July 1972,
at the end of the Exile tour.

*Bob Gruen/www.bobgruen.c*

Me and Gram Parsons at Nellcôte, 1971.

*Dominique Tarlé*

Annie Leibovitz

The *Exile* lineup (except for Charlie), 1972. Left to right: Mick Jagger, Mick Taylor, Bill Wyman, Nicky Hopkins, Bobby Keys, me.

Ken Regan/Camera 5

At the Alamo, Texas, 1975. Ron Wood plays the part.

*Jane Rose*

Angela, aged five, 1977.

*Annie Leibovitz*

Diverting ourselves from the troubles in Toronto, 1977. Marlon and I rig up Scalextrics on the hotel bed.

*Jane Rose*

Born within hours of each other, him in Lubbock, Texas, me in Dartford, Kent. My closest pal, Bobby Keys.

*Annie Leibovitz*

Me and Ron Wood hanging out, 1975.

*Ethan Russell*

The tour of 1972. Somewhere in the USA.

European tour,
1973.

*Michael Putland*

and we were headlining the show until They came on, and then they were headlining the show. And this was Texas, man. This was my stomping ground.

We were all staying at the same hotel in San Antonio, and they were out on the balcony, Brian and Keith, and I think Mick. I went out and listened to them, and there was some actual rock and roll going on there, in my humble opinion. And of course I knew all about it, given it was invented in Texas and me being present at its birth. And the band was really, really good, and they did "Not Fade Away" actually better than Buddy ever did it. I never said that to them or anybody else. I thought maybe I had judged these guys too harshly. So the next day we must have played three shows with them, and about the third time I was in the dressing room with them, they were all talking about the American acts, how before they went on stage they all changed clothes. Which we did. We went on with our black mohair suits and white shirts and ties, which was stupid, because it was nine hundred degrees outside, summertime in San Antonio. They were saying, "Why don't we ever change clothes?" And they said, "Yeah, that's a good idea." I'm expecting them to whip out some suits and ties, but they just changed clothes with each other. I thought that was great.

You got to realize that the vision, the image, according to 1964 US rock-and-roll standards, was mohair suit and tie, and nicey-nicey, ol' boy next door. And all of a sudden here comes this truckload of English jackflies, interlopers, singing a Buddy Holly song! Damn! I couldn't really hear all that well, amplifiers and PAs being what they were, but man, I felt it. I just fucking felt it, and it made me smile and dance. They didn't dress alike, they didn't do sets, they just broke all the fucking rules and made it work, and that is what enchanted the shit out of me. So, being inspired by this, the next day I'd got my mohair suit out and put the trousers on, and my toenails split the seam down the front, and I didn't have anything else to wear. So I wore my shirt and tie and put on Bermuda shorts and cowboy boots. I didn't get fired. I got "What are you … How dare … What is fucking going on, man?" It redefined a lot of stuff for me. The American music scene, the whole set of teenage idols and clean-cut boys from next door and nice little songs, all that went right out the fucking window when these guys showed up! Along with the press, "Would you let your daughter," all that stuff, forbidden fruit.

Anyway, somehow they noticed what I did, and I noticed what they did, and we just kind of met there, really just brushed paths. And then I ran into them again in LA when they were doing the T.A.M.I. show. I discovered that Keith and I had the same birthday, both born 12/18/43. He told me, "Bobby, you know what that means? We're half man and half horse, and we got a license to shit in the streets." Well, that's just one of the greatest pieces of information I'd ever received in my life!

The whole heart and soul of this band is Keith and Charlie. I mean, that's apparent to anybody who's breathing, or has a musical bone in his body. That is where the engine room is. I'm not a schooled musician, I can't read music, I never had any professional training. But I can feel stuff, and when I heard him playing guitar, it reminded me so much of the energy I heard from Buddy and I heard from Elvis. There was something there that was the real deal, even though he was playing Chuck Berry. It was still the real deal, you know? And I'd heard some pretty good guitar players coming out of Lubbock. Orbison came from Vernon, a few hours away, I used to listen to him, and Buddy at the skating rink, and Scotty Moore and Elvis Presley would come through town, so

I'd heard some pretty good guitar players. And there was just something about Keith that immediately reminded me of Holly. They're about the same size; Buddy was a skinny guy, had bad teeth. Keith was a mess. But some folks, they just got a look in their eye, and he looked dangerous, and that's the truth.

There was the stark thing you discovered about America — it was civilized round the edges, but fifty miles inland from any major American city, whether it was New York, Chicago, LA or Washington, you really did go into another world. In Nebraska and places like that we got used to them saying, "Hello, girls." We just ignored it. At the same time they felt threatened by us, because their wives were looking at us and going, "That's interesting." Not what they were used to every bloody day, not some beer-swilling redneck. Everything they said was offensive, but the actual drive behind it was very much defense. We just wanted to go in and have a pancake or a cup of coffee with some ham and eggs, but we had to be prepared to put up with some taunting. All we were doing was playing music, but what we realized was we were going through some very interesting social dilemmas and clashes. And whole loads of insecurities, it seemed to me. Americans were supposed to be brash and self-confident. Bullshit. That was just a front. Especially the men, especially in those days, they didn't know quite what was happening. Things did happen fast. I'm not surprised that a few guys just couldn't get the spin on it.

The only hostility I can recall on a consistent basis was from white people. Black brothers and musicians at the very least thought we were interestingly quirky. We could talk. It was far more difficult to break through to white people. You always got the impression that you were definitely a threat. And all you'd done was ask, "Can I use your bathroom?" "Are you a boy or a girl?" What are you gonna do? Pull your cock out?

Back in England we had a number one album, but out in the middle of America nobody knew who we were. They were more aware of the Dave Clark Five and the Swinging Blue Jeans. In some towns we got some real hostility, real killer looks in our direction. Sometimes we got the sense that an exemplary lesson was about to be taught us, right then and there. We'd have to make a quick getaway in our faithful station wagon with Bob Bonis, our road manager, great guy. He'd been on the road with midgets, performing monkeys, with some of the best acts of all time. He eased us into America, driving five hundred miles a day.

A lot of our gigs in '64, '65, were piggybacked onto these other tours that were already lined up. So for two weeks we'd be with Patti LaBelle and the Bluebelles, the Vibrations and a contortionist called the Amazing Rubber Man. And then we'd switch onto another circuit. The first time I ever saw anybody lip-synch on stage was the Shangri-Las, "Remember (Walkin' in the Sand)." Three New York chicks and they're very handsome and everything like that, but you suddenly realize there's no band, they're actually singing to a tape machine. And there were the Green Men, also Ohio, I think. They actually painted themselves green to perform their duty. Whatever was the flavor of the week or the month. Some of them were damn good players, especially in the Midwest and the Southwest. Those little bands playing any given night in bars, never going to make it and they didn't even want to, that's the beauty of it. And some of them damn good pickers. Wealth of talent out there. Guys that could play much better than I could. Sometimes we were top of the bill, not always but usually. And with Patti LaBelle and the Bluebelles there was young Sarah Dash, who had this woman chaperone, dressed in her Sunday church outfit. If you smiled you got a glare. They used to call her "Inch." She was sweet and short. Twenty years later she'll be back in my story.

And of course, beginning in '65, I'm starting to get stoned — a lifelong habit now — which also intensified my impressions of what was going on. Just smoking the weed at the time. The guys I met on the road were, to me then, older men in their thirties, some in their forties, black bands that we were playing with. And we'd be up all night and we'd get to the gig and there would be these brothers in their sharkskin suits, the chain, the waistcoat, the hair gel, and they're all shaved and groomed, so fit and sweet, and we'd just drag our asses in. One day I was feeling so ragged getting to the gig, and these brothers were so together, and shit, they were working the same schedule we were. So I said to one of these guys, a horn player, "Jesus, how do you look so good every day?" And he pulled his coat back and reached into his waistcoat pocket and said, "You take one of these, you smoke one of those." Best bit of advice. He gave me a little white pill, a white cross, and a joint. This is how we do it: you take one of these and you smoke one of these.

But keep it dark! That was the line I left the room with. Now we've told you, keep it dark. And I felt like I'd just been let into a secret society. Is it all right if I tell the other guys? Yeah, but keep it amongst yourselves. Backstage it had been going on from time immemorial. The joint really got my attention. The joint got my attention so much that I forgot to take the Benzedrine. They made good speed in those days. Oh yeah, it was pure. You could get hold of speed at any truck stop; truck drivers relied upon it. Stop over here, pull over to some truck stop and ask for Dave. Give me a Jack Daniel's on the rocks and a bag. Gimme a pigfoot and a bottle of beer.

2120 South Michigan Avenue was hallowed ground — the headquarters of Chess Records in Chicago. We got there on a last-minute arrangement made by Andrew Oldham, at a moment when the first half of our first US tour seemed like a semidisaster. There in the perfect sound studio, in the room where everything we'd listened to was made, perhaps out of relief or just the fact that people like Buddy Guy, Chuck Berry and Willie Dixon were wandering in and out, we recorded fourteen tracks in two days. One of them was Bobby Womack's "It's All Over Now," our first number one hit. Some people,

Marshall Chess included, swear that I made this up, but Bill Wyman can back me up. We walked into Chess studios, and there's this guy in black overalls painting the ceiling. And it's Muddy Waters, and he's got whitewash streaming down his face and he's on top of a ladder. Marshall Chess says, "Oh, we never had him painting." But Marshall was a boy then; he was working in the basement. And also Bill Wyman told me he actually remembers Muddy Waters taking our amplifiers from the car into the studio. Whether he was being a nice guy or he wasn't selling records then, I know what the Chess brothers were bloody well like — if you want to stay on the payroll, get to work. Actually meeting your heroes, your idols, the weirdest thing is that most of them are so humble, and very encouraging. "Play that lick again," and you realize you're sitting with Muddy Waters. And of course later I got to know him. Over many years I frequently stayed at his house. In those early trips I think it was Howlin' Wolf's house I stayed at one night, but Muddy was there. Sitting in the South Side of Chicago with these two greats. And the family life, loads of kids and relatives walking in and out. Willie Dixon's there....

In America people like Bobby Womack used to say, "The first time we heard you guys we thought you were black guys. Where did these motherfuckers come from?" I can't figure that out myself, why Mick and I in that damn town should come up with such a sound — except that if you soak it up in a damp tenement in London all day with the intensity that we did, it ain't that different from soaking it up in Chicago. That's all we played, until we actually became it. We didn't sound English. And I think it surprised us too.

Each time we played — and I still do this at certain times — I'd just turn round and say, "Is that noise just coming from him there, and me?" It's almost as if you're riding a wild horse. In that respect we're damn lucky we got to work with Charlie Watts. He was playing very much like black drummers playing with Sam and Dave and the Motown stuff, or the soul drummers. He has that touch. A lot of the time very correct, with the sticks through the fingers, which is how most drummers now play. If you try to get savage you're off. It's a bit like surfing; it's OK while you're up there. And because of that style of Charlie's, I could play the same way. One thing drives another in a band; it all has to melt together. Basically it's all liquid.

The most bizarre part of the whole story is that having done what we intended to do in our narrow, purist teenage brains at the time, which was to turn people on to the blues, what actually happened was we turned American people back on to their own music. And that's probably our greatest contribution to music. We turned white America's brain and ears around. And I wouldn't say we were the only ones — without the Beatles probably nobody would have broken the door down. And they certainly weren't bluesmen.

American black music was going along like an express train. But white cats, after Buddy Holly died and Eddie Cochran died, and Elvis was in the army gone wonky, white American music when I arrived was the Beach Boys and Bobby Vee. They were still stuck in the past. The past was six months ago; it wasn't a long time. But shit changed. The Beatles were the milestone. And then they got stuck inside their own cage. "The Fab Four." Hence, eventually, you got the Monkees, all this ersatz shit. But I think there was a vacuum somewhere in white American music at the time.

When we first got to America and to LA, there was a lot of Beach Boys on the radio, which was pretty funny to us — it was before *Pet Sounds* — it was hot rod songs and surfing songs, pretty lousily played, familiar Chuck Berry licks going on. "Round, round get around / I get around," I thought that was brilliant. It was later on, listening to *Pet Sounds,* well, it's all a little bit overproduced for me, but Brian Wilson had something. "In My Room," "Don't Worry Baby." I was more interested in their B-sides, the ones he slipped in. There was no particular correlation with what we were doing so I could just listen to it on another level. I thought these are very well-constructed songs. I took easily to the pop song idiom. I'd always listened to everything, and America opened it all out — we were hearing records there that were regional hits. We'd get to know local labels and local acts, which is how we came across "Time Is on My Side," in LA, sung by Irma Thomas. It was a B-side of a record on Imperial Records, a label we'd have been aware of because it was independent and successful and based on Sunset Strip.

I've talked to guys since like Joe Walsh of the Eagles and many other white musicians about what they listened to when they were growing up, and it was all very provincial and narrow and depended on the local, usually white, FM radio station. Bobby Keys reckons he can tell where someone came from by their musical tastes. Joe Walsh heard us play when he was at high school, and he's told me that it had a huge effect on him simply because nobody he knew had ever heard anything like that because there wasn't anything. He was listening to doo-wop and that was about it. He had never heard Muddy Waters. Amazingly, he was first exposed to the blues, he said, by hearing us. He also decided there and then that the minstrel's life was for him, and now you can't go into any diner without hearing him weaving that guitar of his on "Hotel California."

Jim Dickinson, the southern boy who played piano on "Wild Horses," was exposed to black music through the powerful and only black radio station, WDIA, when he was growing up in Memphis, so when he went to college in Texas he had a musical education that exceeded that of anybody he met there. But he never saw any black musicians, even though he lived in Memphis, except once he saw the Memphis Jug Band with Will Shade and Good Kid on the washboard, when they were playing in the street when he was nine. But the racial barriers were so severe that those kinds of players were inaccessible to him. Then Furry Lewis — at whose funeral he played — and Bukka White and others were being brought out to play via the folk revival. I do think maybe the Stones had a lot to do with making people twiddle their knobs a little more.

When we put out "Little Red Rooster," a raw Willie Dixon blues with slide guitar and all, it was a daring move at the time, November

1964. We were getting no-no's from the record company, management, everyone else. But we felt we were on the crest of a wave and we could push it. It was almost in defiance of pop. In our arrogance at the time, we wanted to make a statement. "I am the little red rooster / Too lazy to crow for day." See if you can get that to the top of the charts, motherfucker. Song about a chicken. Mick and I stood up and said, come on, let's push it. This is what we're fucking about. And the floodgates burst after that, suddenly Muddy and Howlin' Wolf and Buddy Guy are getting gigs and working. It was a breakthrough. And the record got to number one. And I'm absolutely sure what we were doing made Berry Gordy at Motown capable of pushing his stuff elsewhere, and it certainly rejuvenated Chicago blues as well.

I keep a notebook where I write down sketches and song ideas, and it contains this:

### JUKE JOINT... ALABAMA? GEORGIA?

*Finally I'm in my element! An incredible band is wailing on a stage decorated with phosphorescent paint, the dance floor is moving as one, so does the sweat and the ribs cooking out back. The only thing that makes me stand out is that I'm <u>white!</u> Wonderfully, no one notices this aberration. I am accepted, I'm made to feel <u>so</u> warm. I am in heaven!*

Most towns, like white Nashville, for example, by ten o'clock were ghost towns. We were working with black guys, the Vibrations, Don Bradley, I think his name was. The most amazing act, they could do everything. They were doing somersaults while they were playing. "What are you going to do after the show?" This is already an invitation. So, get in the cab and we go across the tracks and it's just starting to happen. There's food going, everybody's rocking and rolling, everybody's having a good time, and it was such a contrast from the white side of town, it always sticks in my memory. You could hang there with ribs, drink, smoke. And big mamas, for some reason they always looked upon us as thin and frail people. So they started to mama us, which was all right with me. Shoved into the middle of two enormous breasts... "You need a rubdown, boy?" "OK, anything you say, mama." Just the free-and-easiness of it. You wake up in a house full of black people who are being so incredibly kind to you, you can't believe it. I mean, shit, I wish this happened at home. And this happened in every town. You wake up, where am I? And there's a big mama there, and you're in bed with her daughter, but you get breakfast in bed.

The first time I stared into a gun barrel was in the men's room of the Civic Auditorium (I believe) in Omaha, Nebraska. It was in the fist of a big grizzled cop. I was with Brian, backstage at a sound check. We used to drink Scotch and Coke at the time. Anyhow, we took our paper cups with us and answered the call of nature, cup in hand. Happily we splashed away. I heard the door open behind us. "OK, turn around slowly," a voice wheezed. "Fuck off," Brian said. "I mean now," came the wheeze. Shaking off the drips, we looked around. A massive cop with a huge revolver in his huge fist fixed us with a menacing regard. Silence ruled as Brian and I stared at the black hole. "This is a public building. No alcoholic beverages allowed! You will tip the contents of your cups into the john. Now! No quick moves. Do it." Brian and I cracked up but did as we were told. He did have the upper hand. Brian said something about heavy-handed overreaction, which only infuriated the old bugger to the point that the barrel began to tremble. So we blabbered about being unaware of the city ordinance, to which he barked out something about ignorance not being a defense in the eyes of the law. I was about to ask how he knew we were drinking booze but thought better of it. We had another bottle in the dressing room.

It was soon after that that I picked up a Smith & Wesson .38 special. It was the Wild West, and still is! I picked it up in a truck stop for twenty-five dollars, plus ammo. Thus began my illicit relationship with that venerable firm. I'm not on their books! Quite a few of the guys we were traveling with were carrying shooters. They were fucking hard cats who I worked with. I remember that other side of it. Pools of blood oozing out of dressing rooms and realizing there's a beating going on and you don't want to get involved. But the biggest horror of all was seeing the cops turn up. Especially backstage. You should have seen some of the bands run, baby. A lot of the cats on the road were on the run for one reason or another. Probably minor offenses, like not paying their alimony or auto theft. You were not working with saints here. They were good players and they could pick up a gig and disappear amongst the minstrels. They were streetwise like motherfuckers. Backstage, a squad of cops would arrive with a warrant for somebody that was playing guitar in some band. It was kind of like the press-gang had arrived. Oh, my God! The panic... You'd see Ike Turner's piano player zooming down the stairs.

By the end of that first American tour, we thought we'd blown it in America. We'd been consigned to the status of medicine shows and circus freaks with long hair. When we got to Carnegie Hall in New York, we were suddenly back in England with screaming teenyboppers. America was coming around. We realized that it was just starting.

Mick and I hadn't come all the way to New York in '64 not to go to the Apollo. So I hooked up again with Ronnie Bennett. We went to Jones Beach with all the Ronettes in a red Cadillac. The desk rang up, "There's a lady downstairs." "Come on, let's go." And it was James Brown's week at the Apollo. Maybe Ronnie should describe what nice English boys we were — contrary to popular belief:

**Ronnie Spector:** The first time Keith and Mick came to America, they weren't successful, they slept on my mother's living room floor up in Spanish Harlem. They had no money, and my mom would get up in the morning and make them bacon and eggs, and Keith would always say, "Thank you, Mrs. Bennett." And then I took them to see James Brown at the Apollo, and that's what made them so determined. Those guys went home and came back superstars. Because I showed them what I did, how I grew up, and how I went to the Apollo Theater when I was eleven years old. I took them backstage and they met all these rhythm and blues stars. I remember Mick standing there shaking when we passed James Brown's room.

The first time I went to heaven was when I awoke with Ronnie (later Spector!) Bennett asleep with a smile on her face. We were kids. It doesn't get any better than that. Just more refined. What can I say? She took me to her parents' house, took me to her bedroom. Several times, but that was the first time. And I'm just a guitar player. You know what I mean?

James Brown had the whole week there at the Apollo. Go to the Apollo and see James Brown, damn fucking right. I mean, who would turn that down? He was a piece of work. So on the button. We thought *we* were a tight band! The discipline in the band impressed me more than anything else. On stage, James would snap his fingers if he thought somebody had missed a beat or hit a wrong note, and you could see the player's face fall. He would signal the fine he had imposed with his fingers. These guys would be watching his hands. I even saw Maceo Parker, the sax player who was the architect of James Brown's band — who I finally got to work with in the Winos — get fined about fifty bucks that night. It was a fantastic show. Mick's looking at his foot moves. Mick took more notice than I did that day — lead singer, dancing, he calls the shots.

Backstage that night, James wanted to show off to these English folk. He's got the Famous Flames, and he's sending one out for a hamburger, he's ordering another to polish his shoes and he's humiliating his own band. To me, it was the Famous Flames, and James Brown happened to be the lead singer. But the way he lorded it over his minions, his minders and the actual band, to Mick was fascinating.

\* \* \*

When we got back to England, the big difference was seeing old friends, mostly musicians, who were already amazed that we were the Rolling Stones, but now "You've been to the States, man." You were suddenly aware that you had been distanced just by the fact that you'd been to America. It really pissed off the English fans. It happened with the Beatles' fans too. You were no longer "theirs." There was a sense of resentment. Never more so than in Blackpool. There, at the Empress Ballroom, a few weeks after our return, we faced the mob again, though this time a rabble army of Scotch drunks baying for blood. They used to have what they called Scotch week. All of the factories in Glasgow shut down and nearly everybody from there went to Blackpool, the seaside resort. We start the gig, and it's jam-packed, a lot of guys, a lot of them very, very pissed, all dressed up in their Sunday best. And suddenly while I'm playing, this little redheaded fucker flobs on me. So I move aside, and he follows me and flobs on me again and hits me in the face. So I stand in front of him again and he spits at me again and, with the stage, his head was just about near my shoe, like a penalty shot in football. I just went *bang* and knocked his fucking head off, with the grace of Beckham. He's never walked the same since. And after that, the riot broke out. They smashed everything, including the piano. We didn't see a piece of equipment that came back any bigger than three inches square with wires hanging out. We got out of there by the skin of our teeth.

In the days after our return from the US we appeared on *Juke Box Jury,* a long-established format presided over by a TV pro called David Jacobs, in which the celebs on the "jury" discussed the records Jacobs played and then voted them hits or misses. This was one of those landmark moments that completely escaped us while it was happening. But in the media later it was seen as a declaration of generational war, the cause of outrage, fear and loathing. On the same day we'd taped a show called *Top of the Pops* to promote our Bobby Womack single "It's All Over Now." I'd gotten used to lip-synching without blushing; that's the way it was done. Very few shows were live. We were getting a little bit cynical about the tripe market. You realized that you were really in one of the sleaziest businesses there is, without actually being a gangster. It was a business where the only time people laughed was when they'd screwed someone else over. I have a feeling that by then we kind of realized the role that we were being cast in, and that there was no fighting it and anyway, nobody had really played it before, and this would be kind of fun. And we didn't give a shit. Andrew Oldham describes our *Juke Box Jury* appearance in his book *Stoned*.

> **Andrew Oldham:** With no prompting from me, they
> proceeded to behave as complete and utter yobos and in
> twenty-five minutes managed to confirm the nation's worst
> opinion of them for once and all. They grunted, they laughed
> among themselves, were merciless towards the drivel that was
> played and hostile towards the unflappable Mr. Jacobs. This
> was no planned press move. Brian and Bill made some effort
> to be polite, but Mick and Keith and Charlie would have none
> of it.

Nobody was particularly witty or anything. We just trashed every record they played. While the record was playing, we were going, "I'm not fit to comment on this," "You can't listen to this stuff. Be serious." And there's David Jacobs trying to cover up the dirt. Jacobs was smarmy, but he was actually quite a nice guy. It had been so easy up until then: Helen Shapiro and Alma Cogan, reliable Variety Club sorts of people, all of those showbiz comfy societies that everybody was roped into, and then we come out of nowhere. I've no doubt that David was thinking, "Thanks a lot, BBC, and I want a raise after working with this lot." It won't get any better. Wait for the Sex Pistols, mate.

The Variety Club was like the inner circle, at the time, in showbiz. You didn't know if it was Freemasons or a charity; it was a clique that basically ran show business. Weirdly archaic, English showbiz mafia. We were thrown into all this in order to tear it apart. They were still playing their game. Billy Cotton. Alma Cogan. But you realized that all these celebs, and really very few of them were talented, had an incredible swing on things. Who got to play where, who would close doors on you and who would open them. And luckily, the Beatles had already shown them all what was what. The writing was on the wall already, so when they had to deal with us, they didn't know quite which way to pussyfoot.

The only reason we got a record deal with Decca was because Dick Rowe turned down the Beatles. EMI got them, and he could not afford to make the same mistake twice. Decca was desperate—I'm amazed the guy still had the job. At the time, just like anything else in "popular entertainment," they thought, it's just a fad, it's a matter of a few haircuts and we'll tame them anyway. But basically we only got a record deal because they could just not afford to fuck up twice. Otherwise they wouldn't have touched us with a barge pole. Just out of prejudice. That whole structure was Variety Club, a nod and a wink here and there. It served its purpose at the time, no doubt, but suddenly they realized, bang, welcome to the twentieth century, and it's 1964 already.

Things happened incredibly fast from the moment Andrew turned up. To me at least, there was a certain feeling that things were running away from us. But you also realize you've just been noosed, honey, and you're going to have to go with it. I was a little bit hesitant to run with it to start with, but Andrew knows it didn't take me long. We were of a very similar mind—let's figure out how to use Fleet Street. This was partly provoked by an incident at a photo session we did, when one of the photographers said to Andrew, "They're so dirty." Andrew's flash point was low, and he decided then that from now on he'd give them what they described. He suddenly saw the beauty of opposites. He'd already done the Beatles stuff with Epstein, so he was a street ahead of me. But he did find a willing partner in me, I must say. Even at that age there was a chemistry between us. Later we became firmer friends, but at the time, I looked at him just as Andrew looked at us — "I can use these bastards."

The media were so easy to manipulate, we could do anything we wanted. We'd get thrown out of hotels, piss on a garage forecourt. Actually that was a total accident. Once Bill wants to take a pee, it doesn't stop for about half an hour. Jesus Christ, where does the little bloke put all that? We went to the Grand Hotel in Bristol deliberately to get thrown out. Andrew called Fleet Street to say if you want to watch the Stones get thrown out of the Grand Hotel, be there at such and such a time — because we were dressed incorrectly. The way Andrew could set them up, we'd have them panting for nothing. And of course it provoked things like "Would you let your daughter marry one?" I don't know whether Andrew planted that idea on somebody or whether it was just one of those Lunchtime O'Booze ideas.

We were obnoxious. But these people were so complacent. They didn't know what hit them. It was blitzkrieg, really, an assault on the whole PR setup. And suddenly you realize there's this landscape out there, these people that need to be told what to do.

While we were pulling all these stunts, Andrew was going around in a Chevrolet Impala driven by Reg, his butch gay chauffeur from Stepney. Reg was a very nasty piece of work. In those days it was a miracle to get four lines from a rock journalist in *New Musical Express,* but it was important because there was very little radio and not much TV. There was a writer at the *Record Mirror* called Richard Green who had used that precious space to write about my complexion. I didn't even suffer from the blemishes he described. But this was the last straw for Andrew. He took Reg and barged into the writer's office. And with Reg holding his hands under the open window, he said to Richard — I quote again from Andrew's memoir:

**Andrew Oldham:** Richard, I got a call this morning from a
very hurt and upset Mrs. Richards. You don't know her, but

she's Keith Richards' mum. She said, "Mr. Oldham, can you do anything to stop what this man keeps saying about my boy's acne? I know you can't stop that rubbish about how they don't wash. But Keith is a sensitive boy, even if he doesn't say so. Please, Mr. Oldham, can you do anything?" So, Richard, this is the story. If you ever again write something about Keith that is out of line, that is hurtful to his mum, because I'm responsible to Keith's mum, your hands will be where they are now, but with one big difference. Reg here will bring that fuckin' window crashing down on your ugly hands, and you will not be writing, you malicious fat turd, for a long fucking time, and you won't be dictating either, 'cause your jaw will be sewn up from where Reg fucking broke it.

And with that, as it goes, they made their excuses and left. I didn't even realize until I read his book that Andrew was still living with his mother while he was pulling off all this derring-do. Maybe that had something to do with it. He was smarter and sharper than the assholes that were running the media, or the people running the record companies, who were totally out of touch with what was happening. You could just run in and rob the whole bank. It was a bit *Clockwork Orange*. There was no great universal "We want to change society"; we just knew that things were changing and that they could be changed. They were just too comfortable. It was all too satisfied. And we thought, "How can we run rampant?"

Of course all of us ran into the brick wall of the establishment. There was an impetus that couldn't be stopped. It was like when somebody says something, and you've got the most fantastic reply. You know you really shouldn't say it, but it has to be said, even though you know that it's gonna get you in shit. It's too good a line not to say. You'd feel that you'd chickened out on yourself if you didn't say it.

Oldham modeled himself to an extent on his idol Phil Spector as a producer as well as a manager, but unlike Spector, he wasn't a natural in the studio. I doubt whether Andrew would call me a liar when I say he was not very musical. He knew what he liked and what other people liked, but if you said E7th to him, you might as well be saying, "What's the meaning of life?" To me, a producer is somebody that at the end of the day comes out with everybody going, yeah, we got it. Andrew's musical input was minimal, and it was usually saved for backup vocals. La la la here. OK, we'll throw some on. He never got in the way of the way we did things, whether he agreed with it or not. But as a fully fledged producer, with knowledge of recording and a knowledge of music, he was on weaker ground. He had good taste for the market, especially once we went to America. The minute we got to America, it took the scales from his eyes as to what we were about, and more and more he let us get on with it. And basically that was the genius, I think, of Andrew's method of producing, to let us make the records. And to provide a lot of energy and enthusiasm. When you've got to take thirty and you're starting to flag a bit, you need that encouragement thing, "Just one more take, come on," unflagging enthusiasm. "We've got it, we're nearly there...."

When I was growing up, the idea of leaving England was pretty much remote. My dad did it once, but that was in the army to go to Normandy and get his leg blown off. The idea was totally impossible. You just read about other countries and looked at them on TV, and in *National Geographic,* the black chicks with their tits hanging out and their long necks. But you never expected to see it. Scraping up the money to get out of England would have been way beyond my capabilities.

One of the first places I remember us going to, after the USA, was Belgium, and even that was an adventure. It was like going to Tibet. And the Olympia in Paris. And then suddenly you're in Australia, and you're actually seeing the world, and they're paying you! But my God, there are some black holes.

Dunedin, for instance, almost the southernmost city in the world, in New Zealand. It looked like Tombstone and it felt like it. It still had hitching rails. It was a Sunday, a wet dark Sunday in Dunedin in 1965. I don't think you could have found anything more depressing anywhere. The longest day of my life, it seemed to go on forever. We were usually pretty good at entertaining ourselves, but Dunedin made Aberdeen seem like Las Vegas. Very rarely did everybody get depressed at the same time; there was usually one to support the others. But in Dunedin everybody was totally depressed. No chance of any redemption or laughter. Even the drink didn't get you pissed. On Sunday, there'd be little knocks on the door, "Er, church in ten minutes..." It was just one of those miserable gray days that took me back to my childhood, a day that will never end, the gloom, and not anything on the horizon. Boredom is an illness to me, and I don't suffer from it, but that moment was the lowest ebb. "I think I'll stand on my head, try and recycle the drugs."

But Roy Orbison! It was only because we were with Roy Orbison that we were there at all. He was definitely top of the bill that night. What a beacon in the southernmost gloom. The amazing Roy Orbison. He was one of those Texan guys who could sail through anything, including his whole tragic life. His kids die in a fire, his wife dies in a car crash, nothing in his private life went right for the big O, but I can't think of a gentler gentleman, or a more stoic personality. That incredible talent for blowing himself up from five foot six to six foot nine, which he seemed to be able to do on stage. It was amazing to witness. He's been in the sun, looking like a lobster, pair of shorts on. And we're just sitting around playing guitars, having a chat, smoke and a drink. "Well, I'm on in five minutes." We watch the opening number. And out walks this totally transformed thing that seems to have grown at least a foot with presence and command over the crowd. He was in his shorts just now; how did he do that? It's one of those astounding things about working in the theater. Backstage you can be a bunch of bums. And "Ladies and gentlemen" or "I present to you," and you're somebody else.

Mick and I spent months and months trying to write before we had anything we could record for the Stones. We wrote some terrible songs whose titles included "We Were Falling in Love" and "So Much in Love," not to mention "(Walkin' Thru the) Sleepy City" (a rip-off of "He's a Rebel"). Some of them were actually medium-sized hits — Gene Pitney, for example, singing "That Girl Belongs to Yesterday," although he improved on the words and on our original title, which was "My Only Girl." I wrote a forgotten gem called "All I Want Is My Baby," which was recorded by P.J. Proby's valet Bobby Jameson; I wrote "Surprise, Surprise," recorded by Lulu. We ended Cliff Richard's run of hits when he recorded our "Blue Turns to Grey" — it was one of the rare times one of his records went into the top thirty instead of the top ten. And when the Searchers did "Take It Or Leave It," it torpedoed them as well. Our songwriting had this other function of hobbling the opposition while we got paid for it. It had the opposite effect on Marianne Faithfull. It made her into a star with "As Tears Go By" — the title changed by Andrew Oldham from the *Casablanca* song "As Time Goes By" — written on a twelve-string guitar. We thought, what a terrible piece of tripe. We came out and played it to Andrew, and he said, "It's a hit." We actually sold this stuff, and it actually made money. Mick and I were thinking, this is money for old rope!

Mick and I knew by now that really our job was to write songs for the Stones. It took us eight, nine months before we came up with "The Last Time," which is the first one that we felt we could give to the rest of the guys without being sent out the room. If I'd gone to the Rolling Stones with "As Tears Go By," it would have been "Get out and don't come back." Mick and I were trying to hone it down. We kept coming up with these ballads, nothing to do with what we were doing. And then finally we came up with "The Last Time" and looked at each other and said, let's try this with the boys. The song has the first recognizable Stones riff or guitar figure on it; the chorus is from the Staple Singers' version, "This May Be the Last Time." We could work this hook; now we had to find the verse. It had a Stones twist to it, one that maybe couldn't have been written earlier — a song about going on the road and dumping some chick. "You don't try very hard to please me." Not the usual serenade to the unattainable object of desire. That was when it really clicked, with that song, when Mick and I felt confident enough to actually lay it in front of Brian and Charlie and Ian Stewart, especially, arbiter of events. With those earlier songs we would have been chased out the room. But that song defined us in a way, and it went to number one in the UK.

Andrew created an amazing thing in my life. I had never thought about songwriting. He made me learn the craft, and at the same time I realized, yes, I am good at it. And slowly this whole other world opens up, because now you're not just a player, or trying to play like somebody else. It isn't just other people's expression. I can start to express myself, I can write my own music. It's almost like a bolt of lightning.

"The Last Time" was recorded during a magical period at the RCA Studios in Hollywood. We recorded there intermittently across two years between June 1964 and August 1966, which culminated in the album *Aftermath,* all of whose songs were penned by Mick and me, the Glimmer Twins, as we later called ourselves. It was the period where everything — songwriting, recording, performing — stepped into a new league, and the time when Brian started going off the rails.

The work was always intensely hard. The gig never finished just because you got off stage. We had to go back to the hotel and start honing down these songs. We'd come off the road and we had four days to cut the tracks for an album, a week maximum. A track would get thirty to forty minutes to get down. It wasn't that difficult, because we're on the road, the band's well oiled. And we've got ten, fifteen songs. But it was nonstop, high-pressure work, which was probably good for us. When we recorded "The Last Time," in January 1965, we'd come back off the road and everyone was exhausted. We'd gone in to record the single only. After we finished "The Last Time," the only Stones left standing were me and Mick. Phil Spector was there — Andrew had asked him to come down and listen to the track — and so was Jack Nitzsche. A janitor had come to clean up, this silent sweeping in the corner of this huge studio, while this remaining group picked up instruments. Spector picked up Bill Wyman's bass, Nitzsche went to the harpsichord, and the B-side, "Play with Fire," was cut with half the Rolling Stones and this unique lineup.

When we first arrived in Los Angeles on that second tour, it was Sonny Bono who was sent to meet us at the airport with a car, because he was the promotion man for Phil Spector then. A year later Sonny and Cher were being feted at the Dorchester, presented to the world by Ahmet Ertegun. But back then, when he knew we were looking for a studio, Sonny put us in touch with Jack Nitzsche, and RCA was the first place he suggested. We went more or less straight there, into the limo-and-pool world, from a three-day tour of Ireland — an almost surreal contrast in cultures. Jack was in and out of the studio, more to get relief from Phil Spector and the enormous amount of work required to make the "wall of sound" than anything else. Jack was the Genius, not Phil. Rather, Phil took on Jack's eccentric persona and sucked his insides out. But Jack Nitzsche was an almost silent — and unpaid for reasons still not clear except he did it for fun — arranger, musician, gluer-together of the talent, a man of enormous importance for us in that period. He came to our sessions to relax and would throw in some ideas. He'd play when the mood took him. He's on "Let's Spend the Night Together," when he took over my piano part while I took over bass. This is just one example of his input. I loved the man.

Somehow we still had no money even by late 1964. Our first album, *The Rolling Stones,* was top of the charts and sold 100,000 copies, which was more than the Beatles initially sold. So where was the money? In fact, we simply figured that if we broke even we were cool. But we also knew we weren't tapping a huge market that we had opened. The system was that you didn't get money from English sales until a year after the record came out, eighteen months later if it was foreign sales. There was no money in any of the American tours. Everyone was rooming with everybody. Oldham used to sleep on Phil Spector's couch. We did the T.A.M.I. show in America late in 1964 — the show where we came on after James Brown — to get us back home. We earned $25,000. So did Gerry & the Pacemakers, and Billy J. Kramer and the Dakotas. That's a bit much, isn't it?

The first real cash I ever saw came from selling "As Tears Go By." I certainly remember the first time I got it. I looked at it! And then I counted it and then I looked at it again. And then I felt it and touched it. I did *nothing* with it. I just kept it in my bin, saying, I've got such a lot of money! Shit! I didn't particularly want to buy anything, or blow it. For the first time in my life, I'd got money. . . . Maybe I'll buy a new shirt, spring for some guitar strings. But basically it was "I don't believe this shit!" There's the queen's face all over it and it's signed by the right man, and you've got more than you've ever had in your hand ever, and more than your dad makes in a year, schlepping and working his fucking arse off. I mean, what to do with it is another thing, because I've another gig to do, and I'm working. But I must say, the first taste of a few hundred crisp new bills was not unsatisfying. What to do with it took some time. But it was the first feeling of being ahead of the game. And all I did was write a couple songs and they gave it to me.

One big setback we had was not being paid by Robert Stigwood for a tour we did with one of his acts. If the homework had been done, we would have known that this was his modus operandi — late paying turned into not paying at all, and we had to go all the way to the High Court. But before that, alas for him, one night at a club called the Scotch of St James, he made the terrible mistake of coming down the stairs as Andrew and I were going up. We blocked off the staircase so I could extract payment. You can't use a boot on a winding staircase, so he got the knee, one for every grand he owed us — sixteen of them. Even then he never apologized. Maybe I didn't kick him hard enough.

And when I got some more money, I took care of Mum. They'd split up, Doris and Bert, a year after I left home. Dad's Dad, but I bought Mum a house. I was always in touch with Doris. But that implied I couldn't be in touch with Bert, because they'd split up. It was like I couldn't take sides. And also I didn't have much time for that because life was getting really exciting. I'm zooming all over the place; I've got other things to do. What Mum and Dad were doing was not at the forefront of my mind.

Then came "Satisfaction," the track that launched us into global fame. I was between girlfriends at the time, in my flat in Carlton Hill, St. John's Wood. Hence maybe the mood of the song. I wrote "Satisfaction" in my sleep. I had no idea I'd written it, it's only thank God for the little Philips cassette player. The miracle being that I looked at the cassette player that morning and I knew I'd put a brand-new tape in the previous night, and I saw it was at the end. Then I pushed rewind and there was "Satisfaction." It was just a rough idea. There was just the bare bones of the song, and it didn't have that noise, of course, because I was on acoustic. And forty minutes of me snoring. But the bare bones is all you need. I had that cassette for a while and I wish I'd kept it.

Mick wrote the lyrics by the pool in Clearwater, Florida, four days before we went into the studio and recorded it — first at Chess in Chicago, an acoustic version, and later with the fuzz tone at RCA in Hollywood. I wasn't exaggerating when I wrote a postcard home from Clearwater that said, "Hi Mum. Working like a dog, same as ever. Love, Keith."

It was down to one little foot pedal, the Gibson fuzz tone, a little box they put out at that time. I've only ever used foot pedals twice—the other time was for *Some Girls* in the late '70s, when I used an XR box with a nice hillbilly Sun Records slap-echo on it. But effects are not my thing. I just go for quality of sound. Do I want this sharp and hard and cutting, or do I want warm, smooth "Beast of Burden" stuff? Basically you go: Fender or Gibson?

In "Satisfaction" I was imagining horns, trying to imitate their sound to put on the track later when we recorded. I'd already heard the riff in my head the way Otis Redding did it later, thinking, this is gonna be the horn line. But we didn't have any horns, and I was only going to lay down a dub. The fuzz tone came in handy so I could give a shape to what the horns were supposed to do. But the fuzz tone had never been heard before anywhere, and that's the sound that caught everybody's imagination. Next thing I know, we're listening to ourselves in Minnesota somewhere on the radio, "Hit of the Week," and we didn't even know Andrew had put the fucking thing out! At first I was mortified. As far as I was concerned that was just the dub. Ten days on the road and it's number one nationally! The record of the summer of '65. So I'm not arguing. And I learned that lesson—sometimes you can overwork things. Not everything's designed for your taste and your taste alone.

"Satisfaction" was a typical collaboration between Mick and me at the time. I would say on a general scale, I would come up with the song and the basic idea, and Mick would do all the hard work of filling it in and making it interesting. I would come up with "I can't get no satisfaction....I can't get no satisfaction....I tried and I tried and I tried and I tried, but I can't get no satisfaction," and then we'd put ourselves together and Mick would come back and say, "Hey, when I'm riding in my car...same cigarettes as me," and then we'd tinker about with that. In those years that was basically the setup. "Hey you, get off of my cloud, hey you..." would be my contribution. "Paint It Black"—I wrote the melody, he wrote the lyrics. It's not that you can say in one phrase he wrote that and he did that. But the musical riff is mostly coming from me. I'm the riff master. The only one I missed and that Mick Jagger got was "Brown Sugar," and I'll tip my hat there. There he got me. I mean, I did tidy it up a bit, but that was his, words and music.

A peculiarity of "Satisfaction" is that it's a hell of a song to play on stage. For years and years we never played it, or very rarely, until maybe the past ten or fifteen years. Couldn't get the sound right, it didn't feel right, it just sounded weedy. It took the band a long time to figure out how to play "Satisfaction" on stage. What made us like it was when Otis Redding covered it. With that and Aretha Franklin's version, which Jerry Wexler produced, we heard what we'd tried to write in the first place. We liked it and started playing it because the very best of soul music was singing our song.

In 1965, Oldham bumped into Allen Klein, the pipe-smoking, smooth-talking manager. And I still think it was the best move Oldham made to put us together with him. Andrew loved the idea that Klein had put to him, that no contract is worth the paper it's written on, which we later found out to be painfully true in our relations with Allen Klein himself. My attitude at the time was that Eric Easton, Andrew's partner and our agent, was just too tired. In fact he was ill. Onward. Whatever happened later with Allen Klein, he was brilliant at generating cash. And he was also spectacular at first in blasting through the record companies and tour managers who had been overpaying themselves and being inattentive to business.

One of the first things Klein did was to renegotiate the contract between the Rolling Stones and Decca Records. And so one day we walked into the Decca office. A stage-managed piece of theater by Klein, the most obvious crass ploy. We got our instructions: "We're going into Decca today and we're going to work on these motherfuckers. We're going to make a deal and we're going to come out with the best record contract ever. Wear some shades and don't say a thing," said Klein. "Just troop in and stand at the back of the room and look at these old doddering farts. Don't talk. I'll do the talking."

We were just there as intimidation, basically. And it worked. Sir Edward Lewis, the chairman of Decca, was behind the desk and Sir Edward was actually drooling! I mean not over us, he was just drooling. And then somebody would come along and pat him with a handkerchief. He was on his last legs, let's face it. We just stood there with shades on. It was really the old guard and the new. They crumbled and we walked out of there with a deal bigger than the Beatles'. And this is where you've got to take your hat off to Allen. These five hoodlums then went back with Allen to the Hilton and glugged down the champagne and congratulated ourselves on our performance. And Sir Edward Lewis, he might have been drooling and everything, but he wasn't stupid. He made a lot of money off of that deal himself. It was an incredibly successful deal for both parties. Which is what a deal is supposed to be. I'm still getting paid off of it; it's called the Decca balloon.

With us, Klein was very much Colonel Tom Parker with Elvis. Hey, I'll make the deals, anything you want, just ask me, you got it — patrician in his dealings with us and with money. You could always get some from him. If you wanted a gold-plated Cadillac, he'd give it to you. When I rang and asked him for £80,000 to buy a house on Chelsea Embankment near to Mick's, so that we could wander back and forth and write songs, it came the next day. You just didn't know the half of it. It was a paternalistic form of management that obviously doesn't rub anymore these days, but it was still flying then. It was a different state of mind to now, where every fucking guitar pick is paid for and accounted for. It was rock and roll.

Klein was magnificent, at first, in the States. The next tour, under his management, was cranked up several gears. A private plane to get us about, huge billboards on Sunset Boulevard. Now we're talking.

One hit requires another, very quickly, or you fast start to lose altitude. At that time you were expected to churn them out. "Satisfaction" is suddenly number one all over the world, and Mick and I are looking at each other, saying, "This is nice." Then *bang bang bang* at the door, "Where's the follow-up? We need it in four weeks." And we were on the road doing two shows a day. You needed a new single every two months; you had to have another one all ready to shoot. And you needed a new sound. If we'd come along with another fuzz riff after "Satisfaction," we'd have been dead in the water, repeating with the law of diminishing returns. Many a band has faltered and foundered on that rock. "Get Off of My Cloud" was a reaction to the record companies' demands for more—leave me alone—and it was an attack from another direction. And it flew as well.

So we're the song factory. We start to think like songwriters, and once you get that habit, it stays with you all your life. It motors along in your subconscious, in the way you listen. Our songs were taking on some kind of edge in the lyrics, or at least they were beginning to sound like the image projected onto us. Cynical, nasty, skeptical, rude. We seemed to be ahead in this respect at the time. There was trouble in America; all these young American kids, they were being drafted to Vietnam. Which is why you have "Satisfaction" in *Apocalypse Now.* Because the nutters took us with them. The lyrics and the mood of the songs fitted with the kids' disenchantment with the grown-up world of America, and for a while we seemed to be the only provider, the soundtrack for the rumbling of rebellion, touching on those social nerves. I wouldn't say we were the first, but a lot of that mood had an English idiom, through our songs, despite their being highly American influenced. We were taking the piss in the old English tradition.

This wave of recording and songwriting culminated in the album *Aftermath,* and many of the songs we wrote around this time had what you might call anti-girl lyrics—anti-girl titles too. "Stupid Girl," "Under My Thumb," "Out of Time," "That Girl Belongs to Yesterday," and "Yesterday's Papers."

> *Who wants yesterday's girl?*
> *Nobody in the world.*

Maybe we were winding them up. And maybe some of the songs opened up their hearts a little, or their minds, to the idea of we're women, we're strong. But I think the Beatles and the Stones particularly did release chicks from the fact of "I'm just a little chick." It was not intentional or anything. It just became obvious as you were playing to them. When you've got three thousand chicks in front of you that are ripping off their panties and throwing them at you, you realize what an awesome power you have unleashed. Everything they'd been brought up not to do, they could do at a rock-and-roll show.

The songs also came from a lot of frustration from our point of view. You go on the road for a month, you come back, and she's with somebody else. Look at that stupid girl. It's a two-way street. I know, too, that I was making unfavorable comparisons between the chicks at home who were driving us mad and the girls we fell in with on the tours who seemed so much less demanding. With English chicks it was you're putting the make on her or she's putting the make on you, yea or nay. I always found with black chicks that wasn't the main issue. It was just comfortable, and if shit happened later, OK. It was just part of life. They were great because they were chicks, but they were much more like guys than English girls were. You didn't mind them being around after the event. I remember being in the Ambassador Hotel with this black chick called Flo, who was my piece at the time. She'd take care of me. Love, no. Respect, yeah. I'd always remember because we'd laugh when we heard the Supremes singing, "Flo, she doesn't know," lying on the bed. And it always made us giggle. You take a little bit out of this one experience, and then a week later you're down the road.

There was certainly that conscious element in those RCA days, from the end of '65 to summer of '66, of pushing the envelope in milder ways. There was "Paint It Black," for example, recorded in March 1966, our sixth British number one. Brian Jones, now transformed into a multi-instrumentalist, having "given up playing the guitar," played sitar. It was a different style to everything I'd done before. Maybe it was the Jew in me. It's more to me like "Hava Nagila" or some Gypsy lick. Maybe I picked it up from my granddad. It's definitely on a different curve to everything else. I'd moved around the world a bit. I was no longer strictly a Chicago blues man, had to spread the wings a bit, to come up with melodies and ideas, although I can't say that we ever played Tel Aviv or Romania. But you start to latch on to different things. With songwriting, it's a constant experiment. I've never done it consciously, like saying, I've got to explore such and such a thing. We were learning about making the album the center of attention — the form for the music instead of just singles. Making an LP usually consisted of having two or three single hits and their B-sides, and then filler. Everything was two minutes twenty-nine seconds for a single, otherwise you wouldn't get played on the radio. I talked with Paul McCartney about this recently. We changed it: every track was a potential single; there was no filler. And if there was, it was an experiment. We'd use the extended time we had with an album just to make more of a statement.

If LPs hadn't existed, probably the Beatles and ourselves wouldn't have lasted more than two and a half years. You had to keep condensing, reducing what it was you wanted to say, to please the distributor. Otherwise radio stations wouldn't play it. Dylan's "Visions of Johanna" was the breakthrough. "Goin' Home" was eleven minutes long — "It ain't gonna be a single. Can you extend and expand the product? Can it be done?" And that was really the main experiment. We said, you can't edit this shit, it either goes out like it is or you're done with it. I've no doubt Dylan felt the same about "Sad-Eyed Lady of the Lowlands" or "Visions of Johanna." The record got bigger — and could anybody listen to that much? It's over three minutes. Can you keep their attention? Can you keep your audience? But it worked. The Beatles and ourselves probably made the album *the* vehicle for recording and hastened the demise of the single. It didn't go away immediately; you always needed a hit single. It just extended you without your even really knowing it.

And because you've been playing every day, sometimes two or three shows a day, ideas are flowing. One thing feeds the other. You might be having a swim or screwing the old lady, but somewhere in the back of the mind, you're thinking about this chord sequence or something related to a song. No matter what the hell's going on. You might be getting shot at, and you'll still be "Oh! That's the bridge!" And there's nothing you can do; you don't realize it's happening. It's totally subconscious, unconscious or whatever. The radar is on whether you know it or not. You cannot switch it off. You hear this piece of conversation from across the room, "I just can't stand you anymore"... That's a song. It just flows in. And also the other thing about being a songwriter, when you realize you are one, is that to provide ammo, you start to become an observer, you start to distance yourself. You're constantly on the alert. That faculty gets trained in you over the years, observing people, how they react to one another. Which, in a way, makes you weirdly distant. You shouldn't really be doing it. It's a little of Peeping Tom to be a songwriter. You start looking round, and everything's a subject for a song. The banal phrase, which is the one that makes it. And you say, I can't believe nobody hooked up on that one before! Luckily there are more phrases than songwriters, *just about*.

Linda Keith was the one that first broke my heart. It was my fault. I asked for it and I got it. The first look was the deepest, watching her, with all her tricks and movements, fearfully, from across the room and feeling that hit of longing, and thinking she was out of my league. I was sometimes in awe of the women I was with at the start, because they were the crème de la crème, and I'd come from the gutter as far as I was concerned. I didn't believe these beautiful women wanted to say hello, let alone lie down with me! Linda and I met at a party given by Andrew Oldham, a party for some forgotten Jagger-Richards–written single. It was the party where Mick first met

Marianne Faithfull. Linda was seventeen, strikingly beautiful, very dark hair, the perfect look for the '60s: a blinder, very self-assured in her jeans and a white shirt. She was in the magazines, she was modeling, David Bailey was photographing her. Not that she was particularly interested. The girl just wanted something to do, to get out of the house.

When I first met Linda I was just astounded that she wanted to come along with me. Once again the girl puts the make on me. She bedded me, I didn't bed her. She made a line straight for me. And I was totally, absolutely in love. We fell for each other. And the other surprise was that I was Linda's first love, the first boy she ever fell for. She had been actively pursued by all kinds of people who she'd rejected. To this day I don't understand it. Linda was the best friend of Andrew Oldham's then almost-wife, Sheila Klein. These beautiful Jewish girls were a powerful cultural force in West Hampstead bohemia, which became my stomping ground, and Mick's too for a couple of years. It centered around Broadhurst Gardens, West Hampstead, near where Decca Records was situated, and a few venues around there where we played. Linda's father was Alan Keith, who for forty-four years presented a program on BBC radio called *Your Hundred Best Tunes*. Linda had been allowed to grow up fairly wild. She loved music, jazz, blues — a blues purist, in fact, who didn't really approve of the Rolling Stones. She never did. She probably doesn't now. She had been hanging out when she was very young at a place called the Roaring Twenties, a black club, when she was wandering around London in bare feet.

The Stones played every night, we were on the road all the time, but still somehow, for a while Linda and I managed to have a love affair. We lived first in Mapesbury Road, then in Holly Hill with Mick and his girlfriend Chrissie Shrimpton, and finally just the two of us in Carlton Hill, the flat I had in St. John's Wood. The rooms there never got decorated: everything piled up around the walls, mattress on the floor, many guitars, an upright piano. We lived, despite all this, almost like a married couple. We used to take the tube before I bought Linda a Mark 2 Jaguar, which had a letterbox 45 player on which she wouldn't play the Stones. We'd hang out in Chelsea at the Casserole, the Meridiana, the Baghdad House. The restaurant we went to in Hampstead is still there — Le Cellier du Midi — and probably still has the same menu after forty years. It certainly looks identical from the outside.

It was bound to unravel with the long absences — through confusion more than anything, the confusion of suddenly living this life that nobody, or certainly nobody that I knew, had a road map for. All of us were pretty young and we were trying to make this thing up as we went along. "I'm going to America for three months. I love you, darling." And meanwhile we're all changing. For one thing, I'd met Ronnie Bennett, and I spent more time on the road with her than I did with Linda. We grew apart slowly. It took a couple of years. We would still hook up, but in those years the band had a total of ten days off for the entire three-year period. Linda and I did manage to have one brief holiday in the South of France, though Linda remembers this as a flight she took away from London, an escape, a job as a waitress in Saint-Tropez, and me following her and installing her in a hotel, giving her a hot bath. Linda also began taking a lot of drugs. For me to disapprove is an irony, but I did disapprove then.

I've seen Linda a couple of times since those days. She's happily married to a very well-known record producer, John Porter. She remembers my disapproval. I was taking little more than weed in those days, but Linda was getting into the heavy stuff, and it was having a dangerous effect on her. That was clear to see. She came with me to New York when we were touring the USA in the summer of 1966, our fifth tour there. I'd put her up at the Americana Hotel, though she spent much of her time with her girlfriend Roberta Goldstein. When I turned up, they'd put all the gear away, the downers, the Tuinals, which I wouldn't have touched — imagine! — and strew wine bottles around to give probable cause if they staggered a bit.

Then she met Jimi Hendrix, saw him play and adopted his career as her mission, tried to get him a recording contract with Andrew Oldham. In her enthusiasm, during a long evening with Jimi, as she tells it, she gave him a Fender Stratocaster of mine that was in my hotel room. And then, so Linda says, she also picked up a copy of a demo I had of Tim Rose singing a song called "Hey Joe." And took that round to Roberta Goldstein's, where Jimi was, and played it to him. This is rock-and-roll history. So he got the song from me, apparently.

We went off on tour, and when I came back, London was suddenly hippie-ville. I was already into that in America, but I wasn't expecting it when I came home to London. The scene had changed totally in a matter of weeks. Linda was on acid and I'd been jilted. You shouldn't expect somebody of that age to hang around for four months with all this stuff going on. I knew it was on the break. It was my presumptuousness to think she was going to sit like a little old lady at home at eighteen or nineteen years old, while I gallivanted around the world doing what I wanted. I found out that Linda had taken up with some poet, which I went bananas about. I went running through the whole of London, asking people, anybody seen Linda? Crying my eyes out from St. John's Wood to Chelsea, screaming, "Bitch! Get out of my fucking way." Fuck the traffic lights. I only remember some very close accidents, nearly getting run over on the way through London to Chelsea. After I'd found out, I wanted to be sure, I wanted to see. I checked with my friends, where does this motherfucker live? I even remember his name, Bill Chenail. Some poet so-called. He was a hip little bugger at the time because he came on with the Dylanesque bit. Couldn't play anything. Ersatz hip, as it's called. I stalked her a couple of times, but I remember thinking, what would I say? I hadn't got that act down yet, how to confront my rival. In the middle of a Wimpy bar? Or some bistro? I even walked to where she was living with him in Chelsea, almost into Fulham, and stood outside. (This is a love story.) And I could see her in there with him, "silhouettes on the shade." And that was it. "Like a thief in the night."

That's the first time I felt the deep cut. The thing about being a songwriter is, even if you've been fucked over, you can find consolation in writing about it, and pour it out. Everything has something to do with something; nothing is divorced. It becomes an experience, a feeling, or a conglomeration of experiences. Basically, Linda is "Ruby Tuesday."

But our story wasn't quite over. After she left me, Linda was in a really bad way, Tuinals had given way to harder stuff. She went back to New York and took up further with Jimi Hendrix, who may have broken her heart, as she broke mine. Certainly, her friends say, she was very much in love with him. But I knew she needed medical help—she was getting very close to the danger line, as she herself acknowledged later, and I couldn't deal with it because I'd burned my boats. I went to see her parents and gave them all the telephone numbers and places where they'd find her. "Hey, your daughter is in distress. She won't admit it, but you've got to do something. I can't. I'm already persona non grata anyway. And this is going to be the final nail in my coffin with Linda, but you've got to do something about her because I'm on the road tomorrow." Linda's father went to New York and found her in a nightclub, brought her back to England, where her passport was removed and she was made a ward of court. She felt that this was a great betrayal on my part, and we didn't speak or see each other again until many years later. She had some close shaves with drugs after that, but she survived and recovered and brought up a family. She now lives in New Orleans.

On a rare day off between tours I did manage to buy Redlands, the house I still own in West Sussex, near Chichester Harbour; the house where we were busted, which burned down twice, the house I still love. We just spoke to each other the minute we saw each other. A thatched house, quite small, surrounded by a moat. I drove up there by mistake. I had a brochure with a couple of houses marked and I'm poncing around in my Bentley, "Oh, I'm going to buy a house." I took a wrong turn and turned into Redlands. This guy walked out, very nice guy, and said, yeah? And I said, oh sorry, we've come to the wrong turning. He said, yes, you want to go Fishbourne way, and he said, are you looking for a house to buy? He was very pukka, an ex-commodore of the Royal Navy. And I said yes. And he said, well, there's no sign up, but this house is for sale. And I looked at him and said, how much? Because I fell in love with Redlands the minute I saw it. Nobody's going to let this thing go, it's too picturesque, ideal. He said twenty grand. This is about one o'clock in the afternoon and the banks are open till three. I said, are you going to be here this evening? He said, yes, of course. I said, if I bring you down twenty grand, can we do the deal? So I zoomed up to London, just got to the bank in time, got the bread — twenty grand in a brown paper bag — and by evening I was back down at Redlands, in front of the fireplace, and we signed the deal. And he turned over the deeds to me. It was like cash on the barrelhead, done in really an old-fashioned way.

By the end of 1966, we were all exhausted. We'd been on the road without a break for almost four years. The crack-ups were coming. We'd already had a wobbler with the formidable but brittle Andrew Oldham in Chicago in 1965, when we were recording at Chess. Andrew was a lover of speed, but this time he was drunk too and very distressed about his relationship with Sheila, his old lady at the time. He started waving a shooter around in my hotel room. This we didn't need. I hadn't come all the way to Chicago to get shot by some wonky public schoolboy whose gun barrel I was staring down. Which looks very ominous at the time, that little black hole. Mick and I got the gun away from him, slapped him around a bit, put him to bed and forgot about it. I don't even know what happened to the shooter, an automatic. Tossed it out the window, probably. We're just getting going. Let's make this a forget-it.

But Brian was a different story. What was comic about Brian was his illusions of grandeur, even before he got famous. He thought it was his band for some weird reason. The first demonstration of Brian's aspirations was the discovery on our first tour that he was getting five pounds more a week than the rest of us because he'd persuaded Eric Easton that he was our "leader." The whole deal with the band was we split everything like pirates. You put the booty on the table and split it, pieces of eight. "Jesus Christ, who do you think you are? I'm writing the songs round here, and you're getting five pounds extra a week? Get outta here!" It started with little things like that, which then exacerbated the friction between us as it went on and he became more and more outrageous. In the early negotiations, it was always Brian who would go to the meetings as our leader. We were not permitted — by Brian. I remember Mick and me once waiting for the results around the block, sitting in Lyons Corner House.

It happened so fast. After we did a couple of TV shows, Brian turned into this sort of freak, devouring celebs and fame and attention. Mick and Charlie and I were looking at it all a bit skeptically. This is shit you've got to do to make records. But Brian — and he was not a stupid guy — fell right into it. He loved the adulation. The rest of us didn't think it was bad, but you don't fall for it all the way. I felt the energy, I knew that there was something big happening. But some guys get stroked and they just can't get over it. Stroke me some more, stroke me some more, and suddenly "I'm a star."

I never saw a guy so much affected by fame. The minute we'd had a couple of successful records, zoom, he was Venus and Jupiter rolled into one. Huge inferiority complex that you hadn't noticed. The minute the chicks started screaming, he seemed to go through a whole change, just when we didn't need it, when we needed to keep the whole thing tight and together. I've known a few that were really carried away by fame. But I never saw one that changed so dramatically overnight. "No, we're just getting lucky, pal. This is not fame." It went to his head, and over the next few years of very difficult road work, in the mid-'60s, we could not count on Brian at all. He was getting really stoned, out of it. Thought he was an intellectual, a mystic philosopher. He was very impressed by other stars, but only because they were stars, not because of what they were good at. And he became a pain in the neck, a kind of rotting attachment. When you're schlepping 350 days a year on the road and you've got to drag a dead weight, it becomes pretty vicious.

We were on a swing through the Midwest, and Brian's asthma had got him and he was in hospital in Chicago. And, hey, when a guy's sick, you double for him. But then we saw pictures of him zooming around Chicago, hanging at a party with so-and-so, fawning over stars with a silly little bow around his neck. We'd done three, four gigs without him. That's double duty for me, pal. There's only five of us, and the whole point of the band is that it's a two-guitar band. And suddenly there's only one guitar. I've got to figure out whole new ways to play all of these songs. I've got to perform Brian's part as well. I learned a lot about how to do two parts at once, or how to distill the essence of what his part was and still play what I had to play, and throw in a few licks, but it was damn hard work. And I never got a thank-you from him, ever, for covering his arse. He didn't give a shit. "I was out of it." That's all I would get. All right, are you gonna give me your pay? That's when I had it in for Brian.

One can get very sarcastic on the road and quite vicious. "Just shut up, you little creep. Preferred it when you weren't here." He had this way of ranting on, saying things that would just grate. "When I played with so-and-so..." He was totally starstruck. "I saw Bob Dylan yesterday. He doesn't like you." But he had no idea how obnoxious he was being. So it would start off, "Oh, shut up, Brian." Or we'd imitate the way he cringed his head into his nonexistent neck. And then it went to baiting him in a way. He had this huge Humber Super Snipe car, but he was a pretty short guy and he had to have a cushion to see over the steering wheel. Mick and I would steal the cushion for a laugh. Wicked, schoolboy sort of stuff. Sitting at the back of the bus, we just let him have it, pretending he wasn't there. "Where's Brian? Shit, did you see what he was wearing yesterday?" It was the pressure of work, and the other side of it was that you hoped that kind of shock treatment would snap him out of it. There's no time to take time off and say let's sort this out. But it was a love-hate relationship with Brian. He could be really funny. I used to enjoy hanging with him, figuring out how Jimmy Reed or Muddy Waters did this or T-Bone Walker did that.

What probably really stuck in Brian's craw was when Mick and I started writing the songs. He lost his status and then lost interest. Having to come to the studio and learn to play a song Mick and I had written would bring him down. It was like Brian's open wound. Brian's only solution became clinging to either Mick or me, which created a triangle of sorts. He had it in for Andrew Oldham, Mick and me, thought there was a conspiracy to roll him out. Which wasn't true at all, but somebody's got to write the songs. You're quite welcome; I'll sit around and write a song with you. What have you come up with? But no sparks flew when I was sitting around with Brian. And then it was "I don't like guitar anymore. I want to play marimbas." Another time, pal. We've got a tour to do. So we got to rely on him *not* being there, and if he turned up, it was a miracle. When he was there and came to life, he was incredibly nimble. He could pick up any instruments that were lying around and come up with something. Sitar on "Paint It Black." The marimbas on "Under My Thumb." But for the next five days we won't see the motherfucker, and we've still got a record to make. We've got sessions lined up and where's Brian? Nobody can find him, and when they do, he's in a terrible condition.

He barely ever played guitar in the last few years with us. Our whole thing was two guitars and everything else wove around that. And when the other guitar ain't there half the time or has lost interest in it, you start getting overdubbing. A lot of those records is me four times. I learned a lot more about recording doing that, and also how to cover unexpected situations. And just by the process of overdubbing, and talking to the engineers, I learned a lot more about microphones, about amplifiers, about changing sounds of guitars. Because if you've got one guitar player playing all the parts, if you're not careful, it sounds like it. What you really want is to make them each sound different. On albums like *December's Children* and *Aftermath,* I did the parts that Brian normally would have done. Sometimes I'd overlay eight guitars and then just maybe use one bar of the takes here and there in the mixing, so at the end of it, it sounds like it's two or three guitars and you're not even counting anymore. But there's actually eight in there, and they're just in and out, in the mix.

Then Brian met Anita Pallenberg. He met her backstage around September 1965 at the show in Munich. She followed us to Berlin, where there was a spectacular riot, and then slowly, over several months, she started going out with Brian. She was working hard as a model and traveling about, but eventually she came to London and she and Brian began their relationship with, soon enough, its bouts of high-volume violence. Brian graduated from his Humber Snipe to a Rolls-Royce—but he couldn't see out of that either.

Acid came into his picture around the same time. Brian disappeared late in 1965 when we were in mid tour with the usual complaints of ill health and surfaced in New York, jamming with Bob Dylan, hanging with Lou Reed and the Velvet Underground, and doing acid. Acid to Brian was something different than to your average drug taker. The dope at the time really wasn't, at least as far as the rest of us were concerned, a big deal. We were only smoking weed and taking a few uppers to keep us going. Acid made Brian feel he was one of an elite. Like the Acid Test. It was that cliquishness; he wanted to be a part of something, could never find anything to be part of. I don't remember anybody else going about saying, "I've taken acid." But Brian saw it as a sort of Congressional Medal of Honor. And then he'd come on like, "You wouldn't know, man. I've been tripping." And he's primping himself, that terrible primping, the hair. The little idiosyncrasies become so annoying. It was the typical drug thing, that they think they're somebody special. It's the head club. You'd meet people who'd say, "Are you a head?" as if it conferred some special status. People who were stoned on something you hadn't taken. Their elitism was total bullshit. Ken Kesey's got a lot to answer for.

I remember well the episode Andrew Oldham describes in his memoir and gives such symbolic weight to—when Brian lay collapsed on the floor of the RCA studio in March 1966, straddling his guitar, which was buzzing and interfering with the sound. Someone had to unplug it, and in Andrew's telling, this was as if Brian were being cast adrift forever. To me it was just an annoying noise, and the concept was not something we were particularly shocked about, because Brian had been toppling over here and there for days. He really loved to take too many downers, Seconals, Tuinals, Desbutals, the whole range. You think you're playing Segovia and think it's going *diddle diddle diddle,* but actually it's going *dum dum dum.* You can't work with a broken band. If there's something wrong in the engine, an attempt has to be made to fix it. In something like the Stones, especially at that time, you can't just say, fuck it, you're fired. At the same time, things couldn't go on with this really rancorous fission. And then Anita introduced Brian to the other lot, the Cammells and that particular set. Of which there will be more bad news.

*Michael Cooper / Raj Prem Collection*

# Chapter Six

In which I get busted in Redlands. Escape to Morocco
in the Bentley. Do a moonlight flit with Anita Pallenberg.
Make my first courtroom appearance, spend a night
in the Scrubs and the summer in Rome.

*No group makes more of a mess at the table. The aftermath of their breakfast with eggs, jam, honey everywhere, is quite exceptional. They give a new meaning to the word untidiness.... The drummer, Keith [sic] of the Stones, an eighteenth-century suit, long black velvet coat and the tightest pants.... Everything is shoddy, poorly made, the seams burst. Keith himself had sewn his trousers, lavender and dull rose, with a band of badly stitched leather dividing the two colors. Brian appears in white pants with a huge black square applied at the back. It is very smart in spite of the fact that the seams are giving way.*

*—Cecil Beaton in Morocco, 1967, from* Self Portrait with
Friends: The Selected Diaries of Cecil Beaton, 1926–1974

Nineteen sixty-seven was the watershed year, the year the seams gave way. There was that feeling that trouble was coming, which it did later, with all the riots, street fighting and all of that. There was a tension in the air. It's like negative and positive ions before a storm, you get that breathlessness that something's got to break. In fact, all it did was crack.

We'd finished touring the previous summer, a grueling American tour, and wouldn't tour there again for two years. In all that time, the first four years of the band, I don't think we ever had more than two days' rest between playing, traveling and recording. We were always on the road.

I felt I'd come to the end of an episode with Brian. At least it couldn't go on as it had while we were touring. Mick and I had gotten incredibly nasty to Brian when he became a joke, when he effectively gave up his position in the band. Things had been bad before that too. There had been tension way before Brian started becoming an asshole. But I was trying to mend fences at the end of 1966. We were a band, after all. I was footloose and fancy-free, having ended my affair with Linda Keith. When Brian wasn't working, it was easier. And naturally I gravitated to Brian's — and Anita's — on Courtfield Road, near Gloucester Road.

We had a lot of fun, becoming friends again, getting stoned together. It was wonderful at first. So I started to move in with them. Brian saw my attempts to bring him back into the center as an opportunity to start a vendetta against Mick. Brian always had to have an imaginary enemy, and around this time he'd decided it was Mick Jagger who had grossly mistreated and offended him. I just hung out as a guest and got a ringside seat on the world that Anita attracted around her — which was an exceptional gang of people. I used to walk back through Hyde Park to St. John's Wood at six in the morning, at first, to pick up a clean shirt, and then I just stopped going home.

In those days on Courtfield Road I had nothing to do with Anita, strictly speaking. I was fascinated by her from what I thought was a safe distance. I thought certainly that Brian had got very lucky. I could never figure out how he got his hands on her. My first impression was of a woman who was very strong. I was right about that. Also an extremely bright woman, that's one of the reasons she sparked me. Let alone that she was so entertaining and such a great beauty to look at. Very funny. Cosmopolitan beyond anyone I'd come across. She spoke three languages. She'd been here, she'd been there. It was very exotic, to me. I loved her spirit, even though she would instigate and turn the screw and manipulate. She wouldn't let you off the hook for a minute. If I said, "That's nice...," she would say, "*Nice?* I hate that word. Oh, stop being so fucking bourgeois." We're going to fight about the word "nice"? How would you know? Her English was still a bit patchy, so she would break out in German occasionally when she really meant something. "Excuse me. I'll have that translated."

Anita, sexy fucking bitch. One of the prime women in the world. It was all building up in Courtfield Gardens. Brian would crash out sometimes, and Anita and I would look at each other. But that's Brian and his old lady and that's it. Hands off. The idea of stealing a band member's woman was not on my agenda. And so the days went by.

The truth was I'm looking at Anita and I'm looking at Brian and I'm looking at her, and I'm thinking, there's nothing I can do about this. I'm going to have to be with her. I'm going to have her or she's going to have me. One way or another. The realization didn't help things. There was this obvious electricity over a few months, and Brian became more and more tangential. It took a lot of patience on my part. I'd stay around there three or four days and once a week I'd walk to St. John's Wood. Better give some space here; it's too transparent what my feelings are. But there were many other people around; it was a continuous party. Brian was desperately in need of attention all the time. But the more he got, the more he wanted.

Also I was getting the flavor of what was going on between Brian and Anita. I would hear the thumping some nights, and Brian would come out with a black eye. Brian was a woman beater. But the one woman in the world you did not want to try and beat up on was Anita Pallenberg. Every time they had a fight, Brian would come out bandaged and bruised. But it was nothing to do with me, was it? I was there only to hang with Brian.

Anita came out of an artistic world, and she had quite a bit of talent herself—she was certainly a lover of art and pally with its contemporary practitioners and wrapped up in the pop art world. Her grandfather and great-grandfather were painters, a family that had gone down, apparently, in a blaze of syphilis and madness. Anita could draw. She grew up in her grandfather's big house in Rome but spent her teens in Munich at a decadent German aristos school where they threw her out for smoking, drinking and—worst of all—hitchhiking. When she was sixteen she got a scholarship to a graphics school in Rome near the Piazza del Popolo, which was when she started hanging out at that tender age in the cafés with the Roman intelligentsia, "Fellini and all those people," as she put it. Anita had a lot of style. She also had an amazing ability to put things together, to connect with people. This was Rome in the *Dolce Vita* period. She knew all the filmmakers—Fellini, Visconti, Pasolini; in New York she'd connected with Warhol, the pop art world and the beat poets. Mostly through her own skills, Anita was brilliantly connected to many worlds and many different people. She was the catalyst of so many goings-on in those days.

If there was a genealogical tree, a tree of genesis of London's hip scene, the one that it was known for in those days, Anita and Robert Fraser, the gallery owner and art dealer, would be at the top, beside Christopher Gibbs, antiques dealer and bibliophile, and a few other major courtiers. And that was mainly because of the connections they made. Anita had met Robert Fraser a long way back, in 1961, when she was tied up with the early pop art world through her boyfriend Mario Schifano, a leading pop painter in Rome. Through Fraser she'd met Sir Mark Palmer, the original Gypsy baron, and Julian and Jane Ormsby-Gore and Tara Browne (subject of the Beatles' "A Day in the Life"), so already a basis is laid for the meeting of music—which played a big part in the art underground from early on—and aristos, though these were not your usual aristos. Here you had three old Etonians, Fraser, Gibbs and Palmer—though it turned out that two of them, Fraser and Gibbs, had been sacked from Eton or left prematurely — and each had special, eccentric talents and a strong personality. They were not born to follow the herd. Mick and Marianne would make pilgrimages with John Michell, a writer and the Merlin of the group, to Herefordshire to observe flying saucers and ley lines and all that. Anita had a Paris life, dancing around nightly and diaphanously in Régine's, where they let her in for free; she had an equally glamorous Roman life. She worked as a model and she got parts in movies. The people she mixed with were hard-core avant-garde in the days when hard core hardly existed.

That was when the drug culture had started to explode. First came the Mandrax with the grass, then the acid in late '66, then the coke sometime in '67, then the smack — always. I remember David Courts, the original maker of my skull ring, still a close friend, coming out to dinner in a pub near Redlands. He'd had some Mandrax and some bevvies and now wanted to rest his head in the soup. I remember it only because Mick carried him on his back to the car. He would never do something like that now — and I realize, remembering that incident, how very long ago it was that Mick changed. But that is another country.

There were some fascinating people. Captain Fraser, who'd had a commission in the King's African Rifles, the strong arm of colonial authority in East Africa, was posted in Uganda, where Idi Amin was his sergeant. He'd turned into Strawberry Bob, floating around in slippers and Rajasthani trousers by night, and gangster-sharp pinstripes and polka-dot suits by day. The Robert Fraser Gallery was pretty much the cutting edge. He was putting on Jim Dine shows, he represented Lichtenstein. He did Warhol's first thing in London, showing *Chelsea Girls* in his flat. He showed Larry Rivers, Rauschenberg. Robert saw all the changes coming; he was very into pop art. He was aggressively avant-garde. I liked the energy that was going into it rather than necessarily everything that was being done — that feeling in the air that anything was possible. Otherwise, the stunning overblown pretentiousness of the art world made my skin crawl cold turkey, and I wasn't even using the stuff. Allen Ginsberg was staying at Mick's place in London once, and I spent an evening listening to the old gasbag pontificating on everything. It was the period when Ginsberg sat around playing a concertina badly and making *ommm* sounds, pretending he was oblivious to his socialite surroundings.

Captain Fraser really loved his Otis Redding and his Booker T. and the MGs. I'd sometimes drop by his flat in Mount Street—the salon of the period—in the morning if I'd been up all night and I'd just got the new Booker T. or Otis album. And there was Mohammed, the Moroccan servant in the djellaba, preparing a couple of pipes, and we'd listen to "Green Onions" or "Chinese Checkers" or "Chained and Bound." Robert was into smack. He had a cupboard full of double-breasted suits, all superbly made, with great fabrics, and his shirts were often handmade bespoke shirts, but the collars and cuffs were always frayed. And that was part of the look. And he used to keep spare jacks, a sixth of a grain—it was six jacks to a grain of heroin—loose in these suit pockets, so he'd always be going to the cupboard and going through all the pockets to find the odd spare jack. Robert's flat was full of fantastic objects, Tibetan skulls lined with silver, bones with silver caps on the end, Tiffany art nouveau lamps and beautiful fabrics and textiles everywhere. He'd float around in these bright-colored silk shirts he'd brought back from India. Robert really liked to get stoned, "wonderful hashish," "Afghani primo." He was a weird mixture of avant-garde and very old-fashioned.

The other thing I really liked about Robert was he had no side on him. He could have easily hidden behind Eton and the patrician style. But he looked around—he deliberately showed works of art by people not in the Royal Academy. And then of course there was the homosexual poofter bit that also put him at odds. He didn't flaunt it, but he certainly didn't hide it. He had a steely eye and I always admired his guts. And I put a lot of that persona of his down to the African Rifles, really. He had his eyes opened in Africa. Captain Robert Fraser, retired. If he wanted to, he could pull rank. But I have the feeling with Robert that he just detested more and more the way that the establishment at that time, as they called it, was still trying to cling on to something that was obviously crumbling. I admired his stand on "this cannot go on." And I think that's why he attached himself to us and the Beatles and the avant-garde artists.

Fraser and Christopher Gibbs had been at Eton together. When Anita first met Gibby, way back, he'd just come out of jail for taking a book from Sotheby's, aged eighteen or something—always a passionate collector and with a very good eye. We linked up with Gibbs again through Robert when Mick decided he wanted to have a country life. Robert was not country inclined and said you'd better get Gibby onto this. So Gibbs started showing Mick and Marianne around England, and they looked at various palaces and estates. I've always loved Gibby in his own way. I used to stay at his apartment in Cheyne Walk on the embankment. He had a great library of books. I could just sit around, look at beautiful first editions and great illustrations and paintings and stuff that I hadn't had time to get into because I'd been working on the road. Very much into flogging the furniture. Very nice pieces. A subtle promoter of his own wares. "I've got this wonderful chest, sixteenth century." He was always flogging something off, or something was always available. At the same time he was crazy, Christopher. He's the only guy I know that would actually wake up and break an amyl nitrate popper under his nose. That even took *me* out. He'd have one by the side of the bed. Just twist that little yellow phial and wake up. I saw him do it. I was amazed. I didn't mind the poppers, but usually later at night.

What Robert Fraser and Christopher Gibbs had in common was nerve and fearlessness—more front than Selfridges. And they were mama's boys. Big mama fear amongst the lot of them. Maybe that's why they were all poofs. Strawberry Bob—he was always scared of his mum. "Oh! My mother's coming." "So what?" Which didn't mean they were soft or pussy whipped. It was the respect for their mothers that was overpowering. Obviously they had very strong mothers, because these guys were very strong guys. Only now have I learned that Gibby's mother was queen of the Girl Guides worldwide, the chief commissioner for overseas. It's not something we talked about in those days. I never realized the influence of this duo back then, but they changed the landscape and greatly influenced the style of the times.

Gibbs and Fraser were only the front names in all that. There were Lampsons and Lambtons, Sykeses, Michael Rainey. There was Sir Mark Palmer, page boy to the queen and inveterate didicoy, bless his heart, him of the gold teeth and the whippets tied to baling twine and the caravans that he used to trundle through the country lanes and park on the estates of his friends. I guess if you're brought up and trained to carry the queen's frock, a Gypsy caravan might look kind of attractive after a while. It was all right before you got hair on your cock. But after that, what do you do? "I haul the queen's frock."

Suddenly we were being courted by half the aristocracy, the younger scions, the heirs to some ancient pile, the Ormbsy-Gores, the Tennants, the whole lot. I've never known if they were slumming or we were snobbing. They were very nice people. I decided it was no skin off of my nose. If somebody's interested, they're welcome. You want to hang, you want to hang. It was the first time I know of when that lot actively sought out musicians in such large numbers. They realized there was something blowin' in the wind, to quote Bob. They felt embarrassed up there, the Knights in Blue, and they felt they were being left out of things if they didn't join in. So there was this weird mixture of aristos and gangsters, the fascination that the higher end of society has with the more brutish end. That was particularly the case with Robert Fraser.

Robert liked to mix with the underworld. Maybe it was his rebellion against the suffocation of his background, the repression of homosexuality. He gravitated towards people like David Litvinoff, who was on the borders of art and villainy, a friend of the Kray brothers, the East End gangsters. There were villains in the story as well. That's how Tony Sanchez came into it, because Tony Sanchez helped Robert out of a tight spot when he had gambling debts. That's how Robert met Tony. So Tony became Robert's conduit, sort of helper-out with villains, and his dealer.

Tony ran a gambling casino for Spanish waiters in London, after-hours. He was a dope dealer and a gangster with a Mark 10 Jaguar, two-tone, all done up pimp-style. His father ran a famous Italian restaurant in Mayfair. Spanish Tony was a hard man. *Biff bang.* One of those. He was a great guy until he became a bad one. His trouble, just like many others', was that you can't be like that and also become a junkie. The two don't mix. If you're going to be a hard man, if you're going to be smart and be on your toes, which is what Tony could have been and was for a while, you can't afford to be on dope. It slows you down. If you're going to be selling it, OK, that's the way it is, but don't sample it. There's a big difference between a dealer and a consumer. To be a dealer, you've got to be way in front, otherwise you slip up, and that's what happened to Tony.

He set me up a couple of times. Without my knowing it—I found out later—he used me as a getaway driver on a hit-and-run jewel theft in the Burlington Arcade. "Here, Keith, I've got this Jag. Want to try it out?" What they wanted was a clean car and a clean driver. And Tony had obviously told these blokes that I was a good night driver. So I waited outside this place, not knowing what was happening. Tony was a good mate of mine, but he used to stitch me up.

Another good friend, Michael Cooper, I used to hang with a lot. Great photographer. He could hang and hang; he could take so much stuff. He was the only photographer I ever knew who actually had a tremor when he was taking pictures, and yet they'd come out right. "How did you do that? Your hands were trembling. The whole picture should be a blur." "I know just when to push." Michael recorded the early Stones life in great detail because he never stopped taking pictures. Pictures were a total way of life for Michael. He was absolutely captured by images, or, more likely, images had captured him.

Michael was Robert's creature in a way. Robert had a Svengali side to him and was strongly attracted to Michael Cooper on all sorts of levels, but he particularly admired Michael's artistry and he promoted him. Michael was a networker. He was the glue between us, all these different parts of London, the aristos and the hoods and the others.

When you take all the stuff we took, you're always talking about everything else rather than what you're working at. Which meant Michael and me sitting around talking about the quality of the dope. Two fiends looking to see if they can get higher than ever before without damaging themselves too much. No talking about the "great work" I'm going to do or you're going to do or anybody else is going to do. That was peripheral. I knew how hard he worked. He was manic, like me, but you took it for granted.

One thing about Michael was he would spiral into deep, ominous depressions. Black dogs. The poet of the lens was a more fragile creature than one imagined. Michael spun slowly towards a bourne from which there was no return. But for now we were basically gangsters. Not that we pulled any jobs, but we were an elite little circle. Flamboyant and outrageous, quite honestly, pushing all the margins because it had to be done.

There's not much you can really say about acid except God, what a trip! Stepping off into this area was very uncertain, uncharted. In the years '67 and '68 there was a real turnover in the feeling of what was going on, a lot of confusion and a lot of experimentation. The most amazing thing that I can remember on acid is watching birds fly — birds that kept flying in front of my face that weren't actually there, flocks of birds of paradise. And actually it was a tree blowing in the wind. I was walking down a country lane, it was very green, and I could almost see every wing movement. It was slowed down to the point where I could even say, "Shit, I could do that!" That's why I understand the odd person jumping out of a window. Because the whole notion of how it's done is suddenly clear. A flock of birds took about half an hour to fly across my vision, an incredible fluttering, and I could see every feather. And they looked at me while they did it like, "Try that on for size." Shit...OK, there's some things I can't do.

You had to be with the right people when you were taking acid, otherwise beware. Brian on acid, for example, was a loose cannon. Either he'd be incredibly relaxed and funny, or he'd be one of the cats that would lead you down the bad road when the good road closes. And suddenly you're going there, down the street of paranoia. And on acid you can't really control it. Why am I going into his black dot? I just don't want to go there. Let's go back to the crossroads and see if the good road opens. I want to see that flock of birds again and have a few astounding ideas for playing and find the Lost Chord. The holy grail of music, very fashionable at the time. There were a lot of Pre-Raphaelites running around in velvet with scarves tied to their knees, like the Ormsby-Gores, looking for the Holy Grail, the Lost Court of King Arthur, UFOs and ley lines.

With Christopher Gibbs you actually couldn't tell whether he was on acid or not, because that's the way he was. Maybe I never knew Christopher off acid, but I must say he was an adventurous lad. He was ready to jump into the unknown, into the valley of death. He was ready to look into it. It was something that had to be done. I never saw Gibbs unbalanced by acid, never saw any sign of a bad trip. My memories of Christopher are that he was somehow always angelically three feet off the ground. As we all were, perhaps.

No one knew much about this; we were tapping in the dark. I found it very interesting, but at the same time I found other people got quite distressed, and that's all you need on that kind of stuff, is to deal with somebody who really is having a bad trip. People could change and become very paranoid or very uptight or very scared. Especially Brian. It could happen to anybody, but that would turn other people into a bad time too. It was the unknown with acid. You didn't know if you'd come back or not. I had a couple of terrible trips. I remember

Christopher talking me down. "Hey, everything is cool. It's all right." He was just like a nurse, a night nurse. I can't even remember what the hell I was going through; it just wasn't pleasant. Paranoia, maybe — the same with a lot of people with marijuana, it makes them paranoid. It's basically fear, but you don't know of what. So you have no defense, and the further you go down there, the bigger it gets. Sometimes you've got to slap yourself.

But it didn't stop me from having another trip. It was the idea of a boundary that had to be pushed. There was a bit of stupidity there as well. Wasn't so good last time? Let's try it again. What, are you chicken now? It was the Acid Test, Ken Kesey's goddamn thing. It meant if you hadn't been there you ain't nowhere, which was really dumb. A lot of people felt obliged to take it even if they didn't want to, if they wanted to stay and hang with the crowd. It was a gang thing. But it could shake you if you weren't careful, and that happened a lot. Even if you've taken it once, it's probably done something to you. It's too volatile.

One epic of that period was an acid-fueled road trip with John Lennon — an episode of such extremes that I can barely piece together a fragment. It took in, I thought, Torquay and Lyme Regis over what seemed like a two- or three-day period with a chauffeur. Johnny and I were so out there that sometimes years later, in New York, he would ask, "What happened on that trip?" With us was Kari Ann Moller, now Mrs. Chris Jagger; I think the Hollies wrote a song about her, or was it about Marianne? Very sweet girl, had a place on Portland Square, where I lived when in town for about two years. Her reminiscences, which I sought out recently for this book, were quite different from mine. But hers were at least not almost a total blank, like mine.

What is clear to me now is that we never thought we were over-worked, but later on you realize you didn't give yourself a break, boy. So when we had three unfamiliar days off, we got a little wild. I remembered going in a chauffeur-driven car. But Kari Ann says we didn't have a chauffeur. We went in a cramped two-door car with one other unidentifiable passenger — so maybe we did have a chauffeur. According to Kari Ann, we started in Dolly's nightclub, the precursor of Tramp, and drove around Hyde Park Corner several times, wondering where to go. We drove to John's house in the country, she says, and said hi to Cynthia, and then Kari Ann decided we'd go and visit her mother in Lyme Regis. What a nice visit for her mother — a couple of flying acid heads who'd been up for a couple of nights. We got there about dawn, so her story goes. One greasy-spoon caff wouldn't serve us. John got recognized. And Kari Ann realized that we couldn't go and visit her mother because we were so out of it. There follow therefore some missing hours, because we didn't get back to John's house until after dark. There were palm trees, so it looks as if we sat on the Torquay palm-lined esplanade for a great many hours, engrossed in a little world of our own. We got home, and so everyone was happy. It was one of those cases of John wanting to do more drugs than me. Huge bag of weed, lump of hash and acid. I usually picked my spots with acid; moving around didn't come into it if you could avoid it.

I liked John a lot. He was a silly sod in many ways. I used to criticize him for wearing his guitar too high. They used to wear them up by their chests, which really constricts your movement. It's like being handcuffed. "Got your fucking guitar under your fucking chin, for Christ's sake. It ain't a violin." I think they thought it was a cool thing. Gerry & the Pacemakers, all of the Liverpool bands did it. We used to fuck around like that: "Try a longer strap, John. The longer the strap, the better you play." I remember him nodding and taking it in. Next time I saw them the guitar straps were a little lower. I'd say, no wonder you don't swing, you know? No wonder you can only rock, no wonder you can't roll.

John could be quite direct. The only rude thing I remember him saying to me was about my solo in the middle of "It's All Over Now." He thought it was crap. Maybe he got out the wrong side of the bed that day. OK, it certainly could have been better. But you disarmed the man. "Yeah, it wasn't one of my best, John. Sorry. Sorry it jars, old boy. You can play it any fucking way you like." But that he even bothered to listen meant that he was very interested. He was so open. In anybody else, this could be embarrassing. But John had this honesty in his eyes that made you go for him. Had an intensity too. He was a one-off. Like me. We were attracted to each other in a strange way. Definitely a two-alpha clash to start with.

"Post-acid" was the prevailing mood at Redlands on a cold February morning in 1967. Post-acid: everybody arrives back with their feet on the ground, so to speak, and you've been with them all day, doing all kinds of nuts things and laughing your head off; you've gone for walks on the beach and you're freezing cold and you're not wearing any shoes and you're wondering why you've got frostbite. The comedown hits everybody in a different way. Some people are going, let's do it again, and others are going, enough already. And you can flash back into full acid drive at any moment.

There's a knock at the door, I look through the window and there's this whole lot of dwarves outside, but they're all wearing the same clothes! They were policemen, but I didn't know it. They just looked like very small people wearing dark blue with shiny bits and helmets. "Wonderful attire! Am I expecting you? Anyway, come on in, it's a bit chilly out." They were trying to read a warrant to me. "Oh, that's very nice, but it's a bit cold outside, come on in and read it to me over the fireplace." I'd never been busted before and I was still on acid. Oh, make friends. Love. Not from me would there be "You cannot come in until I speak to my lawyer." It was "Yeah, come on in!" And then roughly disabused.

While we're gently bouncing down from the acid, they're trampling through the place, doing what they've got to do, and none of us are really taking much notice of them. Obviously there was a shiver of the usuals, but there didn't seem to be much we could do about it at that moment, so we just let them walk about and look in ashtrays. Incredibly enough, what they did come up with was only a few roaches and what Mick and Robert Fraser had in their pockets, which was a minute amount of amphetamine, bought legally by Mick in Italy, and in Robert's case heroin tabs. Otherwise we just carried on.

There was the thing of course of Marianne. Hard day on acid, she had taken a bath upstairs, just finished, and I had this huge fur rug, made of pelts of some kind, rabbit, and she just wrapped herself up in that. I think she had a towel around her too and was lying back on the couch after a nice bath. How the Mars bar got into the story I don't know. There was one on the table — there were a couple, because on acid suddenly you get sugar lack and you're munching away. And so she's stuck forever with the story of where the police found that Mars bar. And you have to say she wears it well. But how that connotation came about and how the press managed to make a Mars bar on a table and Marianne wrapped in a fur rug into a myth is a kind of classic. In fact, Marianne was quite chastely attired for once. Usually when first you said hi to Marianne you started talking to the cleavage. And she knew she was thrusting it. A naughty lady, bless her heart. She was more dressed in this fur bedspread than she'd been all day. So they had a woman police officer who took her upstairs and made her drop the rug. What else do you want to see? From there — it shows you what's in people's minds — the evening paper headlines are "Naked Girl at Stones Party." Info directly from the police. But the Mars bar as a dildo? That's rather a large leap. The weird thing about these myths is that they stick when they're so obviously false. Perhaps the idea is that it's so outlandish or crude or prurient that it can't have been invented. Imagine allowing a group of policemen and -women to see this evidence — keeping it on display as they came tramping through the house. "Excuse me, Officer, I think you may have missed something. Over here."

Others at Redlands that day were Christopher Gibbs and Nicky Kramer, an upper-class drifter and hanger-on who befriended everybody, a harmless enough soul who was innocent of betraying us, although David Litvinoff held him out of a window by his ankles to find out. And of course Mr. X, as he was later referred to in court, David Schneiderman. Schneiderman, who also went by the moniker of Acid King, was the source of that very high-quality acid of the time, such brands as Strawberry Fields, Sunshine and Purple Haze — where do you think Jimi got that from? All kinds of mixtures, and that's how Schneiderman got in on the crowd, by providing this super-duper acid. In those innocent days, now abruptly ended, nobody both-ered about the cool guy, the dealer in the corner. One big happy party. In fact, the cool guy was the agent of the constabulary. He came with this bag full of goodies, including a lot of DMT, which we'd never had before, dimethyltryptamine, one of the ingredients of ayahuasca, a very powerful psychedelic. He was at every party for about two weeks and then mysteriously disappeared and was never seen again.

The bust was a collusion between the *News of the World* and the cops, but the shocking extent of the stitch-up, which reached to the judiciary, didn't become apparent until the case came to court months later. Mick had threatened to sue the scandal rag for mixing him up with Brian Jones and describing him taking drugs in a nightclub. In return they wanted evidence against Mick, to defend themselves in court. It was Patrick, my Belgian chauffeur, who sold us out to the *News of the World,* who in turn tipped off the cops, who used Schnei-derman. I'm paying this driver handsomely, and the gig's the gig, keep schtum. But the *News of the World* got to him. Didn't do him any good. As I heard it, he never walked the same again. But it took us time to piece these little details together. As far as I remember, the atmosphere was fairly relaxed at the time. Shit, anything we'd done we'd done already. It was only later on, the next day when we started to get the letters from solicitors and everything, Her Majesty's Gov-ernment and blah blah blah, we thought, "Ah, this is serious."

\* \* \*

We decided to get out of England and not go back until it was time for the court case. And it would be better to find somewhere where we could get legal drugs. It was one of those sudden things, "Let's jump in the Bentley and go to Morocco." So in early March we did a runner. We've got free time and we've got the best car to do it in. This was Blue Lena, as it was christened, my dark blue Bentley, my S3 Continental Flying Spur—an automobile of some rarity, one of a limited edition of eighty-seven. It was named in honor of Lena Horne—I sent her a picture of it. Having this car was already heading for trouble, breaking the rules of the establishment, driving a car I was definitely not born into. Blue Lena had carried us on many an acid-fueled journey. Modifications included a secret compartment in the frame for the concealing of illegal substances. It had a huge bonnet, and to turn it you really had to swing it about. Blue Lena required some art and knowledge of its contours in tight situations—it was six inches wider at the back than the front. You got to know your car, no doubt about that. Three tons of machinery. A car that was made to be driven fast at night.

Brian and Anita had been to Morocco the previous year, 1966, staying with Christopher Gibbs, who had to take Brian to hospital with a broken wrist after a punch he'd thrown at Anita had hit the metal window frame in the El Minzah Hotel in Tangier. He was never good at connecting with Anita. I learned later just how violent Brian had already become with her, as the downward slide began, throwing knives, glass, punches at her, forcing her to barricade herself behind sofas. It's probably not well known that Anita had a very sporty childhood—sailing, swimming, skiing, outdoor sports of every kind. Brian was no match for Anita, physically or in terms of wit. She was always on top of it. He always came off second best. And she thought, at the start at least, that Brian's rampages were quite funny—but they were becoming unfunny and dangerous. Anita told me later that at Torremolinos on their way to Tangier the previous year, they had had massive fights after which Brian ended up in jail—and Anita too, once, for stealing a car coming out of a club. She was often trying to bail Brian out, screaming at the turnkeys, "You can't keep him in jail. *Let him out.*" All this time they had grown to look like each other; their hair and clothes were becoming identical. They'd merged their personas, stylistically at least.

We flew to Paris, Brian, Anita and I, and met Deborah Dixon, an old friend of Anita, in the Hotel George V. Deborah was a piece of work, a beauty from Texas who had been on every magazine cover in the early '60s. Brian and Anita first met on the Stones tour, but it was in Deborah's house in Paris that they first got together. My new driver to replace the snitch Patrick, Tom Keylock—a tough bloke from north London soon to become the Stones' fixer-in-chief—brought Blue Lena over to Paris, and we set off for the sun.

I sent a postcard to Mum: "Dear Mum, Sorry I didn't phone before I left, but my telephones aren't safe to talk on. Everything will be all right, so don't worry. It's really great here and I'll send you a letter when I get where I'm going. All my love. Your fugitive son, Keef."

Brian, Deborah and Anita occupied the backseat and I sat in the front next to Tom Keylock, changing the 45s on the little Philips car record player. It's hard to know, on this journey, how and why the tension built up in the car as it did. It was helped on by Brian being even more obnoxious and childish than usual. Tom's an old soldier, fought at Arnhem and everything like that, but even he couldn't ignore the tension in that car. Brian's relationship with Anita had reached a jealous stalemate when she refused to give up whatever acting work she was doing to fulfill domestic duties as his full-time geisha, flatterer, punchbag—whatever he imagined, including partaker in orgies, which Anita always resolutely refused to do. On this trip he never stopped complaining and whining about how ill he felt, how he couldn't breathe. No one took him seriously. Brian certainly suffered from asthma, but he was also a hypochondriac. Meanwhile, I was the DJ. I had to keep feeding the goddamn thing with little 45s, the favorite sounds—much Motown at the time. Anita claims that these choices were full of meaning and communication to her, songs of the moment like "Chantilly Lace" and "Hey Joe." All songs are like that. You can take the meaning any way you want.

The first night of our journey through France, we stayed all in the same room, five of us in a kind of dormitory in the top of a house — the only accommodation we could find late at night. Next day, we got to a town called Cordes-sur-Ciel that Deborah wanted to see — a pretty village on top of a hill — and from out of its medieval walls, as we approached, emerged an ambulance, and at this point Brian insisted that we should follow it to the nearest hospital, which was in Albi. There Brian was diagnosed with pneumonia. Well, it was hard to know with Brian — what *was* real and what wasn't. But this meant that he was transferred to a Toulouse hospital, where he would stay for several days, and it was there we left him. I discovered much later that he gave instructions to Deborah not to leave Anita and me alone together. So it was pretty clear to him. We said, "OK, Brian, you're cool. We'll drive down through Spain, and then you fly over to Tangier."

So Anita and Deborah and I drove into Spain and when we reached Barcelona we went out to a famous flamenco guitar joint in the Ramblas. Then it was a rough part of town, and when we came outside, about three in the morning, there was a semi-riot going on. People were throwing things at the Bentley violently, especially when they saw us. Maybe they were anti-rich, anti-us, maybe it was because I was flying the pope's flag that day. I used to have a little flagpole on the car, and I would change the flags around. The cops came, and suddenly I'm in kangaroo court in the middle of the night in Barcelona. A low room with tiles, and a judge presiding over these nocturnal assizes; opposite him a long bench with about a hundred guys all lined up, with me at the end of the row. Then suddenly these cops came in and they started to beat everyone down the line with truncheons around the head. Everyone got one. And they knew what was coming. It looked to me like a pretty normal process. You get into that court at night and you get the usual. And I'm the last cat on the end of this bench. Tom went to get my passport and took hours and when he finally procured it, I flashed it in their face, "Her Majesty Demands." And they did the guy right next to me. After about ninety-nine broken heads, I guessed they were gonna do the whole bench. But they didn't. The judge wanted me to confirm the culprits they had chosen, having rounded up the usual suspects, to charge with smashing the car and causing the riot. But I wouldn't do that. So it came down to a fine for parking in the wrong place: a piece of paper to sign, money to change hands and even then they kept us in jail for the rest of the night.

Next day we got the windscreen fixed and set off with fresh hope but not with Deborah, who had had enough of tension and police cells and wanted to go back to Paris. With no one to watch over us, we drove on to Valencia. And between Barcelona and Valencia, Anita and I found out that we were really interested in each other.

I have never put the make on a girl in my life. I just don't know how to do it. My instincts are always to leave it to the woman. Which is kind of weird, but I can't pull the come-on bit: "Hey, baby, how you doing? Come on, let's get it on" and all of that. I'm tongue-tied. I suppose every woman I've been with, they've had to put the make on me. Meanwhile I'm putting the make on in another way — by creating an aura of insufferable tension. Somebody has to do something. You either get the message or you don't, but I could never make the first move. I knew how to operate amongst women, because most of my cousins were women, so I felt very comfortable in their company. If they're interested, they'll make the move. That's what I found out.

So Anita made the first move. I just could not put the make on my friend's girl, even though he'd become an asshole, to Anita too. It's the Sir Galahad in me. Anita was beautiful too. And we got closer and closer and then suddenly, without her old man, she had the balls to break the ice and say fuck it. In the back of the Bentley, somewhere between Barcelona and Valencia, Anita and I looked at each other, and the tension was so high in the backseat, the next thing I know she's giving me a blow job. The tension broke then. Phew. And suddenly we're together. You don't talk a lot when that shit hits you. Without even saying things, you have the feeling, the great sense of relief that something has been resolved.

It was February. And in Spain it was early spring. Going through England and France it was pretty chill, it was winter. We got over the Pyrenees and within half an hour already it was spring and by the time we got to Valencia, it was summer. I still remember the smell of the orange trees in Valencia. When you get laid with Anita Pallenberg for the first time, you remember things. We stopped in Valencia overnight and checked in as Count and Countess Zigenpuss, and that was the first time I made love to Anita. And from Algeciras, where we checked in as Count and Countess Castiglione, we took the ferry and the car over to Tangier to the El Minzah Hotel. There, in Tangier, were Robert Fraser; Bill Burroughs; Brion Gysin, Burroughs's friend and fellow cutup artist — another of the hip public schoolboys — and Bill Willis, decorator of exiles' palaces. We were greeted by a bundle of telegrams from Brian ordering Anita to come back and collect him. But we weren't going anywhere except the Kasbah in Tangier. For a week or so, it's boinky boinky boinky, down in the Kasbah, and we're randy as rabbits but we're also wondering how we're going to deal with it. Because we were expecting Brian in Tangier. We only dropped him off to have treatment. We were both, I remember, trying to be polite, at least for each other's benefit. "When Brian gets to Tangier we'll do this and that." "Let's make a phone call to see if he's all right." And all of that. And at the same time that was the last thing on our minds. The truth was "Oh God. Brian's going to turn up in Tangier and then we've got to start to play a fucking game." "Yeah, hope he croaks." Suddenly, it's Anita: is she with him or with me? We realized we were creating "an unmanageable situation," maybe threatening the survival of the band. We decided to pull back, to make a strategic retreat. Anita didn't want to abandon Brian. Didn't want to go, tears and crying. She was worried about the effect on the group—that this was the big betrayal and it might bring it all down.

*I just can't be seen with you. . . .*
*It's too dangerous, baby. . . .*
*I just can't be, yes I got to chill this thing with you.*
—a song called "Can't Be Seen"

We visited Achmed, a legendary hashish dealer of those early drug days. Anita had met him first with Chrissie Gibbs on her previous visit, a small Moroccan man with a Chinese jar on his shoulder walking along, looking back at them, leading them through the medina, up the hill towards the Minzah, opening the door into a tiny little shop that was completely empty except for a box with a few pieces of Moroccan jewelry in it and a lot of hashish.

His shop was on the stairs, called the Escalier Waller, going down from the Minzah, little one-story shops on the right-hand side that backed onto the Minzah gardens. Achmed started off with one shop, then he had two above it. There were steps between them—internally, it was a bit of a labyrinth—and the higher ones just had a few brass beds with gaudy-colored velvet mattresses on them, on which one could, having smoked a lot of dope, pass out for a day or two. And then you'd come in and he'd give you some more dope to make you more passed out. It was almost like a basement and it was hung with all of the wonders of the East, caftans, rugs and beautiful lanterns... Aladdin's cave. It was a shack, but he made it look like a palace.

Achmed Hole-in-Head, we used to call him, because he said his prayers so often he had a hole in the middle of his forehead. He was a good salesman. First thing, he gets the mint tea, and then a pipe. He was somewhat on the spiritual side, and as he gave you your pipe he would usually tell you some thrilling adventure of the Prophet in the wilderness. He was a good ambassador for his faith and a cheerful soul. Also a typical Moroccan little shyster. He had gaps in his teeth, and he had this great smile that never left. Once he started smiling, it was there all the time. And he kept looking at you. But he had such good shit, you kind of went to the land of milk and honey there. And after a few rounds of this, it was almost as if you were on acid. In and out he went, bringing sweetmeats and candies. And it was very difficult to get out. You think you're going to have a quick one and then do something else, but very rarely would you do anything else. You could stay there all day, all night; you could live there. And always Radio Cairo, with static, slightly off the tuning.

The Moroccan specialty was kef, the leaf cut up with tobacco, which they smoked in long pipes — sebsi, they called them — with a tiny little bowl on the end. One hit in the morning with a cup of mint tea. But what Achmed had in large quantities and which he imbued with a new glamour was a kind of hash. It was called hash because it came in chunks, but it wasn't hash strictly speaking. Hash is made from the resin. And this was loose powder, like pollen, from the dried bud of the plant, compressed into shape. Which was why it was that green color. I heard that a way of collecting it was to cover children in honey and run them naked through a field of herb, and they came out the other end and they scraped 'em off. Achmed had three or four different qualities, decided by which kind of stocking he put it through. There would be the coarser ones, and there would be the twenty-four denier, very close to the dirham, the money. The high-quality one went through the finest, finest silk. It was just powder by then.

That was my first touch of Africa. Within the short buzz from Spain over to Tangier, you were in another world. It could have been a thousand years ago, and you either went, "How weird," or you went, "Wow! This is great." And we loved to be transported. We were already heavy-duty smokers. One could say we were going round as hash inspectors. We used to do so much of it. "We must reconsider our ideas on drugs," wrote Cecil Beaton in his diary. "It seems these boys live off them, yet they seem extremely healthy and strong. We will see."

Anita's dilemma, apart from the guilt of this betrayal and her passionate and destructive attachment to Brian, was that Brian was still very wobbly and sick and she felt she should look after him. So Anita went back to get Brian, took him from Toulouse to London for more medical attention and then, with Marianne, who was coming to join Mick in Marrakech for the weekend, brought him, at first, to Tangier. Brian had been doing a lot of acid and he was in a weak physical state from his pneumonia, so to stiffen him up, Anita and Marianne, the nursing sisters, gave him a tab of acid on the plane. Anita and Marianne had both been up all the previous night on acid and, according to Anita, when they finally got to Tangier, some incident at Achmed's in which Marianne found her sari (the only item of clothing she had packed) unraveling and herself suddenly exposed naked in the Kasbah caused panic to set in — especially in Brian, who ran back to the hotel, seized with fear. There they huddled in the corridors of the Minzah Hotel, on straw mats, grappling with hallucinations. Not a good beginning to Brian's recuperation.

We went to Marrakech, the whole troupe, including Mick, who was waiting there for Marianne. Beaton was twitching about us, admiring our breakfast arrangements and my "marvelous torso." Beaton was mesmerized by Mick ("I was fascinated with the thin concave lines of his body, legs, arms . . .").

When Brian, Anita and Marianne got to Marrakech, Brian must have sensed something, although Tom Keylock, who was the only person who knew about Anita and me, wouldn't have told him. And we're pretending barely to know each other. "Yeah, we had a great trip, Brian. Everything was cool. Went to the Kasbah. Valencia was lovely." The almost unbearable tension of the situation. That was recorded by Michael Cooper in one of his most revealing photographs (which is at the head of this chapter), and a chilling image in retrospect, the last picture of Anita and Brian and me together. It has a tension about it that still radiates — Anita staring straight at the camera, me and Brian looking grimly away in different directions, a joint in Brian's hand. Cecil Beaton took one of

Mick and me and Brian, who is clutching his Uher tape recorder, bags under his eyes, malevolent and sad. It's not surprising that little or no work was done. I don't remember doing or composing anything with Mick in Morocco, which was rare at the time. We were too occupied.

It was obvious that Brian and Anita had come to the end of their tether. They'd beaten the shit out of each other. There was no point in it. I never really knew what the beef was. If I were Brian, I would have been a little bit sweeter and kept the bitch. But she was a tough girl. She certainly made a man out of me. She had had almost nothing but turbulent, abusive relationships, and she and Brian had always been fighting, she running away screaming, being chased, in tears. She had been used to this for so long, it was almost reassuring and normal. It's not easy to get out of those destructive relationships, to know how to end them.

And of course Brian starts his old shit again, in Marrakech in the Es Saadi hotel, trying to take Anita on for fifteen rounds. His reaction to whatever he sensed between Anita and me was more violence. And once again he breaks two ribs and a finger or something. And I'm watching it, hearing it. Brian was about to sign his own exit card and help Anita and me on our way. There's no point to this noninterference anymore. We're stuck in Marrakech, this is the woman I'm in love with, and I've got to relinquish her out of some formality? All of my plans of rebuilding my relationship with Brian are obviously going straight down the drain. In the condition he was in, there was no point in building anything with Brian. I'd done my best. . . . Now it was just unacceptable. Then Brian dragged two tattooed whores — remembered by Anita, incidentally, as "really hairy girls" — down the hotel corridor and into the room, trying to force Anita into a scene, humiliating her in front of them. He started to fling food at her from the many trays he'd ordered up. At that point Anita ran to my room.

I thought Anita wanted out of there, and if I could come up with a plan, she would take it. Sir Galahad again. But I wanted her back; I wanted to get out. I said, "You didn't come to Marrakech to worry that you've beaten up your old man so much he's lying in the bath with broken ribs. I can't take this shit anymore. I can't listen to you getting beaten up and fighting and all this crap. This is pointless. Let's get the hell out of here. Let's just leave him. We're having much more fun without him. It's been a very, very hard week for me knowing that you're with him." Anita was in tears. She didn't want to leave, but she realized that I was right when I said that Brian would probably try and kill her.

And so I planned the moonlight flit. When Cecil Beaton took that picture of me lying beside the pool at the hotel, I was actually figuring out an escape route. I was thinking, "Right, tell Tom to get the Bentley ready, suggest somewhere after sunset, we're getting out of here." The great moonlight flit from Marrakech to Tangier was in motion.

We set Brion Gysin up, had Tom Keylock order him to take Brian into Marrakech into the Square of the Dead, with the musicians and acrobats, to do some recording with his Uher tape recorder, to avoid what Tom had told him was an invasion of press hunting for Brian. And in the meantime, Anita and I drove to Tangier. We left late at night, Anita and I, with Tom at the wheel. Mick and Marianne had already left. In some written work, Gysin recorded the devastating moment when Brian got back to the hotel and called him: "Come quickly! They've all gone and left me. Cleared out! I don't know where they've gone. No message. The hotel won't tell me. I'm here all alone, help me. Come at once!" Gysin writes, "I go over there. Get him into bed. Call a doctor to give him a shot and stick around long enough to see it take hold on him. Don't want him jumping down those ten stories into the swimming pool."

Anita and I got back to my little pad in St. John's Wood, which I'd hardly used since I'd moved into it with Linda Keith. It was quite a difference for Anita after Courtfield Gardens. We were hiding out from Brian there, and that took a while. Brian and I still had to work together, and Brian made desperate attempts to get Anita back. There was no chance of that happening. Once Anita makes up her mind, she makes up her mind. But there was still this intense period of hiding out and negotiating with Brian, and he just used that as an even bigger excuse to get more and more out there. It's said that I stole her. But my take on it is that I rescued her. Actually, in a way, I rescued him. Both of them. They were both on a very destructive course.

Brian went to Paris and fell onto Anita's agent—howling that everyone had left him, fucked off and left him. He never forgave me. I don't blame him. He quickly got himself a chick, Suki Poitier, and we did somehow manage to tour together in March and April.

Anita and I went to Rome that spring and summer, between the bust and the trials, where Anita played in *Barbarella,* with Jane Fonda, directed by Jane's husband Roger Vadim. Anita's Roman world centered around the Living Theatre, the famous anarchist-pacifist troupe run by Judith Malina and Julian Beck, which had been around for years but was coming into its own in this period of activism and street demos. The Living Theatre was particularly insane, hard-core, its players often getting arrested on indecency charges—they had a play in which they recited lists of social taboos at the audience, for which they usually got a night in the slammer. Their main actor, a handsome black man named Rufus Collins, was a friend of Robert Fraser, and they were a part of the Andy Warhol and Gerard Malanga connection. And so it all went round in a little avant-garde elite, as often as not drawn together by a taste for drugs, of which the LT was a center. And drugs were not copious in those days. The Living Theatre was intense, but it had glamour. There were all those beautiful people attached, like Donyale Luna, who was the first famous black model in America, and Nico and all those girls who were hovering around. Donyale Luna was with one of the guys from the theater. Talk about a tiger, a leopard, one of the most sinuous chicks I've ever seen. Not that I tried or anything. She obviously had her own agenda. And all backlit by the beauty of Rome, which gave it an added intensity.

One night when she was doing *Barbarella,* Anita ended up in prison. She was with some guys from the Living Theatre when she was pulled over for drugs, and the police thought she was a transvestite. They put her into the tank, and as soon as they opened the door everybody went, "Anita! Anita!" Everyone knew her—talk about connections. And she's hissing, "Shut up!" because her story was she was the Black Queen and she couldn't be arrested—a bit of a theatrical number that she thought would appeal to the enlightened Romans, or somehow divert them. She'd had to swallow a whole lump of hash when they caught her, so by then she was pretty high. They put her in a room with all the other queens. And eventually the next morning someone bailed her out. Those were days when police didn't really know how to handle the gender-bender varieties. They didn't really know what was going on.

Anita's friends were, as ever, a hip crowd of the period—people like the actor Christian Marquand, who directed *Candy,* the next film Anita worked on that summer, which starred, among a large cast of stars, Marlon Brando, who kidnapped her one night and read her poetry and, when that failed, tried to seduce Anita and me together. "Later, pal." There were Paul and Talitha Getty, who had the best and finest opium. I fell in with some other reprobates, like the writer Terry Southern, with whom I got on well, and the picaresque, scarcely believable figure of the period "Prince" Stanislas Klossowski de Rola, known as Stash, son of the painter Balthus. Stash was an Anita connection from Paris who had been sent by Brian Jones to try and get Anita back. Instead he fell in with the poacher—me. Stash had the bullshit credentials of the period—the patter of mysticism, the lofty talk of alchemy and the secret arts, all basically employed in the service of leg-over. How gullible were the ladies. He was a roué and a playboy, liked to look upon himself as Casanova. What an amazing creature to sweep through the twentieth century. He played with Vince Taylor, an American rock and roller who came over to England and never quite made it, but had a big success in France. Stash was in his band, playing tambourine with one black glove. He loved his music. He loved to dance, in this weird aristocratic way. I was always convinced Stash was going to break out into a minuet. He wanted to be one of the lads. But he could also do "I'm Prince Blah-blah." All hot air.

We lived together in this magnificent palace, the Villa Medici, with its formal gardens, one of the most elegant buildings in the world, that Stash had managed to pull off. His father, Balthus, had an apartment there, some diplomatic role via the French Academy, which owned the building. Balthus was away, so we had his place to ourselves. Down the Spanish Steps for lunch. Nightclubs, hanging out at the Villa Medici, going to the gardens of the Villa Borghese. It was my version of the Grand Tour. There was also this undercurrent of revolution in the air, a lot of political undertones, all half-assed except for the Red Brigades later. Before the riots in Paris the following year, the students started a revolution at the University of Rome, which I went to. They barricaded it, they sneaked me in. They were all flash-in-the-pan revolutionaries.

Me, I had nothing to do, really. Sometimes I'd go to the studio and see Fonda and Vadim at work. Anita went to work and I didn't. Like some sort of Roman pimp or something. Send the woman to work, and hang about. It was weird. I was enjoying it, but at the same time there was that sort of itch. Shouldn't I be doing something? Meanwhile, Tom Keylock is there with my Bentley. Blue Lena had loudspeakers in the grille, and Anita used to terrorize the Romans by putting on a woman policeman's voice, reading out their number plates and ordering them to turn immediately to the right. The car flew a Vatican flag with the keys of Saint Peter.

Marianne and Mick stayed with us for a while. Hear Marianne on the subject.

**Marianne Faithfull:** Now that's a trip I'll never forget. Me and Mick and Keith and Anita and Stash. On acid, at night in the full moon at the Villa Medici. It was just utterly beautiful. And Anita's smile I remember. I mean, her wonderful smile in those days, which promised everything. When she was having a good time, she was so full of promise. She gave this incredible smile, which was quite frightening too, all those teeth. Like a wolf, like a cat that got the cream. If you were a man, it must have been very powerful. She was gorgeous because she was so beautifully dressed, always in the perfect costume.

Anita had a huge influence on the style of the times. She could put anything together and look good. I was beginning to wear her clothes most of the time. I would wake up and put on what was lying around. Sometimes it was mine, and sometimes it was the old lady's, but we were the same size so it didn't matter. If I sleep with someone, I at least have the right to wear her clothes. But it really pissed off Charlie Watts, with his walk-in cupboards of impeccable Savile Row suits, that I started to become a fashion icon for wearing my old lady's clothes. Otherwise it was plunder, loot that I wore — whatever was thrown at me on stage or what I picked up off stage and happened to fit. I would say to somebody, I like that shirt, and for some reason they felt obliged to give it to me. I used to dress myself by taking clothes off other people.

I was never really interested very much in my look, so to speak, although I might be a liar there. I used to spend hours stitching old pants together to give them a different look. I'd get four pairs of sailor pants, I'd cut them off at the knee, get a band of leather and then put another color from the other pair of pants and stitch them in. Lavender and dull rose, as Cecil Beaton says. I didn't realize he was keeping an eye on that shit.

I did enjoy hanging out with Stash and his degenerates — look who's talking. They'd cover my fucking arse. I had no particular desire to get into that area of society, European bullshit high society. I'd use them when I could. I don't want to knock the man; I always liked to hang with him. And, yes, I could say he's so shallow you couldn't paddle in it, and Stash would know exactly what I mean, and he knows he deserves it, little snipe. He got enough out of me, and I let him get away with a few things. I know exactly how tough he is. One kick up the bum and he's gone.

I used to believe in law and order and British Empire. I thought Scotland Yard was incorruptible. Wonderful, I fell for the whole shtick.

The coppers I came up against taught me what it was really about. Amazing to think now that I was shocked, but I was. The busts we were subjected to were set against the background of massive corruption in the Metropolitan Police at the time and for the next few years, which culminated in the commissioner publicly firing a great many CID officers and prosecuting others.

It was only by getting busted that we realized how fragile the structure really was. They're shitting themselves with fear now, because they've busted us and they don't know what to do with us. It was sort of eye-opening. What had they got at Redlands? Some Italian speed that Mick had on script anyway, and they found some smack on Robert Fraser, and that was it. And because they found a few roaches in the ashtray, I got done for allowing people to smoke marijuana on my premises. It was so tenuous. They got nothing out of it. In fact, what they got was a big black eye.

On the day, almost on the hour, that Mick and I were charged, on May 10, 1967, Brian Jones was simultaneously busted in his apartment in London. The stitch-up was orchestrated and synchronized with rare precision. But due to some small glitch of stage management, the press actually arrived, television crews included, a few minutes *before* the police knocked on Brian's door with their warrant. The police had to push through the army of hacks that they had summoned to get to the door. But this collusion was barely noticeable in the farce that unfolded.

The Redlands trial, in late June, was in Chichester, which was still in 1930 when it came to the judicials. On the bench was Judge Block, who was probably sixty-odd, about my age now, at the time. This was my first ever show in court, and you don't know how you're going to react. In fact I had no choice. He was so offensive, obviously trying to provoke me so that he could do what he wanted. He called me, for having used my premises for the smoking of cannabis resin, "scum" and "filth," and said, "People like this shouldn't be allowed to walk free." So when the prosecutor said to me that surely I must have known what was going on, what with a naked girl wrapped in a rug, which is basically what I was being done for, I did not just say, "Oh, sorry, Your Honor."

The actual exchange went as follows:

**Morris (The Prosecutor):** There was, as we know, a young woman sitting on a settee wearing only a rug. Would you agree, in the ordinary course of events, you would expect a young woman to be embarrassed if she had nothing on but a rug in the presence of eight men, two of whom were hangers-on and the third a Moroccan servant?
**Keith:** Not at all.
**Morris:** You regard that, do you, as quite normal?
**Keith:** We are not old men. We are not worried about petty morals.

It got me a year in Wormwood Scrubs. I only did a day, as it turned out, but that was what the judge thought of my speech — he gave me the heaviest sentence he thought he could get away with. I found out later that Judge Block was married to the heiress of Shippam's fish paste. If I'd known about his fishwife, I could have come out with a better one. We'll leave it at that.

That day, June 29, 1967, I was found guilty and sentenced to twelve months in prison. Robert Fraser was given six months and Mick three months. Mick was in Brixton. Fraser and I went to the Scrubs that night.

What a ludicrous sentence. How much do they hate you? I wonder who was whispering in the judge's ear. If he had listened to wise information, he would have said, I'll just treat this as twenty-five quid and out of here; this case is nothing. In retrospect, the judge actually played into our hands. He managed to turn it into a great PR coup for us, even though I must say I didn't enjoy Wormwood Scrubs, even for twenty-four hours. The judge managed to turn me into some folk hero overnight. I've been playing up to it ever since.

But the dark side of this was discovering that we'd become the focal point of a nervous establishment. There's two ways the authorities can deal with a perceived challenge. One is to absorb and the other is to nail. They had to leave the Beatles alone because they'd already given them medals. We got the nail. It was more serious than I thought. I was in jail because I'd obviously pissed off the authorities. I'm a guitar player in a pop band and I'm being targeted by the British government and its vicious police force, all of which shows me how frightened they are. We won two world wars, and these people are shivering in their goddamn boots. "All of your children will be like this if you don't stop this right now." There was such ignorance on both sides. We didn't know we were doing anything that was going to bring the empire crashing to the floor, and they were searching in the sugar bowls not knowing what they were looking for.

But it didn't stop them trying again and again and again, for the next eighteen months. It coincided with their learning about drugs. They'd never heard of them before. I used to walk down Oxford Street with a slab of hash as big as a skateboard. I wouldn't even wrap it up. This was '65, '66—there was that brief moment of total freedom. We didn't even think that it was illegal, what we were doing. And they knew nothing about drugs at all. But once that came on the menu in about '67, they saw their opportunity. As a source of income or a source of promotion or another avenue to make more arrests. It's easy to bust a hippie. And it got very easy to plant a couple of joints on people. It was just so common that you expected it.

Most of the first day of the prison sentence was induction. You get in with the rest of the inductees and take a shower and they spray you with lice spray. Oh, nice one, son. The whole place is meant to intimidate you to the max. The Scrubs wall is daunting to look at, twenty feet, but someone tapped me on the shoulder and said, "Blake got over it." Nine months earlier the spy George Blake's friends had dropped a ladder over the wall and spirited him away to Moscow—a sensational escape. But having Russian friends to spirit you away is another thing. I walked around in an orderly circle with so much rabbit going on it took me a while to get a touch on the back. "Keef, you got bail, you sod." I said, "Any messages? Give 'em to me now." I had to deliver about ten notes to families. Tearful. There were some mean mothers there and most of them were warders. The head bugger said to me as I got in the Bentley, "You'll be back." I said to him, "Not on your time, I won't."

Our lawyers had filed an appeal and I'd been released on bail. Before the appeal hearing, the *Times,* great champion of the underdog, came unexpectedly to our assistance. "There must remain a suspicion," wrote William Rees-Mogg, the *Times* editor, in his piece "Who Breaks a Butterfly on a Wheel?," "that Mr. Jagger received a harsher sentence than would ever have been handed down to an unknown defendant." I.e., you've cocked it up and made British justice look bad. In actual fact we got saved by Rees-Mogg, because, believe me, I felt like a butterfly at the time and I'm going to be broken. When you look back at the brutality of the establishment in the Profumo affair—something as dirty as any John le Carré story, in which inconvenient players were framed and hounded to their death—I'm quite amazed it didn't get more bloody than it did. In that same month my conviction was overturned and Mick's was upheld but his sentence quashed. Not so lucky Robert Fraser, who had pleaded guilty to heroin possession. He had to do his porridge. I think that the experience in the King's African Rifles had more effect on him than Wormwood Scrubs. He'd thrown loads of guys into jankers — army for the glasshouse — which is slopping out the bogs or digging new latrines. It wasn't as if he had no idea about confinement and punishment. I'm sure Africa was a bit rougher than anywhere else. He went in very bold. Never flinched. I thought he came out very bold too, bow tie, cigarette holder. I said, "Let's get stoned."

The same day we were released, the strangest TV discussion ever filmed took place between Mick — flown in by helicopter to some English lawn — and representatives of the ruling establishment. They were like figures from *Alice,* chessmen: a bishop, a Jesuit, an attorney general and Rees-Mogg. They'd been sent out as a scouting party, waving a white flag, to discover whether the new youth culture was a threat to the established order. Trying to bridge the unbridgeable gap between the generations. They were earnest and awkward, and it was ludicrous. Their questions amounted to: what do you want? We're laughing up our sleeves. They were trying to make peace with us, like Chamberlain. Little bit of paper, "peace in our time, peace in our time." All they're trying to do is retain their positions. But such beautiful English earnestness, this concern. It was astounding. Yet you know they're carrying weight, they can bring down some heavy-duty shit, so there was this underlying aggressiveness in the guise of all this amused curiosity. In a way they were begging Mick for answers. I thought Mick came off pretty well. He didn't attempt to answer them; he just said, you're living in the past.

Much of that year we struggled haphazardly to make *Their Satanic Majesties Request*. None of us wanted to make it, but it was time for another Stones album, and *Sgt. Pepper's* was coming out, so we thought basically we were doing a put-on. We do have the first 3-D record cover of all time. That was acid too. We made that set ourselves. We went to New York, put ourselves in the hands of this Japanese bloke with the only camera in the world that could do the 3-D. Bits of paint and saws, bits of Styrofoam. We need some plants! OK, we'll go down to the flower district. It coincided with the departure of Andrew Oldham—dropping the pilot, who was now in a bad way, getting shock treatment for some insurmountable mental pain to do with women trouble. He was also spending a lot of time with his own label, Immediate Records. Things might have run their course, but there was something between Mick and him that couldn't be resolved, that I can only speculate on. They were falling out of sync with each other. Mick was starting to feel his oats and wanted to test it out by getting rid of Oldham. And to be fair to Mick, Andrew was getting big ideas. And why not? A year or two before, he was nobody; now he wanted to be Phil Spector. But all he's got is this five-piece rock-and-roll band to do it with. He would spend an inordinate amount of time, once a couple of hits had rolled in, trying to make these Spector-type records. Andrew wasn't concentrating on the Stones anymore. Added to that, we could no longer create coverage in the way Oldham had done; we were no longer writing the headlines, we were ducking them, and that meant another of Oldham's jobs had gone. His box of tricks was exhausted.

Anita and I went back to Morocco for Christmas in 1967, with Robert Fraser, soon after he'd got out of jail. Chrissie Gibbs took a house belonging to an Italian hairdresser in Marrakech. It was a house with a big garden that had run wild, and the garden was full of peacocks and white flowers coming up through weeds and grass. Marrakech gets very dry, and when the rains come all this vegetation comes piercing through. It was cold and wet, so there was a lot of making of fires in the house. And we were also smoking a lot of dope. Gibbs had a big pot of majoun, the Moroccan candy made of grass and spices, that he'd brought from Tangier, and Robert was very keen about this person who Brion Gysin had put us all onto, who was also a maker of majoun, Mr. Verygood, who worked in the "mishmash"—the jam—factory and made us apricot jam in the evening.

We had dropped in on Achmed in Tangier on the way. His shop was now decorated with collages of the Stones. He'd cut up old seed catalogues, and our faces peered out from a forest of sweet peas and hyacinths. This was the period when dope could be mailed in various ways. And the best hash, if you could get any, was Afghani primo, which used to come in two shapes: like flying saucers, with a seal on it, or in the shape of a sandal, or the sole of a sandal. And it used to have white veins in it that were apparently goat shit, part of the cement. And over the next couple of years Achmed would send out large quantities of hashish sealed in the bases of brass candlesticks. Soon he had four shops in a row and big American cars with Norwegian au pair girls falling out the back. All kinds of wonderful things happened to him. And then a couple of years later, I heard he was in the slammer with everything taken from him. Gibbs looked after him and kept in touch with him until he died.

Tangier was a place of fugitives and suspects, marginal characters acting other lives. On the beach in Tangier on that trip we saw these two strange beach boys walking along, dressed in suits, looking like the Blues Brothers. It was the Kray twins. Ronnie liked little Moroccan boys, and Reggie used to indulge him. They'd brought a touch of Southend with them, handkerchief knotted on the corners over the head and trousers rolled up. And those were the days when you were reading about how they'd murdered the axman, and all those people they'd nailed to the floor. The rough mixed with the smooth. Paul Getty and his beautiful and doomed wife, Talitha, had just bought their huge palace at Sidi Mimoun, where we stayed one night. There was a character called Arndt Krupp von Bohlen und Halbach, whose name I remember because he was the gaily painted heir to the Krupp millions, and a degenerate even by my standards. I believe he may have been in the car during one of the most terrifying moments I've had in a motorcar and one of my closest shaves with mortality.

Certainly Michael Cooper was in the car, and maybe Robert Fraser, and one other, who might have been Krupp. And had it been the heir to the munitions empire, it would have been ironic what nearly befell us. We'd gone on a trip to Fez in a rented Peugeot, and left at night to go back to Marrakech, across the Atlas Mountains. I was driving. Up there among the hairpin bends, halfway down, round the corner right in front of me, without any by-your-leave, coming at us there were these two motorcycles, military I realized by the uniforms, and they were covering all of the road. So he managed to swerve there, I managed to get round here, but down below is half a mile of forget-about-it. So I pull back in and swerve around, and in front of me now is this huge truck, with more motorcycle outriders, and I ain't going over, so I clipped one of the motorcyclists and I went right by the thing. They went bananas. And as we were passing by it, there's a huge missile, a rocket on the truck. We're going round the bend and we've just made it — I've got one wheel over the abyss; I just managed to save us. What the fuck is this doing in the middle of the road? And seconds later, *booom*. It went over. We hear this huge crash and explosion. It was so fast I don't think they knew what happened. This was a long, big motherfucker, an articulated truck. But how we got away with it I don't really know. Just drove on. Foot down. Deal with the hairpins. My night-driving abilities were famous at that time. We changed cars when we got down to Meknes. I went to the garage and said, "This car isn't working very well. Can we rent another one?" We just got the hell out of there. I was expecting NATO on my tail or something, at least an immediate military response, helicopters and searchlights. The next day we're looking in the papers. Not a mention. Falling down a cliff into an abyss astride a third world rocket would have been a sad end, perhaps the only fitting send-off for the heir to the Krupp armaments fortune.

I was suffering from hepatitis on that trip and virtually crawled out of there, but, my luck still holding, into the welcoming arms of one of medicine's great Dr. Feelgoods, Dr. Bensoussan, in Paris. Anita took me to Catherine Harlé. She was a model agent, a Sufi, an incredible woman who had a great range of contacts. She was like Anita's spiritual mother, and took her in when she was ill or in trouble. It was she who Brian Jones went to when Anita left, to try and get her back. It was Catherine who put me in touch with Dr. Bensoussan. Already the name, Algerian probably, gave me the hope of something other than conventional medicine. Dr. Bensoussan used to go to Orly Airport and meet sheikhs and kings and princes who were just stopping off on their way to somewhere else, and he would go and fix them up, whatever the time of day or night. In my case it was heavy-duty hepatitis, and it was really sucking me out. I had no strength. I went to visit Dr. Bensoussan, who gave me this shot that took twenty minutes to go in. And it was basically a concoction of vitamins, everything that's good for you, and then something else very nice. I'd crawl into his store and just manage to get my ass in there, and half an hour later I'd walk back, "Forget the car." An amazing shot, amazing cocktail concoction. Whatever it was, I've got to take my hat off. I mean, in six weeks he had me rockin'. And not only did he deal with the hepatitis, he built me up and made me feel good at the same time. But I also have an incredible immune system. I cured myself of hepatitis C without even bothering to do anything about it. I'm a rare case. I read my body very well.

The only trouble was that with these preoccupations and interruptions, the legal problems, the flights abroad, the wobbling of our relationship with Oldham, we had been temporarily distracted from what was now alarming and evident: the Rolling Stones had run out of gas.

Robert Altman / altmanphoto.com

# Chapter Seven

In which, in the late 1960s, I discover open tuning, and heroin.
Meet Gram Parsons. Sail to South America. Become a father.
Record "Wild Horses" and "Brown Sugar" in Muscle Shoals.
Survive Altamont, and re-meet a saxophonist named Bobby Keys.

W e'd run out of gas. I don't think I realized it at the time,
but that was a period where we could have foundered —
a natural end to a hit-making band. It came soon after *Satanic Majesties*, which was all a bit of flimflam to me. And this is where Jimmy
Miller comes into the picture as our new producer. What a great collaboration. Out of the drift we extracted *Beggars Banquet* and helped
take the Stones to a different level. This is where we had to pull out
the good stuff. And we did.

I remember our first meeting with Jimmy. Mick was instrumental
in getting him involved. Jimmy came from Brooklyn originally, grew
up in the West — his father was entertainment director of the Vegas
gambling hotels the Sahara, the Dunes, the Flamingo. We turned up
at Olympic Studios and said, we'll have a run-through and see how
things go. We just played — anything. We weren't trying to make a
track that day. We were feeling the room, feeling Jimmy out; and
Jimmy was feeling us out. I'd like to go back and be a fly on that wall.
All I remember is having a very, very good feeling about him when
we left the session, about twelve hours later. I was playing the stuff,

going into the control room, the usual old trek, and actually hearing on the playback what was going on in the room. Sometimes what you're playing in the room is totally different from what you hear in the control room. But Jimmy was hearing the room, hearing the band. So I had a very strong thing with him from that first day. He had a natural feel for the band because of what he'd been doing, working with English guys. He'd produced things like "I'm a Man" and "Gimme Some Lovin'" by the Spencer Davis Group; he'd worked with Traffic, Blind Faith. He'd worked a lot with black guys. But most of all it was because Jimmy Miller was a damn good drummer. He understood groove. He's the drummer on "Happy"; he was the original drummer on "You Can't Always Get What You Want." He made it very easy for me to work, mainly for me to set the groove, set the tempos, and at the same time, Mick and Jimmy were communicating well. It gave Mick confidence to go along with him too.

Our thing was playing Chicago blues; that was where we took everything that we knew, that was our kickoff point, Chicago. Look at that Mississippi River. Where does it come from? Where does it go? Follow that river all the way up and you'll end up in Chicago. Also follow the way those artists were recorded. There were no rules. If you looked at the regular way of recording things, everything was recorded totally wrong. But what is wrong and what is right? What matters is what hits the ear. Chicago blues was so raw and raucous and energetic. If you tried to record it clean, forget about it. Nearly every Chicago blues record you hear is an enormous amount over the top, loading the sound on in layers of thickness. When you hear Little Walter's records, he hits the first note on his harp and the band disappears until that note stops, because he's overloading it. When you're making records, you're looking to distort things, basically. That's the freedom recording gives you, to fuck around with the sound. And it's not a matter of sheer force; it's always a matter of experiment and playing around. Hey, this is a nice mike, but if we put it a little closer to the amp, and then take a smaller amp instead of the big one and shove the mike right in front of it, cover the mike with a towel, let's see what we get. What you're looking for is where the sounds just melt into one another and you've got that beat behind it, and the rest of it just has to squirm and roll its way through. If you have it all separated, it's insipid. What you're looking for is power and force, without volume — an inner power. A way to bring together what everybody in that room is doing and make one sound. So it's not two guitars, piano, bass and drums, it's one thing, it's not five. You're there to create one thing.

Jimmy produced *Beggars Banquet, Let It Bleed, Sticky Fingers* — every Stones record through *Goats Head Soup* in 1973, the backbone stuff. But the best thing we ever did with Jimmy Miller was "Jumpin' Jack Flash." That song and "Street Fighting Man" came out of the very first sessions with Jimmy at Olympic Studios for what would become *Beggars Banquet,* in the spring of 1968 — the May of street fighting in Paris. Suddenly between us this whole new idea started to blossom, this new second wind. And it just became more and more fun.

Mick was coming up with some great ideas and great songs, like "Dear Doctor" — I think probably Marianne had something to do with that — and "Sympathy for the Devil," although it was not in the way he envisioned it when it started. But that's in the Godard movie — I'll deal with Godard later — where you hear and see the transformation of the song. "Parachute Woman," with that weird sound area like a fly buzzing in your ear or a mosquito or something — that song came so easily. I thought it was going to be difficult because I had that concept of that sound and wasn't sure it would work, but Mick jumped on the idea just like that, and it took little time to record. "Salt of the Earth," I think I came up with the title of that and had the basic spur of it, but Mick did all the verses. This was our thing. I'd spark the idea, "Let's drink to the hardworking people, let's drink to the salt of the earth," and after that, Mick, it's all yours. Halfway through he'd say, where do we break it? Where do we go to the middle? Where's the bridge? See how long he would take this one idea before he turned to me and said, we've got to go somewhere else now. Ah, the bridge.

Some of that is technical work, a matter of discussion, and usually very quick and easy.

There was a lot of country and blues on *Beggars Banquet:* "No Expectations," "Dear Doctor," even "Jigsaw Puzzle." "Parachute Woman," "Prodigal Son," "Stray Cat Blues," "Factory Girl," they're all either blues or folk music. By then we were thinking, hey, give us a good song, we can do it. We've got the sound and we know we can find it one way or another if we've got the song—we'll chase the damn thing all around the room, up to the ceiling. We know we've got it and we'll lock on to it and find it.

I don't know what it was in this period that worked so well. Maybe timing. We had barely explored the stuff where we'd come from or that had turned us on. The "Dear Doctor"s and "Country Honk"s and "Love In Vain" were, in a way, catch-up, things we had to do. The mixture of black and white American music had plenty of space in it to be explored.

We also knew that the Stones fans were digging it, and there were an awful lot of them by then. Without thinking about it, we knew that they'd love it. All we've got to do is what we want to do and they're gonna love it. That's what we're about, because if *we* love it, a certain thing comes across from it. They were damn good songs. We never forget a good hook. We've never let one go when we've found it.

I think I can talk for the Stones most of the time, and we didn't care what they wanted out there. That was one of the charms of the Stones. And the rock-and-roll stuff that we *did* come out with on *Beggars Banquet* was enough. You can't say apart from "Sympathy" or "Street Fighting Man" that there's rock and roll on *Beggars Banquet* at all. "Stray Cat" is a bit of funk, but the rest of them are folk songs. We were incapable of writing to order, to say, we need a rock-and-roll track. Mick tried it later with some drivel. It was not the interesting thing about the Stones, just sheer rock and roll. A lot of rock and roll on stage, but it was not something we particularly recorded a lot of, unless we knew we had a diamond like "Brown Sugar" or "Start Me

Up." And also it kind of made the up-tempo numbers stand out even more, against a lovely bedrock of really great little songs like "No Expectations." I mean, the body of work was not to smash you between the eyes. This was not heavy metal. This was music.

"Flash!" Shit, what a record! All my stuff came together and all done on a cassette player. With "Jumpin' Jack Flash" and "Street Fighting Man" I'd discovered a new sound I could get out of an acoustic guitar. That grinding, dirty sound came out of these crummy little motels where the only thing you had to record with was this new invention called the cassette recorder. And it didn't disturb anybody. Suddenly you had a very mini studio. Playing an acoustic, you'd overload the Philips cassette player to the point of distortion so that when it played back it was effectively an electric guitar. You were using the cassette player as a pickup and an amplifier at the same time. You were forcing acoustic guitars through a cassette player, and what came out the other end was electric as hell. An electric guitar will jump live in your hands. It's like holding on to an electric eel. An acoustic guitar is very dry and you have to play it a different way. But if you can get that different sound electrified, you get this amazing tone and this amazing sound. I've always loved the acoustic guitar, loved playing it, and I thought, if I can just power this up a bit without going to electric, I'll have a unique sound. It's got a little tingle on the top. It's unexplainable, but it's something that fascinated me at the time.

In the studio, I plugged the cassette into a little extension speaker and put a microphone in front of the extension speaker so it had a bit more breadth and depth, and put that on tape. That was the basic track. There are no electric instruments on "Street Fighting Man" at all, apart from the bass, which I overdubbed later. All acoustic guitars. "Jumpin' Jack Flash" the same. I wish I could still do that, but they don't build machines like that anymore. They put a limiter on it soon after that so you couldn't overload it. Just as you're getting off on something, they put a lock on it. The band all thought I was mad, and they sort of indulged me. But I heard a sound that I could get out of there.

And Jimmy was onto it immediately. "Street Fighting Man," "Jumpin' Jack Flash" and half of "Gimme Shelter" were all made just like that, on a cassette machine. I used to layer guitar on guitar. Sometimes there are eight guitars on those tracks. You just mash 'em up. Charlie Watts's drums on "Street Fighting Man" are from this little 1930s practice drummer's kit, in a little suitcase that you popped up, one tiny cymbal, a half-size tambourine that served as a snare, and that's really what it was made on, made on rubbish, made in hotel rooms with our little toys.

That was a magic discovery, but so were these riffs. These crucial, wonderful riffs that just came, I don't know where from. I'm blessed with them and I can never get to the bottom of them. When you get a riff like "Flash" you get a great feeling of elation, a wicked glee. Of course, then comes the other thing of persuading people that it is as great as you actually know it is. You have to go through the pooh-pooh. "Flash" is basically "Satisfaction" in reverse. Nearly all of these riffs are closely related. But if someone said, "You can play only one of your riffs ever again," I'd say, "OK, give me 'Flash.'" I love "Satisfaction" dearly and everything, but those chords are pretty much a de rigueur course as far as songwriting goes. But "Flash" is particularly interesting. "It's allllll right now." It's almost Arabic or very old, archaic, classical, the chord setups you could only hear in Gregorian chants or something like that. And it's that weird mixture of your actual rock and roll and at the same time this weird echo of very, very ancient music that you don't even know. It's much older than I am, and that's unbelievable! It's like a recall of something, and I don't know where it came from.

But I know where the lyrics came from. They came from a gray dawn at Redlands. Mick and I had been up all night, it was raining outside and there was the sound of these heavy stomping rubber boots near the window, belonging to my gardener, Jack Dyer, a real country man from Sussex. It woke Mick up. He said, "What's that?" I said, "Oh, that's Jack. That's jumping Jack." I started to work around the phrase on the guitar, which was in open tuning, singing the phrase "Jumping Jack." Mick said, "Flash," and suddenly we had this phrase with a great rhythm and ring to it. So we got to work on it and wrote it.

I can hear the whole band take off behind me every time I play "Flash"—there's this extra sort of turbo overdrive. You jump on the riff and it plays you. We have ignition? OK, let's go. Darryl Jones will be right next to me, on bass. "What are we on now, 'Flash'? OK, let's go, one two three..." And then you don't look at each other again, because you know you're in for the ride now. It'll always make you play it different, depending what tempo you're in.

Levitation is probably the closest analogy to what I feel—whether it's "Jumpin' Jack" or "Satisfaction" or "All Down the Line"—when I realize I've hit the right tempo and the band's behind me. It's like taking off in a Learjet. I have no sense that my feet are touching the ground. I'm elevated to this other space. People say, "Why don't you give it up?" I can't retire until I croak. I don't think they quite understand what I get out of this. I'm not doing it just for the money or for you. I'm doing it for me.

The big discovery late in 1968 or early 1969 was when I started playing the open five-string tuning. It transformed my life. It's the way of playing that I use for the riffs and songs the Stones are best known for—"Honky Tonk Women," "Brown Sugar," "Tumbling Dice," "Happy," "All Down the Line," "Start Me Up" and "Satisfaction." "Flash" too.

I had hit a kind of buffer. I just really thought I was not getting anywhere from straight concert tuning. I wasn't learning anymore; I wasn't getting some of the sounds I really wanted. I'd been experimenting with tunings for quite a while. Most times I went into different tunings because I had a song going and I was hearing it in my head but I couldn't get it out of the conventional tuning no matter any way I looked at it. Also I wanted to try to go back and use what a lot of old blues guitarists were playing and transpose it to electric but keep the same basic simplicity and straightforwardness—that pumping drive that you hear with the acoustic blues players. Simple, haunting, powerful sounds.

And then I found out all this stuff about banjos. A lot of five-string playing came from when Sears, Roebuck offered the Gibson guitar in the very early '20s, really cheap. Before that, banjos were the biggest-selling instrument. Gibson put out this cheap, really good guitar, and cats would tune it, since they were nearly all banjo players, to a five-string banjo tuning. Also, you didn't have to pay for the other string, the big string. Or you could save it for hanging the old lady or something. Most of rural America bought their stuff from the Sears catalogue. Rural America was where it was really important. In the cities, you could shop around. In the Bible Belt, rural America, the South, Texas, the Midwest, you got your Sears, Roebuck catalogue and you sent away. That's how Oswald got his shooter.

Usually that banjo tuning was used, on the guitar, for slide playing or bottleneck. An "open tuning" simply means the guitar is pretuned to a ready-made major chord—but there are different kinds and configurations. I'd been working on open D and open E. I learned then that Don Everly, one of the finest rhythm players, used open tuning on "Wake Up Little Susie" and "Bye Bye Love." He just used the barre chord, the finger across the neck. Ry Cooder was the first cat I actually saw play the open G chord—I have to say I tip my hat to Ry Cooder. He showed me the open G tuning. But he was using it strictly for slide playing and he still had the bottom string. That's what most blues players use open tunings for, they use it for slide. And I decided that was too limiting. I found the bottom string got in the way. I figured out after a bit that I didn't need it; it would never stay in tune and it was out of whack for what I wanted to do. So I took it off and used the fifth string, the A string, as the bottom note. You didn't have to worry about bashing that bottom string and setting up harmonics and stuff that you didn't need.

I started playing chords on the open tuning — which was new ground. You change one string and suddenly you've got a whole new universe under your fingers. Anything you thought you knew has gone out the window. Nobody thought about playing minor chords in an open major tuning, because you've got to really dodge about a bit. You have to rethink your whole thing, as if your piano was turned upside down and the black notes were white and the white notes were black. So you had to retune your mind and your fingers as well as the guitar. The minute you've tuned a guitar or any other instrument to one chord, you've got to work your way around it. You're out of the realms of normal music. You're up the Limpopo with Yellow Jack.

The beauty, the majesty of the five-string open G tuning for an electric guitar is that you've only got three notes — the other two are repetitions of each other an octave apart. It's tuned GDGBD. Certain strings run through the whole song, so you get a drone going all the time, and because it's electric they reverberate. Only three notes, but because of these different octaves, it fills the whole gap between bass and top notes with sound. It gives you this beautiful resonance and ring. I found working with open tunings that there's a million places you don't need to put your fingers. The notes are there already. You can leave certain strings wide open. It's finding the spaces in between that makes open tuning work. And if you're working the right chord, you can hear this other chord going on behind it, which actually you're not playing. It's there. It defies logic. And it's just lying there saying, "Fuck me." And it's a matter of the same old cliché in that respect. It's what you leave out that counts. Let it go so that one note harmonizes off the other. And so even though you've now changed your fingers to another position, that note is still ringing. And you can even let it hang there. It's called the drone note. Or at least that's what I call it. The sitar works on similar lines — sympathetic ringing, or what they call the sympathetic strings. Logically it shouldn't work, but when you play it, and that note keeps ringing even though you've now changed to another chord, you realize that that is the root note of the whole thing you're trying to do. It's the drone.

I just got fascinated by relearning the guitar. It really invigorated me. It was like a different instrument in a way, and literally too. I had to have the five-string guitars made for me. I've never wanted to play like anybody else, except when I was first starting, when I wanted to be Scotty Moore or Chuck Berry. After that, I wanted to find out what the guitar or the piano could teach me.

The five-string took me back to the tribesmen of West Africa. They had a very similar instrument, sort of a five-string, kind of like a banjo, but they would use the same drone, a thing to set up other voices and drums over the top. Always underneath it was this underlying one note that went through it. And you listen to some of that meticulous Mozart stuff and Vivaldi and you realize that they knew that too. They knew when to leave one note just hanging up there where it illegally belongs and let it dangle in the wind and turn a dead body into a living beauty. Gus used to point it out to me: just listen to that one note hanging there. All the other stuff that's going on underneath is crap, but that one note makes it sublime.

There's something primordial in the way we react to pulses without even knowing it. We exist on a rhythm of seventy-two beats a minute. The train, apart from getting them from the Delta to Detroit, became very important to blues players because of the rhythm of the machine, the rhythm of the tracks, and then when you cross onto another track, the beat moves. It echoes something in the human body. So then when you have machinery involved, like trains, and drones, all of that is still built in as music inside us. The human body will feel rhythms even when there's not one. Listen to "Mystery Train" by Elvis Presley. One of the great rock-and-roll tracks of all time, not a drum on it. It's just a suggestion, because the body will provide the rhythm. Rhythm really only has to be suggested. Doesn't have to be pronounced. This is where they got it wrong with "this rock" and "that rock." It's got nothing to do with rock. It's to do with roll.

Five strings cleared out the clutter. It gave me the licks and laid on textures. You can almost play the melody through the chords, because of the notes you can throw in. And suddenly instead of it being two guitars playing, it sounds like a goddamn orchestra. Or you can no longer tell who is playing what, and hopefully if it's really good, no one will care. It's just fantastic. It was like scales falling from your eyes and from your ears at the same time. It broke open the dam.

Ian Stewart used to refer to us affectionately as "my little three-chord wonders." But it is an honorable title. OK, this song has got three chords, right? What can you do with those three chords? Tell it to John Lee Hooker; most of his songs are on one chord. Howlin' Wolf stuff, one chord, and Bo Diddley. It was listening to them that made me realize that silence was the canvas. Filling it all in and speeding about all over the place was certainly not my game and it wasn't what I enjoyed listening to. With five strings you can be sparse; that's your frame, that's what you work on. "Start Me Up," "Can't You Hear Me Knocking," "Honky Tonk Women," all leave those gaps between the chords. That's what I think "Heartbreak Hotel" did to me. It was the first time I'd heard something so stark. I wasn't thinking like that in those days, but that's what hit me. It was the incredible depth, instead of everything being filled in with curlicues. To a kid of my age back then, it was startling. With the five-string it was just like turning a page; there's another story. And I'm still exploring.

My man Waddy Wachtel, guitar player extraordinaire, interpreter of my musical gropings, ace up the sleeve of the X-Pensive Winos, has something to say on this topic. Take the floor, Wads.

**Waddy Wachtel:** Keith and I come to the guitar with a very similar approach. It's funny. I sat with Don Everly one night, Don was a real drinker at that point, and I said, "Don, I've got to ask you something. I've known every song you guys have ever done"—that's why I got the job in their band; I know every vocal part, I know every guitar part—"except," I said, "there's something I've never understood on your first single, 'Bye Bye Love,' and that is the intro. What the fuck is that sound? Who's playing that guitar that starts that song?" And Don Everly goes, "Oh, that was just this G tuning that Bo Diddley showed me." And I went, "Excuse me, I'm sorry, what did you say?" And he had a guitar, so he's putting it in the open G tuning and he goes, "Yeah, it was me," and he plays it and I go, "Oh, my fucking word, that's it! It's you! It was you!"

I remember when I discovered this weird tuning—as it seemed to me then—Keith had adopted. In the early '70s, I went to England with Linda Ronstadt. And we walked into Keith's house in London and there's this Strat sitting on a stand with five strings on it. And I'm like, "What happened to that thing? What's wrong with that?" And he goes, "That's my whole deal." What is? He goes, "The five-string! The five-string open G tuning." I went, "Open G tuning? Wait a minute, Don Everly told me about an open G tuning. You play open G tuning?" Because growing up and playing guitar, you're learning Stones songs to play in bars, but you know something's wrong, you're not playing them right, there's something missing. I'd never played any folk music. I didn't have that blues knowledge. So when he said that to me, I said, "Is that why I can't do it right? Let me see that thing." And it makes so many things so easy. Like "Can't You Hear Me Knocking." You can't play that unless it's in the tuning. It sounds absurd. And in the tuning, it's so simple. If you lower the first string, the highest string, one step, then the fifth is always ringing through everything, and that's creating that jangle. The inimitable sound, at least the way Keith plays it.

Those two strings he travels up and down on, you can do a lot with them. We got on stage with the Winos one night and we're about to do "Before They Make Me Run," and he goes to do the intro and he starts to hit it and goes . . . "Argh, I don't know which one it is!" Because he has so many introductions that are all based on the same form. The B string and the G string. Or the B string and the D string. He just went, "Which one are we doing, man? I'm lost in a sea of intros." He's got so many of them, a whirling dervish of riffs, open G intros.

When I fell in with Gram Parsons in the summer of 1968, I struck a seam of music that I'm still developing, which widened the range of everything I was playing and writing. It also began an instant friendship that already seemed ancient the first time we sat down and talked. It was like a reunion with a long-lost brother for me, I suppose, never having had one. Gram was very, very special and I still miss him. Early that year he'd joined the Byrds, "Mr. Tambourine Man" and all that, but they'd just recorded their classic *Sweetheart of the Rodeo,* and it was Gram who had totally turned them around from a pop band into a country music band and expanded their whole being. That record, which bemused everybody at the time, turned out to be the incubator of country rock — a major influence. They were touring, on their way to South Africa, and I went to see them at Blaises Club. I expected to hear "Mr. Tambourine Man." But this was so different, and I went back to see them and met Gram.

"Got anything?" was probably the first question he asked me, or the more discreet "Erm, anywhere, erm . . . ?" "Sure, come back to . . ." I think we went back to Robert Fraser's to hang out, do some stuff. I was taking heroin by this time. He wasn't unfamiliar with it. "Doodgy" was his word for it. It was a musical friendship, but also there was a similar love of a similar substance. Gram certainly liked to get out of it — which made two of us at the time. He also, like me, liked to go for the highest quality — he had better coke than the Mafia, did Gram. Southern boy, very warm, very steady under the drugs, calm. He had a troubled background, a lot of Spanish moss and Garden of Good and Evil.

At Fraser's that night we started to talk about South Africa, and

Gram asked me, "What's this drift I'm getting since I got to England? When I say I'm going to South Africa, I get this cold stare." He was not aware of apartheid or anything. He'd never been out of the United States. So when I explained it to him, about apartheid and sanctions and nobody goes there, they're not being kind to the brothers, he said, "Oh, just like Mississippi?" And immediately, "Well, fuck that." He quit that night — he was supposed to leave the next day for South Africa. So I said, you can stay here, and we lived with Gram for months and months, certainly the rest of that summer of 1968, mostly at Redlands. Within a day or two I thought I'd known him all my life. There was an immediate recognition. What we could have done if we'd known each other earlier. We just sat around one night, and five nights later we were still sitting up talking and catching up on old times, which was five nights ago. And we played music without stopping. Sat around the piano or with guitars and just went through the country songbook. Plus some blues and a few ideas on top. Gram taught me country music — how it worked, the difference between the Bakersfield style and the Nashville style. He played it all on piano — Merle Haggard, "Sing Me Back Home," George Jones, Hank Williams. I learned the piano from Gram and started writing songs on it. Some of the seeds he planted in the country music area are still with me, which is why I can record a duet with George Jones with no compunction at all. I know I've had a good teacher in that area. Gram was my mate, and I wish he'd remained my mate for a lot longer. It's not often you can lie around on a bed with a guy having cold turkey in tandem and still get along. But that is a later story.

Of the musicians I know personally (although Otis Redding, who I didn't know, fits this too), the two who had an attitude towards music that was the same as mine were Gram Parsons and John Lennon. And that was: whatever bag the business wants to put you in is immaterial; that's just a selling point, a tool that makes it easier. You're going to get chowed into this pocket or that pocket because it makes it easier for them to make charts up and figure out who's selling. But Gram and John were really pure musicians. All they liked was music, and then they got thrown into the game. And when that happens, you either start to go for it or you fight it. Some people don't even realize how the game works. And Gram was a bold man. This guy never had a hit record. Some good sellers, but nothing to point to, yet his influence is stronger now than ever. Basically, you wouldn't have had Waylon Jennings, you wouldn't have had all of that outlaw movement without Gram Parsons. He showed them a new approach, that country music isn't just this narrow thing that appeals to rednecks. He did it single-handed. He wasn't a crusader or anything like that. He loved country music, but he really didn't like the country music business and didn't think it should be angled just at Nashville. The music's bigger than that. It should touch everybody.

Gram wrote great songs. "A Song for You," "Hickory Wind," "Thousand Dollar Wedding," great ideas. He could write you a song that came right round the corner and straight in the front, up the back, with a little curve on it. "I've been writing about a guy that builds cars." And then you listen to it and it's a story—"The New Soft Shoe." Written about Mr. Cord, innovative creator of the beautiful Cord automobile, built on his own dime and deliberately crushed out by the triumvirate of Ford, Chrysler and General Motors. Gram was a storyteller, but he also had this unique thing that I've never seen any other guy do: he could make bitches cry. Even hardened waitresses in the Palomino bar who'd heard it all. He could bring tears to their eyes and he could bring that melancholy yearning. Guys he could rub pretty hard too, but his effect on women was phenomenal. It wasn't boo-hoo, it was heartstrings. He had a unique hold on that particular string, the female heart. My feet were soaking from walking through tears.

I remember well the trip with Mick and Marianne and Gram to Stonehenge under Chrissie Gibbs's leadership early one morning, a jaunt photographed by Michael Cooper. The pictures are also a record of the early days of my friendship with Gram. Gibby recalls it thus:

**Christopher Gibbs:** We started off very early from some
club in South Kensington; set off about two or three in the
morning in Keith's Bentley. And we walked from where
Stephen Tennant lived, from Wilsford, across a sort of track to
Stonehenge in order to approach it in a properly reverent
manner, and watched the dawn come up there. And we were
all gibbering with acid. We had breakfast in one of the
Salisbury pubs, lots of acid freaks trying to dismember
kippers, get the spine out. Imagine that if you can. And like
all these things one does on acid, it seemed to take a very long
time but actually it took about thirty seconds. No one's ever
got a kipper cleaner or more swiftly.

It's difficult to put those middle and late '60s together, because
nobody quite knew what was happening. A different kind of fog
descended and much energy was around and nobody quite knew
what to do with it. Of course, being so stoned all the time and experimenting, everybody, including me, had these vague, half-baked ideas.
You know, "Things are changing." "Yeah, but for what, for where?"
It was getting political in 1968, no way to avoid that. It was getting
nasty too. Heads were getting beaten. The Vietnam War had a lot to
do with turning it around, because when I first went to America, they
started drafting the kids. Between '64 and '66 and then '67, the attitude of American youth was taking drastic turns. And then when you
got the killings at Kent State in May of 1970, it turned really sour. The
side effects hit everybody, including us. You wouldn't have had "Street
Fighting Man" without the Vietnam War. There was a certain reality
slowly penetrating.

Then it became a "them against us" sort of thing. I could never
believe that the British Empire would want to pick on a few musicians. Where's the threat? You've got navies and armies, and you're
unleashing your evil little troops on a few troubadours? To me it was
the first demonstration of how insecure establishments and govern-

ments really are. And how sensitive they can get to something that is trivial, really. But once they perceive a threat, they keep looking for the enemy within, without realizing that half the time, they're it! It *was* an assault upon society. We had to assault the entertainment business, and then later the government took us seriously, after "Street Fighting Man."

A flavor of the period is contained in *The True Adventures of the Rolling Stones,* by our friend Stanley Booth — our writer in residence on the early tours. He picked up a flyer in Oakland, back in the late '6os or early '7os, that proclaimed: "The Bastards hear us playing you on our little transistor radios and know that they will not escape the blood and fire of the Anarchist revolution. We will play your music, dear Rolling Stones, in rock and roll marching bands as we tear down the jails and free the prisoners and arm the poor. Tattoo Burn, Baby, Burn on the asses of the wardens and generals."

Taking "Street Fighting Man" to the extremes, or "Gimme Shelter." But without a doubt it was a strange generation. The weird thing is that I grew up with it, but suddenly I'm an observer instead of a participant. I watched all these guys grow up; I watched a lot of them die. When I first got to the States, I met a lot of great guys, young guys, and I had their phone numbers, and then when I got back two or three years later, I'd call them up, and he's in a body bag from Nam. A whole lot of them got feathered out, we all know. That's when that shit hit home with me. Hey, that great little blondie, great guitar player, real fun, we had a real good time, and the next time, gone.

Sunset Strip in the '6os, '64, '65 — there was no traffic allowed through it. The whole strip was filled with people, and nobody's going to move for a car. It was almost off-limits. You hung out in the street, you just joined the mob. I remember once Tommy James, from the Shondells — six gold records and blew it all. I was trying to get up to the Whisky a Go Go in a car, and Tommy James came by. "Hey, man." "And who are you?" "Tommy James, man." "Crimson and Clover" still hits me. He was trying to hand out things about the draft that day.

Because obviously he thought he was about to be fucking drafted. This was Vietnam War time. A lot of the kids that came to see us the first time never got back. Still, they heard the Stones up the Mekong Delta.

Politics came for us whether we liked it or not, once in the odd personage of Jean-Luc Godard, the great French cinematic innovator. He somehow got fascinated with what was happening in London in that year, and he wanted to do something wildly different from what he had done before. He probably took a few things he shouldn't have, not being used to it, just to get himself in the mood. Nobody, I think, has ever quite honestly been able to figure out what the hell he was aiming at. The film *Sympathy for the Devil* is by chance a record of the song by us of that name being born in the studio. The song turned after many takes from a Dylanesque, rather turgid folk song into a rocking samba — from a turkey into a hit — by a shift of rhythm, all recorded in stages by Jean-Luc. The voice of Jimmy Miller can be heard on the film, complaining, "Where's the groove?" on the earlier takes. There wasn't one. There are some rare instrumental switches. I play bass, Bill Wyman plays maracas, Charlie Watts actually sings in the *wooo-woooo* chorus. As did Anita and maybe Marianne too. So far so good. I'm glad he filmed that, but Godard! I couldn't believe it; he looked like a French bank clerk. Where the hell did he think he was going? He had no coherent plan at all except to get out of France and score a bit of the London scene. The film was a total load of crap — the maidens on the Thames barge, the blood, the feeble scene of some brothers, aka Black Panthers, awkwardly handing weapons to one another in a Battersea scrap yard. Jean-Luc Godard up until then made very well-crafted, almost Hitchcockian work. Mind you, it was one of those years when anything was flyable. Whether it would actually take off was another thing. I mean, why, of all people, would Jean-Luc Godard be interested in a minor hippie revolution in England and try to translate it into something else? I think somebody slipped him some acid and he went into that phony year of ideological overdrive.

Godard at least managed to set Olympic Studios on fire. Studio one, where we were playing, used to be a cinema. To diffuse the light, he had tissue paper taped up under these very hot lights on the ceiling. And halfway through — I think there are some outtakes where you can actually see this — all of this tissue paper and the whole ceiling caught alight at ferocious speed. It was like being inside the Hindenburg. All of the heavy light rigging started to crash to the floor because it had burned through the cables; lights going out, sparks. Talk about sympathy for the fucking devil. Let's get the fuck out of here. It was the last days of Berlin, down to the bunker. The end. *Fin.*

I wrote "Gimme Shelter" on a stormy day, sitting in Robert Fraser's apartment in Mount Street. Anita was shooting *Performance* at the time, not far away, but I ain't going down to the set. God knows what's happening. As a minor part of the plot, Spanish Tony was trying to steal the Beretta they were using as a prop off the set. But I didn't go down there, because I really didn't like Donald Cammell, the director, a twister and a manipulator whose only real love in life was fucking other people up. I wanted to distance myself from the relationship between Anita and Donald. Donald was a decadent dependent of the Cammell shipyard family, very good-looking, a razor-sharp mind poisoned with vitriol. He'd been a painter in New York, but something drove him mad about other clever and talented people — he wanted to destroy them. He was the most destructive little turd I've ever met. Also a Svengali, utterly predatory, a very successful manipulator of women, and he must have fascinated many of them. He would sometimes take the piss out of Mick for his Kentish accent and sometimes me, Dartford yokel. I don't mind a good putdown now and again; I come up with a few. But putting people down was almost an addiction for him. Everybody had to be put in their place. Anything you did in front of Cammell was up for his ridicule. He had a fairly developed sense of inferiority in there somewhere.

When I first heard of him, he was in a ménage à trois with Deborah Dixon and Anita, long before Anita and I were together, and they were all jolly jolly. He was a procurer, an arranger of orgies and threesomes — in a pimpish way, though I don't think Anita saw it like that.

One of the first things that happened between Anita and me was the shit of *Performance*. Cammell wanted to fuck me up, because he had been with Anita before Deborah Dixon. Clearly he took a delight in the idea that he was screwing things up between us. It was a setup, Mick and Anita playing a couple. I felt things through the wind. I knew Mouche — Michèle Breton, the third one in the bath scene in the movie; I'm not totally out of this frame — who used to be paid to "perform" as a couple with her boyfriend. Anita told me Michèle had to have Valium shots before every take. So he was basically setting up third-rate porn. He had a good story in *Performance*. He got the only movie of any interest in his life because of who was in it, and Nic Roeg, who shot it, and James Fox, who he drove round the bend. The normally pukka-voiced Fox couldn't stop talking like a gangster from Bermondsey on and off the set until he was rescued by the Navigators, a Christian sect that claimed his attention for the next two decades.

Donald Cammell was more interested in manipulation than actually directing. He got a hard-on about intimate betrayal, and that's what he was setting up in *Performance,* as much of it as he could engineer. He made only four films, and three of them ended the same way — with the main character getting shot or shooting someone they were very close to. Always the watcher. Michael Lindsay-Hogg, director of *Ready Steady Go!* in its early days and later of the Stones' *Rock and Roll Circus,* told me that when he was shooting *Let It Be,* the rooftop swan song of the Beatles, he looked over to another nearby roof and there was Donald Cammell. In at the death, again. The final film Cammell made was a real-life video of him shooting himself, the last scene in *Performance* again, prepared elaborately and filmed over many minutes. The person he was very close to in this case was his wife, who was in the next room.

I met Cammell later in LA, and I said, you know, I can't think of anybody, Donald, that's ever got any joy out of you, and I don't know if you've ever got any joy out of yourself. There's nowhere else for you to go, there's nobody. The best thing you can do is take the gentleman's way out. And this was at least two or three years before he finally topped himself.

I didn't find out for ages about Mick and Anita, but I smelled it. Mostly from Mick, who didn't give any sign of it, which is why I smelled it. The old lady comes back at night complaining about the set and about Donald and blah blah blah. But at the same time, I know the old lady, and the odd time she didn't come home at night, I'd go round somewhere and see another girlfriend.

I never expected anything from Anita. I mean, hey, I'd stolen her from Brian. So you've had Mick now; what do you fancy, that or this? It was like Peyton Place back then, a lot of wife swapping or girlfriend swapping and . . . oh, you had to have him, OK. What do you expect? You've got an old lady like Anita Pallenberg and expect other guys not to hit on her? I heard rumors, and I thought, if she's going to be making a move with Mick, good luck to him; he can only take that one once. I've got to live with it. Anita's a piece of work. She probably nearly broke his back!

I'm not that jealous kind of guy. I knew where Anita had been before, and where she'd been before that with Mario Schifano, who was a successful painter. And with this other guy who was an art dealer in New York. I didn't expect to put any reins on her. It probably put a bigger gap between me and Mick than anything else, but mainly on Mick's part, not mine. And probably forever.

I gave no reaction at all to Mick about Anita. And decided to see how things would pan out from there. It wasn't the first time we'd been in competition for a bird, even for a night on the road. Who's going to get that one? Who's Tarzan round here? It was like two alphas fighting. Still is, quite honestly. But it's hardly the basis for a good relationship, right? I could have given Anita shit for it, but what was the point? We were together. I was on the road. By then I was so cynical about that stuff. I mean, if I'd stolen her off Brian, I didn't expect Mick not to knock her off, under the direction of Donald Cammell. I doubt whether it would have happened without Cammell. But, you know, while you were doing that, I was knocking Marianne, man. While you're missing it, I'm kissing it. In fact, I had to leave the premises rather abruptly when the cat came back. Hey, it was our only time, hot and sweaty. We were just there in, as Mick calls it in "Let Me Down Slow," the afterglow, my head nestled between those two beautiful jugs. And we heard his car drive up, and there was a big flurry, and I did one out the window, got my shoes, out the window through the garden, and I realized I'd left my socks. Well, he's not the sort of guy to look for socks. Marianne and I still have this joke. She sends me messages: "I still can't find your socks."

Anita's a gambler. But a gambler sometimes makes the wrong bets. The idea of status quo to Anita, in those days, was verboten. Everything must change. And we're not married, we're free, whatever. You're free as long as you let me know what's going on. Anyway, she had no fun with the tiny todger. I know he's got an enormous pair of balls, but it doesn't quite fill the gap, does it? It didn't surprise me. In a way I kind of expected it. That's why I was sitting in Robert Fraser's flat, writing, "I feel the storm is threatening my very life today." He had rented us his flat while Anita was shooting the movie, but in the end he never moved out, so when Anita went to work, I stayed there with Strawberry Bob and Mohammed, who were probably the first people I played it to. "War, children, it's just a shot away..."

It was just a terrible fucking day and it was storming out there. I was sitting there in Mount Street and there was this incredible storm over London, so I got into that mode, just looking out of Robert's window and looking at all these people with their umbrellas being blown out of their grasp and running like hell. And the idea came to me.

You get lucky sometimes. It was a shitty day. I had nothing better to do. Of course, it becomes much more metaphorical with all the other contexts and everything, but at the time I wasn't thinking about, oh my God, there's my old lady shooting a movie in a bath with Mick Jagger. My thought was storms on other people's minds, not mine. It just happened to hit the moment. Only later did I realize, this will have more meaning than I thought at the time. "Threatening my very life today." It's got menace, all right. It's scary stuff. And those chords are Jimmy Reed inspired—the same haunting trick, sliding up the fret board against the drone of the E note. I'm just working my way up A major, B major, and I go, hello, where are we ending up? C-sharp minor, OK. It's a very unlikely guitar key. But you've just got to recognize the setups when you hear them. A lot of them, like this one, are accidents.

At the same time, Anita and I had drifted into heroin. We just snorted it for a year or two, along with pure cocaine. Speedballs. A beautifully bizarre law of that time, when the National Health started, was that if you were a junkie, you registered with your doctor, and that would register you with the government as being a heroin addict, and then you would get pure little heroin pills, with a little phial of distilled water to shoot it up with. And of course any junkie is going to double how much he says he needs. Now, at the same time, whether you wanted it or not, you got the equivalent in cocaine. The theory being that the coke would counteract the junk and maybe make the junkies useful members of society, on the grounds that if they take just the junk, they'll lie down and meditate and read things and then shit and stink. And the junkies of course would sell off their cocaine. They doubled their actual need for heroin, so they've got half their heroin stash to sell off, plus all of the cocaine. A beautiful scam! And it was only when the program stopped that you really began to have a drug problem in the UK. But the junkies couldn't believe it. We want to go down, you know? And they're giving us these pure ups. Every junkie's rent was made out of selling off their coke. Very few were interested at all in cocaine, and if they were, they kept a bit back to give them a boost. That's when I first got in touch with cocaine, pure May & Baker, right out of the bottle. It used to say on it "pure fluffy crystals." On the label! And then a skull and crossbones saying "poison." It was a beautifully ambiguous label. That's how I got into all this — with Spanish Tony, Robert Fraser. That's where it all started. Because they had the connection with all these junkies. And the reason I'm here is probably that we only ever took, as much as possible, the real stuff, the top-quality stuff. Cocaine I only got into because it was pure pharmaceutical — *boom*. When I was introduced to dope, it was all pure, pure, pure. You didn't have to worry about what's it cut with and go through all that street shit. Sometimes, eventually, you would have to drift to the bottom — by the time the dope had got you by the scruff of the neck. With Gram Parsons I really went low. Mexican shoe scrapings. But basically my introduction to drugs was all crème de la crème.

So of course everybody eventually had their own pet junkie. Steve and Penny were a registered junkie couple. I'd probably been taken round by Spanish Tony when we used to score from them in London. They were living in a shabby basement flat in Kilburn. And after we'd been round there for a couple of months, they were saying, "I'd like to get out of here. I'd like to live in the country." I said, "I've got a cottage!" So Anita and I installed them in the cottage across from Redlands, which was where I was living at the time. And once a week, "Steve!" Into Chichester, pop into Boots for a minute, go back home and then I'd have half of his smack. Steve and Penny were a very sweet, shy, unassuming couple. They weren't some lowlifes. He was very ascetic, with a little beard. He was a philosopher, always reading Dostoyevsky and Nietzsche. Big, tall, thin bloke with ginger hair, mustache and glasses. He looked like a fucking professor, though he didn't smell like one. It must have gone on for about a year. They were such a sweet and gentle couple. "Can we make you a cup of tea?" Nothing that you think about "junkies." It was all very civilized. Sometimes I'd go to the cottage and—because they were mainliners—say, "Penny, is Steve still alive?" "I think so, darling. Anyway, have a cup of tea and then we'll wake him up." It was all so genteel. For every stereotypical junkie, I can point to ten others who live perfectly ordered lives, bankers and whatever.

That was the golden era. At least until '73, '74, it was all perfectly legal. After that, they knocked it on the head and it was methadone, which is worse, or certainly no better. Synthetic. One day the junkies woke up and they only got half their script in pure heroin and half in methadone. And then that turned it into a bit more of a market, the era of the all-night drugstore in Piccadilly. I used to park around the corner. But there was always a queue of people outside waiting for their pet junkies to come out with the stuff and then split it. The system couldn't really support it anymore against the voracious demands. We were creating a nation of junkies!

I have no clear recollection of the first time I had heroin. It was probably slipped in with a line of coke, in a speedball—a mixture of coke and smack. If you were around people who were used to doing that in one line, you didn't know. You found out later on. "That was very interesting last night. What was that? Oh." That's how it creeps up on you. Because you don't remember. That's the whole point of it. It's suddenly there.

They don't call it "heroin" for nothing. It's a seductress. You can take that stuff for a month or so and stop. Or you can go somewhere where there isn't any and you're not really that interested; it's just something you were taking. And you might feel like you've got the flu for a day, but the next day you're up and about and you feel fine. And then you come into contact again, and you do it some more. And months can pass. And the next time, you've got the flu for a couple of days. No big deal, what are they talking about? That's cold turkey? It was never in the front of my mind until I was truly hooked.

It's a subtle thing. It grabs you slowly. After the third or fourth time, then you get the message. And then you start to economize by shooting it up. But I've never mainlined. No, the whole delicacy of mainlining was never for me. I was never looking for that flash; I was looking for something to keep me going. If you do it in the vein, you get an incredible flash, but then you want more in about two hours. And also you have tracks, which I couldn't afford to show off. Furthermore, I could never find a vein. My veins are tight; even doctors can't find them. So I used to shoot it up in the muscles. I could slap a needle in and not feel a thing. And the spank, the smack, is, if you do it right, more of a shock than the actual injection. Because the recipient reacts to that and meanwhile the needle has come and gone. Especially interesting on the butt. But not politically correct.

That was a very productive and creative period, *Beggars Banquet, Let It Bleed*—some good songs were written, but I never thought drugs per se had very much to do with whether I was productive or not. It might have changed a few chords, a few verses here and there, but I never felt any diminishment or any extra lift as far as what I was doing was concerned. I didn't look upon smack as an aid or a detraction from what I was doing. I would probably have written "Gimme Shelter" whether I was on or off the stuff. It doesn't affect your judgment, but in certain cases it helps you be more tenacious about something and follow it further than you would have, than if you just threw up your hands and said, oh, I can't figure this one out right now. On the stuff sometimes you would just nag at it and nag at it until you'd got it. I've never believed that bullshit like all those saxophone players who went on dope because they thought that's what made Charlie Parker so great. Like anything else in this world, it's either good for you or it's bad for you. Or at least it has a use for you. A lump of heroin sitting on the table is totally benign. The only difference is, will you take any? I took loads of other drugs I really didn't like and never went back to.

I suppose heroin made me concentrate on something or finish something more than I would normally. This is not a recommendation. The life of being a junkie is not recommended to anybody. I was on the top end, and that was pretty low. It's certainly not the road to musical genius or anything else. It was a balancing act. I've got loads of things to do, this song's interesting, and I want to make copies of all of this stuff, and I'd be doing it for five days, perfectly balanced on this equilibrium of cocaine and heroin. But the thing is that after about six or seven days, I'd forget what the balance was. Or I'd run out of one side of the balance or the other. Because I was always having to think about supplies. The key to my survival was that I paced myself.

I never really overdid it. Well, I shouldn't say *never;* sometimes I was absolutely fucking comatose. But I think it really became to me like a tool. I realized, I'm running on fuel and everybody else isn't. They're trying to keep up with me and I'm just burning. I can keep going because I'm on pure cocaine, none of that shit crap, I'm running on high octane, and if I feel I'm pushing it a little bit, need to relax it, have a little bump of smack. It sounds ridiculous now in a way, but the truth is that was my fuel, that speedball. But I have to impress on anyone who reads this that this was the finest, finest cocaine and the purest, purest heroin, this was no crap off the street, no Mexican shoe scrapings. This was the real shit. I felt very Sherlock Holmes about it all at the time. In order to deal with one's morbidity, or in order to deal with one's levity, it was like a balancing act. And it could keep me going for days and days without realizing that in fact I was wearing guys ragged.

I got to know John Lennon longer and better further down the line. We'd hang for quite a while; he and Yoko would pop by. But the thing was with John—for all his vaunted bravado—he couldn't really keep up. He'd try and take anything I took but without my good training. A little bit of this, a little bit of that, couple of downers, a couple of uppers, coke and smack, and then I'm going to work. I was freewheeling. And John would inevitably end up in my john, hugging the porcelain. And there'd be Yoko in the background, "He really shouldn't do this," and I'd go, "I know, but I didn't force him!" But he'd always come back for more, wherever we were. I remember one night in the Plaza Hotel, he came by my room — and then he disappeared from the room. I'm talking to the chicks, and their mates are all saying, I wonder where John went? And I go to the john, and there he is, hugging the parquet, on the tiles. Too much red wine and some smack. Technicolor yawn. "Don't move me; these tiles are beautiful" — his face a ghastly green. Sometimes I thought, are these guys just coming to see me or is there some sort of race on that I don't know about? I don't think John ever left my house except horizontally. Or definitely propped up.

Maybe the frenetic pace of life had something to do with it. I would take a barbiturate to wake up, a recreational high compared to heroin, though just as dangerous in its own way. That was breakfast. A Tuinal, pin it, put a needle in it so it would come on quicker. And then take a hot cup of tea, and then consider getting up or not. And later maybe a Mandrax or quaalude. Otherwise I just had too much energy to burn. So you wake up slow, since you have the time. And when the effect wears off after about two hours, you're feeling mellow, you've had a bit of breakfast and you're ready for work. And sometimes I used to take downers to keep going. When I'm awake, I know that it's not going to put me to sleep, because I've obviously slept. What it's going to do is smooth my path into the next three or four days. I've no intention of going to sleep again for a while, and I know there's enough energy in me that if I don't slow it down, I'm going to burn it up before I finish what I think I'm going to finish, in a studio, for instance. I would use drugs like gears. I very rarely used them for pleasure. At least, that's my excuse. They smoothed my path into the day.

Don't try this at home. Even I can't do it anymore; they don't make them the same. They suddenly decided in the mid-'70s that they would make downers that would put you to sleep without the high. I would raid the lockers of the world to find some more barbiturates.

No doubt somewhere in the Middle East, in Europe, I could find some. I love my downers. I was so hyper all the time that I needed to suppress myself. If you didn't want to go to sleep and just enjoy the buzz, you just stood up for a little bit and listened to some music. It had character. That's what I would say about barbiturates. Character. Every man who is worth his salt in downers knows what I'm talking about. And even that wouldn't put me down; that would keep me on a level. To me, the sensible drugs in the world are the pure ones. Tuinals, Seconals, Nembutals. Desbutal was probably one of the best that there ever was, a capsule in a weird red and cream color. They were better than later versions, which acted on the central nervous system. You could piss them out in twenty-four hours; they didn't hang on to your nerve endings.

In December 1968, Anita, Mick, Marianne and I took a ship from Lisbon to Rio, maybe ten days at sea. We thought, let's go to Rio and let's do it in the old style. If any of us had been seriously hooked by then, we wouldn't have taken that form of transport. We were still dabbling, except perhaps for Anita, who was going to the ship's surgeon to ask for morphine from time to time. There was nothing to do on the boat, so we'd go around filming Super 8—the footage still exists. I think it may even show Spiderwoman, as we called her. This was a refrigeration ship, but it had passengers as well. And it was all very '30s—you expected Noël Coward to walk in. The Spiderwoman was one of those with all the bangles and the perm and the expensive dresses and the cigarette holder. We used to go down and watch her act at the bar. Buy her a drink now and again. "Fascinating, darling." She was kind of like a female Stash, full of shit. The bar was crowded with these upper-class English people, all drinking like mad, pink gins and pink champagne, all prewar conversation. I was dressed in a diaphanous djellaba, Mexican shoes and a tropical army hat, deliberately outlandish. After a while they discovered who we were and became very perturbed. They started asking questions. "What *are* you trying to do? Do try to explain to us what this whole thing is about." We never answered them, and one day Spiderwoman stepped forward and said, "Oh, do give us a hint, just give us a glimmer." Mick turned to me and said, "We're the Glimmer Twins." Baptized on the equator, the Glimmer Twins is the name we used later for ourselves as producers of our own records.

We already knew Rupert Loewenstein, who soon started to run our affairs, by this time, and he checked us into the best hotel in Rio. And suddenly Anita was mysteriously going through the phone book. I said, what are you looking for? She said, I'm looking for a doctor.

"A doctor?"

"Yeah."

"What for?"

"Don't worry about it."

When she came back later that afternoon, she says, I'm pregnant. And that was Marlon.

Oh, well...great! I was very happy, but we didn't want to stop the trip now. We were headed for the Mato Grosso. We lived for a few days on a ranch, where Mick and I wrote "Country Honk," sitting on a veranda like cowboys, boots on the rail, thinking ourselves in Texas. It was the country version of what became the single "Honky Tonk Women" when we got back to civilization. We decided to put "Country Honk" out as well, on *Let It Bleed,* a few months later in late '69. It was written on an acoustic guitar, and I remember the place because every time you flushed the john these black blind frogs came jumping out — an interesting image.

Marianne went home to get medical help for her child Nicholas, who had been sick on the boat and confined to his cabin for most of the journey. So Mick and Anita and I worked our way to Lima, Peru, and then up to Cusco, which is eleven thousand feet. Everybody's been a bit short of breath, and we get to the hotel lobby, and it's lined wall to wall with these huge oxygen tanks. We get to our rooms, and in the middle of the night, Anita finds that the john's not working. So she takes a pee in the sink, and in the middle of the pee, the sink collapses to the floor and water comes shooting out of a huge pipe. Real Marx Brothers, slapdash, carry on...stuff some rags down there, call the people. The sink was shattered, lying in pieces, but the weird thing is that when they finally arrived in the middle of the night, the Peruvians were very nice. They didn't go, "What are you doing! How did you break the sink!" They just mopped it up and gave us another room. I thought they were going to bring the cops with them.

Next day Mick and I went for a walk, sat on a bench and did what you do in the daytime, started chewing coca leaves. When we got back to the hotel, we found a card delivered, as if from the British consul: "General So-and-so...It would be fortuitous to meet." The general in question was the military governor of Machu Picchu, who had invited us to his home for dinner, and you can't very well say no to that. He did run the area, and he gave out the permissions and travel passes. Obviously he was very bored in this province, so he summoned us to his villa outside of Cusco. He was living with a German DJ, a blond boy. I'll never forget the decor; it had all been ordered from Mexico or straight from the States. He was one of those guys that kept the furniture wrapped in plastic covers, probably because the insects would eat everything the minute you unwrapped it. All terrible furniture, but the actual villa was very nice, like an old Spanish mission, as far as I can remember. The general was charming and a great host and we had good food. And then came the pièce de résistance, performed by his boyfriend, the German DJ. They put on these terrible twist records, phony soul—and this was '69—and then he orders this poor boy to demonstrate how to do the swim, a dance already so old I could barely remember it. He lay on the floor and started rolling around doing the breaststroke. Mick and I looked at each other. Where the fuck? How do we get out of here? It was almost impossible to not burst out laughing, because the guy's doing his best, he thinks he's doing the best swim south of the border. Yeah, get down, man! And he would do anything the general ordered him to do. "Now do the mashed potato," and he would instantly obey. We really thought we'd gone back a hundred years or so.

We traveled to Urubamba, a village not far from Machu Picchu on a river of the same name. Once you got out there, you were out there, man. There was nothing there. No hotel, certainly. This place was not on the tourist map. The only white people they ever saw were lost. In fact we were, basically (lost). But eventually we found this bar and had a nice meal, shrimps and rice and beans, and we said, well, we've only got this car; any chance of some *dormir?* And at first a lot of no's went around the room, but they noticed we had a guitar with us, so Mick and I serenaded them for about an hour, trying to come up with any old thing we could think of. It seemed to me you needed a majority vote to get invited to sleep on the premises. And Anita being pregnant, I did want to give her a bed for the night. We must have done all right. I did a few bits of "Malagueña" and a few other songs that sounded vaguely Spanish that Gus had taught me. And finally the landlord said we could have a couple of rooms upstairs. The only time Mick and I sang for a bed.

It was a good writing period. Songs were coming. "Honky Tonk Women," which came out as a single before the next album, *Let It Bleed,* in July 1969, was the culmination of everything we were good at at the time. It's a funky track and dirty too; it's the first major use of the open tuning, where the riff and the rhythm guitar provide the melody. It's got all that blues and black music from Dartford onwards in it, and Charlie is unbelievable on that track. It was a groove, no doubt about it, and it's one of those tracks that you knew was a number one before you'd finished the motherfucker. In those days I used to set up the riffs and the titles and the hook, and Mick would fill it in. That was basically the gig. We didn't really think too much or agonize. There you go, this one goes like this, "I met a fucking bitch in somewhere city." Take it away, Mick. Your job now, I've given you the riff, baby. You fill it in and meanwhile I'll try and come up with another one. And he can write, can Mick. Give him the idea and he'll run with it.

We also composed using what we called vowel movement — very important for songwriters. The sounds that work. Many times you don't know what the word is, but you know the word has got to contain this vowel, this sound. You can write something that'll look really good on paper, but it doesn't contain the right sound. You start to build the consonants around the vowels. There's a place to go *ooh* and there's a place to go *daah*. And if you get it wrong, it sounds like crap. It's not necessarily that it rhymes with anything at the moment, and you've got to look for that rhyming word too, but you know there's a particular vowel involved. Doo-wop is not called that for nothing; that was all vowel movement.

"Gimme Shelter" and "You Got the Silver" were the first tracks we recorded in Olympic Studios for what became *Let It Bleed* — the album that we worked on throughout the summer of '69, the summer that Brian died. "You Got the Silver" was not the first solo vocal I recorded with the Stones — that was "Connection." But it was one of the first ones I wrote entirely by myself and laid on Mick. And I sang it solo simply because we had to spread the workload. We'd always sung harmony, like the Everlys, so it wasn't as if I'd suddenly started to sing. But like all my songs, it never felt like my creation. I'm a damn good antenna to pick up songs zooming through the room, but that's all. Where did "Midnight Rambler" come from? I don't know. It was the old days trying to knock you on the back of the head. "Hey, don't forget us, pal. Write a damn good blues. Write one that takes the form in another way, just for a bit." "Midnight Rambler" is a Chicago blues. The chord sequence isn't, but the sound is pure Chicago. I knew how the rhythm should go. It was in the tightness of the chord sequence, the D's and the A's and the E's. It wasn't a blues sequence, but it came out like heavy-duty blues. That's one of the most original blues you'll hear from the Stones. The title, the subject, was just one of those phrases taken out of sensationalist headlines that only exist for a day. You just happen to be looking at a newspaper, "Midnight Rambler on the loose again." Oh, I'll have him.

The fact that you could get that kind of tasty bite into the lyrics by mixing in contemporary stories or headlines or just what appeared to be mundane daily narrative was so far away from pop music and also from Cole Porter or Hoagy Carmichael. "I saw her today at the reception" was just very plain. No dynamics, no sense of where it was going. I think Mick and I looked at each other and said, well, if John and Paul can do it ... The Beatles and Bob Dylan to a great extent changed songwriting in that way and people's attitudes towards voice. Bob has not got a particularly great voice, but it's expressive and he knows where to put it, and that's more important than any technical beauties of voice. It's almost anti-singing. But at the same time what you're hearing is real.

"You Can't Always Get What You Want" was basically all Mick. I remember him coming into the studio and saying, I've got this song. I said, you got any verses? And he said, I have, but how is it going to sound? Because he'd written it on guitar, it was like a folk song at the time. I had to come up with a rhythm, an idea.... I'd float it around the band and just play the sequence here and there. And maybe Charlie decides which to go for. It's all experimentation. And then we added the choir on the end, very deliberately. Let's put on a straight chorus. In other words, let's try and reach them people up there as well. It was a dare, kind of. Mick and I thought it should go into a choir, a gospel thing, because we'd played with black gospel singers in America. And then, what if we got one of the best choirs in England, all these white, lovely singers, and do it that way, see what we can get out of them? Turn them on a little bit, get them into a little sway and a move, you know? "You caaarnt always..." It was a beautiful juxtaposition.

In early June, when we were working every day in Olympic Studios on these tracks, I turned over the Mercedes with Anita in it when she was seven months pregnant with Marlon. Anita broke her collarbone.

I took her to St Richard's, and they patched her up within half an hour while I sat around — really brilliant people looking after us — only to walk out straight into the arms of the Brighton CID, who then took us to Chichester police station and started to interrogate us. I've got a pregnant woman with a broken collarbone, for Christ's sake, it's three in the morning, and they don't give a shit. The more I deal with cops, especially British cops, I must say, something's wrong with the training. My attitude probably didn't help, but what am I going to do, roll over for them? Get outta here. They suspected drugs. Of course there were drugs involved. They should have looked in the oak tree around the corner. They start with "How did the car turn over? You must have been out of it." Actually no. On a corner, close to Redlands, a red light came on in the car and nothing would work. A hydraulic fault. Brakes wouldn't work, steering wouldn't work, it just teetered on a patch of slippery grass and then rolled over. It was a convertible, and it was three tons rolling on the windscreen and on the struts that hold up the canvas. The miracle was that the windscreen held up. I only found out later it was because the car was built in 1947 out of panzer parts and armored steel, immediately postwar, German scrap lying around the battlefield — whatever they could get their hands on. This shit was heavy-duty steel. Basically I was riding a tank with a canvas roof. No wonder they swept through France in six weeks. No wonder they almost took Russia. The panzers saved my life.

My body left the car. I watched it all happen from twelve, fifteen feet above. You can leave your body, believe me. I'd been trying all my life, but this was the first real experience of it. I watched that thing roll over in slow motion three times, very dispassionate, very cool about it. I was an observer. No emotion involved. You're already dead; forget about it. But meanwhile, before the lights actually went out...I noticed the underside of the car, and I noticed it was built with these diagonal riveted struts underneath. Very solid-looking things. It all appeared to be slow motion. You're holding a very long breath. And I know that Anita is in the car, and I'm wondering in another part of my mind if Anita is also watching from above. I'm more concerned about her than I am myself, because I'm not even in the car. I've escaped, in the mind, or wherever you think you are when things like that happen in a split second. But then it came pounding rubber side down, after three turns, into this hedge. And suddenly I'm back behind the wheel.

So Marlon had his first car crash two months before he was born. No wonder he has never driven, never obtained a driving license. Marlon's full name is Marlon Leon Sundeep. Brando called up while Anita was in hospital, to compliment her on *Performance*. "Marlon, that's a good name. Why don't we call him Marlon?" The poor kid was forced through this religious ceremony when he arrived home in Cheyne Walk, the rice and the flower petals and the chanting and all of that shit. Well, Anita's the mother, right? Who am I to say no? Anything you like, Mother. You've just given birth to our son. So the Bauls of Bengal came, courtesy of Robert Fraser. And Robert had a crib made, beautiful little one that rocked. So that's his full name, Marlon Leon Sundeep Richards. Which is the most important bit. The rest is mere pretext.

It's strange, given the fact that we'd had to pull the plug on Brian in the studio three years earlier, when he was lying in a coma beside his buzzing amp, to be reminded that he was still playing on tracks early in 1969, the year of his death. Autoharp on "You Got the Silver," percussion on "Midnight Rambler." Where did that come from? A last flare from the shipwreck.

By May we were playing in his replacement, Mick Taylor, at Olympic Studios — playing him in on "Honky Tonk Women," on which his overdub is there for posterity. No surprise to us, how good he was. He seemed just to step in naturally at the time. We had all heard Mick, and we knew him because he'd played with John Mayall and the Bluesbreakers. Everybody was looking at me, because I was the other guitar player, but my position was, I'd play with anybody. We could only find out by playing together. And we did the most brilliant stuff together, some of the most brilliant stuff the Stones ever did. Everything was there in his playing — the melodic touch, a beautiful sustain and a way of reading a song. He had a lovely sound, some very soulful stuff. He'd get where I was going even before I did. I was in awe sometimes listening to Mick Taylor, especially on that slide — try it on "Love in Vain." Sometimes just jamming, warming up with him, I'd go, whoa. I guess that's where the emotion came out. I loved the guy, I loved to work with him, but he was very shy and very distant. I'd get close to him when we were working out stuff and playing, and when he let his hair down he was extremely funny. But I always found it very difficult to find any more than the Mick Taylor I'd met the first time. You can see it on the screen in *Gimme Shelter* — his face has no animation. He was fighting himself somewhere inside. There's not a lot you can do about that, with guys like that; you can't bring them out. They've got to fight their own demons. You'd bring him out for an hour or two, for an evening or a night, but the next day he was brooding again. Not a barrel of laughs, let's put it like that. Well, you give certain people their space. You realize, some guys you can spend a day with them and basically you've learned all you're ever going to know about them. Like Mick Jagger in exact reverse.

We'd already fired Brian two or three weeks before he died. It had come to a head and Mick and I had been down to Winnie-the-Pooh's house. (Cotchford Farm had belonged to author A. A. Milne, and Brian had recently bought it.) Mick and I didn't fancy the gig, but we drove down together and said, "Hey, Brian... It's all over, pal."

We were in the studio when we got the phone call not long afterwards, cutting with Mick Taylor. There exists one minute and thirty seconds of us recording "I Don't Know Why," a Stevie Wonder song, interrupted by the phone call telling us of Brian's death.

I knew Frank Thorogood, who made a "deathbed confession" that he'd killed Brian Jones by drowning him in the swimming pool, where Brian's body was found some minutes after other people had seen him alive. But I'm always wary of deathbed confessions because the only person there is the person he's supposed to have said it to, some uncle, daughter, or whatever. "On his deathbed he said he killed Brian." Whether he did or not I don't know. Brian had bad asthma and he was taking quaaludes and Tuinals, which are not the best things to dive under water on. Very easy to choke on that stuff. He was heavily sedated. He had a high tolerance for drugs, I'll give him that. But weigh that against the coroner's report, which showed that he was suffering from pleurisy, an enlarged heart and a diseased liver. Still, I can imagine the scenario of Brian being so obnoxious to Thorogood and the building crew he had working on Brian's house that they were just pissing around with him. He went under and didn't come up. But when somebody says, "I did Brian," at the very most I'd put it down to manslaughter. All right, you may have pushed him under, but you weren't there to murder him. He pissed off the builders, whining son of a bitch. It wouldn't have mattered if the builders were there or not, he was at that point in his life when there wasn't any.

Three days later, July 5, we performed our first concert in over two years, in Hyde Park, a free concert to which something like half a million people came, and it was an amazing show. The all-important thing for us was it was our first appearance for a long time and with a change of personnel. It was Mick Taylor's first gig. We were going to do it anyway. Obviously a statement had to be made of one kind or another, so we turned it into a memorial for Brian. We wanted to see him off in grand style. The ups and downs with the guy are one thing, but when his time's over, release the doves, or in this case the sackfuls of white butterflies.

\* \* \*

We went touring in the USA in November '69 with Mick Taylor. B.B. King and Ike and Tina Turner were opening acts, which was a hot show just by itself. Added to that, it was the first tour that the open-tuning riffs — the big new sound — were let loose on audiences. The most powerful effect was on Ike Turner. The open tuning fascinated him the way it had fascinated me. He dragged me into his dressing room basically at gunpoint, I believe in San Diego. "Show me that five-string shit." And we were there for about forty-five minutes, and I showed him the basics of it. And the next thing was *Come Together,* that beautiful album that Ike and Tina did, and all of it was five-string. He got the hang of it in forty-five minutes, picked it up like that. But to me the amazing thing is, I'm showing Ike Turner shit? With musicians there's this weird crossing over between awe and respect and being accepted. When other guys come to you and go, hey, man, show me that lick, and they're guys that you've been listening to for years, that's when you know that you're amongst men now. OK, I can't believe it, but I'm part of the front line, top hands. And the other great thing about musicians, or most of them, is the reciprocation, the generosity they show to one another. Have you got that little pop? Yeah, it goes like this. Mostly there are no secrets; everybody swaps ideas. How did you get that? And he shows you and you realize it's really simple.

Oiled up and running hot, in early December we ended up at Muscle Shoals Sound Studios in Sheffield, Alabama, at tour's end (or not quite end, since the Altamont Speedway track loomed in the distance, some days away). There we cut "Wild Horses," "Brown Sugar" and "You Gotta Move." Three tracks in three days, in that perfect eight-track recording studio. Muscle Shoals was a great room to work, very unpretentious. You could go in there and do a take, none of this fiddling about: "Oh, can we try the bass over there?" You just went in, hit it and there it was. It was the crème de la crème, except it was just a shack in the middle of nowhere. The people that put the studio together — great bunch of southern guys, Roger Hawkins and Jimmy

Johnson and a couple of others owned it—were famed musicians, part of the Muscle Shoals Rhythm Section who had been in the house band at Rick Hall's FAME Studios, previously situated in Muscle Shoals proper. That setup already had a legendary ring because some great soul records had been coming out of there for several years— Wilson Pickett, Aretha Franklin, Percy Sledge's "When a Man Loves a Woman." So to us, it was on a par with going to Chess Records, even though it was out of the way and we had wanted to record in Memphis. But you should hear the late Jim Dickinson, piano player on "Wild Horses," tell what happened. He was a southern boy and a good storyteller.

**Jim Dickinson:** This is the part of the story nobody knows, because even in Stanley Booth's book he for whatever reason chose not to tell it. But the way they got to Muscle Shoals was Stanley. He was traveling with them for the biography, and he called me in the middle of the night. My wife and I had met him down in Auburn and seen the show, thinking that would be it. And he calls maybe a week, week and a half later and says, is there anywhere in Memphis the Stones could record? They've got three days at the end of their tour, and they've been on the road playing together and they're hot, they've got some new material. Now, at the time, from the American Federation of Musicians, you could get a touring permit or a recording permit as a foreign band, but you couldn't get both. And they had been barred from recording in Los Angeles. The way I heard it, Leon Russell tried to set up a session for them in LA and was fined by the musicians union. Anyway, they were looking for a place that would be under the union radar. And they thought about Memphis. Well, the Beatles had tried to record in Memphis, at Stax, and had been refused for insurance reasons, or for whatever reason, and there really wasn't anyplace in Memphis that they could have safely

recorded anonymously. And I told Stanley that, and it made
Stanley mad. He said, well, what the hell am I supposed to tell
'em? I said, tell them to go to Muscle Shoals; nobody will even
know who they are, which in fact nobody did. And Stanley
responded negatively. He said, well, I don't know any of those
rednecks down there. How am I supposed to... I said, call
Jerry Wexler. He'll set it up. But what I didn't know, what
nobody knew at that point, was that the Stones' contract with
EMI was run down. Well, you can bet Wexler knew it; he put
it together in a heartbeat. And I didn't hear any more about it
for another week or ten days, and then Stanley calls in the
middle of the night. He says, be in Muscle Shoals on
Thursday. The Stones are going to record. And he says, don't
tell anybody. So I didn't use my car; I took my wife's car so
nobody would recognize it. I drove down there, and the old
studio was across the highway from the cemetery. The old
studio had actually been a coffin factory. It was a real small
building. So I go to the door, and Jimmy Johnson opens the
door just a crack and he looks at me and says, Dickinson, what
do you want? And I said, I've come down for the Stones
session. And he says, oh hell, does everyone in Memphis
know? I said, no, nobody knows, Jimmy. It's cool, don't worry.
And nobody was there at this point, they hadn't showed up
yet. When they showed up, it was the biggest plane that ever
landed in the Muscle Shoals airport. Because I was with
Stanley, I got to stay. And you'll hear different people claim
they were there. There was no one there. I've been asked
several times if Gram Parsons was there. Well, hell, if Gram
Parsons had been there, I certainly would never have played
the piano; it would have been him. So there was literally no
one from the outside there. And Keith and I hit it off right
away, and waiting for Jagger and whoever else, we started
jamming. They still to this day think I'm a country piano

player. I'm not sure why, because I can barely play country music. I had a couple of licks from Floyd Cramer's stuff. But I think it was because of Gram Parsons. They had just got to be buddies with Gram, and I think Keith was kind of fascinated by country music. So we sat around that afternoon, playing Hank Williams songs and Jerry Lee Lewis songs, and they let me stay.

And as Mick was singing "Brown Sugar," the pickup line into the refrain was different in every verse. I was in the control room with Stanley, and I said, Stanley, he's leaving out a great line. And right then, I heard this voice come from behind the console where there was a couch. Charlie Watts was sitting there, and I hadn't seen him in the room or I wouldn't have said it. And Charlie says, tell him! And I said, I'm not going to tell him! And Charlie reaches over to the console, punches the talk-back button and he says, tell him! So I said, OK... Mick, you're leaving a line out. You were singing "hear him whip the women just around midnight" in the first verse. Which is a great line. And Jagger kind of halfway laughed and said, oh yeah, who said that, is that Booth? And Charlie Watts said, no, it's Dickinson. And Jagger said, same thing. I'm not sure what he meant by that. I guess just another wise-ass southern guy. So if I have a footnote to rock-and-roll history, that's it, because by God, "hear him whip the women" is in there because of me.

Dickinson was a beautiful piano player. Probably at the time I did take him for a country player, just because he was a southern guy. I found out later he was far more wide-ranging. Playing with guys like that was a break because you got stuck in this "star" thing, and there were all these musicians you'd heard about and wanted to play with but you never got the chance to. So working with Dickinson, and just getting the feel, really, of the South, and the way we were automatically accepted down south, was wonderful. They'd say, you're from London? How the hell do you play like that?

Jim Dickinson, who was the only other musician there apart from the Rolling Stones and Ian Stewart, was perplexed when on the third day we started running through "Wild Horses" and Ian Stewart took a backseat. "Wild Horses" started in a B-minor chord, and Stu didn't play minor chords, "fucking Chinese music." That's how Dickinson got the gig of playing on the track.

"Wild Horses" almost wrote itself. It was really a lot to do with, once again, fucking around with the tunings. I found these chords, especially doing it on a twelve-string to start with, which gave the song this character and sound. There's a certain forlornness that can come out of a twelve-string. I started off, I think, on a regular six-string open E, and it sounded very nice, but sometimes you just get these ideas. What if I open tuned a twelve-string? All it meant was trans-late what Mississippi Fred McDowell was doing — twelve-string slide — into five-string mode, which meant a ten-string guitar. I now have a couple custom built for that. It was one of those magical moments when things come together. It's like "Satisfaction." You just dream it, and suddenly it's all in your hands. Once you've got the vision in your mind of wild horses, I mean, what's the next phrase you're going to use? It's got to be "couldn't drag me away." That's one of the great things about songwriting; it's not an intellectual experience. One might have to apply the brain here and there, but basically it's capturing moments. Jim Dickinson, bless him — he died August 15, 2009, while I was writing this book — will say later on what "Wild Horses" was "about." I'm not sure. I never thought about songwriting as writing a diary, although sometimes in retrospect you realize that some of it is like that.

What is it that makes you want to write songs? In a way you want to stretch yourself into other people's hearts. You want to plant your-self there, or at least get a resonance, where other people become a bigger instrument than the one you're playing. It becomes almost an obsession to touch other people. To write a song that is remembered and taken to heart is a connection, a touching of bases. A thread that runs through all of us. A stab to the heart. Sometimes I think songwriting is about tightening the heartstrings as much as possible without bringing on a heart attack.

Dickinson reminded me of the speed with which we did things in those days. We were well rehearsed from being on the road. Nevertheless, he remembered that both "Brown Sugar" and "Wild Horses" were done in two takes—unheard of later, when I would comb through forty or fifty versions of a song, looking for the spark. The thing about eight-track was it was punch in and go. And it was a perfect format for the Stones. You walk into that studio and you know where the drums are going to be and what they sound like. Soon after that, there were sixteen and then twenty-four tracks, and everyone was scrambling around these huge desks. It made it much more difficult to make records. The canvas becomes enormous, and it becomes much harder to focus. Eight-track is my preferable means of recording a four-, five-, six-piece band.

Here's one last observation from Jim on that in some ways historic recording session, since we're still playing those same songs:

> **Jim Dickinson:** They started running down "Brown Sugar" the first night, but they didn't get a take. I watched Mick write the lyrics. It took him maybe forty-five minutes; it was disgusting. He wrote it down as fast as he could move his hand. I'd never seen anything like it. He had one of those yellow legal pads, and he'd write a verse a page, just write a verse and then turn the page, and when he had three pages filled, they started to cut it. It was amazing!
>
> If you listen to the lyrics, he says, "Skydog slaver" (though it's always written "scarred old slaver"). What does that mean? Skydog is what they called Duane Allman in Muscle Shoals, because he was high all the time. And Jagger heard somebody

say it and he thought it was a cool word so he used it. He was writing about literally being in the South. It was amazing to watch him do it. The same thing happened with "Wild Horses." Keith had "Wild Horses" written as a lullaby. It was about Marlon, about not wanting to leave home because he'd just had a son. And Jagger rewrote it, and it's, perceptibly, about Marianne Faithfull, and Jagger was like a high school kid about it and he wrote the song about her. He took a little more time with it, but not much more, maybe an hour.

The way he did it, Keith had some words and then he grunted and he groaned. And somebody asked Mick, do you understand that? And Jagger looked at him and said, of course. It was like he was translating, you know?

They were unbelievable, the raw vocals. They both stood at the microphone together with the fifth of bourbon, passing it back and forth, and sang the lead and the harmony into one microphone on all three songs, pretty much as quick as they could do it on the last night.

And so we went from Muscle Shoals to the Altamont Speedway, from the sublime to the ridiculous.

Altamont was strange, particularly because we were pretty laid back after touring and cutting tracks. Sure, we'll do a free concert, why not? Thank you very much, everybody. And then the Grateful Dead got involved; we invited them in because they were the ones that did this all the time. We just hooked into their pipeline and said, do you think we could put one together in the next two or three weeks? Thing is that Altamont wouldn't have been at Altamont at all if it wasn't for the absolute stupidity of the boneheaded, hard-nosed San Francisco council. We were going to put it on in their version of Central Park. They'd put the stage up, and then they'd withdrawn the license, the permits, and they'd torn it down. And then it was, oh, you can have this joint. And we were in Alabama somewhere, cutting records, so we said, well, we'll leave it to you guys and we'll turn up and play.

So it ended up that the only place left was this speedway track in Altamont, which is way, way beyond the boondocks. No security whatsoever except for the Hells Angels, if you can call that secure. But it was '69 and there was a lot of rampant anarchy. Policemen were very thin on the ground. I think I saw three cops for half a million people. I've no doubt there were a few more, but their presence was minimal.

Basically it was one huge commune that sprang out of the ground for two days. It was very medieval in look and feel, guys with bells on, chanting, "Hashish, peyote." You can see it all in *Gimme Shelter*. A culmination of hippie commune and what can happen when it goes wrong. I was amazed that things didn't go more wrong than they did.

Meredith Hunter was murdered. Three others died accidentally. With a show that size sometimes the body count is four or five people trampled or suffocated. Look at the Who, playing a totally legit gig, and eleven people died. But at Altamont it was the dark side of human nature, what could happen in the heart of darkness, a descent to cave-man level within a few hours, thanks to Sonny Barger and his lot, the Angels. And bad red wine. It was Thunderbird and Ripple, the worst fucking rotgut wines there are, and bad acid. It was the end of the dream as far as I was concerned. There was such a thing as flower power, not that we saw much of it, but the drive for it was there. And I've no doubt that living in Haight-Ashbury from '66 to '70, and even beyond, was pretty cool. Everybody got along and it was a different way of doing things. But America was so extreme, veering between Quaker and the next minute free love, and it's still like that. And now the mood was antiwar, and basically leave us alone, we just want to get high.

When Stanley Booth and Mick went back to the hotel after we'd walked the grounds at Altamont, I stayed. It was an interesting environment. I'm not going to go back to the Sheraton and then come back here tomorrow. I'm here for the duration; that's the way I felt. I've got how many hours to tune in to what's happening here. It was fascinating. You could feel it in the air, that anything could happen. California being what it is, it was pretty nice during the day. But once the sun went down it got really cold. And then a Dante's hell began to stir. There were people, hippies, trying desperately to be nice. There was almost a desperation about love and "come on," trying to make it work, trying to make it feel right.

That was where the Angels certainly didn't help. They had their own agenda, which was basically to get as out of it as possible. Hardly an organized security force. Some of those guys, their eyes are rolling, they're chewing their lips. And the deliberate provocation of parking their choppers in front of the stage. Because you can't touch an Angel's chopper, apparently. It's absolutely verboten. They put up a barrier of their Harleys and defied people to touch them. And with the crowd pressing forward it was unavoidable. If you watch *Gimme Shelter,* one Angel face says it all. He's basically foaming at the mouth, he's got tattoos, the leathers and the ponytail, and he's just waiting for somebody to touch his chopper so he can go to work. They were pretty tooled up — the cut-off pool sticks, and they were all carrying knives, of course, but then so was I. But whether you pull it out and use it is another thing. It's the last resort.

As the evening went dark and we went on stage, the atmosphere became very lurid and hairy. As Stu said — he was there — "Getting a bit hairy, Keith." I said, "We've got to brass it out, Stu." Such a big crowd, we could only see in front of our immediate circle, with lights, which are already in your eyes, because stage lights always are. So you're virtually half blinded; you can't see and judge everything that's going on. You just keep your fingers crossed.

Well, what can you do? The Stones are playing, what can I threaten you with? "We're not playing." I said, "Calm down or we ain't going to play no more." What's the point of traipsing your ass all the way out here and not seeing anything? But by then certain things were set.

It wasn't long after that before the shit hit the fan. In the film you can see Meredith Hunter waving a pistol and you can see the stabbing. He had a pale lime green suit on and a hat. He was foaming at the mouth too; he was as nuts as the rest. To wave a shooter in front of the Angels was like, well, that's what they're waiting for! That's the trigger. I doubt the thing was loaded, but he wanted to be flash. Wrong place, wrong time.

When it happened, nobody knew he'd been stabbed to death. The show went on. Gram was there too, he was playing that day with the Burritos. We all piled into this overloaded chopper. It was like getting back from any other gig. Thank God we got out of there, because it *was* hairy, though we were used to hairy escapes. This one was just on a bigger scale in a place we didn't know. But it was no hairier than getting out of the Empress Ballroom in Blackpool. In actual fact, if it hadn't been for the murder, we'd have thought it a very smooth gig by the skin of its fucking teeth. It was also the first time "Brown Sugar" was played to a live audience—a baptism from hell, in a confused rumble in the Californian night. Nobody knew what had happened until we'd gotten back to the hotel later or even the next morning.

Mick Taylor being in the band on that '69 tour certainly sealed the Stones together again. So we did *Sticky Fingers* with him. And the music changed—almost unconsciously. You write with Mick Taylor in mind, maybe without realizing it, knowing he can come up with something different. You've got to give him something he'll really enjoy. Not just the same old grind—which is what he was getting with John Mayall's Bluesbreakers. So you keep looking for ways. Hopefully turning the musicians on translates into turning the audience on. Some of the *Sticky Fingers* compositions were rooted in the fact that I knew Taylor was going to pull something great. By the time we got back to England, we had "Sugar," we had "Wild Horses" and "You Gotta Move." The rest we recorded at Mick's house, Stargroves, on our new "Mighty Mobile" recording studio, and some at Olympic Studios in March and April 1970. "Can't You Hear Me Knocking" came out flying—I just found the tuning and the riff and started to swing it and Charlie picked up on it just like that, and we're thinking, hey, this is some groove. So it was smiles all around. For a guitar player it's no big deal to play, the chopping, staccato bursts of chords, very direct and spare. Marianne had a lot to do with "Sister Morphine." I know Mick's writing, and he was living with Marianne at the time, and I know from the style of it there were a few Marianne lines in there. "Moonlight Mile" was all Mick's. As far as I can remember, Mick came in with the whole idea of that, and the band just figured out how to play it. And Mick can write! It's unbelievable how prolific he was. Sometimes you'd wonder how to turn the fucking tap off. The odd times he would come out with so many lyrics, you're crowding the airwaves, boy. I'm not complaining. It's a beautiful thing to be able to do. It's not like writing poetry or just writing down lyrics. It's got to fit what has already been created. That's what a lyricist is—a guy that has been given a piece of music and then sets up how the vocals are going to go. And Mick is brilliant at that.

Around now we started to gather musicians to play on tracks, the so-called supersidemen, some of whom are still around. Nicky Hopkins had been there almost since the beginning; Ry Cooder had come and almost gone. On *Sticky Fingers* we linked up again with Bobby Keys, the great Texan saxophone player, and his partner Jim Price. We'd met Bobby very briefly, the first time since our first US tour, at Elektra Studios when he was recording with Delaney & Bonnie. Jimmy Miller was working there on *Let It Bleed* and called Bobby in to play a solo on "Live with Me." The track was just raw, straight-ahead, balls-to-the-wall rock and roll, tailor-made for Bobby. A long collaboration was born. He and Price put some horns on the end of "Honky

Tonk Women," but they're mixed down so low you can only hear them in the very last second and a half on the fade. Chuck Berry had a saxophone just for the very end of "Roll Over Beethoven." We loved that idea of another instrument coming in just for the last second.

Keys and Price came over to England to play some sessions with Clapton and George Harrison, and Mick bumped into them in a nightclub. So it was get 'em while they're here. They were a hot section and Mick felt that we needed a horn section, and it was all right with me. The Texan bulldog gave me a look. "We've played before," he Texaned. "We have? Where?" "San Antonio Teen Fair." "Oh, you were there?" "Damn fucking right." Then and there I said, screw it, and let's rock. A huge warm grin, a handshake to crush a rock. You're a motherfucker! Bobby Keys! That was the session in December '69 when Bobby blew his stuff on "Brown Sugar"—as much a blast for the times as anything else on the airwaves.

I did a couple of cleanups with Gram Parsons at this time—both unsuccessful. I've been through more cold turkeys than there are freezers. I took the fucking hell week as a matter of course. I took it as being a part of what I was into. But cold turkey, once is enough, and it should be, quite honestly. At the same time I felt totally invincible. And also I was a bit antsy about people telling me what I could put in my body.

I always felt that no matter how stoned I was, as far as I was concerned, I could cover what I was doing. And I was bigheaded in that I thought I could control heroin. I thought I could take it or leave it. But it is far more seductive than you think, because you can take it or leave it for a while, but every time you try and leave it, it gets a little harder. You can't, unfortunately, decide the moment when you've got to leave it. The taking of it is easy, the leaving of it hard, and you never want to be in that position when suddenly someone bursts in and says, come with me, and you realize that you've got to leave it, and you're in no condition to go to the police station and start cold turkey. You've got to think about that and say, hey, there's one simple way of never being in that position. Don't take it.

But there's probably a million different reasons you do. I think it's maybe to do with working on the stage. The high levels of energy and adrenaline require, if you can find it, a sort of antidote. And I saw smack as just becoming part of that. Why do you do it to yourself? I never particularly liked being that famous. I could face people easier on the stuff, but I could do that with booze too. It isn't really the whole answer. I also felt I was doing it not to be a "pop star." There was something I didn't really like about that end of what I was doing, the blah blah blah. That was very difficult to handle, and I could handle it better on smack. Mick chose flattery, which is very like junk—a departure from reality. I chose junk. And also I was with my old lady Anita, who was as avid as I was. I think we just wanted to explore that avenue. And when we did, we only meant to explore the first few blocks, but we explored it to the end.

Off of Bill Burroughs, I got apomorphine, along with Smitty, the vicious nurse from Cornwall. The cure that Gram Parsons and I did was total anti-heroin aversion therapy. And Smitty loved to administer it. "Time, boys." There's Parsons and me in my bed, "Oh no, here comes Smitty." Gram and I needed to take a cure just before the farewell tour of 1971, when he and his soon-to-be wife, Gretchen, came over to England and we went about our usual ways. Bill Burroughs recommended this hideous woman to administer the apomorphine that Burroughs talked endlessly about, a therapy that was pretty useless. But Burroughs swore by it. I didn't know him that well, except to talk about dope—how to get off or how to get the quality you're after. Smitty was Burroughs's favorite nurse and she was a sadist and the cure consisted of her shooting you up with this shit and then standing over you. You do as you're told. You don't argue. "Stop sniveling, boy. You wouldn't be here if you hadn't screwed up." We took this cure in Cheyne Walk, and it was Gram and me in my four-poster bed, the only guy I ever slept with. Except that we kept falling off the bed because we were twitching so much from the treatment. With a bucket to throw up in, if you could stop twitching for enough seconds to get near it. "You got the bucket, Gram?" Our only outlet, if we could stand up, would be to go down and play the piano and sing for a bit, or as much as possible to kill time. I wouldn't recommend that cure to anybody. I wondered if that was Bill Burroughs's joke, to send me to probably the worst cure he'd ever had.

It didn't work. It's a long seventy-two hours, and you've been shitting yourself and pissing yourself and twitching and spasms. And after that, your system's washed. When you take the stuff you put all the other stuff—your endorphins—to sleep. They think, oh, he doesn't need us, because something else is in there. And they take seventy-two hours to wake up and go back to work. But usually as soon as you've finished, you go back on it. After all that, after a week of that shit, I need a fix. And there you go, the number of times I've cold turkeyed, only to go straight back on. Because the cold turkey is so rough.

The powers that be couldn't break the butterfly on the wheel, but they tried again and again at my house in Cheyne Walk in the late '60s and early '70s. I got quite used to being thrown up against my own doorposts, coming home from a club at three in the morning. Just as I reached my front gate, out of the bushes would leap these people with truncheons. Oh OK, here we go again, assume the position. "Up against the wall, Keith." That fake familiarity annoyed me. They wanted to see you cringe, but I've been there, pal. "Oh, it's the Flying Squad!" "We're not flying as high as you, Keith," and all that bullshit. They wouldn't have a warrant, but they were playing their own game.

"Oh, I've got you this time, my boy, flash ol' sod"—their glee in thinking they'd pinned me. "Oh, what have we got here, Keith?" and I know I've got nothing on me. They come on heavy because they want to see if they can make a big rock-and-roll star quiver in his boots. You'll have to do better than that. Let's see how far you want to go. Officers walking in and out and looking at bits of paper, confused as to what's going to happen when the newspapers hear that I've been pulled in again, and wondering whether Detective Constable Constable has made the right move tonight in his fervor to clear the world of junkie guitarists.

It was also a real drag to wake up every day with these bluebottles around your door, these bobbies, to wake up realizing you're a criminal. And you start to think like one. The difference between waking up in the morning and saying, "Oh, nice day," and peering through the curtains to see if the unmarked cars are still parked outside. Or waking up grateful that during the night there wasn't a knock at the door. What a mind-bending distraction. We're not destroying the virtue of the nation, but they think we are, so eventually we're drawn into a war.

It was Chrissie Gibbs who linked Mick up with Rupert Loewenstein when it was clear that we had to try and sever ourselves from the wiles of Allen Klein. Rupert was a merchant banker, very pukka, trustworthy, and although I didn't actually get to speak to him for about a year after he started working for us, I got on well with him from then on. He discovered I liked reading, and one book led to a library's worth over the years, sent by Rupert.

Rupert didn't like rock and roll; he thought "composing" was something done with a pen and paper, like Mozart. He'd never even heard of Mick Jagger when Chrissie first talked to him. We brought seven lawsuits against Allen Klein over seventeen years, and eventually it was a farce, with both sides waving and chatting in the courtroom — like a normal day at the office. So Rupert at least learned the jargon of the business, even if he never got emotionally involved in the music.

It had taken us a while to discover what Allen Klein had helped himself to and what wasn't ours anymore. We had a company in the UK called Nanker Phelge Music, which was a company we all shared in. So we get to New York and sign this deal to a company into which everything is to be channeled henceforth, also called Nanker Phelge, which we presume is our same company with an American name,

Nanker Phelge USA. Of course after a while we discovered that Klein's company in America bore no relation to Nanker Phelge UK and was wholly owned by Klein. So all the money was going to Nanker Phelge USA. When Mick was trying to buy his house on Cheyne Walk, he couldn't get the money out of Allen Klein for eighteen months because Allen was trying to buy MGM.

Klein was a lawyer manqué; he loved the letter of the law and loved the fact that justice and the law had nothing to do with each other; it was a game for him. He ended up owning the copyright and the master tapes of all our work — anything written or recorded in the time of our contract with Decca, which was to end in 1971. But it ended in fact with *'Get Yer Ya-Ya's Out!'* in 1970. So Klein owned unfinished and uncompleted songs up to the '71 limit, and that was the tricky part. The fight was about whether the songs between that record and '71 belonged to him. In the end we conceded two songs, "Angie" and "Wild Horses." He got the publishing of years of our songs and we got a cut of the royalties.

He still owns the publishing to "Satisfaction" too, or his heirs do; he died in 2009. But I don't give a shit. He was an education. Whatever he did, he blew us up the river, he put it together, although "Satisfaction" certainly helped at that moment. I've made more money by giving up the publishing on "Satisfaction," and my idea has never been to make money. Originally it was, do we make enough to pay for the guitar strings? And then later on, do we make enough to put on the kind of show we want to put on? I'd say the same about Charlie, and Mick too. Especially initially, hey, we don't mind making the money, but most of it's plowed back into what it is we want to do. So the basic flavor of it is that Allen Klein made us and screwed us at the same time.

Marshall Chess, who climbed the ladder from the mail room to become president of Chess after his father died, had just sold the company and was looking to start a new label. Together we founded Rolling Stones Records in 1971 and made a deal with Atlantic Records to distribute, which is where Ahmet Ertegun came in. Ahmet! An elegant Turk who with his brother, Nesuhi, drove the music business into a total re-think of what it was that people could hear. The echoes of the Stones' idealism (juvenile as it was) resonated. Shit, I miss the mother. The last time I saw him was backstage at the Beacon Theatre in New York. "Where's the fucking john?" I showed him the way. He snapped the lock. I went on stage. After the show I found out he had slipped on the tiles. He never recovered. I loved the man. Ahmet encouraged talent. He was very much hands-on. It wasn't like an EMI or a Decca, some huge conglomerate. That company was born and built up out of love of music, not business. Jerry Wexler too, it was a whole team, a family thing in a way. Need I go through the roster? Aretha...Ray...too many to mention. You felt like you'd joined the elite.

But in 1970 we had a problem.

We were in the ludicrous situation where Klein would be lending us money that we could never afford to repay because he hadn't paid the tax and anyway we'd spent the money. The tax rate in the early '70s on the highest earners was 83 percent, and that went up to 98 percent for investments and so-called unearned income. So that's the same as being told to leave the country.

And I take my hat off to Rupert for figuring a way out of massive debt for us. It was Rupert's advice that we become nonresident—the only way we could ever get back on our feet financially.

The last thing I think the powers that be expected when they hit us with super-super tax is that we'd say, fine, we'll leave. We'll be another one not paying tax to you. They just didn't factor that in. It made us bigger than ever, and it produced *Exile on Main St.,* which was maybe the best thing we did. They didn't believe we'd be able to continue as we were if we didn't live in England. And in all honesty, we were very doubtful too. We didn't know if we would make it, but if we didn't try, what would we do? Sit in England and they'd give us a penny out of every pound we earned? We had no desire to be closed down. And so we upped and went to France.

*Dominique Tarlé*

# Chapter Eight

In which we leave for France in spring of 1971 and I rent Nellcôte, a
house on the Riviera. Mick gets married in Saint-Tropez. We set up
our mobile truck to record *Exile on Main St.* and settle into a prolific
nighttime recording schedule. We motorboat to Italy for breakfast in
the *Mandrax.* I hit my stride on the five-string guitar. Gram Parsons
comes and Mick gets possessive. I insulate myself with drugs; we get
busted. I hang out for the last time with Gram in LA and get badly
hooked on second-rate dope. I flee to Switzerland with Anita for a
cure, undergo cold-turkey horrors and compose "Angie" while
recovering.

When I first saw Nellcôte, I thought that I could probably
handle a spell of exile. It was the most amazing house,
right at the base of Cap Ferrat, looking out over Villefranche Bay. It
had been built around the 1890s by an English banker, with a large
garden, a little overgrown, behind the great iron gates. The proportions were superb. If you felt a little ragged in the morning, you could
walk through this glittering château and feel restored. It was like a
hall of mirrors, with twenty-foot ceilings and marble columns, grand
staircases. I'd wake up thinking, this is my house? Or, about bloody
time someone's got it right. This was the grandeur we felt we deserved
after the shabbiness of Britain. And since we'd committed ourselves
to living abroad, how hard really was it to sit in Nellcôte? We'd been
on the road forever, and Nellcôte was a lot better than the Holiday

Inn! I think everybody felt a sense of liberation compared to what had been going on in England.

It was never our intention to record at Nellcôte. We were going to look around for studios in Nice or Cannes, even though the logistics were a little daunting. Charlie Watts had taken a house miles away in the Vaucluse, several hours' drive. Bill Wyman was up in the hills, near Grasse. He was soon hanging out with Marc Chagall, of all people. The most unlikely couple I can think of, Bill Wyman and Marc Chagall. Neighbors, pop round for a cup of Bill's terrible tea. Mick lived first in the Byblos hotel in Saint-Tropez while he waited for his wedding day, then rented a house belonging to Prince Rainier's uncle and then a house owned by someone called Madame Tolstoy. Talk about falling in with the cultural Euro trash, or they with the white trash. They, at least, welcomed us with open arms.

One of the features of Nellcôte was a little staircase down to a jetty, to which I soon attached the *Mandrax 2,* a very powerful twenty-foot motorboat, a Riva, built of mahogany, the crème de la crème of Italian speedboats. *Mandrax* was an anagram of its original name; all I had to do was knock off a couple of letters and move a couple around. It was irresistible to call it that. I bought it off a guy, renamed it and set off. No skipper's license or pilot's license. There wasn't even the formal "Have you ever been on the water before?" Now I'm told you have to take exams to drive a boat in the Mediterranean. It required the companionship of Bobby Keys, not long coming, Gram Parsons and others to put the *Mandrax* to the test on the glassy Mediterranean, to strike out for the Riviera and adventure. But this was later. First there was the matter of Mick's wedding to Bianca, his Nicaraguan fiancée, which came up in May, four weeks after our arrival. Marianne had gone from his life in 1970, the previous year, and into the beginning of a lost decade.

Mick arranged what he saw as a quiet wedding, for which he chose Saint-Tropez at the height of the season. No journalist stayed at home. In these presecurity days, the couple and the guests wrestled their way through the streets against photographers and tourists, from the church to the mayor's office — hand-to-hand combat, like trying to get to the bar in a rowdy club. I slid off, leaving Bobby Keys, who was a close friend of Mick's in those days, to act as assistant best man or whatever. Roger Vadim was best man.

Bobby's role is mentioned here because Bianca's bridesmaid was the very pretty Nathalie Delon, estranged wife of the French movie star Alain Delon, and Bobby took a great and dangerous fancy to her. She and Delon had been in the center of a scandal that had embroiled the French prime minister Georges Pompidou and his wife, as well as the crime underworld from Marseilles to Paris. Delon's Yugoslav bodyguard, with whom Nathalie had had a brief affair, had been shot, his body found in a garbage dump on the outskirts of Paris. No one was ever convicted of killing him. Delon had left Nathalie and taken up with the actress Mireille Darc. It was a big mess and wrapped in considerable danger. Behind Delon and Nathalie were powerful figures from the Marseilles milieu a few miles down the road, as well as a band of Yugoslav toughs. There was clearly a lot of bad feeling and some major political blackmail flying about — Nathalie herself had had the wheels loosened on her car. Not a great moment, maybe, to become her new beau.

Bobby, knowing nothing of all this, developed an instant fascination with Nathalie and blew his heart out at the party that night to attract her attention. He couldn't take his eyes off her. He went back to London before returning to work on the music at Nellcôte. And when he got back, Nathalie was still there, staying with Bianca. What happened then? Well, they're both still alive as I write, but I'm not sure why. Weeks would pass before that trouble became real.

When I slid off at the wedding, it was towards a cubicle in the john of the Byblos, and I'm taking a leak and in the next cubicle I hear sniffing. "Keep it down," I say, "or break it out." And a voice comes back, "Want some?" And that's how I met Brad Klein, who became a great friend of mine. His forte was transshipment, rerouting dope from here to there. He was a very well-educated, clean-cut-looking boy and used this persona to brass his way through. He did get into dealing coke later and got more involved than he should have, but when I met him it was the smoke. Brad's dead now. It was the usual old story. If you're dealing in this shit, don't dabble in it. He dabbled and he always wanted to stay in the game a little longer. But on that day of our meeting, Brad and I went off together to hang and left the wedding to itself.

I only got to know the qualities of Bianca later on. Mick never wants me to talk to his women. They end up crying on my shoulder because they've found out that he has once again philandered. What am I gonna do? Well, it's a long ride to the airport, honey; let me think about it. The tears that have been on this shoulder from Jerry Hall, from Bianca, from Marianne, Chrissie Shrimpton ... They've ruined so many shirts of mine. And they ask *me* what to do! How the hell do I know? I don't fuck him! I had Jerry Hall come to me one day with this note from some other chick that was written backwards — really good code, Mick! — "I'll be your mistress forever." And all you had to do was hold it up to a mirror to read it. "Oh, what a bastard that guy is." And I'm in the most unlikely role of consoler, "Uncle Keith." It's a side a lot of people don't connect with me.

At first I thought Bianca was just some bimbo. She was also quite aloof for a while, which didn't endear her to anybody around us. But as I got to know her, I discovered that she's bright and, what really impressed me later on, a strong lady. She became a mouthpiece for Amnesty International and a sort of roving ambassador for her own human-rights organization, which is some achievement. Very pretty and everything like that, but a very forceful character. No wonder Mick couldn't handle it. The only drawback was that she was never one for a joke. I'm still trying to think of something to make her laugh. If she'd had a sense of humor, *I'd* have married her!

Mick's taking up with Bianca did coincide with our leaving England. So there was a definite schism in place already, a fault line.

Bianca brought with her a whole load of baggage and society that Mick got into that nobody else was at all interested in and I've no doubt Bianca by now is no longer interested in either. Even then I had nothing against her personally, it was just the effect of her and her milieu on Mick that I didn't like. It distanced him from the rest of the band, and Mick's always looking to separate himself from the band. Mick would disappear for two weeks on vacation; he would commute from Paris. Bianca was pregnant, and their daughter, Jade, was born in the fall, when Bianca was in Paris. Bianca didn't like Nellcôte life, and I don't blame her. So Mick was torn.

In those early days at Nellcôte we'd do our promenades down by the harbors, or to the Café Albert in Villefranche, where Anita would drink her pastis. We were obviously conspicuous in those parts, but we were also pretty hardened and unworried by what people thought. Violence happens when you least expect it, though. Spanish Tony, who came down early on, saved my life a couple of times — either literally or not — and in the town of Beaulieu, on one of those outings near Nellcôte, he saved my hide. I had an E-Type Jaguar that I drove down to Beaulieu harbor with Marlon and Tony aboard and parked in what was pointed out to us — by what appeared to be two harbor officials — as the wrong place. One came across and said, "Ici," beckoning me and Tony into the harbor office, so Tony and I wandered over, leaving Marlon in the car for what we imagined would be a couple of minutes, and we could see him.

Tony smelled it before I did. Two French fishermen, older guys. One had his back to us. He was locking the door, and Tony looked at me. He just said, "Watch my back." He moved like a flash, shoved a chair into my hand, jumped on the table with another chair and tore into them, splinters everywhere. These guys were wined out of their heads; they'd had a big lunch, some of it still on the table. I just trod on the neck of one of them while Tony did the other one in. Then Tony came back for my one, who was scared shitless, so Tony gave him another smack around the head. "Let's get out of here." Kicked the door open. It was over in a matter of seconds. They're on the floor moaning and whining, claret everywhere, broken furniture. The last thing they were expecting was an assault—they were big sailors, no pussyfooting, and they were going to fuck around with us, slap us about. They were planning to have some fun with the longhairs. Marlon's sitting in the Jaguar. "Where you been, Dad?" "Don't worry about it." *Vroom vroom.* "Let's go." What moves from Spanish Tony. It was a ballet; it was his finest moment. That day Douglas Fairbanks had nothing on him. It was the swiftest move that I've seen happen, and I've seen a few. I took a lot of leaves out of Tony's book that day — when you smell that trouble coming, act. Don't wait for it to start.

Three days later, cops turned up at the house. They had warrants on me only, because Tony wasn't known and had gone back to England by now. A whole lot of rigmarole went down with examining magistrates, but by the time it got to the second or third level, they realized that these guys didn't have a leg to stand on. When the facts came out that they'd intimidated us, that I'd had a child in the car, that there was no reason for us to be hauled into the office in the first place, suddenly, miraculously, the charges wafted away. I've no doubt it cost me a bit of money with the lawyer, but in the end, these guys chose not to get up in court and say they'd been done in their own office by two insane Englishmen.

I was not totally clean when I got to Nellcôte. But there's a difference between being not clean and being hooked. Hooked is when you're not going to do anything until you get your hands on the stuff. All your energy goes into that. I'd brought a small maintenance dose with me, but as far as I was concerned, I'd just cleaned up. Sometime in May, not that long after our arrival, we went to a go-kart track in Cannes, where my car flipped over on me and rushed me fifty yards down the tarmac on my back, stripping off my skin like bark. I scraped it almost to the bone. And this when I was just about to make a record. All I needed. I was advised by the doctor, "This is going to be very painful, monsieur. The wound must be kept clean. I'll send a nurse to you every day to dress it and check it." There arrived each morning a male nurse who had been a frontline medic for the French army. He'd been at Dien Bien Phu, the last stand of the French army in Indochina; he'd been in Algeria; he'd seen plentiful blood, and his style was accordingly robust. Little wizened guy, hard as nails. He gave me a shot of morphine each day, and I needed morphine badly. Each time, after he'd fixed me, he would throw the syringe as a dart, always at the same spot, at a painting, right in the eye. Then of course the treatment stopped. But now I'm on the morphine because of this wound, just when I'd cleaned up off the dope. So, first things first, I need some shit.

Fat Jacques was our cook, who now doubled as the heroin dealer. He was the Marseilles connection. He had a bunch of sidekicks, this team of cowboys who we decided were safer on the payroll than off it, who were good at running "errands." Jacques emerged because I said, "Who knows how to get some shit around here?" He was young, he was fat and he was sweaty, and one day he went to Marseilles on the train and he brought back this lovely little bag of white powder and this huge supply, almost the size of a cement bag, of lactose, which was the cut. And he explained to me in his bad English and my even worse French—he had to write it down—mix ninety-seven percent lactose with three percent heroin. This heroin was pure. Normally when you bought it it was premixed. But this stuff you had to mix very precisely. Even at these proportions, it was incredibly powerful. And so I'd be in the bathroom with these scales, going ninety-seven to three; I was scrupulous in my weighing out. You had to be careful; the old lady was taking it and a couple of other people. Ninety-six to four and you could croak on it. One hit of it pure and *boom*. Good-bye.

There were obvious advantages to buying in such quantity. The price was not phenomenal. It was coming straight from Marseilles to Villefranche, just down the road. There were no transport costs, just Jacques's train ticket. The more times you have to score, the more things are likely to screw up. But you also have to really try not to overdo it, because the bigger the score, the more people are interested. Just get enough to get settled for a couple of months, so you don't have to go out and scrabble around for it. This bag, however, never seemed to disappear. "Well, once we finish this bag we can straighten out...." Let's put it this way: it lasted from June to November, and we still left some behind.

I had to trust the orders that came with it. And they must have been correct, because every time I tried it, it was perfectly fine, and no one complained. I posted the formula on the wall so I wouldn't forget it. Ninety-seven to three. (Of course I thought of writing a song with that title, but then I thought there was no point advertising myself.) I would be up there half the afternoon getting it right. I had these great old scales, big brass things, very, very fine, and this big scoop for the lactose. Ninety-seven grams. Put that aside and then you take a little spoon out of the heroin bag, three grams. Then you put the two together and mix 'em up. You've got to shake it. I remember being up there often, so I didn't ever mix a lot together at once. I would do a couple of days' worth, or a little more.

We looked at studios in Cannes and elsewhere, reckoned up how much money the French were going to suck out of us. Nellcôte had a large basement and we had our own mobile studio. The Mighty Mobile, as we called it, was a truck with eight-track recording machines that Stu had helped to put together. We'd thought of it quite separately from any plan to move to France. It was the only independent mobile recording unit around. We didn't realize when we put it together how rare it was—soon we were renting it out to the BBC and ITV because they only had one apiece. It was another one of those beautiful, graceful, fortuitous things that happened to the Stones.

So one day in June it trundled through the gates and we parked it outside the front door and plugged in. I've never done any different since. When you've got the equipment and the right guys, you don't need anything else in terms of studios. Only Mick still thinks you have to take things into "real" recording studios to really make a real record. He got proved totally wrong on our latest — at the time of writing — album, *A Bigger Bang,* especially, because we did it all in his little château in France. We had got the stuff worked up, and he said, "Now we'll take it into a real recording studio." And Don Was and I looked at each other, and Charlie looked at me. . . . Fuck this shit. We've already got it down right here. Why do you want to spring for all that bread? So you can say it was cut in so-and-so studio, the glass wall and the control room? We ain't going nowhere, pal. So finally he relented.

The basement in Nellcôte was big enough, but it was divided into a series of bunkers. Not a great deal of ventilation — hence "Ventilator Blues." The weirdest thing was trying to find out where you'd left the saxophone player. Bobby Keys and Jim Price moved around to where they could get their sound right — mostly standing with their backs to the wall at the end of a narrow corridor, where Dominique Tarlé took one of his pictures of them with microphone cables snaking away around the corner. Eventually we ended up painting the microphone cable to the horn section yellow. If you wanted to talk to the horns, you followed the yellow cable until you found them. You wouldn't know where the hell you were. It was an enormous house. Sometimes Charlie would be in a room, and I'd have to tramp a quarter of a mile to find him. But considering that it was basically a dungeon, it was fun to work there.

All the characteristics of that basement were discovered by the other guys. For the first week or so we didn't know where Charlie was set up because he'd be trying different cubicles every night. Jimmy Miller encouraged him to try down the end of the corridor, but Charlie said, I'm half a mile down the damn road, it's too far away, I need to be closer. So we had to check out every little cubicle. You didn't want to add electronic echo unless you had to; you wanted natural echo, and down there you found some really weird ones. I played guitar in a room with tiles, turning the amp round and pointing it at the corner of the room to see what got picked up on the microphone. I remember doing that for "Rocks Off" and maybe "Rip This Joint." But as weird as it was to record there, especially at the beginning, by the time we were into it, within a week or two, it was totally natural. There was no talk amongst the band or with Jimmy Miller or the engineer Andy Johns, "what a weird way to make a record." No, we've got it. All we've got to do is persevere.

We would record from late in the afternoon until five or six in the morning, and suddenly the dawn comes up and I've got this boat. Go down the steps through the cave to the dockside; let's take *Mandrax* to Italy for breakfast. We'd just jump in, Bobby Keys, me, Mick, whoever was up for it. Most days we would go down to Menton, an Italian town just inside France by some quirk of treaty making, or just beyond it to Italy proper. No passport, right past Monte Carlo as the sun's coming up with music ringing in our ears. Take a cassette player and play something we've done, play that second mix. Just pull up at the wharf and have a nice Italian breakfast. We liked the way the Italians cooked their eggs, and the bread. And with the fact that you had actually crossed a border and nobody knew shit or did shit about it, there was an extra sense of freedom. We'd play the mix to the Italians, see what they thought. If we hit the fishermen at the right time, we could get red snapper straight off the boats and take it home for lunch.

We'd pull into Monte Carlo for lunch. Have a chat with either Onassis's lot or Niarchos's, who had the big yachts there. You could almost see the guns pointed at each other. That's why we called it *Exile on Main St.* When we first came up with the title it worked in American terms because everybody's got a Main Street. But our Main Street was that Riviera strip. And we were exiles, so it rang perfectly true and said everything we needed.

The whole Mediterranean coast was an ancient connection of its own, a kind of Main Street without borders. I've hung in Marseilles, and it was all it was cracked up to be and I've no doubt it still is. It's like the capital of a country that embraces the Spanish coast, the North African coast, the whole Mediterranean coast. It's basically a country all its own until a few miles inland. Everybody that lives on the coast—fishermen, sailors, smugglers—belongs to an independent community, including the Greeks, the Turks, the Egyptians, the Tunisians, the Libyans, the Moroccans, the Algerians and the Jews. It's an old connection that can't be broken by borders and countries.

We'd piss about; we'd go to Antibes. We used to go to Saint-Tropez to score all the bitches. This boat could kick through. It had a big engine. And the Mediterranean when it's smooth is a quick ride. The summer of '71 was one of those Mediterranean summers where every day was perfect. You hardly needed to know any navigation; you'd just follow the coastline. I never had charts. Anita refused ever to board this boat on the grounds of my lack of familiarity with the submerged rocks. She would wait and watch for the distress flares as we ran out of petrol. I just figured if they could get an aircraft carrier into the damn bay, I should be able to navigate it. The only bit I did check out was the landing, the dockside. Land is always the dangerous thing for a boat. The only time I thought about the actual art of boatmanship was docking. Otherwise it was a laugh.

Villefranche harbor is very deep and was a big hang for the American navy, and one day, suddenly, there was this huge aircraft carrier in the middle of the bay. The navy on a courtesy call. They did all the flag-waving around the Mediterranean during the summer. And as we were pulling away from our dock, we got this whiff of marijuana on a large scale blowing out of the portholes. Out of their brains. I had Bobby Keys with me. So we went to have breakfast, and when we came back we circled around the aircraft carrier, and there were all these sailors there who were glad they weren't in Vietnam. And I was in my little *Mandrax*. And we sniffed. "Oh, hi, guys. I smell..." And they threw us a bag of weed. And in exchange we told them which were the best whorehouses in town. The Cocoa Bar, the Brass Ring was a good 'un.

When the fleet was in, all of these damn dark streets in Ville-franche would suddenly burst with lighting as if it were Las Vegas. It's the "Café Dakota" or the "Nevada Bar"—they'd put anything that sounded American on it: the "Texan Hang." The streets of Ville-franche would come alive with neon and fairy lights. All the bitches from Nice would come in, and Monte Carlo, all the whores from Cannes. The crew of an aircraft carrier is two thousand–odd men, randy and ready to serve. It was enough to attract the whole south coast. Otherwise, when they weren't in town, Villefranche was dead as a doornail.

It's amazing that the music we made down in that basement is still going, given that the record wasn't even that highly rated when it first came out. The *outtakes* of *Exile on Main St.* were released as part of a reissue in 2010. The music was recorded in 1971, nearly forty years ago as I write. If I had been listening to music that was forty years old in 1971, I would have been listening to stuff that was barely recordable. Maybe some early Louis Armstrong, Jelly Roll Morton. I suppose a world war in between changes the perception.

"Rocks Off," "Happy," "Ventilator Blues," "Tumbling Dice," "All Down the Line"—that's five-string, open tuning to the max. I was starting to really fix my trademark; I wrote all that stuff within a few days. Suddenly, with the five-string, songs were just dripping off my fingers. My first real exercise on five-string was "Honky Tonk Women" a couple of years before. At that time it was, well, this is interesting. There was "Brown Sugar" too, which came out the month we quit England. By the time we got to working on *Exile,* I was really starting to find all these other moves, and how to make minor chords and suspended chords. I discovered that the five-string becomes very interesting when you add a capo. This limits your room to maneuver drastically, especially if you've placed the capo up on the fifth or the seventh fret. But also it gives a certain ring, a certain resonance that can't be obtained really any other way. But it's when to use it and when not to overdo it.

If it's Mick's song to start with, I won't start it off with five-string. I'll start on a regular tuning and just learn it or feel my way around it, classico style. And then if Charlie ups the rhythm a little bit or gives it a different feel, I'll say let me put this to five-string for a moment and just see how that alters the structure of the thing. Obviously, doing that simplifies the sound, in that you're limiting yourself to a set thing. But if you find the right one, like "Start Me Up," it creates the song. I've heard millions of bands try and play "Start Me Up" with regular tuning. It just won't work, pal.

We brought a lot of stuff to Nellcôte that had been incubating for a while. I would farm out the title or the idea. "This is called 'All Down the Line,' Mick. *I hear it coming, all down the line…* Off you go." I was coming up with a couple of new songs a day. And one would work and one wouldn't. Mick kept up with the writing at this phenomenal pace — very canny rock-and-roll lyrics, with those catchy phrases and repetitions. "All Down the Line" came directly out of "Brown Sugar," which Mick wrote. Most of what I had to do was to come up with riffs and ideas that would turn Mick on. To write songs he could handle. They had to be good records but translatable to being played on stage. I was the butcher, cutting the meat. And sometimes he didn't like it. He didn't like "Rip This Joint" — it was too fast. I think we might have popped it once since then, but "Rip This Joint," in terms of beats per minute, is something like a world record. Maybe Little Richard had done something faster, but in any case, nobody was looking to beat the world record. Some of the titles of the songs we wrote that never made it onto the album are bizarre: "Head in the Toilet Blues," "Leather Jackets," "Windmill," "I Was Just a Country Boy," "Dancing in the Light." That must have been one of Mick's. "Bent Green Needles," "Labour Pains," "Pommes de Terre" — well, we were in France at the time.

We wrote "Torn and Frayed," which is not often played and has some topical interest:

*Joe's got a cough, sounds kinda rough*
*Yeah, and the codeine to fix it*
*Doctor prescribes, drugstore supplies*
*Who's gonna help him to kick it?*

Apart from "Sister Morphine" and a few odd references to coke, we never really wrote songs about drugs. They would only crop up in songs as they did in life, here and there. There were always rumors and folklore about songs, who they were written for, what they were really about. "Flash" was supposed to be about heroin, and I see the connotation, the reference to "Jack"—but "Jumpin' Jack Flash" has nothing to do with heroin. The myths go deep, though. Whatever you write, somebody is going to interpret it in some other way, see codes buried in the lyrics. That's why you have conspiracy theories. Somebody croaked. Oh, my God! Who they going to blame this one on? When the guy just keeled over! The lifeblood of good conspiracies is that you'll never find out; the lack of evidence keeps them fresh. No one's ever going to find out if I had my blood changed or not. The story is well beyond the reach of evidence or, if it never happened, my denials. But then, read on. I have stood back for many years from honestly addressing that burning topic.

"Tumbling Dice" may have had something to do with the gambling den that Nellcôte turned into—there were card games and roulette wheels. Monte Carlo was around the corner. Bobby Keys and cats did go down there once or twice. We did play dice. I credit Mick with "Tumbling Dice," but the song had to make the transition from its earlier form, which was a song called "Good Time Women." You might have all of the music, a great riff, but sometimes the subject matter is missing. It only takes one guy sitting around a room, saying, "throwing craps last night..." for a song to be born. "Got to roll me." Songs are strange things. Little notes like that. If they stick, they stick. With most of the songs I've ever written, quite honestly, I've felt there's an enormous gap here, waiting to be filled; this song should have been written hundreds of years ago. How did nobody pick up on that little space? Half the time you're looking for gaps that other people haven't done. And you say, I don't believe they've missed that fucking hole! It's so obvious. It was there staring you in the face! I pick out the holes.

I realize now that *Exile* was made under very chaotic circumstances and with innovative ways of recording, but those seemed to be the least of the problems. The most pressing problem was, do we have songs and do we get the sound? Anything else that went on was peripheral. You can hear a load of my outtakes ending, "Oh well, run out. That's the story so far." But you'd be surprised when you're put right on the ball and you've got to do something and everybody's looking at you, going, OK, what's going to happen? You put yourself up there on the firing line — give me a blindfold and a last cigarette and let's go. And you'd be surprised how much comes out of you before you die. Especially when you're fooling the rest of the band, who think you know exactly what you're going to do, and you know you're blind as a bat and have no idea. But you're just going to trust yourself. Something's going to come. You come out with one line, throw in a guitar line and then another line's got to come out. This is where supposedly your talent lies. It's not in trying to meticulously work out how to build a Spitfire.

Maybe I would crash out, if I crashed out at all, around ten in the morning, get up around four in the afternoon, subject to the usual variations. Nobody's going to arrive until sunset anyway. So then I had a couple of hours to think about or play back what we did last night so I could pick it up where we left off. Or if we had it already, it was a matter of what to do when the guys arrived a little later. And you sometimes start to panic when you realize you have nothing to offer them. It's always that feeling when these guys are expecting material as if it comes from the gods, whereas the reality is it comes from Mick or me. When you see the documentary on *Exile,* it gives an impression of jamming away spontaneously for hours in the bunker until we've got something, until we're ready to go for a take, as if we're

trusting to incoming from the ether. That's the way it's been portrayed, and some of it might have happened that way, but ask Mick.
He and I would look at each other, what do we give them today?
What ammo do we put in today, baby? Because we know everybody
is going to go along with this as long as there's a song, there's something to play. We might have occasionally lapsed and decided to overdub something we did yesterday. But basically Mick and I both felt it
was our duty to come up with a new song, a new riff, a new idea, or
two, preferably.

We were prolific. We felt then that it was impossible that we
couldn't come up with something every day or every two days. That
was what we did, and even if it was the bare bones of a riff, it was
something to go on, and then while they were trying to get the sound
on it or we were trying to shape the riff, the song would fall into place
of its own volition. Once you're on a roll with the first few chords, the
first idea of the rhythm, you can figure out other things, like does it
need a bridge in the middle, later. It was living on a knife edge as far
as that's concerned. There was no preparation. But that's not the point;
that's rock and roll. The idea is to make the bare bones of a riff, snap the
drums in and see what happens. And it was the immediacy of it that
in retrospect made it even more interesting. There was no time for too
much reflection, for plowing the field twice. It was "It goes like this"
and see what comes out. And this is when you realize that with a good
band, you only really need a little sparkle of an idea, and before the
evening's over it will be a beautiful thing.

We did dry up. "Casino Boogie" came out of when Mick and I
had just about run ourselves ragged. Mick's looking at me, and I go, I
don't know. And it came to my mind, the old Bill Burroughs cut-up
method. Let's rip headlines out of newspapers and pages out of a book
and then throw 'em on the floor and see what comes up. Hey, we're
obviously in no mood to write a song in the usual fashion, so let's use
somebody else's method. And it worked on "Casino Boogie." I'm surprised we haven't used it since, quite honestly. But at the time, it was

desperation. One phrase bounces off another, and suddenly it makes sense even though they're totally disconnected, but they have the same feel about them, which is a fair definition of writing a rock or pop lyric anyway.

*Grotesque music, million dollar sad*
*Got no tactics, got no time on hand*
*Left shoe shuffle, right shoe muffle*
*Sinking in the sand*
*Fade out freedom, steaming heat on*
*Watch that hat in black*
*Finger twitching, got no time on hand.*

I remember being a little dismayed that Charlie had decided to live three hours away. I would have loved to have Charlie around the corner so I could call him and say, got an idea; can you pop by? But the way Charlie wanted to live and where he wanted to live was in fact about 130 miles away, in the Vaucluse, above Aix-en-Provence. So he would come down from Monday till Friday. So then I had him there, but I could have used a little more. And Mick was a lot of the time in Paris. The only thing I was afraid of on *Exile* was that with people living so far away, it would break their concentration. And once I'd got them there, I wanted them for the duration. I'd never lived on top of the work before, but once I was, I said, damn it, the rest of you better get used to it. Fuck it, I'm doing it, and I've committed my house to it. If I can do it, you can all get a little closer. To Charlie it was an absolute no-no. He has an artistic temperament. It's just uncool for him to live down on the Côte d'Azur in summer. Too much society going on and too much blah blah. I can understand totally. Charlie's the kind of guy that would go down in winter when it's horrible and empty. He found where he wanted to live and it certainly wasn't on the coast, and it certainly wasn't Cannes, Nice, Juan-les-Pins, Cap Ferrat or Monte Carlo. Charlie cringes from places like that.

One sublime example of a song winging in from the ether is "Happy." We did that in an afternoon, in only four hours, cut and done. At noon it had never existed. At four o'clock it was on tape. It was no Rolling Stones record. It's got the name on it, but it was actually Jimmy Miller on drums, Bobby Keys on baritone and that was basically it. And then I overdubbed bass and guitar. We were just waiting for everybody to turn up for the real sessions for the rest of the night and we thought, we're here; let's see if we can come up with something. I'd written it that day. We got something going, we were rocking, everything was set up and so we said, well, let's start to work it down and then we'll probably hit it with the guys later. I decided to go on the five-string with the slide and suddenly there it was. Just like that. By the time they got there, we had it. Once you have something, you just let it fly.

> Well, I never kept a dollar past sunset
> Always burned a hole in my pants
> Never made a school mama happy
> Never blew the second chance, oh no
> I need a love to keep me happy.

It just came, tripping off the tongue, then and there. When you're writing this shit, you've got to put your face in front of the microphone, spit it out. Something will come. I wrote the verses of "Happy," but I don't know where they came from. "Never got a lift out of Learjet / When I can fly way back home." It was just alliteration, trying to set up a story. There has to be some thin plot line, although in a lot of my songs you'd be very hard-pressed to find it. But here, you're broke and it's evening. And you want to go out, but you ain't got shit. I'm busted before I start. I need a love to keep me happy, because if it's real love it will be free! Don't have to pay for it. I need a love to keep me happy because I've spent the fucking money and I have none left, and it's nighttime and I'm looking to have a good time, but I ain't got shit.

So I need love to keep me happy. Baby. Baby, won't you keep me happy.

I'd have been happier if more came like "Happy": "It goes like this." Great songs write themselves. You're just being led by the nose, or the ears. The skill is not to interfere with it too much. Ignore intelligence, ignore everything; just follow it where it takes you. You really have no say in it, and suddenly there it is: "Oh, I know how this goes," and you can't believe it, because you think that nothing comes like that. You think, where did I steal this from? No, no, that's original — well, about as original as I can get. And you realize that songs write themselves; you're just the conveyor.

Not to say that I haven't labored. Some of them had us on our knees. Some are about thirty-five years old and I've not quite finished them yet. You can write the song, but that's not the whole deal. The thing is what kind of sound, what tempo, what key and is everybody really into it? "Tumbling Dice" took a few days to get right. I remember working on that intro for several afternoons. When you're listening to music, you can tell how much calculation has gone into it and how much is free-flow. You can't do the free-flow all the time. And it's really a matter of how much calculation and how little you can put into it. Rather than the other way round. Well, I've got to tame this beast one way or another. But how to tame it? Gently, or give it a beating? I'll fuck you up; I'll take you twice the speed I wrote you! You have this sort of relationship with the songs. You talk to the fuckers. You ain't finished till you're finished, OK? All that sort of shit. No, you weren't supposed to go *there*. Or sometimes you're apologizing: I'm sorry about that. No, that was certainly not the way to go. Ah, they're funny things. They're babies.

But a song should come from the heart. I never had to think about it. I'd just pick up the guitar or go to the piano and let the stuff come to me. Something would arrive. Incoming. And if it didn't, I'd play somebody else's songs. And I've never really had to get to the point of saying, "I'm now going to write a song." I've never ever done that.

When I first knew I could do it, I wondered if I could do another one. Then I found they were rolling off my fingers like pearls. I never had any difficulty in writing songs. It was a sheer pleasure. And a wonderful gift that I didn't know I had. It amazes me.

Sometime in July, Gram Parsons came to Nellcôte with Gretchen, his young bride-to-be. He was already working on the songs for his first solo record, *GP*. I had been hanging with him for a couple of years by then and I just had the feeling that this man was about to come out with something remarkable. In fact, he changed the face of country music and he wasn't around long enough to find out. He recorded his first masterpieces with Emmylou Harris a year later, with "Streets of Baltimore," "A Song for You," "That's All It Took," "We'll Sweep Out the Ashes in the Morning." Whenever we were together we played. We played all the time; we'd write stuff. We'd work together in the afternoons, sing Everly Brothers songs. It's hard to describe how deeply Gram loved his music. It was all he lived for. And not just his own music but music in general. He'd be like me, wake up with George Jones, roll over and wake up again to Mozart. I absorbed so much from Gram, that Bakersfield way of turning melodies and also lyrics, different from the sweetness of Nashville — the tradition of Merle Haggard and Buck Owens, the blue-collar lyrics from the immigrant world of the farms and oil wells of California, at least that's where it had its origins in the '50s and '60s. That country influence came through in the Stones. You can hear it in "Dead Flowers," "Torn and Frayed," "Sweet Virginia" and "Wild Horses," which we gave to Gram to put on the Flying Burrito Brothers record *Burrito Deluxe* before we put it out ourselves.

We had plans, or at least great expectations, Gram and I. You work with somebody that good and you think, we've got years, man, no rush, where's the fire? We can put some really good stuff together. And you expect it to evolve. Once we get over the next cold turkey, we'll really come out with some good shit! We thought we had all the time in the world.

Mick resented Gram Parsons. It took me a long time to discover that people around me were much more conscious of this than I was. They describe how he made life uncomfortable for Gram, hitting on Gretchen to put pressure on him, making it plain he wasn't welcome. Stanley Booth remembers Mick being like a "tarantula" around Gram. That I was writing and playing with somebody else seemed to him to be a betrayal, though he could never put it in those terms. And it never occurred to me at the time. I'm just expanding my club. I'm getting around, meeting people. But it didn't stop Mick from sitting around and playing and singing with Gram. That's all you wanted to do around Gram. It would just be song after song after song.

Gram and Gretchen left under some bad feeling, although it must be said that Gram wasn't in great physical shape. I really don't remember the circumstances of his departure clearly. I had insulated myself against the dramas of the crowded household.

I've no doubt, in retrospect, that Mick was very jealous of me having other male friends. And I've no doubt that that was more of a difficulty than women or anything else. It took me a long time to realize that any male friend I had would automatically get the cold shoulder, or at least a suspicious reception, from Mick. Any guys I got close to would tell me, sooner or later, "I don't think Mick likes me." Mick and I were very tight friends and we'd been through a lot. But there is a weird possessiveness about him. It was only a vague aura to me, but other people pointed it out. Mick doesn't want me to have any friends except him. Maybe his exclusivity is bound up with his own siege mentality. Or maybe he thinks he's trying to protect me: "What does that asshole want from Keith?" But quite honestly, I can't put my finger on it. People he thought were getting close to me, he would preempt them, or try to, as if they were girlfriends rather than just friends.

But back then with Gram, was Mick feeling excluded? It wouldn't have occurred to me at the time. Everybody was moving around, meeting different people and experiencing things. And I don't know if Mick would even agree with this. But I have the feeling that Mick thought that I belonged to him. And I didn't feel like that at all. It's taken me years to even think about that idea. Because I love the man dearly; I'm still his mate. But he makes it very difficult to be his friend.

Most guys I know are assholes, I have some great asshole friends, but that's not the point. Friendship has got nothing to do with that. It's can you hang, can you talk about this without any feeling of distance between you? Friendship is a diminishing of distance between people. That's what friendship is, and to me it's one of the most important things in the world. Mick doesn't like to trust anybody. I'll trust you until you prove you're not trustworthy. And maybe that's the major difference between us. I can't really think of any other way to put it. I think it's something to do with just being Mick Jagger, and the way he's had to deal with being Mick Jagger. He can't stop being Mick Jagger all the time. Maybe it's his mother in him.

Bobby Keys was installed in an apartment not far from Nellcôte, where one day he caused a disturbance by throwing his furniture out of the window in a moment of Texan self-expression. But he was soon tamed into French customs by the beautiful Nathalie Delon. She was staying with Bianca up the road after the wedding. It all seemed very recent to Bobby when I asked him to recall what happened when they got to know each other.

> **Bobby Keys:** I don't know why she was still there. Maybe she was dodging bullets. Mick had a house north of Nice, where he and Bianca stayed, and I would ride out on my newly purchased motorcycle to see Nathalie. Mick and I went down to get motorcycles at the same time. He got the 500 or 450 or whatever the hell it was, and then I saw the 750, which

had seven cylinders, four fucking tailpipes. "Give me that
four-piped one, man. I need four tailpipes because I got a
French movie star I want to sit back here!" We would melt the
Côte d'Azur, screaming up and down the Moyenne Corniche
between Nice and Monaco, on that motorcycle, with Nathalie
in just a little bit of nothing, like a couple of Kleenex, me with
a yard of hard and a keg full of gas! I mean rock and roll,
good God almighty, can it get any better? We'd just take off
and drive into the interior, the little French villages, a bottle of
wine, a sandwich, while Nathalie taught me some French.
Those are the things that stay with you your whole life, going
on those back country roads in France. It was just such a
wonderful match. She was very funny, in a quiet sort of way,
and also we used to smack each other in the butt with a
syringe, just a little touch. It was like being in an adult
Disneyland. She was a beauty. She stole my heart. I still love
her. How can you not?

It should be added that Bobby was married at the time, though
not for long, to one of his many wives, and this wife was staying at
their apartment while Bobby was out romancing Nathalie. Bobby
must have broken some marital record by staying out four nights in a
row while everybody's telling his wife where he was.

But the romance came to an abrupt end some months later, when
Nathalie told Bobby it was over and told him never to call or try to get
in touch. Bobby's heart was broken; he'd never had such a rejection,
with no explanation, from someone he'd been so close to. He carried
the mystery around for decades, until recently a journalist who had
been close to the case explained to Bobby that it would have been too
dangerous for Nathalie and Bobby to have walked out publicly. Her
son, Anthony, was protected by bodyguards; Nathalie too had had
police protection. Nobody was sure who had killed the bodyguard
Nathalie had slept with; she had since been systematically harassed by

his Yugoslav buddies. Bobby remembered that she had mentioned something about the danger, but he hadn't listened. If Nathalie had had affection for Bobby, she wouldn't have prolonged their romance, was the explanation Bobby got. When Bobby heard this he considered it a revelation. He was staying in my house, and when he came down to breakfast the next day he was feeling good, all grateful now to Nathalie for saving his life and glad she hadn't told him the real circumstances at the time, otherwise he would have taken the unwise position of "Who are these goddamn frog motherfuckers? I'm from Texas. I'll fucking eat 'em for dinner," as he put it, which wouldn't have worked. Bobby lived to blow his heart out on many more "Brown Sugar"s, though he continued to live dangerously, as will be seen.

How was all that music produced—two songs a day written on a heroin habit, on what appeared to be high energy? For all of its downsides—I'd never recommend it to anybody—heroin does have its uses. Junk really is a great leveler in many ways. Once you're on that stuff, it doesn't matter what comes your way; you can handle it. There was the business of trying to get the whole Rolling Stones operation into this one house in the South of France. We had a record to cut and knew that if we failed, then the English would have won. And this house, this Bedouin encampment, contained anywhere from twenty to thirty people at a time, which never bothered me, because I have the gift of not being bothered or because I was focusing, with assistance, on the music.

It did bother Anita. It drove her up the wall. She was one of the few people who spoke French, and German to the Austrian housekeeper. So she became the bouncer, getting rid of people sleeping under beds and overstaying their welcome. There were tensions, no doubt, and paranoia—I have heard her accounts of her nightmare spell as doorkeeper—and there were of course a lot of drugs. There were many people to feed, and one day some holy men in orange robes came to visit and sat at the table with us and within two seconds, diving for the food, they'd cleaned us out, eaten everything. In terms of staff relations, Anita was reduced to going into the kitchen and making throat-cutting gestures; she felt very threatened by the cowboys who surrounded us.

Fat Jacques lived around the corner in the cookhouse, which was separated from the main building. One day we heard this enormous explosion, a big dull thud. We were all sitting around the great dining room. And suddenly there at the entrance is Jacques, with his hair singed and soot over his face, like a comic-book illustration. He's blown up the kitchen. Left the gas on too long before lighting it. He announces that there is no dinner. It has, literally, he says, gone through the roof.

The smack helped my siege mentality. It was my wall against all of that daily stuff, because rather than deal with it, I shut it out, to concentrate on what I wanted to do. You could go out and about, totally insulated. Without it, in certain cases you wouldn't have walked into that room at that time to deal with something. With it, you could go in there, brazen it off and be very smooth. And then go back and get the guitar out and finish what it was you were doing. It made everything possible. Whereas straight, I don't know, there were too many things going on. While you're insulated like this, you live in a world where other people go round with the sun and the moon. They wake up, go to sleep.... If you break that cycle and you've been up for four, five days, your perception of these people who have just got up, who have crashed out, is very distant. You've been working, writing songs, transferring tape to tape, and these people come in and they've been to bed and everything! They've even eaten stuff! Meanwhile, you're sitting at this desk with a guitar and this pen and paper. "Where the fuck you been?" It got to the point where I'd be thinking, how can I help these poor people who have to sleep every day?

For me there's no such thing as time when I'm into recording. Time changes. I only realize that time's come into it when the people around me are dropping. Otherwise I'd go on and on. Nine days was my record. Obviously, eventually, you hit the deck. But that perception of time — Einstein is pretty right: it's all relative.

It's not only to the high quality of the drugs I had that I attribute my survival. I was very meticulous about how much I took. I'd never put more in to get a little higher. That's where most people fuck up on drugs. It's the greed involved that never really affected me. People think once they've got this high, if they take some more they're going to get a little higher. There's no such thing. Especially with cocaine. One line of good coke and you should be popped all night. But no, within ten minutes they're going to take another one and another one. That's crazy. Because you're not going to get any higher. Maybe that's a measure of control, and maybe I'm rare in that respect. Maybe there I have an advantage.

I was a taskmaster. Especially in those days, I was a maniac for not letting up. If I've got the idea and if it's right, it has to be put down *now*. I might lose it in five minutes. Sometimes I found it was better if I turned up and appeared pissed off without anybody knowing why. I'd get more out of them. It made them go, wow, he's weird; he's gone a bit eccentric or cantankerous. But at the end of the day, what I was looking for in a track or in a song came to fruition. It was a trick I only pulled if I thought it necessary. Also, it gave me forty minutes in the john to shoot up while they considered what I'd said.

I suppose the schedule was rather strange. It became known as Keith Time, which in Bill Wyman's case made him a little cranky. Not that he said anything. At first we were going to start at two p.m., but that never happened. So we said we'd start at six p.m., which usually meant around one a.m. Charlie didn't seem to mind. Bill was particularly sensitive to it. I can understand that. I'd be famous. I'd go down to the john and I'd be thinking about the song and I'd take a shot, and forty-five minutes later I'm still sitting there, trying to work out what I'm doing. I should have said, hey, take some time off, I'm thinking about this. That's what I didn't do. It was rude of me, thoughtless.

My saying "I'll just go and put Marlon to bed" was, it appears, the signal for my disappearance for several hours. A story is told by Andy Johns of Mick and Jimmy Miller and him standing at the bottom of the stairs, going, "Who's gonna wake him up? I've had enough of this." "I'm not fucking going up there. Why don't you do it, Andy?" "I'm just little Andy. Come on, you guys. I can't be dealing with this." All I can say is, it got worse in the later '70s on tour, when Marlon became the only one permitted to wake me up.

But it worked — somehow. Let Andy, the tireless engineer in the Mighty Mobile, give a testimonial.

> **Andy Johns:** We were working on "Rocks Off," and
> everyone else had left. Keith said, "Play that back for me,
> Andy." And it was four or five in the morning, and he went to
> sleep while the playback was on, and I thought, great! I can
> get out of here. So I went all the way back to this villa that
> Keith had been kind enough to rent for me and Jim Price. Just
> getting to sleep and *ring, ring, ring, ring* . . . "Where the fuck
> are you? I've got this great idea." It was a half-hour drive. "Oh
> sorry, Keith. I'll be right back." So I jumped in the car, went
> back, and he played this other Telecaster part, which is why
> the two-guitar interchange happens on "Rocks Off," which is
> still stunning to me. And he just went right through it in one
> take. Bang, done. And I'm so glad that it went that way.

Then the circus left, and I was there in Nellcôte with Anita and Marlon and a few skeleton crew into the late autumn, when the clouds roll in and it gets stormy and gray and the colors change, and then into the winter, which was pretty miserable, especially when you remembered the summer. It also became menacing. The *brigade des stupéfiants,* as the drugs squad was called, was on our back. Gathering evidence, collecting statements from their usual suspects about the admittedly heavy activity at Nellcôte, not just mine and the cowboys', but that of all the other consumers of *stupéfiants* in the group. They had been snooping and spying, and it wasn't that difficult. In October we were burgled and my guitars, a great many of them, were stolen. We would have fled, but the French authorities wouldn't let us go. We were told we were officially under investigation on a number of heavy charges and we'd have to go to a hearing in Nice in front of an investigating magistrate—when all the gossip and accusations from disgruntled or police-pressured informants at Nellcôte would be aired. We were in some bad trouble. There was no habeas corpus in France to speak of; the state had total power. We could be locked up for months while the investigations took place, if the judge thought the evidence was strong enough, and maybe if he didn't. And this is where the—at that time fledgling—structure created by our manager Prince Rupert Loewenstein came into play. Later on he would set up a global network of lawyers, of top-ranking legal gunslingers, to protect us. For now he managed to acquire the services of a lawyer called Jean Michard-Pellissier. You couldn't have reached higher. He had been a lawyer for de Gaulle and he had just been named as cabinet adviser to Prime Minister Jacques Chaban-Delmas, who was his bosom friend. Furthermore, our mouthpiece was also the legal adviser to the mayor of the Antibes region. And if that wasn't enough, the gifted Mr. Michard-Pellissier was a friend of the prefect of the region, who was in charge of the police. Nice one, Rupert. The hearing took place in Nice, with Rupert interpreting for us. I remember after it was over Rupert describing as "terrifying" the stuff that the police were leveling at us. But it was also very comic. It was, in fact, hilarious—a Peter Sellers French comedy, a movie in which a detective was solemnly and slowly typing while the judge got everything radically wrong. He was convinced that we were running a huge ring of prostitutes, that dope was being bought and sold by sinister people with German accents and this English guitarist. "He wants to know whether you know a Mr. Alphonse Guerini." Or whatever. "Never heard of him." "Non, il ne le connaît pas." Whoever was grassing us up had had to dress up the information with ludicrous exaggerations and inventions to oblige the gendarmerie. So what came out was nothing but false information. Loewenstein had to point out that no, no, this was a man trying to buy things, not sell them, and the crooks were trying to work out how they could charge him double or treble the rate. In the meantime, the wheels of Michard-Pellissier were turning. So instead of the prospect of being in jail, even for a few years, a real possibility, Anita and I got one of several skin-of-teeth legal agreements that I've received in my time. It was decreed that we should leave French territory until I was "allowed back," but I had to keep renting Nellcôte as some kind of bond, at $2,400 a week.

It had reached the papers that the Stones were under investigation for dealing heroin, which began a whole long saga; the cat, as it were, was out of the bag. Aha, a heroin problem in the group and in the music industry at large. It came with the standard slanders, such as Anita peddling heroin to minors; many witches' tales went into circulation about bad things going on at Nellcôte. The story wasn't over in France. We went to LA, but in our absence, in the middle of December, the police raided Nellcôte and found what they were looking for, though it took them a full year to bring charges and a warrant for the arrest of Anita and me. When it came, they found us guilty of drug possession, fined us and banned us from entering France for two years. All those peddling charges had been dropped, and finally I could stop paying the rent on Nellcôte, tearing up thousand-dollar bills.

What we brought to LA from France was only the raw material for *Exile,* the real bare bones, no overdubs. On almost each song we'd said, we've got to put a chorus on here, we've got to put some chicks in there, we need extra percussion on that. We were already planning ahead without noting it down. So LA was basically to put the flesh on. For four or five months in LA in early 1972, we mixed and overdubbed *Exile on Main St.* I remember sitting in the parking lot of Tower Records or Gold Star Studios, or driving up and down Sunset, listening at precisely the moment when our favorite DJ was teed up to play an unreleased track, so that we could judge the mix. How did it sound on radio? Was it a single? We did it with "Tumbling Dice," "All Down the Line" and many others, called up a DJ at KRLA and sent him a dub. Fingers burning from the last cut and we'd just take the car out and listen to it. Wolfman Jack or one of several other DJs in LA would put it on, and we'd have a guy standing over him to take it back again. *Exile on Main St.* had a slow start. It was the kiss of death to make double albums, according to the lore of record companies and their anxieties about pricing and distribution and all that. The fact that we stuck to it, saying, look, that's what it is, that's what we've done here, and if it takes two albums, that's what we're going to do, was a bold move, and totally against all business advice. At first it seemed that they'd been proven right. But then it just kept going and going and getting bigger and bigger, and it always had incredible reviews. And anyway, if you don't make bold moves, you don't get fucking anywhere. You've got to push the limits. We felt we'd been sent down to France to do something and we'd done it, and they might as well have it all.

When that finished, Anita and I lived in Stone Canyon and I hooked back up with Gram, for the last time I saw him. Stone Canyon was nice, but there was still the dope to get. There's a photograph of Gram on his Harley motorcycle, me on the back wearing Biggles glasses, and we're off to score. "Hey, Gram, where we going?" "Through the cracks of the city." He'd take me to places in LA I never knew existed. In fact, a lot of the dealers I remember going to were chicks. Female junkies. FJs, as they were known in the trade. Once or twice it was a guy, but otherwise Gram's connections were female. He thought they were cooler than guys as far as dealing dope and being available. "Got the shit, but I ain't got a fix." "Oh, I know a chick...." He had a few bitches living up at the Riot House, the Continental Hyatt House on Sunset—very popular with bands, cheap and you could park your bus. And there'd be some very pretty chick, total junkie, who'd lend you her needle. This was before the days of worrying about AIDS. It wasn't around then.

This was when Gram was hanging with Emmylou Harris for the first time, though it was over a year before he recorded his great duets with her. Mind you, I bet it didn't start out as an idea to vocalize. He was a randy son of a bitch. Otherwise the bad news was the dearth of any high-grade smack anywhere on the West Coast. We were reduced to Mexican shoe scrapings, MSS as we used to call it. This is really street shit, brown, came over from Mexico. It looked like shoe scrapings, and sometimes it was and sometimes you'd have to do a test on it. You'd burn a little in a spoon first just to see whether it liquefied or not, and smell it. There's a definite smell to it when you burn it. And you didn't mind if the smell you got was the smell of the cut, because old heroin, street heroin, was cut with lactose. But this stuff was thick. Sometimes you could hardly push it through the needle. It was a pretty low life.

I never usually let it get to where I would be left without clean shit. And street dope, that's where I drew the line. I decided to quit. This is not the stuff; this is not where it's at. All it's doing is keeping the motor going.

One day you wake up and there's been a change of plans, you've got to go somewhere unexpected, and you realize that the first thing you think about is, OK, how do I handle the dope? The first thing on the list isn't your underwear, isn't your guitar, it's how do I hook up? Do I carry it with me and tempt fate? Or do I have phone numbers where I'm going, where I know that it's definitely there? Around now, with a tour coming up, was the first time it really hit me. I'd reached the end of the rope. I didn't want to be stuck in the middle of nowhere with no stuff. That was the biggest fear. I'd rather clean up before I went on the road. It's bad enough cleaning up by yourself, but the idea of putting the whole tour on the line because I couldn't make it was too much, even for me.

My visa had run out for America, so I had to get out of there anyway. It was also time for Anita and me to leave LA. She was pregnant with Angela; it was time to clean up, girl. I don't think Anita was particularly hooked; she didn't need it at the time. And obviously our robust Angela proves there was no serious health risk. Anita would have a hit now and again. It was me that was hooked big-time. It was pretty dire. We lived on the edge. But I don't think Anita or I had any doubt that we could pull this off. It was just a matter of doing it. I can't remember any sense of fear or apprehension about quitting. It was just, this is what has to be done, and it has to be done now. We couldn't do it in England or France, because I couldn't go into either of those countries, so Switzerland became our destination.

I loaded well up before we got on the plane, because I would go straight into cold turkey by the time I arrived, with no provisions for supplies in Switzerland. In fact it was pretty bad. There was confusion when we got there. I don't remember it, but I was taken in an ambulance from the hotel to the clinic. June Shelley, who had looked after all our affairs at Nellcôte and was overseeing this episode as well, wrote in her memoir that she thought I was going to die in the ambulance; I looked like it, anyway. I have no recollection of that; I was just being pushed around from pillar to post. Get me to the joint, let's cut it out and go through the shit. Dope me up so I can sleep through as much of seventy-two hours of hell as possible.

I was being cleaned up by a Dr. Denber in a clinic in Vevey. He was American. He looked Swiss, close shaven and rimless glasses, Himmleresque; he spoke with a midwestern twang. In actual fact Dr. Denber's treatment was useless for me. Dodgy little bugger too. I'd have rather cleaned up with Smitty, Bill Burroughs's nurse, that hairy old matron. But Dr. Denber was the only one that spoke English. There was nothing I could do about it. You have a guy in cold turkey, you've got him where you want him.

I can't imagine what other people think cold turkey is like. It is fucking awful. On the scale of things, it's better than having your leg blown off in the trenches. It's better than starving to death. But you don't want to go there. The whole body just sort of turns itself inside out and rejects itself for three days. You know in three days it's going to calm down. It's going to be the longest three days you've spent in your life, and you wonder why you're doing this to yourself when you could be living a perfectly normal fucking rich rock star life. And there you are puking and climbing walls. Why do you do that to yourself? I don't know. I still don't know. Your skin crawling, your guts churning, you can't stop your limbs from jerking and moving about, and you're throwing up and shitting at the same time, and shit's coming out your nose and your eyes, and the first time that happens for real, that's when a reasonable man says, "I'm hooked." But even that doesn't stop a reasonable man from going back on it.

While I was in the clinic, Anita was down the road having our daughter, Angela. Once I came out of the usual trauma, I had a guitar with me and I wrote "Angie" in an afternoon, sitting in bed, because I could finally move my fingers and put them in the right place again, and I didn't feel like I had to shit the bed or climb the walls or feel manic anymore. I just went, "Angie, Angie." It was not about any particular person; it was a name, like "ohhh, Diana." I didn't know Angela was going to be called Angela when I wrote "Angie." In those days you didn't know what sex the thing was going to be until it popped out. In fact, Anita named her Dandelion. She was only given the added name Angela because she was born in a Catholic hospital where they insisted that a "proper" name be added. As soon as Angela grew up a little bit, she said, "Never again do you call me Dandy."

Ethan Russell

# Chapter Nine

We embark on the great tour of 1972; Dr. Bill opens his medicine bag, and Hugh Hefner has us to stay; I meet Freddie Sessler. We move to Switzerland, then to Jamaica. Bobby Keys and I get in trouble on the road and are saved by Hawaii's Pineapple King. I buy a house in Jamaica; Anita is jailed there and expelled. Gram Parsons dies, and I am put on the most-likely-to list. Ronnie Wood joins the band.

*The Stones' big, ugly 1972 tour started on June 3. You can see how a sensitive person like Keith might need medication, but none of this stuff cheered me up. I hoped for better things. The idealism of the 1969 tour had ended in disaster. The cynicism of the 1972 tour included Truman Capote, Terry Southern (would have included William S. Burroughs if the* Saturday Review *had come up with Bill's price), Princess Lee Radziwill, and Robert Frank. Featured sideshows on the tour involved a traveling physician, hordes of dealers and groupies, big sex-and-dope scenes. I could describe for you in intimate detail the public desecrations and orgies I witnessed and participated in on this tour, but once you've seen sufficient fettuccine on flocked velvet, hot urine pooling on deep carpets, and tidal waves of spewing sex organs, they seem to run together. So to speak. Seen one, you seen 'em all. The variations are trivial.*
— *Stanley Booth,* Keith: Standing in the Shadows

*I have never been on anything like this. I have been on trips with extraordinary people before but they were always directed outward.... This totally excludes the outside world. To never get out, to never know what city you are in ... I cannot get used to it.*
— *Robert Frank, photographer and director,* Cocksucker Blues

The '72 tour was known by other names—the Cocaine and Tequila Sunrise tour or the STP, Stones Touring Party. It was mythologized along the lines of Stanley Booth's list of excesses, above. Personally I never saw anything like this. Stanley must have been exaggerating or he was a very innocent boy. It was the case nevertheless that by this time we couldn't get a reservation in any hotel above a Holiday Inn. It was the beginning of the booking of whole hotel floors, with no one else allowed up, so that some of us—like me— could get privacy and security. It was the only way we could have a degree of certainty that when we decided to party, we could control the situation or at least get some warning if there was trouble.

The whole entourage had exploded in terms of numbers, of roadies and technicians, and of hangers-on and groupies. For the first time we traveled in our own hired plane, with the lapping tongue painted on. We had become a pirate nation, moving on a huge scale under our own flag, with lawyers, clowns, attendants. For the guys running the operation there was maybe one battered typewriter and hotel or street phones to run a North American tour through thirty cities. A feat of organization on the part of our new tour manager, Peter Rudge, a four-star general among the anarchists. We never missed a show, though we came near it. The guy that opened for us, in almost every city, was Stevie Wonder, and he was barely twenty-two.

I remember stories about Stevie when we were on tours in Europe with his great band. They'd say, "The motherfucker can see! We walk into a brand-new hotel, he picks up his key, heads straight for the elevator." I found out later that he'd memorized the plan of a Four Seasons Hotel. Five steps up here, two steps to the elevator. . . . It was no big deal to him. He only did it to fuck them up.

The band was rocking on that tour. Better to hear an impression from another resident writer, Robert Greenfield. There were so many writers on that tour—it had become like a political campaign in terms of coverage. Our old friend Stanley Booth retired, disgusted by the new mob of socialites and famous authors who had diluted the once pure patch, "the ballrooms and smelly bordellos / And dressing rooms filled with parasites." But we played on.

**Robert Greenfield:** In Norfolk and Charlotte and Knoxville, the set seems to fly from beginning to end, the musicians completely locked into one another and on time, like a championship team in its finest, most fluid moments. But only people who listen, like Ian Stewart, and the Stones themselves and their supporting musicians, are aware of the magic that's going down. Everyone else is either worrying about logistics or trying to find a way to get off.

The traveling physician mentioned by Stanley we'll call Dr. Bill, to give it a Burroughsian ring. His specialty was billed as emergency medicine. Mick, who was getting appropriately nervous about people trying to get at him—there were threats and there were freaks fixated on him; people would walk up and hit him; the Angels wanted him dead—wanted a doctor around who could keep him alive if he got shot on stage. Dr. Bill was there, however, primarily for the pussy. And being quite a young, good-looking doctor, he got plenty.

He printed these cards, "Dr. Bill," as it were, "Physician of the Rolling Stones." He would scout the audience before we went on and give out twenty or thirty of those cards to the most foxy, beautiful girls, even if they were with a guy. He wrote on the back, the name of our hotel, the suite number to call. And even girls with guys would go home and come back. They'd give this to the guard, and Dr. Bill knew that out of the six or seven girls who would come, there were one or two who he could get by saying he would introduce them to us. He was into getting laid every night. And he also had this case of every kind of substance, Demerol, anything you wanted. He could write scripts in every city. We used to send chicks to his room and take his medicine bag. There would be a line waiting in the room with a waste bag of syringes while he was giving out the Demerol.

In Chicago there was an acute shortage of hotel rooms, to add to our problem of unpopularity with booking clerks. There was a hardware convention, a McDonald's convention, a furniture convention, the lobbies were full of name badges. So Hugh Hefner thought it would be a laugh to invite some of us to stay in the Playboy Mansion. I think he regretted it. Hugh Hefner, what a nut. We've worked the lowest pimps to the highest. The highest being Hefner, a pimp nonetheless. He threw the place open for the Stones and we were there for over a week. And it's all plunges in the sauna, and the Bunnies, and basically it's a whorehouse, which I really don't like. The memory, however, is very, very hazy. I know we did have some fun there. I know we ripped it up. Hefner had been shot at just before our visit, and the place resembled the state house of some Caribbean dictatorship, with heavily armed security everywhere. But Bobby and I avoided that, and the tourists who had come to watch us playing in the Playboy Mansion, and retreated into our own entertainment.

We had the doc there, and we'd get in one of the Bunnies for him. The deal was "We get free dibs on your bag and you can have Debbie." I felt the script had been written, play it to the hilt. Bobby and I played it a little far when we set fire to the bathroom. Well, we didn't, the dope did. Not our fault. Bobby and I were just sitting in the john, comfortable, nice john, sitting on the floor, and we've got the doc's bag and we're just smorgasbording. "I wonder what these do?" *Bong.* And at a certain point... talk about hazy, or foggy, Bobby says, "It's smoky in here." And I'm looking at Bobby and can't see him. And the drapes are smoldering away; everything was just about to go off big-time. To the point where I can't see him, he's disappeared in this fog. "Yes, I guess it *is* a bit smoky in here." It was a really delayed reaction. And then suddenly a flurry at the door and the fire alarms start going, *beep beep beep.* "What's that *noise,* Bob?" "I don't know. Should we open the window?" Someone shouts through the door, "Are you all right?" "Oh yeah, we're fucking great, man." So he just turns away, and we don't know exactly what to do. Maybe if we're quiet and walk out and we pay for the reconstruction? And then a little later there was a thumping on the door, waiters and guys in black suits bringing buckets of water. They get the door open and we're sitting on the floor, our pupils very pinned. I said, "We could have done that ourselves. How dare you burst in on our private affair?" Hugh decamped soon after that and moved to LA.*

Some of my most outrageous nights I can only believe actually happened because of corroborating evidence. No wonder I'm famous for partying! The ultimate party, if it's any good, you can't remember it. You get these brief vignettes of what you did. "Oh, you don't remember shooting the gun? Pull up the carpet, look at those holes, man." I feel a bit of shame and embarrassment. "You can't remember *that*? When you got your dick out, swinging from the chandelier, anybody up for grabs, wrap it in a five-pound note?" Nope, don't remember a thing about it.

It's very hard to explain all that excessive partying. You didn't say, OK, we're going to have a party tonight. It just happened. It was a search for oblivion, I suppose, though not intentionally. Being in a band, you are cooped up a lot, and the more famous you get the more of a prison you find yourself in. The convolutions you go through just to not be you for a few hours.

I can improvise when I'm unconscious. This is one of my amazing tricks, apparently. I try and stay in contact with the Keith Richards I know. But I do know there's another one that lurks, occasionally, about. Some of the best stories about me relate to when I'm not actually there, or at least not consciously so. I am obviously operating, because I've had it corroborated by too many people, but I can reach a point, especially on cocaine after a few days, where I just crack, where I think I'm totally crashed out and asleep, but in actual fact I'm doing things that are quite outrageous. This is called pushing the envelope. But

---

* He recorded in his Little Black Book from a memo dated 6/28/72: "For your information, the following is a list of damage that resulted from the visit of the Rolling Stones: The White rug in the Red and Blue Room bathroom was burnt and needed to be replaced; the toilet seat was also burnt and had to be replaced; two bath mats and four towels were also burnt; Red Room chair and couch are stained, possibly to the point of needing reupholstering; Red Room bedspread is badly stained. We are hoping it will come out in cleaning."

nobody showed me how big the envelope is. There is a certain point where suddenly everything cuts off because you've been pushing it too far, but it's just too much fun and you're writing songs, and then there's some bitches and you go to that rock-and-roll thing and loads of friends are coming by and refueling you, and there is a point where the switch does go off and you still keep moving. It's like another generator kicks in, but the memory and the mind have totally gone. My friend Freddie Sessler would have been a mine of information about this, God rest his soul.

Chandeliers do produce one memory, which might be classed as a close shave. I wrote it in a notebook under the heading "A Celestial Shotgun."

> *A lady (nameless) whom I was entertaining was so grateful, she insisted on entertaining me. She stripped naked and leaped up and grasped the huge chandelier, then proceeded to perform some very athletic convolutions as the light beams dazzled around the room. It was very entertaining. Then, with the nimbleness of an acrobat, she let go and landed on the couch beside me. At that moment the chandelier detached itself from its moorings and shattered on the floor. We both huddled together under a blast of crystal, laughing hysterically as it rained down on us. Then it got even more entertaining.*

We had some sport with Truman Capote, author of *In Cold Blood,* one of the group of Mick's society friends who had attached themselves to the tour and who included Princess Lee Radziwill, Princess Radish to us, as Truman was just Truby. He was on assignment from some high-paying magazine, so he was ostensibly working. Truby said something bitchy and whiny backstage—he was being an old fart, actually complaining about the noise. It was just some snide, queenie remark and sometimes I don't give a damn, other times it just gets up my nose. This happened after a show and I was already on cloud nine. Motherfucker needed a lesson. I mean, this snooty New York attitude.

You're in Dallas. It got a little raucous. I remember, back at the hotel, kicking Truman's door. I'd splattered it with ketchup I'd picked up off a trolley. Come out, you old queen. What are you doing round here? You want cold blood? You're on the road now, Truby! Come and say it out here in the corridor. Taken out of context, it sounds like I'm some right sort of Johnny Rotten, but I must have been provoked.

What was hilarious was how Truman for some unknown reason took a shine to Bobby. Truman was on the Johnny Carson show at the end of his little stint with the Stones, and Johnny asked him, what do you think about all this rock-and-roll hoopla and bizarre stuff you've been doing? Oh yes, I've been on the road with the Rolling Stones. And Bobby is watching this on TV, of course. Johnny said, well, tell us some of your experiences. Who did you meet? Oh, I met this delightful young man from Texas. And Bobby's going, no! Don't do it! And Bobby's phone started ringing immediately from the Texas League of Gentlemen: ah, you and Truman, huh?

I remember the gig in Boston on July 19, 1972, for two reasons. The first was the motorcade the Boston police provided to get us to the stadium when their buddies in Rhode Island had wanted to lock us up. We'd landed in Providence from Canada, and while they were searching all the baggage, I was sleeping on the fender of a fire truck, one of those nice, curved old-fashioned ones with the mudguards. I felt a sudden explosion of heat—a flashbulb right in my face—and I just leaped up and grabbed the camera. Fuck off. Kicked the photographer. And I got arrested. And Mick and Bobby Keys and Marshall Chess demanded to be arrested with me. I've got to give that to Mick. But in Boston that day the Puerto Ricans got pissed off in their section of town and they were kicking up shit. And the mayor of Boston was saying, you let those fuckers go right now, because I've got to deal with this riot, and don't give me a Rolling Stones riot on the same day. And so we were sprung, and these cops escorted us to Boston posthaste, with outriders and civic fanfare.

The other big event that day was the knock on my hotel room door that led to my facing Freddie Sessler for the first time. I don't know how he got there, but back then everybody would come to my room. It doesn't happen anymore—I couldn't stand the pace—but in this case I wasn't busy at the moment and he looked intriguing. Jewish to the max, dressed in ridiculous clothes. What a character. "I've got something you'll like," he said. And he pulled out this full ounce, with a still-unbroken seal, of pure Merck cocaine. The real deal. "This is a gift. I love your music." This is the stuff that when you open it, it almost flies out the bottle, *swoosh*. And I liked my cocaine off and on up until then, but apart from the cocaine you got from junkies in England, it was street shit; you never knew if it was amphetamine. And from now, once a month, Freddie would deliver a full ounce of pure cocaine. No money changed hands. Freddie never wanted to be labeled as a "supplier." He wasn't a dealer you could call up and ask, "Hey, Fred, you got any...?"

It was beyond that. Freddie and I just hit it off. He was an incredible character. He was twenty years older than me. His history, even by the average experience of any Jew who lived through the Nazi invasion of Poland, was a story of horror and almost miraculous survival. Only three of the fifty-four of his relatives in Poland survived. A story not unlike that of the young Roman Polanski, having to fend for himself and evade the Nazis who had taken the rest of his relations to the camps. I didn't find out the details of this for a while, but in the meantime Freddie quickly became a fixture on tour. He took on the role of my second dad for ten or fifteen years after that, probably without realizing it. I recognized something in Freddie almost immediately. He was a pirate and an adventurer and an outsider, though at the same time one with extraordinarily good contacts. He was incredibly funny, sharp as a razor with all the experience behind it. He'd made a fortune about five times over, blown it each time and made it again—the first one out of pencils. He said, what gets shorter every time you use it? He made a fortune out of office supplies. And then he got another idea, flying round New York in a holding pattern for an hour, looking at all the buildings and the lights. Whoever supplies those lightbulbs is making a fucking fortune. Two weeks later it's him. Very simple ideas. Some others were not so simple, or successful. Snake venom for curing multiple sclerosis. He put a lot of money into the doomed Amphicar, the amphibious vehicle that was described, in one review, as "the car that may revolutionize drowning." It never quite made it. Dan Aykroyd has one, but who apart from him needs a car that can cross rivers when you've got bridges? Freddie was like a Leonardo of sorts, but running these businesses? Forget about it. The minute it worked he was bored to death and he'd blow it.

Of course Mick didn't take to Freddie, nor did a lot of other people. He was too loose a cannon. Gram probably drove a bigger wedge between Mick and me than Freddie did because that was music. But Mick despised Freddie. He only put up with him because to annoy Freddie would be to annoy me. I think Freddie and Mick did have a couple of good times together, but they were rare. Freddie would do things for Mick and not even let me know, put him in touch with this whore or this bitch. He would grease Mick's path. Mick would get in touch with Freddie when he wanted something, and Freddie would oblige.

People would knock Freddie, say he was crude, insulting, vulgar, and why not? You could think anything you wanted of him, but Freddie was one of the best men I ever met. Totally horrible, revolting. Absolutely over the top, stupid at times, but solid. I can't think of another bloke that was solid all the way. I was stupid in those days and over the top too. I'd dare Freddie to be more outrageous than he really wanted to be, which was my fault, but I knew there was a thing in the man. He didn't care; he didn't give a shit. He thought he'd died at fifteen. "I'm dead anyway, even if I'm still alive. Everything else from here on is gravy, even if it's shit. Let's make the shit into gravy if we can." And that's the way I took Freddie's basic "fuck it" attitude. Fifteen was when he watched his grandfather, the most revered figure in his life, and his uncle being tortured and then shot by two Nazi officers in broad daylight in the main square of their town, while he held on to his terrified grandmother. His grandfather was selected for this horrifying punishment because he was the leader of the Jewish community in the area. Then Freddie too was picked up, and that was the last he saw of any member of his family then living in Poland. All were taken off to the camps.

Freddie left an autobiographical manuscript dedicated to me, which is embarrassing because the other dedicatee is Jakub Goldstein, the grandfather whom he watched being murdered. The horrors are described, but it's also a fascinating story of survival, very Pasternak in subject matter, and it explains what made this man I came to be so close to. He tells first, for example, of a well-off middle-class Jewish family in Kraków in 1939, going to their summer home outside the town, with its stables and barns, smokehouses and mowed lawns, and a Gypsy woman comes across the poppy fields and says, I'll read your fortune, cross my palm with silver and all of that. And she predicts doom for the entire family, except specifically three members, two of them absent from Poland, the third being Freddie, who she says will go east to Siberia.

The Germans came in September 1939. Freddie was sent to a labor camp in Poland, a hastily organized prison from which he escaped. He spent several weeks running at night and hiding in the frozen forest, stealing from farmhouses, heading eastward to the Russian-occupied sector of Poland. He crossed a frozen river at night with bullets landing around him and ran straight into the arms of the Red Army. These were the days of the Hitler-Stalin pact, but anything was better than Germans. Freddie was sent to a Siberian Gulag, as the fortune-teller had predicted.

Freddie was sixteen. The plot, of unremitting punishment and desperation, is something like *Candide,* as are the descriptions of the Siberian conditions that Freddie managed to survive. In later life Freddie would wake up screaming with nightmares about it.

He and the few of his Polish fellow prisoners who were still alive were released when Germany invaded Russia. With thousands of released prisoners from other camps, Freddie started out to reach the railhead, a distance of a hundred miles or so. Only three hundred made it. Freddie joined the Polish army in Tashkent, contracted typhoid, got discharged and joined the Polish navy in 1942. His job was watching radar for long hours. The ship's doctor introduced him to pharmaceutical cocaine. After that things began to get a little better.

Fred's brother Siegi, the only other surviving member of his family of seven children, was in Paris at the Sorbonne when the Germans invaded Poland. He joined the Polish army and later managed to get to England. Freddie joined him in London after the war. Siegi became a famous club owner and restaurateur, co-owner of Les Ambassadeurs, which quickly became a hangout for four-star generals and Hollywood stars who came to entertain US troops. When he opened Siegi's Club in Charles Street, Mayfair, in 1950, he'd become personal friends with the likes of Frank Sinatra, Ronald Reagan and Bing Crosby. It became the hangout of Princess Margaret, the Aga Khan and the like. So Siegi and by proxy Freddie, who knew Sinatra and Marilyn Monroe, were very well connected. It served Freddie well on at least two occasions I know of. Once when he was coming through a New York airport and was arrested for some gear in his briefcase and they were going to put him away and somehow they didn't—the whole incident disappeared. And much later in 1999, on the No Security tour, he was arrested for possession in Las Vegas, taken to the cells, the whole caboodle. Freddie made one call—this was witnessed by Jim Callaghan, my muscle at the time—and three hours later he had a letter of apology from the mayor's office, and the gear and the money were handed back.

When I met Freddie he had his Hair Extension Center in New York—inspired by his own woven hair attachments. Cocaine and Quaaludes were his favorite drugs and he had access to the very best of them. (A scheme in Miami to treat obesity with appetite suppressants and Quaaludes, which turned into the Miami Venom Institute to treat degenerative diseases with snake venom, was closed down by the

FDA. Freddie moved it to Jamaica, where he came seriously a cropper with the government.) Freddie actually owned drugstores. And he owned doctors too. He had them strategically positioned across New York, and they would write prescriptions to his drugstores. He bought a stationery business and set up this tired old doctor with a script pad, and during any one week there was $20,000 worth of pharmaceuticals coming in and going out of Freddie's various businesses. He never sold "recreational" drugs, but he did like to give his friends the same access he had; he liked to relieve them, he said, from getting it on the street. It gave him great satisfaction to contribute to someone's pleasure or to the greater glory of rock and roll.

Freddie's costumes were terrible. He would wear cowboy boots with a leisure suit tucked into them. "How do you like this? Pretty cool, eh?" Silk fucking jacket and little hipster pants with a great big arse sticking out the back. Freddie's sense of fashion was absolutely unbelievable. It was Polish. He would have these girlfriends, and they would deliberately dress him up ridiculously and say, "You look great!" A Hawaiian shirt and a brown Nudie suit tucked into some cowboy boots, and they'd put a bowler hat on him. But Freddie didn't give a damn; he knew what was going on. He was always trawling for young girls and groupies down in the lobby. Sometimes he disgusted and revolted me. Three what looked like underage chicks in the room. "Freddie, get them out. We're not going there, baby."

One time in Chicago there was a big party in my room and loads of bimbos, Freddie's groupies. They'd been there for twelve hours and I was getting sick of it, and I kept telling them to go and they wouldn't. I wanted to clear the room and no one would listen to me. Get the fuck out. For five minutes I tried. So *boom,* I fired a shot through the floor. Ronnie and Krissie, his first wife, were also there, so I knew that there was nobody down in their room, which was directly below mine. And that cleared the room in a cloud of dust and skirts and bras. What amazed me was after that, I was stuffing the shooter, waiting for security to come up or the cops, and nothing fucking happened!

The times guns have gone off in hotel rooms and never, ever has security or cops or anybody arrived. Not in America, at least. I have to say I was using guns too much, but I was pretty out of it at the time. I gave them up when I got clean.

A lot of people didn't like Freddie; management hated him. "This guy's bad for Keith." People like Peter Rudge, the manager, and Bill Carter, the lawyer, saw Freddie as a big risk. But Freddie wasn't just getting high and bent on self-gratification. He had the weird, beautiful vision of let's be who we are, it doesn't matter. Freddie was part of the '60s thing in a way, and he had that fearlessness: let's just break the boundaries. Who are we to bow to every goddamn cop, every accepted social correctness? (Which has got even worse. Freddie would have hated it now.) It was just scratch the surface, let's see what's underneath these people. And mostly you'd find there's very little substantial conviction behind them, if you just take 'em on. They crumble.

Freddie and I knew what we had to offer each other. Freddie offered me protection. He had a way of filtering people out of the traveling gang. I can understand people seeing Freddie Sessler as a threat. First off, he was very close to me, which meant he couldn't be reined in that easily. And that was basically ninety percent of the barrier. Then I always heard the stories of how Freddie was ripping me off, scalping tickets and so on. So fucking what? Compared to the spirit and friendship? Go ahead, pal, scalp as much as you fucking like.

Switzerland was my base for the next four years or so. I couldn't live in France for legal reasons or in Britain for tax reasons. In 1972, we moved up to Villars, in the hills above Montreux, east of Lake Geneva—a very small and secluded place. You could ski—I did ski—right up to the back door. The place was found for me by Claude Nobs, a mate of mine who started the Montreux Jazz Festival. I made other connections: Sandro Sursock became a solid friend. He was the godson of the Aga Khan, a lovely bloke. There was another one called

Tibor, whose father was connected to the Czechoslovakian embassy. Your typical goddamn Slav. Randy little bastard. He lives in San Diego now and raises dogs. Sandro and he were friends. They waited around the exit of the local girls' college and they'd take their pick. They were rolling in it. And we'd all roar around in cars — in my case an E-Type Jaguar.

I made a statement at that time in an interview that is worth recording here. "Up until the mid-1970s, Mick and I were inseparable. We made every decision for the group. We'd get together and kick things around, write all our songs. But once we were split up, I started going my way, which was the downhill road to dopesville, and Mick ascended to jet land. We were dealing with a load of problems that built up, being who we were and what the sixties had been."

Mick would come and visit me occasionally in Switzerland and talk about "economic restructuring." We're sitting around half the time talking about tax lawyers! The intricacies of Dutch tax laws vis-à-vis the English tax law and the French tax law. All of these tax thieves were snapping at our heels. I was trying to wish it away. Mick was a bit more practical on that point: "The decisions we make now will affect blah blah blah." Mick picked up the slack; I picked up the smack. The cures didn't always stick through the periods off the road, when I wasn't working.

Anita had cleaned up when she was pregnant, but the minute she had the baby, she was straight back on it, more, more, more. At least we could be on the road together, with the children, when we took off for Jamaica to cut *Goats Head Soup* in November 1972.

I had first gone to Jamaica for a few days off at a place called Frenchman's Cove in 1969. You could hear the rhythm going around. Free reggae, rock steady and ska. In that particular area you're not very close to the population, you're all white guys there, isolated from local culture unless you really want to go out and look for it. I met a few nice guys. I was listening to a lot of Otis Redding at the time and had guys coming up, saying, "That's so fine." I discovered that in

Jamaica they were getting two radio stations from the US that could reach that far with a very clear signal. One was out of Nashville, which played country music, obviously. And the other one was from New Orleans, which also had an incredibly powerful beam. And when I came back to Jamaica at the end of 1972, I realized that what they'd been doing was listening to these two stations and stacking them together. Listen to "Send Me the Pillow That You Dream On," the reggae version that came out then by the Bleechers. The rhythm section is New Orleans, the voice and song are Nashville. You had basically the rockabilly, the black and the white stuck together in an amazing fashion. The melodies of one with the beat of the other. It was that same mixture of white and black that brought you rock and roll. And I said, well, blimey, I'm halfway there!

Jamaica in those days was not the Jamaica it is now. By 1972 the place was blooming. The Wailers were signed to Island Records. Marley was just sprouting his locks. Jimmy Cliff was in the cinemas with *The Harder They Come*. In Saint Ann's Bay the audiences shot the screen as the titles rolled, in a familiar (to me) surge of rebellious glee. The screen was already perforated — perhaps from spaghetti westerns, which were the rage in those times. Plenty of gunmen in Kingston. The town was rife with an exotic form of energy, a very hot feeling, much of which was coming from the infamous Byron Lee's Dynamic Sounds. It was built like a fortress, with a white picket fence outside, as it appears in the film. The track "The Harder They Come" was cut by Jimmy Cliff in the same room we used to record some of *Goats Head Soup,* with the same engineer, Mikey Chung. A great four-track studio. They knew where the drums were exactly right, and to prove it, *bang bang,* they nailed down the stool!

We were all shacked up at the Terra Nova Hotel, which used to be Chris Blackwell's family residence in Kingston. Neither Mick nor I could get visas to the United States at that moment, which partly explains why we were in Jamaica. We went to the American embassy in Kingston. The ambassador was one of Nixon's boys and he obviously had his orders and also he hated our guts. And we were just trying to get a visa. The minute we walked in, we knew that we weren't going to get it but, even so, we had to listen to this guy's stream of venom. "People like you..." We got a lecture. Mick and I were looking at each other: have we not heard this before? We discovered later from the visa negotiations that Bill Carter conducted on our behalf that what they had in the files was very primitive—a few tabloid cuttings, a couple of screaming headlines, a story of us pissing against a wall. The ambassador pretended to go through the papers, talked of heroin, rubbed it all in.

*Goats Head Soup* meanwhile took some cranking up, despite Dynamic Sounds and the fervor of the moment. I think Mick and I were a little bit dried up after *Exile*. And we had just been on the road in the US and then here comes another album. After *Exile,* such a beautifully set up list of songs that all seemed to go together, it was difficult for us to get that tightness again. We hadn't been in the studio for a year. But we had some good ideas. "Coming Down Again," "Angie," "Starfucker," "Heartbreaker." I enjoyed making it. Our way of doing things changed while we were recording it, and slowly I became more and more Jamaican, to the point where I didn't leave. There were some downsides. By now Jimmy Miller's on the stuff too, so is Andy Johns, and I'm watching this happen and I'm, oh fuck... You're supposed to do as I say, not as I do. I was still on the dope myself, of course. Of "Coming Down Again," I said not long ago that I wouldn't have written it without heroin. I don't know if it was *about* dope. It was just a mournful song—and you look for that melancholy in yourself. I'm obviously looking for great grooves, great riffs, rock and roll, but there's the other side of the coin that still wants to go where "As Tears Go By" came from. And by then I'd worked a lot in the country field, especially with Gram Parsons, and that high-lonesome melancholy has a certain pull on the heartstrings. You want to see if you can tug 'em a little harder.

Some people think "Coming Down Again" is about me stealing

Anita, but by then that's all water under the fucking bridge. You get highs and lows. I would have been most of the time very, very up, but when it got low, it got very, very low. I remember joy and happiness and a lot of hard work. But when shit did hit the fan, it always hit it very solidly. You get exhausted. You get busted. For a long stretch, I was either on trial or had a case pending, or we were going through visa problems. That was always the backdrop. It was sheer pleasure to get in the studio and lose yourself, forget about it for a few hours. You knew when it was over you were going to be facing some shit one way or another.

Once the recording was over, having decided to stay in Jamaica, Anita, Marlon, Angie and I moved to the north coast, to Mammee Bay, between Ocho Rios and Saint Ann's Bay. We ran out of dope. Cold turkey in paradise, par for the course. If you're gonna clean up, there are worse places. (Still, it was only slightly warmer turkey.) Nevertheless, all things must pass, and before long we began to act as human beings again and then met some of the Rasta brethren of the coast. First one guy, Chobbs—Richard Williams on the birth certificate—he was one of those full-of-brass, full-on guys you met on the beach. He was selling coconuts, rum and anything else he could flog off. And he used to take the children out in his boat. As usual it was "Hey, man, any chance of some bush?" So it started from there. Then I met Derelin and Byron and Spokesy, who was later killed in a motorcycle accident. They worked the tourists in Mammee Bay and lived mostly in Steer Town. And slowly they all sort of gravitated around and we started to talk music. Warrin (Warrin Williamson), "Iron Lion" Jackie (Vincent Ellis), Neville (Milton Beckerd), a dreadlock man who still lives in my house in Jamaica. There was Tony (Winston "Blackskull" Thomas) and Locksley Whitlock, "Locksie," who was the leader, so to speak, the Boss Man. They called him Locksie because he had a severe attack of dreadlocks. Locksley could have been a first-class cricketer. He was a wicked batsman. I had a picture of him somewhere, at the crease. He was invited to join the

Jamaican top team, but he refused to cut his locks off. The only one who actually made a profession of music was Justin Hinds. The King of Ska. Late lamented. A beautiful singer — Sam Cooke reincarnated. One of his biggest records, called "Carry Go Bring Come," Justin Hinds and the Dominoes, was a huge hit in Jamaica in 1963. In the few years before he died in 2005, he recorded albums with his band the Jamaica All Stars. And he was still very much one of the brethren of Steer Town, a fearsome place just inland into which I never would have ventured — let's say I wouldn't have been welcome there — before I knew them. I was eased in gently, via Chobbs, and eventually I was allowed to go up to the Covenant, which is what they used to call their moveable gathering .

"Come to the Covenant, you're welcome, brother." I mean, Jesus Christ, I don't know how important this is in their terms, but if I'm asked to go, I'll go. Quite honestly you couldn't see a thing, the place would be covered in smoke. They used to smoke the chalice, a coconut with a huge earthenware jar on top and about half a pound of weed in it and a rubber pipe coming out the end. It was a question of who could smoke more than anybody else. The daring chaps would fill the coconut with white rum like a hubbly bubbly and smoke it through the rum. You set the earthenware container ablaze, bursting into flames with clouds of smoke. "Fire burn, Jah wonderful!" Who was I to defy local custom? OK, I'll try and hang in here. This is powerful weed. Funnily enough, I never flaked out. That's why I think I impressed them. I was a smoker for quite a few years before that, but never that amount. It was just like a dare, in a way. You know, watch whitey fall to the floor. And I was telling myself, not gonna go to the floor, not gonna go to the floor. I stood up and stayed with them. Mind you, I fell to the floor later, when I got out of there.

It seemed the whole population of Steer Town was musicians whose music consisted of beautifully reworked hymns chanted by voices and drums. I was in heaven. They used to sing in unison, there was no concept of singing harmonies, and they played no instruments except these drums—a very powerful sound. Just drums and voices. The words and the chants were already a century old or more, old hymns and psalms that they would rewrite to suit their tastes. But the actual melodies were straight out of the church, and many churches in Jamaica used drums as well. They'd go all night for it. Hypnotic. Trance. Relentless beat. And they'd keep coming out with more and more songs. Some of them cutting-edge songs too. The drums belonged to Locksley, with a bass drum that could be so loud it was believed it could kill you, like a massive stun grenade. In fact there were many witnesses to the story of a cop who unwisely ventured into a house in Steer Town, and Locksley looked at him—they were in a small room—and said, "Fire burn," meaning hit the drum, giving others warning to protect their ears. Then he hit the bass drum, and the cop fell unconscious, was stripped of his uniform and ordered never to return.

Steer Town was a Rasta town at that time. Now it's a much bigger junction, but then to go up there you had to have a pass, in a way. It was on a main road from Kingston; it had the crossroads and many shacks and a couple of taverns. But you didn't poke your nose in. Because even if you said, "Oh, I know him and I know him," other cats might not know who you were and just slash you up. It was their bastion and they had no shame with that machete. And they had reason to be fearful. So fearful that they had to make themselves fearsome so that no cops were ever gonna walk into Steer Town. It wasn't long ago that the cops would ride down the street and if they saw two Rastas, they'd shoot one and leave the other to drag the body away. These guys stood up in front of fire. I've always admired them for that.

Rastafarianism was a religion, but it was a smokers' religion. Their principle was "ignore their world," live without society. Of course they didn't or couldn't—Rastafarianism is a forlorn hope. But at the same time, it's such a beautiful forlorn hope. When the grid and the iron and the bars closed in on societies everywhere, and they got tighter and tighter, the Rastafarians loosened themselves from it. These guys just figured out their little way of being spiritual about it and at the same time not joining in. They would not accept intimidation. Even if they had to die. And some of them did. They refused to work within the economic system. They're not going to work for Babylon; they're not going to work for the government. For them that was being taken into slavery. They just wanted to have their space. If you get into the theology, you can get a little lost. "We're the lost tribe of Judah." OK, anything you say. But why this bunch of black Jamaicans consider themselves to be Jewish is a question. There was a spare tribe that had to be filled and that one would do. I have the feeling it was like that. And then they found a spare deity in the unreal medieval figure of Haile Selassie, with all his biblical titles. The Lion of Judah. Selassie, I. If there was a clap of thunder and lightning, "Jah!" everybody got up, "Give thanks and praises." It was a sign that God was working. They knew their Bible back to front—they could quote phrase after phrase of the Old Testament. I loved their fire about it, because whatever the religious ins and outs, they were living on the edge. All they had was their pride. And what they were engaged in was not, in the end, religion. It was one last stand against Babylon. Not all of them hung to the tenets of the Rastafarian law. They were very flexible. They had all these rules that they would gladly break. It was amazing to watch them when they got into arguments amongst themselves over a point of doctrine. There was no parliament or senate or tribunal of elders. Rasta politics—"fundamental reasoning"—was very like the bar at the House of Commons, in this case with a lot of stoned people and huge amounts of smoke.

What really turned me on is there's no you and me, there's just I and I. So you've broken down the difference between who you are and who I am. We could never talk, but I and I can talk. We are one. Beautiful.

That time was when the Rastas were almost at their most serious. Just when I thought I was shacking up with this really weird, unknown sect, Bob Marley and the Wailers happened and Rastas suddenly became fashionable all over the world. They went global just within that year. Before Bob Marley became a Rastafarian, he was trying to be one of the Temptations. Like anybody else in the music business, he'd had a long career already, in rock steady, ska, etc. But others said, "Hey, Marley didn't have no fucking locks, you know? He weren't a Rasta until it became cute." The first time the Wailers went to England, soon after this, I caught them by chance up in Tottenham Court Road. I thought they were pretty feeble compared to what I'd been hearing in Steer Town. But they certainly got their act together real quick. Family Man joined in on the bass, and Bob obviously had all of the stuff required.

I respond instinctively to kindness with no side attached. In those days when I hung in Steer Town, I could walk in any door and my every need would be satisfied. I was treated as family and I acted like family. Not acted! I behaved like family, became family. Me sweep the yard, me mash up coconuts, me make chalice for the sacramental smoking. Man, I was more Rasta than they. I'd fallen in with just the right bunch of guys, and their old ladies. It was another one of those across-the-tracks things — just being accepted and welcomed into something I didn't even know existed.

I also learned some useful Jamaican skills with the ratchet, the working knife used for paring and cutting but also for fighting or protecting yourself, "with a ratchet in your waist," as Derrick Crooks of the Slickers sang it in "Johnny Too Bad." I've almost always carried a knife, and this one requires a special technique. I've used it to make a point — or to get myself heard. The ratchet has a ring to lock the blade; just a little pressure and you can flick it out. You've got to be quick in this game. The way it was explained to me, if you're going to use a blade, the winner is the one who can make a quick horizontal cut across the other's forehead. The blood will fall like a curtain, but you don't really hurt the cat that much, you just put an end to the fight because he can't see. The blade's back in your pocket before anybody knows about it. The big rules of knife fighting are (a) do not try it at home, and (b) the whole point is *never, ever* use the blade. It is there to distract your opponent. While he stares at the gleaming steel, you kick his balls to kingdom come—he's all yours. Just a tip!

Eventually they brought the drums down to the house, which was a major break with the sacred conventions, though I didn't realize it at the time. And we began to record there, just on cassettes, and play all night. Naturally I'd pick up the guitar and stroke away, find out what chords might fit, and they, they kind of broke their own rules and turned round and said, "Hey, man, that's nice." So I wormed my way in. I suggested maybe a harmony here could help, and I crept in with a guitar. They could have told me to fuck off or not. So I left it to them, basically. But when they heard what they were sounding like coming back on a cassette recorder, they loved it—loved to hear themselves played back. Damn right, you're good. You're fucking unique, motherfuckers!

I went down there for years and years after that. We would just record in the room. If I had some tape and we had a machine, we'd put it down, but if not, it didn't matter. If it ran out of tape, it didn't matter. We weren't there to record, we were there to play. I felt like a choirboy. I would just stroke a little bit behind them and hope that I didn't annoy them. One frown, I'd shut up. But I kind of got accepted. And then they told me that I was not actually white. To the Jamaicans, the ones that I know, I'm black but I've turned white to be their spy, "our man up north" sort of thing. I take it as a compliment. I'm as white as a lily with a black heart exulting in its secret. My gradual transition from white man to black was not unique. Look at Mezz Mezzrow, a jazzman from the '20s and '30s who made himself a naturalized black man. He wrote *Really the Blues,* the best book on the subject. It was my mission in a way to get these guys recorded. Finally, when we were together around 1975, we schlepped everybody down to Dynamic Sounds, but they couldn't handle the studio situation. It wasn't their milieu. "You move over there, you go there..." The idea of being told what to do, for them, was incomprehensible. And it was a dismal failure, really. Even though it was a good studio. That's when I realized, if you want to record these guys, it's got to be in the front room. It's got to be up at the house, where they're all feeling comfortable and they're not thinking about being recorded. We had to wait twenty years for that to happen, to get the take we wanted, which is when they became known as the Wingless Angels.

I cleaned up for tours, but in the middle of a long tour, somebody would give me some shit and then I'd want some more. And I'd say, well, I've got to get some more now, because I need to wait until I have some time off to clean up. I've had some lovely junkie babes on the road, ones that saved my life, got me off the hook here and there. And most of them not lowlife bitches. A lot of them very sophisticated, very smart women who were into it themselves. It wasn't like you had to go to the gutters or the whorehouses to find it. You could be at some backstage party or go and visit these society people, and a lot of the shit I've scored is because they offered it, these debutante junkies, bless their hearts.

Even then I could never get being with a woman I didn't genuinely like, even if it was just for a night or two, or just a port in the storm. Sometimes they were taking care of me, sometimes I was taking care of them, and a lot of it had nothing to do with lust. A lot of times I've ended up in bed with a woman and never done anything, just cuddled and slept. And I've loved loads of them. I've always been so impressed that they actually loved me in return. I remember a chick in Houston, my junkie friend, I think on the '72 tour. I'm out, fucked up, and I'm cold turkey. Bumped into her in a bar. She gave me some stuff. For a week I loved her and she loved me and she saw me through a hard time. I'd broken my own rule and gotten strung out. And this sweet girl came to my rescue, moved in with me. I don't know how I found her. Where do angels come from? They know what's what and they can see through you, cut through the bullshit look in your eyes and say, "You've got to do this." From you, I'll take it. Thank you, sister.

Another was in Melbourne, Australia. She had a baby. Sweet, shy, unassuming, she was on the scuppers; the old man had left her with the kid. She could get me pure cocaine, pharmaceutical. And she kept coming to the hotel to deliver, so I went, hey, why don't I just move in? Living in the suburbs of Melbourne for a week with a mother and child was kind of weird. Within four or five days I was like a right Australian old man. Sheila, where's my fucking breakfast? Here's your breakfast, darling. It was like I'd been there forever. And it felt great, man. I can do this, just a little semidetached. I'd take care of the baby; she went to work. I was husband for the week. Changed the baby's diapers. There's somebody in a suburb in Melbourne who doesn't even know I wiped his ass.

Then there was the stopover Bobby and I made with two girls we picked up in Adelaide. Lovely girls who took care of us very well. These chicks had some acid, and I'm not a big acid head, but we had a couple of days off in Adelaide, and they were fine-looking babes and they had a little hippie bungalow up in the hills, drapes and candles and incense and sooty oil lamps. So OK, take me away. We'd been living in hotels, we'd been on the road forever, and just to be taken out of our context was a huge relief. When we had to leave, because we had to go from Adelaide to Perth, which is the other end of the fucking continent, we said, why don't you come with us? So they did, but we were still all fucking high as kites. We got on the plane, and somewhere halfway to Perth, Bobby and I were in the front seat, both girls burst out of the john seminaked. They'd been having it off together and they came tumbling out, giggling. They were outrageous Australian Sheilas. We were laughing. "Go on, get 'em out," and we heard this collective gasp from the rest of the tube behind us. We figured we were on our own plane; we'd forgotten about the other passengers. And we turned around and there were two hundred shocked faces behind us, Australian businessmen and matrons. Their gasps took the air out of the whole cabin. Some of them started laughing and some went to see the captain and demanded immediate reprisals. So we were threatened with arrest at Perth airport. We were all corralled for a bit when we landed. It was a close call, but somehow we talked our way out of it. Bobby and I were saying, what have we got to do with it? We were just sitting in our seats. The two girls explained they were "exchanging frocks." I don't know how they got away with it.

They came with us to Perth, we did the gig, and then we left on our own plane, a cargo plane, a Super Constellation. Leaking oil, no soundproofing, and all your own kit, bring a mattress or two to lie on. We spent fifteen hours from Perth to Sydney. You could raise your voice; it wouldn't matter. It was like being in a World War II bomber, without the Benzedrine. And we obviously made the most of it. We knew these chicks a week. This happens on the road a lot. Very fierce relationships form and then they're gone; it's almost a flash. "I was really close to her, I really liked her, I almost remember her name."

It's not like I was collecting — I'm not Bill Wyman or Mick Jagger, noting down how many I've had. I'm not talking about shagging here. I've never been able to go to bed with a woman just for sex. I've no interest in that. I want to hug you and kiss you and make you feel good and protect you. And get a nice note the next day, stay in touch. I'd rather jerk off than just have a piece of pussy. I've never paid for it in my life. I've *been* paid for it, though. Sometimes there's a backhander — "I love you too, *and here's some smack!*" Sometimes I'd get into it just for fun. Can you pull her? Let's see if you can. Try your best line. Usually I was more interested in chicks who weren't slavering and falling all over me. I'd be hanging out and go, let's try the wife of the banker....

I remember once in Australia, I had a room opposite Bill Wyman's. And I found out he had a deal with the doorman, because there were something like two thousand chicks outside the hotel. "That one in the pink. No, not *that* one in the pink, *that* one in the pink." He had loads of chicks up there that day, and none of them stayed more than ten minutes. I don't think any of them got much more than the insipid cup of tea that Bill likes — some hot water with a little milk in it and a dip of a tea bag. It was just too short for anything to happen and get dressed again. None of them emerged disheveled, so to speak. But then it would go down in the book: had that one! I counted nine in four hours. He wasn't shagging them, so I presume he was auditioning them. "You from around here?" Bill was just blatantly like that. The weird thing is that, as different as they seem, Bill Wyman and Mick Jagger were actually very similar. That would rankle Mick like a motherfucker, me saying that. But if you saw them together on the road or read their diaries, they were basically the same. Except Mick's got a bit of class, standing at the front, being the lead singer and la la la. But if you saw them off stage and what they were doing, "How many did you have tonight?" they were the same.

Different from teenyboppers or the queues of chicks waiting for tea with Bill Wyman were the groupies. I'd like to vindicate them as the fine young ladies they were, who knew what they wanted and knew what to provide. There were a few blatant opportunists, like the plaster casters who went around trying to get an impression of every rock-and-roll player's cock. They didn't get mine. I won't go through that. Or the butter queens, rivals to the plaster casters. I've got to admire their moxie. But I don't like professionals who go around predatorily, had him, had him...like a Bill Wyman in reverse. I was never interested in that lot. I would deliberately not fuck 'em. I'd tell them to get undressed and go, OK, you can leave now. Because you knew you were gonna be chalked up on scoreboards.

But there were loads of groupies out there that were just good old girls who liked to take care of guys. Very mothering in a way. And if things got down to that, OK, maybe go to bed, have a fuck. But it wasn't the main thing with groupies. Groupies were friends and most of them were not particularly attractive. They were providing a service. You got into town, Cincinnati, Cleveland, and there would be one or two chicks who you knew would come by and make sure that you were OK, take care of you, make sure you ate properly. They banged on the door, and you'd look through the little hole and say, oh, it's Shirley.

The groupies were just extended family. A loosely framed network. And what I really liked was there was no jealousy or possession involved in any of it. In those days there was a kind of circuit. Play Cincinnati, next you're going to be playing Brownsville, then you're going down to Oklahoma; there was a sort of route. And they'd just pass you on to their next friend down the road. You go in there and ask for help. Baby, I'm dying out here! I've done four shows, I'm croaking. And they were nurses, basically. You could look upon them more like the Red Cross. They'd wash your clothes, they'd bathe you and stuff. And you're going, why are you doing this for a guitar player? There's a million of us out there.

Flo, who I've already mentioned, was one of my favorites, lived in LA, one of a band of black chicks. Flo had another three or four groupies around her. If I was a bit short of weed or whatever, she would send her crew out. We slept together many times, never fucked, or very rarely. We just crashed out or stayed up and listened to music. A lot of it was to do with music. I had the best sounds, and they would bring me their local sounds that had just come out. Whether you ended up in bed together was immaterial, really.

Bobby Keys and I got into further trouble at the end of the Far East tour in early 1973. In fact, Bobby got into such bad trouble he might still be doing time now but for a deus ex machina of intervention. It was pineapples this time that came to his rescue.

We had played Honolulu as the first gig of the tour. Honolulu was the point of exit and reentry into the United States for this tour, which had taken us to New Zealand and Australia. You had to register musical instruments on the way out of Hawaii and have the list checked on the way back to prove you weren't importing goods.

Bobby should tell the story, since he is the main protagonist.

**Bobby Keys:** Keith and I and the Rolling Stones tour Australia and the Far East, early in 1973. That's back when Dr. Bill used to travel with us, and there were concessions of self-medication for Keith and me to relieve the stress of the road. We're on our way back and we go through customs in Hawaii. I've got all my saxophones with me, and they want to check the serial numbers to make sure they're the same horns I took out. So the guy's got to turn the horn upside down because the serial numbers are printed upside down. Well, the minute this guy turns the saxophone around, I hear this rattling sound. Oh God, I know what that is! *BOINNNGGG,* right on the desk out comes a syringe. And sticks in the desk in front of the customs guy. So one thing naturally leads to another. Keith is there with me; we're in the same line. They separate us immediately, take me away and give me the whole rubdown and find these large capsules full of smack and what have you. They're just soaking it up. The booking guy has made his fucking year's quota now! He's just rattling that typewriter. "Oh boy, we nailed a Kingfish and his sidekick now, buddy! This is it, yeah, we got the menu on these boys!" And they do. They've just taken our pictures and we've given them our prints, and they're just having so much fun out there—hee hee, ten years! Ten years! Being the very end of the tour, there wasn't really an entourage at all, everybody had split. I was allowed one phone call.

Meanwhile, they've got me and they've got nothing. I was traveling clean. They'd gone through me with a fine-tooth comb. I'm presuming that Bobby is now definitely in the clink. There's no way you can have a syringe come flying out and get away with it. I need a phone call, because I know Bobby's going to need a lawyer. So I'm going through pains to call Frisco, LA, to get him a mouthpiece. Finally they let me on the next connection to Frisco. I get in the queue to get on the plane, and who's fucking there ahead of me but Bobby bloody Keys! What the fuck are you doing here, baby? They just put me through the goddamn grinder! How come you're here before me? Says Bobby, "I made a phone call." "You made a phone call? Who to?" "To Mr. Dole."

**Bobby:** This man Mr. Dole was the big pineapple exporter, the Pineapple King of Hawaii. You ever opened up a can of Dole pineapples, you know who he is. And he also owned the franchise of a professional football team of the World Football League. And Keith and I somehow had run into his daughter when we played Hawaii on the way to Australia. And she invited us up to the house for an afternoon with her and some of her friends, lovely, lovely ladies, all tanned, tanned and rich. Everything was nice and friendly, and phone numbers were exchanged, and we had an enjoyable evening that went on into the night, and I got real friendly with Mr. Dole's pretty daughter and I'm sure we drank lots of pineapple juice. This was before security; we were let loose on the world on our own then, so all sorts of shit happened. We're here Dole-ing it out at the mansion, and in the morning Mr. Dole comes in and there's this sort of embarrassed, "Oh, Daddy!" He sees this bacchanal scene in his lounge, with Keith Richards and me. And his daughter says, "Let me introduce you to my new friends." Keith's just out the door like a shadow, but Mr. Dole, instead of calling the dogs and saying, "Eat these people!," says, "Very happy to meet you." Daddy is actually gracious. This is uncomfortable as hell, because I'm screwing the

Pineapple Princess. Mr. Dole gives me his card, saying, "Well, obviously you're my daughter's friends. If there's ever anything I can do for you if you're passing through Hawaii, give me a call. Here's my private number, goes straight through." So I take Mr. Dole's card, put it in my wallet and don't think any more about it.

Now, on the verge of many years of hard labor in the Texas sun, I have my one phone call and I don't have any numbers to contact anybody. Nobody from the Stones party knows where the hell we are. Then I find Mr. Dole's card in my wallet, the only card I have and the only number I have. So I call this number, and I amazingly get through to Mr. Dole. And I say, "Mr. Dole, do you remember that scantily clad guy and that half-dead-looking Englishman who were in your living room the other day? Well, this is half of them." "Oh hello, Bobby, how are you?" I say, we've had a little problem here. They found this and that, and syringes, and... we don't know what to do. And he says, "Where are you, what happened exactly? What flight were you on?" And I tell him, and he says, "Well, I'll see what I can do," and he hangs up. I don't know what's happening to Keith but I'm scared to death. I thought we were really going to Leavenworth. I was just waiting for the guys to come with the chains and take us away. So I'm sitting back there, partitioned off by this mirrored glass from these clowns that have booked us. And all of a sudden the phone rings at this guy's desk, the one who's been talking all this shit at us, and you can tell, just by the change in his posture, that something has got him going. He looks back at me, looks back at the phone, hangs the phone up, and he just kind of shakes his head very slowly and tears up the charge sheet. They give the shit back, put us on the plane and say, "Don't ever do this again!" And we fly happily off into the sunset.

But it doesn't finish there. We get on the plane, and I'm going, fuck, man. Better make some phone calls to get some shit for Frisco when we get there. Know anybody in Frisco? Who do we call? Now, for some reason I pull out my wallet, I immediately feel these two unfamiliar bumps under its skin. Unmistakable. In there are two double-O caps full of smack, which is a damn good whack of pure heroin. The caps came from the chicks in Adelaide, our Sheilas. Customs had been through me like a dose of salts, they'd searched me, they'd been up my ass! If I'd been busted I would never have got back in the country again. How did they miss them? You find that a lot with customs people. If you think you're clean, you are. And I was totally convinced I had cleaned out my shit. So I immediately went to the bathroom. And suddenly everything went rosy. We'll share one cap now — snort it because we don't have any needles. That will keep us going and then we can make phone calls when we get there. Another close shave. The dog that didn't bark in the night.

Bobby and I seem to be lucky in combination, especially at airports in those years. Once, going through security in New York, Bob was taking care of the baggage. One bag of mine had to go in the hold; it couldn't go through checks. It had a shooter, my .38 special, in it, with five hundred rounds of ammunition. I used to carry a lot of heat. None of my guns were legal. I'm not allowed to own firearms; I'm a convicted felon. In the hold it would have been cool as part of the general baggage. And Bobby got it fucking wrong, and I saw the bag with the shooter in it going through the X-ray. Fuck! No! I yelled out, "BOB!" and everybody that's looking at the machinery turned round and looked at me and took their eyes off the screen. They didn't see it go through.

I went straight back to Jamaica, where I'd left Anita and the children. We stayed in Mammee Bay that spring of 1973. It was already getting a little rough in some ways. Anita was beginning to act in unpredictable ways; she began to suffer from paranoia, and during my absence on tour began to collect a lot of people who took her hospitality for granted—a bad combination. Even when I was there we had a pretty rowdy house. Without realizing it, we were shocking the neighborhood. White man with a big house and everybody knew that Rastas were round there every night, recording, playing music. The neighbors wouldn't have minded *over the weekend* or something. But not on a Monday or a Tuesday. We were starting to do it every damn night. And also the pong coming out of that house! These guys were burning weed by the pound in the chalice. The smoke would go for a mile. It didn't suit the neighbors. I learned later that Anita had also sorely pissed a few people off. She'd been warned a few times, and she'd been excessively rude to the constabulary or anyone who complained. They were calling her rude girl. They called her, more comically, Mussolini, because she spoke Italian. Anita can be rough. I was married to her (without being married to her). And she was in trouble.

I left for England, and the cops hit the house at night, almost before I'd landed in London—many cops in plain clothes. There were shots, one of them apparently fired by an Officer Brown when Anita threw a pound of weed past him into the garden. They took Anita, after a lot of struggling, to jail in Saint Ann's and left the kids. Marlon was barely four and Angela was one year old, and Marlon, at least, watched this. Scary shit. Me, I'm in London finding out what's happened. My immediate reaction was to take the first flight back to Jamaica. But I was persuaded that it was better to put the pressure on from London. If I'd gone there they'd have probably popped me too. The brothers and sisters had taken the kids and whisked them up to Steer Town before the authorities had thought, "What are we gonna do about these two children?" And they lived up there while Anita was in jail, and the Rastas took perfect care of them. And that was very important to me. It was a huge relief to know they were safe and protected, safer than if they'd been whipped off to a foster home.

Angie and Marlon up there with their playmates — who still remember them, who are now great big guys. Then I could concentrate on springing Anita.

There are myths and rumors about Anita in jail, mostly originated by Spanish Tony and his tabloid ghostwriter in Tony's book about me and copied faithfully by other book writers. That Anita was raped in jail, that I had to pay a very large sum of money to spring her, that it was all a conspiracy by the white nabobs of Jamaica and so on. But none of this happened. The cells in the Saint Ann's slammer weren't nice — there was nothing to sleep on, Anita was barely allowed to wash, and it was crawling with cockroaches. None of which did much to calm the bouts of paranoia and hallucination that she suffered then. And they mocked her — "rude girl, rude girl." But she wasn't raped, and I didn't have to pay a bribe. The bust was simply punishment for ignoring their warnings. All this was explained to the lawyer, Hugh Hart, who came to spring her. He discovered that the police were relieved to be rid of her. They didn't know what to do with her. They hadn't yet charged her with any offense. Hart got her out by promising to get her off the island. So she was driven home to collect the children and then to a plane for London. Anita was not making a lot of the right moves at the right time. At the same time, Anita's Anita. You don't take her on for nothing. I still loved her and she was the mother of my kids. I don't let go; I have to be kicked out. But Anita and I were starting to be no good together.

My Jamaican roots, by contrast with Anita's expulsion, would only get deeper, even though I wasn't able to get back there for a few years. Before Anita's bust I had already realized I needed a little more protection, that we were getting exposed on the beach at Mammee Bay. I already loved Jamaica enough to look for a really nice house there. I didn't want any more rent-a-houses. So we went touring with our landlord at the time, Ernie Smatt, who showed me Tommy Steele's house tucked away up in the hills above Ocho Rios. Its name was Point of View and I still own it to this day. This house had a perfect location, sitting on a small cliff looking out over the bay, in fairly dense hillside woodland. Its location had been picked with the greatest care by an Italian prisoner of war called Andrea Maffessanti, who had been shipped out to Jamaica with a bunch of other Italian POWs. Maffessanti was an architect, and while he was a prisoner he was also looking around for perfect spots to build houses. And he either got them made or he sold his drawings, because many houses there are attributed to him. He was there for two or three years, studying wind and weather, which is why the house is slightly L shaped. During the day you get the breeze off of the sea, from the front, where you're over-looking the harbor. At six o'clock in the evening, the breeze changes and comes down from the mountain. He had it shaped so the cool breeze comes down past the kitchen, from the land. A brilliant piece of architecture. I got it for eighty grand. The house was kind of dark, with air-conditioning machines, which I tore out immediately. Because of Maffessanti's design, the house is naturally ventilated. We just put some more fans in, and it's always worked that way since then.

I bought it and left it on the vine. It was a very busy period, and also I was on the dope.

We toured Europe in September and October 1973, after the release of *Goats Head Soup.* The lineup now included, almost perma-nently until 1977, Billy Preston playing keyboards, usually organ. He'd already had a meteoric career, playing with Little Richard and with the Beatles almost as a fifth member of the band, and writing and churning out his own number one hits. He was from California, born in Houston, a soul and gospel musician who ended up playing with almost everybody who was good. We now toured with two trumpets, two saxophones and two keyboards — Billy's organ alongside Nicky Hopkins's piano — as sidemen.

Billy produced a different sound for us. If you listen to the records with Billy Preston, like "Melody," he fit perfectly. But all the way through a show with Billy, it was like playing with somebody who was going to put his own stamp on everything. He was used to being a star in his own right. There was one time in Glasgow when he was playing so loud he was drowning out the rest of the band. I took him backstage and showed him the blade. "You know what this is, Bill? Dear William. If you don't turn that fucking thing down right now, you're going to feel it." It's not Billy Preston and the Rolling Stones. You are the keyboard player with the Rolling Stones. But most of the time I never had a problem with it. Certainly Charlie quite enjoyed the jazz influence, and we did a lot of good stuff together.

Billy died of complications brought about by various kinds of over-indulgence, in 2006. And there was no reason for him to have gone that way. He could have gone up and up. He had all the talent in the world. I think he'd been in the game too long; he'd started very young. And he was gay at a time when nobody could be openly gay, which added difficulties to his life. Billy could be, most of the time, a bundle of fun. But sometimes he would get on the rag. I had to stop him beating up his boyfriend in an elevator once. Billy, hold it right there or I'll tear your wig off. He had this ludicrous Afro wig. Meanwhile, he looked perfectly good with the Billy Eckstine look underneath.

I was taking a pee with Bobby Keys in Innsbruck, just after a show, and Bob usually has a joke or two at these moments. But he's very quiet. And he goes, "Ah, I got bad news....GP's dead." It was like a kick to the solar plexus. I looked at him. Gram, dead? I thought he was straight, I thought he was on the ups. Story later, says Bobby. All I've heard is that he's dead. Oh, my man. You never know quite how it's going to affect you; it never hits you at once. Another good-bye to another good friend.

We heard later that Gram was clean when he went overboard. He took a normal-sized dose. "Oh, just one..." But cold turkey had already wiped out his body's resilience against it, and *boom*. There's that fatal mistake with junkies. When you've cleaned up, the body's just been through that shock. They think, I'll just use one little hit, but they give themselves the same shot that they were taking the week before, to which they've built up a tolerance in amazing proportions, which is why the comedown is so heavy. And the body just says, well, fuck it, I give up. If you're going to do things like that, you should try and remember the amount you took the first time you ever took it. Start again. A third less. A pinch.

In order to deal with Gram's death, I said, I can't stay in Innsbruck tonight. I'm going to rent a car, and we're going to Munich and we're going on an impossible task. We're going to look for one woman. Because I knew about her, I'd seen her once or twice, and she fascinated me. I know this is pointless, but we're going to go into Munich to look for her. Let's go tonight. Let's just forget about it and go do something else. I hate all that crying shit, and moping. There's nothing you can do about it. The fucker's dead and all you do is get mad at him for dying. So you take your mind off it. I'm going to look for one of the most beautiful women in the world. I'll never find her, but that's what we'll go for. A focus. A target. And Bobby and I rented a BMW, this was one in the morning, and took off.

The target was Uschi Obermaier. If there was one thing that could soothe my soul, it was her. She was beautiful. She was quite famous in Germany as a model who had graduated into an icon of the student protest movement that was traumatizing relations between the generations in Germany and threatening to tear the country apart. She was the poster girl of the left; her picture was everywhere. She was a mad rock-and-roll fan, which is how she'd found her way to Mick at first and how I'd met her, very briefly, once. Mick had invited her to come to Stuttgart and she was looking for him in the hotel. She ran into me instead and I took her to Mick's door. But I'd seen her picture on posters and in magazines, and there was something about her that got to me. Uschi's boyfriend, a guy called Rainer Langhans, had been one of the founders of Commune 1, a public live-in designed to wage war against the nuclear family and the authoritarian state. She'd been co-opted into Commune 1 when she took up with Rainer, but Uschi's other title, of which she was proud, was the Bavarian Barbarian. She had never taken the ideology seriously, openly drinking banned Pepsi-Cola and smoking menthol cigarettes and upsetting other Commune dictates. She was photographed naked by *Stern* magazine rolling joints; she was certainly wholehearted in her desire to outrage the German bourgeoisie. But when the commune world hardened up into two camps — terror groups like Baader-Meinhof on one hand and the Greens on the other — Uschi retired from the fray, at least retired from Rainer, and went back to Munich. Her road is littered with guys who tried to tame her. They tried to tame something that's untamable. She's the best bad girl I know.

Anyway, that night we checked into the Bayerischer Hof, where everybody's got a Rembrandt over his bed, a real one. Bob said, right, what are we going to do now, Keith? I said, Bob, now we're going down to Schwabing and hit the strip, the club circuit. Let's do what Gram would have done if we'd croaked. I said, we've got to look for Uschi Obermaier in this city. I've got to have a target. No particular reason — it was the only thing I knew in Munich to aim at. I didn't even know if she was in town. So we buffed ourselves up a bit and started to hit the clubs. And things were rocking, but it wasn't what we were looking for. And by about the fifth or sixth club, there's some damn good records being played, so I went up and talked to the DJ, who I happened to know, George the Greek. And on top of that he happened to know the Obermaier.

But even if I find her, what am I going to do? I'm in no condition to put the make on her, and there's not much time anyway. So...OK, well, we've actually found someone who knows her, this is already a miracle, but I'm lost for a plan. George says, I know her address, but she's with her old man. I said, George, let's go round there. And we parked opposite the flat, and I said, George, will you go up and say that KR's looking for her? I was determined to make the full circle with GP dying. And George goes up and knocks on her door, and out she struts, just to the window, and goes, who are you? Why? I don't know why, a friend of mine's just died, and I'm pretty fucked up. I just want to say hello. You were the target, and we found you. We'll leave it at that. Then she came down and gave me a kiss and went back upstairs. But hey, we actually pulled it off! Mission accomplished.

The second time I tried to get in touch with Uschi, I got Freddie Sessler to track her down on the phone. He called her agency. And the agent said, "I'm not allowed to give those numbers out," and there's Freddie greasing the line and Freddie could grease like nobody. Freddie was versed in many languages. Uschi and I didn't speak each other's language. When I got her number and she answered she said, "Hi, Mick." I said, "No, it's Keith." She was living in Hamburg at the time and I sent a car round to drive her to Rotterdam. She basically had to do a runner from her old man. They had a fight; she got in the car and came to Rotterdam. She ripped my earring out that night in the bed. We were in this Japanese-style hotel in Rotterdam—next morning I realize my ear is stuck with my own blood to the pillow. As a result of which I have a permanent malformation of the right earlobe.

With Uschi Obermaier, especially at that time, it was lust, pure and simple. And then she grew on me and entered my heart. We'd draw pictures or use sign language. But even if we couldn't talk to each other, I'd found a friend. As simple as that, really. And I loved her dearly. We dabbled around off and on with each other in the '70s, and then she took off with her new love, boyfriend Dieter Bockhorn, to Afghanistan, and she slipped from my mind and my heart. And then I heard that she'd died, of a miscarriage somewhere in Turkey. Which was almost true, but it turned out she was smarter than that. I found out the real story many years later on a beach in Mexico, on the most important day of my life.

This was a terrible period for casualties. Towards the end of that summer, Gus, my granddad, died; Michael Cooper, my deep mate, committed suicide—a fragile psyche, I'd always seen it as a potential.

All the good ones die on you. And where does that leave me? The only answer is to make new friends. But then some of the live ones dropped off the active list. We wore out Jimmy Miller, who slowly succumbed to the dope and ended up carving swastikas into the mixing board while he worked on his swan song album for us, *Goats Head Soup*. Andy Johns lasted until late 1973. We were cutting "It's Only Rock 'n' Roll" in Munich when he got fired for the same reason — hitting the hard stuff too hard. (He survived and worked ever after.) And then my buddy Bobby Keys — I couldn't save him from his own rock-and-roll shipwreck around that same time.

Bobby went down in a tub of Dom Pérignon. Bobby Keys, so the story goes, is the only man who knows how many bottles of it it takes to fill a bath, because that's what he was floating in. This was just before the second-to-last gig on the '73 European tour, in Belgium. No sign of Bobby at the band assembly that day, and finally I was asked if I knew where my buddy was — there had been no reply from his hotel room. So I went to his room and said, Bob, we gotta go, we gotta go right now. He's got a cigar, bathtub full of champagne and this French chick in with him. And he said, fuck off. So be it. Great image and everything like that, but you might regret it, Bob. The accountant informed Bobby afterwards that he had earned no money at all on the tour as a result of that bathtub; in fact he *owed*. And it took me ten goddamn years or more to get him back in the band, because Mick was implacable, and rightly so. And Mick can be merciless in that way. I couldn't answer for Bobby. All I could do was help him get clean, and I did.

As for me, I was now put on the death list by a cheering press, starting with the music papers. A new angle. Not interested so much in the music, early in 1973. *New Musical Express* drew up a top ten of rock stars most likely to die, and put me at number one. I'm also the Prince of Darkness, the world's most elegantly wasted man and so on — these titles that have stuck to me were coined then and were good forever. I often felt wished to death in this period, even by well-meaning people. At first you were a novelty. But then that's what they thought about rock and roll, even into the '60s. And then they wished you to fuck off. And then when you didn't fuck off, they wished you to death.

Ten years I was number one on that list! It used to make me laugh. That was the only chart on which I was number one for ten years in a row. I was kind of proud of that position. I don't think anybody's held that position as long as I have. I was really disappointed when I went down the charts. Finally dropping down to number nine. Oh my God, it's over.

These necromantics were given a boost by the story that I went to Switzerland to get my blood changed — perhaps the one thing everybody seems to know about me. OK for Keith, he can just go and have his blood changed and carry on. It's said to have been some transaction with the devil deep under the stones of Zurich, face white as parchment, a kind of vampire attack in reverse and the rosiness returns to his cheeks. But I never changed it! That story comes from the fact that when I was going to Switzerland, to the clinic to clean up, I had to land at Heathrow and change planes. And there's the Street of Shame following me, "Hey, Keith." I said, "Look, shut the fuck up. I'm going to have me blood changed." Boom, that's it. And then off to the plane. After that, it's like it's in the Bible or something. I just said it to fob them off. It's been there ever since.

I can't untie the threads of how much I played up to the part that was written for me. I mean the skull ring and the broken tooth and the kohl. Is it half and half? I think in a way your persona, your image, as it used to be known, is like a ball and chain. People think I'm still a goddamn junkie. It's thirty years since I gave up the dope! Image is like a long shadow. Even when the sun goes down, you can see it. I think some of it is that there is so much pressure to be that person that you become it, maybe, to a certain point that you can bear. It's impossible not to end up being a parody of what you thought you were.

There is something inside me that just wants to excite that thing in other people, because I know it's there in everybody. There's a demon in me, and there's a demon in everybody else. I get a uniquely ridiculous response — the skulls flow in by the truckload, sent by well-wishers. People love that image. They imagined me, they made me, the folks out there created this folk hero. Bless their hearts. And I'll do the best I can to fulfill their needs. They're wishing me to do things that they can't. They've got to do this job, they've got this life, they're an insurance salesman . . . but at the same time, inside of them is a raging Keith Richards. When you talk of a folk hero, they've written the script for you and you better fulfill it. And I did my best. It's no exaggeration that I was basically living like an outlaw. And I got into it! I knew that I was on everybody's list. All I had to do was recant and I'd be all right. But that was something I just couldn't do.

The dope, and the cops on our back, had gotten to a low point. This is going down the tube. But I never felt that *I* was. I thought, I can handle this. This is the way things are going, this is the way things are thrown at me, all I have to do is get through. I might have all this shit hitting me from this direction, but I know there's a lot of people out there going, go, Keith. In a way it's an election without a ballot. Who wins? The authorities or the public? And there's me in the middle, or the Stones in the middle. At the time, I suppose sometimes I did wonder, is it just fun for everybody? Oh, Keith busted again. Woken up in the fucking early morning with your kids around and you've only been asleep for two hours, if that. I don't mind a polite arrest. It was their manners. They barge in like a SWAT team. It really pissed me off. And you can't do anything about it at the particular time; you've just got to swallow it. You know you're being stitched up. "Mr. Richards says you shoved him up against the gate and said assume the position and kicked him in the ankles?" "Oh, no, no, no, wouldn't have done that. Mr. Richards is exaggerating."

Nonresident in the UK meant, in those days, that we could spend three months or so each year at home. In my case at Redlands and my house in Cheyne Walk, in London. In 1973, that address was under twenty-four-hour surveillance. It wasn't just me. They had their eyes on Mick too, and busted him a couple of times. Most of that summer I couldn't go to Redlands. It burned in July when we were there with the children. A mouse ate through the electrical wiring — stripped away the insulation. It was Marlon, aged four, who discovered it, screaming, "Fire, fire."

It was mostly because of Marlon — Angela was too young to notice it — that I had started to feel a little more serious about the endless cop harassment. He would say, "Dad, why you looking out the window?" and I'd say, "I'm looking for the unmarked car," and he'd go, "Why, Dad?" and I thought, oh fuck. I can play this game solo, but it's starting to affect my kids. "Why are you frightened of the policemen, Daddy?" "I ain't frightened of them. I'm just keeping an eye out for them." But every day it would be an automatic thing to see whether they were parked across the street. Basically you were at war. All I had to do was stop taking the stuff. But I thought, first let's win the war, then we'll decide. Which was probably a really stupid attitude, but that's the way it was. I wasn't gonna bow to these motherfuckers.

They busted us soon after we got back from Jamaica in June 1973, when Marshall Chess was staying with us. They found cannabis, heroin, Mandrax and an unauthorized gun. This was perhaps the most famous bust because I faced many, many charges. There were burnt spoons with residue, needles, shooters, marijuana. Twenty-five charges.

I also had a brilliant lawyer in the person of Richard Du Cann. He was formidable looking, lean, austere. He had famously defended the publisher of D. H. Lawrence's *Lady Chatterley's Lover* from prosecution by the government for obscenity. He was, soon after my case — in spite of it, perhaps — made chairman of the Bar. He told me, there's nothing we can do about this evidence; you just have to plead guilty and I'm going to plead mitigation. "Guilty, Your Honor, guilty." You get a bit hoarse after fifteen. And the judge is getting bored with this, because now he's waiting for Du Cann's speech. But the police had added at the last moment a twenty-sixth charge, a sawn-off shotgun, which was an automatic year in jail. And I suddenly said, "Not guilty, Your Honor." And the wig went, "What?" The judge was ready for lunch; I was already done for. He said, "Why do you say not guilty to this charge?" And I said, "Because if it was sawn-off, Your Honor, why is there a sight on the end of the barrel?" It was an antique miniature, a kid's shotgun that was made for bird hunting by some nobleman in France in the 1880s. Lovely inlay work and everything like that, but it was not sawn-off. And the judge looked at the cops, and I could see the cops' faces drain as they realized they'd gone over the top. They'd tried one too many. It was a beautiful moment for me. You can't get gleeful because you know you've just hit them right in the balls. The judge looks at them with a glare that says, "We had him. You idiots." Then Du Cann goes into this amazing Shakespearean speech about artists and let's face it, the gentleman here is being persecuted. This hardly seems to be necessary. A mere minstrel, etc. And the judge agreed, apparently, because he turned around and said £10 a charge, £250 in all. I'll never forget the judge's contempt for the police. He wanted to show them up with this light sentence because it was obvious they were trying to stitch me up. And so to lunch, Du Cann and I.

After lunch I headed for the Londonderry Hotel to celebrate. There, unfortunately, the bedroom caught fire. The corridor filled with smoke and my little family were ushered out, and indeed banned forever from our favorite hotel. The fire broke out in my room, and Marlon was asleep in my bed, and I leaped through the flames, plucked the boy out and then waited for the ruckus. It wasn't dangerous and reckless behavior — as would be assumed by the tabloids — it was faulty wiring in the room. But who would believe that?

\* \* \*

Ronnie Wood came into the picture in late 1973. We'd bumped into each other but we weren't particularly mates. I knew him as a good guitar player with the Faces. I was at Tramps, one of those ongoing clubs at the time, and this blonde came over to me and said, hey, I'm Krissie Wood, Ronnie Wood's old lady. I said, oh, nice to meet you. How you doing, girl? How's Ronnie? And she said, he's down in Richmond at the house and he's recording there. Do you want to come along? I said, I'd like to see Ronnie, so let's go. So I went down with Krissie to Richmond, to their house, called the Wick, and I stayed for weeks. At the time, the Stones had some time off, Mick was mixing vocals on "It's Only Rock 'n' Roll," I kind of felt like playing anyway. When I got there I saw these top men, Willie Weeks on bass, Andy Newmark on drums and Ian McLagan, Ronnie's buddy from the Faces, on keyboards. I just started to play along. Ronnie was making his first solo album, *I've Got My Own Album to Do* — a *great title,* Ronnie — and I walked in on that session and they gave me a guitar. So that first meeting with Ronnie started over a couple of hot guitars. The next day Ronnie says, let's finish that off, and I say yes but I've got to get home, back to Cheyne Walk. No, just bring some clothes down. Ronnie had bought the Wick from the actor John Mills and he had a studio put downstairs in the basement. It was the first time I'd seen a studio deliberately constructed in somebody's house (and I do advise against living on top of a factory — I know; I did it for *Exile*). But the house was beautiful, the garden sloping down to the river. I had John Mills's almost equally famous actress daughter Hayley's bedroom, not that I used it much, but when I did I found myself reading a lot of Edgar Allan Poe. Staying down there got me away from the Chelsea surveillance, although they cottoned on eventually. Anita didn't mind. She came down too.

There was an extraordinary flow of players and talent concentrated in that time and place, gathered around Woody's record. George

Harrison walked in one night. Rod Stewart would pop in occasionally. Mick came and sang on the record, and Mick Taylor played. After not hanging about much on the London rock-and-roll scene for a couple of years, it was nice to see everybody and not have to move. They'd come to you. There was always jamming. Ronnie and I hit it off straight-away, day in, day out, we had a load of good laughs. He said, I'm run-ning short of songs, so I knocked up a couple of songs for him, "Sure the One You Need" and "We Got to Get Our Shit Together."

That's where I first heard "It's Only Rock 'n' Roll," in Ronnie's studio. It's Mick's song and he'd cut it with Bowie as a dub. Mick had gotten this idea and they started to rock on it. It was damn good. Shit, Mick, what are you doing it with Bowie for? Come on, we've got to steal that motherfucker back. And we did, without too much diffi-culty. Just the title by itself was so beautifully simple, even if it hadn't been a great song in its own right. I mean, come on. "It's only rock and roll but I like it."

Overlapping with Ronnie's record, in December 1974, we went to Munich to record *Black and Blue,* to lay the basic tracks of songs like "Fool to Cry" and "Cherry Oh Baby." That was when Mick Taylor dropped his bombshell on us, telling us he was leaving the band and that he had other furrows to plow, which none of us could believe. We were just then planning our US tour of 1975, and he kind of left us in the lurch. Mick could never explain why he left. He doesn't know why. I always asked him, why did you leave? He said, I don't know. He knew how I felt. I always want to keep a band together. You can leave in a coffin or with dispensations for long service, but otherwise you can't. I can't second-guess the man. It might have had something to do with Rose, his wife. But the proof that he didn't really fit in is that he left. He didn't want to fit in, I don't think. I guess he felt that with his credentials from being with the Stones, he'd be able to write songs, produce. But he didn't do anything.

\* \* \*

So early in '75 we were looking for guitar players and we were in Rotterdam laying more tracks for *Black and Blue* — the time of "Hey Negrita," "Crazy Mama," "Memory Motel" and of the embryonic "Start Me Up," the reggae version that we couldn't make work despite forty or fifty takes. We would be nagging at it again two years later, then four years after that — the slow birth of a song whose perfect non-reggae nature we had discovered in one passing take without realizing it, even forgetting we'd done it. But that's for laters.

We'd been living with Ronnie at the Wick for quite a while, Anita and me and the kids, when I had to go to Rotterdam to record. By this time we'd discovered policemen in the trees with binoculars, in the style of the *Carry On* comedies. And I wasn't hallucinating. Absurd though it was, it was equally serious. We were being watched now all the time. Surrounded. And I'm on my usual dose. So I told Anita, we're going to have to slide out at night. But first I have to call Marshall Chess, who's already in Rotterdam. Marshall was also hooked. We're in this together. We would score together. I said to Marshall, make sure you've got the shit. I'm not moving until I know that you've got it, because what's the point of Rotterdam and working and cold turkey? As I left he said, "Yeah, yeah, I've got it. It's right here. I've got it in my hand." OK. But when I get to Rotterdam, Marshall has this sad, sad look on his face. It's cat litter. They sold him cat litter instead of smack. In those days you had brown, usually Mexican or South American, smack. Brown or beige crystals, which actually looked very much like some cat litter. I was livid. But what's the point of killing the pilot? These fucking Surinamese had sold him cat litter. And we'd paid top price for it.

Instead of being able to zoom along to the studio and start work, we're scrabbling for dope. It makes a man out of you, at least. We spent a nasty couple of days. When you're cold turkey and trying to make a deal at the same time, you're not in a very strong position. The fact that we actually went back to the Surinamese bar is proof of the point. We went down to the depths of the dock area, an almost Dickensian place—like an old illustration, shacks and brick buildings. We looked at the guy behind the bar Marshall thought had sold it to him, and he goes—that famous pose—"Gotcha. Sorry." And they're laughing. What you going to do about it?

Forget about it. It's cold turkey, pal. But I didn't say sorry to the Stones. Hey, just warm up, get a sound, give me another twenty-four hours. Everybody knows what's what. Until I'm in the right condition, I won't appear.

Ronnie wasn't necessarily a shoo-in as our new guitarist, despite our closeness at the time. He was still, for one thing, a member of the Faces. We tried other players before him—Wayne Perkins, Harvey Mandel. Both great players, both of them are on *Black and Blue*. Ronnie turned up as the last one, and it was really a toss-up. We liked Perkins a lot. He was a lovely player, same style, which wouldn't have ricocheted against what Mick Taylor was doing, very melodic, very well-played stuff. Then Ronnie said he had problems with the Faces. So it came down to Wayne and Ronnie. Ronnie's an all-rounder. He can play loads of things and different styles, and I'd just been playing with him for some weeks, so the chips fell there. It wasn't so much the playing, when it came down to it. It came down to the fact that Ronnie was English! Well, it is an English band, although you might not think that now. And we all felt we should retain the nationality of the band at the time. Because when you get on the road, and it's "Have you heard this one?," you've all got the same backgrounds. Because of being London-born, Ronnie and I already had a built-in closeness, a kind of code, and we could be cool together under stress, like two squaddies. Ronnie was damn good glue for the band. He was a breath of fresh air. We knew he'd got his chops, we knew he could play, but a big decider was his incredible enthusiasm and ability to get along with everybody. Mick Taylor was always a bit morose. You'll not see Mick Taylor lying on the floor, holding his stomach, cracking up with laughter for anything. Whereas Ronnie would have his legs in the air.

If you sit Ronnie down, take his mind off everything else, just concentrate all the bits, he's an incredibly sympathetic player. He can surprise you at times. I enjoy playing with him still, very, very much. We were doing "You Got the Silver," and I said, well, I can sing it, but I can't sing and play at the same time. You've got to do my bit. And he got it down so much, it was beautiful. He's a lovely slide player. And he genuinely loves his music. It's innocent, totally pure; there are no angles on it. He knows Beiderbecke, he knows his history, his Broonzy, he's solidly grounded. And he was perfectly adapted to the ancient form of weaving, where you can't tell rhythm from lead guitar, the style I'd developed with Brian, the old bedrock of the Rolling Stones sound. The division between guitar players, rhythm and lead, that we had with Mick Taylor melted away. You have to be intuitively locked to do that, and Ronnie and I are like that. "Beast of Burden" is a good example of the two of us twinkling felicitously together. So we said let's get it on. It was going to be temporary and let's see how it works. So Ronnie came on the 1975 tour of the USA, even though he wasn't officially a member of the band.

Ronnie is the most malleable character I've ever met and a real chameleon. He doesn't really know who he is. It's not insincere. He's just looking for a home. He has a sort of desperation for brotherly love. He needs to belong. He needs a band. Ronnie's a very tight family man. He's had a bit of a rough time—his mum and dad and both of his brothers have died in the past few years. It's tough. You say, hey, Ron, sorry about that. He says, well, what do you expect? Everyone has their time. But Ronnie sometimes doesn't let it out. He holds it in for a long time. Without his mum, Ronnie is sort of lost. Being the youngest in the family, he was Mum's boy. And I know I'm the same way. Ronnie holds it in a lot. He's a tough little sod, fucking Gyppo. The last family of water Gypsies to come onto dry land, some fantastic moment of evolution, though sometimes I don't think Ronnie's shed his fins. Perhaps that's why he's always falling off the wagon. He doesn't like being dry; he wants to get back into the wet.

One difference between Ronnie and me is he was an over-the-top man. He had no control whatsoever. I'm a bit of a drinker, let's say, but Ronnie was everything to the max. I can get up and take a drink, but Ronnie's breakfast used to be a White Cloud tequila and water. If you gave him real cocaine he didn't like it, because what he'd been taking was speed. Except he paid cocaine prices for it. And you'd try and drill it into his head: you're not taking coke, you're taking speed. You've just been sold speed at cocaine prices. At the same time, it's not as if he was discouraged from these habits in his new job.

There was one memorable initiation of Ronnie just before the USA tour at the end of March 1975. We were rehearsing the band in Montauk, Long Island, and we decided to pay a visit to Freddie Sessler, who was living then in Dobbs Ferry, just up the Hudson River from Manhattan. Freddie dared us to consume an ounce of pharmaceutical there and then. It was basically like ripping three pages out of your diary. Freddie's notes enlighten us about this, because I remember very little:

Freddie Sessler: I was deeply asleep about five a.m. when I heard an enormous knock at the front door of my house. With my eyes closed I managed to open the door. I was immediately greeted and awakened to Keith's sense of humor. "What the fuck are you doing sleeping while we are working our asses off and just drove one hundred miles to visit you?" "OK," I said, "I'm up. Just let me wash my face," and I grabbed an orange juice for myself and handed a bottle of Jack Daniel's to Keith. At once he inserted a cassette in the deck of the stereo of some reggae music, at full blast of course, and it was party time. Within a few moments I asked Keith and Ronnie if they would care to join in a wake-up toast. I was holding in my hand a one-ounce bottle of Merck, went into the bedroom, reached for a painting framed in glass and decided to play a game of my own devising. One of my biggest pleasures has always been the ritual of opening a sealed bottle of cocaine.

Just looking, staring at it, breaking the seal, I would get an instant rush, euphoria. It was a bigger pleasure than actually consuming the cocaine itself. As I broke the seal I emptied on the glass two-thirds of the bottle. Then I prepared two equal piles of about eight grams each for Keith and myself and about four grams for Ronnie.

When completed, I said the following to Keith:

"Keith, I would like to test you. What kind of man you are," knowing very well he would stand up to any challenge. I made two lines, grabbed a straw and with swift action snorted my share of eight grams. "Now, let me see if you can do that." In my entire adult life I had never, ever seen anyone indulging in a quantity of this magnitude. Keith looked, stared, grabbed the straw and duplicated my effort with no difficulties. I passed the four grams to Ronnie, saying, "You are a junior. That's all you get. Do it." He did it.

Pharmaceutical cocaine cannot be compared in any way to cocaine produced in Central or South America. It is pure, does not bring on depression or lethargy. A totally different type of euphoria, one of creativity, exists immediately when it is absorbed by the central nervous system. There are absolutely no withdrawal symptoms.

As I passed the line to Ronnie, I was ready to hit the ceiling, an enormous rush. Oh shit, what a sensation. Absolutely nothing I knew of could compare. As I offered Ronnie his line, those were the last words to come out of my mouth for the next six hours. We embarked on a journey to Woodstock.

Pure cocaine. Are you going to go for it or not? Then jump in the car and drive. We had no idea where we went. It was kind of like the drive I did with John Lennon, we just went. I've no idea how we got anywhere. Obviously I drove, and very responsibly, never got pulled over. We gassed up, we did everything, but in another head. I had sketchy reports that we stayed overnight in Bearsville with the Band, probably with Levon Helm. I don't know if there was any aim in going there. Did we want to go and see somebody? I don't think Bob Dylan was living up there at the time. We made it back to Dobbs Ferry eventually. I have a weird feeling that Billy Preston was there, but he didn't come on the drive.

The 1975 tour on which we were about to embark was fueled by Merck cocaine. It was when we initiated the building of hideaways behind the speakers on the stage so that we could have lines between songs. One song, one bump was the rule between Ronnie and me. Even then, three years after the STP tour, it was an extraordinarily ramshackle affair by today's standards. How was it done then? Listen to Mary Beth Medley. She was the tour coordinator, she put the dates together and did the deals with the promoters across the USA. She was twenty-seven, working under Peter Rudge. She had no staff.

**Mary Beth Medley:** It was done on 3 × 5 index cards. I tell this to people and they look at me like I'm talking Swahili. A Rand McNally highway mileage guide, a map of the United States. No fax, no cell phone, no FedEx, no computer. A Rolodex, but nothing other than a regular phone line and telex to Europe to the office. As to the rock-and-roll lifestyle, you might have thought we'd have learned the lessons of caution after the incident in Fordyce. But there was another incident after that, at the end of the tour in August 1975, that's never been related as far as I know. It involves Keith, but it involves everybody. We were in Jacksonville, Florida, and we were going to Hampton, Virginia, and Bill Carter had heard that the plane was going to be searched when we got there. He had these police connections all over the place. We had gone through this scare once in Louisville, Kentucky, where they just came on the plane. And so to avoid that, we collected everyone's contraband. Everyone's guns, knives, drugs, anything that could be considered illegal, and packed it in two suitcases, and I took a private plane from Jacksonville to Hampton, Virginia, with these two suitcases and drove to the hotel. The plane ride I wasn't worried about. With private planes, you didn't even have to fill out a manifest in those days. I think I went anonymously. The drive was nerve-racking. I was going fifty miles an hour. Just me. And then I got to the hotel, I went into a room, not mine, and put it all out on the bed. And as they came in a couple of hours later they all picked up their stuff. Annie Leibovitz has a picture somewhere of the treasure that was in those suitcases.

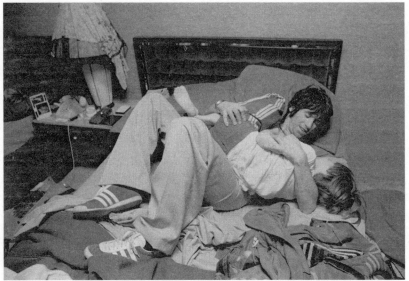

*Annie Leibovitz*

# Chapter Ten

In which Marlon becomes my road companion. Our son Tara dies. We
move in with John Phillips and family in Chelsea. I get busted in
Toronto and charged with trafficking. I give up heroin with the help of
a black box and Jack Daniel's. The Stones record *Some Girls* in Paris.
I meet Lil Wergilis, who helps me clean up. I am given probation in
1978, on condition I give a concert for the blind. Anita's boyfriend
shoots himself playing Russian roulette, and she and I finally part.

There had been so many close shaves. The bust at Fordyce during the 1975 tour was potentially the most lethal. I had used up
all my cat lives. No use counting. Closer shaves were to come, busts
and stray bullets and cars flying off the road. Some escapes had a measure of luck about them. But there was a darkness in the air — a storm
coming. I saw Uschi again — she joined the tour in San Francisco for
a week, and then disappeared for many years. The Rolling Stones
spent some time that autumn in Switzerland, since that was my home,
working more on the album *Black and Blue* — the album whose promotion featuring a half-naked, bruised and bound woman led to a
call for a boycott of Warner Communications. We worked on songs
such as "Cherry Oh Baby," "Fool to Cry" and "Hot Stuff." In Geneva
in March of 1976, Anita gave birth to our third child, a boy we named
Tara.

He was barely a month old when I left Anita to go on a long European tour that was to run from April until June. I took Marlon with

me as my road buddy. He was seven years old. Anita and I had become two junkies living separate existences, except trying to bring up kids. Most of it was actually not that difficult for me because I was on the road so much, and now Marlon was usually with me. But it was not a pleasant atmosphere. It's very difficult living with your old lady who's also a junkie, in fact a bigger one than you are. The only thing Anita ever said to me then was "Has it arrived?" The only important thing in life was the stuff. And she had started to get really far out. A crash in the middle of the night and she'd have thrown a whole bottle of cranberry juice or wine down the wall of the rent-a-house we'd just moved into. "Oh, do you need some stuff, darling?" I understood, but it needn't include redecorating the fucking house. By now she wasn't touring with us or coming to recording sessions; she was more and more isolated.

The more the shit hit the fan, the more I kept the boy with me. I'd never had a son before, so it was a great thing to watch him grow up, to say, I need your help, boy. So Marlon and I became a team. Angela in 1976 was still too young for the road.

We took ourselves to the gigs in this great car of mine. Marlon was my navigator. In those days there were countries; it wasn't just border-less Europe. I gave him a position, a job to do. Here's the map. Tell me when we get to the border. To get from Switzerland to Germany, we went through Austria. So you're talking Swiss border, boom, into Austria, bang, fifteen miles through Austria, bang, into Germany. You're talking a lot of borders just to get to Munich. So you had to be very precise, especially in the snow and ice. Marlon was on the case. He would say, "Fifteen clicks from the border, Dad." That was when to pull over, have a shot and either dump it or re-sort your shit. Sometimes he'd give me a nudge and say, "Dad, time to pull over. You're falling, you're slipping." He acted beyond his age. Necessary when we were being busted. "Er, Dad?" "Yeah?" (He's waking me up, shaking me.) "The men in the blue suits are downstairs."

It wasn't that often that I was late for a show, and I never missed one — but when I was late I was spectacularly late. And it was usually a great show anyway. In my experience, crowds don't mind waiting as long as you turn up, you deliver. It was that half-hippie fog, dope fog. In the '70s, showtime was when I woke up. I might have been three hours late, but there was no such thing as curfews for shows. If you went to see a show, you would be there for the whole night. Nobody said it would start on time. If I was late, sorry, but it was just the right time for the show. Nobody left. But I didn't push my luck. I kept these late shows to a minimum.

Usually if I was late it was because I was deeply asleep. I remember Marlon having to wake me up. It became a habit, actually. Jim Callaghan and the security knew I had a shooter under the pillow and they didn't want to wake me up. Half an hour before we were due on stage they'd send Marlon, shove him into the room. "Dad . . ." Marlon got the hang of it real quick. He knew what to say. "Dad, it really is time." Things like that. "That means two more hours, doesn't it?" "Dad, I held 'em off." He was a great minder.

I was a bit unpredictable in those days, or they thought I was. I never shot anybody, but there was always that fear that I might wake up in one of those moods and grab the gun, thinking I was being robbed. It's not as if I haven't nurtured that a bit; it comes in handy. I never meant to stick people up, but it was a rough schedule, I had a kid with me on the road and I was pretty fucked up.

Usually when I got on stage, I'd just got up. Getting out of bed is one thing, waking up is another. It takes me three or four hours. Then I've got to put the rig on. The shortest time between getting out of bed and getting on stage was probably one of those where I was supposed to be on stage an hour ago. "What am I wearing?" "Pajamas, Daddy." "OK, quick, where's me fucking pants?" Usually I had crashed out in what I was wearing to play anyway. Half an hour later, it's "Ladies and gentlemen, the Rolling Stones." It's an interesting wake-up call.

Let Marlon tell it.

**Marlon:** The '76 tour was in Europe and that's why I went
on the tour with them for the whole summer and ended up at
the Knebworth concert in August, when they played with
Zeppelin. They'd ask me to wake Keith up, because he did
have a bad temper; he didn't like being woken up. So Mick or
someone would come to me and say, we've got to leave in a
few hours, why don't you wake your dad up. I was the only
one capable of doing it without getting my head bitten off. I'd
say, Dad, get up, you've got to get on the road, you've got to
leave, got to get on the plane, and he'd do it. He was very
sweet. We'd go to gigs and then come back. I don't really
remember too much bacchanal, really. We shared a room with
two beds. I'd wake him up and order breakfast from room
service. Ice cream for breakfast or cake. And the waitresses
would often be very condescending to me — oh, poor little
boy — and I'd tell them to fuck off. I found that really
annoying. And I got wise pretty quick to the hangers-on and
people who'd try to get to Keith through me. I got very used
to getting rid of them too, saying, look, I don't want to see you
here, go away. Keith would say, oh, I've got to put Marlon to
bed, to get rid of people. And to some girls or dodgy types, I'd
say, fuck off, Dad's asleep, leave us alone. They wouldn't say
anything to a kid, so they would obey.

I do remember Mick on that tour was quite sweet. We
were in Germany, Hamburg, and Keith was asleep and Mick
invited me to his room. I'd never had a hamburger, and he
ordered me one. "You've never had a hamburger, Marlon?
You've got to have a hamburger in Hamburg." So we sat there
and had dinner. He was very friendly and charming at that
time. He really got to Keith too. He was very nurturing; he
took care of him. That stood out. And at that point Keith was
in such a state.

Keith would always read me stories. We used to love

Tintin and Asterix, but he couldn't read French, and they
were French editions, so he'd make the whole bloody thing
up. It was only after years that I realized when I read a Tintin
that he didn't know what the hell the story was about; he'd
bluffed his way through the whole thing. Given all the smack,
nodding out and that sort of thing, that is quite remarkable. I
do recall I only had one pair of shoes and one pair of trousers,
and I just wore them to death for the whole tour.

There were the bodyguards, Bob Bender and Bob
Kowalski, the two Bobs. They were both six foot and they
were huge guys, walls, mountains. One was blond and one
was dark haired, and they were like bookends. I used to play
chess with them in the hallway, because that's what they'd do,
sit out in the hallway and play chess to pass the time. It was
really fun. That whole time it didn't seem traumatic, it
seemed like a laugh going to concerts every night in a different
city. I'd be up until five in the morning sometimes, go to sleep
till three in the afternoon. It was all on Keith's routine.

I was never even curious about drugs. I found all those
people bloody ridiculous; I just found it really silly what they
were doing. Anita tells me I did smoke lots of spliffs when I
was four or so in Jamaica, but I don't believe that at all; that
sounds like an Anita story. I found the drugs repulsive, but I
did learn to clean it up and not to touch it and not to leave it
lying around. If I saw it, I'd put it away. And there was always
the occasion where I'd pick up a magazine or a book, and
lines of blow would be on it and would go all over the place.
Keith wouldn't get too mad.

At the end of that tour we had a car crash, driving back
from Knebworth. That's the one when Keith was arrested. He
fell asleep and plowed into a tree. Seven of us were in the car
and no one was seriously hurt because, luckily again, that was
the Bentley. That car's actually felt quite a bit. Until five or six

years ago there was still my bloody handprint on the backseat. And on the dashboard there was still the dent where my nose hit it. I was impressed having a dent in the dashboard and disappointed when it was repaired.

I'm a good driver. I mean, nobody's perfect, right? Somewhere I lost it, fell asleep. I just passed out. We skidded off the road. All I hear is Freddie Sessler in the back going, "Jesus fucking Christ!" But I managed to get it off the road and into a field, which is after all the sensible thing to do. At least we didn't hit anybody, we didn't kill anybody, we didn't even hurt ourselves. Then the cops found acid in my jacket. How did I get out of this one? We'd just finished a show. The jackets we were wearing were like band jackets, same shape but different colors. It could have been Mick Jagger's one; it could have been Charlie's that I picked up. It could have been anybody's jacket. That was my defense.

I did make some speech along the lines of, this is my life, this is the way we live and shit happens. You don't live like me. I do what I have to do. If I fuck up, I'm very sorry. I'm just living a peaceful life. Let me get to the next gig. In other words, "Hey, it's only rock and roll." But tell that to a bunch of Aylesbury plumbers. Maybe "he charmed the jurors"—so one report said. It's hard to believe, because my attitude was, I need a jury that's at least half full of rock-and-roll guitar players to have anybody know what the fuck I'm talking about. A jury of my peers would be Jimmy Page, a conglomeration of musicians, guys that have been on the road and know what's what. My peers are not some lady doctor and a couple of plumbers. As far as that's English law, I respect it very much. But do me a favor. And they basically got that. No one, it seems, this time, was trying to teach me a lesson, and they let me off with a fine and a slight slap on the wrist.

I was in Paris, with Marlon, on tour when I got the news that our little son Tara, aged just over two months, had been found dead in his cot. I got the phone call as I was getting ready to do the show. And it's a "Sorry to tell you...," which hits you like a gunshot. And "No doubt you're going to want to cancel the show." And I thought about it for a few seconds and I said, of course we're not canceling. It would be the worst possible thing because there was nowhere else to go. What am I going to do, drive back to Switzerland and find out what didn't happen? It's happened already. It's done. Or sit there and mope and go bananas and get into, what? Why? I called Anita, of course, and she was in tears, and the details were all confusing. Anita had to stay there and take care of the cremation, and all of the argy-bargy from the Swiss coroners, before she could come to Paris, and all I could do then was to protect Marlon from it, try not to bounce everything onto him. The only thing that kept me going through that was Marlon and the day-to-day work of taking care of a seven-year-old on the road. I don't have enough time to cry about this, I've got to make sure this kid is all right. Thank God he was there. He was too young to really get the drift on it. The only upside in this respect is at least Marlon and I were away from the immediate grief. I had to go on stage that night. After that it was plowing on through the tour with Marlon and keeping that separated. It made Marlon and me tighter, no matter what. I've lost my second son, I ain't going to lose the first.

What happened? I know very little about the circumstances. All I knew about Tara was this beautiful little boy in the cradle. Hey, little bugger, I'll see you when I get back off the road, right? He seemed perfectly robust. He looked like a miniature Marlon. Never knew the son of a bitch, or barely. I changed his nappy twice, I think. It was respiratory failure, cot death. Anita found him in the morning. I wasn't about to ask questions at the time. Only Anita knows. As for me, I should never have left him. I don't think it's her fault; it was just a crib death. But leaving a newborn is something I can't forgive myself for. It's as if I deserted my post.

Anita and I, to this day, have never talked about it. I dropped it because I didn't want to open old wounds. If Anita wanted to sit around and talk to me about it, I might, but I couldn't bring it up. It's too painful. Neither of us, I'm sure in her case too, have got over it.

You don't get over these things. At the time it certainly further eroded our relationship, and Anita descended further into fear and paranoia.

There's no question that losing a child is the worst thing that can ever happen, which is why I wrote to Eric Clapton when his son died, knowing something of what he was going through. When that happens you go totally numb for a while. It's only very slowly that the possibilities of your love for the little chap emerge. You can't deal with it all at once. And you can't lose a kid without it coming to haunt you. Everything's supposed to go in its natural order. I've seen my mum and my dad off, and that's the natural order. But seeing a baby off is another thing. It never lets you rest. Now it's a permanent cold space inside me. Just selfishly, if it had to happen, I'm glad it happened then. When he was too young to form a relationship. Now he bangs into me once a week or so. I have a boy missing. Could have been a contender. I wrote in my notebook when I was working on this book, "Once in a while Tara invades me. My son. He would be thirty-odd now." Tara lives inside me. But I don't even know where the little bugger is buried, if he's buried at all.

That same month that Tara died, I looked at Anita and saw that there was only one place Angela could go while we sorted this out—to my mother. And by the time we could even think about her returning to us, she was ensconced in Dartford with Doris. So I thought, better leave her with Mum. She's got a settled life, no more of this madness for her, she can grow up a normal kid. And she has, and brilliantly. Doris was in her fifties and she could bring up another kid. Given the chance and the possibility, she took it on. She and Bill did it together. I knew I was going to be busted again and again and again, and what was the point of bringing up a daughter, knowing that the cops were at the door? At least I knew there was a shelter for Angela in my mad world. And Angela stayed with Doris for the next twenty years. I kept Marlon with me, on the road, until the tour ended that August.

\*  \*  \*

I packed all my stuff up at the Wick when Ronnie Wood emigrated for tax reasons to America that year, 1976. We couldn't go back to Cheyne Walk because of the twenty-four-hour patrols and the "Oh hello, Keith." If we stayed there, it was with windows closed and curtains closed, a hermetic existence, a real siege, drawn into ourselves.

We were just trying to stay alive and stay one step ahead of the law all the time. Always traveling, a phone call in front, can you get needles there? Mundane fucking junkie shit. It was a prison of my own making. We lived for a while at the Ritz Hotel in London until we were forced to flee on account of our room being in need of refurbishment courtesy of Anita. Marlon began going to school for the first time properly, to Hill House, a school where they wore orange uniforms and seemed to spend much time walking in crocodile lines through the streets of London. The boys of Hill House were a London institution, like the Chelsea pensioners. Marlon, needless to say, found this a profound shock, or what he terms in retrospect a "bloody nightmare."

At this moment John Phillips, of the disbanded Mamas and Papas, was living in London. He and his new wife, the actress Geneviève Waïte, and his small child, Tamerlane, had a house in Glebe Place, Chelsea. And we took refuge there for a time. We moved in. There were already plans to work together, for Rolling Stones Records to produce John's solo album, with Ronnie, Mick, Mick Taylor and me playing on it. Ahmet Ertegun was funding it from Atlantic Records. Good idea too—on paper. John was a great guy, really funny and interesting to work with (although he was nuts). He'd written almost all those songs for the Mamas and others that defined a certain period, some with his ex-wife Michelle Phillips—"California Dreamin'," "Monday, Monday," "San Francisco (Be Sure to Wear Flowers in Your Hair)."

Phillips was amazing. I've never known anybody to be so hooked on dope so quick, and I had something to do with it. The night Ronnie was leaving the Wick, John had called up and said, I've got a bottle of this stuff called Merck. And he said, does anybody have some use for it? I don't do that stuff. I said I would drop by on my way out of Ronnie's. I left the Wick and went straight to John's joint. We were playing and everything, and he'd shown me the bottle. We were there two or three hours and I said, John, can I use your john? I've got to take a hit. So I went in the john, shot up. I mean, I didn't want to pull it in front of the family or anything like that. And when I came out, John said, what was that you were doing? I said, John, it's called smack. And I did the thing I never, or very rarely, did. I think it was the only time. You don't turn other people on; you keep it to yourself. He'd just given me this cocaine, and I felt, well, you want to know what I'm doing? Here we go. So I shot him up. Just in the muscle.

I always felt responsible for John because I turned him on to smack. Within a week, he's got a pharmacy under control and he's become a dealer. I've never seen a guy become a junkie that quick. Usually it takes months, sometimes years, for a guy to get hooked hooked hooked. But John, ten days later, he's running the show. It changed his life. He moved back to New York, and so did I, the following year, when even greater madness took place, but more of that later. The music we played together with Mick and others was released after John's death in 2001, with the title *Pay Pack & Follow*.


**A**nita, **M**arlon and **I** moved around. We stayed in Blakes Hotel. We didn't last long there either, so we moved into a rented house in Old Church Street in Chelsea, recently vacated by Donald Sutherland. It was here, in this house, where Anita really lost it with me. She had become delusional, very paranoid. It was one of her darkest periods and it developed with the dope. Wherever we went, she was convinced that someone had left a stash before doing a runner. She'd take the whole place apart looking for it. The bathroom at the Ritz, sofas, wallpaper, paneling. I remember once I took her in the car and told her to concentrate on the number plates, something mundane to try and calm her, connect her to reality. We made a pact, at her request, that I would never take her to the nuthouse.

I like a high-spirited woman. And with Anita, you knew you were taking on a Valkyrie — she who decides who dies in battle. But she went right off the rails, became lethal. Anita had rage whether there was dope or not, but if there was no dope she'd go crazy. Marlon and I used to live in fear of her sometimes, of what she would do to herself, let alone to us. I used to take him downstairs to the kitchen and we'd hunker down and say, wait for Mum to get over it. She was slinging shit about, which might have hit the kid. You'd come back to the house, and the walls were covered in blood or wine. You didn't know what was going to happen next. We would be there just hoping that she'd stay asleep and not wake up in one of her screaming fits, raging at the top of the stairs like Bette Davis, throwing glass objects at you. She was a tough bitch. No, there wasn't a lot of fun for a while with Anita in the middle '70s. She became unbearable. She was a real bitch to me, a bitch to Marlon, she was a bitch to herself. And she knows it, and I'm writing it here in this book. Basically I was looking at how the hell do I get out of there without screwing it up with the kids. I loved her dearly. I don't get that involved with women if I don't love them dearly. I always feel it's my failure if it doesn't work, if I can't pull it together and make it all right. But with Anita I couldn't make it right. She was unstoppably self-destructive. She was like Hitler; she wanted to take everything down with her.

I tried to clean up loads of times, but not Anita. She would go the other way. Any suggestion of it and she would go into rebellion mode and if anything take more. Domestic duties, at this point, were not something she took on gladly. I said, what the fuck am I doing? OK, she's the mother of my children. Swallow it. I loved the woman; I'd do anything. She's got a problem? I'll take over. I'll help out.

"Unscrupulous" is not a bad word for her. I don't mind flinging it in her face right now, and she knows it. It's up to her to live with. I just did what I had to do. Anita will still have to wonder how the hell she screwed up. I'd still be with her right now! I'm never one to change, especially with the kids. Anita and I can now sit around at Christmastime with our grandchildren and give each other a bemused smile; hey, you silly old cow, how you doing? Anita is in good shape. She's become a benign spirit. She's a marvelous granny. She's survived. But things could have been better, baby.

I sealed myself off much of the time from Anita, or she didn't care to join us in the studio at the top of the house. She spent most of her time in the Donald Sutherland memorial bedroom, which had massive chains hanging from the wall, purely decorative but giving an overall S&M feel to the room. The regulars came by — Stash, Robert Fraser. I was seeing a lot of the Monty Python people at the time, particularly Eric Idle, who used to come up and hang.

It was in this Church Street period that I achieved my longest feat of Merck-assisted wakefulness — a nine-day epic of no sleep. I was still going on the ninth day. I may have had a couple of snoozes, but no more than twenty minutes. I was busy doing my sounds, transferring this to that, making notes, writing songs, and I'd become manic, basically a hermit. But over the nine days lots of people came to visit the cave. Everybody I knew in London at the time dropped by day by day, but to me it was just one long day. They'd been doing other things, whatever they had to do. They'd slept and brushed their teeth and shit, and I'm up there writing songs, reorganizing my sounds and making double copies of everything. This was all on cassette in those days. And then I would get into artistically decorating the labels. The reggae one had a beautiful Lion of Judah.

It was into the ninth day and I was still, as far as I was concerned, in fine form. I remember I was going to copy one cassette onto another. I'd got it all down, noted which track, *boom,* pushed play. I turned around and fell asleep on my feet for three-tenths of a second, then I fell forward and hit the JBL speaker. Which woke me up, but worse than that, I couldn't see a thing. It was just a curtain of blood. There were three steps, I still remember them now, and I managed to miss every one, and I rolled over and fell asleep on the floor. I woke up with an encrusted face, maybe a day later. Eight full days, and on the ninth day, he fell.

The band was waiting for me in Toronto early in 1977. I put off going for many days. They sent me telegrams: "Where are you?" We had a gig at the El Mocambo, which would provide more tracks for our *Love You Live* album. We needed some days of rehearsal. I couldn't, apparently, extract myself from the rituals of Old Church Street. And I had to get Anita on the road too, which was just as difficult. But finally we flew there on February 24. The gigs—two nights at the club—were scheduled for ten days later. I took a hit on the airplane and somehow the spoon ended up in Anita's pocket. They found nothing on me at the airport, but they found the spoon on Anita and busted her. Then they bided their time. They went to great effort to prepare the big bust of me in the Harbour Castle Hotel, knowing that they'd find something—just follow the junkies. They had intercepted a package of stuff I'd sent ahead. Alan Dunn, the longest-serving Stones man, the logistics and transport supremo, discovered later that the regular personnel who worked in the hotel suddenly found themselves working alongside many extra people, who had been hired mostly as telephone and television engineers. The police were setting it up: massive resources against one guitar player. The hotel manager would have known, but of course nobody tipped us off. To save money, Peter Rudge, the tour manager, had taken any personnel off the floor. So the police came straight to the room. Marlon would not normally have let in any policemen, but they were dressed as waiters. They couldn't wake me up. By law you have to be conscious to be arrested. It took them forty-five minutes—I'd been up for five days and I'd had a heavy-duty shot and I was out. This was my last rehearsal day, and I'd been asleep for about two hours. My memory of it is waking up and them going slap slap, two Mounties dragging me about the room slapping me. Trying to get me "conscious." *Bang bang bang bang bang.* Who are you? What's your name? Do you know where you are and do you know why we're here? "My name's Keith Richards, and I'm in the Harbour Hotel. What you're doing here I have no idea." Meanwhile they'd found my stash. And it was about an ounce. Quite a lot. No more than a man needs. I mean, it wouldn't feed the city. But obviously they knew their shit, like I knew my shit, and it was clearly not the Canada smack. It had come from England. I'd put it in the flight case.

So they arrest me, take me to this Mountie police station, and it's really not my time of day. They put me through the books and everything. And because of the amount they found, they decided to charge me with trafficking, which is an automatic jail sentence for a very long time, in Canada. I said, OK, fine. Give me a gram back. "Oh, we can't do that." I said, so what are you going to do now? You know I need it and that I'm going to have to get it. What are you going to do? Follow me and bust me again? Is that your game? How are you going to play this? Give me some back till I figure this out. "Oh no, no." And that was when Bill Wyman came through. Bill was the first one to come around and say, is there anything I can do? And I said quite honestly, I'm out of shit and I need some shit. And of course that's not Bill's area, but he said, I'll see what I can do. And he found somebody. We'd been working at the El Mocambo club, so we had local connections. Bill came through and got some shit to get me off the hook, over the hill. And that was a big risk for Bill, considering the attention I was getting. That was about the closest emotional thing that I can remember with Bill.

The Mounties never did try to bust me again. I was quoted as saying, "What is on trial is the same thing that's always been on trial. Dear old *them and us*. I find this all a bit weary. I've done my stint in the fucking dock. Why don't they pick on the Sex Pistols?" Yet again someone was seriously after my ass, and the situation was further complicated by Margaret Trudeau, the wife of Prime Minister Pierre Trudeau, moving into the hotel as a Stones appendage, offering a double-big tabloid story. The prime minister's young wife with the Stones, and you throw in drugs, you're looking at a three-month run. In the end it may have played in my favor, but at the time it was the worst combination of circumstances. Margaret Trudeau was twenty-two and Trudeau was fifty-one when they got married. It was a bit like Sinatra and Mia Farrow—the power and the flower child. And now Trudeau's bride—and this was exactly their sixth wedding anniversary—was seen walking in our corridors in a bathrobe. So then the story was that she had left him. She had, in fact, moved into the room next to Ronnie, and they were hitting it off really well, or, as Ronnie put it so nicely in his memoirs, "We shared something special for that short time." She flew to New York to escape the publicity, but Mick flew to New York as well, so it was assumed they too were an item. Worse and worse. She was a groupie, that's all she was, pure and simple. Nothing wrong with that. But you shouldn't be a prime minister's wife if you want to be a groupie.

I'm out on a bond of many dollars, but they took my passport and I'm released only to the hotel. So I'm trapped. And I'm still waiting to see if they're going to jail me. They're shooting fish in a barrel. At another hearing they added a charge of cocaine possession and revoked bail, but we got off that on a technicality. I would have loved to have dared them to put me in jail. It was all bullshit. They didn't have the balls. They weren't feeling confident. The rest of the band left Canada out of caution, and quite wisely so. I was the first one to say, you fuckers get out of here; they're only going to involve you. Let me take the heat. It's my heat.

It was quite likely that jail time was on the cards. I was facing a probable two years, according to my lawyers. It was Stu who suggested that I should use the waiting time to put down some tracks of my own—put something down to remember the man by. He hired a studio, a beautiful piano and a microphone. The result has been doing the circuit for a while—*KR's Toronto Bootleg*. We just did all the country songs, nothing different from what I do any other night, but there was a certain poignancy about it because at that moment things looked a bit grim. I played the George Jones, Hoagy Carmichael, Fats Domino songs I'd played with Gram. Merle Haggard's "Sing Me Back Home" is pretty poignant anyway. The warden is taking the prisoner down the hall to his execution.

*Sing me back home with a song I used to hear...*
*Sing me back home before I die.*

Once again it was Bill Carter who came to my rescue. Carter's problem was that in 1975 he had assured the visa-issuing authorities that there were no problems with drugs. Now I'm busted in Toronto for drug *trafficking*. Carter had flown straight to Washington. Not to visit his friends in the State Department or Immigration, who had told him that I would never be allowed into America again. To the White House. First he had assured the Canadian court when he posted my bond that I had a medical problem and that I needed to be cured of my heroin addiction. He made the same case to his contacts in the White House, where Jimmy Carter was president, using all the political muscle he could work, talking to one counsel there who was Carter's drug policy man, fortunately charged, at the time, with finding solutions more effective than punishment. He told them that his client had fallen off the wagon, had a medical problem, and Bill was asking their mercy to grant me a special visa to come to the United States. Why the United States and not Borneo? Well, there was only one woman who could cure me and she was called Meg Patterson and she did a "black box cure" with electric vibrations. She was in Hong Kong and needed a sponsor doctor in the United States. These were the lengths Bill Carter went to. And it worked. Miraculously, his White House contacts instructed Immigration to grant me a visa, and he got permission from the Canadian court for me to fly to the United States. We were allowed to rent a house in Philadelphia, where Meg Patterson would treat me every day for three weeks. From there, after her prescribed cure, we moved to Cherry Hill, New Jersey. I was not allowed to move outside a twenty-five-mile radius from Philadelphia, which included Cherry Hill. A deal worked out between the doctors and lawyers and the immigration department. This wasn't so great for Marlon, however.

**Marlon:** They let him in to clean up, which is when we went to New Jersey. And I lived with this doctor's family, this very religious family. That was actually the most traumatic thing, moving from this hotel with all the Stones and everyone into this house in New Jersey with a right-wing Christian American family, a white picket fence and skateboards, and I started going to an American school where you had to say prayers every day. That was really shocking. And I would go and visit Keith and Anita, who were down the road, every few days. I couldn't wait to get out of there. I was a right brat, I think. This family thought I was wild. I had long hair, I didn't wear shoes, I barely ever wore clothes, I used the worst language you can imagine for a seven-year-old, and I think they were just very pitying of me. It was a bit pathetic. I didn't like that family at all; they were trying to turn me into a good little American boy. And I'd never been to America. I still thought America was full of bloody Indians, loads of buffalo wandering around, and suddenly I was in New Jersey. I thought, oh my God, I'm gonna be scalped if I go outside.

Although I was getting clean under Meg Patterson's care, a cure imposed by the authorities lacks conviction in the heart. Meg's method was supposed to be the painless way out. Electrodes attached to your ear released endorphins, which, theoretically, canceled the pain. Meg also believed in alcohol — in my case Jack Daniel's, which is a strong brew — as a substitute, a diversion, let's say. So I drank heartily under Meg's maternal guidance. I was quite interested in Patterson's method. It did certainly help, but it was still no fun. After it was finished, in a matter of two weeks or so, Immigration announced that they'd have to monitor me for another month. I'm clean, all right? And I'm getting antsy and restless, stuck in this nice suburb. I felt like I was in jail and I just got sick of it. Meg Patterson made her report to the State Department and Immigration that I was following the medical treatment, and, to cut a long story short, I got reinstated: as far as Immigration was concerned, the slate was wiped clean. No offenses appeared on my record. Times were different then. There was more of a belief in rehabilitation than there is now. The visa, which was originally a medical visa, overrode everything. It was extended from three to six months, from single to multiple entries. There were waivers for touring and working on the grounds that I was confirmed as clean and curing myself. As you clean up, you go up another level and another until you get to full clean status, according to my understanding of it. And I've always been very grateful to the US government for allowing me to come to America to get help to come off the stuff.

So we sprung Marlon and moved out of New Jersey to a rented house in South Salem, New York, called Frog Hollow — a classic Colonial-style wooden house, although haunted, according to an increasingly haunted Anita, who saw the ghosts of Mohican Indians patrolling the hilltop. It was down the road from George C. Scott. He used to crash regularly into our white wooden fence, pissed out of his brain, driving at ninety miles an hour. But that's where we ended up — near Mount Kisco, in Westchester County.

It was at this time that Jane Rose, who is now my manager, started unofficially looking after me. Jane was working mostly for Mick, but Mick had asked Jane to stay in Toronto and help me when everybody left. And she's still here, my secret weapon thirty years later. I have to say that during the bust in Toronto, in fact during all busts, Mick looked after me with great sweetness, never complaining. He ran things; he did the work and marshaled the forces that saved me. Mick looked after me like a brother.

Jane described herself at this time as the meat in the sandwich — between Mick and me. She witnessed the first sign of a rift between us when I came out of the junk fog and the mental fog that accompanies it and started to want to take care of business, at least musical business. Mick would come up to Cherry Hill and hear my selection of tracks for *Love You Live,* which we'd been working on all this time sporadically. And he'd go back and bitch to Jane about them. Collaboration was giving way to struggle and disagreement. It's a two-disc album, and the result is that one disc was Mick's and the other was mine. I started talking about things, about business, things we had to settle, which I imagine for Mick was unfamiliar, shocking. I'd kind of risen from the dead after the will had been read. But this was a skirmish, a sign only of what was to come in later years.

It took nineteen months from the bust in March 1977 in Toronto to the trial in October 1978. But at least now I was living in striking distance of New York. The visas were of course not without conditions. I had to travel back and forth to Toronto for various hearings. I had to prove that I'd cleaned up and had been following a steady course of rehab. And I was obliged to attend psychiatric evaluation and treatment in New York. I had this doctor in New York City who would say, "Oh, thank God you're here. I've been dealing with other people's brains all day." She would open the drawer and pull out a bottle of vodka. She'd say, "Let's sit here for half an hour and have a drink. You look all right." I'd say, "I'm feeling pretty good." But she helped me. She was doing her job. She made sure the program worked.

John Phillips called me one day when I was in South Salem and said, "I've got one. Get your ass down here and I'll show you, proof positive, I've got one!" He was into the coke bugs. I thought, I'll drive down, give my friend a hand, you know, if he's *got one.* People had been calling him mad for weeks because he was convinced that he was infected by bugs. So I went down there, and he pulled out a napkin, a Kleenex with a little bloody hole in it. "See? I've got one." John, are you serious? You'll have to reconsider, baby. And I'd driven an hour and a half down there to see. He'd picked himself to bits. I mean, he was covered in scabs. But this time he was convinced he'd got one. He looked at the Kleenex and said, "Oh shit, it got away!" John had taken over a pharmacy. Who didn't in those days? Freddie Sessler used to own drugstores. And John was in a state. In the bedroom he had a medical bed, one of those bendy beds; only half of it worked. His mirror in the john was held together with gaffer tape. It was a shattered image any way you looked at it. Needles were stuck in the wall where he'd used them as darts. But we'd play, never starting before midnight, sometimes not until two a.m., with other musicians. I survived that without smack. John's solo project was stopped by Ahmet Ertegun because John was in no condition to go on.

The sessions for *Some Girls* always had a following wind from the moment we started rehearsing in the strangely shaped Pathé Marconi studios in Paris. It was a rejuvenation, surprisingly for such a dark moment, when it was possible that I would go to jail and the Stones would dissolve. But maybe that was part of it. Let's get something down before it happens. It had an echo of *Beggars Banquet* about it — a long period of silence and then coming back with a bang, and a new sound. You can't argue with seven million copies and two top ten singles out of it, "Miss You" and "Beast of Burden."

Nothing was prepared before we got there. Everything was written in the studio day by day. So it was like the earlier times, at RCA in Los Angeles in the mid-'60s — songs pouring out. Another big difference from recent albums was that we had no other musicians in with us — no horns, no Billy Preston. Extra stuff was dubbed later. If anything the buildup of sidemen had taken us down a different path in the '70s, away from our best instincts on some occasions. So the record was down to us, and it being Ronnie Wood's first album with us, down to our guitar weaving on tracks like "Beast of Burden." We were more focused and we had to work harder.

The sound we got had a lot to do with Chris Kimsey, the engineer and producer who we were working with for the first time. We knew him from his apprenticeship at Olympic Studios, and so he knew our stuff backwards. And he would, on the basis of this experiment, engineer or coproduce eight albums for us. We had to pull something out—not make another Stones-in-the-doldrums album. He wanted to get a live sound back and move away from the clean and clinical-sounding recordings we'd slipped into. We were in the Pathé Marconi studios because they were owned by EMI, with whom we'd just made a big deal. This one was way on the outskirts of town in Boulogne-Billancourt, near the Renault factory; nothing around like restaurants or bars. It was a car ride, and I remember that I was listening to Jackson Browne's *Running on Empty* on a daily commuter basis. At first, we'd booked into this enormous rehearsal studio like a soundstage, with a tiny control room that fitted barely two people and with a primitive 1960s console and a basic sixteen-track. The shape was odd because the console faced the window and a wall, which held the speakers, but the wall went off at an angle, so one speaker was always farther away from you than the other during playbacks. The adjoining studio had a much bigger desk and generally more sophisticated equipment, but for the moment we got playing in this warehouse, sitting around in a semicircle, fencing off space with screens. We hardly went into the control room for the first few days—there wasn't enough space.

Kimsey spotted immediately that this studio had truly great sound properties. Because it was a rehearsal room, we'd rented it cheap, which was lucky because we spent a long time on this record and never moved into the proper studio next door. The primitive mixing desk turned out to be the same kind of soundboard designed by EMI for Abbey Road Studios — very humble and simple, with barely more than a treble and bass button but with a phenomenal sound, which Kimsey fell in love with. Uprooted relics of these desks are apparently muso collectors' items. The sound it got had clarity but dirtiness, a real funky, club feel to it that suited what we were doing.

It was a great room to play in. So, despite Mick doing his usual "Let's move to a proper studio," that's where we stayed, because in a recording session, especially with this kind of music, everything has to feel good. There's no swimming upstream; you're not salmon. We're looking to glide, and if you've got problems with the room, you start to lose confidence in what's going to be captured by the microphones and you start shifting things about. You know it's a good room when a band is smiling. What a lot of *Some Girls* was down to was this little green box I used, this MXR pedal, a reverb-echo. For most of the songs on there I'm using that, and it elevated the band and it gave it a different sound. In a way, it came down to a little bit of technology. It was kind of like "Satisfaction," a little box. On *Some Girls* I just found a way of making that thing work, at least through all of the fast songs. And Charlie was on with it, and Bill Wyman too, I've got to say. There was a certain sense of renewal. A lot of it was, we've got to out-punk the punks. Because they can't play, and we can. All they can do is be punks. Yes, that might have been a certain thorn in the side. The Johnny Rottens, "these fucking kids." I love every band that comes along. That's why I'm here, to encourage guys to play and get bands together. But when they're not playing anything, they're just spitting on people, now come on, we can do better than that. There was also an extra urgency because of this grim prospect of the trial and also because after all the palaver, the bust, the noise, the cleaning up, I needed to prove that there was something behind all this — some purpose to this kind of suffering. And it came together very nicely.

Because we hadn't been together for a while, we needed to get back our old form of writing and collaborating — doing it all on the day, there and then, composing from scratch or semi-scratch. We jumped straight in, back to our old ways with remarkable results. "Before They Make Me Run" and "Beast of Burden" were basically collaborations. "When the Whip Comes Down" I did the riff. Mick wrote it and I looked around and said, shit, he's finally written a rock-and-roll song. By himself! "Some Girls" was Mick. "Lies" too. Basically he'd say, I've got a song, and then I'd say, what if we do it this way or that way?

We didn't think much of "Miss You" when we were doing it. It was "Aah, Mick's been to the disco and has come out humming some other song." It's a result of all the nights Mick spent at Studio 54 and coming up with that beat, that four on the floor. And he said, add the melody to the beat. We just thought we'd put our oar in on Mick wanting to do some disco shit, keep the man happy. But as we got into it, it became quite an interesting beat. And we realized, maybe we've got a quintessential disco thing here. And out of it we got a huge hit. The rest of the album doesn't sound anything like "Miss You."

Then we had trouble with the cover, from Lucille Ball, of all people, who didn't want to be included, and there were loads of lawsuits going on. On the original cover you could pull out and change the faces with one of those cards. There was every famous woman in the world in there, everybody we fancied. Lucille Ball? You don't like it? Fine! The feminists didn't like it either. We always like to piss them off. Where would you be without us? And there is the offending line "Black girls just wanna get fucked all night" from "Some Girls." Well, we've been on the road with a lot of black chicks for many years, and there's quite a few that do. It could have been yellow girls or white girls.

I made a damn good attempt at cleaning up in 1977 with my black box and Meg Patterson and the rest, but for a brief time it didn't stick. While working on *Some Girls,* I'd go to the john from time to time and shoot up. But it had its method. I'd think about what I was gonna do in there. I would be in there meditating about this track that was really nice but only half finished, and where it could go and what was going wrong with it, and why we'd done twenty-five takes and were still stumbling on the same block every time. When I came out, it was, "Listen, it goes a little faster, and we cut out the keyboards in the middle." And sometimes I was right, sometimes I was wrong, but it had only been, hey, forty-five minutes. Better than forty-five minutes when everybody is putting their oar in at once — "Yeah, but what about if we do *this?*" Which is, to me, murder. Very occasionally I would go on the nod while we were playing. Still upright, but removed from present concerns, only to pick it up a few bars on. This did waste time because the take, if there was one, would have to be scrapped.

For sheer longevity — for long distance — there is no track that I know of like "Before They Make Me Run." That song, which I sang on that record, was a cry from the heart. But it burned up the personnel like no other. I was in the studio, without leaving, for five days.

> *Worked the bars and sideshows along the twilight zone*
> *Only a crowd can make you feel so alone*
> *And it really hit home*
> *Booze and pills and powders, you can choose your medicine*
> *Well here's another goodbye to another good friend.*
>
> *After all is said and done*
> *Gotta move while it's still fun*
> *Let me walk before they make me run.*

It came out of what I had been going through and was still going through with the Canadians. I was telling them what to do. Let me walk out of this goddamn case. When you get a lenient sentence, they say, oh, they let him walk.

"Why do you keep nagging that song? Nobody likes it." "Wait till it's finished!" Five days without a wink of sleep. I had an engineer called Dave Jordan and I had another engineer, and one of them would flop under the desk and have a few hours' kip and I'd put the other one in and keep going. We all had black eyes by the time it was finished. I don't know what was so difficult about it; it just wasn't quite right. But then you get guys that'll hang with you. You'll be standing there with a guitar round your neck and everybody else is conked out on the floor. Oh no, not another take, Keith, please. People brought in food, *pain au chocolat*. Days turned into nights. But you just can't leave it. It's almost there, you're tasting it, it's just not in your mouth. It's like fried bacon and onion, but you haven't eaten it yet, it just smells good.

By the fourth day, Dave looked like he'd been punched in both eyes. And he had to be taken away. "We got it, Dave," and somebody got him a taxi. He disappeared, and when we were finally finished, I fell asleep under the booth, under all the machinery. I woke up eventually, how many hours I never counted, and there's the Paris police band. A bloody brass band. That's what woke me up. They're listening to a playback. And they don't know I'm under there, and I'm looking at all these trousers with red stripes and "La Marseillaise" going on, and I'm wondering, when should I emerge? And I'm dying for a pee, and I've got my shit with me, needles and stuff, and I'm surrounded by cops that don't know I'm there. So I waited a bit and thought, I'll just be very English, and I sort of rolled out and said, "Oh, my God! I'm terribly sorry," and before they knew it, I was out, and they were all *zut alors*–ing and there were about seventy-six of them. I thought, they're just like us! They're so intent on making a good record they didn't bust me.

When you get into it that much, you can lose the drive of it, but if you know it's there, it's there. It's manic, but it's like the Holy Grail. Once you're in, you're going to go for it. Because there's no turning back, really. You've got to come out with something. And eventually you get there. That's probably the longest I've done. There have been others that were close— "Can't Be Seen" was one—but "Before They Make Me Run" was the marathon.

There's a postscript to these *Some Girls* sessions, which I should let Chris Kimsey tell.

**Chris Kimsey:** "Miss You" and "Start Me Up" were actually recorded on the same day. When I say on the same day, "Miss You" took about ten days to get the final master, and then when it was done they went and did "Start Me Up." "Start Me Up" had been a reggae song recorded in Rotterdam three years earlier. When they started playing it this time, it wasn't a reggae song, it was what we know today as the great "Start Me Up." It was Keith's song; he just changed it. Maybe after the disco thing of "Miss You," he went to it with a different approach. And it was the only occasion I've ever recorded two masters on the same session. It didn't take long to get down. And when we got the take that everyone felt, oh, that was good, Keith came in and listened to it, and he said, it's all right, it sounds like something I've heard on the radio, it should be a reggae song. Wipe it. He was still toying with it, but he didn't like it. I remember Keith saying at one point that he would prefer to wipe all the masters after they'd been done and released. So no one could go back and fiddle with them. So of course I didn't wipe it. And it became the big song on *Tattoo You* three years later.

Once again, everything revolved around the stuff. Nothing could be done or organized without first organizing the next fix. It got more and more dire. Elaborate arrangements had to be made, some of them more comic than others. I had a man, James W, who I would call up when I was going from London to New York. I would stay at the Plaza Hotel. James, this sweet young Chinese man, would meet me in the suite, the big one preferably, and I'd hand him the cash, he'd give me the shit. And it was always very polite. Give my regards to your father. It was difficult in the '70s to get hypodermics in America. So when I traveled I would wear a hat and use a needle to fix a little feather to the hatband, so it was just a hat pin. I would put the trilby with the red, green and gold feather in the hat bag. So the minute

James turned up, I got the shit. OK, but now I need the syringe. My trick was, I'd order a cup of coffee, because I needed a spoon for cooking up. And then I'd go down to FAO Schwarz, the toy shop right across Fifth Avenue from the Plaza. And if you went to the third floor, you could buy a doctor and nurse play set, a little plastic box with a red cross on it. That had the barrel and the syringe that fitted the needle that I'd brought. I'd go round, "I'll have three teddy bears, I'll have that remote-control car, oh, and give me two doctor and nurse kits! My niece, you know, she's really into that. Must encourage her." FAO Schwarz was my connection. Rush back to the room, hook it up and fix it.

By then I've ordered up coffee, so I've got the teaspoon. You fill the spoon and hold a lighter to it, and you watch it and it should burn clear and turn to treacle. It shouldn't go black; that means there's too much cut in it. James never let me down on that; it was always high-quality stuff. I'm not looking for weight, I'm looking for sustenance. I'm strung out. I've got to have some dope. But never look for a huge amount. Quarter ounces. Because also, the quality could change over a week or so. You don't want a whole bag of useless, rotten dope. You watch the market. James W was my man. "Look, this is the best we've got right now. I don't suggest you buy any more of this. Next week, we're getting some high quality." Absolutely reliable was James. And a great sense of humor, very straight up, straight business, price on the button. The only thing we'd laugh about was "Have you been over to the toy store yet?"

Once you're a junkie, your smack's your daily bread. You don't really get off anymore that much. There's junkies that keep upping their dosage, and that's why you get ODs. To me, it just became maintenance. It was to set the trend for the day. Then came all those agonizing moments when there was a drought on, and the old lady's going, I want some stuff! So do I, honey, but we've got to wait. Waiting for the man. When there was a heroin drought it was a bit rough. They really used to put the screws on. There'd be people in the room in dire straits, throwing up. You'd be treading over bodies. And there's sometimes really no drought; it's only to jack the price up. And it doesn't really matter how much money you've got. I'm not going to say, "Do you know who I am?" I'm just another junkie.

When there's no shit at all, then you've got to go down to the pits, and you know it's going to be like a fucking pool of piranhas down there. It happened to me a couple of times on the East Side in New York and in LA. We knew the trick — you'd score upstairs, and on your way down the other bunch would take it back off you again. Most of the time you'd hear it going on while you were waiting for your turn. The thing was to leave quietly, and if you saw anybody outside — because you never knew if it was going to happen or not — usually you'd give them a kick in the balls. But a couple of times, fuck it, OK, let's go for it. You cover me. You stay down there, and as I come down with the shit I'll go bang, and they'll go bang and then you go bang. Shoot out the lightbulbs and put a few bullets around and do the run, sparks flying. Then with a bit of luck we're out of there. The statistics are well on your side against being hit when you're a moving target. If you look at the odds, one thousand to one, you're going to win. You have to be very close and you have to have good eyesight to shoot out a lightbulb. And it's dark. Flash, bang, wallop and get out of there. I loved it. It was real OK Corral stuff. Only did it twice.

It was a very time-consuming routine. I'd wake up in the morning, and the first thing is go to the bathroom to have a shot. You don't brush your teeth. And then, oh, fuck it, I've got to go to the kitchen and get the spoon. Those stupid rituals that you go through. Shit, last night I should have brought a spoon up so that I didn't have to go down to the kitchen. Every time it got progressively harder and harder to kick. And the desire to go back on the minute you were off got stronger. Oh, just one, now that I'm clean. Just that fatal one more, that celebration, is a killer. And on top of that, you've come out of it, you're off the stuff, but all your friends are junkies. If somebody cleans up, that somebody has escaped the circle. And whether they like you or love you or hate you or not, the first thing they want to do is to pull you back in. "This is really good shit, here." Certain pressures within junkiedom have it that if somebody cleans up and actually stays clean, it's like they've failed somehow. Failed at what, I don't know. How many cold turkeys can you go through? It's ludicrous, but you never realize it when you're on dope. Several times on cold turkey I was convinced there was a safe behind the wall that was full of the shit and it had everything ready to go, spoon and all. And finally I'd crash out, and when I woke up I'd see bloody fingernail marks down the wall where I'd actually been trying to get in there. Is this really worth it? In fact my decision then was, yep.

I can be as bigheaded as Mick, and flighty and everything, but you can't do that when you're a junkie. There are certain realities that come into play that really keep your feet in the gutter, even lower than you need to be. Not even on the sidewalk — in the gutter. And obviously that was the period when Mick and I went off on almost perfect 180s. He had no time for me and my supposedly stupid state. I remember being at a disco once in Paris and I was supposed to meet the man, and I was sick. People were dancing around little glitter balls, and I'm under the benches, just hiding and throwing up because the man hasn't arrived. And I'm also wondering, will he find me under here? If he does arrive, he might look around and fuck back off. I was in a distressed frame of mind, let's put it like that. Luckily he did find me. But being in that position, and at the same time you're like numero uno in the world, you realize where you've sunk to. Just getting yourself in that position leaves a sense of self-loathing that takes a while to rub off. You son of a bitch, you'd do anything for the shit. But I'm my own man, I say. Nobody can tell me what to do. And yet you realize you've put yourself in the position where you're in the hands of a dealer, and that's disgusting. Waiting for this cunt, and begging him?

That's where the self-loathing comes in. Any way you look at it, junkies are people waiting for the man. Your world gets diminished to dope. Just that, by itself, becomes the whole world.

Most junkies become idiots. That's really what finally turned me around. We've only got one subject in mind, which is the dope. Can't I be a little more smart about it? What am I doing hanging around with these dregs? They're just boring people. Worse, a lot of these are very bright people, and we all kind of know that we've been hoodwinked, but then... why not? Everybody else is hoodwinked by something, and at least we *know* we're fooling ourselves. No one's a hero just for taking dope. You might be a hero for getting off it. I loved the shit. But enough was enough. Also, it narrowed one's horizons, and eventually all you know are junkies. I had to move to broader horizons. You only know all this, of course, once you've gotten out of there. That's what that stuff does. It's the most seductive bitch in the world.

The Canadian case went on and on. I was flying up and down from New York to Toronto on a weekly basis. But it didn't stop me taking the shit at the time. There was a little airport out of which I flew back to New York from Toronto on a private plane. On one of these trips, in the airport before taking off, I went to the john to have a fix. I'm in the cubicle, and just as I'm cooking up the spoon, from beneath the door I see this ominous set of spurs. There's a fucking Mountie in the whole goddamn rig. He wants to take a pee. And he's going to be smelling this dope; it's just flaring up.... *Clink, clink* and I'm a goner. And we're down the hole. And *clink clink clink* and the spurs walk out. How many chances have I got left? I'd pulled my string too long. There was already a permanent black cloud of expecting the shit to hit the fan. I'm facing three charges: trafficking, possession and importing. I'm going to be doing some hard fucking time. I'd better get ready.

Which is one of the reasons I finally cleaned up. I didn't want to

Suit bought with difficulty on a Sunday for my trial in Toronto, October 1978.

*Jane Rose*

Limo drivers on the New Barbarians tour, 1979.

*Henry Diltz/Morrison Hotel Gallery*

*Henry Diltz/Morrison Hotel Gallery*

Waiting to go on with Ron Wood and the New Barbarians, Los Angeles, May 1979, with Joseph "Zigaboo" Modeliste, drums (next to Ronnie), and Stanley Clarke, bass (next to me).

*Michael Halsband/Landov*

Ian Stewart, "Stu," our founder. "Rightful heir of Pittenweem." On tour in 1981.

The bed that I lie on: me and Charlie, 1982.

*Denis O'Regan*

Patti and me, 1982.

Me and Patti on the beach in Barbados, 1982.

*Jane*

With, from left, Woody, Robbie Shakespeare, Sly Dunbar, Joseph "Zigaboo" Modeliste, 1979.

*Jane*

Visiting Mick in Mustique, 1980.

*Jane Rose*

Playing with Muddy Waters at the Checkerboard Lounge, Chicago, November 22, 1981.

*Michael Halsband/Landov*

Christmas 1982 at Doris's house, Dartford, with Doris, Bill Richards, Patti, Angela.

*Jane*

Wingless Angels, Jamaica. Left to right: me, Locksley Whitlock, Winston Thomas, Justin Hinds, Jackie Ellis, Warrin Williamson, Maureen Fremantle.

*Jane Rose*

Wedding song, Cabo San Lucas, December 18, 1983.

*Jane Rose*

My daughter Theodora, 1985.

A visit from John Lee Hooker during the
X-Pensive Winos tour, San Francisco, 1993.

*Paul Natkin/Photo Reserve*

The best Chuck Berry
live you'll ever get:
concert at Saint Louis's
Fox Theatre, October
16, 1986, for the film
*Hail! Hail! Rock 'n' Roll.*

*Paul Natkin/Photo Reserve, Inc.*

X-Pensive Winos triumphant, Aragon Ballroom,
Chicago, 1988.

Glimmer Twins. Somewhere between Spain and Portugal, 1990.

Claude Gassian

My father, Bert, 1997.

*Max Vadr*

Annie Leibovitz

Patti and me with our daughters Alexandra (left) and Theodora (right), Connecticut, 1992.

Patti Hansen

Alexandra at Ronnie Wood's house in Ireland, 1993.

*Kevin Mazur*

Driving across the Brooklyn Bridge to the press conference for the Bridges to Babylon tour, August 1997.

Pierre de Beauport, guitar tech and backline crew chief, Forty Licks tour, Ford Center, Oklahoma City, January 28, 2003.

*Jane R*

Blondie Chaplin (left) and Lisa Fischer (right), on the Forty Licks tour, 2003.

*Jane Rose*

*Kevin Mazur*

Charlie, Mick, and me, recording *Bridges to Babylon,* July 1997, Ocean Way studios, Hollywood.

Meeting with my manager Jane Rose, and her dog Delilah, 1999.

*Patti Hansen*

Jane Rose

Paul McCartney on one of his daily visits along the beach at Parrot Cay in January 2005.

Jane Rose

Tom Waits visiting the Stones tour, 2003.

With Johnny Depp at the Matthew Rolston *Pirates of the Caribbean* photo shoot for *Rolling Stone* magazine, 2006.

Jane Rose

Top: Loyal inmates, Parrot Cay, 2008. Left to right: Steve Crotty, me, James Fox.

Left: The dog Rasputin (Raz), rescued from the streets of Moscow, now in Parrot Cay.

Bottom: The Richards family. From left on couch: Patti, Angela, Lucy (wife of Marlon), Orson (their son), me, Marlon, Ida (daughter of Lucy and Marlon), and Ella (their elder daughter). Seated in front: Alexandra, Theodora.

My library in Connecticut.

*Christopher Sy*

cold turkey in jail. I wanted to leave time for my nails to grow. They're the only weapons you're left with when you go to jail. Also, attached to the junk as I was, I was putting myself slowly into a position where it would be impossible to move around the world and work. There was a tour coming up in one month, in June of 1978, for *Some Girls*. I knew I'd have to get clean for it. Jane Rose had been asking me, "When are you going to get clean?" and I'd say tomorrow. I had done it the year before, fucked up and gotten hooked again. And this was the last time. I didn't want to hear about another dope deal. Been there. You get about ten years and you stop; you take your medal and retire. And Jane stuck with me, bless her fucking heart. The old Jugs—which is her nickname—came through. It must have been horrendous for her. Far worse for me. But for her to witness what goes on when you're climbing the walls, shitting yourself, going bananas. How could she plow through that? At this moment the Stones were gathered at Bearsville Studios, in Woodstock, New York, to rehearse for the tour. I was at home with Anita. Jane better tell the moment when I gave up heroin.

**Jane Rose:** I had basically become the courier—I would bring money or drugs from New York to Westchester County for Keith. He still wouldn't clean up, and his habit was bad now. And he would not admit it. And I couldn't stand the calls to Westchester anymore. I went up there, and Antonio and Anna Marie were there, friends of Anita's who lived in Keith's apartment in Rue Saint-Honoré, in Paris. (Antonio later became Antonia.) So they were in the house, and Keith was waiting for money or drugs. Anita was there. I went up to the house, and they said, "Where's the money?" and I said, "I don't have the money." I said, "It's in New York." They flipped out, and Anita got in the car; she was furious. And I said, "Keith, today is tomorrow." Because he was always saying, tomorrow I'll clean up, and this was right before the tour, in

May. He and Anita had a huge fight later that day. Keith went upstairs; he was furious. Anna Marie and Antonio looked at this Jewish chick from New York and said, this girl is going to be dead. How could she come out here without the money? Then there was silence, and I went upstairs to the bedroom, the four-poster bed, and I said hello. And he had kicked off his shoes, and he said, "OK, I'm going to do it. I've got my machine; I'm going to kick." And I said, "Want to go to Woodstock? That's where the rehearsals are going to be. Get away, do it. I'll go with you." And after three hours, he said OK. So we were getting ready to go before Anita came back, because I just knew it had to be that way. And she came back before we left. There was a big row and somebody went flying down the stairs. In the end Keith sat in the car and we went to Woodstock. Anita had her drugs or her money. And Keith went to Woodstock and he went cold turkey, with his machine. Mick and Jerry [Hall] came up for two days to be there with me. And I stayed with him twenty-four hours, I stayed in the room, I was there. I don't know for how many days after that, or if I even talked to anybody. I had a conviction that he was going to get better. I just believed in him.

If you want to get something out of anybody, I'd say put them on dope for a month or two and just withdraw it, and they'll talk. Jane got me through the seventy-two hours. She watched me climb the walls, which is why I don't like wallpaper anymore. You're barely able to control your muscle spasms. And you're really ashamed of yourself. And you've got to do it. I didn't go back for another shot, because after coming out of there, I just locked myself in a room. Jane was with me. And Jane just cleaned me up. And that was the last time. I ain't going there again.

Anita, on the other hand, was no help. She wouldn't do the deal. If we're going to stay together, we've got to do it together. And she didn't. We were spinning out of control. By now I couldn't live in the house with somebody who was still on junk. It's a chemical reaction to the body, but it's also in your relationship to other people. That's where the difficult bit is. I would have stayed with Anita probably forever, but when it came to that very important time when dope was out of the picture from now on, she didn't stop. She'd never stopped, in fact. When we did it for several months in 1977, she'd be sneaking stuff round the back. I knew that she was on it; you can just tell by the eye-balls. So now I couldn't even go and see her. And that was where I said, oh well...that's Anita. That's where it blew.

I was clean and we were rehearsing for the 1978 tour in Woodstock, New York, at Bearsville Studios. One day out of the clouds, by heli-copter, there came Lil. She had come with her friend Jo Wood, Ronnie's soon-to-be wife, for Woody's birthday. It was about ten days before we went on the road and it was almost miraculous timing to find such a new friend. Her real name is Lil Wergilis, although she's always been written about as Lil "Wenglass" or Lil Green — her mar-ried name. Swedish she is, although she was more of a London girl than you'd believe after a decade there. And talked like one, "Oh, fuckin' naff" and all that. She was a brilliant Swedish blonde in the bloom of her life. When I first met Lil she was like Marilyn Monroe. Dazzling. Pink Lurex tights and blond hair. But she was also very smart and strong hearted. She was a lovely girl, a beautiful lover, and I'd just got off the stuff and Lil came along and made me laugh. She laughed me out of it. She really brought me out of the abyss. It's not so easy to kick that shit as I pretend it is, after ten years on the stuff and five or six cold turkeys. And staying off the stuff is another thing, and Lil, bless her heart, took my mind off it totally. We just fell into each other's arms for a year or so. We had a great time together. Lil was like a breath of fresh air. Lighthearted, loads of fun, outrageous. Up for anything. Incredibly funny, very witty, and a great lay. She was energetic; she did things. Like cook breakfast and make sure I was up on time. And I needed a bit of that. Not popular with Mick; not your Studio 54 girl was Lil. He couldn't think what I was doing with her. It was a turbulent time for our marriages or non-marriages. Bianca had sued him for divorce. He now had Jerry Hall on his arm, and I got on well with Jerry.

I took Lil on tour with me, where she was my accomplice in another of my fate-cheating close shaves — the list now too long to be taken lightly. This time it was from fire in our rented house in Laurel Canyon, LA. Lil and I had gone to bed, and Lil, so she said later, heard this distant bang and got up and opened the curtain a little and it was strangely bright outside. Not right. She opened the bathroom door and fire exploded into the room. And we had a few seconds to jump out of the window. I'm dressed in a short T-shirt only and Lil is naked. And we're exposed — people are gathered, freaking out, trying to put the fire out — and this is a big story as soon as the press gets here. Up pulls a car and we get in gratefully. Amazingly, it's a cousin of Anita! We are in a state of shock. We go to her house, borrow some clothes, go to a hotel. The next day someone went round to have a look and there was a large sign stuck in the blackened grass that read, "Thanks a lot, Keith."

My trial was finally heard in Toronto in October 1978. We knew it might sink us all, but in the face of it, some of us were looking on the bright side. "I don't think it's gonna be as bad as *that*," said Mick. "You've got to say if the worst happens and Keith gets put in an open prison with Mrs. Trudeau for life, that I am still gonna go on the road. Maybe we could play a tour of Canadian prisons. Ha ha ha."

The longer the process went on, the clearer it was that the Canadian government wanted to wriggle out of it. The Mounties and their allies were thinking, "Oh, great! Wonderful job! We've delivered him to the Canadian government with a hook in his mouth." And the Trudeaus were thinking, "Uh-uh, pal, this is the last thing we need."

There were five to six hundred people outside every time I turned up in court, chanting, "Free Keith, free Keith." And we knew that the enemy camp, if you want to call the Canadian government at the time the enemy, our persecutors, were unsure of their footing. Whereas I didn't mind. I figured the harder they hit me, the easier I would get out. The Mounties, or at least the prosecution, didn't want to wriggle out at all. But, as Bill Carter observed, in almost every one of these cases brought against us at that time, the law had its hands dirty. They knew I wasn't trafficking, but they wanted to railroad it through a jury to get a long and historic jail sentence. There they made a mistake. Look at Keith Richards. He's not selling drugs. He's got all the money he needs. The allegation of trafficking, just to get a stiff sentence, is absurd. He's a hopeless addict. He has a medical problem. My lawyers wrote a report that showed that according to all legal precedent and local case histories, if I weren't Keith Richards, I would probably have gotten no more than a suspended sentence. Only at the last minute did they change the trafficking charge to possession, adding a cocaine charge. But this shift weakened and exposed them, exposed more about the Canadian government than anything to do with "Oh, guess what? Keith Richards is on smack." What else is new? The idea of the prime minister's wife buzzing around the hotel trying to get laid was another thing. So one thing overwhelmed the other, so to speak. I certainly felt that whatever the charge was, I was definitely in way above my head, or below it, any way you look at it. Who knows what really goes on? It's called politics. It's one of the scrubbiest games in town.

So we knew it was dead in the water. Now it was, how long will it take for them to get me out of here? They walked themselves into it, now they don't want to know about it, and how will they find their way out of it? We were waiting to watch the Canadian government melt.

The Canadian people were the ones that got me off the hook. But really, the mastery of it was coordinating the faux pas of Margaret

Trudeau. If they had hit me hard and quick, they probably could have got me just for importing. But when it came to court, clearly the new judge had said, get this thing off the hook. We don't want any more to do with this; it's causing us more embarrassment and money than it's worth. On the day of reckoning I arrived in court, this courtroom that had the air of England in the 1950s, with a portrait of the queen hanging strangely on the wall. The actor Dan Aykroyd, who I'd met when we did *Saturday Night Live* just before this, was on standby as a Canadian and a character witness. The producer of the show, its Canadian founder, who still produces it, Lorne Michaels, spoke in court about my role as a slinger of hash in the great cultural kitchen. He did a very elegant job of it. I was not in the slightest intimidated by the court. I knew by now that they had a real problem. I knew too, from other moments like this, that most of the governments of the world were out of touch with their subjects and that's what I knew I could exploit. Sometimes you can smell defeat even with all of that artillery arranged against you, and this was one such occasion.

The verdict was guilty, but the judge concluded, "I will not incarcerate him for addiction and wealth." He must be freed, said the judge, to get on with his treatment, with a condition. He will perform a concert for the blind. Very intelligent, I thought. The most Solomon-like judgment that had been handed down in many a year. And this was to do with a blind girl who had followed the Stones everywhere on the road. Rita, my blind angel. Despite her blindness, she hitchhiked to our shows. The chick was absolutely fearless. I'd heard about her backstage, and the idea of her thumbing in the darkness was too much for me. I hooked her up with the truck drivers, made sure she got a safe lift and made sure she got fed. And when I was busted, she actually found her way to the judge's house and told him this story. And this is how he arrived at the concert for the blind. The love and devotion of people like Rita is something that still amazes me. So aha! A way was found.

From that appearance on *Saturday Night Live,* Lil and I used to hang with Dan Aykroyd and Bill Murray and John Belushi in their club, the Blues Bar, in New York, around 1979. Belushi was an over-the-top man. You can say *that* again. I said to John once, as my father says, there's a difference between scratching your arse and tearing it to bits. John was hilarious, and nuts to hang with. Belushi was an extreme experience even by my standards. A case in point.

When I was a kid, I'd pop round to Mick's house. You want something to drink. Open the fridge, there's nothing in it except maybe half a tomato. Big fridge. Thirty years later, walk into Mick's apartment, open the fridge, it's an even bigger fridge, what's in there? Half a tomato and a bottle of beer. One night around this time, when we'd been hanging out with John Belushi in New York, we'd been in session all night and Ronnie and Mick and I had gone back to Mick's apartment. There's a knock at the door, and there's Belushi, dressed in a porter's uniform, and he's got a trolley. And he's got twelve fucking boxes of gefilte fish. And he ignores us all, trundles it straight to Mick's fridge, bundles all the gefilte fish into the fridge and says, "Now it's full."

Riding high on the success of *Some Girls* and on the outcome of the court case, we repaired to Nassau in the Bahamas, to Compass Point Studios. There were ripples of argument between Mick and me that would grow into a rumble soon, but not quite yet. We got playing and composing songs for *Emotional Rescue*. While we were doing this, Pope John Paul II paid an unexpected visit to Nassau on a refueling stop. The Bahamas are strongly Catholic, at least while the pope's there, and it was announced that he would conduct a public blessing in a football stadium. I decided that since Alan Dunn, our road manager, was a Catholic and eligible for a blessing by the pope, he should take the tapes we were making up to the stadium and have them blessed too. Why not? You never know. Alan got a ticket through the local school and took the tapes up in the heat—big two-inch tapes that weighed a ton, and weighed even more when the handles of the straw basket he was carrying them in broke, so he told me. He clutched them to his chest as the pontiff waved his blessing over them and over Alan. It certainly worked for Alan, who was miraculously rescued out at sea a few days later when his dinghy carried him and his girlfriend across the reef and into deep water. He had a broken outboard and no oars. It should have meant certain death, but Alan's mother reckons that the passing boat that rescued them was a gift from God, via the pope.

One of the great sessions I have played on happened around this time, when Lil and I went to Jamaica and I fell in with Sly Dunbar and Robbie Shakespeare, who were making a Black Uhuru album. Sly and Robbie were one of the best rhythm sections in the world. We did seven tracks together in one night, and one of them, called "Shine Eye Gal," became a great big hit and a classic. Another was an instrumental called "Dirty Harry" for Sly's album *Sly, Wicked and Slick*. And I've still got the rest. All done on four-track at Channel One, Kingston. We played anything anybody felt like playing. Most of it was just made out of riffs, but it was a supreme band: Sly and Robbie; Sticky and Scully, who were Sly's percussion men and did all the little fiddly bits; Ansell Collins on organ and piano; me on guitar; another guitar player, might have been Michael Chung. It was a brilliant night. At the time, we said, let's split the tracks, I'll take three and you take three, but they made a big hit out of "Shine Eye Gal." They came touring with us in the next couple of years.

Mick didn't want to tour in 1979, but I did. I was put out and frustrated. But it meant I could shoot off. Ronnie was going on the road, and he put together the New Barbarians, which was an incredible band — Joseph "Zigaboo" Modeliste on drums, one of the best ever. And that's why I immediately jumped in. Drummers from New Orleans, of which Ziggy is one of the giants, are great readers of the song and how it goes; they feel it, tell the way it's going even before you do. I'd known Ziggy when the Meters worked with the Stones for several tours. George Porter on bass. The Meters had a big influence on my appreciation of funk. They are uniquely New Orleans in rhythm and the use of space and time. New Orleans is the most different city in America, and it shows in the music. I've worked with George Recile, who is now Bob Dylan's drummer, another one from that city. Bobby Keys was there with the New Barbarians. Ian McLagan on keyboards. On bass was the great jazz player Stanley Clarke. It was a fun tour and we had a lot of laughs. I didn't have to worry about the things I usually do on tours; I didn't have to bear responsibility. To me, it was a ball, a riot. I was basically just a sideman hired for the tour. I can't even remember much of it, it was so much fun. To me, the important thing was that, shit, I'd managed to avoid doing hard time, and at the same time I was doing what I love to do. And I had Lil with me, the good-time girl for all seasons. Then Lil's mother got ill, and she had to fly back to Sweden. And I had a temporary lapse in her absence. I bought some Persian brown from a woman named Cathy Smith in Los Angeles. I described myself at the time as "reliving a second rock-and-roll childhood." Cathy Smith was also the downfall of Belushi. It was just too strong for Belushi. Basically he was a very strong bloke, but he just pushed it over the limit. Also he wasn't in shape. He was freebasing, as Ronnie had started doing at this time. There was a high death rate among the cast of *Saturday Night Live*. John died at the Chateau Marmont. He'd been up too many days, too many nights, which he used to do regularly. Too many nights and too much weight to carry.

Maybe it was the coming off dope, the slow resurfacing of buried impulses or feelings. I don't know. But when I went back to Paris to finish *Emotional Rescue* at Pathé Marconi, again with Lil, my finger was on the hair trigger, metaphorically speaking. My reactions were certainly quicker, and my anger too. There are times when my blood gets heated and I get irate. A red curtain falls before my eyes, and I'm going to do anything. It's a horrific thing. I hate the person who puts me in that position where force comes up. You're almost more scared of yourself than you are of whoever it is on the other side. Because you know that you've gone to the point of no return and you could do anything, you could kill, just like that, and then have to wake up and say, "What happened?" "Well, you ripped his throat out." When it has happened to me, I'm scared of myself. It may be something to do with getting used to taking beatings when I was a kid, being the smallest guy in the class. It's certainly a very old thing.

My security man and friend Gary Schultz was there with me once in a nightclub in Paris, and this little French fucker was really being obnoxious. He was just out of it. And I was with Lil, bless her heart. He was trying to pull a number on Lil, and I just went, "What did you say?" "What?" And I had a wineglass with a long stem. I cracked off the base so I had the stem. And I put him down. I had him on his knees with the stem of this wineglass at his throat. And I'm hoping I'm not going to crush the bowl of the glass because right now, I've got the advantage. Because he was with a whole lot of friends, I was dealing with not just him but his buddies, so it was just a matter of being really overdramatic. "Take him away." And they did; otherwise his mates would have done us all.

The blade should be used to play for time only, the shooter to make sure you get your point across sometimes. But you've got to be convincing. For example—in one incident I remember from this period—when you're trying to get a cab in Paris and you're a foreigner. There's twenty cabs in the line all just waiting there doing nothing. So you go to the first one, and he'll send you to the one behind, and then he'll send you to the front again. And then you realize, oh, business isn't important, then, you just want to fuck with people, and that's where you can start to growl objectionably, kick up some sand. It's their idea of fun just to piss around with foreigners, and I've seen them do it to old ladies too. I'd been through that enough. I put the blade to one of them and said, "You're taking me." Only later did I realize they're even worse to French people from the provinces.

It was in Paris that I realized I had finally said good-bye to heroin. I went to dinner in Paris a year or so later with Wonder Woman

Lynda Carter and Mick and some others. I don't know why Mick did this. He's weird this way. He said, "Come with me to the Bois de Boulogne. I'm going to meet this guy." Mick thought he was getting cocaine. So we did the deal in the park, the party broke up and we went home. And the bag was full of heroin, not coke. Typical Mick Jagger. He didn't know. Mick, this ain't coke, man. And I looked at it, this great big beautiful bag of smack. And it was raining outside the apartment in Rue Saint-Honoré. I looked at it, I admit I took a gram out and put it in a little packet, and then I just tossed the rest onto the street. And that's when I figured that I was really no longer a junkie. Even though I'd been basically off the stuff for two or three years, the fact that I could do that meant I was out of its power.

Things went beyond any point of return with Anita when her young boyfriend blew his brains out in our house, on the bed. I was three thousand miles away, in Paris making a record, but Marlon was there and he heard Anita screaming and then saw her running down the stairs covered in blood. The boy had shot himself in the face, playing Russian roulette, the story goes. I had met him. He was this crazy little kid, aged seventeen, Anita's boyfriend. I said to her, listen, baby, I'm leaving, we're over, we're finished, but this is not the guy for you. And he proved it. The reason she went with this guy, who was an absolute prick, was, I think, to piss me off. By then, I wasn't actually living with her anyway. I would pop up to get my crap out of there, or come to see Marlon. I saw the guy once, playing with Marlon, when I came back, and I warned him off, and he certainly resented that. And I said to Anita, dump this fucker, but I didn't mean it that way.

**Marlon:** The movie *The Deer Hunter* was recently out. And there's the Russian roulette scene, and that's what he was doing, he was playing Russian roulette. Very dark. He was about seventeen. He kept telling me—a really nasty kid—he

kept saying he was going to shoot Keith, and that upset me, so
I was kind of relieved when he shot himself.

I remember the date, July 20, 1979, vividly because it
was the tenth anniversary of the moon landing. I remember
he was only around for a few months, but Anita was being
very self-destructive. This was the time Keith was off with
Lil, so Anita was like, right, I'm gonna show him, get her
own back so to speak. So she flaunted him quite blatantly;
Keith met him, actually. I was watching the anniversary
of the lunar landings and I heard one pop. It didn't really
sound like a bang or anything, it was a pop. And then
Anita comes running down the stairs, covered in blood,
screaming.

I went, my God, Jesus Christ. I had to have a little peek, so
I did go up and saw all this brain matter all over the walls.
And then the cops came pretty damn quickly. Larry Sessler,
one of the Sessler boys, was there to sort it all out, and the next
morning I left. I went to Paris and met Keith. And poor Anita
had to stay and deal with that. There were all these stories in
the press at the time saying that she was a witch, that people
were having Black Sabbaths. They were saying all sorts of
things.

It literally was just bad luck. I don't think he intended to
shoot himself, really, just an idiot of seventeen who was
stoned, angry, playing with a pistol. Anita didn't recognize it
as a shot, but she turned round and heard this gargling noise,
she said. She saw there was blood coming from his mouth and
her first instinct was to pick up the gun and put it on the desk,
so it had her fingerprints all over it. One bullet in the chamber,
one bullet in the mouth, and that's it; it wasn't like it was fully
loaded. But then we had to move out of that house quite
sharpish. Anita was in the papers every day and had to hide in
a hotel in New York.

When the cops found out, they wanted first to question me, but I was in Paris. Hey, damn good shot with a Smith & Wesson from Paris. And Anita? I was going to make sure she didn't go to jail when they lost interest in me. It was a miracle how that case just disappeared. I believe it was to do with the fact that the gun was traced back to the police, bought in some gun market in the parking lot of a police station. Suddenly it wasn't an issue. The case was put down as suicide. The boy's parents tried to bring a case for corruption of a minor, which didn't stick. So Anita moved to New York, to the Alray Hotel, and began a different kind of existence. That was the final curtain for me and Anita, apart from trips to see the children. It was the end. Thanks for the memories, girl.

Jane Rose

# Chapter Eleven

In which I meet Patti Hansen and fall in love. I survive a disastrous
first meeting with her parents. Grief is brewing with Mick. I fight with
Ronnie Wood and dig out my dad after twenty years. Marlon's tale of
Gatsby mansions on Long Island. Marriage in Mexico.

Studio 54 in New York was a big hangout of Mick's. It wasn't my
taste — a tarted-up disco club or, as it appeared to me at the
time, a room full of faggots in boxer shorts, waving champagne bottles
in your face. There were crowds round the block trying to get in, the
little velvet rope saying you're in or out. I knew they were dealing dope
round the back, which is why they all got busted. As if they weren't
coining enough. But they were having a good time; they were just
boys partying, basically. The weird thing is, the first time I met Patti
Hansen was in Studio 54. John Phillips and I had run in there because
Britt Ekland was chasing me. She had the hots for me. And hey, Britt,
I love you, you're a nice girl and everything like that — sweet, shy and
unassuming — but my agenda is full, if you get my meaning. But she
wouldn't let go; she was chasing me all over fucking town. So we
thought, the one place to hide, Studio 54! It was the most unlikely
place to find me. And it happened to be Saint Patrick's Day, March 17,
which is Patti's birthday. The year was 1979.

So we're hiding away, saying Britt will never find us here. And

Shaun, one of Patti's mates, came over and said, it's my friend's birthday today. I said, which one? And she pointed out this blond beauty dancing with wild hair flying. "Dom Pérignon immediately!" I sent over a bottle of champagne and just said hello. I didn't see her again for a while, but the vision stayed in my mind.

Then in December it was my birthday, my thirty-sixth, for which, in accordance with the craze of the moment, we repaired to the Roxy roller rink in New York for a party. Jane Rose had kept Patti on her radar all those months, having noticed, apparently, some spark that first night, and made sure Patti was invited. So I caught sight of Patti again, and she caught sight of me catching sight of her. And she left. And a few days later I called her and we got together. I wrote in my notebook in January 1980, a few days after that:

> *Incredibly I've found a woman. A miracle! I've pussy at the snap of a finger but I've met a woman! Unbelievably she is the most beautiful (physically) specimen in the WORLD. But that ain't it! It certainly helps but it's her mind, her joy of life and (wonders) she thinks this battered junkie is the guy she loves. I'm over the moon and peeing in my pants. She loves soul music and reggae, in fact everything. I make her tapes of music which is almost as good as being with her. I send them like love letters. I'm kicking 40 and besotted.*

I was amazed that she was willing to hang out with me. Because I was hanging with a bunch of guys and all we did was go up to the Bronx and Brooklyn to these bizarre West Indian places and record stores. Nothing of interest to supermodels. My friend Brad Klein was there; I think Larry Sessler, Freddie's son, was there. Gary Schultz, my minder, was there too. He was always known as Concorde, a nickname derived from Monty Python ("Brave, brave Concorde! You shall not have died in vain!" "I'm not quite dead, sir," etc.). Jimmy Callaghan, my muscle for many years; Max Romeo, reggae star; and a few other cats. Nice to meet you, nice to know you, you want to hang with this bunch of assholes? Up to you, you know? But she was there every day. And I know something's happening, but how it happens and when and who pulls the spring is another thing. That's how we hung for days and days. I never put the hammer on hard. I didn't make a move. I could never put the make on. I could just never find the right line, or one that hadn't been used before. I just never had that thing with women. I would do it silently. Very Charlie Chaplin. The scratch, the look, the body language. Get my drift? Now it's up to you. "Hey, baby" is just not my come-on. I've got to lay back and see the tension build to a point where something's got to happen. And if they can hang through that tension, then we're OK. They call it the reverse molecular version, the RMV, as it's known. Finally, after an astonishing number of days, she lay down on the bed and said, come on.

At the time I was living with Lil. Suddenly I disappeared for ten days and took a room at the Carlyle, and Lil was wondering where the hell I'd gone. She got the message pretty quick. I'd been with Lil eighteen months by then, and we were quite handsomely ensconced in a nice apartment. She's a great girl and I just dumped her.... I had to make it up to Lil.

I wanted to hear Patti's version of these events, long ago.

**Patti Hansen:** I didn't know anything about Keith. I didn't follow his music. Of course listening to the radio, you know who the Rolling Stones are, but it wasn't music I listened to. It's March '79 and it's my birthday and I'm in Studio 54 and I had just broken up with some guy I had been with for a few years. I was dancing with my girlfriend Shaun Casey, who saw Keith arrive and sit down in a little booth. It was after last call, and she said, it's my best friend's birthday, would you please give her a bottle of champagne because they won't sell us any. And she said, oh, by the way, I'm a good friend of Bill Wyman, and she introduced Keith and me very briefly. I barely remember. And I went back to the dance floor. It was probably three in the morning. I don't think he had ever been to Studio 54 or ever went back again; that was my place. And so he spotted me.

And then it was December '79 and I was working with Jerry Hall at Avedon's studio, and she said, there's a big party for Keith Richards coming up and he'd like you to come. Jerry and I didn't hang out; we did modeling together. I didn't really know her and Mick. And I drank some vodka with a friend of mine and said, let's go to this party at the Roxy and see this guy. Most of my boyfriends were gay, so it was nervous-making meeting some guy who wanted to meet me. Also it's a setup, a little bit cheesy and whorey. But it's also the end of the '70s and I was twenty-three. So we went up and there was a wonderful awkward butterfly-filled-tummy moment, sitting there with him watching me, and all these people around him. The sun was coming up and my friend Billy and I decided to walk home. We went back to my place, and I guess I had given Keith, somewhere along the night, my number. And a few days later he called at two o'clock in the morning and said, what happened to you? And he said, hey, how about meeting me at Tramps? Some band was playing. One of my gay friends said, don't do it! Don't go. Don't go, Patti. I said, I'm going; this is great.

And I was up with him for five days straight from Tramps on. We were in a car, we went to apartments, we went to Harlem looking at record shops. I remember on the fifth day, when I finally started seeing things flying, I think we went to Mick's house; Mick was having a huge party. It was a big modeling time for me, I was on the cover of *Vogue* a lot, but I still didn't like socializing, and it was pretty A-list at Mick's place, and I said to Keith, I think I'm gonna go home now; this is it for me. After that I guess he went on with his usual biz and I the same.

Then the next thing I knew, I was out in Staten Island and I spent New Year's Eve with my family. And I remember getting in my car and zooming as fast as I could back to my apartment in the city after midnight, to find blood dripping up to my apartment on the stairs. He was waiting, leaning against my door. I don't know what he did, he had cut his foot or something. My apartment was at Fifth Avenue and Eleventh Street. And I think at that point he had been working at Eighth Street. We must have said we were going to meet there. And it was lovely.

He decided to fix us up at the Carlyle hotel. And I remember Keith making everything just right, lighting the place, putting curtains up, beautiful scarves on the lights. There were two single beds in there. Sex wasn't a big thing. It was there, but it was very slow moving. On the other hand, I have boxes and boxes of love letters from the first day we met. He would do drawings in his blood. And I still look forward to those notes I get. Very charming and very witty.

All those first moments were so great. Then little by little, people started raising red flags. Keith was going back and forth, leaving me in the middle of the night to go back to Long Island. You have a family? You have a family in Long Island, you have a child? It was nerve-racking. I didn't know he was with Anita, and I definitely didn't know he had a girlfriend named Lil Wergilis at the time. A guy asks me to come to a party, I assume he's single. I didn't know he had all this stuff and history. I remember just feeling this guy needed a place to stay. People began telling me what I was doing wrong, what I was saying wrong. Oh, don't make Keith those kind of eggs, don't say this to him, don't do this to him. It was very odd. Then my family would get horrible letters about Keith and they started worrying, but they always had trust in my judgment. I gave him the keys to my place and I went off to Paris to work for a few weeks. And I was wondering, is this happening? I really wanted to hang on to him; I really liked him. And I was excited when he called me in Paris, when are you coming home? And around March 1980, I went out to California and started doing a film with Peter Bogdanovich. But that was insane, having a relationship with Keith and trying to be a professional actress for the first time. And even Bogdanovich sent a letter to my family warning them about Keith, which I think now he regrets.

And if I didn't know much about Keith, my Lutheran family in Staten Island knew even less. My brothers and sisters grew up on the other side of the '60s, the '60s of Doris Day. My older sisters wore beehives, the French twist. They missed that hippie era. I think my brothers tried marijuana, but I don't think anyone did any kind of drugs in the family, even though they're not teetotalers. They all have their own issues; we're a heavy-drinking family. When Keith finally went to introduce himself at home at Thanksgiving, in the autumn of 1980, it was a disaster.

The first time I went up to Staten Island to meet Patti's family I'd been up for days. I had a bottle of vodka or Jack Daniel's in my hand, and I thought I'd just walk in the house with it, la-la-la-la, I ain't lying to you, this is your prospective son-in-law. I was way over the top. I'd brought along Prince Klossowski, Stash. Hardly your best backup, but I needed some charm, and bringing a prince into their home, I thought for some reason, gave me the perfect cover. A real live prince. The fact that he's a real live asshole was neither here nor there. I needed a buddy along. I knew that Patti and I would end up together anyway, it was just a question of getting the family blessing, which would make it a lot easier for Patti.

I pulled out the guitar, gave them a bit of "Malagueña." "Malagueña"! There's nothing like it. It will get you in anywhere. You play that, they think you're a fucking genius. So I played that beautifully and imagined I'd gotten all the women, at least, on my side. They made a very nice dinner, and we were noshing away and everything was polite. But to Big Al, Patti's father, I was just kind of weird. He was a Staten Island bus driver and I was an "international pop star." And then they were talking about that, about being a "pop star." I said, oh, it's just a disguise and all that. Stash has the story on this. He remembers it better because I was already pissed out of my brains. He recalls one of the brothers saying, "So what's *your* scam, then?" I remember that suddenly I felt under the grill. Stash particularly remembers that one of Patti's sisters said something like, "I think you've drunk too much to play that." And then *bang,* I went berserk. I said something like, enough of this. And smashed my guitar on the table. Which takes some force. It could have gone either way. I could have been banished forever, but the amazing thing about this family is that they weren't offended. A little startled maybe, but by then everybody had had a tipple. My apologies were very abject the following day. In the case of the old man, big old Al, a great guy, I think at least he saw that I was willing to take a chance, and he kind of liked that. He was a Seabee attached to a construction battalion in the Aleutian Islands in the war. He was supposed to be there building a runway and ended up fighting Japs because there was nobody else around. Eventually I took Big Al on at pool at his local favorite bar, and I let him think that he'd drunk me under the table. "I got ya, sonny!" "You certainly did, sir." But it was Beatrice, Patti's mum, who was the key to my acceptance. She was always for me, and I had great times with her later on.

This is how it looked for Patti the day she introduced me to her family.

**Patti Hansen:** I just remember being upstairs, crying, when the shit hit the fan. Something must have happened prior to that, because I remember I wasn't at the table with them when it happened. I must have seen he was out of it and just wanted to go and crawl in a hole. It was a holiday dinner. Something was said and a guitar flew across the table at my parents. I don't know what happened to him. He suddenly became this rock star, this person none of us had ever been around. And my mother said, something's wrong, Patti, something's very wrong. I know they were terrified, so worried about me. My father was a bus driver; he's a quiet man anyway and he was recovering from a heart attack, and that was the first time he met Keith, with his leather jacket and his skinny little legs. I'm their baby, the youngest out of seven children. Who knows what Keith was doing, but it was mostly downers and alcohol, and I remember crying on the steps and him crying in my arms, and my family watching. They had never been around all this kind of stuff. They did handle it pretty well. We had other family there, my sisters, and then we had some neighbors. It's always a full house. The next thing I know, my mom is holding me in her arms and telling me Keith was going to take care of me, it's OK, he's a good boy. And then Keith was so dreadfully upset with himself. He was so apologetic and sent my mother this beautiful note saying he was very sorry for his behavior. I don't know how she could have trusted him after that, but she did. I couldn't stay. I went back with him in the car. And they must have been terrified that I was getting in the car with this violent nut. My other brothers were in California that night, but Keith went up against them later. He would puff out his chest to me. "Choose me, Patti, or them." I said, I choose you! He would always do that to me. Just to make sure.

As to Patti's three brothers, the toughest challenge was Big Al Jr., and he really, at the time, did not like me *at all*. He wanted to fight; he wanted an OK Corral. So one day at his house in LA I said, let's cut the crap, Al, let's go outside, let's take it on, let's do it now. You're six-foot-what, and I'm five-foot-this. You'll probably kill me, but you'll never walk the same again because I'm fast. Before you kill me I'll sever you and your sister. Your sister will hate you forever. He threw in the towel. I knew that was the kicker. The rest about the macho bullshit didn't mean anything. That was his way of testing me.

Greg took a little longer. He's a nice guy, he's got eight kids, he's working hard for a living and keeps having babies. This is a religious family that I'm married into; they go to church, they form prayer circles. We have different ideas on religion. I've never found heaven, for example, a particularly interesting place to go. In fact, I take the view that God, in his infinite wisdom, didn't bother to spring for two joints — heaven and hell. They're the same place, but heaven is when you get everything you want and you meet Mummy and Daddy and your best friends and you all have a hug and a kiss and play your harps. Hell is the same place — no fire and brimstone — but they just all pass by and don't see you. There's nothing, no recognition. You're waving, "It's me, your father," but you're invisible. You're on a cloud, you've got your harp, but you can't play with nobody because they don't see you. *That's* hell.

Rodney, the third brother, was a naval chaplain at the time I met Patti, so I took him on on theology. Who actually wrote this book, Rodney? Is it the word of God or is it the edited version? Has it been tampered with? And of course he's got no answer to that, and we still love to joust about these things. It's very important to him. He likes the challenge. He'll come back with another thing the next week, "Well, the Lord says…" "Oh, he does, does he?" I had to fight my way into Patti's family, but once you're in, they'd die for you.

It was good that I had such a distraction of the heart at that time because there was a bitter current beginning to flow between me and Mick. Its onset seemed quite sudden, and it was shocking to me. It dated from the time I finally kicked heroin. I wrote a song called "All About You," which was on *Emotional Rescue* in 1980 and on which I sang one of my then-rare vocals. It's usually taken by the lyric watchers to be a song of parting from Anita. It seems like an angry boy-girl song, a bitter love song, a throwing in of the towel:

> *If the show must go on*
> *Let it go on without you*
> *So sick and tired*
> *Of hanging around with jerks like you.*

There's never one thing a song's about, but in this case if it was about anything, it was probably more about Mick. There were certain barbs aimed that way. It was at that time when I was deeply hurt. I realized that Mick had quite enjoyed one side of my being a junkie — the one that kept me from interfering in day-to-day business. Now here I was, off the stuff. I came back with the attitude of, OK, thanks a lot. I'll relieve you of the weight. Thank you for carrying the burden for several years while I was out there. I'll make recompense in time. I'd never fucked up; I'd given him some great songs to sing. The only person it fucked up was me. "Got out of there, Mick, by the skin of my teeth," and he'd got out of a few things by the skin of his teeth too. I think I expected this burst of gratitude: sort of, thank God, mate.

But what I got was, I'm running this shit. It was that rebuff. I would ask, what's happening here, what are we doing with this? And I'd get *no reply*. And I realized that Mick had got all of the strings in his hands and he didn't want to let go of a single one. Had I really read this right? I didn't know power and control were that important to Mick. I always thought we'd worked on what was good for all of us. Idealistic, stupid bastard, right? Mick had fallen in love with power while I was being . . . artistic. But all we had was ourselves. What's the point of struggling between us? Look how thin the ranks are. There's Mick, me and Charlie, there's Bill.

The phrase from that period that rings in my ears all these years later is "Oh, shut up, Keith." He used it a lot, many times, in meetings, anywhere. Even before I'd conveyed the idea, it was "Oh, shut up, Keith. Don't be stupid." He didn't even know he was doing it — it was so fucking rude. I've known him so long he can get away with murder like that. At the same time, you think about it; it hurts.

At the time I was cutting "All About You," I took Earl McGrath, who was nominally running Rolling Stones Records, to look at the wonderful view of New York from the roof of Electric Lady Studios. I said, if you don't do something about this, you see that pavement down there? It's yours. I virtually picked him up. I said, you're supposed to be the go-between with Mick. What's going on? You can't control this. Earl's a lovely bloke, and I realized he wasn't cut out to do some of this stuff between Mick and me on a bad night. But I wanted to let him know how I was feeling about this. I couldn't bring Mick up there and throw him off, and I had to do something.

I was losing Ronnie too, but temporarily and for other reasons. More to the point, Ronnie was getting lost. He was freebasing. He and Jo were living up in Mandeville Canyon, around 1980, and he had a little gang, a clique that did it with him. Crack cocaine, this stuff's worse than smack. I never did it. Never, never. I didn't like the smell of it. And I didn't like what it did to people. Once in Ronnie's house, he and Josephine and everybody else around him were freebasing. And when you're doing that, that's it, that's all there is in the world. There were all these fawning people around Ronnie, stupid blokes in straw Stetsons with feathers. I went into his john, and he was in there with loads of hangers-on and snide little dealers, and they're all on the phone in the john, trying to get more of whatever crap it is they're freebasing. There's somebody else flaming up in the bath. I walked in, sat down and took a crap. Hey, Ron! Not a word. It was like I wasn't there. Well, that's it, he's gone. Now I know what I've got to do; I've got to treat the man differently from now on. I said to Ronnie, what are you doing this for? Oh, you wouldn't understand. Oh, really? I heard that phrase from potheads many years ago. And then I think, OK, well, I'll understand or not, but I'll make up my own mind.

Everybody had wanted Ronnie off the US tour in '81 — he was just getting too out of it — but I said, no, I'll guarantee him. That meant I personally guaranteed to insure the tour and promised that Ronnie would not be misbehaving. Anything to get the Stones on the road. I figured I could handle him. And then in Frisco, the middle of October 1981, we're on the tour, the J. Geils Band along with us, and we're at the Fairmont Hotel, which looks a bit like Buckingham Palace, with an east wing and a west wing. I was in one wing and Ronnie was in the other. And I heard there was a big freebase party going on in Ronnie's room. He was being irresponsible to the max. He had promised me he wouldn't be doing that shit on the road. The red curtain came down. So I went downstairs, marched through the central lobby of the Fairmont. Patti was saying, don't go mad, don't do it. By then she'd torn my shirt off. I said, fuck it, he's putting me and the band's life on the line. If anything went wrong it was going to cost me a few mil and blow everything. I got there, he opened the door and I just socked him. You cunt, *boom.* So he fell backwards over the couch and the rest of my punch carried me over on top of him, the couch fell over and we both nearly fell out the window. We scared ourselves to death. The couch was going over and both of us were looking at the window, thinking, we could be going through here! After that I don't really remember much. I'd made my point.

Ronnie's been in and out of rehab many times since then. I put a sign on Ronnie's dressing room on tour not long ago that read, "Rehab is for quitters." You could take it any way you want. To mean keep going to these joints that actually do nothing for you, all you're doing is paying a lot of money and you walk out and do the same thing. They have rehabs for gamblers, which is the one Ronnie went to. Ronnie's idea of rehab was mainly a strategy to get away from the pressure. In recent times, he's found a smooth little rehab place — he tells me these stories, this is straight out of the horse's mouth. I've got this great one in Ireland. Oh yeah, what do they do there? It's great, nothing. I walked in and said, well, what's the regime? "Mr. Wood, there isn't one." The only rule is, there's no phone calls and no visitors. This is perfect! You mean I don't have to do anything? No. In fact, they let him go down the pub for three hours every night. And he's in there with people that are in for gambling, people that are actually hiding, like he is, just to get the day-to-day living off their back.

Once when he'd come back from rehab, I said, "He's OK now. I've known him stoned out of his brain and I've known him straight and sober. Quite honestly it makes little difference. But there's a bit more focus on him now." I stand by that, basically. That was the weird thing about it, when you come down to it. All this shit and money he'd spent on this crap and on getting off of it, and no bloody difference. He'd just look you in the eye a little more maybe. In other words, it's not about the shit, it's something else. "You wouldn't know, man."


I've been out in all weathers with Ronnie, and it shows. One rare occasion a year after our fight, after he'd laid down the crack pipe, required him to be in perfect order, to put no foot wrong. And he duly stepped up and he did a great job. I asked him to come with me to Redlands to be there when I met my dad again for the first time in twenty years.

I was scared to meet Bert. To me he was still the guy I'd left twenty years earlier, when I was a teenager. I had some idea over the years that he was OK from relations who had seen him, who told me that he was hanging out at his local pub. I was scared to meet him because of what I'd done in the meantime. That's why it took me twenty years to get round to it. In my mind, I was an absolute reprobate to my father—the guns, the drugs, the busts. The shame, the degradation for him. I had humiliated him. That was my thought—that I'd really let him down. Every headline that hit the goddamn newspapers,

"Richards Busted Again," made it even more difficult for me to get in touch with my dad. I thought he was better off not seeing me.

There aren't a lot of blokes that scare me anymore. But during my childhood, to disappoint my dad was devastating for me. I was frightened of his disapproval. I wrote earlier how the thought of it—the idea of not living up to his expectations—could still reduce me to tears, because when I was a child, his disapproval would totally isolate me, make me almost disappear. And that stuff was just frozen in time. Gary Schultz, who told me his regrets at not making amends with his dad before he died, talked me into it, although I'd always known I had to do it.

It wasn't difficult to track him down through relations. He'd been living in the back room of a pub in Bexley for all those years, never apparently needing anything from me, or certainly never asking. So I wrote to him.

I remember I was sitting on the bed in my hotel room in Washington, DC, in December 1981, near my birthday, scarcely able to believe that I was reading his reply. We couldn't meet until the European tour of 1982, a few months after that. And Redlands was the appointed place. In the meantime, I wrote to him.

> *I am really looking forward to seeing your ugly mug after all these years!! I bet you'll still scare the shit out of me. All my love, your son Keith.*
>
> *P.S. I also have a couple of your grandchildren to show you. Soon come*
>
>                                      *K*

I had brought Ronnie with me as a humorous buffer, clown, just a sidekick, a friend, because I didn't think I could handle it by myself. I sent a car to the pub in Bexley to bring Bert to me. Gary Schultz was there at Redlands too, and he remembers me, very nervous, counting down the time—he'll be here in two hours; he'll be here in half an hour. And then he arrived. And out got this little old bloke. We looked at each other and he said, "Hello, son." He was completely different. It was a shock to see him. Bandy legs, limping a bit with his war wound. It was like looking at some old rascal; he looked like a retired pirate. What twenty years can do! Silver curly locks, an amazing combo of gray sideburns with mustache. He always had one.

This was not my *dad*. I didn't expect him to be the same as I had left him, a sturdy middle-aged chap, stocky, well built. But he was a completely different person. "Hello, son." "Dad." That breaks the ice, I can tell you. Bert walked away a little bit at one point, and Gary Schultz tells me that I said to him, "You never knew I was the son of Popeye, did you?" So it was "Come in, Dad." And once he was in, couldn't get rid of him. Still a pipe man, smoking St. Bruno flake, the same dark tobacco I remember as a kid.

The weird thing is my dad turned out to be a great piss artist. Not when I was growing up, then it was maybe one beer a night, or on the weekends if we were out socializing. Now he was one of the greatest rummies I'd ever met, I mean, Jesus Christ, Bert! There are still stools commemorated to him in several pubs, especially in Bexley. Rum was his drink. Dark Navy rum.

All he said about those headlines of mine was "You've been a bit of a bugger, haven't you?" So now we could talk like grown men. And suddenly I had another friend. I had a dad again. I'd given that up; a father figure didn't come into it anymore. It was a full circle. We became conspiratorial and friendly and we found out that we really liked each other. We started to hang and decided it was time for him to travel. I wanted him to see the world from the top. Showing off, I suppose. He devoured the whole bloody globe! He wasn't in awe of it, he absorbed it. So then we began to have all the fun we hadn't had the time for. World traveler Bert Richards, who'd never been in an airplane, never been anywhere except Normandy up until that point. His first flight was to Copenhagen. The only time I saw Bert scared. As the engines were revving up, I saw his knuckles whiten. He was clutching his pipe, about to break it. But he brassed it out, and once we were in the air he loosened up. The first takeoff is hairy no matter who you are. So then he started chatting up the stewardess and he was on his way.

Next thing I know he's on the tour and we're traveling down to Bristol, me and my friend the writer James Fox in the back, my minder Svi Horowitz and Bert forward. Svi says to Bert, would you like a drink, Mr. Richards? And Bert goes, I think I'll have a light ale, thank you, Svi. And I wind down the partition and say, what? On the Sabbath, Dad? and I fall back laughing at the irony of all this. And then in Martinique he's got Brooke Shields on his knee. I couldn't get a word in edgeways. They were all over my dad, three or four top starlets. Where's Dad? Where do you think? He's down the bar surrounded by the latest batch of beauties. He had some energy. I remember him playing dominoes with five or six of us right through the night, and everybody else was down under the table, and he was knocking back neat rum at the same time. He'd never get drunk. Always steady. He was kind of like me, and that's the problem. You can drink more because it doesn't really do much. It's just something you do, like waking up or breathing.

Anita meanwhile, a fugitive from the press for a while after the boy shot himself on the premises, had holed up in the Alray Hotel in New York on 68th Street, with Marlon. Larry Sessler, Freddie's son, was there to look after them. Marlon's life revolved not around schooling, at least not of the conventional kind, but around Anita's new friends, the post-punk world centered on the Mudd Club, which was the anti–Studio 54 on White Street in New York. The world of Brian Eno, the Dead Boys and Max's Kansas City was Anita's hangout. Nothing, of course, had changed with Anita, and she probably remembers it as the worst of times for her, or counts herself lucky to be alive. It was very dangerous in New York at that time, not just from

AIDS. Shooting up in Lower East Side hotels is no joke. Nor is the fourth floor of the Chelsea Hotel, specializing in angel dust and heroin.

To try and provide some stability, I took over Mick Taylor's rented house in Sands Point, Long Island, for them — the first of a series of mad movie-like mansions on Long Island that they lived in during this period. I would come to visit when I could, to see Marlon. I came out for Anita's birthday in 1980 and found Roy "Skipper" Martin, one of a bunch of people Anita would bring out from the Mudd Club. Roy had a nightly spot there doing some extreme kind of stand-up comedy. Roy had cooked this huge meal: roast lamb, Yorkshire pudding and all that stuff — and then apple crumble and custard. I asked him, is this real custard? And he said yes, and I said, no, it's not, you got it out of a tin. And he said, I fucking made it, it came out of a packet, Bird's vanilla, that you make with milk. So we had a set-to. I remember I threw a glass at him across the table.

I usually make an instant connection with my long-term, solid friends; I can spot them straightaway — some sense that we're going to trust each other. It's a binding contract. Roy is one of them, from that first night. Once I've made a connection, to me it's the biggest sin to let a friend down. Because that means you don't understand the whole meaning of friendship, comradeship, which is the most important thing. You'll hear more of Roy because as well as being a good friend of mine, he's still taking care of biz at my house in Connecticut. He's been on a family retainer, for want of a better term, ever since about a year after that meeting.

I'd be nowhere without my mates: Bill Bolton, my distant muscle on the road, built like a brick shithouse; Tony Russell, my minder for the past many years; Pierre de Beauport, guitar tech and musical adviser. The only trouble with true friends like that is we keep jumping in front of each other to save each other. Me, no, me, I'll take the hit. True friends. Hardest thing to find, but you never look for them — they find you; you just grow into each other. I can go nowhere without knowing I have some solid backup. Jim Callaghan in the past, and Joe Seabrook, who croaked a couple of years before I wrote this, were just that. Bill Bolton's married to Joe's sister, so it's all in the family. Cats that I've been through thick and thin with are very important to me.

For some reason all my close friends have been jailbirds at one time or another. I hadn't taken this in until I saw them on a list together with their thumbnail CVs. What does that tell us? Nothing, because each circumstance is so different. Bobby Keys is the only one who's been to jail several times, for, as he says, crimes he didn't even know he committed. We all stick together, me and my dastardly crew. We just want to do what we want to do without being bothered by all of that other crap. We love "The Adventures of Keith Richards." It'll come to a sticky end, I've no doubt. It's like a Just William,* really. Roy, for example, ran away to sea at fifteen years old, from Stepney in the East End of London, which tells you a lot. He went into gold smuggling in the early '60s. A free spirit, Roy. He used to buy the gold in Switzerland and put it in special jackets and around his knickers, forty kilos of it, and fly it to the Far East, Hong Kong, Bangkok. Heavy gold bars made by Johnson Matthey, .999. One day when Roy got out of the taxi after flying for twenty-five hours, he couldn't get up because of the weight. He was on his knees at the taxi door, and the hotel doormen had to rush out and help him in. Roy was banged up, for other reasons, in the famous Arthur Road prison in Bombay, as it appears in the book *Shantaram*. No charge, no trial. Defence of India Regulations. And he escaped. He wanted to be an actor, and he was an actor in fringe theater for a while, which is probably why he was doing stand-up in the Mudd Club. Roy is one of the funniest guys I know, and occasionally he went out of control with manic energy, and it *is* manic energy. Nobody else going to do it? I'll show you. Once, in the Mayflower Hotel, there were loads of people after a show and sud-

* The boys' adventure series written by Richmal Crompton.

denly I hear this knock at the window, this is about sixteen stories up, and there's Roy clinging to the sill, knocking on the window, going, "Help, help." There's police cars going by and people below calling, "Hey, up there. Someone's got a jumper." *That's not funny, Roy.* Get your ass in. Underneath him there was a very narrow brick ledge. He just had his toes on it. There are guys who should not be alive.

After the '81 tour I persuaded Roy to look after Marlon and Anita full-time. One of his briefs was to see whether he could get Marlon to go to school. Bert joined them after the 1982 European tour. What a ménage à trois that was. Bert, Marlon and Roy, living in the Gatsby mansions with Anita coming and going. Bert always thought Anita was nuts. And yes, she was pretty far out; she just carried on, out of her brain all this time. It was like some crew stranded on half pay in a series of huge, deserted mansions. Harold Pinter meets Scott Fitzgerald. Roy was a sailor anyway. Bert and Marlon weren't, but they were all adrift, let's put it that way, in this foreign country, though Marlon was so used to foreign countries he didn't really care which one he was in. Roy lived with Bert from 1982 until he died. I put them there while I was on the road. I only ever visited there off and on, pop in and say hi. So I should have Marlon describe what gothic adventures came to pass in those lost years on the shores of Long Island.

**Marlon:** The worst part was growing up in New York, because in the late '70s it was a scary place. I didn't go back to school for all of 1980. We lived in the Alray Hotel, in the middle of Manhattan, which wasn't too bad. It was like Eloise at the Plaza. We went to movies. Anita used to take me round to see Andy Warhol, William Burroughs. I think he lived in the men's showers at the Chelsea Hotel. It was all tiled, and there were washing lines with used condoms on them, hanging across the room. Very strange man.

From there we moved to the Mick Taylor–vacated house on Sands Point, Long Island, for about six months. The first

filmed version of *The Great Gatsby* was shot there, in which
Sands Point is East Egg, with many acres of lawns and a huge
beachfront and a saltwater pool, all decaying. We used to hear
'20s jazz music coming from the gazebo, dinner parties and
clinking glasses and laughter that dissipated as you walked
towards it. There were certainly mob connections in this
house. I found family snaps in the attic of Sinatra and Dean
Martin, all the Rat Pack, hanging out there in the '50s. This
was where Roy first turned up, before he came to live with us
for good, this crazy Englishman who Anita brought from the
Mudd Club, where his act was to drink a whole bottle of
cognac on stage while telling jokes and blabbering on and
reciting a poem by Shel Silverstein called "The Perfect High,"
about a boy called Gimmesome Roy, and slowly peeling off
his clothes. All for two hundred dollars and a bottle of cognac.
Anita brought him home to the big house, and we put him up
in the attic at first, but he completely wrecked the room in a
drunken rant. He was terrifying. We had to kick him out of
the house, essentially. He would drink a bottle of cognac in
the morning and sing, so we just shifted him into the
doghouse, which was like a shed. He had an affinity for the
Labrador at the time and he would spend the hours singing
away with the dog. It was a mild spring, so it wasn't too bad.

Anita collected other fringe acts too. The writer and beat
poet Mason Hoffenberg often used to live there with us. This
little bearded Jewish gnome who would sit naked out in the
garden and sort of spew down at people who drove by. He was
going through his naturist stage, which was a bit terrifying for
Long Island. We called him the garden gnome. He stayed for
quite a while that summer.

Roy became a permanent fixture in late '81, having been
on tour with Keith, a kind of official minder to us when we
moved to Old Westbury, another huge mansion where we

lived from 1981 until 1985. It was an enormous place with only the four of us living there and semi-derelict, absolutely no furniture and no heating but with a beautiful ballroom I used to roller-skate around, its walls hand painted on canvas in the 1920s but now peeling. In fact, by the end of our stay the whole edifice, with its two main staircases and two wings, looked like Miss Havisham's.

The only furniture was a big white Bösendorfer piano that Roy used to play on and do his Liberace routine. And I had my drum kit at the other end of the ballroom, so we sort of jammed. We had a good sound system and all Keith's records, so we'd put a record on and mess about and then Roy would open a tin for dinner. What tin do you want tonight, Spam or...? So I became a vegetarian after that. No, I don't want any more Spam, Roy, thanks a lot.

Anita was going through a very self-destructive period at this time. She was in a dark place. If she went to New York she would drink a lot when she got back to calm whatever she had taken and go into violent alcoholic rages. Despite this, interesting people were coming all the time via Anita — Basquiat, Robert Fraser came down, and Anita's punk friends, like the fellows from the Dead Boys and some of the guys from the New York Dolls. It was quite crazy. I don't think Anita got any credit for the fact that she did contribute to the punk movement. A lot of them, at least New York ones, would come and spend weekends at our house. She'd come back from the Mudd Club and CBGBs with a car full of pink-haired nutters. Nice people generally, just nerdy Jewish kids, really.

Every now and again Roy would go up to the office in New York with receipts and come back with big envelopes full of hundred-dollar bills, and that would be the money for the month. It was hilarious. So when I got my allowance, what did I do with this brand-new crisp hundred-dollar bill? I just wanted to go and buy some comic books, and I was waving this thing around.

They got quite used to us in Long Island. Roy would go ninety miles an hour everywhere, screaming. And he drove huge Lincoln Continentals, those big pimpmobiles we used to rent. Roy would write them off once every two months and we'd get another one. He used to have his two days off, where he'd say, right, I'm going away for two days, don't bother me. And he'd just go off on a drinking binge and he'd come back with bruises or all cut up. On one spectacular outing Roy got into some argument in a bar in Long Island. He left the bar, came back ten minutes later and drove the car right through the bar windows, crashed three cars outside and a bunch of motorcycles. He then got out of the car, walked back into the bar he'd just wrecked to make a telephone call. Next day he was arrested and put in jail and we bailed him out. But Bert was very patient with all that. Oh, Roy in trouble again? Luckily for Roy, it was a town with a private police force, so every time Roy would get into a car crash they'd just sort of drop him off at home. Bert used to go down in the evening to a Hells Angels bar by the train station in Westbury. And he'd sit there with all these Hells Angels, these guys with the caps and the leather, for hours and hours and hours. He'd sit there with Roy, and Roy would entertain everyone, yodeling and screaming.

Bert, on the other hand, lived a life of strict routine. He used to get up and have a swim, fix his own breakfast. He had these very set meals, now cooked by Roy. He always had a glass of Harveys Bristol Cream at seven bells. Because *Wheel of Fortune* came on at seven thirty. He always watched *Wheel of Fortune*. He had a thing for Vanna White, used to cheer her on, yell at people who were rude to her. And then at eight o'clock he'd have dinner and then watch TV till midnight, drinking Bass and dark Navy rum.

Thank God the houses were large enough that sometimes I could just disappear and I didn't have to see people. One person could have a wing to himself, and basically I wouldn't know what the hell they were doing for weeks on end. People say, oh, remember when Jean-Michel Basquiat visited for a week? No! Maybe I was in the east wing then. We used to change bedrooms every few months, just to make it interesting. I wouldn't see Roy for two weeks. I didn't know where his bedroom was.

The landlord never did any maintenance on the place, so it was just getting worse and worse and worse. Once my bedroom became too decrepit, I would move into another one — luckily there were about fifteen of them — until eventually I moved all the way to the attic. It was the last place left! A huge attic space, the size of a cathedral up there, and I had my bed and a TV and my desk, and I would just lock the door and not let anyone else up there. By then we said, we can't stay here anymore; it's falling down. Or we've destroyed it. So that's why we moved to the final mansion at Mill Neck, on the edge of Oyster Bay.

Around '83, Anita moved back to England because of visa problems and stayed there, coming over only for the occasional visit. So she wasn't there for this last gigantic house with twelve or thirteen bedrooms, so incredibly cold in the winter. We had a fireplace in one living room. Roy's room was heated, Bert's room was heated, and we would all sort of meet up sometimes in the kitchen. If you walked in the hallway, you had to put an overcoat on. This house had an elevator up to the rooms we lived in. One day the elevator broke down and we didn't go out for two weeks. Then we discovered that the front door had been left open and the whole ground floor had frozen into an ice ballroom, icicles hanging from the chandeliers. It was like Narnia. It was like Gormenghast. I came upon the African frogs we had as pets frozen solid in their tank, many years pre Damien Hirst.

Around this time I asked Keith if I could have guitar lessons. "No son of mine is going to be a guitar player," he said. "Certainly not. I want you to grow up to be a lawyer or accountant." He was joking, of course, but very dry, and I was quite traumatized.

The amazing thing is that I went to school, Portledge, a posh local school in Locust Valley, driven by Roy. But intermittently, let's put it that way. My attendance record wasn't very good. I didn't really mind all this self-sufficiency. I was kind of happy to not have everyone around, really, because it was exhausting with Anita and Keith. I just wanted to go to school as best I could and get things done and have some sort of normal life, and I felt I could do that much better by myself. Or at least with Roy. Eventually I got kicked out of the Locust Valley school for not showing up, not doing my homework, and I just gave up on school, really. Keith was getting advice from one of his relations saying that I was a complete delinquent and I should go to military academy. There was even a move to convince Keith to send me off to West Point. I wouldn't have minded, actually. But Keith said, well, what do you want to do? He said, do you want to just give up school altogether, and I said, well, no, I want to get my education; I want to go to England because I can't do it in America. So I came over to England in 1988 and moved in across the street from Anita on Tite Street in Chelsea and got a flat. And lest it be forgotten, I got four A levels.

For Marlon himself, and for me, it was the defining point. It was his decision to go back to England. He said to me, all I'm going to get is Long Island bullshit. And that's when I took my hat off to Marlon. He could take his choice, he could be the Long Island brat, but thank God he's smarter than that and got out of there and managed to cope. Maybe Bert was one of the first solid anchors. Maybe he became the steadying force. The proof is in the pudding. I'm sure things could have been done far better, but we were on the run. And Marlon had a unique upbringing. Far from normal. Hence, probably, why he's bringing up his own kids in a very secure way, hands on all the time. Because he never got that. By now Marlon understands; it was the times, and the circumstances, that made it tough on him. It was very difficult to be one of the Rolling Stones and take care of your kids at the same time.

As for Anita, she survived too. Now she is the benign grandmother to Marlon's three children. She's a kind of elder and icon in the fashion world, in which she involves herself; people see her as a source of inspiration. And she's developed her green thumb lately. I know a bit about gardening, but I think she knows more than I do. She took care of my trees in Redlands. She chopped off the ivy. The trees were being choked to death by ivy, several of them. I gave her a machete. And the trees are blooming again; the ivy's gone. She knows what to do. She has an allotment somewhere in London that she cultivates; rides down on her bicycle.

Patti and I had been together for four years by December 1983. I loved her soul and I knew in my heart I wanted to make this thing legitimate. And I was coming up to my fortieth birthday. What was more appropriate? We'd been shooting videos in Mexico City, for "Undercover of the Night," with Julien Temple, who shot many of our videos in those days. We shot three or four movies in Mexico while we were there. And at the end I decided, right, fuck it, time off, go down to Cabo San Lucas, then a small town with two hotels on the beach, one of which was the Twin Dolphin.

We have "conferences," me and my friends scattered across the globe, group meetings — sitting conferences, like bishops' conferences, ready to be convened at any time. There's the Eastern and the Western in the USA, which are straightforward, but the one that was nuts was the Southwestern conference, much of which took place in New Mexico. The names of its members: Red Dog; Gary Ashley, who's now dead and gone; Stroker, real name Dicky Johnson. They're called the Southwestern conference because you'd never see them east of the Mississippi. They're a solid bunch, absolute madmen, all of them. They brook no interference from sanity, bless their hearts. I'd hung with these guys on many occasions. I got to Cabo San Lucas on this trip, and within a week, I'd met Gregorio Azar, who had a house there. Gregorio's father owns Azar nuts, which was the biggest nut business in the Southwest. He'd heard I was staying at the Twin Dolphin, which is one of the few hotels there. I didn't know him at the time, but he knew all of the other Southwest conference guys, came out with the right names at the right time. A friend of Gary Ashley and Red Dog? Cool, come on in. And so we started to hang and he was co-opted.

I proposed to Patti on the rooftop of Gregorio's house in Cabo San Lucas. Come on, let's get married on my birthday. She said, do you mean it? I said yeah. Immediately she jumped on my back. I didn't feel anything, but I just heard something go snap and I looked down and there's two beautiful fountains of blood coming out from behind my toenail. Within five seconds of me saying, yeah, I mean it, she broke my toe. Next time it'll be the heart, right? Half an hour later it had started to throb and then I was on a crutch for the next two weeks. A few days before our wedding day, I found myself running through the Mexican desert on a crutch with a black coat and chasers on. We'd had a fight, Patti and I, some premarriage thing, I don't know what it was about, but here I was, hobbling through cacti, chasing her into the desert, "Come here, you bitch!" like Long John Silver.

On the day before the wedding, Gregorio says to me, by the way, have you heard about this German chick with the big Mercedes bus and the tepee? And I went chilled. She's German? Big Mercedes bus? Tepee? Get out of here. The bus was parked on a beach in Cabo San Lucas. I knew from magazines that Uschi Obermaier had been traveling the hippie trail through Afghanistan, Turkey and India in recent years, with this huge bus, fur lined and with a sauna in it. She was traveling with her husband, Dieter Bockhorn. I knew for sure that she was in Cabo San Lucas when I opened the door of my room in the Twin Dolphin, which is right on the beach, and there was this little vase of flowers outside. There could have been no stranger or weirder coincidence than this — for us to meet on the eve of my wedding in this remote part of Mexico, about as far as you could get from Afghanistan or Germany or anywhere Uschi had been. What was she doing here? And then Uschi and Dieter came by, and I told her I was getting married and I was very much in love with Patti. We talked about the intervening years, rumors of her demise — and the reality, which was her travels in her bus through the world, through India and Turkey and God knows where. A few nights later, on New Year's Eve, Dieter was killed on his motorcycle, his severed head, still in his helmet, on one side of the road; his body had gone over the bridge. I went to see Uschi. There was a big black dog barking in the doorway. Who's there? I said, it's the Englishman. The door opened. I've heard what's happened. Is there anything I can do to help? She said, thank you but no, I have friends and everything is being taken care of. So I left Uschi in these bizarre and tragic circumstances, our most unlikely meetings having been framed by shock and grief, first mine and then hers.

Doris and Bert came for our wedding ceremony, the first time they'd met in twenty years, and Angela locked them in a room and forced them to talk to each other. Marlon came; Mick was the best man. Four years Patti and I had been together, four years of road testing, and I'd expended enough sperm to fertilize the whole world, and no babies. Not that I really expected to have children by Patti. "I can't have babies," she'd said. Well, I guess you can't! But it's not the reason

I'm gonna marry you. Put that little curtain ring round her finger and in six months guess what? "I'm pregnant." So the dungeon that we were planning, no, it's going to be a nursery now. All right, paint it pink and put a cot in, take the chains off the walls, get the mirrors down. I thought by then I'd done my fathering bit, with Marlon and Angela. They're growing up all right, we've done it and we've made it. No more diapers. But no! Here comes another one. Her name's Theodora. And then a year later another one, Alexandra. Little T&A. And they weren't even a gleam in my eye when I wrote that song.

*Jane Rose*

# Chapter Twelve

---

Secret solo deals and skulduggery. World War III breaks out—
between the Glimmer Twins. I ally myself with Steve Jordan and make
a difficult film with Chuck Berry, then cut loose and form the
X-Pensive Winos. Reunion with Mick in Barbados; Voodoo, the
rescued cat (opposite), and his lounge; rebirth of the Stones and the
start of the megatours with Steel Wheels. *Bridges to Babylon*
and four songs with a parallel narrative.

I t was the beginning of the '80s when Mick started to become unbearable. That's when he became Brenda, or Her Majesty, or just Madam. We were in Paris, back at Pathé Marconi, in November and December of 1982, working on songs for *Undercover*. I went to WHSmith, the English bookshop on the Rue de Rivoli. I forget the title of the book, but there it was, some lurid novel by Brenda Jagger. Gotcha, mate! Now you're Brenda whether you know it or like it or not. He certainly didn't like it. It took him ages to find out. We'd be talking about "that bitch Brenda" with him in the room, and he wouldn't know. But there's a terrible thing that starts, and it's very much like the way Mick and I behaved towards Brian. Once you release that acid, it begins to corrode.

This situation was a culmination of things that had been going on for several years. The immediate problem was that Mick had developed an overriding desire to control everything. As far as he was concerned, it was Mick Jagger and *them*. That was the attitude that we all got. It didn't matter how much he tried, he couldn't stop appearing, to himself at least, as numero uno. Now there was Mick's world, which was a socialite world, and our world. This didn't work at all well with keeping a band together or keeping them happy. Oh dear me, after all these years, the swollen head's arrived. He'd gotten to where it wouldn't fit through the doorway. The band, including myself, were now basically hirelings. That had always been his attitude to everyone else, but never to the band. When it dripped over onto us, that was it.

An inflated ego is always very difficult in a band, especially a band that's been going a long time, and is tight, and really relies upon, at least amongst its members, a certain bizarre integrity. The band is a team. It's very democratic in a way. Everything has to be decided between us — it's so much for a left leg from the top of the knee, and so much for your testicles. Anybody that tries to elevate himself above the others endangers himself. Charlie and I would raise our eyes to the ceiling. Do you believe that? And for a while we just put up with it when Mick tried to take the whole thing over. When you think about it, we'd been together twenty-five years or so before the shit really hit the fan. So the view was, this was bound to happen. This happens to all bands eventually, and now's the test. Does it hold together?

It must have been pretty bad for anyone around us who worked on *Undercover*. A hostile, discordant atmosphere. We were barely talking or communicating, and if we were, we were bickering and sniping. Mick attacking Ronnie, me defending him. Eventually, in the Pathé Marconi studios in Paris, trying to finish the album, Mick would come in from midday until five p.m. and I'd appear from midnight until five a.m. It was only the early skirmishing, the phony war. The work itself wasn't bad, somehow; the album did well.

Well, Mick got very big ideas. All lead singers do. It's a known affliction called LVS, lead vocalist syndrome. There had been early symptoms, but it was now rampant. A video display in the stadium in Tempe, Arizona, where the Stones were performing and Hal Ashby was shooting *Let's Spend the Night Together* announced, "Mick Jagger and the Rolling Stones." Since when? Mick was a controller of every detail, and it was no producer's oversight. The shots were excised.

If you combine congenital LVS with a nonstop bombardment of flattery every waking moment over years and years, you can start to believe the incoming. Even if you're not flattered by flattery or you're anti-flattery, it will go to your head; it will do something to you. And even if you don't completely believe it, you say, well, everybody else does — I'll roll with it. You forget that it's just part of the job. It's amazing how even quite sensible people like Mick Jagger could get carried away by it. Actually believe they were special. I've had problems ever since I was nineteen with people saying, you're fantastic, and you know you ain't. Downfall, boy. I could see how other people were sucked in so easily; I became a puritan in that respect. I will never go that way. I'll disfigure myself. Which I did, by letting some teeth fall out. I'm not playing this game. I'm not in show business. Playing the music is the best I can do, and I know it's worth a listen.

Mick had become uncertain, had started second-guessing his own talent — that seemed, ironically, to be at the root of the self-inflation. For many years through the '60s, Mick was incredibly charming and humorous. He was natural. It was electrifying the way he could work those small spaces, as a singer and as a dancer; fascinating to watch and work with — the spins, the moves. He never thought about it. That performance was exciting without him appearing to do anything. And he's still good, even though to my mind it's dissipated on the big stages. That's what people have wanted to see: spectacle. But it's not necessarily what he's best at.

Somewhere, though, he got unnatural. He forgot how good he was in that small spot. He forgot his natural rhythm. I know he disagrees with me. What somebody else was doing was far more interesting to him than what he was doing. He even began to act as if he wanted to be someone else. Mick is quite competitive, and he started to get competitive about other bands. He watched what David Bowie was doing and wanted to do it. Bowie was a major, major attraction. Somebody had taken Mick on in the costume and bizarreness department. But the fact is, Mick could deliver ten times more than Bowie in just a T-shirt and a pair of jeans, singing "I'm a Man." Why would you want to be anything else if you're Mick Jagger? Is being the greatest entertainer in show business not enough? He forgot that it was he who was new, who created and set the trends in the first place, for years. It's fascinating. I can't figure it out. It's almost as if Mick was aspiring to be Mick Jagger, chasing his own phantom. And getting design consultants to help him do it. No one taught him to dance, until he took dance lessons. Charlie and Ronnie and I quite often chuckle when we see Mick out there doing a move that we know some dance instructor just laid on him, instead of being himself. We know the minute he's going plastic. Shit, Charlie and I have been watching that ass for forty-odd years; we know when the moneymaker's shaking and when it's being told what to do. Mick's taken up singing lessons, but that may be to preserve his voice.

Coming back after a few months apart, I realized that Mick's taste in music had often changed quite drastically. He wanted to lay on me the latest hit he heard at a disco. But it's already been done, pal. At the time we were doing *Undercover* in 1983, he was just trying to out-disco everybody. It all sounded to me like some rehash of something he heard in a club one night. Already five years earlier, on *Some Girls,* we'd got "Miss You" out of it, which was one of the best disco records of all time. But Mick was chasing musical fashion. I had a lot of problems with him trying to second-guess the audience. This is what they're into this year. Yeah, what about next year, pal? You just become one of the crowd. And anyway, that's never the way we've worked. Let's just do it the way we've always done it, which is do we like it? Does it pass our test? When it comes down to it, Mick and I wrote our

first song in a kitchen. That's as big as the world is. If we'd been thinking about how the public was going to react, we'd never have made a
record. I also understood Mick's problem, because lead singers always
get into this competition: what's Rod doing, what's Elton doing, David
Bowie, what's he up to?

It gave him a spongelike mentality when it came to music. He'd
hear something in a club and a week later he'd think he wrote it. And
I'd say, no, that's actually a total lift. I've had to check him on that. I've
played him songs that I've come up with, ideas...He says, that's nice,
and we fiddle about for a bit and leave it alone. A week later he'll
come back and say, look, I've just written this. And I know it's totally
innocent, because he wouldn't be that dumb. The writers' credits
under "Anybody Seen My Baby?" include K.D. Lang and a cowriter.
My daughter Angela and her friend were at Redlands and I was playing the record and they start singing this totally different song over it.
They were hearing K.D. Lang's "Constant Craving." It was Angela
and her friend that copped it. And the record was about to come out
in a week. Oh shit, he's lifted another one. I don't think he's ever done
it deliberately; he's just a sponge. So I had to call up Rupert and all of
the heavy-duty lawyers, and I said, have this checked out right now,
otherwise we're going to be sued. And within twenty-four hours, I got
a phone call: you're right. We had to include K.D. Lang in the writing
credits.

I used to love to hang with Mick, but I haven't gone to his dressing
room in, I don't think, twenty years. Sometimes I miss my friend.
Where the hell did he go? I know when the shit hits the fan, I can
guarantee he'll be there for me, as I would be for him, because that's
beyond any contention. I think over the years Mick has become more
and more isolated. I can understand it in a way. I try and avoid isolat-
ing myself, but even so, you often need to *insulate* yourself from what's
going on. In recent years, if I ever watch an interview with Mick, at
the base of it he's going, what do you want out of me? A defensive
charm comes on. What do they want from you? They want some

answers, obviously, to some questions. But what are you so scared of giving away? Or is it just the act of giving away something for free? And you can imagine how, if you were Mick at that time, in his high days, everybody wanted a piece, and how difficult it was. But his way of dealing with it was that he would start to slowly treat everybody that defensive way. Not just strangers, but his best friends. Until it came to the point where I would say something to him and I could tell from that look in his eyes that he was wondering, what's Keith's gain? And I didn't have one! The siege mentality builds up. Now you've built the wall, but can you get out?

I don't know quite how to put the finger on where and when this all happened. He used to be a lot warmer. But not for many, many years. He put himself in the fridge, basically. First it was, what do other people want out of me? and then he closed the circle until I was on the outside too.

For me it's very painful, because he still is a friend of mine. Jesus Christ, he's given me enough grief over my life. But he's one of my mates, and to me it's a personal failure not to have been able to turn him around to the joys of friendship and just bring him down to earth.

We've been through so many different periods together. I love the man dearly. But it was a long time ago that we could be that close. We have a respect, I guess, for now, with a deeper, under-rooted friendship. Do you know Mick Jagger? Yeah, which one? He's a nice bunch of guys. It's up to him which one you meet. He chooses on the day whether he's going to be distant or flippant or "my mate," which doesn't ever come off very well.

And I think maybe in recent years he's realized that he's become isolated. He actually talks to the crew at times! In years past he wouldn't even know their names or bother to learn them. When he got on the plane on tour, crew members would say, "How you doing, Mick?" and he just walked straight by. Me and Ronnie and Charlie too. He was famous for it. Yet these people were the ones that could make you sound and look great or like crap if they wanted to. In that sense he made things difficult, but if Mick wasn't making things difficult you'd think he was ill.

Just when he was at his most insufferable, a bombshell was dropped onto our assembled gathering. In 1983, we were a growing concern. There was a multi-record deal with CBS and its president, Walter Yetnikoff, for twenty-odd million dollars. What I didn't know until a good while later was that on the back of that deal, Mick had made his own deal with CBS for three solo records for millions of dollars, without a word to anybody in the band.

I don't care who you are, you don't piggyback on a Rolling Stones deal. Mick felt free to do that. It was total disregard for the band. And I'd rather have found out about it before it went down. I was incensed. We didn't build this band up to stab each other in the back.

It became clear how much earlier the plans had been laid. Mick was the big star, and Yetnikoff and others were fully behind the idea of him taking off on a solo career — all of which flattered Mick and encouraged his takeover plans. In fact, Yetnikoff let it be known later that everyone at CBS was thinking that Mick could be as big as Michael Jackson and they were actively promoting it, and Mick was going along with it. So the real purpose of the Rolling Stones deal was for Mick to ride in on top of it.

I thought it was just a dumb move, basically. He didn't realize that by doing something else he was breaking a certain image in the public mind that is very fragile. Mick was in a unique position as lead singer of the Stones, and he should have read a little more into what that actually meant. Anybody can get bigheaded once in a while and think, I can do this with any old band. But obviously he proved it's not true. I can understand somebody wanting to kick the traces. I like to play with other people and do something else, but in his case he had nothing really in mind except being Mick Jagger without the Rolling Stones.

The way it was done was just so tacky. I could have maybe

understood it if the Stones were flopping, like the rat leaving the sinking ship. But the fact is the Stones were doing very well and all we had to do was keep it together. Instead of losing four, five years in the wilderness and then having to pull it all together again. Everybody felt betrayed. What happened to the friendship? He couldn't have told me from the beginning that he was thinking of doing something else?

What really pissed me off at the time was Mick's compulsion to cultivate buddy relationships with CEOs, in this case Yetnikoff. Incessant telephone calls to impress them with his knowledge, letting them know that he was on top of it, when actually no one guy's on top of it. And annoying everyone with his constant interference in places where people who are paid fortunes know how to do it better than he does.

Our only strength was in distance, in a united front. That's how we did the Decca deal. We just stood there in shades and intimidated them into one of the best record deals of all time. My theory on working with record people is never to talk to them personally except on social occasions. You never get that close to them; you never get involved in the daily da da da — you pay somebody to do that. Asking about budgets for advertising and ... "Hey, Walter, where's the ... ?," making yourself personally available to the guy you're working with? You reduce yourself, diminish your power. You reduce the band. Because it's "Jagger's on the phone again." "Oh, tell him to call me later." That's what happens. I like Walter very much; I think he's great. But Mick actually pulled the rug from under us by getting too familiar with him.

There was a rare moment, in late 1984, of Charlie throwing his drummer's punch — a punch I've seen a couple of times and it's lethal; it carries a lot of balance and timing. He has to be badly provoked. He threw this one at Mick. We were in Amsterdam for a meeting. Mick and I weren't on great terms at the time, but I said, c'mon, let's go out. And I lent him the jacket I got married in. We got back to the hotel about five in the morning and Mick called up Charlie. I said, don't call him, not at this hour. But he did, and said, "Where's my drummer?"

No answer. He puts the phone down. Mick and I were still sitting there, pretty pissed — give Mick a couple of glasses, he's gone — when, about twenty minutes later, there was a knock at the door. There was Charlie Watts, Savile Row suit, perfectly dressed, tie, shaved, the whole fucking bit. I could smell the cologne! I opened the door and he didn't even look at me, he walked straight past me, got hold of Mick and said, "Never call me your drummer again." Then he hauled him up by the lapels of my jacket and gave him a right hook. Mick fell back onto a silver platter of smoked salmon on the table and began to slide towards the open window and the canal below it. And I was thinking, this is a good one, and then I realized it was my wedding jacket. And I grabbed hold of it and caught Mick just before he slid into the Amsterdam canal. It took me twenty-four hours after that to talk Charlie down. I thought I'd done it when I took him up to his room, but twelve hours later, he was saying, "Fuck it, I'm gonna go down and do it again." It takes a lot to wind that man up. "Why did you stop him?" My jacket, Charlie, that's why!

By the time we gathered in Paris to record *Dirty Work* in 1985, the atmosphere was bad. The sessions had been delayed because Mick was working on his solo album, and now he was busy promoting it. Mick had come with barely any songs for us to work on. He'd used them up on his own record. And he was often just not there at the studio.

So I began writing a lot more on my own for *Dirty Work*, different kinds of songs. The horrendous atmosphere in the studio affected everybody. Bill Wyman almost stopped turning up; Charlie flew back home. In retrospect I see that the tracks were full of violence and menace: "Had It with You," "One Hit (to the Body)," "Fight." We made a video of "One Hit (to the Body)" that more or less told the story — we nearly literally came to blows, over and above our acting duties. "Fight" gives some idea of brotherly love between the Glimmer Twins at this juncture.

> *Gonna pulp you to a mess of bruises*
> *'Cos that's what you're looking for*

*There's a hole where your nose used to be*
*Gonna kick you out of my door.*

*Gotta get into a fight*
*Can't get out of it*
*Gotta get into a fight.*

And there was "Had It with You":

*I love you, dirty fucker*
*Sister and a brother*
*Moaning in the moonlight*
*Singing for your supper*
*'Cos I had it I had it I had it with you*
*I had it I had it I had it with you....*

*It is such a sad thing*
*To watch a good love die*
*I've had it up to here, babe*
*I've got to say goodbye*
*'Cos I had it I had it I had it with you*
*And I had it I had it I had it with you.*

That was the kind of mood I was in. I wrote "Had It with You" in Ronnie's front room in Chiswick, right on the banks of the Thames. We were waiting to go back to Paris, but the weather was so dodgy that we were stranded until the Dover ferry started rolling again. Peter Cook and Bert were hanging about. There was no heating, and the only way to keep warm was to turn on the amps. I don't think I'd ever written a song before, apart maybe from "All About You," in which I realized I was actually singing about Mick.

Mick's album was called *She's the Boss,* which said it all. I've never listened to the entire thing all the way through. Who has? It's like

*Mein Kampf.* Everybody had a copy, but nobody listened to it. As to his subsequent titles, carefully worded, *Primitive Cool, Goddess in the Doorway,* which it was irresistible not to rechristen "Dogshit in the Doorway," I rest my case. He says I have no manners and a bad mouth. He's even written a song on the subject. But this record deal of Mick's was bad manners beyond any verbal jibes.

Just by the choice of material, it seemed to me he had really gone off the tracks. It was very sad. He wasn't prepared not to make an impact. And he was upset. But I can't imagine why he thought it would fly. This is where I felt Mick had lost touch with reality.

No matter what Mick's doing or what his intentions are, I'm not sitting around festering, nurturing venom. My attention, anyway, was turned suddenly and forcibly, in December 1985, to the shattering news that Ian Stewart had died.

He died of a heart attack, aged forty-seven. I was waiting for him that afternoon in Blakes Hotel off the Fulham Road. He was going to meet me after he'd seen his doctor. Around three in the morning, I got a call from Charlie. "Are you still waiting for Stu?" I said yes. "Well, he's not coming" was Charlie's way of breaking the news. The wake was held at his golf course at Leatherhead, Surrey. He'd have appreciated the joke that this was the only way he'd ever get us there. We played a tribute gig to Stu at the 100 Club—the first time we'd been on stage together in four years. Stu was the hardest hit I had ever had, apart from my son dying. At first you're anesthetized, you go on as if he's still there. And he did remain there, turning up one way or another for a very long time. He still does. The things that go through your mind are the things that make you laugh, that keep you close, like his jutting-jawed way of speaking.

He looms still, as when I remember how he cracked over Jerry Lee Lewis. At the beginning my love for "the Killer's" playing diminished me in Stu's soul. "Bloody fairy pounding away" comes to mind as a typical Stu response. Then, about ten years later, Stu came to me one night and said, "I must admit some redeeming factors in Jerry

Lee Lewis." Out of the blue! And this between takes. Now that's *looming*.

He never broached the subject of life and death except if somebody else croaked. "The silly sod. Asking for it." When we went up to Scotland for the first time, Stu pulled over and asked someone, "Can you nae tell me the way to the Odeon?"—Stu being a very proud Scotsman, from Kent. Stu was a law unto himself, in his cardigans and polo shirts. When we had expanded into the mega stadiums and satellite television, thousands in the audience, he'd come on stage in his Hush Puppies, with his cup of coffee and his cheese sandwich, which he put on the piano while he played.

I got really mad at him for leaving me, which is my normal reaction when a friend or somebody I love croaks when they're not supposed to. He left many legacies. Chuck Leavell, from Dry Branch, Georgia, who had been in the Allman Brothers, was a Stu protégé and appointee. He first played keyboards on tour with us in 1982 and became a permanent fixture on all subsequent tours. By the time Stu died, Chuck had been working with the Stones for several years. If I croak, God forbid, said Stu, Leavell's the man. Maybe when he said that, he knew he was ill. He also said, "Don't forget that Johnnie Johnson is alive and well and still playing in Saint Louis." And it was all in the same year. Maybe a doctor had told him, you've got so long to go.

D*irty* W*ork* came out in early 1986, and I badly wanted to tour with it. So, of course, did the other band members, who wanted to work. But Mick sent us a letter saying he wouldn't tour. He wanted to get on with his solo career. Soon after the letter came, I read in one of the English tabloids of Mick saying the Rolling Stones are a millstone around my neck. He actually said it. Swallow that one, fucker. I had no doubt that some part of his mind was thinking that, but saying it is another thing. That's when World War III was declared.

Unable to tour, I thought on Stu's remark about Johnnie Johnson. Johnson was Chuck Berry's original piano player and, if Chuck was honest, the cowriter of many Chuck Berry hits. But Johnson wasn't playing much in Saint Louis. Ever since Chuck had told him to hasten down the wind, more than a decade before this, he'd been a bus driver, ferrying old folks around, almost entirely forgotten. It wasn't just his partnership with Berry that distinguished Johnnie Johnson. He was one of the best-ever players of blues piano.

When we were cutting *Dirty Work* in Paris, the drummer Steve Jordan came to hang out in the studio, and then played on the album, filling in for Charlie, who was having a wobble of his own, carried away for a time on various *stupéfiants,* as the French have it. Steve was around thirty then, and a very gifted all-round musician and singer. He had come to Paris to record, getting some leave from his job playing in the David Letterman show band. Before that he had played with the *Saturday Night Live* band and toured with Belushi and Aykroyd in their Blues Brothers band. Charlie had picked him out as a drummer back in 1978 when he was playing on *Saturday Night Live,* and remembered him.

Aretha Franklin called up because she was making a movie called *Jumpin' Jack Flash,* with Whoopi Goldberg, and she wanted me to produce her title track for it. I remembered Charlie Watts saying, if you ever work outside of this frame, Steve Jordan's your man. And I thought, well, if I'm going to do *Jumpin' Jack Flash* with Aretha, I've got to put a band together. I've got to start again. I knew Steve anyway, so that's how we forged ourselves—on Aretha's soundtrack. Which was a great session. And in my mind it was lodged that if I'm going to do anything else, it's with Steve.

I inducted Chuck Berry as one of the first musicians in the Rock and Roll Hall of Fame, in 1986, and it happened that the band that played behind Chuck and all the other musicians jamming with him that night was the David Letterman band, with Steve Jordan on drums. Next thing I knew, Taylor Hackford asked me to be musical director for a feature film he was making for Chuck Berry's sixtieth birthday, and suddenly Stu's words were echoing: Johnnie Johnson is alive. The first problem, I realized the minute I thought about it, was that Chuck Berry had been playing with pickup bands for so long, he'd forgotten what it was like to play with top hands. And especially with Johnnie Johnson, who he'd not played with since they broke up in the early 1970s. When Chuck turned around and said, in his inimitable fashion, Johnnie, fuck off, he cut off a hand and a half.

He thought he'd have hits forever. Was he too suffering from LVS, even though he played guitar? In fact he never had a hit record after he split that band up, apart from his biggest record ever, "My Ding-a-Ling." Go, Chuck! With Johnnie Johnson he had had the perfect unit. It was made in heaven, for Christ's sake. Oh no, says Chuck, it's only me that counts. I can find another pianist, and anyway, I can get them cheaper too. It's basically the cheapness he was concerned about.

When I went with Taylor Hackford to see Chuck at his home in Wentzville, just outside Saint Louis, I waited until the second day to slide the question. They're all talking about lighting, and I just said to Chuck, I don't know if this is a good question because I don't know your relationship, but is Johnnie Johnson still about? And he said, I think he's in town. But more importantly, said I, could you two play together? Yeah, he said. Shit, yeah. A tense moment. Suddenly I've put Johnnie Johnson back together with Chuck Berry. The possibilities are endless. Chuck rolled right in there, and it was a good decision, because he got a great movie out of it and a great band.

One of those fabulous ironies now took place — and the joke was on me. I'd wanted Charlie to play the drums. Steve Jordan had wanted to do it, but I thought he wouldn't know the music well enough — and I was wrong there, but then I still didn't know him that well. So I told Steve, thanks, mate, but Charlie's up for it. Then on another visit, Chuck wanted to play me something quite urgently. He put on a video of the jam at the end of Chuck's induction into the Hall of Fame —

and there was Steve, whacking away on the drums, though the camera angle cut his head off. But it's rocking, and Chuck says, man, I like that drummer. Who's that drummer? I want that drummer on the film. So I had to call up Steve and say, um, ah, there may be an opening. No doubt Steve enjoyed that. But there was a kicker. He'd better tell it.

> **Steve Jordan:** Chuck flies down to meet us in Jamaica and stay at the house in Ocho Rios, and we go to pick Chuck up at the airport. It's a hot day, it's like ninety plus, very hot. And everybody's coming off the plane in shorts or bikinis, because they know they're coming into sweltering weather. Chuck gets off the plane with a blazer, polyester flares and a briefcase. It was hysterical. Then we're sitting around in the living room, and the drums are set up, and we're supposed to play together. We have just a couple of little Champ amps and a couple of guitars so we can start banging out some stuff, and Chuck says, so where's the drummer? And I had dreadlocks, I'm looking like Sly Dunbar. And Keith says, this is the drummer, it's Steve, he's the drummer. And Chuck goes, he's my drummer? He looked at my dreadlocks and goes, he ain't my drummer! Because there was no shot of my head [in the video he'd seen], and he didn't know I had dreadlocks at the time. He was thinking I was some reggae drummer and he didn't want to play with me. Then we started playing and he was fine.

I asked Johnnie Johnson, how did "Sweet Little Sixteen" and "Little Queenie" get written? And he said, well, Chuck would have all these words, and we'd sort of play a blues format and I would lay out the sequence. I said, Johnnie, that's called songwriting. And you should have had at least fifty percent. I mean, you could have cut a deal and taken forty, but you wrote those songs with him. He said, I never thought about it that way; I just sort of did what I knew. Steve and I did the forensics on it, and we realized that everything Chuck wrote was in E-flat or C-sharp—piano keys! Not guitar keys. That was a dead giveaway. These are not great keys for guitar. Obviously most of these songs started off on piano and Chuck joined in, playing on the barre with his huge hands stretching across the strings. I got the sense that he followed Johnnie Johnson's left hand!

Chuck's hands are big enough; he's got the stretch for all that barre chord playing. Very long, slender hands. It took me a couple of years to figure out how it was possible to sound like that with smaller hands. It was by going to see *Jazz on a Summer's Day,* where Chuck plays "Sweet Little Sixteen." I watched his hands, where they were moving and where the fingers were going, and discovered that if I transposed this into guitar keys, something with a root note, I could get my own swing on it. Just the way Chuck did. And the beautiful thing about Chuck Berry's playing was it had such an effortless swing. None of this sweating and grinding away and grimacing, just pure, effortless swing, like a lion.

It was fantastic, to say the least, to put Chuck and Johnnie together. What was interesting was the way they reacted off each other. They hadn't done it together for so long. Just by being there, Johnnie reminded Chuck of how it really went, and Chuck had to come up to Johnnie's mark. He'd been playing with slouches for years, with the cheapest band in town, just going in and out with a briefcase. To a musician, playing below your mark is soul destroying, and he had been doing that for ages, to the point where he was completely cynical about the music. When Johnnie was rocking, Chuck would say, hey, remember this one? and switch to something really out of left field. It was weird and funny to watch Chuck catching up to Johnnie, and also with the band, because now he's got Steve Jordan on drums, and he ain't played with a drummer like that since goddamn '58. I put a band together that came to find Chuck Berry, as much as that was possible. To present him with a band that was as good as his original. And I think we did it, in our own way, although he's an elusive mother-fucker. But I'm used to working with elusive motherfuckers.

One really brilliant thing that came out of that movie: I gave Johnnie Johnson a new life. He got a chance to play in front of people on a good piano. And for the rest of his life, he was playing all over the world and being liked. He had gigs; he was recognized. And more important than anything else, he had self-respect again, and he was seen for what he was, a brilliant player. He never thought anybody knew it was him on all those incredible records. His credits and royalties as a composer eluded him. Maybe it wasn't Chuck's fault; maybe it was Chess Records. It wouldn't have been the first time. Johnnie never asked, so it was never given to him. Johnnie Johnson had another fifteen years of being heard, doing what he should have been doing and getting his kudos, not croaking behind a wheel.

I don't knock people much (outside my intimate circle), but I've got to say Chuck Berry was a big disappointment. He was my numero uno hero. Shit, I thought, the cat's got to be great to play like that, write like that, sing like that, sling the hash like that. He's got to be a great cat. When we put his equipment together with ours for the film, I found out later that he charged the production company for the use of his amps. From the first bar of that first night of the show at the Fox Theatre in Saint Louis, Chuck threw all our carefully laid plans to the wind, playing totally different arrangements in different keys. It didn't really matter. It was the best Chuck Berry live you're ever going to get. As I said when I inducted him into the Hall of Fame, I've stolen every lick he ever played. So I owed it to Chuck to bite the bullet when he was at his most provocative, to play rope-a-dope to see it through. And he sure pushed me hard—you can see it in the film. It's very difficult for me to allow myself to be bullied, and that is what Chuck was doing to me and to everybody else.

Yet what I think about Chuck deep down is what I wrote in a fax to him one day after hearing him on the radio for the millionth time:

Dear MR. BERRY,
Let me say that despite our
UPS & DOWNS I love you so!
your work is so precious
& beautifully Timeless,
I'm still in AWE!
I'm hoping they don't make
another like you. I couldn't
take the heat!
You may feel the same way
about me!!
My Love to you
brother!
For what it is
worth.

as your english
is better
than
mine!

`05

The big betrayal by Mick, which I find hard to forgive, a move that seemed almost deliberately designed to close down the Rolling Stones, was his announcement in March 1987 that he would go on a tour with his second solo album, *Primitive Cool*. I had been assuming we would tour in 1986 and was already frustrated by Mick's delaying tactics. And now it all came clear. As Charlie put it, he'd folded up twenty-five years of the Rolling Stones. That's what it looked like. The Stones didn't tour at all from 1982 to 1989, and didn't go into the studio together from '85 to '89.

Said Mick, "The Rolling Stones…cannot be, at my age and after spending all these years, the only thing in my life.…I certainly have earned the right to express myself in another way." And he did. The way he expressed himself was to go on tour with another band singing Rolling Stones songs.

I really believed that Mick wouldn't dare tour without the Stones. It was too hard a slap in the face to deliver to us. It was a death sentence, pending appeal. And for what? But I was wrong and I was outraged and hurt. Mick was touring.

So I let him have it, mostly in the press. An opening shot was, if he doesn't want to go out with the Stones and then goes out with Schmuck and Ball's band instead, I'll slit his fuckin' throat. And Mick responded loftily, "I love Keith, I admire him…but I don't feel we can really work together anymore." I can't recall all the jibes and barbs I let loose — Disco Boy, Jagger's Little Jerk Off Band, why doesn't he join Aerosmith? — that's the kind of stuff I fed the grateful tabloids. It got really bad. One day a reporter asked me, "When are you two going to stop bitching at each other?" "Ask the bitch," I replied.

Then I thought, let the guy have his play. I took it like that. Let him go out there and fall flat on his face. He'd shown a total lack of friendship, of camaraderie, of everything that's necessary to hold a band together. It was a dump. Charlie felt even worse about it than I did, I think.

I saw a clip of Mick's show, and he had Keef look-alike guitar players stepping in tandem, doing guitar hero moves. When it was on the road, I was asked what I thought, and I said it was sad that a high percentage of his show was Rolling Stones songs. I said, if you're going to do something on your own, do stuff off the two albums you did. Don't pretend you're a solo artist and have two chicks prancing around doing "Tumbling Dice." The Rolling Stones spent a lot of time building up integrity, as much as you can get in the music industry. And the way

Mick handled his solo career jeopardized all that, and it severely pissed me off.

Mick had misjudged something by a hundred miles. He took it for granted that any bunch of good musicians would be as compatible with him as the Rolling Stones. But he didn't sound like himself. He had great players, but it's kind of like the World Cup. England's not Chelsea or Arsenal. It's a different game, and you've got to work with a different team. Now you've hired the best hands around and you've got to form a relationship with them. Which is not Mick's forte. He could certainly strut around and have the star on his dressing room door and treat the band like hirelings. But you can't get good music that way.

After that I decided, fuck it, I want a band. I was determined to make music in Mick's absence. I wrote a lot of songs. I began to sing in a new way on songs like "Sleep Tonight." It was a deeper sound, one I'd never had before, and it worked well for the kind of ballads I had started writing. So I called in guys I'd always wanted to work with, and I knew the man to start with. You could almost say a collaboration had begun between me and Steve Jordan even back in Paris during the making of *Dirty Work*. Steve encouraged me; he heard something in my voice that he thought could make records. If I had a melody I was working on, I'd get him to sing it. And I thrive on collaboration—I need a reaction to think anything I've done is any good. So back in New York we started to hang, and we wrote a lot of songs together. Then, with his buddy and collaborator Charley Drayton, mainly a bass player but also another superbly gifted drummer, we started to jam at Woody's house. Then Steve and I hung in Jamaica for a while, and he became my buddy. And Steve and I found, hey, we can write too! He's the only one. It's either going to be Jagger/Richards or Jordan/Richards.

Steve will tell how we came together.

**Steve Jordan:** Keith and I were very close during those times when we were writing, before we put together a band, when there was just the two of us. We went into a studio called Studio 900, which was right around the corner from where I lived and up the street from where he lived in New York. And we would go in there and hunker down. The first time we went in there, we played twelve hours straight. Keith didn't even go out and take a piss! It was unbelievable. It was just sheer love of music that bound us. But it was clearly liberating for him. He had so many ideas he wanted to get out. And certainly he was upset, or, at least when it came to writing, wearing his heart on his sleeve. Much of the music was very specific. It was about his old partner. "You Don't Move Me" was a classic of its kind, which ended up on the first solo album, *Talk Is Cheap*.

All I had was the title, "You don't move me anymore." And I had no idea which way to shift it; I could be a guy talking to a chick or a chick talking to a guy. But then, when I got to the first verse, I realized where my mind was going. I suddenly had a focus, and it was Mick. Trying to be gracious at the same time. But *my* version of graciousness.

> *What makes you so greedy*
> *Makes you so seedy.*

Steve and I thought we ought to make a record and started to put together the core of the X-Pensive Winos — so named later on when I noticed a bottle of Château Lafite introduced as light refreshment in the studio. Well, nothing was too good for this amazing band of brothers. Steve asked me who I wanted to play with, and first up, on guitar I said Waddy Wachtel. And Steve said, you took the words, brother. I had known Waddy since the '70s and I'd always wanted to play with him, one of the most tasteful, simpatico players I know. And he's completely musical. Understanding of it, empathetic, nothing ever needing to be explained. He's also got the most uncanny ultrasonic ear, still tuned high after years of bandstands. He was playing with Linda Ronstadt and he was playing with Stevie Nicks—chick bands—but I knew my man wanted to rock. So I called him and said simply, "I'm putting a band together, and you're in it." Steve agreed that Charley Drayton should be the bass player, and I think it was just a general consensus that Ivan Neville, from Aaron Neville's family from New Orleans, should be the piano player. There was no audition process whatsoever.

The Winos were put together very slyly. Almost everybody in that band can play anything. They can switch instruments; they can virtually all sing. Steve can sing. Ivan's a fantastic singer. This core band, from the first few bars we ever played, took off like a rocket. I've always been incredibly lucky with the guys I've played with. And there's no way you can stand in front of the Winos without getting off. It's a surefire high. It was so hot you could hardly believe it. It brought me back to life. I felt as if I'd just gotten out of jail. As engineer we had Don Smith, who Steve had picked out. He had cut his teeth at Stax in Memphis and worked with Don Nix, who wrote "Going Down." He also worked with Johnnie Taylor, one of my earliest heroes. He'd hung out in the juke joints of Memphis with Furry Lewis. He loved his music.

Waddy describes our journey, and bears flattering witness to my improvement as a singer from the early thwarted promise of the Dartford boy soprano.

> **Waddy Wachtel:** We went up to Canada and did the whole of the first record, *Talk Is Cheap,* there. I think the second track we cut was "Take It So Hard," which is a magnificent composition. And I just thought, I get to play on this? Let's go. And we played it a few times. I guess you could call it rehearsing. And there's one take that is just a great pass. It's just ridiculously good. It was the second tune of the night, and it was this killer fucking take of our strongest tune. I went back to the house going, we've conquered Everest already?

These other mountains we can climb easily if we've got the big one down. And Keith didn't want to believe it; he was going, I don't want these guys thinking they're that good. He made us do a retake. I don't know why. The take was shouting, hey, dude, I'm the take. I think Keith just did it to make sure people stayed in focus. But it never sounded as good as that first take. When you've got it, you've got it. When we were putting the sequence of the album together, I insisted "Big Enough" should be the first song. Because the first time you hear Keith sing on that, that first line is amazing, his voice sounds so beautiful. He delivers it effortlessly. I said, people when they hear this, they're not going to believe it's fucking Keith Richards singing. And then we'll hit 'em with "Take It So Hard."

In fact, on *Talk Is Cheap* it's not just our band. We looked high and low. We went down to Memphis and recruited Willie Mitchell and put the Memphis Horns on "Make No Mistake." Willie Mitchell! He engineered, arranged, produced and wrote all the Al Green stuff, either with Al Green or with Al Jackson or both. So we went down to the studio where he did all Al Green's records and we had him do a horn arrangement. We tried for everybody we wanted, and we got most of them: we had Maceo Parker playing, we had Mick Taylor, William "Bootsy" Collins, Joey Spampinato, Chuck Leavell, Johnnie Johnson, Bernie Worrell, Stanley "Buckwheat" Dural, Bobby Keys, Sarah Dash. And we had Babi Floyd singing with us on tour. Great singer, great voice, one of the best. Babi Floyd used to do "Pain in My Heart" on our tour and do the whole Otis bit, getting down on his knees. On the last night of the Winos tour, we shackled him by his ankle to the microphone stand, because we thought he was a little overdoing it. How do you shackle him without him knowing it? It's done very carefully.

I'd never really written with anybody on a long-term basis except Mick, and I wasn't really writing much with Mick anymore. We were writing our own songs. And I didn't realize until I worked with Steve Jordan how much I'd missed that. And how important it was to collaborate. When the band was assembled in the studio, I often composed the songs there, just standing up and voweling, hollering, whatever it took, a process that was unfamiliar to Waddy at first.

**Waddy Wachtel:** It was very funny. Keith's concept of writing was this. "Set up some mikes." "Huh? OK." He goes, "OK, let's go sing it." "Go sing what?" And he goes, "Go sing it!" "What are you talking about? Go sing what? We don't have anything." And he goes, "Yeah, right, let's go make something up." And this is it. This is the routine. So Steve and I are standing up there with him and every so often he'd go, "What the fuck . . . that feels good," trying to come up with lines. Throw everything at the wall, see if it sticks. And that was basically the routine. It was amazing. And we got some lines out of it too.

I did start writing as well as singing songs differently. For one thing, I wasn't writing for Mick — songs that he'd have to deliver on stage. But mostly I was learning to sing. First off I put the songs in a lower key, which allowed me to get my voice down from high-pitched songs like "Happy." The melodies, too, were different from the Stones melodies. And I was learning to sing into the microphone rather than waving in and out while I played air guitar, which I used to do while I sang on stage. Don Smith rigged the mikes and compressors so that I heard it very loud in the headphones, which meant I couldn't sing loud and scream, which used to be the way I'd do it. I got writing quieter songs, ballads, love songs. Songs from the heart.

We went on tour. Suddenly I was the front man. *OK, we're going to do this.* It made me far more sympathetic to some of Mick's more loony things. When you have to sing every goddamn song, you have to develop your lungs. You're doing an hour-odd show every day, not only singing but prancing around and playing guitar, and that brought my voice on. Some people hate it, some people love it. It's a voice with character. Pavarotti it ain't, but then I don't like Pavarotti's voice. When you sing lead in a band, it's an exhausting business. Just the breathing involved. Singing song after song is enough to knock most people on their ass. It's an incredible amount of oxygen you're going through. So we would do shows and we'd come off stage and I'd go to bed! Sometimes, of course, we'd be up till the next show, but a lot of times it would be forget it! We had the time of our lives touring with the Winos. We had standing ovations at almost every show, we did small theaters, sellouts, we broke even. The caliber of musicianship across the stage was astonishing. Fabulous playing every night, the music flowing like crazy. We were flying. It was really magic.

In the end neither Mick nor I sold a lot of records from our solo albums because they want the Rolling bleeding Stones, right? At least I got two great rock-and-roll records out of it, and credibility. But Mick went out there trying to be a pop star on his own. He got out there and hung his flag and had to pull it down. I'm not gloating about what happened, but it didn't surprise me. In the long run he had to come back to the Stones to reidentify himself—for redemption.

So here come the Millstones, brother, to save you from drowning. I was not going to put the first feeler out. I was over it. I was not interested in being with the Stones under these conditions. By then I had a very good record under my belt and I was enjoying myself. I would have done another Winos record right then. There was a phone call; there was some shuttle diplomacy. The meeting that followed wasn't easy to organize. Blood had been spilt. Neutral territory had to be found. Mick wouldn't come to Jamaica, where I was—this is now early January in 1989. I wouldn't go to Mustique. Barbados was the choice. Eddy Grant's Blue Wave studios were down the road.

The first thing we did was to say this has got to stop. I'm not using the *Daily Mirror* as my mouthpiece. They're loving this; they're eating us alive. There was a little sparring, but then we started laughing about the things we'd called each other in the press. That was probably the healing moment. I called you a *what*? We hit it off.

Mick and I may not be friends — too much wear and tear for that — but we're the closest of brothers, and that can't be severed. How can you describe a relationship that goes that far back? Best friends are best friends. But brothers fight. I felt a real sense of betrayal. Mick knows how I feel, although he may not have realized my feelings went so deep. But it's the past I'm writing about; this stuff happened a long time ago. I can say these things; they come from the heart. At the same time, nobody else can say anything against Mick that I can hear. I'll slit their throat.

Whatever has happened, Mick and I have a relationship that still works. How else, after almost fifty years, could we be contemplating — at the time of writing this — going out on the road again together? (Even if our dressing rooms do have to be a mile distant for practical reasons — he can't stand my sounds, and I can't listen to him practicing scales for an hour.) We love what we do. When we meet up again, whatever antagonisms have been whipped up in the meantime, we drop them and start talking about the future. We always come up with something when we're alone together. There's an electromagnetic spark between us. There always has been. That's what we look forward to and that's what helps turn folks on.

That's what happened at that meeting in Barbados. It was the beginning of the détente of the '80s. I let water go under the bridge. I may be unforgiving, but I can't work a grudge that long. As long as we've got something going, everything else becomes peripheral. We're a band, we know each other, we'd better refigure this, refigure our relationship with each other, because the Stones are bigger than any of us when it comes down to the nitty-gritty. Can you and I get together and make some good music? That's our thing. The key, as ever, was to have no one else there. There is a marked difference between Mick and me alone and Mick and me when there's somebody else — anybody else — in the room. It could just be the housemaid, the chef, anybody. It becomes totally different. When we're alone we talk about what's happening, "Oh, the old lady's kicked me out of the house," a phrase will come up and we start working on that phrase. It very quickly falls into piano, guitar, songs. And the magic returns. I pull things out of him; he pulls things out of me. He can do things in a way that you wouldn't think of, you wouldn't plan, they just happen.

Pretty soon everything was forgotten. Less than two weeks after that first meeting we were recording our first new album in five years, *Steel Wheels,* at AIR Studios in Montserrat, with Chris Kimsey back as coproducer. And the Steel Wheels tour, the biggest circus yet, was planned to start in August 1989. Having nearly dissolved the Stones forever, Mick and I were now faced with a further twenty years on the road.

I knew that this was about starting over again. Either this thing was going to break and all the wheels would fall off, or we'd survive. Everybody else had swallowed the pill and got over it. We wouldn't have been able to start it up otherwise. So it was kind of amnesia of the immediate past, although the bruises still showed.

We prepared with care. We rehearsed for two solid months. It was a massive new operation. The set, designed by Mark Fisher, was the biggest stage ever constructed. Two stages would leapfrog each other along the route, the trucks carrying a moveable village with spaces for everything from rehearsal rooms to the pool table where Ronnie and I warmed up before shows. No longer a pirate nation on the road. This was the changeover in both personality and style from Bill Graham to Michael Cohl, who'd been a promoter for us in Canada. This time I realized how big a spectacle I was involved in — huge, enormous — a new kind of deal.

The Stones only started to make money through touring in the '80s — the tour of '81–'82 was the start of the big stadium venues and broke box office records for rock shows. Bill Graham was the promoter. He was the king of rock concerts at the time, a big backer of the counterculture, of unknown artists and good causes, as well as bands like the Grateful Dead and Jefferson Airplane. But that last tour was a rather dodgy period—a lot of bits were going missing. The mathematics weren't adding up. To put it more simply, we needed to get control of our shows again. Rupert Loewenstein had reordered the finances so that, basically, we didn't get cheated out of eighty percent of the takings, which was nice. On a fifty-dollar ticket, up till then, we'd get three dollars. He set up sponsorship and clawed back merchandising deals. He cleaned out the scams and fiddles, or most of them. He made us viable. I loved Bill dearly, he was a wonderful guy, but his head was beginning to turn. He was getting too big for his boots, as they all do when they've been doing it for too long. Separate from Bill, his business partners were stealing money from us and openly bragging about it—one of them telling how he bought a house with it. The inside machinations are nothing to do with me. Eventually I'm going to end up on stage playing. That's why I pay other people. The whole point is that I can only do what I do if I have the space to do it in. That's why you work with people like Bill Graham or Michael Cohl or whoever. They take this weight off your shoulders, but you're going to get a good cut of it. All I've got to do is have somebody on my staff like Rupert or Jane who makes sure at the end of the day that the right shekels end up in the right pot. There was a big meeting on one of the islands when we threw in our lot with Michael Cohl, and he then did all our tours up to *A Bigger Bang* in 2006.

Mick does have a talent for discovering good people, but they can get discarded or left lying about. Mick finds them, Keith keeps them, is the motto in our troupe, and it's borne out by the facts. There were two people particularly that Mick had picked up for his solo stuff, and without knowing it, he actually put me in contact with some of the best—guys I wouldn't let go of again or ever. Pierre de Beauport, who came to Barbados as Mick's sole assistant when Mick and I met up again, was one. He had taken a summer job out of college to learn to make records in New York, and Mick brought him along on his solo tour. Pierre can not only mend anything from tennis rackets to fishing nets, he's a genius at guitars and amplifiers. When I came to Barbados, all I'd brought with me was one old Fender tweed amp, which was barely working and sounded terrible. Pierre of course, as a rookie working for Mick, had been warned never to cross the cold war battle lines, as if it was North and South Korea, when all it was was East and West Berlin. One day Pierre, cutting through all that, got hold of the Tweedie, stripped it, reassembled it and made it work perfectly. He got a hug from me. It wasn't very long before I knew that he's the man. Because also—and he hid it for a long time—he can play guitar like a motherfucker. He can play this shit better than I can. We fell in through our total infatuation with and obsessive love of the guitar. After that, he was backstage for me, handing me the guitars. He's the guitar curator and trainer. But we're a team music-wise too, to the point where now, if I think I've got a good song, I'll play it to Pierre before I'll play it to anybody else.

All these guitars Pierre presides over have nicknames and personalities. He knows their different sounds and properties. Most of the people who made them in '54, '55, '56 are dead and gone. If they were forty or fifty years old then, they would now be well over a hundred. But you can still read the names of the checkers, the ones who gave them the seal of approval, inside the guitars. So the guitars get their nicknames from their checkers. On "Satisfaction" I play a lot of Malcolm, a Telecaster, while on "Jumpin' Jack Flash" I play Dwight, another Telecaster. Micawber is a real all-rounder. Micawber's got a lot of highs; Malcolm's got more bottom on it. And Dwight's an in-betweener.

I take my hat off to Pierre and the rest of his backline crew. On stage, things go wrong suddenly. They have to be prepared for a guitar with a broken string to come back for a restring and have one ready that's going to sound similar and fling it over the guy's neck in ten seconds. In the old days, fuck it, if you broke your guitar, you just walked off and let everybody else carry on until you'd sorted it yourself. With all this film and video, everything is under scrutiny. Ronnie's a string breaker. Mick is actually the worst. When he plays guitar, he thrashes the thing with his pick.

The second new arrival was Bernard Fowler, singer with the band ever since, along with Lisa Fischer and Blondie Chaplin, who came a few years later. Bernard too was working with Mick on his solo stuff. Bernard has since sung on my solo records and on every song I've written since he arrived on the scene. The first thing I said to Bernard when he was doing some backup vocals in the studio was "You know, I didn't want to like you." "Why not?" "You're one of *his* guys." Bernard cracked up, and the ice was broken. I felt I stole him, in a way, from Mick. But I wanted to get out of this embattled idea anyway, and we sing good together. So all that shit went out of the way.

I smuggled Bobby Keys back into the band in 1989 for the Steel Wheels tour, but it wasn't easy. He'd been out for ten years or so, apart from some one-night gigs. It took me that long to get him back in. And when I did, I didn't tell anyone at first. We were rehearsing for the new tour at the Nassau Coliseum. We were getting to the dress rehearsals, and I wasn't too happy with the horns, so I rang Bobby and said, get on a plane and hide yourself when you get here. So we're going to play "Brown Sugar," and Bobby was in, but Mick didn't know he was there. I just told Bobby, when we play "Brown Sugar," come in on the solo. So it was solo time, and Mick looked round at me and said, "What the fuck . . . ?" I just said, "See what I mean?" And when it was over, Mick looked at me like, well, you can't argue with that. I mean, baby, that is rock and roll. But it took me years to grease Bobby back into the band. As I said, some of my friends can really fuck up, but so can I, and so can Mick, so can anybody. If you can't fuck up, where's your halo? My life is full of broken halos. Mick didn't speak one word to Bobby for the whole tour. But he stayed.

I added one more member to the Richards gang in the person of Steve Crotty — one of those people who just find me, who become instant friends. Steve comes from Preston, Lancashire. His dad was a butcher and a rough man, which is why Steve left home at fifteen for a life of pretty rough adventure. I met Steve in Antigua, where he ran a famous restaurant, a big hangout for musicians and yachtsmen called Pizzas in Paradise. Anyone recording at George Martin's AIR Studios in Montserrat would come back to Antigua, so Steve knew many people in the business. We used to stay at Nelson's Dockyard, which was not far from his restaurant.

I struck up immediately with Steve, recognizing a kindred spirit. A jailbird, of course. My mates go to the most distinguished jails. In Steve's case, he'd recently been released from the prison outside Sydney, Australia, in Botany Bay, where Captain Cook landed. He was there, sentenced to hard labor, for eight years, of which he did three and a half, locked up twenty-three hours a day. Part of the reason Steve survived its brutalities untouched was that it was known he had kept his mouth shut and taken the rap for two friends who got away. That's the kind of bloke he is. For such a sweet-natured man, hard though he is, Steve's taken a lot of beatings. One day Spanish sailors, cracked out of their heads, came into his bar at three a.m., and he told them he was closing. They nearly killed him. He was in a coma for some days, suffered aneurysms, lost nine teeth, couldn't see for two weeks. Why had they beat him so badly? The last bit of dialogue exchanged was Steve saying, "Come back later today and I'll buy you a drink." He turns to the bar and hears, "I fuck your mother." So Steve says, "Well, somebody did. What do you want me to do, call you Daddy?" He suffered for that.

When Steve had recovered, I asked him to come and look after my place in Jamaica, where he is today as sheriff of the Caribbean conference. While this book was being written, a guy came armed with a pistol to rob my house there. Steve floored him with an electric guitar. The guy's elbow hit the floor and his gun went off. The bullet went in an inch from Steve's willy, missed all the major arteries and went out. What you call a clean shot. The guy that broke in was shot dead by the police.

There was one time the blade was called for while we were rehearsing in Montserrat. We were recording a song called "Mixed Emotions." One of our engineers was there and witnessed it, and he had better tell it. I don't include it just to brag about how accurate I am with a throwing knife (although it's lucky I made my mark on this occasion), but to show the kind of thing that triggers the red mist — in this case someone coming into the studio who didn't play an instrument, who knew fuck all about what I was doing and tried to tell me how to improve the track. Yap, yap, yap. As this eyewitness remembered:

Some bigwig figure in the music business, invited by Mick, came to Montserrat to discuss some contract to do with touring. He obviously fancied himself for his producing abilities, because we're standing in the studio area, playing back "Mixed Emotions," which was going to be the first single. And Keith is standing there with his guitar on and Mick's standing there and we're listening to it. The song finishes, and the guy says, Keith, great song, man, but I tell you, I think if you arranged it a little bit differently it would be so much better. So Keith went to his doctor's bag and pulled out a knife and threw it, and it landed right between the bloke's legs, *boinggg.* It was really like William Tell; it was great. Keith says, listen, sonny, I was writing songs before you were a glint on your father's dick. Don't you tell me how to write songs. And he walked out. And then Mick had to smooth it over, but it was fantastic. I'll never forget.

The great Steel Wheels tour was all set to go when I got a visit from Rupert Loewenstein — not from Mick, who should have come himself — to say that Mick would not do the tour if Jane Rose was on it. Jane Rose was, and still is, as I write, my manager, last heard of in these pages heroically sticking by me during my last cleanup in the days after the Toronto bust in 1977, and all through the months, years, of the court cases in Canada that followed. She is an unseen presence on the page in much of the narrative since then. We were in the summer of 1989, ten years after those events, and Jane had certainly become a thorn in Mick's side — though he put the thorn there himself. Jane had worked jointly for Mick and me for what now seems like an impossibly long time, from that Toronto period up to 1983, though for a while her working for me was unofficial—she was delegated by Mick to stick by me and help me out. In 1983, Mick decided he wanted to get rid of her and dismissed her from the Rolling Stones. He didn't tell me. And when I found out, I wouldn't have it. Not me, pal. I'm not going to throw off Jane Rose. I believed in her; she stayed with me in Toronto, she went through all this stuff with me and also she'd been acting as my manager. I rehired her that same day.

Jane immediately became a force to be reckoned with. When Mick had refused to tour in 1986, Jane started setting up projects for me—first an ABC television special with Jerry Lee Lewis, then *Jumpin' Jack Flash* with Aretha Franklin, then a record deal with Virgin, which had newly arrived in the United States, to make the Winos record. It was me and Jane, and Jane was driven. So now Mick wanted to insist that she couldn't come on the tour. It was the same old problem—someone getting too close to me, making it difficult to control me, and now someone who kept thwarting Mick's plans for controlling the whole shebang. Jane is tenacious; she's my bulldog. She just will not let go. And she usually wins it. In this case she was fighting simply to have me consulted on important stuff, which Mick was always avoiding. So she flew directly in the face of Mick's desire to command. Worse for her in this situation, and she's had a doubly hard task because of it, she's a chick.

But Jane did some major things for me, from the Winos deal to my appearance in *Pirates of the Caribbean,* which she pulled off by sheer tenacity. After she'd done the deal with Virgin for me, Rupert asked her if she thought the Stones might switch to the label, and in 1991 we signed an enormous deal with them. Jane can be annoying at times, bless her heart. And she's inflicted bruises—often people bump into her expecting her to give way and find a rock in their path. I have a tiger in disguise here, and a devoted one. When Mick gave his ultimatum to ban her back in 1989, he had been incensed by my slipping

Bobby Keys back into the lineup, defying his ban on Bobby, used as he was to running everything. Maybe this was his way of getting back at me. But my response to his ultimatum was predictable: if you won't tour with Jane Rose, no tour. So the tour went ahead with Jane on it, and in some ways I don't think Mick got over it. But he chose his ground badly.

There are comic sides to all this — one of which was Mick's pathological inability to consult me before executing his Great Ideas. Mick always thought he needed more and more props and effects. Piling on the gimmicks. The inflatable cock was great. But because a couple of things worked, every tour we started, I'd have to send acts home. I think you're better off without any props. Or the minimum. Many times I cut down the props projects on these tours. He wanted stilt walkers. Luckily, at dress rehearsals it was raining, and all the stilt walkers fell over. I had to fire thirty-five dancers who were going to appear for about thirty seconds on "Honky Tonk Women." Sight unseen, I sent them all home. Sorry, girls, go hoof it somewhere else. That was a hundred thousand dollars down the sink. Mick had got used to the fait accompli in the '70s, believing I wouldn't notice his decisions. I almost always did, even then, especially when it came to music. My weary faxes would go like this:

*Mick, how is it that the Stones tracks are being mixed and about to be issued without a by your leave? I find this odd to say the least. Terrible mixes anyway. If you don't know that by now ... this is thrown at me as a fait accompli. How could you be so clumsy? Who chose the tracks? Who chose the mixing? Why do you imagine that it is your decision? Will you never realize that you cannot piss around with me?*

It wasn't Mick any more than the rest of us who conceived these megatours: Steel Wheels, Voodoo Lounge, Bridges to Babylon, Forty Licks, A Bigger Bang — these great traveling shows that kept us on the road for many months at a time from 1989 to 2006. It was basically public demand that expanded them to this size. People say, why do you keep doing this? How much money do you need? Well, everyone likes making money, but we just wanted to do shows. And we're working in an unknown medium. You felt drawn to it like a moth to a flame because it was there and they wanted it. And what can you say? That must be right. You've asked for it; you got it. I prefer theaters, but where are you going to put everybody? We never realized just what the scale of this thing would become. How did it get so big when we're not doing anything much different than what we did in 1963 in the Crawdaddy Club? Our usual set list is two-thirds standard Stones numbers, the classics. The only thing that's different is the audiences have grown and the show's gotten longer. All any top act would do was twenty minutes when we started. The Everly Brothers did maybe half an hour. When you're talking about a tour, you're talking cold-blooded arithmetic: it's how many bums on seats, how much does it cost to put the show on — it's an equation. You could say that Michael Cohl was the one who expanded things to this scale, but he did it by judging the demand — after eight years without a tour — and taking a risk. We hadn't known for sure whether the demand was still that high, though it was clear Cohl had got it right when tickets went on sale that first day in Philadelphia and could have sold out three times.

Touring was the only way to survive. Record royalties barely paid overheads; you couldn't tour behind a record like the old days. Megatours were, in the end, the bread and butter of keeping this machinery running. We couldn't have done it on a smaller scale and been sure to do more than break even. The Stones were a rarity in this market in that the show that filled the stadium was still based on the music — nothing else. You're not going to see dance routines or get a tape playing. You'll just hear the Stones, and see them.

There were aspects of these tours that would have been unthinkable in the '70s. There were shocked murmurings that we'd become a corporate enterprise and an advertising medium through all the sponsorship deals. But this too was part of the bread and butter, the equation. How do you finance a tour? And as long as it's a fair deal to the audience and to yourselves, that's the way they figure it out. There were the corporate "meet and greet" sessions — where people come in and shake our hands and get their pictures taken — that were part of our contract. In actual fact, it's fun. They're just loads of pissed people lined up going, "Hey, how you doing, baby?" "Oh, I love you." "Hey, brother." It's pressing the flesh. These people work for these companies that sponsor us. It's also part of the buildup. Oh, we're actually starting to do the work. Finished the snooker game, meet-and-greet time. And in a way, it's reassuring. It means it's two hours before we go on. So you know where you are. Everybody likes a bit of a routine, especially when you're in a new city every day.

Our biggest problem with the huge stadiums and sets, the open-air venues, was the sound. How do you convert a stadium into a club? A perfect rock-and-roll theater would be a really large garage, made of brick, with a bar at the end. There is no such thing as a rock-and-roll venue; there's not one in the world that's made to play this kind of music as an ideal form. You work and wedge yourself into spots that are made to do other things. What we love is a controlled environment. There are some theaters like the Astoria, really good ballrooms like Roseland in New York, the Paradiso in Amsterdam. There's a good Chicago joint called the Checkerboard. There's an optimum size and space. But when you're playing outdoors on those big stages, you never quite know what's in store for you.

There's another guy that joins the band on outdoor stages — God. Either he's benign or he can come at you with wind from the wrong direction and the sound is swept out of the park, and somebody is getting the best Stones sound in the world, but they're two miles away and they don't want it. Luckily, I have the magic stick. Before the shows start, we come and do a sound check and I traditionally have one of my rods in my hand and make some cabalistic signs in the sky and on the floor of the stage. OK, the weather's gonna be cool. It's a fetish, but if I come to an open-air gig without a stick, they think I'm ill. The weather usually comes around by showtime.

Some of our best gigs have been in the worst conditions that you'd want to play in. In Bangalore, our first gig in India, their monsoon actually came down in the middle of the opening song and pissed down throughout the show. You couldn't see the fret board for rain splashing and squirting all over the place. Monsoon in Bangalore, that's what we still call it, it was a famous show. But it was a great show. Sleet, snow, rain or anything, the audience always stays there. If you stay there with them, under the worst conditions in the world, they'll stay there and rock and forget about the weather. The worst ones are when there's a cold snap. That's really hard to work, when the fingers are freezing. There are very few of them — we try and avoid them — and Pierre will have guys backstage to give us little heat bags to put on for a few minutes until the next song starts, just trying to keep our fingers from freezing.

There's a scar I have from burning my finger to the bone while playing the very first number one night. It was my fault. I told everybody, stand back, there's a big pyro to start with, and then I forgot. I went out there, the fireworks were going off, and a lump of white phosphorus settled on my finger. And it's steaming and burning. And I know I can't touch it — if I touch it, I'm going to spread it. I'm playing "Start Me Up" and I've just got to let my finger burn through to the bone. I'm watching my white bone for the next two hours.

I remember a show in Italy where I really knew that I was losing it. It was in Milan, in the '70s, and I could barely stand; I couldn't breathe. The air was totally dead, it was hot and I started to feel myself going. Mick was just about holding himself up. Charlie always has some shade, but I was out in the pollution of Milan, the heat and the chemicals there in the brutal sun. There have been a couple of shows like that. Sometimes I've woken up with a temperature of one hundred and three, but I'm going to go on. I can handle it; I'll probably sweat it out on stage. And most times I do. I've had terrible fevers going on and I'm totally cured at the end of the show, just because of the nature of the job. Sometimes I should have canceled the show and stayed in bed. But if I think I can totter up there, I will. And with a bit of sweating, I'll pull through. There are occasions when I've actually been sick on stage. How many times I've turned round behind the amplifiers and chucked up, you wouldn't believe! Mick pukes behind the stage. Ronnie pukes behind the stage too. Sometimes it's the conditions: not enough air, too much heat. Throwing up is not such a big deal. It's in order to make you better. "Where's Mick gone?" "He's chucking up backstage." "Well, me next!"

When you play these big stadiums, you're hoping that when you first hit it, it fills the room and doesn't come out like a bat whisper. Something that you played yesterday in a little rehearsal room sounded fantastic, and you take it out on the big stage and it sounds like three mice caught in a trap. In the Bigger Bang tour we had Dave Natale, the best live-sound man I've ever worked with. But even with skill like that, in a big stadium you can never test the sound until it's filled up with bodies, so you never know what it will be like on the first night. And when Mick gets away from the band, walking down some ramp, you can never trust that what he's hearing out there is the same as what we're hearing. It might be off just a fraction of a second, but the beat's gone. And now he's singing the song Japanese-style unless we put a brake on it for a second. And that is a real art. You need cats that are so together they know how to turn the whole beat around so that he'll end up on the right place. The band has changed from off beat to on beat and back twice in order to do that, but the audience wouldn't know it. I'll wait for Charlie to look at Mick to readjust to his body talk, not to the sound, because that's echoing and you can't trust it. Charlie will just do a little stutter and watch where Mick's gonna come down, and bang and I'm in.

You feel this need to run down these ramps, and it's not doing anything for the music, because you can't play very well on the run. And then you get there and you've got to run back. And you think, why am I doing this? What we've learned is that it doesn't matter how big the stadium is, if you focus the band all around one spot, you can pretend it's small. With the TV screens now, the audience can see four or five guys really tight together. That's a far more powerful image than us dispersed all over the place, running around. The more we do it, the more we realize it's the screen they're watching. I'm like a matchstick; I'm only five-foot-ten and I can't get any bigger any way you look at it.

When you go on the road on these grueling tours you become a machine; your whole routine is geared to the gig. From the moment you wake up, you're preparing for the show; your whole mind's on it all day, even if you think you know what you're going to do. Afterwards you have a few hours free if you want, if you're not knackered. Once I start a tour it takes me two or three shows to find my line, to get to the groove I'm in, then I can work it forever. Mick and I have different ways of approaching it. Mick has a lot more physically to do than I do, except that I am carrying five or six pounds of guitar. So it's a different concentration of energy. He does lot of training. All I do to train and preserve energy is keep breathing. The grind is the traveling, the hotel food, whatever. It's a hard drill sometimes. But once I hit the stage, all of that miraculously goes away. The grind is never the stage performance. I can play the same song again and again, year after year. When "Jumpin' Jack Flash" comes up again it's never a repetition, always a variation. Always. I would never play a song again once I thought it was dead. We couldn't just churn it out. The real release is getting on stage. Once we're up there doing it, it's sheer fun and joy. Some long-distance stamina, of course, is needed. And the only way I can sustain the impetus over the long tours we do is by feeding off the energy that we get back from an audience. That's my fuel. All I've got is this burning energy, especially when I've got a guitar in my hands. I get an incredible raging glee when they get out of their seats. Yeah, come on, let it go. Give me some energy and I'll give you back double. It's almost like some enormous dynamo or generator. It's indescribable. I start to rely on it; I use their energy to keep myself going. If the place was empty, I wouldn't be able to do it. Mick does about ten miles, I do about five miles with a guitar around my neck, every show. We couldn't do that without their energy, we just wouldn't even dream of it. And they make us want to give our best. We'll go for things that we don't have to. It happens every night we go on. One minute we're just hanging with the guys and oh, what's the first song? and oh, let's have another joint, and suddenly we're up there. It's not that it's a surprise, because that's the whole reason to be there. But my whole physical being goes up a couple of notches. "Ladies and gentlemen, the Rolling Stones." I've heard that for forty-odd years, but the minute I'm out there and hit that first note, whatever it is, it's like I was driving a Datsun and suddenly it's a Ferrari. At that first chord I play, I can hear the way Charlie's going to hit into it and the way Darryl's going to play into that. It's like sitting on top of a rocket.

Four years went by between Steel Wheels and Voodoo Lounge, which kicked off in 1994. It gave me and everyone else time for other music, for solo records and guest spots, tribute albums and idol worship of various kinds. Eventually I played with almost all the survivors among my childhood heroes, like James Burton, the Everlys, the Crickets, Merle Haggard, John Lee Hooker and George Jones, with whom I recorded "Say It's Not You." The award I was proudest of was when Mick and I were inducted into the Songwriters Hall of Fame in 1993, because it was signed by Sammy Cahn on his deathbed. It took me years to appreciate just how great was the art of Tin Pan Alley writing—I used to dismiss it or it went straight through me. But when I became a songwriter I could appreciate the construction and the skill of those guys. I held Hoagy Carmichael in the same high esteem, and I will never forget him calling me six months before he died.

Patti and I were in Barbados, hiding away for a couple of weeks, and one evening the housekeeper comes in, "Mr. Keith! There's Mr. Michael on the phone." So immediately I think it's Mick. Then she said, I think it was Carmichael. I said, Carmichael? I don't know any Carmichael. And then this sort of frisson went through me. I said, ask him his first name. And she comes back and says Hoagy. And I'm looking at Patti. It's like being summoned by the gods. Such a weird feeling. Hoagy Carmichael's calling me? Somebody's putting me on. So I get to the phone and there it is, it's Hoagy Carmichael. He'd heard a version I'd done of the song "The Nearness of You," which I'd given to our lawyer Peter Parcher. Peter liked my record and the piano playing and he'd sent it to Hoagy. My treatment of it is barrelhouse; it really flips the song on its back, deliberately so. I can't play piano well and I was improvising to say the least, just sort of making do. And here's Carmichael on the phone, and he says, "Hey, man, when I heard that version, shit, that's the way I was hearing it when I was writing it." I had always thought Carmichael was so right-wing, I doubted whether he'd ever approve of me or of me doing his song. So I couldn't believe it when he rang and said he liked the way I'd done it. And to hear this from ... Whoa! I've died and gone to heaven, right? In one sweet slice. He said, "You in Barbados? You oughtta go to the bar and get some corn 'n' oil." That is a drink made of dark blackstrap rum and falernum, the sweet syrup made of sugarcane. I drank nothing else for two weeks — corn 'n' oil.

At the tail end of the Steel Wheels tour we liberated Prague, or so it felt. One in Stalin's eye. We played a concert there soon after the revolution that ended the communist regime. "Tanks Roll Out, Stones Roll In" was the headline. It was a great coup by Václav Havel, the politician who had taken Czechoslovakia through a bloodless coup only months earlier, a brilliant move. Tanks were going out, and now we're going to have the Stones. We were glad to be a part of it. Havel is perhaps the only head of state who has made, or would imagine making, a speech about the role that rock music played in political events leading to a revolution in the Eastern Bloc of Europe. He is the one politician I'm proud to have met. Lovely guy. He had a huge brass telescope in the palace, once he was president, and it was focused on the prison cell where he did six years. "And every day I look through there to try and figure things out." We lit the state palace for him. They couldn't afford to do it, so we asked Patrick Woodroffe, our lighting guru, to relight the huge castle. Patrick set him up, Taj Mahal'd him. We gave Václav this little white remote control with a tongue on it. He walked around lighting up the palace, and suddenly statues came alive. He was like a kid, pushing buttons and going, whoa! It's not often you get to hang with presidents like that and say, Jesus, I like the cat.

In any band, you're learning how to play together all the time. You always feel that you're getting tighter and better. It's like a close family. If one person leaves, it's a bereavement. When Bill Wyman left, in 1991, I got extremely stroppy. I really did have a go at him. I wasn't very nice. He said he didn't like to fly anymore. He had been driving to every gig because he'd developed a fear of flying. That's not an excuse — get outta here! I couldn't believe it. I'd been in some of the most ramshackle aircraft in the world with that guy and he'd never batted an eyelid. But I guess it's something that one can develop. Or maybe he did a computer analysis. He was very into that. Bill had one of the first. It satisfied that meticulous mind of his, I suppose. He probably got something out of the computer, like the odds against you after flying so many miles. I don't know why he's so worried about dying. It's not a matter of avoiding it. It's where and how!

But then what did he do? Having freed himself by luck and talent from the constraints of society, that one-in-ten-million chance, he goes back into it, into the retail trade, putting his energy into opening up a pub. Why would you leave the best band in the fucking world to open a fish-and-chip shop called Sticky Fingers? Taking one of our titles with him. It seems to be doing well.

Not so Ronnie's similarly inexplicable foray into the catering trade, always a nightmare of keeping people's fingers out of the till. Josephine's dream was to have a spa. They opened it, it was a disaster, it fell apart and went down in a blaze of insolvency proceedings.

We didn't tell the world that Bill had left until 1993, when we found a replacement, which took a while, and thank God we found a guy totally sympathetic. In the end we didn't have to look far. Darryl Jones is very closely related to the Winos — great friends with Charley Drayton and Steve Jordan. So he was on the periphery. Darryl, in my estimation, is a giant, beautiful, an all-round man. And of course Darryl's playing five years with Miles Davis certainly didn't hurt Charlie Watts, who schooled himself on the great jazz drummers. And Darryl melted into the band real quick. I do enjoy playing with Darryl; he's always provoking me. We have tremendous fun on stage. You want to go there? Fine, let's go a little further. We know Charlie's got it nailed. Let's fuck around. Let's sling some hash! And Darryl's never let me down.

Despite their dispersal, the X-Pensive Winos left trails of smoke in the popular culture with their hot licks, like their appearance on the *Sopranos* soundtrack with "Make No Mistake," along with the Stones' "Thru and Thru." We were ready for a comeback, and we convened in New York to stage it — a slightly more ragged gang than the fresh-faced musicians who had first obeyed the call to arms five years earlier. Wine had long ago given way to Jack Daniel's as the favored band beverage. When we went to Canada to make the first record, we were out in the country, in the woods, and we drank every bottle of Jack Daniel's in a fifty-mile radius! This was towards the end of the first week. We'd cleaned out all the stores. We had to send out to Montreal to buy some more. Now when we gathered for our second act, the Jack flowed again and other stuff too, and it got a little disjointed and it began to take what seemed a long time. To the point where I, Keith Richards, ordered a ban on Jack Daniel's at the sessions. That was my official moment of switchover from Jack to vodka, and the ban did lighten things up. Two, maybe three members of the band gave up drinking after that and haven't taken a drop since.

Before I put them on short rations, we had to listen to a sudden outburst of wrath from Doris at what she saw, through the studio glass, as our dilatory approach to our work. She was in New York visiting and came by the studio. Don Smith showed her in. Don died while I was writing this book and he's much lamented. He had recalled Doris's visit like this:

**Don Smith:** Keith and the guys are out in the studio to record background vocals, and they are just blabbering away instead for about twenty minutes or so. Doris asks me what's all this about and then asks how she could talk to them. I show her the talk-back button, and she presses it and starts screaming, "You boys stop messing around out there and get to work.... This studio is costing money, and you're standing out there talking about nothing and nobody understands a thing you're saying anyway, so get to bloody work. I've flown all the way from bloody England. I don't have all night to sit around listening to you yapping about nothing." In fact it was much longer and stronger. She actually scared them for a tiny minute and they all laughed, but they got to work fast.

So thanks to Doris we renewed our labors. And it became a punishing regimen, which Waddy must describe.

**Waddy Wachtel:** We started first at seven at night and we'd go for twelve hours at least. Then, as it went on, we'd go, oh, let's go in at eight, let's go in at nine, let's go in at eleven. So all of a sudden, and I swear to God this is how it wound up, finally we'd go in to work at one in the morning, three in the morning. We're in the car one morning and Keith's sitting there with his drink and his shades on, it's bright sun, and he goes, hey, wait a minute! What time is it? And we said, it's eight in the morning. And he said, turn around! I'm not going to work at eight in the morning! He'd completely turned his day around.

We were there for weeks trying to finish this record. We were in New York, it was during the summer, I never saw the sun once. We'd come out in the morning, it would be gray. I'd get back to my room, sleep all day, get up at night and go back to the studio. To give an idea of how long it took us: I was a total chain-smoker and I had this little mini Bic lighter. Jane Rose had said we had a month and a half until we were supposed to be finished. And I said to Keith, "Well" — and I was lighting a cigarette — "you know, these lighters, they last about a month and a half. So when this pink lighter is empty, we should be done." He goes, "All right, man, cool, we'll watch the lighter." So a month and a half is gone. I buy another pink lighter and I don't say anything. And now it's almost two months. Every time he has a cigarette, I'm making sure I'm lighting it with a pink lighter. And he's looking. We still have time, you know? So three lighters later, my wife, Annie, comes to New York to visit. I say, honey, I've got an assignment for you. I want you to go out and find every little pink Bic lighter you can. Because we're heading into mix mode. Finally we're mixing the last song, "Demon," and it came out really nice. And for the last three or four days, I went with a pocketful of pink lighters, at least a dozen of them stuffed in my pocket. We finally finished "Demon," and Keith comes in the room and he's really happy and he goes, ahhh, I'll have a cigarette. And I go, oh, let me light that for you, and I reached in and brought all these lighters out. And he's, "You motherfucker! I knew something was going on!"

Even just getting to those sessions could be an ordeal. There was a little misunderstanding in a bar in New York when I was having a drink with Don on the way to the studio. It's happened to me so often that some fucker tries to wind me up because of who I am — and this time it was the sheer dumb stupidity that pissed me off. Don was a witness.

**Don Smith:** I used to meet Keith down at the apartment and we'd walk to work and we'd stop at this bar and have a drink. And this DJ who was in the bar, as soon as we came in, a few minutes later he started playing Stones songs. And after the second one, Keith walked up and politely said, could you not do that? We're just having a drink on the way to work. So the guy puts on another one and another one. Keith walks up, jumps across, grabs the guy and already has him on the ground with his knee on him. And we're like, hey, Keith, we should go? Yeah, OK.

We did another riotous Winos tour, including to Argentina, where we were greeted with a pandemonium not seen since the early '60s. The Stones had never been there, so we walked into full-scale Beatlemania, frozen in time and released for our arrival. We played the first gig in a stadium with forty thousand people, and the noise, the energy, was unbelievable. I convinced the Stones that this was definitely a market where there were lots of people who really liked us. I took Bert and we lived in Buenos Aires, in this great hotel, one of my favorites in the world, the Mansion, in a fine suite of rooms with lovely proportions. Bert would wake up and chuckle every morning, he'd be hearing "Olé, olé, olé, Richards, Richards…" This was the first time his family name had been beaten out on a drum to wake him up for breakfast. He said, "I thought they were chanting for me."

Mick and I had mostly learned to live with our disagreements, but diplomacy was still required to drag us together in 1994. Barbados was again the place to see whether we could get on well enough to make another album. It went well as it usually did when we were alone. I only brought Pierre, now working with me. We lived in a compound on a lemongrass plantation and I acquired a companion who gave his name to the album and to the tour that followed—*Voodoo Lounge*.

A storm had come in, one of those tropical downpours, and I was doing a quick rush to get some cigarettes. Suddenly I heard a sound and thought it was one of those huge toads that inhabit Barbados, which make catlike sounds. I looked and at the other end of this sewer pipe on the walkway was a sodden little kitten. Bit my hand. I knew there were loads of cats down there. Oh, you come from down the pipe, where your mother lives? So I shoved him back in, and I turned around and he shot back up. He was not welcome, in other words. I tried it again. I said, come on, you know your own kid, and he shot back out again. And he was looking at me, this little runt. And I said, fuck it, all right, come on. Put him in my pocket and I rushed home, by now I'm drowning like a rat. I appear at the door in this sodden floor-length leopard bathrobe, an obeah man under a fire hose, holding a small cat. Pierre, we've got a slight side trip. It was pretty clear that if we didn't take care of him, he'd be dead by morning. So Pierre and I tried the basic thing, got a saucer of milk, shoved his head in it, and he went for it. So we have a strong one here, all we've got to do is keep him going. All we've got to do is grow him up. We called him Voodoo because we were in Barbados and his survival was against the odds — Voodoo luck and charm. And always this little cat followed me everywhere. So the cat became Voodoo and the terrace became Voodoo's Lounge — I put up signs around the perimeter. And the cat was always on my shoulder or nearby. I had to protect him from all the tomcats round there for weeks. The tomcats, they wanted his ass, they didn't want another tom on the scene. I'm throwing rocks at these toms, and they're all gathered like some lynch mob. "Give me that little fucker!" Voodoo ended up at my house in Connecticut. We weren't going to be parted after that. He disappeared only in 2007. He was a wild cat.

We all decamped to Ronnie's house in Ireland, in County Kildare, to start work on *Voodoo Lounge,* and all went well and then one day we found out that Jerry Lee Lewis was down the road, hiding from the IRS or something. It's only an hour or two away, so we asked him, do you want to come up and play? But apparently from Jerry's point of view at the time, or the way it got to him, he was going to make a Jerry Lee Lewis album with the Stones backing him. But we were just saying come up and play, it was just like a jam: we're pretty loose, we've got the studio set up, let's rock and roll. So we did a lot of stuff, a lot of great stuff too, and it's all there on tape somewhere. Then we were listening to playbacks later on, and Jerry's going, hey, the drummer's a bit slow there. He's starting to pick the band apart. Hey, that guitar is... And I looked at him and I said, Jerry, we just did a playback, you know what I mean, we ain't cutting. We were just playing. A red mist was falling, and I said if you want to tear my band apart, your name's Lewis, right? You're from Wales. I said, my name's Richards; we're both Welsh. So I'll look into your little baby blue eyes and you look into these two black motherfuckers, and if you want to take it outside, let's deal with it. Don't fucking chop my band up. And I left, I just stormed off and actually wrote "Sparks Will Fly" out of it, watching the bonfire outside. Our longtime crew chief Chuch Magee said Jerry just turned around and said, "Well, it usually works." But the stuff we did with him that night was amazing. And it was a real honor for me to play in that sort of situation, where we'd say, Jerry, what you got? OK, let's do "House of Blue Lights." Brilliant. That's where Jerry and I met on the level that guys like us have to meet, and since then he's been a brother.

The new meat in the sandwich, between Mick and me, was Don Was, who became our producer. He was too clever to get eaten. Don possessed a mix of finely honed diplomatic skills and musical insight. Not swayable, certainly not by fashion. And if something ain't happening, he'll say, I don't think this is happening, which very few people do. They just sort of let us carry on not happening. Or in a polite way, they say, let's leave this one alone for now; let's go on to something else and come back. With all these skills, Don brilliantly survived the next four albums, including this one, *Voodoo Lounge*. He's held high in the business as a gifted producer; he's worked with a long list of the best musicians, but mainly he's a musician, which makes it a lot easier. On top of that he was personally hardened in psychological band warfare, of which Mick and I are some of the oldest practitioners. Don had a band called Was (Not Was) and he started with a guy he'd grown up with; they'd never had an argument until they became successful, and they went for six years without speaking to each other until it collapsed in a storm of acrimony. Sound familiar? With Don, too, the band and the friendship survived. His understanding of the DNA code in all bands is that sooner or later the two principals will turn on each other because one of them will be driven crazy by the knowledge that to be at their best they need to perform with the other person and therefore they need that other person to be successful, or even to be heard. It makes you hate that person. Well, it didn't in my case, because I wanted us to depend on each other and carry on.

Let Don describe what things had come to when we were mixing in LA.

**Don Was:** When we did *Voodoo Lounge,* Keith and Mick would exchange pleasantries about a football match for maybe thirty seconds and then go to opposite corners of the room. And then they'd play, but the degree of interaction with each other was part of a group thing. Throughout the making of that whole record, I assumed that they were calling each other at five in the morning to talk about what was going to happen the next day and all of that. And it was only when we got to the end that I found out they never talked to each other. The only time either of them called the other guy was, Mick told me, when Keith hit a speed dial wrong at the Sunset Marquis and Mick was staying at a rented house in the hills and he called Mick and asked for more ice. He thought it was room service.

Nevertheless, Don was rocked off balance very early on by a sudden and apparently terminal row that erupted in the studio, Windmill Lane in Dublin, between Mick and me, out of the blue, despite our apparent peace terms. It came from sheer nonexistent communication, the building up of festering rages. It was the culmination of a lot of things, but mostly, I think, the control freak business that I found so wearing to digest and deal with. Ronnie and I had come back into the studio, and Mick was playing some imitation riffs on a brand-new Telecaster. It was one of his songs, called "I Go Wild," and he was strumming, sitting down. I'm told I said, "There's only two guitar players in this band and you're not one of them." I probably threw it out as a joke, but it didn't connect to the funny bone for Mick — he took it the wrong way, and then it got deeper. I just laid into him, and once again, according to eyewitness accounts, we hammered each other about everything from Anita to contracts to betrayals. It was pretty wild, hurling one-liners at each other. "What about this?" "Well, what about that?" And everyone else ran, the assistants and Ronnie and Darryl and Charlie and everyone, all scuttled into the control room. I don't know if they were listening on a microphone or not, but several people heard the slanging match. Don Was, electing himself arbitrator, tried to do a shuttle diplomacy act, because we'd both gone to other ends of the building. "But you're both saying the same thing," one of those. Old trick. Don told me he genuinely believed that if one more word was uttered, everybody was going to get on planes and the show would be over forever. What he underestimated was that we'd been conducting this slanging match for thirty years. In the end, after maybe an hour and a half, we hugged and carried on.

It was Mick who had originally got hold of Don Was. Mick had always wanted to work with Don because Don is a groove producer. It's groove, dance hall music. And when we'd finished with *Voodoo Lounge,* Mick said he wouldn't work with Don again because he'd hired him to be a groove producer and Don wanted to make *Exile on Main St.* And Mick wanted to make Prince, *The Black Album* or something. Mick, again, wanted what he heard in the club last night.

Mick's biggest fear at the time, as he kept on telling the press, was to be pigeonholed, as he put it, to *Exile on Main St.* But Don was more interested in protecting the legacy of what was good about the Stones; he didn't want to do anything that was below the standard of that stuff from the late '60s and early '70s era. Why did Mick fear *Exile*? It was too good! That's why. Whenever I heard "Oh, we don't want to go back and re-create *Exile on Main St.,*" I thought, I wish you fucking could, pal!

So when it came to Bridges to Babylon, a tour and a record later in 1997, Mick wanted to make sure we made cutting-edge music of the moment. Don Was was still on board as producer despite Mick's frustrations, because he was so good and worked so well with both of us, but this time Mick had what seemed at first like not a bad idea to get different producers to work under Don on different tracks. But when I got to LA to go to work, I found that he'd just hired who he wanted without asking. He'd hired a team of all these people who had won Grammys and were all cutting-edge. The only problem was none of it worked. I did try to accommodate one of these arrivals. If they asked for a retake, I did one, however good the take was, and another, until I realized they weren't getting it. They didn't know what they wanted. And that was it. Then Mick realized his mistake and said get me out of here. It wasn't promising to discover that one of these producers had looped Charlie Watts — just put him on a drum machine on a loop. Well, that didn't sound like the Stones. Ronnie Wood, lying on the couch, was heard to moan, "All that's left is the ghost of Charlie's left foot."

Mick went through three or four producers. There was no consistency in what he wanted to do. So with all these producers and musicians, including a total of eight bass players, it got out of hand. We actually ended up for the first time almost making separate records — mine and Mick's. Everybody was playing on the record except the Stones half the time. At one point — when things were really strained between me and Mick — collaboration consisted of Don Was sitting and hammering out lyrics with Mick. Don's like my lawyer, representing me, and he's reading out all the scribbles of my improvised lyrics that were taken down by some Canadian girl while I was blabbering into a mike, and he's using these notes as input when they're looking for a rhyme or whatever line. A long way from Andrew Oldham's kitchen — a collaboration without us actually being together.

Mick had hired everybody he wanted to work with, and I wanted Rob Fraboni as well. No one knew who was doing what, and Rob has this annoying habit of turning round to guys and saying, "Well, of course you know that if that goes through the M35 microphone it's absolutely useless," and, in fact, they *don't* know this.

Nevertheless, I still very much like *Bridges to Babylon;* there's some interesting stuff on it. I still like "Thief in the Night," "You Don't Have to Mean It" and "Flip the Switch." Rob Fraboni had introduced me to Blondie, real name Terence Chaplin, when we were mixing *Wingless Angels* in Connecticut, and Blondie came along to do some extra work in the studio. He's from Durban. His father is Harry Chaplin, who was a top banjo player in South Africa and used to work the Blue Train from Jo'burg to Cape Town. Together with Ricky Fataar, the drummer who works a lot with Bonnie Raitt, and Ricky's brother, Blondie had a band called the Flames. They were the biggest band in South Africa, in spite of the fact that Blondie was classified as "colored" with the rest of his band, though he passed as white in other respects. Such was apartheid. When they came to the US, they were taken up by the Beach Boys and moved to LA. Blondie became Brian Wilson's stand-in and sang the vocal on the Beach Boys hit "Sail On, Sailor," and Ricky became the drummer. Fraboni produced the album *Holland* for the Beach Boys and so another musical family tree spread some branches. Blondie began to hang, at my request, around the *Bridges to Babylon* rehearsal period, and we've been close ever since. These songs I was developing were very much based on the work I was doing with Blondie and Bernard — their background vocals were part of the composing process. Now he works with me all the time. One of the best hearts I've known.

It's often in the songs and their composition that a parallel narrative takes place — the story beside the story. So here are a few that have tales attached.

"Flip the Switch" was a song on *Bridges to Babylon* that I wrote almost as a joke but that, as soon as I'd written it, turned out to have a chilling prescience.

*I got my money, my ticket, all that shit*
*I even got myself a little shaving kit*
*What would it take to bury me?*
*I can't wait, I can't wait to see.*

*I've got a toothbrush, mouthwash, all that shit*
*I'm looking down in the filthy pit*
*I had the turkey and the stuffing too*
*I even saved a little bit for you.*

*Pick me up — baby, I'm ready to go*
*Yeah, take me up — baby, I'm ready to blow*
*Switch me up — baby, if you're ready to go, baby*
*I've got nowhere to go — baby, I'm ready to go.*

*Chill me freeze me*
*To my bones*
*Ah, flip the switch.*

Ninety miles away in San Diego, just after I finished this song — maybe three days later — a mass suicide took place of thirty-nine members of a UFO cult called Heaven's Gate, who decided that the Earth was about to be destroyed and they'd better link up with the incoming UFO that was following the fatal comet. The boarding card was phenobarbital, applesauce and vodka, administered in relays. Then lie down in your uniform and await transport. These guys were actually doing it, and I had no idea until I woke up the next day and heard that these people had topped themselves, all laid out neatly, waiting to go to this new planet. It was, to say the least, a bizarre situé of which I don't relish a repeat. The cult leader looked like something out of *E.T.*, and his name was Marshall Applewhite.

I wrote jauntily:

> *Lethal injection is a luxury*
> *I wanna give it*
> *To the whole jury*
> *I'm just dying*
> *For one more squeeze.*

There's a brothel near Ocho Rios, where my house is in Jamaica, called Shades, run by a bouncer I used to know from the Tottenham Court Road. It looks like a classic house of ill repute, with balconies and archways and a dance floor with a cage and poles and a large supply of local beauties. All silhouettes and mirrors and blow jobs on the floor. I went down there one night and hired a room. I needed to get out of my house. I was having a beef with the Wingless Angels, who weren't playing properly, and the electricity had gone. So I left them alone to sort the shit out, took Larry Sessler and Roy and went down to Shades. I wanted to work on a song, so I asked the proprietor to bring me two of his best chicks. I didn't want to do anything with them, just have a place to hang and be comfortable. I'll give you my best, he said. So I installed myself in one of his rooms, with the fake-mahogany bed, one plastic light against the wall, broom cupboard, red bedcover, a table, a chair, a red, green, and gold couch, low red lighting. I had my guitar, a bottle of vodka and some slosh, and I told the girls to imagine we were there forever, together, and how would they decorate the place. Leopard skin? Jurassic Park? What did they say to the Canadians who came? Oh, they're all over in two seconds, they said. You say anything — say you love them. Don't have to mean it. Then the chicks slept, breathing quietly in little bikinis. This was not the normal gig for them, and they were tired. If I couldn't think of a lyric, I would wake them up and we'd talk more, I'd ask them questions. What do you think of it so far? OK, you go back to sleep now. So I wrote "You Don't Have to Mean It" that night at Shades.

> *You don't have to mean it*
> *You just got to say it anyway*
> *I just need to hear those words for me.*

> *You don't have to say too much*
> *Babe, I wouldn't even touch you anyway*
> *I just want to hear you say to me.*

> *Sweet lies*
> *Baby baby*
> *Dripping from your lips*
> *Sweet sighs*
> *Say to me*
> *Come on and play*
> *Play with me, baby.*

Love has sold more songs than you've had hot dinners. That's Tin Pan Alley for you. Though it depends if people know what love is. It's such a common subject. Can you come up with a new twist, a new expression of it? If you work at it, it's contrived. It can only come from the heart. And then other people will say to you, is that about her? Is that about me? Yeah, there's a little bit about you, the second bit of the last verse. Mostly it's about imaginary loves, a compilation of women you've known.

> *You offer me*
> *All your love and sympathy*
> *Sweet affection, baby*
> *It's killing me.*

*'Cause baby baby*
*Can't you see*
*How could I stop*
*Once I start, baby.*

"How Can I Stop." We were in Ocean Way studios, in Los Angeles. Don Was was producer and he's on keyboard. He put a lot of hints and helps in on it. As the song developed, it became more and more complex, and then — how the hell do we get out of here? And we had Wayne Shorter, who Don had brought in, maybe the greatest living jazz composer, let alone sax player, on the planet, who had grown up playing in Art Blakey's and Miles Davis's bands. Don has a great connection with musicians of all stripes, shapes, sizes and colors. He's produced most of them — almost all the good ones. And also LA's been his hometown for many years. Wayne Shorter, a jazzman, said he was going to get ribbed for coming down and playing what they call duty music. Instead he took off onto this wonderful solo. I thought I'd come in and play duty music, he said, and I'm wailing my ass off. Because for that last bit on the song, I said, feel free, go any way you want, take it. And he was fantastic. And Charlie Watts, who is the best jazz drummer of the goddamn century, was playing with him. It was a brilliant session. "How Can I Stop" is a real song from the heart. Perhaps everyone's getting old. What's different from those earlier songs is how it exposes feelings, wears them on the sleeve.

I always thought that's what songs are really about; you're not supposed to be singing songs about hiding things. And when my voice got better and stronger, I was able to communicate that raw feeling, and so I wrote more tender songs, love songs, if you like. I couldn't have written like that fifteen years ago. Composing a song like that, in front of a mike, is like holding on to a friend in a way. You lead me, brother, I'll follow behind and we'll sort the bits out later. It's like you've been taken for a blind ride. I might have a riff, an idea, a chord sequence, but I've no idea what to sing over it. I'm not agonizing for days with poems and shit. And what I find fascinating about it is that when you're up there on the microphone and say, OK, let's go, something comes out that you wouldn't have dreamt of. Then within a millisecond you've got to come up with something else that adds to what you've just said. It's kind of jousting with yourself. And suddenly you've got something going and there's a framework to work with. You're going to screw up a lot of times doing it that way. You've just got to put it on the mike and see how far it can go before you run out of steam.

"Thief in the Night" had a dramatic, deadline-busting journey to the mastering studio. I got the title from the Bible, which I read quite often; some very good phrases in there. It's a song about several women and actually starts when I was a teenager. I knew where she lived and I knew where her boyfriend lived, and I would stand outside a semi-detached house in Dartford. Basically the story goes on from there. Then it was about Ronnie Spector, then it was about Patti and it was also about Anita.

> *I know where your place is*
> *And it's not with him....*

> *Like a thief in the night*
> *I'm gonna steal what's mine.*

Mick put a vocal on the song, but he couldn't feel it, he couldn't get it, and the track sounded terrible. Rob couldn't mix it with this vocal, so we tried to fix it one night with Blondie and Bernard, barely able to stand from fatigue, snatching sleep in turns. We came back and found the tape had been sabotaged in the meantime. All kinds of skulduggery went on. Eventually Rob and I had to steal the two-inch master tapes of the half mixes of "Thief in the Night" from Ocean Way studios in LA, where we'd recorded it, and fly them to the East Coast, where I had now returned homewards to Connecticut. Pierre found a studio on the north shore of Long Island where we remixed it to my liking for two days and two nights, with my vocal. Sometime during one of those nights Bill Burroughs died, so in homage to his work I sent angry Burroughsian cut-ups to Don Was, the producer in the middle — you rat, this is going to be finished my way, nobody else's way, with screaming headline cuttings and headless torsos. Batten down the hatches; we're going to war. I just had a beef with Don. I love the man and we got over it right away, but I was sending him terrible messages. When you're coming to the end of a record, anybody who gets in the way of what you want to do is the Antichrist. This was near to the deadline, so the quickest way to get the tapes back to LA was to take them by speedboat from Port Jefferson, Long Island, to Westport, the nearest harbor to my house on the Connecticut coast. We did this at midnight, under a very nice moon, roaring across the Long Island Sound, successfully avoiding the lobster pots with a swerve here and a shout there. Next day Rob got them to New York and they were flown back to LA to the mastering studio to be inserted into the album.

Exceptionally for a Stones song, Pierre de Beauport got a writing credit on the track, along with me and Mick.

The big problem now was that it was looking as if I was going to be singing three songs on the album, which was unheard-of. And to Mick unacceptable.

**Don Was:** I firmly believed in Keith's right to have a third vocal on the record, but Mick was having none of it. I'm sure Keith is totally unaware of all that it took to get "Thief in the Night" on that record. Because it was a total standoff between these two guys, neither one was backing down, and we were going to miss the release date and the tour was going to start without a new album out there. And the night before the deadline, I had a dream, and I called Mick up and I said, I know your point about him singing three songs, but if two were at the end of the record and they were together as a medley, if there wasn't a lot of space between the two songs, then they would be seen as one big Keith thing at the end of the record. And for the people you're concerned about, who don't love Keith songs, they could just stop after your last vocal, and for those people who love Keith stuff, it would be one last Keith, so view it not as a third song, but as a medley, and we'll leave a space before it begins, and we'll leave very little space between the two songs. And he went with that. And I'm sure Keith has no idea, or Jane, no one knows what happened. So that gave Mick an out, basically, because it was a standoff. And so those two became one song. However, the song that it got paired up with is "How Can I Stop," which is one of the best Rolling Stones songs ever.

It's amazing . . . Keith absolutely at his best, and Wayne Shorter, what an odd pairing, to have Wayne Shorter just blowing, it turns into Coltrane at the end, it turns into "A Love Supreme" at the end. There was something about it. There were like ten people playing at once, and it was a magical session. There were no overdubs to that thing; it just came out like that. And the other thing was, that night, when we cut it, Charlie was leaving, it was the end, it was the last track we cut for that album. They were tearing down the instruments the next day. And Charlie had a car waiting out in the alley. And so he does this big flourish at the end, that's the last take, and it's like a grand hurrah, and the way everyone was feeling at the end of that record, I didn't think they'd ever make another. And so I saw "How Can I Stop" as the coda. I thought it was the last thing they were ever going to cut, and what a great way to end it. How can I stop once I've started? Well, you just stop.

Peter Pakvis / Getty Images

# Chapter Thirteen

---

Recording the Wingless Angels in Jamaica. We set up a studio in my
home in Connecticut, and I break some ribs in my library.
A recipe for bangers and mash. A hungover safari in Africa.
Jagger's knighthood; we work and write together again.
Paul McCartney comes down the beach. I fall from a branch
and hit my head. A brain operation in New Zealand.
*Pirates of the Caribbean,* my father's ashes, and Doris's last review.

T wenty-odd years after I began playing with local Rastafarian
musicians, I went back to Jamaica with Patti for Thanksgiving
1995. I'd invited Rob Fraboni and his wife to come and stay with us—
Rob had originally met this crew in 1973, when I first knew them.
Fraboni's holiday was canceled on day one because it turned out that
at this moment all the surviving members were present and available,
which was rare; there had been a lot of casualties and ups and downs
and busts, but this was a once-in-a-lifetime opportunity to record
them. Fraboni somehow had bits of recording equipment available
courtesy of the Jamaican minister of culture and promptly offered to
record the setup. That was a gift from the gods!

A gift because Rob Fraboni is a genius when you want to record
things outside the usual frame. His knowledge and his ability to
record in the most unusual places are breathtaking. He worked as a
producer on *The Last Waltz;* he remastered all the Bob Marley stuff.
He's one of the best sound engineers you can ever meet. He lives round

the corner from me in Connecticut, and we've done a lot of recording together in my studio there, of which I'll write more. Like all geniuses, he can be a pain in the arse, but it goes with the badge.

I christened the group the Wingless Angels that year from a doodle I made — which is on the album cover — of a figure like a flying Rasta, which I'd left lying around. Somebody asked me what's that, and just off the top of my head I said, that's a wingless angel. There was one new addition to this group, in the person of Maureen Fremantle, a very strong voice and the rare presence in Rasta lore of a female singer. This is how we came together, as she tells it.

> **Maureen Fremantle:** One night Keith was with Locksie in Mango Tree bar in Steer Town, and I was passing that night, so Locksie says, sister Maureen, come in, come and have a drink. And I go in and I meet this guy. Keith hug me and says, this sister look like a real sister. And then we started to have a drink; I was having rum and milk. And then it was like...I don't know, the power of Jah. I just start to sing. Yes, just start to sing. And Keith said, this lady have to come by me. And it never turned back from then. I just start to sing. And I was reeling. And I started to sing, love, peace, joy, happiness, and it burst into one thing. It was something else.

Fraboni had a microphone in the garden, and at the beginning of the recording you hear the crickets and frogs, the ocean beyond the veranda. There are no windows in the house, just wooden shutters. You can hear people playing dominoes in the back. It has a very powerful feel, and feel is everything. We took the tapes back to the US and began to figure how to keep the intrinsic core. That's when I met Blondie Chaplin, who came along to the sessions with George Recile, who became Bob Dylan's drummer. George is from New Orleans, and there are many different races in there — he's Italian, black, Creole, the whole lot. What's startling is the blue eyes. Because with those blue eyes, he can get away with anything, including crossing the tracks.

I wanted to bring the Angels into a more global mood, and guys from everywhere began to show up at the Connecticut overdubbing sessions. The incredible fiddler Frankie Gavin, who founded De Dannan, the Irish folk group, came in with his great Irish humor, and a certain feel began to emerge. This was obviously not a record of great commercial appeal, but it had to be done, and I'm still very proud of it. So much so that there was another on the way as I was writing this.

Very soon after *Exile,* so much technology came in that even the smartest engineer in the world didn't know what was really going on. How come I could get a great drum sound back in Denmark Street with one microphone, and now with fifteen microphones I get a drum sound that's like someone shitting on a tin roof? Everybody got carried away with technology and slowly they're swimming back. In classical music, they're rerecording everything they rerecorded digitally in the '80s and '90s because it just doesn't come up to scratch. I always felt that I was actually fighting technology, that it was no help at all. And that's why it would take so long to do things. Fraboni has been through all of that, that notion that if you didn't have fifteen microphones on a drum kit, you didn't know what you were doing. Then the bass player would be battened off, so they were all in their little pigeonholes and cubicles. And you're playing this enormous room and not using any of it. This idea of separation is the total antithesis of rock and roll, which is a bunch of guys in a room making a sound and just capturing it. It's the sound they make together, not separated. This mythical bullshit about stereo and high tech and Dolby, it's just totally against the whole grain of what music should be.

Nobody had the balls to dismantle it. And I started to think, what was it that turned me on to doing this? It was these guys that made records in one room with three microphones. They weren't recording every little snitch of the drums or the bass. They were recording the room. You can't get these indefinable things by stripping it apart. The enthusiasm, the spirit, the soul, whatever you want to call it, where's the microphone for that? The records could have been a lot better in the '80s if we'd cottoned on to that earlier and not been led by the nose by technology.

In Connecticut, Rob Fraboni created a studio, my "Room Called L"—because it was L-shaped—in the basement of my house. I had a year off during 2000 and 2001, and I worked with Fraboni to build it up. We put a microphone facing the wall, not pointed at an instrument or an amplifier. We tried to record what was coming off of the ceiling and off of the walls rather than dissecting every instrument. You don't, in fact, need a studio, you need a room. It's just where to put the microphones. We got a great eight-track recorder made by Stephens, which is one of the smoothest, most incredible recording machines in the world, and it looks like the monolith in Kubrick's *2001*.

The only track I've put out from "L" so far is "You Win Again," on the Hank Williams tribute album *Timeless,* which got a Grammy. Lou Pallo, who was Les Paul's second guitar player for years, maybe centuries, played guitar on it. Lou was known as "the man of a million chords." Incredible guitar player. He lives in New Jersey. "What's your address, Lou?" "Moneymaker Road," he says. "It doesn't live up to its name." George Recile played drums. We had the makings of a house band, and anyone that was around could come and play. Hubert Sumlin would come by, Howlin' Wolf's guitar player, of whose music Fraboni later made a very good record called *About Them Shoes.* Great title. On September 11, 2001, we were cut short in the middle of recording with my old flame Ronnie Spector, a song called "Love Affair."

You can get into a bubble if you just work with the Stones. Even with the Winos it can happen. I find it very important to work outside of those areas. It was inspiring to work with Norah Jones, with Jack

White, with Toots Hibbert—he and I have done two or three versions of "Pressure Drop" together. If you don't play with other people, you can get trapped in your own cage. And then, if you're sitting still on the perch, you might get blown away.

Tom Waits was an early collaborator back in the mid-'80s. I didn't realize until later that he'd never written with anyone else before except his wife, Kathleen. He's a one-off lovely guy and one of the most original writers. In the back of my mind I always thought it would be really interesting to work with him. Let's start with a bit of flattery from Tom Waits. It's a beautiful review.

> **Tom Waits:** We were doing *Rain Dogs.* I was living in New York at the time, and someone asked if there was anybody I wanted to play on the record. And I said, how about Keith Richards? I was just kidding around. It was like saying Count Basie or Duke Ellington, you know? I was on Island Records at the time, and Chris Blackwell knew Keith from Jamaica. So somebody got on the phone, and I said no, no, no! But it was too late. Sure enough, we got a message: "The wait is over. Let's do it." So he came to RCA, a huge studio with high ceilings, with Alan Rogan, who was his guitar valet, and about 150 guitars.
>
> Everybody loves music. What you really want is for music to love you. And that's the way I saw it was with Keith. It takes a certain amount of respect for the process. You're not writing it, it's writing you. You're its flute or its trumpet; you're its strings. That's real obvious around Keith. He's like a frying pan made from one piece of metal. He can heat it up really high and it won't crack, it just changes color.
>
> You have your own preconceived ideas about people that you already know from their records, but the real experience, ideally, hopefully, is better. That certainly was the case with Keith. We kind of circled each other like a couple of hyenas,

looked at the ground, laughed and then we just put something on, put some water in the swimming pool. He has impeccable instincts, like a predator. He played on three songs on that record: "Union Square," we sang on "Blind Love" together, and on "Big Black Mariah" he played a great rhythm part. It really lifted the record up for me. I didn't care how it sold at all. As far as I was concerned it had already sold.

Then a few years later we hooked up in California. We got together every day at this little place called Brown Sound, one of those funky old rehearsal places with no windows and carpet on the wall, smells like diesel. We started writing. You have to get relaxed enough around someone to be able to throw out any kind of twisted idea that might test your mind, that comfort zone. I remember on my way to the studio, I taped a Sunday gospel brunch Baptist preacher coming right out of the radio. And the title of the sermon was "The Carpenter's Tools"! It was all about the carpenter's tools, how he went into his bag and pulled out all these tools.... We laughed about that for a long time. And then Keith played me a copy he had of "Jesus Loves Me," sung by Aaron Neville, something he'd sung in a rehearsal, just a cappella. So he likes diamonds in the rough, he likes Zulu music, Pygmy music, the arcane, obscure and impossible to categorize music. We wrote a whole bunch of songs, one was called "Motel Girl" and another was "Good Dogwood." And that's where we wrote "That Feel" — I put that on *Bone Machine*.

One of my favorite things that he did is *Wingless Angels*. That completely slayed me. Because the first thing you hear is the crickets, and you realize you're outside. And his contribution to capturing the sounds on that record just feels a lot like Keith. Maybe more like Keith than I had contact with when we got together. He's like a common laborer in a lot of ways. He's like a swabby. Like a sailor. I found some things they say about music that seemed to apply to Keith. You know, in the old days they said that the sound of the guitar could cure gout and epilepsy, sciatica and migraines. I think that nowadays there seems to be a deficit of wonder. And Keith seems to still wonder about this stuff. He will stop and hold his guitar up and just stare at it for a while. Just be rather mystified by it. Like all the great things in the world, women and religion and the sky... you wonder about it, and you don't stop wondering about it.

In 1980, Bobby Keys, Patti, Jane and I paid a visit to the remaining Crickets in Nashville. Must have been something special, because we hired a Learjet to get there. We went to see Jerry Allison, alias Jivin' Ivan, the Crickets' drummer, the one who actually married Peggy Sue (though it didn't last long), at his place he calls White Trash Ranch just outside of Nashville in Dickson, Tennessee. There was Joe B. Mauldin, bass player with Buddy. Don Everly was around on that trip, and to play *with* him, sitting around... these were the cats I was listening to on the goddamn radio twenty years ago. Their work had always fascinated me, and just to be in their house was an honor.

There was another wonderful expedition to record a duet with George Jones at the Bradley Barn sessions, "Say It's Not You," a song that Gram Parsons had turned me on to. George was a great guy to work with, especially when he had the hairdo going. Incredible singer. There's a quote from Frank Sinatra, who says, "Second-best singer in this country is George Jones." Who's the first, Frank? We were waiting and waiting for George, for a couple of hours, I think. By then I'm behind the bar making drinks, not remembering that George is supposed to be on the wagon and not knowing why he was so late. I've been late many times and so no big deal. And when he turns up, the pompadour hairdo is perfect. It's such a fascinating thing. You can't take your eyes off it. And in a fifty-mile-an-hour wind it would still have been perfect. I found out later that he'd been driving around because he was a bit nervous about working with me. He'd been doing some reading up and was uncertain of meeting me.

On the country end, Willie Nelson and I are close, and Merle Haggard too. I've done three or four TV shows with Merle and Willie. Willie's fantastic. He has a guy with a turned-over Frisbee, rolling, rolling, rolling. A beautiful weedhead, is Willie. I mean straight out of bed. At least I *wait* ten minutes in the morning. What a songwriter. He's one of the best. From Texas too. Willie and I just get along. I know that he's very concerned about the agriculture of America and the small farmer. Most of the stuff that I've done with him has been in that cause. The conglomerates are taking over, that's what he's fighting and he's putting up a damn good fight. Willie's a true heart. Unfazed, unswerving and true to his cause, no matter what. I slowly realized I grew up listening to his music, because he was a songwriter way before he started performing—"Crazy" and "Funny How Time Slips Away." I've always been slightly in awe, in a way, to be asked by people like that, that I've already been on my knees before, "Hey, you want to play with me?" Are you kidding?

A case in point was the great sessions at Levon Helm's home in Woodstock, New York, in 1996 to play on *All the King's Men,* with Scotty Moore, Elvis's guitar player, and D. J. Fontana, his drummer on the early Sun recordings. This was serious stuff. The Rolling Stones are one thing, but to hold your own with guys that turned you on is another. These cats are not necessarily very forgiving of other musicians. They expect the best and they're going to have to get it—you really can't go in there and flake. Bands that work behind George Jones and Jerry Lee Lewis, these are top, top hands. You have to be on your mark. I love that. I don't often work in the country area. But that's been the other side of it to me; there's been blues and there's been country music. And let's face it, those are the two vital ingredients of rock and roll.

Another great singer and a girl after my own heart—as well as my bride in a rock-and-roll "marriage"—is Etta James. She'd been making records from the early '50s, when she was a doo-wop singer. She's expanded into every range since then. She has one of those voices that when you heard it on the radio, or you saw an Etta James record in the store, you bought it. She'd sold you. And on June 14, 1978, we played together. She was on a bill with the Stones at the Capitol Theatre, Passaic, New Jersey. Now, Etta had been a junkie. So we found a certain reciprocation almost immediately. At the time she was clean, I think. But that doesn't really matter. It takes one look in the eye for one to know another. Incredibly strong, Etta, with a voice that could take you to hell or take you to heaven. And we hung in a dressing room, and like all ex-junkies, we talked about the junk. And why did we do this, the usual soul-searching. This culminated in a backstage wedding, which in show business terms is like, you get married but you're not really married. You exchange vows and stuff, on the top of the backstage stairs. And she gave me a ring, I gave her a ring and actually that's where I decided her name's Etta Richards. She'll know what I mean.

W hen Theodora and Alexandra were born, Patti and I were living in an apartment on Fourth Street in New York City, and it seemed to us that Fourth Street was not the place to bring up children. So we headed for Connecticut and started building a house on land I'd bought. The geology is not unlike Central Park in New York — great flat slabs and boulders of gray slate and granite emerging from the earth, all enclosed by lush woodland. We had to blast tons of rock to build the foundation, hence my name for the house — Camelot Costalot. We didn't move in until 1991. The house sits alongside a nature preserve that is an old Indian burial ground, a happy hunting ground of the Iroquois, and the woods have a primeval serenity about them that would suit the ancestral spirits. I have a key that unlocks a gate from my garden into the forest, and we go for walks there and roam about.

There's a very deep lake in these woods with a waterfall coming down. I was there one day with George Recile when we were working together around 2001. And you're not supposed to go fishing there, so we're like Tom Sawyer and Huckleberry Finn, and we're trying to catch these incredible fish, called oscars, big and very tasty. George is an expert fisherman and he said, they're not supposed to be anywhere north of Georgia. So I said, let's put in another hook! And suddenly I'm getting this incredible tug on the line. And this enormous snapping turtle, as big as an ox, green and slimy, comes lumbering out with my fish in its mouth! It was like confronting a dinosaur. The look of horror on my face and George's, I wish I'd had a camera. This guy's about ready to pop and snap — his neck can come out three or four feet — he's enormous; he must be about three hundred years old. George and I reverted to cavemen. My God! This motherfucker's serious. I dropped the rod, picked up this rock and cracked him on the shell with it. "Goddamn, it's you or me, pal." They're vicious. They can bite your foot off. And he went back down. Creatures that lurk in the deep, immense and old, are truly frightening, to chill your bones. He's probably been down there so long the last time he came up he was meeting Iroquois.

Aside from poaching, which I haven't done since then, I lead a gentleman's life. Listen to Mozart, read many, many books. I'm a voracious reader. I'll read anything. And if I don't like it, I'll toss it. When it comes to fiction, it's George MacDonald Fraser, the Flashmans, and Patrick O'Brian. I fell in love with his writing straightaway, at first with *Master and Commander*. It wasn't primarily the Nelson and Napoleonic period, more the human relationships. He just happened to have that backdrop. And of course having characters isolated in the middle of the goddamn sea gives more scope. Just great characterizations, which I still cherish. It's about friendship, camaraderie. Jack Aubrey and Stephen Maturin always remind me a bit of Mick and me. History, in particular the British Navy during that period, is my subject. The army wasn't up to much then. It was the navy and the guys that got roped into it against their will, the press-gang. And to make this machine work, you had to weld this bunch of unwilling people into a functioning team, which reminds me of the Rolling Stones. I've always got some historical work on the go. The Nelson era and World War II are near the top of my list, but I do the ancient Romans too, and a certain amount of British colonial stuff, the Great Game and all that. I have a fine library furnished with these works, with dark wooden shelves reaching to the ceiling. This is where I hole up and where one day I came to grief.

Nobody believes that I was looking for a book on anatomy by Leonardo da Vinci. It's a big book, and the big books are way up on the top shelf. I got a ladder and went up there. There are little pins that hold these shelves up, and heavy, heavy volumes up there. And as I touched the shelf, a pin fell out and every fucking volume came down on my face. *Boom.* I hit the desk with my head and I went out. Woke up I don't know how much time later, maybe half an hour, and it's hurting. It's an ouch. I'm surrounded by huge tomes. I would have laughed at the irony, except I couldn't because it was hurting too much. Talk about "you wanted to find out about anatomy..." I crawled up the stairs, gasping for air. I just thought, I'll get up to the old lady and see what's what in the morning. The morning was even worse. Patti asked, "What's the matter?" "Oh, I just fell over. I'm OK." I was still gasping. It took me three days to say to Patti, "Darling, I've got to have this checked out." And I wasn't OK—I'd punctured a lung. Our European tour, set to open in Berlin in May 1998, was delayed a month—one of the only times I've held up a tour.

A year later, I did the same to the other side. We'd just arrived in Saint Thomas in the Virgin Islands and I'd put on some sun oil. Gaily I leapt up on some earthenware pot to look over the fence, and the oil did me in. I slipped—*crack, bang.* The wife had some Percodan, so I just took a load of painkillers. And I didn't know that I'd fractured three ribs on one side and perforated the other lung until a month later, when I had to do a medical for a tour. You've got to be checked out, do all the tests on the treadmill and all that crap. And then they X-ray you—"Oh, by the way, you fractured three ribs and perforated a lung on the right side. But it's all healed now, so it doesn't matter."

When I'm at home I cook for myself, usually bangers and mash (recipe to follow), with some variation on the mash but not much. Or some other basic of English nosh. I have quite solitary eating habits at odd hours, born out of mealtimes on the road being the opposite of everyone else's. I only eat when I feel like it, which is almost unheard-of in our culture. You don't want to eat before you go on stage, and then when you get off, you've got to give it an hour or two before the adrenaline subsides, which is usually around three in the morning.

You've got to hit it when you're hungry. We've been trained from babyhood to have three square meals a day, the full factory–industrial revolution idea of how you're supposed to eat. Before then it was never like that. You'd have a little bit often, every hour. But when they had to regulate us all, "OK, mealtime!" That's what school's about. Forget the geography and history and mathematics, they're teaching you how to work in a factory. When the hooter goes, you eat. For office work or even if you're being trained to be a prime minister, it's the same thing. It's very bad for you to stuff all that crap in at once. Better to have a bit here, a mouthful there, every few hours a bite or two. The human body can deal with it better than shoving a whole load of crap down your gob in an hour.

I've been cooking bangers all my life and I only just found out from this lady on TV that you have to put bangers in a cold pan. No preheating. Preheating agitates them, that's why they're called bangers. Very slowly, start them off cold. And then just be prepared to have a drink and wait. And it works. It doesn't shrivel them up; they're plump. It's just a matter of patience. Cooking is a matter of patience. When I was cooking *Goats Head Soup,* I did it very slowly.

## My Recipe for Bangers and Mash

1. First off, find a butcher who makes his sausages *fresh*.
2. Fry up a mixture of onions and bacon and seasoning.
3. Get the spuds on the boil with a dash of vinegar, some chopped onions and salt (seasoning to taste). Chuck in some peas with the spuds. (Throw in some chopped carrots too, if you like.) Now we're talking.
4. Now, you have a choice of grilling or broiling your bangers or frying. Throw them on low heat with the simmering bacon and onions (or in the cold pan, as the TV lady said, and add the onions and bacon in a bit) and let the fuckers rock gently, turning every few minutes.
5. Mash yer spuds and whatever.
6. Bangers are now fat free (as possible!).
7. Gravy if desired.
8. HP sauce, every man to his own.

My granddad Gus made the best egg and chips you'd ever believe in the world. I'm still trying to get up to the mark on that, and shepherd's pie, which is an ongoing art. Nobody's actually made the quintessential, absolute shepherd's pie; they all come out different. My way of doing it has evolved over the years. The basic thing is just great ground meat and throw in some peas, some carrots, but the trick I was taught by, bless his soul, he's gone now, Big Joe Seabrook, who was my minder, is before you spread the spuds on the top, you chop up some more onions, because the onions you've used to cook with the meat have been reduced, and he was damn right—it just gives you that extra je ne sais quoi.... Just a tip, folks.

Tony King, who has worked with the Stones, and with Mick, and on and off as a publicist since we began in the '60s, records the last occasion when somebody ate my shepherd's pie without asking.

**Tony King:** In Toronto, on the Steel Wheels tour, there was a shepherd's pie delivered to the lounge and the security guys all tucked into it, and Keith arrived and he realized that someone had broken the crust ahead of him. He demanded to know the names of all the people who had eaten the shepherd's pie. So Jo Wood's running around going, "Did you eat the shepherd's pie?" and everyone's denying all knowledge, except the security people, of course, who'd had loads of it and couldn't deny it. I denied all knowledge too, even though I'd had a piece. Keith said, "I'm not going on stage until another one is produced." So they had to send out for another shepherd's pie to be cooked and delivered. I had to say to Mick, "Your show is running late because Keith doesn't want to go on stage until he gets a shepherd's pie." Mick said, "You can't be serious." And I said, "I think I can on this occasion." There was this scene in the backstage area, where on the walkie-talkies somebody actually said, "The shepherd's pie is in the building!" And it got carried through the lounge and dropped into Keith's dressing room, with some HP sauce, naturally. And he just stuck a knife in it and didn't bother eating any of it and went on stage. Just wanted to cut the crust. Ever since then he's always had his own delivered to his dressing room so he doesn't have to worry.

It's now famous, my rule on the road. Nobody touches the shepherd's pie until I've been in there. Don't bust my crust, baby. It's written into the contract. If you come into Keith Richards's room and he's got a shepherd's pie on the warmer, bubbling away, if it's still pristine, the only one that can bust the crust is me. Greedy motherfuckers, they'll come in and just scoop up anything.

I put that sort of shit about just for fun, quite honestly. Because I very rarely eat before I go on stage. It's the worst thing you can do, at least for me. Barely digested food in your stomach and you've got to head out there and do "Start Me Up" and another two hours to go. I just want it there in case I realize I haven't eaten that day and I might need a bit of fuel. It's just my particular metabolism; I've just got to have enough fuel.

When my daughter Angela married Dominic, her Dartford fiancé, in 1998, we had the party at Redlands, a big and wonderful celebration. Dominic had come to Toronto to ask my permission to marry Angela, and I kept him guessing for two weeks. Poor guy. I knew what he wanted, but he didn't know I knew he was going to ask and he could never get an opportunity — I'd always create a diversion, or he couldn't get it up to make his case. And after that I was going on tour. And each morning, even after Dominic had been up past dawn, Angela would say, have you asked him? and he'd say no. Finally, one dawn when the time was running out, I said, for fuck's sake, of course you can marry her, and threw him a skull bracelet to remember the moment.

At Redlands we put marquees up all over the garden and the paddocks and they looked so good I kept them up for a week afterwards. It was the widest mixture of people you could bring together: all Angie's friends from Dartford, the tour people, the crew, Doris's family — people we hadn't seen for years. There was a steel band playing to start it off, and then Bobby Keys, who Angie's known all her life, played "Angie" as she walked down the aisle, and Lisa and Blondie sang, and Chuck Leavell played piano. Bernard Fowler read the Confirmation — a little shocked that he wasn't asked to sing, but Angie said she loved his speaking voice. Blondie sang "The Nearness of You." We all got up, Ronnie, Bernard, Lisa, Blondie and me, and we played and sang.

Then there was the Incident of the Spring Onions — the spring onions that were supposed to be topping the mash to go with the bangers I was making for myself. Except someone swiped them from under my nose. There were many witnesses to what happened, including Kate Moss, who will give an account of the manhunt that followed.

**Kate Moss:** Food of the kind he likes is one of the few
comforts Keith has, whereas everything else is all over the
shop. And because the hours are erratic, he makes his own
food a lot of the time. That's what he was doing the night of
Angela's wedding. It was about three in the morning.
Everyone was partying, it was a beautiful evening, everyone
was outside drinking, dancing, it was a big wedding, still
going strong. And Patti and I were in the kitchen, and Keith
was making his sausages and mash. And he had his spring
onions. The sausages were on, the potatoes were boiling, I was
standing by the Aga, talking to Patti, and he turned round
and said, where have my spring onions gone? And we were
like, what? He said, I just had them, they were just there,
where have they gone? Oh God, we thought, he's out of it. But
he was so indignant, we started going through the dustbins.
He was saying, they were *definitely* here, so we're looking
everywhere, under the tables… "I'm *sure* they were there."
And he was getting really angry. And we said, maybe you
didn't put them there, maybe you put them somewhere else?
No, I fucking put them there. And everyone thought he was
going mad. And a friend of Marlon's walked through the door
and went, Keith, what's the matter? And Keith said, I'm
looking for my fucking spring onions, and he was almost
deranged, going through rubbish, and I looked up and it was
like those accident scenes in slow motion. You think,
noooooooo! Don't do it! This guy had the spring onions
behind his ears. I mean, why would you do that? To get
attention, obviously, but the wrong kind of attention. And
Keith looked up and saw them too. Explosion. In Redlands
he's got those sabers over the fireplace. He grabbed them both
and went running off into the night, chasing this kid. Oh my
God, he's going to kill him! Patti was really worried. We all
went running after him, Keith, Keith, and he came back and

he was raging. The guy spent most of the night in the bushes. He came back to the party later with a balaclava on so that Keith wouldn't recognize him.

I's strange, given my vocation, that I have had dogs since 1964. There was Syphilis, a big wolfhound I had before Marlon was born. And Ratbag, the dog I smuggled in from America. He was in my pocket. He kept his trap shut. I gave him to Mum, and he lived with her for many, many years. I'm away for months, yet the time you spend with pups binds you forever. I now have several packs, all unknown to one another due to the size of the oceans, although I sense they scent the others on my clothes. In rough times I know I can count on canines. When the dogs and I are alone, I talk endlessly. They're great listeners. I would probably die for one.

At home in Connecticut we have an assembly of dogs — one old golden Labrador called Pumpkin, who comes swimming with me in the sea in Turks and Caicos, and two young French bulldogs. Alexandra picked one up as a puppy and called her Etta, in honor of Etta James. Patti fell in love with her, so we bought her sister, who had been left behind in her cage in the pet shop, and called her Sugar. "Sugar on the Floor," one of Etta James's great records. Then there's a famous dog — famous in the Stones back line — called Raz, short for Rasputin, a little mutt of extraordinary charisma and charm, and I've known a few. His history is murky — after all, he's Russian. It seems that along with three or four hundred other strays, he was working the garbage cans of Dynamo Stadium, Moscow, when we toured there in 1998. Russia had gone into a severe economic downslide and dogs were being dumped all over town. It was a dog's life! Somehow, while our crew was setting up the stage, he made himself noticed by the riggers and others. They took him in and he became a kind of mascot in a very short time. From the crew, he worked his way into the kitchen, and from there into the wardrobe and makeup departments. From his daily fights for food, he wasn't looking his best (I know the feeling), yet he touched hard hearts.

When the Stones arrived for sound check, I got a pull from Chrissy Kingston, who works in the wardrobe department, who gushed about this amazing mongrel. The crew had seen him taking kickings and beatings and still coming back. They admired his relentless balls and took him in. "You really must see him," said Chrissy. I was doing our first gig in Russia, and dogs were not on my agenda. But I knew Chrissy. Something about her intensity, her urgency, the little tears welling in her eyes, checked me. We're all pros, and I felt that I should take her seriously. Chrissy doesn't throw you curveballs. Theo and Alex were there, and the infallible "Oh, Dad, Dad, do see him, please" melted even this dog's heart. I smelled a setup, but I had no defense against it. "OK, bring him in." Within seconds Chrissy returned with the mangiest jet-black terrier I've ever set eyes on. A cloud of fleas surrounded him. He sat down in front of me and fixed me with a stare. I stared back. He didn't flinch. I said, "Leave him with me. Let's see what can be done." Within minutes a deputation of the crew came into "Camp X-ray" (my room), big guys, all beards and tattoos, with moist eyes, thanking me. "He's a hell of a mutt, Keith." "Thanks, man, he got to us all." I had no idea what I would do with him. But at least the show could go on. The mutt seemed to sense victory and licked my fingers. I was sold. Patti looked at me with love and despair. I shrugged. There was an immense operation to get him shots and papers and visas and the rest, and finally he flew into the United States, a lucky dog. He lives as czar of Connecticut, where he coexists with Pumpkin and the cat, Toaster, and the bulldogs.

I once had a mynah bird, and it wasn't a pleasant experience. When I put music on, it would start yelling at me. It was like living with an ancient, fractious aunt. The fucker was never grateful for anything. Only animal I ever gave away. Maybe it got too stoned; there were a lot of guys smoking weed. To me it was like living with Mick in the room in a cage, always pursing its beak. I have a poor record with caged birds. I accidentally disposed of Ronnie's pet parakeet. I thought it was a toy alarm clock that had gone wrong. It was hanging in a cage at the end of his house and the fucking thing just sat there and didn't react to anything, except to make this repetitive squawk. So I got rid of it. Too late I realized my mistake. "Thank Christ for that" was Ronnie's reaction. He hated that bird. I think the truth is that Ronnie's not a real animal lover, despite being surrounded by them. He's a horse fancier. In Ireland he has stables, four or five colts there, but you say, "Let's go for a ride, Ron," he won't go near them! Likes them from a distance, especially when the horse he's bet on is crossing the finishing line first.

So why is he living with all this shit and dung and three-legged fillies? He says it's a Gypsy thing. Romany. In Argentina once, Bobby Keys and I were going for a ride and we roped Ronnie in for a third. They were nice quarter horses. If you haven't ridden for a while, it does hurt your arse, without a doubt. And we went around the pampas, and Ronnie's hanging on for fucking dear life. "But you own horses, Ronnie! I thought you loved them." And Bobby and I are cracking up. "Here comes Geronimo. Let's kick it up a bit."

Connecticut is where Theo and Alex were brought up, leading as normal a life as possible, going to the local high school. Patti has many relations within striking distance. There's my niece-in-law Melena, who's married to Joe Sorena. We've made wine in their garage, ending up in that scene where you're all in the tub with your socks off, pounding away on these grapes, going, "This is going to be the vintage." It's fun to do. I've done it in France once or twice, and there's something about squishing grapes between your toes. We even went occasionally on "normal" holidays. There's a fully equipped and battle-hardened Winnebago parked near my virgin tennis court to prove it. The Hansen family are very big on family reunions, and they're also very big on camping, and they pick somewhere ludicrous like Oklahoma. I've only done it two or three times. But you just drive out of New York and...go to Oklahoma. On one of these trips, thank God I went along or they'd have drowned and had no fire. There was an incredible flash flood and we nearly got washed away—all the usual things, in other words, that happen on camping trips. I was never recognized because I was always drenched in rain. And my Boy Scout training came in very handy. Cut that wood! Get those tent pegs in! I'm a great fire builder. I'm not an arsonist, but I am a pyromaniac.

Entry in my notebook, 2006:

> *I am married to a most beautiful woman. Elegant, graceful and as down to earth as you can get. Smart, practical, caring, thoughtful and a very hot horizontal consideration. I presume that a lot of luck is involved. I must say that her practicality and logic confound me because she makes sense out of my discursive way of life. Which sometimes goes against my nomadic traits. Applying logic goes against my grain but how I appreciate it. I bow as gracefully as I can.*

There was a memorable weekend safari with the children in South Africa, when I nearly got my hand bitten off by a crocodile—a close call for early retirement. We were there only two or three days, in the middle of the Voodoo Lounge tour, and we took along Bernard Fowler and Lisa Fischer. We were in a safari park where all of the employees were white former prison guards. And obviously most of the prisoners had been black. You could see it on the barman's face when Bernard or Lisa ordered a double shot of Glenfiddich. It was hardly welcoming. Mandela had been released five years earlier. Lisa and Bernard went out to seek this moment and do their roots thing, and they came back really pissed off. All they got was blacks not welcome. Nothing seemed to have changed from the old apartheid attitudes.

One morning, we'd been up all night and I'd been asleep about an hour and I really wasn't ready for it, but they scooped me up and put me in the back of this open safari truck. I wasn't in the best of moods to start with, jolting around in the back, and it wasn't "Oh my God, it's Africa," it was just scrub and bush. Suddenly we come to a halt on a little side turn. Why are we stopping now? There are some rocks and a cave mouth. At that very moment, out comes my image of Mrs. God — a warthog. It's got a mud pack all over its face and it stands there snorting steam right in front of me. This is all I need now — these tusks — and it just looks at me with its little red eyes.... It was the ugliest creature I'd ever seen, especially at that time of day. That was my first encounter with African wildlife. Mrs. God, the one you don't want to meet. Excuse me, could I see God, please? Maybe I could come back tomorrow? Talk about coming home and getting the rolling pin. I started to see curlers and one of those old housecoats. Steaming with energy and venom at the same time. Which is wonderful to watch, but not when you've slept for an hour and have a terrible hangover.

Now we're jolting down the track again, and a very nice cat, a black guy called Richard, is perched on the back of the Land Rover, spotting things, and there's this huge pile of something, and Richard says, hey, watch this. He chops off the top of this pile, and out flies a white dove. It was elephant crap. There are these white birds that follow elephants and eat the seeds that they haven't digested. Their feathers are covered in an oil so they're not actually covered in crap. And they can breathe under that pile for hours and hours. In fact they eat their way out. But it was pristine, like the dove of peace, totally immaculate, as it flapped away. Next we go round this bend and there's an elephant, big bull, right across the road. And he's busily tearing down two trees about thirty feet tall, he's wrapping them up together, and we stop, and he sort of gives us one look, like "I'm busy," and he carries on ripping out these trees.

Then one of my daughters said, "Oh, Daddy, he's got five legs," and I said, "Six including the trunk." His cock was on the ground, eleven foot long. Humbled, I was humbled. I mean, this gun was loaded. In fact, on the way back, Richard said, look at the tracks there, and there were these huge elephant tracks and a line down the middle which was its cock trailing on the ground. We saw some cheetahs. How do we know they're around? Because there's an antelope in the goddamn tree, dangling. A cheetah has dragged it and stashed it up there. Next the water buffaloes, three thousand of them in a marsh. These things are amazing. One of them decides to have a shit, and before it hits the ground, another has come up behind and caught it and eaten it. They're drinking their own pee. And then, to cap it all, let alone the flies, suddenly in front of us is a female giving birth, and all of the bulls are having a bash at the placenta! What more can we stand! We get out of there, and on the way back, the stupid driver stops beside this puddle, pulls out a stick and goes, hey, look at this! And he pokes this puddle. And I'm just sort of hanging around the back, I've got my hand dangling over the edge, and I feel this hot breath, and I hear this snap, and the jaws of this croc must have missed me by a goddamn inch. I almost killed the guy. Crocodile breath. You don't want to feel it.

We did bump into some hippos, which I loved. But in one day, how many of God's creatures am I going to bump into before I get some sleep? I can't really say it was fabulous. It's a retrospective pleasure. What riled me up was the way the whites were treating Bernard and Lisa. It just soured me for the whole visit.

Maybe I should have read the signs of Mick putting on civic chains when he ushered in the millennium by opening the Mick Jagger Centre at his old school Dartford Grammar. I had heard rumors, which turned out to be unfounded, that a Keith Richards wing had been opened, without my permission, at Dartford Tech. I was preparing to go by helicopter and daub EXPELLED on the roof. It wasn't too long after Mick's ribbon cutting that he called me to say, I've got to tell you this now: Tony Blair is insisting that I accept a knighthood. You can turn down anything you like, pal, was my reply. I left it at that. It was incomprehensible for Mick to do it; he'd blown his credibility. I rang Charlie. What's all this shit about a knighthood? He said, you know he's always wanted one. I said, no, I didn't know. It never occurred to me. Had I misread my friend? The Mick that I grew up with, here's a guy who'd say shove all your little honors up your arse. Thank you very much, but no thanks. It's a demeaning thing to do. It's called the honors list, but we've been honored enough. The public has honored us. You're going to accept an honor from a system that tried to put you in jail for nothing? I mean, if you can forgive them for that... Mick's class consciousness had become more and more evident as we went along, but I never knew he'd fallen for this shit. It may have been another attack of LVS.

Instead of the queen, there was a muddle about the dates and Mick got Prince Charles, the heir to the throne, to tap him on the shoulders, which I think makes him a cur instead of a sir. At least, unlike some others newly knighted, he doesn't insist on being called Sir Mick. But we do chuckle about it behind his back. As for me, I won't be Lord Richards, I'll be fucking King Richard IV, with that IV pronounced *eye-vee.* It would be appropriate. Keep it coming, keep it coming. I'd have my own button to pump it.

Despite that, or maybe because of its relaxing effect on Mick, the following year, 2004, was the best year I'd spent with him in God knows how long. He'd become a lot looser, I don't know why. Maybe it's just growing up and realizing this is really what you've got. I think a lot of it was to do with what happened with Charlie. I'd gone to Mick's house in France in 2004 to start writing together for a new record — the first in eight years — which would become *A Bigger Bang.* Mick and I were sitting together the first or second day I got there, with acoustic guitars, just trying to start some songs. And Mick said, oh dear, Charlie's got cancer. There was a pregnant pause, like, what do we do? It was as big a shock to me as any, because he was saying, do we put this on hold and wait for Charlie and see what happens? And I thought for a minute and said, no, let's start. We're starting to write songs, so we don't need Charlie right now. And Charlie would be very pissed if we stopped just because he was incapacitated for the moment. It wouldn't be good for Charlie and, shit, we've got some songs to write. Let's write a few, send Charlie the tapes so he can have a listen to where we're at. That's the way we did it.

Mick's château is very nice, the Loire about three miles away, with beautiful vineyards above it, with caves beneath it that were made to store the wine at forty-five degrees, year in year out. A real Captain Haddock château, very Hergé. We were tight together, got some good stuff working. There was less of the moodiness. When you've got a sense of really wanting to work together, rather than, OK, how do we pin this, it's totally different. I mean, shit, if you work with a guy for forty-odd years, it's not all going to be plain sailing, is it? You've got to go through the bullshit; it's like a marriage.

My retreat away from Jamaica became Parrot Cay, a place in the Turks and Caicos Islands, north of the Dominican Republic. It's got nothing on Jamaica, but Jamaica had become unpopular with my family because of a number of scares and incidents. The peace of Parrot Cay, by contrast, is never disturbed—least of all by parrots. There's never been a parrot anywhere near Parrot Cay, and the name was obviously changed from Pirate Cay by the nervous investors of yesteryear. Here my children and my grandchildren come and go, and I spend long periods. I listen to US radio stations that specialize in genre music—'50s rock will be on twenty-four hours a day until I feel it's time for the bluegrass channel, which is pretty damn good, or your pick of hip-hop, retro rock, alternative. I draw the line at arena rock. It reminds me too much of what I do.

I wrote in my notebook:

> *After being here a month or so a strange cycle becomes*
> *apparent. For a week squadrons of dragonflies do a show worthy*
> *of Farnborough, then—vanish. Within a few days, however,*

*flocks of small orange butterflies begin to pollinate the flowers.*
*There seems to be some scheme. I live here with several species.*
*Two dogs, one cat, Roy (Martin) and Kyoko, his Japanese lady (or*
*in reverse, Kyoko with Roy her East End diamond). Then Ika,*
*the beautiful (but untouchable) butler(ess). Bless her! Balinese!*
*Mr. Timothy, a sweet black local man who does the garden and*
*from whom I purchase his wife's basketry and palmweaving. Oh,*
*then innumerable geckos (all sizes) and probably a rat or two.*
*Toaster, the cat, works for a living. He does big moths! Then there*
*are the Javanese and Balinese barmen (wicked). Local sailors add*
*local color. But manana I go back to the fridge. I have to pack*
*once again. Wish me luck.*

This was written at the beginning of January 2006, after a break
in the Bigger Bang tour for Christmas. I was packing to go back on
the road, to play first the Super Bowl in February and then one of
the biggest rock-and-roll concerts ever staged, in Rio, to more than
a million people, two weeks later. A busy start to the year. Exactly a
year earlier, while I was walking along the beach, climbing rocks,
along the shore came Paul McCartney, just before he played the
Super Bowl that year. It was certainly the strangest place for us to
meet after all the years, but certainly the best, because we both had
time to talk, maybe for the first time since those earliest days when
they were flogging songs before we were writing them. He just
turned up, said he'd found out where I lived from my neighbor
Bruce Willis. He said, "Oh, I just came down. I hope it's OK. Sorry I
didn't ring." And since I don't answer the phone anyway, it was the
only way he could do it. I sensed with Paul that he really was looking for some time off. That beach is long, and of course these things
come in hindsight: there was something wrong there already. His
breakup with Heather Mills, who was with him on that trip, was
not long coming.

Paul started to turn up every day, when his kid was sleeping. I'd
never known Paul that well. John and I knew each other quite well,

and George and Ringo, but Paul and I had never spent much time together. We were really pleased to see each other. We fell straight in, talking about the past, talking about songwriting. We talked about such strangely simple things as the difference between the Beatles and the Stones and that the Beatles were a vocal band because they could all sing the lead vocal, and we were more of a musicians' band—we only had one front man. He told me that because he was left-handed, he and John could play the guitars like mirrors opposite each other, watching each other's hands. So we started playing like that. We even started composing a song together, a McCartney/Richards number whose lyrics were pinned on the wall for many weeks. I dared him to play "Please Please Me" at the Super Bowl, but he said they needed weeks of warning. I remembered his hilarious takeoff of Roy Orbison singing it, so we started singing that. We got into discussions about inflatable dog kennels designed like the dogs inside them—spotted ones for Dalmatians and so on. Then we went off on one about a special project we were going to develop, sun-dried celebrity turds, purified with rainwater—get celebrities to donate them, coat them with shellac and get a major artist to decorate them. Elton would do it; he's a great guy. George Michael, he'll go for it. What about Madonna? So we just had a good laugh. We had a good time together.

Now, a year later, we headed, two weeks after playing the Super Bowl, to Copacabana Beach for the free concert paid for by the Brazilian government. They built a bridge over the Copacabana Road that went right down to the stage on the beach from our hotel, just for us to get there. When I looked at the video of that show, I realized I was concentrating like a motherfucker. I mean, grim! What had to be right was the sound, pal; didn't matter about the rest. I'd turned into a bit of a nursemaid, just making sure everything was going right. And understandably so, because we were playing to a million people, and half of them were in another bay round the corner, so I was wondering if it was projecting that far, or if it ended up in a muddle somewhere in the middle. We could only see a quarter of the audience. They had screens set up for two miles. That might have been the triumphant exit, apart from a couple of shows in Japan, to a long career slinging the hash. Because soon after that I fell off my branch.

The four of us had flown to Fiji and were staying on a private island. We'd gone for a picnic on a beach. Ronnie and I went for a swim while Josephine and Patti were organizing lunch. There was a hammock, and I think Ronnie had the hammock — he got in quick — and we were just drying off after a swim. And there was this tree. Forget any palm tree. This was some gnarled low tree that was basically a horizontal branch.

It was obvious that people had sat there before, because the bark was worn away. And it was about, I guess, seven feet up. So I'm just sitting there on the branch, waiting for lunch and drying off. And they said, "Lunch is ready." There was another branch in front of me, and I thought, I'll just grab hold of that and drop gently to the ground. But I forgot that my hands were still wet and there was sand and everything on them, and as I grabbed this branch, the grip didn't take. And so I landed hard on my heels, and my head went back and hit the trunk of the tree. Hard. And that was it. It didn't bother me at the time. "Are you all right, darling?" "Yeah, fine." "Whoa, don't do that again."

Two days later, I was still feeling fine, and we went out in this boat. The water was like a mirror until we got out into the sea a little, and these huge Pacific swells started coming in. Josephine was at the front and she said, oh, look at this. So I went up to the bow, and a swell came in and I fell back down, just onto the seat, and suddenly something went. A blinding headache came on. We've got to turn round now, I said. Still, I thought that was that. But this headache got worse and worse. I never have headaches, and if I do, it's an aspirin and it's gone. I'm not a headache man. I always feel sorry for people like Charlie who have migraines. I can't imagine what they're like, but this was probably pretty close.

I found out later I was lucky that that second jolt happened. Because the first one had cracked my skull and that could have gone on for months and months before being discovered, or before killing me. It could have kept on bleeding under the skull. But the second blow made it obvious. That night I took a couple of aspirin for the headache, which is the wrong thing to do because aspirin thins the blood — the things you learn when you're killing yourself. And apparently in my sleep I had two seizures. I don't remember them. I thought I had a bad choking cough and woke up to Patti saying, "Are you all right, darling?" "Yes, I'm fine." And then I had another one, and that's when I saw Patti running around the room, "Oh, my God," making calls. By now she was in a panic, but a controlled one; she still operated. Fortunately the same thing had happened to the island's owner a few months before, and he recognized the symptoms, and before I knew it I was on this plane to Fiji, the main island. In Fiji they checked me out and said, he's got to go to New Zealand. The worst flight I've ever had in my life was the flight from Fiji to Auckland. They strapped me in, in basically a straitjacket on a stretcher, and put me on this plane. I couldn't move and it was a four-hour flight. I mean, forget the head, I can't move. And I'm, "Shit, can't you give me something?" "Well, we could have before we took off." "Why didn't you?" I was cursing like a motherfucker. "Give me painkillers, for Christ's sake!" "We can't do it in the air." Four hours of this claptrap. Finally they got me to the hospital in New Zealand, where Andrew Law, neurosurgeon, was waiting for me. Luckily he was a fan of mine! Andrew didn't tell me until later that when he was growing up he had my picture at the foot of his bed. After that I was in his hands and I don't really remember much about that night. They put me on the morphine. And I woke up after that, feeling all right.

I was there for maybe ten days, very nice hospital, very nice nurses. I had this lovely night nurse from Zambia, she was great. For about a week, Dr. Law gave me tests every day. And I said, well, what happens now? And he said, you're stabilized. You can fly to your doctor in New York or London or wherever. There was just the presumption that I'd want the pick of the world's medical attention. I don't want to fly, Andrew! By now I'd gotten to know him pretty well. "I ain't flying." "Yeah, but you've got to have the operation." I said, "I'll tell you what. You're going to do it. And you're going to do it now." He said, "Are you sure about that?" I said, "Absolutely." I wanted to suck the words back into my mouth. Did I really say that? I'm inviting someone to cut my head open. But yes, I knew it was the right thing to do. I knew he was one of the best; we'd had him well checked out. I didn't want to go to somebody I didn't know.

So Dr. Law came back in a few hours with his anesthetist Nigel, a Scotsman. And I thought my really smart move was to say, Nigel, I'm really hard to put out. Nobody's been able to put me out yet. He said, watch this. And within ten seconds, I'm bye-bye gone. And two and a half hours later, I woke up feeling great. And I said, well, when are you going to start? Law said, it's all done, mate. He had opened up the skull, sucked out all the blood clots and then put the bone back on like a little hat with six titanium pins to connect the hat back to its skull. I was fine except that when I came out of it, I found myself attached to all these tubes. I've got one down the end of my dick, one coming out of here, one coming out of there. I said, what the fuck is all this shit? What's that for? Law says, that's the morphine drip. OK, we'll keep that one. I wasn't complaining. And actually, I've never had a headache since. Andrew Law did a wonderful job.

I was in there for about another week. And they brought me a little extra morphine. They were really nice, very cool. In the end they want you to be comfortable; that's what I found. I seldom asked for the drugs, but when I did, it was, OK, here you go. The guy I was next to had a very similar injury. He'd done his on a motorcycle without a helmet, and he was moaning and groaning. And the nurses stayed with him for hours, talking him down. Very calm voices.

Meanwhile, I was pretty much healed and I was going, I know the feeling, pal.

And then a month in a wee Victorian boardinghouse in Auckland, and all my family came out, bless their hearts. And I had messages from Jerry Lee Lewis, from Willie Nelson too. Jerry Lee sent me a signed 45 of "Great Balls of Fire," first pressing. Goes on the wall. Bill Clinton sent me a note, get well soon, my dear friend. The opening line of my letter from Tony Blair was "Dear Keith, you've always been one of my heroes..." England's in the hands of somebody who I'm a hero of? It's frightening. I even got one from the mayor of Toronto. It gave me an interesting preview of my obituaries, the general flavor of what's to come. Jay Leno said, why can't we make planes like we make Keith? And Robin Williams said, you can bruise him, you can't break him. I got a few good lines out of knocking myself on the head, added to all the other knocks.

What was amazing to me was what the press dreamed up. Because it's Fiji, it must be a palm tree I fell out of, and I had to be forty feet off the ground, going for a coconut. And then Jet Skis came into the story, which are things I really dislike intensely because they're noisy and stupid and disruptive to the reefs.

Here's how Dr. Law remembers it all.

**Dr. Andrew Law:** I got a call Thursday, April 30, three a.m. They rang me from Fiji, where I do work for a private hospital, saying they had someone with an intracranial hemorrhage, and it was quite a prominent person, could I cope with that? And they said it's Keith Richards from the Rolling Stones. I remember having his poster on my wall when I was at university, so I was always a Rolling Stones fan and a Keith Richards fan.

All I knew was that he was conscious, that the scan showed an acute cerebral hematoma, and his history with regards to the fall from the tree and the episode in the boat. So

I knew he would need to be under neurosurgery care, but at that stage I didn't know whether he would need surgery. That means you've got pressure from one side of the brain pushing the midline across to the other side.

That first night I got lots of phone calls from neurosurgeons around the world, from New York and LA, people who wanted to be involved. "Oh, just wanted to check. I've spoken to such and such a person, and you've got to be sure you do this and that and this and that." And the next morning I said, look, Keith, I can't cope with this. I'm being woken in the middle of the night by people trying to tell me how to do a job that I do every day. And he said, you talk to me first and you can tell everyone else to get fucked. Those were the actual words. And that took all the weight off me. It was easy then, because we could make the decisions together, and that's exactly what we did. Each day we talked about how he was. And I made it very clear what the signs would be for when we'd have to operate.

In some people with acute subdurals, the blood clot will dissolve over about ten days and you can remove it through little holes rather than a big window. And that was what we were trying to do, because he was well. We were trying to manage him conservatively or with the simplest operation. But the scan showed a decent-sized blood clot, with some shift in the midline of his brain on that first scan.

I didn't do anything, I just waited, and then Saturday night, after he'd been here a week, I went for dinner with him and he was just not looking good. The next morning he rang me, saying, I've got a headache. I said, we'll arrange a scan on Monday. And by Monday morning he was much worse, very headachy, starting to slur his words, starting to have some weakness. And the repeat scan showed that the clot had got bigger again, and there was quite significantly more midline shift. So it was an easy decision, and he wouldn't have survived if he hadn't had it removed. He was really quite sick by the time he went to theater. I think we operated about six or seven o'clock that night, 8 May. And it was quite a big clot, about a centimeter and a half thick at least, maybe two. Like thick jelly. And we removed it. There was an artery that was bleeding. I just corked that artery, washed it up and put it back together. And then he woke up straight afterwards and said, "God, that's better!" He quickly had relief of pressure and felt much better after surgery, immediately, on the operating table.

In Milan, the first concert he did after the surgery, he was nervous and I was nervous. Language was what worried me most, both receptive and expressive language. Some people say the right temporal lobe plays more on musical ability, but it's the dominant hemisphere of your brain, the eloquent part of your brain. The left side in a right-handed person. We were all worried. He might not remember how to do it, he could have a fit on stage. We were all very tense that night, everyone. Keith didn't let on, but he came off the stage euphoric because he'd proved he could do it.

They said you won't be able to work for six months. I said six weeks. Within six weeks I was back on stage. It was what I needed to do. I was ready to go. Either you become a hypochondriac and listen to other people, or you make up your own mind. If I felt that I couldn't make it, I'd be the first one to say so. They say, what do you know? You're not a doctor. And I say, I'm telling you I'm all right.

When Charlie Watts miraculously appeared back on the scene within a couple of months after his cancer treatment, looking more perfitz than ever, and sat down behind the drums and said, no, it really goes like this, it was like a huge sigh of relief across the room. Until I got to Milan and played that first gig, they were also holding their breath. I know that because they're all friends of mine. They're thinking, he might be all right, but can he still deliver? The audience were waving inflatable palm trees, bless their hearts. They're wonderful, my crowd. A bit of a smirk and an in-joke. I fall out of a tree, they give me one.

I was put on a drug called Dilantin, which thickens the blood, which is why I've not taken bump since, because cocaine thins the blood, aspirin too. Andrew told me about that in New Zealand. Whatever you do, no more bump, and I said OK. Actually, I've done so much bloody blow in my life, I don't miss it an inch. I think it gave me up.

By July, I was back on tour. In September, I played my debutante role as a cameo actor, playing Captain Teague in *Pirates of the Caribbean* 3 — Johnny Depp's father, as it were — a project that started off with Depp asking me if I minded his using me as a model for his original performance. All I taught him was how to walk around a corner when you're drunk — never moving your back away from the wall. The rest was his. I never felt I had to act with Johnny. We were confident with each other, just looked each other straight in the eyes. In the first shot they gave me, two of these guys were having a conference around this huge table, all these candles, some guy says something, and I walk out of this doorway and shoot the motherfucker dead. That's my opening. "The code is the law." They made me feel very welcome. I had a great time. I got famous for being two-take Richards. And later that year Martin Scorsese shot a documentary based on two nights of the Stones at the Beacon Theatre in New York, which became the film *Shine a Light*. And we were rocking.

I can rest on my laurels. I've stirred up enough crap in my time and I'll live with it and see how somebody else deals with it. But then there's that word "retiring." I can't retire until I croak. There's carping about us being old men. The fact is, I've always said, if we were black and our name was Count Basie or Duke Ellington, everybody would be going, yeah yeah yeah. White rock and rollers apparently are not supposed to do this at our age. But I'm not here just to make records and money. I'm here to say something and to touch other people, sometimes in a cry of desperation: "Do you know this feeling?"

In 2007, Doris began to sink from a long illness. Bert had died in 2002, but his memory was revived a few weeks before Doris died in a big press story generated by a journalist reporting that I'd claimed to have snorted some of my father's ashes along with a line of bump. There were headlines, editorials, there were op-eds on cannibalism, there was some of the old flavor of Street of Shame indignation at the Stones. John Humphrys on prime-time radio was heard to ask, "Do you think Keith Richards has gone too far this time?" What did he mean *this* time? There were also articles saying this is a perfectly normal thing, it goes back to ancient times, the ingestion of your ancestor. So there were two schools of thought. Old pro that I am, I said it was taken out of context. No denying, no admitting. "The truth of the matter" — read my memo to Jane Rose when the story threatened to get out of hand — "is that after having Dad's ashes in a black box for six years, because I really couldn't bring myself to scatter him to the winds, I finally planted a sturdy English oak to spread him around. And as I took the lid off of the box, a fine spray of his ashes blew out onto the table. I couldn't just brush him off, so I wiped my finger over it and snorted the residue. Ashes to ashes, father to son. He is now growing oak trees and would love me for it."

While Doris lay dying, the Dartford council was naming the streets in a new estate close to our old home in Spielman Road — Sympathy Street, Dandelion Row, Ruby Tuesday Drive. All that in a lifetime. The streets named for us only a few years after we were being shoved up against the wall. Maybe the council changed their minds again after Dad's ashes. I haven't checked. In the hospital, my mum was very cheeky with the doctors and everything, but getting weaker. And Angela said, we know what's happening, the girl's going, we all know that, it's just a matter of what day, really. So Angela said, take up a guitar, play to her. Good idea, I hadn't really thought about it. You get a bit confused when your mother's dying. So our last night together, I took the guitar up there and I sat on the foot of her bed, and she's lying there, and I said, "How you doing, Mother?" And she says, "This morphine's not bad." She asked me where I was staying. I said Claridge's. She said, "We are going up in the world, aren't we?" She was drifting in and out of this opiate state, and I played a few licks for her of "Malagueña" and the other stuff that she knew that I knew, that I'd played since I was a kid. She drifted off to sleep, and the next morning my assistant Sherry, who looked after my mother with love and devotion, went to see her, like she did every morning, and she said, "Did you hear Keith playing for you last night?" And Doris said, "Yeah, it was a bit out of tune." That's my mother for you. But I have to defer to Doris. She had unerring pitch and a beautiful sense of music, which she got from her parents, from Emma and Gus, who first taught me "Malagueña." It was Doris who gave me my first review. I remember her coming home from work. I was on the top of the stairs, playing "Malagueña." She went through to the kitchen, did something with pots and pans. She began to hum along with me. Suddenly she came to the foot of the stairs. "Is that you? I thought it was the radio." Two bars of "Malagueña" and you're in.

# Acknowledgments

---

My thanks to the following for their help with *Life,* then and now:

Jerry Ivan Allison
Shirley Arnold
Gregorio Azar
Neville Beckford
Heather Beckwith
Georgia Bergman
Chris Blackwell
Stanley Booth
Tony Calder
Jim Callaghan
Lloyd Cameron
Gretchen Parsons Carpenter
Bill Carter
Seymour Cassel
Blondie Chaplin
Barbara Charone
Bill Chenail
Marshall Chess
Alan Clayton
David Courts
Steve Crotty
Fran Curtis
David Dalton
Sherry Daly
Pierre de Beauport
Stash Klossowski de Rola
Johnny Depp
Jim Dickinson
Deborah Dixon

Bernard Doherty
Charley Drayton
Sly Dunbar
Alan Dunn
Loni Efron
Jackie Ellis
Jane Emanuel
Ahmet Ertegun
Marianne Faithfull
Lisa Fischer
Patricia Ford
Bernard Fowler
Rob Fraboni
Christopher Gibbs
Kelley Glasgow
Robert Greenfield
Patti Hansen
Hugh Hart
Richard Heller
Barney Hoskyns
Sandra Hull
Eric Idle
Dominic Jennings
Brian Jobson
Andy Johns
Darryl Jones
Steve Jordan
Eve Simone Kakassy
James Karnbach

# ACKNOWLEDGMENTS

Vanessa Kehren
Linda Keith
Nick Kent
Bobby Keys
Chris Kimsey
Tony King
Hannah Lack
Andrew Law
Chuck Leavell
Fran Lebowitz
Richard Leher
Annie Leibovitz
Kay Levinson
Michael Lindsay-Hogg
Elsie Lindsey
Prince Rupert Loewenstein
Michael Lydon
Roy Martin
Paul McCartney
Earl McGrath
Mary Beth Medley
Lorne Michaels
Barry Mindel
Haleema Mohamed
Kari Ann Moller
Kate Moss
Marjorie Mould
Laila Nabulsi
David Navarrete
Willie Nelson
Ivan Neville
Philip Norman
Uschi Obermaier
Andrew Oldham
Anita Pallenberg
Peter Parcher
Beatrice Clarke Payton
James Phelge
Michael Pietsch
Alexandra Richards
Angela Richards

Bill Richards
Doris Richards
Marlon Richards
Theodora Richards
Lisa Robinson
Alan Rogan
Jane Rose
Peter Rudge
Tony Russell
Daniel Salemi
Kevin Schroeder
Gary Schultz
Martin Scorsese
Simon Sessler
Robbie Shakespeare
June Shelley
Ernest Smatt
Don Smith
Joyce Smyth
Ronnie Spector
Maurice Spira
Trevor Stephens
Dick Taylor
Winston Thomas
Nick Tosches
Betsy Uhrig
Ed Victor
Waddy Wachtel
Tom Waits
Joe Walsh
Don Was
Nigel Waymouth
Dennis Wells
Lil Wergilis
Locksley Whitlock
Vicki Wickham
Warrin Williamson
Peter Wolf
Stephen Yarde
Bill Zysblat

# Index

The abbreviation KR in subheadings refers to Keith Richards.

# INDEX